DATE DUE			

COMMAND DECISION
AND THE PRESIDENCY

Books by R. Gordon Hoxie:

John W. Burgess, American Scholar
Frontiers for Freedom
A History of the Faculty of Political Science
The White House: Organization and Operations
The Presidency of the 1970's
Command Decision and the Presidency

****

COMMAND DECISION AND THE PRESIDENCY

*A Study in National Security
Policy and Organization*

R. GORDON HOXIE

Center for the Study of the Presidency

****

READER'S DIGEST PRESS

*Distributed by
Thomas Y. Crowell Company, New York, 1977*

Dedicated to
HARRY S TRUMAN, SOLDIER, SENATOR, STATESMAN,
   and
DWIGHT D. EISENHOWER, SOLDIER, EDUCATOR, STATESMAN,
   Builders of Our National Security Policy and Organization

LIBRARY OF CONGRESS CATALOGING IN PUBLICATION DATA

ISBN 0-88349-162-1
LC: 77-88416
10 9 8 7 6 5 4 3 2 1

CONTENTS

ACKNOWLEDGMENTS

This study on national security policy and organization originated in 1948, when General of the Army Dwight D. Eisenhower came to Morningside Heights in New York City as Columbia University president. I had the rare opportunity of earning my administrative apprenticeship under his guidance.

In 1950, Eisenhower regretfully left Columbia to accept appointment as the first Supreme Allied Commander of NATO. With characteristic loyalty to those who had served under him, he gave me encouragement throughout the following years as I pursued a dual academic-military career as a university chancellor and Air Force reservist. A memorandum written shortly before he died inspired the founding of the Center for the Study of the Presidency, of which his widow, Mamie Doud Eisenhower, is honorary chairman.

Although the earliest inspirations for this volume came through the person of Dwight David Eisenhower, President Harry S Truman also made an indelible impression through his statesmanlike national security policy programs. In 1952, on the invitation of the Social Science Foundation of the University of Denver, I served as editor of the volume *Frontiers for Freedom*. In compiling the material for that book, I was struck by certain observations of President Truman. As an early advocate of the United Nations and a principal architect of NATO and other regional alliances, Truman offered a profound truth when he declared, "No one nation can find protection in a selfish search for a safe haven from the storm."[1] Looking toward lesser-developed lands, he entered upon his Point Four Program. "For the first time in history," Truman asserted, "humanity possesses the knowledge and the skill to relieve the suffering of these people."[2]

These, then, were my early impressions of two remarkable leaders who forged our post–World War II national security policies as the United States embarked on a new course of world leadership. Years in the Air Force Reserve quickened my interest both in the President's role as Commander in Chief and in defense organization. Accordingly, when the Center for the Study of the Presidency established its fellowship program for outstanding undergraduate and graduate students, I suggested to one of the first such fellows, Michael J. Nizolek, then a senior at Fordham University, that he undertake a study on the origins of the National Security Act of 1947. Later, when I discussed that study with Dr. Thomas Belden, then chief historian of the Office of Air Force History, he suggested that I carry the story forward. This I did with the cordial support of the successive chiefs of the Office of Air Force History, Major General Robert N. Ginsburgh, Brigadier General Brian S. Gunderson, and Brigadier General Earl G. Peck. Deputy Chief Air Force historian Max Rosenberg gave considerable guidance to the study, as did Carl Berger, Eugene P. Sagstetter, Murray Green, David Schoem, and other staff members.

Although a portion of the work was written during my tours of duty as an Air Force reservist, it does not in any way purport to represent the official views of the U.S. Air Force, nor is there any implication of Air Force concurrence with its contents or conclusions.

The Department of Defense offered considerable help with this study; so also did the Department of State and the White House. In 1969 I accepted an appointment on a board at the Department of State. This was the beginning of a productive relationship with Elliot L. Richardson, then Under Secretary of State, who has read the manuscript and given me the benefit of his unique perspective. It was Richardson who, while serving as Secretary of Defense in 1973, advised the Congress and the American people that "the military balance, at this crucial junction in world affairs, is very delicately poised. We have," he further counseled, "a great stake in maintaining that balance while we continue to pursue ways to give it greater stability." [3] At the White House, Gerald Ford's Assistant for National Security Affairs,

Lieutenant General Brent Scowcroft, provided considerable insight on my discussion of recent policy.

Thanks also go to Dr. Louis Koenig, professor of politics, New York University, and Dr. Curtis P. Nettels, professor emeritus of history, Cornell University, for reading portions of the manuscript. Dr. Koenig gave particular insight through his expertise in the area of crisis management. Dr. Nettels, my mentor since my earliest days as a graduate student, provided considerable historical perspective.

I would like to express my appreciation to Dr. James Tracy Crown for having made available a number of taped interviews relating to the Kennedy Presidency and crisis management. Also my appreciation to the late Dr. Kenneth W. Colegrove and Dr. Kenneth E. Davison, of the Center for the Study of the Presidency, and Marianna Hof, of the Oyster Bay–East Norwich, New York, Public Library, for their help in bibliographical materials, and to Nancy Kelly, my editor at Reader's Digest Press, for all her expertise and grace.

Other distinguished students of the Presidency, who were most helpful, and who are quoted in this study, include former Under Secretaries of State Robert D. Murphy, William J. Casey, and L. Dean Brown; Eisenhower's Special Assistant for National Security Affairs, Gordon Gray; Counselor to the State Department Helmut Sonnenfeldt; and former State Department historian Dr. William M. Franklin. Especially warm thanks must go the remarkable James C. Hagerty, President Eisenhower's press secretary, who read the manuscript with keen perception and exhorted me to its completion. It is understandable how President Eisenhower affectionately referred to Jim as "my Good Man Friday."

Finally, there are those unsung heroines who typed the manuscript: Sue Cockrell, Selma Shear, Margaret Peters, and Elizabeth Schwartzmann at the Office of Air Force History; and Sheila Halpin, Deborah Carroll, Emily Geoghegan, Janice Jacobsen, and Gay Orde at the Center for the Study of the Presidency. Last, but not least, my wife, Louise, gave much-needed encouragement.

To all these people, I am deeply grateful.

RGH

AUTHOR'S PREFACE

In this study governmental structure is not viewed as separate from governmental policy, but rather as a means to achieve better instruments for decisionmaking and decision implementation; our primary view herein is from the office of the Presidency. No other office is so concerned with the shaping of American strategy.

There are those who would ask whether there is, indeed, an American strategy: a national strategy. Viewed in terms of the volume of literature on the subject and the penchant of virtually every American to be his own armchair strategist, one would answer in the affirmative. The greatest of the nineteenth- and twentieth-century strategists have been identified with their own particular concept: Mahan with sea power, Douhet with air power, Mao with guerrilla warfare, and the father of modern strategy, Clausewitz, with what has been termed the "continental doctrine."

What we are concerned with here, however, might be better termed grand strategy; we are concerned with the interplay of the total resources of a nation in identifying and achieving an objective. "Strategy," Robert Strausz-Hupé recounted, "is formulated on the basis of an estimate of resources, that is, of power factors."[1] We are concerned with the special relationships, which Clausewitz recognized, among political, economic, diplomatic, military, moral, spiritual, and psychological factors. Of all of these, the least stable, and often the most crucial, is the psychological. Taken with the moral and spiritual, it comprises the national will. In the darkest days of World War II, Churchill offered the British people "blood, sweat and tears." So also Stalin, when it appeared that the German military was invincible, exhorted the Russian people not with Marxist doctrine but rather with extolling "Mother Russia."

Here in the United States the conductor of this interplay of national resources is the President. Certain Presidents have excelled in this regard. President Lincoln was particularly skillful in orchestrating these resources toward the attainment of his primary goal, the preservation of the Union. For example, he needed and sought the psychological factor of a military victory before announcing his Emancipation Proclamation; late in 1862, he found that military posture in the Battle of Antietam. A year later in his memorable Gettysburg Address he used an even more notable victory to eulogize the moral principles of the nation's founding. Beyond this, his second Inaugural Address masterfully set forth a national strategy for the future based upon reconciliation.

As ardent students of history and political science, Presidents Theodore Roosevelt and Woodrow Wilson also recognized this interplay of national resources or "power factors." Franklin D. Roosevelt, a consummate politician, further recognized the relationship of both external and internal political factors and of public opinion in seeking to shape an effective strategy. So also did President Kennedy, acting in the Cuban missile crisis confrontation with the Soviet Union. Concerning that action, Henry A. Kissinger, then a Harvard professor, wrote that Kennedy had "boldly seized an opportunity given few statesmen: to change the course of events by one dramatic move."[2] Such "command decisions" play a profound role in a nation's life, and events such as Washington's crossing the Delaware on Christmas night 1776 are cherished more for their daring than for their military importance. Today, within the constitutional guidelines, there is an ever-increasing commingling of Congressional and Presidential authority, in foreign as well as in domestic affairs. The War Powers Act of 1973 pointed up that commingling. More than that, however, this act, passed during the Watergate crisis, is a severe statutory challenge to Presidential authority. Indeed, it not only fixes timetables for termination of combat operations unless Congress has authorized the engagement, but it also provides Congressional means to countervene orders of the Commander in Chief.

On May 14, 1975, President Ford, in the rescue of the *Mayagüez* and its crew, demonstrated, as Kissinger expressed it, "that initiative creates its own consensus."[3] A nation whose pride had been diminished by the events of Southeast Asia and Watergate, for a fleeting second saw that pride restored. Technically it was in accordance with the War Powers Act, and the President reported to the Congress at the time of the incident: " This operation was ordered and conducted pursuant to the President's constitutional executive power and his authority as Commander in Chief. . . ."[4]

In the course of this volume the "authority as Commander in Chief" is traced from the origins of that office in the Constitutional Convention of 1787 to the present. Particular attention is given to the years 1945–1961, for the basic organization for the conduct of our present national security policy was established during that period; systems of alliances were conceived and forged, and present weapon systems came off the drawing boards. It was also the most productive period for the writing of strategic doctrine. Moreover, the doctrines bearing the names of the two Presidents during those years, Truman and Eisenhower, provided new approaches to foreign policy. As President Ford recently expressed it, in the years since 1961, there have been "changes of course but not of destination."[5]

With the Communist triumph in South Vietnam and Cambodia in the spring of 1975, the United States began an agonizing reappraisal of its national security policy. At this historic juncture it is appropriate both to look back and to look ahead. In the decade of the 1970s, Congress has, by inquiry and by law, sought to define and delimit the parameters of Presidential authority in national security policy.

The full meaning of this Congressional endeavor to delimit the Presidential role in national security policy has, to date, received but little attention. A distinguished exception is Richard E. Neustadt of Harvard, who served as an adviser to President Kennedy on national security affairs during the period of the Cuban missile crisis. Recently Professor Neustadt warned of the dangers in diminishing the President's ability "to function effectively."[6] Dr. Neustadt also served President Truman, who concluded, "I sit here all day trying to persuade people to do the things they ought to have sense enough to do without my persuading them. . . . That's all the powers of the President amount to."[7] Although Truman emphasized the vital importance of command decisions, Neustadt, in his classical study, *Presidential Power,* found this function of Presidential authority limited. "Evidently some commands are effective," Neustadt observed. "Some results can be gained simply by giving orders; some actions do get taken without argument." But, Neustadt concluded, "Command is but a method of persuasion, not a substitute and not a method suitable for everyday employment."[8]

To grasp the meaning of the title of this book, *Command Decision and the Presidency,* one must understand that I share Neustadt's view that the Presidency, far from being imperial, is and always has been of limited authority, or, as he so well expressed it, "Command is but a method of persuasion." Many careful students of the Presidency have, like Neustadt, found Presidential power limited. Perspective on this subject has recently been given by Richard Rose of the University of Strathclyde, Scotland, who finds the American President "a chief but not an executive." As Professor Rose perceives it, it is only in the area of national security policy, "where the President uniquely enjoys the position as Commander in Chief," that Presidents have had "unchallenged authority," that Presidents have, as Rose termed it, actually been engaged in "executing programs."[9]

But this so-called "unchallenged authority" of the Commander in Chief, as Neustadt points out, never did exist except in times of gravest national emergency, as in the Civil War. Moreover, Commander in Chief authority has been severely tried and curtailed since the early 1970s. Such curtailment has not been limited to blocking Presidential actions such as impoundment of funds and exercise of executive privilege in the witholding of information (a privilege which every President from Washington through Nixon had exercised). These have been negative Congressional actions. But Congress, from 1973 to 1976, has also engaged in positive actions. It has legislated unto itself operational authority in the traditional areas of the Commander in Chief. In legislation of dubious constitutionality it has, for example, authorized by joint resolution Congressional withdrawal of troops while engaged in combat and Congressional termination of declarations of national emergency.

It is noteworthy that President Ford in his final State of the Union Address urged the Congress to "re-examine its constitutional role in international affairs. . . . There can be only one commander-in-chief," he asserted. "In these times crises cannot be managed and wars cannot be waged by committee. Nor can peace be pursued solely by parliamentary debate."[10]

Our strongest Presidents have always been zealous guardians of their role as Commander in Chief. This was true of both men to whom this volume is dedicated. Their styles were different. Truman was more assertive; Eisenhower more seeking of Congressional views. "Yet," as Professor Rose has written of Eisenhower, "when his prerogative powers were involved, as in foreign affairs, he was ready to act on his own initiative."[11] President Ford acted in the tradition of both these men, and it was accordingly appropriate as well as a signal honor to invite him to write the Foreword to this book.

This Preface was written just after our nation had completed its bicentennial year. Discounting all the rhetoric, the pessimism of the recent past appears to have been replaced by a rededication and an increased optimism. Moreover, as Herman Kahn has written, "the world seems [now] to be steadily moving into a much more confident and self-assured mood."[12] Indeed, perhaps it is too self-assured in the light of (1) the perilous state of the strategic balance; (2) the enormous Soviet arms and civil defense buildup; (3) the restiveness both in the Soviet Union and its satellites over the human rights issue; and (4) the world's continuing tinderbox areas, including the Korean Peninsula, the Middle East, and southern Africa.

With these mounting perils there is no substitute for strength—economic, military, moral, and spiritual—as the nation, with a new President, charts its course in a competitive, demanding world. As chief diplomat, as Commander in Chief, he must be able to conduct American foreign policy and make his command decisions with the confidence and support of the Congress and the American people.

In his first seven months in office, Jimmy Carter, a President in a hurry, made more than his quota of command decisions, ranging from an announced United States troop withdrawal on the Korean peninsula to two Panama Canal treaties, which would require either Congressional or Senatorial approval for their fulfillment. Only time would tell, for example, whether his controversial decision of June 30, 1977, opposing present production of the B-1 bomber, which surprised the Congressional leadership of his own party, had enhanced or impaired this "confidence and support," the sine qua non for national security.

It is possible that we are entering upon an era which historians may, in retrospect, term "Pax Americana." But in the effort for a more peaceful, secure world, we cannot go it alone. Statesmen of recent date have been referring to a so-called interdependence. Contemplating this, I reread the manuscript, sent to me twenty-five years ago, by the late British statesman Anthony Eden. Eden concluded, regarding the foreign policies of the industrial democracies, "We must be bold and vigilant lest daily cares cloud our longer vision of the task that lies ahead and of the fair fortunes at our command . . . .But this unity, this understanding, this sense of interdependence is the heart of the business. Without it we shall make no headway. With it there is no fair ambition we cannot realize."[13] That "fair ambition" was perhaps best enunciated by Washington in his Farewell Address: ". . . to maintain inviolate the relations of Peace and amity towards other Nations."[14]

R. GORDON HOXIE
New York City
August 15, 1977

FOREWORD

It is appropriate that this volume tracing national security policy from the origins of our nation to the present is dedicated to both Dwight David Eisenhower and Harry S Truman. It was during their Presidencies that the foundations for today's national security policies were established with the Truman Doctrine and the Eisenhower Doctrine.

The period of their Presidencies, 1945–1961, saw both men play key roles in the establishment of a bipartisan foreign policy, the free world's security programs, and organizations such as NATO. This period marked the development of aid to underdeveloped countries as well as military assistance to our allies. Strong personalities loom large in these years: Dean Acheson, George C. Marshall, Douglas MacArthur, Arthur H. Vandenberg, Robert A. Taft, and John Foster Dulles, to name but a few. These are the years in which we trace the origins of the Cold War, marked by such crises as the Berlin airlift and the Korean War. They are the years in which such high-level decisionmaking and information-gathering instruments as the National Security Council and the Central Intelligence Agency were formed. They are the years, characterized by intense interservice rivalry, in which our present defense establishment was consolidated by Truman and reorganized by Eisenhower.

Few persons could differ more in their personalities and in their approach to the high office they occupied than Harry S Truman and Dwight D. Eisenhower. Yet both were characterized by courage, dedication, and integrity. When the mantle of the Presidency came upon Harry Truman, it could not have been a surprise. Roosevelt had been gravely ill. Yet, few other Vice Presidents ever acceded to the Presidency in the face of such enormous problems—especially in the national security area—with so little counsel or direction from their predecessors. Truman sought to fulfill Roosevelt's goals. Yet, assuming the Presidency in the final fast-moving months of World War II, he had to be his own man with little prior orientation. His command decisions were marked by resolution and judgment.

A vigorous President, a student of history, he sought to act as he believed a Jefferson or a Lincoln would have acted, and he must stand in history as one of our most resolute Presidents. His greatest years may have been the period 1947–1950 when, as Gordon Hoxie recounts in this volume, heroic strides were made in the European Recovery Program and in meeting the challenge of Communism throughout the world. Perhaps the differing approach to the Presidency of Harry S Truman and Dwight D. Eisenhower is best characterized by their respective use of the National Security Council. Always on guard for the prerogatives of the Presidential office, Harry Truman at first dealt with the NSC rather reluctantly and at arm's length. On the other hand, believing in the most thorough staff study prior to making command decisions, Eisenhower perfected, like none of his predecessors, this and other staff support in the Presidential office.

Historical judgments of the Eisenhower administration have been consistently and increasingly favorable, though it often seemed in the 1950s that only his public admired his performance in office. Criticism of the Eisenhower years as being a time of unfocused leadership was—and still is—a mistaken assessment of both the man and the era.

Eisenhower was first in his class at the Command and General Staff School, was instrumental in the founding of the Industrial College of the Armed Forces, and was marked early in his military career for major command. General Douglas MacArthur chose him for his personal staff. Those who worked with him found him very bright, tough, and commanding. But Ike liked to put it in softer language:

> Leadership is a word and a concept that has been more argued than almost any other I know. I am not one of the desk-pounding type that likes to stick out his jaw and look like he is bossing the show. I would far rather get behind and,

> recognizing the frailties and the requirements of human na-
> ture, I would rather try to persuade a man to go along—
> because once I have persuaded him, he will stick. If I scare
> him, he will stay just as long as he is scared, and then he is
> gone.[1]

Another source of misunderstanding that few of his critics realized was that the habits of a lifetime in the military had given President Eisenhower a military concept of organization. He used it extensively. He delegated authority and trusted the judgment of his subordinates—leaving him precious time to scan the broader horizons of national and international policy, to look further down the road, to think, to plan, to lead.

This book provides valuable insights into command decisions in the national security area in the 1945–1961 period. Truman's White House years were, as he titled his writings about those days, "Years of Trial and Hope," while those of Eisenhower were aptly termed "Waging Peace." This book is another volume that will contribute to setting right the proper image of both Harry S Truman and Dwight D. Eisenhower.

Beyond that, however, Gordon Hoxie has identified constitutional issues which concerned me during my Presidency and which continue to concern me as a private citizen. The first dozen years of the national experience pointed to the need for a strong executive, particularly as related to foreign policy and national security affairs. That is why the framers of the Constitution made the President both the nation's chief diplomat and its Commander in Chief. With characteristic candor President Truman declared, "I make American foreign policy,"[2] echoing President Jefferson's claim that the conduct of foreign affairs is "executive altogether."[3]

Both are overstatements. Congress has a constitutional responsibility to shape foreign policy, and as I said in my third State of the Union Message, that responsibility "should be jealously guarded." Nonetheless, the responsibilities of the Commander in Chief are indivisible. Furthermore, once a foreign policy is arrived at, the world listens for one clear voice to enunciate it. As I stated in my 1977 State of the Union Message, the President "and his emissaries must not be handicapped in advance in their relations with foreign governments as has sometimes happened in the past."

It seems to me, and I am glad that Gordon Hoxie's study points this up, that in the last few years the Congress has become too minutely involved in the day-by-day operation of foreign policy, that bipartisanship in foreign policy is fast becoming a relic of the past. Moreover, I do question the constitutionality of any legislation authorizing the Congress, by joint resolution, to direct the withdrawal of the armed forces of the United States while engaged in combat or to terminate a declaration of national emergency. As I put it in my State of the Union Message, "There can be only one Commander in Chief."

I am glad to see the concern of this volume for a clear enunciation of national goals, purpose, and strategy, for a definition of areas critical to the maintenance of peace, of a concern for both East-West and North-South relationships, and for our particular relations with the other industrial democracies and the developing nations. Peace through strength remains our national goal. It is the special responsibility of the President as Commander in Chief to see that we remain strong. That is why in my two and one-half years as President, I set high priority on reversing the decade-long trend toward lower and lower rates of military spending.

Recognizing the dramatic buildup of Soviet armed forces, the Congress supported my recommendations to arrest the dangerous downturn in our defense effort. The strategic balance must never tilt against the United States and our allies. We must maintain the capability and the determination to negotiate from strength. Looking to our nation's security in the next decade, I have advocated land, sea, and air missile launching systems: the Trident submarine, the B-1 bomber, and a more advanced intercontinental ballistic missile. Indispensable as these strategic nuclear forces are, we must have air, ground, and sea conventional forces prepared, with our NATO and other allies, to repel any nonnuclear regional attack.

As President and as Commander in Chief I have also been concerned with securing a comprehensive program to preclude the worldwide spread of nuclear weapons. Early in his first administration, President Eisenhower announced his statesmanlike Atoms for Peace program, to be conducted under the auspices of the United Nations. Later, the United States began to export its nuclear technology unilaterally for peaceful purposes. Ominous recent developments, including the 1973 oil crisis and the 1974 nuclear test in India, which exhibited for the first time the dramatic misuse of nuclear material supplied for civil purposes, prompted me to take swift corrective action. First, I proposed to the United Nations General Assembly stronger safeguards against explosive utilization of nuclear exports. Second, I initiated a conference of nuclear suppliers in London, which developed a set of principles governing such exports. Third, I ordered a comprehensive policy review from which, on October 28, 1976, I announced major steps to inhibit the spread of nuclear weapons. These included immediate termination of United States' nuclear assistance for violators. The faithful adherence to these principles can ensure that our nuclear capacity remains the fulfillment of a promising dream—not a threatening nightmare.

Finally, I am glad that this volume concludes on a moral and a spiritual note, for in this realm is found the sustaining strength of a free people. President Eisenhower said it best: "America is not good because it is great. America is great because it is good."

GERALD R. FORD
Palm Springs, California
August 22, 1977

"There can be only one Commander in Chief."

President Gerald Ford's
State of the Union Message,
January 12, 1977

PART ONE

****

THROUGH THE TRUMAN YEARS

I
****

CONGRESS AND THE PRESIDENCY

> ... of all the President's functions that of Commander in Chief has grown the most in importance and in its demands upon the incumbent.
> HARRY S TRUMAN

> A nation's global policy comprises the world wide objectives of the government and the basic methods and programs developed for achieving them.
> DWIGHT D. EISENHOWER

> We must achieve a rational division of labor between Congress' defining of broad national commitments and the Executive's constitutional responsibility for tactics, the execution of policy, and the conduct of negotiations.
> HENRY A. KISSINGER, *November 24, 1975*

In the Beginning

The United States, in its bicentennial year, stood at an historic crossroads. Through the years, the relationship between the Congress and the Presidency has involved an ebbing and flowing of authority. The gravity of national emergency in the Civil War brought a short-lived Presidential domination. Only in the twentieth century, with the emergence of the United States as a world power under the assertive Presidency of Theodore Roosevelt, was Presidential primacy in foreign affairs—or in national security policy, as it is more generally termed in this book––again reaffirmed. This Presidential dominance from 1901 to 1919 was, with the rejection of Woodrow Wilson's foreign policies (notably the League of Nations), to be followed by twenty years of Congressional domination, 1919–1939, in the spirit of isolationism.

Again, a grave emergency, the advent of World War II in 1939, inaugurated a period of Presidential dominance that extended until 1973. During the last six years of that period, when President Lyndon B. Johnson's role as Commander in Chief came under increasing attack, the pressures for Congressional supremacy mounted. In 1973 the Nixon administration became discredited, and after this explosion, the very real question for Nixon's successor, Gerald R. Ford, was whether the Presidency still had enough primacy in national security policy to meet the perils of a superpower in a nuclear age.

The foundations for our present national security policies and the organization for their implementation were essentially the work of the Truman and Eisenhower administrations and Congresses with which they worked from 1945 to 1961. What they accomplished should be instructive today as the nation and its policymakers face an uncertain future. While this book traces national security policy and organization from the beginnings of our nation through the beginning of the Carter administration, greatest attention is given to the Truman-Eisenhower years.

The American nation was born without a chief executive and commander in chief. Under the Articles of Confederation, Congress exercised limited executive and legislative functions in a loose confederation of states—a parliamentary form of government of sorts, but without a prime minister. By the grace of God, the resoluteness of General George Washington, the diplomatic skill of Benjamin Franklin, and the help of the French, the bold foreign policy enunciated in Thomas Jefferson's Declaration of Independence was successfully consummated in the Treaty of Paris of 1783, which recognized the United States of America as an independent nation.

By 1787 it was apparent that if these United States were to survive as a nation, they must, as the Preamble to the Constitution set forth, not only "form a more perfect union" but also "provide for the common defence...." They would need to delegate more authority to a central government and a strong chief executive. In the Constitutional Convention they created an unprecedented office: a head of state called, for the first time, the "President." Actually, they created two presidencies, a president for domestic affairs and a president for foreign affairs, who would exercise his direction in foreign affairs as three chiefs: as chief of state, as chief diplomat, and as commander in chief.

The founding fathers had waged a war against three tyrannies: a tyranny of kings, a tyranny of courts, and a tyranny of parliaments; now they determined to check and balance their creations: their Congress, their Courts, and their President. Also they emphasized that the federal principle of powers not granted to the federal government were reserved to the states and to the people. Only in external affairs was the federal government to be dominant. In that area no branch of government would have exclusive authority. Thus they established an admixture in foreign and national security policy as Constitution framers.

The President was designated in Article II, Section 2, as the "commander in chief of the army and navy of the United States, and of the militia of the several states, when called into the actual service of the United States. . . ." As Samuel P. Huntington has pointed out, this clause is more than a nice distinction: it is "unique in the Constitution in granting authority in the form of an *office* rather than in the form of a *function.*"[1] Rather than having the President carry out defined duties of commanding the armed forces, the Constitution created for the President an office, a position, of undefined and thereby expandable authority. But by Article I, Section 8, it was the Congress, not the President, that was to "provide for the common defence" and was therefore empowered "to declare war . . . ; to raise and support armies . . . ; to provide and maintain a navy . . . ; [and] to provide for calling forth the militia to execute the laws of the Union. . . ." Moreover, in herently distrustful of standing armies—since they had occupied certain American cities from 1765 until independence had been achieved—the constitutional fathers limited specific appropriation acts for the armed services to two years. The initiation of all such acts, as with all other appropriation bills, was to be lodged in the House of Representatives.

According to Article II, Section 3, the President, as chief diplomat, was to "receive ambassadors and other public ministers. . . ." By the same section, he was to "commission all the officers [both civilian and military] of the United States." But the preceding section made clear that such commissions and the appointment of "ambassadors, other public ministers and consuls," would be "with the advice and consent of the Senate. . . ." The Congress would exercise its discretion in designating, from time to time, lesser officers whom "the President alone," the courts, or "the heads of departments" might appoint.

The Congress, under Article I, Section 8, was "to regulate commerce with foreign nations. . . ." Arthur M. Schlesinger, Jr., has speciously argued that Washington's emphasis in his 1796 Farewell Address on "extending our commercial relations . . . with . . . as little political connections as possible" signified Congressional primacy in foreign relations.[2] Washington's counsel of commercial rather than political connections with foreign states was related more to his determination to steer a neutral course in the Anglo-French War than it was a reflection of the view of the constitutional fathers ten years before. Moreover, the Farewell Address was principally written for Washington by Hamilton, who more than any other person advanced the concept of a strong Presidency.

Finally, while the President, under Article II, Section 2, was empowered "to make treaties," it was to be "by and with the advice and consent of the Senate" and with the proviso that "two-thirds of the Senators present concur." Taking the Constitution literally, early in his first term President Washington entered the Senate chamber to seek advice about a treaty with the Southern Indian tribes. The Senators frostily made clear to the President that his presence was not required for their deliberations. According to Senator William Maclay, Washington then withdrew "with sullen dignity."[3] Never again did a President so seek Senatorial advice.

The reaction Washington experienced provided early encouragement to alternative arrangements to treaties in foreign relations. Stemming from both the commander in chief role and the chief diplomat role, these were to take the form of executive agreement. All Presidents have on their own authority entered upon executive agreements. These have included surrenders and armistices and such historic agreements as that of 1817 demilitarizing the Great Lakes (Rush-Bagot) and the Boxer Protocol of 1900 providing indemnities and exacting guarantees following the Boxer uprising in China.

With the passage of time, executive agreements were increasingly utilized, especially in the World War II and post–World War II eras. They were rationalized in terms of both secrecy and dispatch. Nonetheless Congressional concern over executive agreements has been manifested on several occasions in our national history, most especially in the 1966–1976 decade.

Just as there were early alternatives to the Senate's treaty-making role, so also alternatives early became operative for Congress to declare war. Commencing with Adams, in the undeclared naval war of 1798–1800 with France, Presidents have taken the view that if a *casus belli* existed, they would respond with force in their role as Commander in Chief. It was thus that fame came to *The Constitution*, "Old Ironsides," when it destroyed the French *L' Insurgente*. Jefferson, not a party to the Constitutional Convention or ratification, distrusted the authority given the President. As the nominal first Secretary of State (when, in fact, the first Secretary of the Treasury, Hamilton, was virtually Washington's prime minister in both foreign and domestic affairs), Jefferson was aghast at Hamilton's views of Presidential primacy in treatymaking and warmaking. During the debate over Washington's 1793 proclamation of neutrality in the war between Britain and France, Jefferson entreated Madison to respond to Hamilton's views: "For God's sake, my dear Sir, take up your pen, select the most striking heresies and cut him to pieces in face of the public."[4] Similarly, he applauded James Monroe's *View of the Conduct of the Executive of the United States*, published in 1797, because it revealed "the duplicity of the administration here."[5] In a paper that I delivered in 1974 at the National Archives, I recalled the admirable stoicism of Washington, whom Byron termed "the Cincinnatus of the West":

> So long as he was in office, Washington, despite the abusive attacks, believed that he should preserve the confidentiality of conversations with his advisors and of his official correspondence. Accordingly, he exercised great restraint in not personally responding to such criticisms. However, he clearly valued the verdict of history which the Presidential papers would provide. Hence he took them with him to Mount Vernon, as well as lesser impedimenta and such animate objects as a dog and a parrot.[6]

Recollecting how Washington "in his second term was reviled and belittled," former President Dwight D. Eisenhower, in 1968, when President Lyndon Johnson was under great pressure, especially for his Commander in Chief role, concluded that no President "since [Washington] has escaped." Philosophically, this most popular of our post–World War II Presidents added, "By the very nature of the Presidency any one occupying the position becomes a controversial figure."[7]

Jefferson lavishly criticized Washington's and Adams's foreign policies, but he had no hesitation in far exceeding Congressional advice in the Louisiana Purchase treaty or in engaging in covert operations seeking to overthrow (in Tripoli) a head of state. Nor did he hesitate to refuse to expend funds appropriated by the Congress for the buildup of the Navy, thereby commencing a tradition of Presidential impoundment. Jefferson's frugality in building small gunboats instead of the proud frigates of the *Constitution* class inspired a special toast from his Federalist critics. When one gunboat was washed into a cornfield during a severe storm, a Federalist wag declared, "Here's to Jefferson's navy. First on land, if not on the sea." Using the Federalist-built frigates, Jefferson had no trepidations about waging an undeclared punitive war (1801–1805) against the Barbary pirates; nor did his successor, Madison, in the Second Barbary War (1815). Nor did his, Monroe, in sending Andrew Jackson into Spanish Florida in 1818 to chastise marauders on the Georgia frontier. The Mexican-American clashes of 1914–1917 were also undeclared, when President Wilson sent General John J. Pershing's command into Mexico in search of the elusive Pancho Villa.

John Adams, Jefferson, Madison, Monroe, and Wilson acted in accordance with the Hamiltonian conception that the Constitution intends "that it is the peculiar and exclusive province of Congress, when the nation is at peace, to change that state into a state of war," but, "when a foreign nation declares or openly and avowedly makes war upon the United States, they are then by the very fact already at war and any declaration on the part of Congress is nugatory...." Under such circumstances, Hamilton concluded, "it is at least unnecessary."[8]

Polk took a Hamiltonian view in 1846 in the war with Mexico. He ordered Brigadier General Zachary Taylor into disputed territory along the Rio Grande, then asked the Congress, when Taylor's forces were attacked, *not* to declare war, but rather to recognize the *existence* of war "by the act of the Republic of Mexico."[9] Former President John Quincy Adams, serving in the Congress, endeavored to make a distinction between Congressional *recognition* of war and a *declaration* of war. Emotionally aroused, the Congress voted overwhelmingly as Polk had asked. "It is now established as an irreversible precedent," Adams warned, "that the President of the United States has but to declare that War exists, with any Nation upon Earth, by the act of that Nation's Government, and the War is essentially declared."[10]

One of the fourteen Congressmen who had voted against the resolution was the then little-known Abraham Lincoln, who introduced his "spot" resolution, demanding to know where on American soil American blood had been shed. Writing to his law partner, W. H. Herndon, Lincoln warned against Presidential preemptive as well as defensive war action. Using an absurd example, the danger that Britain would invade the United States, Lincoln complained to Herndon, "You may say to him [the President], 'I see no probability of the British invading us', but he will say to you 'be silent; I see it, if you don't.'"[11]

But if Jefferson and Polk expanded their conception of Presidential authority upon assuming office, Lincoln went further. Confronted by secession, he acted decisively and immediately in his *office* as Commander in Chief to suppress the rebellion by the armed forces, and he augmented that force by a call for volunteers. Further, like Hamilton had suggested to Washington at the time of the Whisky Rebellion, he acted, as he interpreted it, under his authority as contained in Article II, Section 3: ". . . he shall take care that the laws be faithfully executed. . . ." In the twelve weeks between the firing on Fort Sumter and the convening of Congress in special session on July 14, 1861, Lincoln enlarged the armed forces, directed their deployment against the Confederate forces, and ordered a blockade of southern ports. He even suspended the writ of habeas corpus (the constitutional protection of the citizenry against arbitrary arrest) for persons engaged in or contemplating "treasonable practices." Lincoln later invited the Congress to "ratify" his actions, which it did, recognizing not merely his primacy but his supremacy in the grave national emergency.

Lincoln, more than any other President, advanced the authority of the office of President and the office of Commander in Chief. Long before he assumed those offices, Congress had accepted, if it had not become reconciled to, Presidential primacy in foreign and national security policy. Although, as a federal circuit court member and as Chief Justice, John Marshall was subsequently to challenge areas of Presidential authority, his opinion as Congressman in 1800 was generally accepted: that the President is "the sole organ of the nation in its external relations, and its sole representative with foreign nations."[12]

Reechoing that sentiment 136 years later in *U.S.* v. *Curtiss-Wright Corporation*, the Supreme Court held that, by contrast with domestic affairs, the Presidency had primacy in external affairs as "necessary concomitants of sovereignty." In this 1936 opinion, the Court, under Chief Justice Charles Evans Hughes (Secretary of State under Harding and Coolidge), further opined that "premature disclosure" to the Congress of delicate international negotiations could be productive of harmful results." In this opinion written by Justice George Sutherland, long before the advent of the CIA, the Court declared that the President "not the Congress has the better opportunity of knowing the conditions which prevail in foreign countries. . . ."[13]

World War II, the Cold War, and Presidential Primacy

Franklin D. Roosevelt won his 1932 Presidential election and his 1936 reelection by landslide margins, with overwhelming majorities for his own party in the Congress. Nevertheless, he was painfully aware that in a democracy the President can exceed or be out ahead of public opinion in the area of foreign policy only to a limited extent. By nature and philosophy an internationalist, he was seemingly hapless in the isolationist sentiment rampant in the United States in the mid-1930s. His biographer, James MacGregor Burns, regretfully concludes, "At this crucial juncture Roosevelt offered little leadership."[14]

The result was that Congress tied the hands of the President with the Neutrality Act of 1935. Not until well after the outbreak of the war in Europe and the fall of Poland did Roosevelt denounce the act. Even then he acted cautiously, looking to William Allen White's "Non-partisan Committee for Peace Through Revision of the Neutrality Law" to lead public opinion.[15] With the swing in public opinion led by the Republican "nonpartisan" sage of Emporia, Roosevelt acted skillfully in establishing bipartisanship in foreign policy for the first time. In 1940 he named Republicans to two key defense posts: Frank Knox, Landon's 1936 Vice Presidential running mate and the publisher of the Chicago *Daily News,* as Secretary of the Navy, and Henry L. Stimson, Taft's Secretary of War and Hoover's Secretary of State, as Secretary of the War Department (Army).

That same year Roosevelt began to enter upon a bold series of executive agreements. He turned over fifty old United States destroyers to the hard-pressed British in exchange for the right to lease (that is, defend) British bases in Newfoundland, British Guiana, and several Caribbean islands. Roosevelt promptly reported the contents of all these agreements to the Congress, although it is doubtful whether the Senate would have sanctioned them if they had been entered upon as treaties. It was not until the Yalta Conference that Roosevelt, in the last three months of his life, entered upon certain secret agreements which he did not disclose to the Congress.

What Alexander Hamilton, John Marshall, and other Federalists had viewed in the eighteenth century as the necessities for Presidential primacy in national security policy appeared the more self-evident 150 years later, as the United States became a world leader in a nuclear age. "I don't want some young colonel to drop an atomic bomb," President Truman insisted.[16] With the President as the only person who could give the awesome order to release nuclear weapons, who else could direct national security policy? This was the pragmatic question the nation faced at the end of World War II. In a sense it began six years before, when Albert Einstein and Alexander Sachs advised Roosevelt of the horrendous power of nuclear fission. Sachs had further advised of the ominous research in that field in Nazi Germany. The Manhattan Project then became a race to beat Germany in producing the ultimate weapon, the nuclear bomb.

The United States emerged from World War II with nuclear and economic strength. Every other major power in the world was economically prostrate. The United States alone had the economic resources for world rebuilding, and the United States alone possessed the ultimate weapon. What then went wrong in the long path of frustrations commencing with Poland in 1945 and culminating with Vietnam in 1975? What led to the relative decline of American power and prestige?

It is now quite clear that we could not rebuild the world in our own image. It is now popular to find the wrong turn at Yalta, where in February of 1945 three of the most remarkable leaders of modern history, Winston Churchill, Joseph Stalin, and Franklin Roosevelt, came together. With the war nearing an end, Roosevelt had both a pragmatic and an idealistic view. He shared the view of his military advisers that it was crucial to bring Russia into the war against Japan. Beyond the war he looked to his ideal, the United Nations, through which he would work with his wartime allies in building a peaceful world—an ideal not unlike that of Wilson in his League of Nations. But Roosevelt had not reckoned with the irrevocable determination of the tough and wily Stalin, and Roosevelt would not be around to deal with him. On the day of his death three months later, he suggested that the spirit of Yalta was being betrayed by the Soviets. Nonetheless, he counseled Churchill to "minimize the general Soviet problems as much as possible, because these problems, in one form or another, seem to arise every day and most of them straighten out. . . ."[17]

What Roosevelt did not reckon with was the basic distrust, fear, ingrained sense of inferiority, and suspicion of the Soviets. When Churchill and Roosevelt talked about free elections for Poland, part of the Yalta agreement, Stalin could not fathom the meaning: he had been born a peasant with no Western Democratic experience. More than that, like the Czars who had preceded Lenin and himself, he sought to secure Russia's western boundaries, the historic invasion route, by the control of eastern Europe. The Russian armies occupied these territories, and Stalin did not intend to give them up. Roosevelt's successor, Harry S Truman, and his advisers never comprehended this. At Yalta, Stalin demanded, among other things, what the Czars had also sought: warm-water ports (Darien and Port Arthur) at the end of the Trans-Siberian railroad. In turn, Stalin would not only enter the war against Japan but also pledge support to Chiang's China.

Five months after Yalta the world looked much different. Japan was about to surrender, and the atom bomb, which had earlier been viewed as a tactical weapon to help in the invasion of Japan, would now instead be the coup de grace. Russia was anxious to get in before it was over, and Truman and the United States wanted no part of it. There would be no repetition of the European experience in the occupation of Japan, and Truman had already determined that General Douglas MacArthur would play a large role.

At war's end, with pressures at home to immediately demobilize the most powerful military force in history, there was a precarious balance between the United States atomic bomb and the Red Army. The bomb might destroy Russian population centers, but the Russians could overrun western Europe. As long as the Reds had a massive army, the United States would be distrustful. As long as the United States had the nuclear bomb and they did not, the Soviets would be distrustful. Henry L. Stimson, culminating a remarkable career of public service under four Presidents, proposed a bold solution to this dilemma. He recognized the vast difference between Soviet autocracy and American democracy. "I believe that the change in attitude towards the individual in Russia will come slowly and gradually," he wrote President Truman, "and I am satisfied that we should not delay our approach to Russia in the matter of the atomic bomb until that process has been completed."[18]

But the proposal for United Nations control of atomic energy, as developed by the Truman administration (even when served up by the park-bench sage Bernard Baruch), was bound to be unacceptable to the Soviets. That the United States would not give up its stockpile of bombs was understandable. On the other hand, the War Department correctly estimated that the Soviets making this demand would never submit to unrestricted inspection or waiving the veto against penalties for violations of the prohibition of nuclear weapon production. Only with these provisions would the United States eventually destroy its stockpile. In this posture President Truman had the counsel of Dwight D. Eisenhower, then serving as the Army Chief of Staff. "If we enter too hurriedly into an international agreement to abolish all atomic weapons," Eisenhower warned, "we may find ourselves in the position of having no restraining means in the world capable of effective action if a great power violates the agreement."[19]

Stimson had been right in his prediction that inevitably, whether it was five or twenty years, the Soviets would develop the know-how for the bomb. The time span was foreshortened to four years by espionage. In the interim, Stimson speculated, "relations may be perhaps irretrievably embittered."[20] This posted difficult command decisions for Truman and Eisenhower.

If the bomb did not thwart the aggressive Soviet foreign policy, neither did the promise of economic aid, either at war's end or three years later in the Marshall Plan. A tough protagonist, Stalin grimly determined that the Russian people should go it their own way, with their own Five-Year Plan, augmented by such reparations and loot as they could exact from the occupied areas and the wartime axis, Germany, Italy, and Japan.

Did the United States have a national strategy for the post–World War II era? Although its diplomacy was to be dominated by economics and the bomb, there was, prior to 1949, no comprehensive national strategy. Universal Military Training (UMT) kept popping up during this period, but it was no strategy. Besides, as General Alfred Gruenther pointed out, UMT was no answer for the Red Army, which could complete the occupation of Europe before such a reserve force could be in position.[21] America in these postwar years was groping for a strategy of deterrence to complement a policy of containment.

The Truman Doctrine and the Marshall Plan have a masterful tone, although they were *regional,* not comprehensive, programs. The very term "containment," when it was first enunciated by George F. Kennan in 1947, was imprecise and vague. Later Kennan was increasingly embittered as the emphasis went increasingly from economic to military assistance. What then was the "counterforce" of which Kennan wrote? Was it simply a mystical belief in the eventual triumph of democratic institutions? Where and how was this counterforce applied? Quite correctly, Walter Lippmann observed that it could lead to a "strategic monstrosity."[22] Moreover, although Kennan is viewed almost as a prophet by many contemporary Congressional critics of Presidential conduct of foreign policy, they overlook his 1947 pronouncement, in which he ignored the duality in our Constitutional system: the role of Congress as well as that of the executive branch in foreign policy.

Not until the eve of the Korean War did the nation have its first comprehensive formalized national security statement of worldwide policy and strategy. National Security Council Memorandum Number 68—NSC-68, as it was termed—was merely being considered by President Truman at the time of the North Korean attack. Without that attack, the worldwide policy of countering Communist imperialism with something approaching an adequate military posture would probably never have occurred. Even so, with the exception of the Korean War years, the military budgets of the 1950s, almost as much as the first five years after World War II, were characterized by severe economic constraint.

Changes in the national view were far more significant than budgetary increases. The role was thrust upon us and reluctantly accepted, but there has been a virtual revolution in American foreign policy when contrasted with the isolationism of the 1930s. When, on the eve of World War II, President Roosevelt suggested that our first line of defense might be the Rhine, it aroused a furor in an isolationist-minded Congress and public. Twenty years later most Americans agreed with President Eisenhower that our defense lines did, indeed, extend from the Mekong to the Elbe to the Tigris-Euphrates Valley. Only the frustrating, protracted war around the Mekong caused second thoughts on the part of many concerning such parameters of interest.

The loss of Congressional power in national security policy has been a phenomenon not so much of World War II as it has been of the post–World War II nuclear age. As late as 1945, General George C. Marshall, as Army Chief of Staff, was pleading with the Congress regarding force levels. Beginning in 1947, however, with the passage of the National Security Act, which was followed by several amendments, a rapid evolution began. Both the formulation and the virtual authorization of military programs passed to the several instrumentalities of that Act: the National Security Council, the Secretary of Defense, and the Joint Chiefs of Staff. This is not to say that the successors to Marshall, Eisenhower, and the other service chiefs gave up their importunate visits, hat in hand, to Capitol Hill, or to the Budget Bureau (since 1971 the Office of Management and Budget), or indeed to the White House. But the National Security Act of 1947 and its amendments established the framework for the essential decisions on building, maintaining, and modernizing a nuclear retaliatory force; on designing and updating the continental defense system; on creating a body of doctrine and forces for limited war; and on total force levels, as well as on formulating national strategy policies.

Likewise, during this period the vital decisions on Berlin, Korea, Taiwan, Lebanon, and Indochina all came from the executive branch. An assessment of such facts caused one distinguished scholar to conclude in 1961: "The military and diplomatic conditions of the mid-twentieth century made obsolete the Congressional declaration of war." Indeed, Samuel P. Huntington (then from Columbia University's Institute of War and Peace Studies, subsequently Frank G. Thomson Professor of Government at Harvard) concluded: "In a small scale intervention or limited war a congressional declaration was unnecessary and undesirable; in a general war it would in all probability be impossible."[23]

The critical watershed in Congressional-Presidential relations, however, occurred more than two decades before the War Powers Act, in two 1950–1951 initiations of the Truman administration. The first of these two unprecedented actions of the Commander in Chief was the deployment of United Nations Armed Forces to the Korean Peninsula and their engagement there in the first full-scale United States war without a Congressional declaration. It was also the first war conducted by a multinational peacekeeping organization, the United Nations. The President found his authority under Article XLIII of the United Nations Charter. During the conflict—a "police action," as he termed it—the President served as Commander in Chief not only of the United States forces but of all the United Nations forces engaged, since he was serving as the executive agent for the United Nations.

The second unprecedented action was the deployment, again without Congressional action, of United States armed forces to Europe in early 1951 to form the military foundation for NATO. Since the first Supreme Allied Powers Commander Europe (SACEUR), Dwight D. Eisenhower, was an American nominated by the President (as has been each succeeding SACEUR), this has been an extension of the Presidential Commander in Chief role. Although not without precedent, the President's third watershed act of 1950–1951 was his declaration of a state of national emergency.

Looking back on this accretion of power, particularly
through the Commander in Chief role, the late Clinton Rossiter observed in his classic work *The American Presidency:*
"We have placed a shocking amount of military power in the
President's keeping, but where else . . . could it possibly have
been placed?"[24]

Writing in a similar vein in the *Cornell Law Review* in the fall
of 1961, Senator J. W. Fulbright declared, ". . . for the existing requirements of American foreign policy we have hobbled the President by too niggardly a grant of power. . . ."[25]
How different things would look to Senator Fulbright in a
few years.

Congress vs. the Presidency

With but few notable exceptions, Congress during the
twenty-year period 1945–1965 rarely challenged Presidential
primacy in foreign relations. Three times during this period,
first in 1947 and again in 1959–1962 and in 1962–1965, Congress studied these issues and concluded that the President
should be more vigorous in his pursuit of foreign policy objectives. Indeed, when a brave young President was inaugurated in 1961, both Truman and Eisenhower were being
criticized for lack of initiative regarding national security
proposals and for failure to arouse public concern and support in a critical nuclear age. The Congress and the public
were caught up in the inspiring rhetoric of the Kennedy
inaugural: "We shall pay any price, bear any burden, meet
any hardship, support any friend, oppose any foe to assure
the survival and the success of liberty." Fourteen years later,
on the eve of our national bicentennial, we were talking
about "selected responsibilities." And we were doing so in
an atmosphere which seemed to be rejecting our Presidential
system. Only a few persons were asking the troublesome
question: Who will determine these "selected responsibilities"?[26] Only a few of Congressman John B. Anderson's
colleagues recognized with him that there is danger "of executive emasculation in the present mood."[27]

How did this complete reversal come about? Adolf A.

Berle, by scholarship, study, and experience one of the soundest students of the Presidency, examined the dilemma in
some detail in 1970, a year before his death. Contrary to the
prevalent view of the time, Berle, who had been one of
Roosevelt's closest advisers, a member of the so-called Brain
Trust, as well as a longtime professor of public law at Columbia University,[28] concluded that "the rumpus kicked up
was not because the Presidents in question misused their
powers. It was," Berle declared, "because they used their
powers legitimately to act and achieve objectives their critics
did not want."[29]

Senator Fulbright, as chairman of the Senate Foreign Relations Committee, completely differed with Dr. Berle's
view—and, indeed, his own view of ten years before. Speaking more like a professor than had Professor Berle, Fulbright,
the former Rhodes scholar, enjoyed lecturing his Senatorial
colleagues. Thus, in addressing the Senate during the Nixon
administration, he looked back studiously on the Commander in Chief roles of Roosevelt, Truman, Eisenhower,
Kennedy, and Johnson. He was a bit concerned with
Eisenhower, who had "reigned with paternal benignancy"
and with "the Kennedys . . . on white chargers with promises of Camelot," but he was more disturbed by the
Roosevelt, Truman, and Johnson uses of the Commander in
Chief role: Roosevelt had in 1941 "circumvented the war
power of the Congress—by engaging in an undeclared naval
war in the Atlantic. . . ." He found "FDR's deviousness in a
good cause made it much easier for LBJ to practice the same
kind of deviousness in a bad cause" (Southeast Asia). But it
was the Truman roles of 1950–1951, and the never to be
forgotten admonition of his Secretary of State, Dean Acheson, to the Senate that they should not be quibbling about
"who has the power to do this, that, or the other thing" that
in retrospect worked Fulbright up to his finest prose about
the President's "vainglorious role as Commander in
Chief. . . ." Should such be the case, he told his Senatorial
colleagues, "we are all about as secure as gazelles in a tiger
cage; our only hope," Fulbright concluded, "is that the tiger
may not be hungry at the moment."[30]

Listening to Fulbright's persuasive oratory, veteran observer Thomas G. Corcoran, the "Tommy the Cork" of early New Deal fame, noted, "Fulbright is trying to re-establish that relationship between the Foreign Relations Committee of the Senate . . . and the Presidency that . . . Borah achieved when he took on Wilson—which Roosevelt reversed."[31] Truman's Congressional critics' efforts to "re-establish that relationship" in the midst of the Korean War had been feeble and ineffective. Recalling the ineffectual policies of Congressional hegemony in national security policy during the 1919–1939 period, neither the Congress nor the President wanted a return.

Chairman of the Senate Foreign Relations Committee, Tom Connally, voiced the majority view when he responded to Senator Taft's challenge to the President's authority in sending troops to NATO: "The authority of the President as Commander in Chief to send the Armed Forces to any place required by the security interests of the United States has often been questioned," Connally acknowledged, "but never denied by authoritative opinion."[32] The Senate resolution in 1951 approved Truman's having sent the four divisions, but did state that no others should be sent "without further Congressional approval." This mild challenge, led by Taft, has never been tested, since the United States force level in NATO has not since been significantly raised.

Truman's more severe challenge came a year later in the steel mill seizure, when Justice Jackson referred to "a zone of twilight in which [the President] and the Congress may have concurrent authority, or in which its distribution is uncertain."[33]

Truman's successor, Eisenhower, scarcely recognized for the consummate politician that he was, perceptively insisted that military excursions be by joint Congressional and Presidential authority. When Eisenhower asked Congress for authority to use the armed forces, if need be, to defend Formosa and the Pescadores, the Congress agreeably added the phrase "as he deems necessary." In this instance Senator Fulbright arose to express his concern lest any Congressional resolution might tend to reduce the President's powers as Commander in Chief to defend the "vested interests" of the nation.[34] In like manner, in a plea for the Senate to get back to its concern for basic principles, this "earlier" Fulbright lamented that "we have tended to snoop and pry in matters of detail, interfering in the handling of specific problems in specific places. . . ."[35]

In the instance of the 1955 Formosa resolution, which Eisenhower had requested, Speaker Sam Rayburn of the House avowed, "If the President had done what is proposed here without consulting the Congress, he would have had no criticism from me."[36]

During the same period, without raising a ripple of protest, Eisenhower used the CIA to help overthrow a pro-Communist government in Iran (1953) and to install the present Shah. The following year the CIA at Eisenhower's direction did the same thing in Guatemala. In such operations Allan Dulles, director of the CIA, worked closely both with his brother, Secretary of State John Foster Dulles, and with the President. Indeed, in both the Truman and the Eisenhower administrations the CIA played its most constructive, effective, and influential advisory role—in contrast to its role in subsequent administrations.

Further, unlike their successors, Sidney Souers, Robert Cutler, and Gordon Gray, as President Truman's and President Eisenhower's Assistants for National Security Affairs, acted most ably in seeking out the broadest and soundest areas of advice for the President. Although they may not have had the foreign policy experience of McGeorge Bundy, Walt Rostow, and Henry Kissinger, they served their Presidents well and not with a highly personalized advisory system.

One of the hallmarks of success of both Truman and Eisenhower in handling national security affairs was in their own commonsense approach to problems and their adherence to principles. Unlike Johnson, who as a politician was always seeking a consensus, which increasingly eluded him, Truman, somewhat stubbornly, and Eisenhower, more skillfully, adhered to their principles. Moreover, unlike Kennedy and Nixon, both Truman and Eisenhower had to work their way up through lower and middle levels of management. This gave them an understanding both of problems and of people and of the relations between the two. Unlike Ken-

nedy and Nixon, neither Truman nor Eisenhower was vulnerable to eager and persuasive but young and inexperi-
enced advisers. Each in his own way had been around and
was not readily susceptible to flattery. They gathered about
them mature men of judgment in national security matters:
Acheson, Marshall, Lovett, the Dulles brothers, and Admiral
Radford.

Eisenhower made the most significant effort of any
modern President to restore the active advisory role of the
President's Cabinet. A student of history, he recalled that in
1793 Washington had called the Cabinet into being from
among his executive department heads to deliberate and
give him their best advice on the crisis arising over America's
neutral course in the Franco-British War. Eisenhower's efforts to restore the importance of the Cabinet met with some
success. As long as he was President, the pyramidal structure going up to the President through the executive departments continued. His successor, Kennedy, placed emphasis instead on the White House staff, creating an organization in which the President was more like the hub of a
wheel. That configuration has been continued by all Presidents in the 1961–1977 period[37] and has led to the insulation
of the Presidential office by an overly protective staff.

Further, as a student of history Eisenhower appreciated
full well the challenge of the so-called Bricker Amendment,
which was thrust on his doorstep in the first days of his
administration. Bricker and other conservative Republicans
tried to assure Eisenhower that their constitutional amendment in no way was inspired by his own actions, but the much
disturbed President was not assuaged. He was as well acquainted as the Senators with the extensive utilization of executive agreements in the 1940s by Presidents Truman and
Roosevelt: the 1940 old-destroyer transfer to Britain was followed by the 1941 agreement with Denmark for Greenland's
defense and with Iceland for its defense. Then had come in
rapid succession the agreement with the principal wartime
allies: the Atlantic Charter (1942); the Cairo Conference, the
Moscow Declaration and the Tehran Conference Declaration
(1943); and the Yalta and Potsdam agreements (1945). Eisenhower had personally participated only in the Cairo and Pots-

dam conferences, but he fully appreciated that all of them had represented the chief diplomat and Commander in Chief roles of the President. These and the climactic Truman Acts of 1950–1951, deployment of troops to Korea and NATO, which Eisenhower staunchly defended, had inspired the Bricker Amendment. By it, and in its several versions, Congress would be empowered "to regulate all executive and other agreements with any foreign power or international organization."[38]

Eisenhower, to the surprise of even his Secretary of State, John Foster Dulles, had a keen grasp of the proposed amendment's implications. After rereading *The Federalist,* he asserted that the Bricker proposal would "put us back" into the kind of government, characterized by a weak executive, of the Articles of Confederation.[39] He further asserted that it "would be notice to our friends as well as our enemies abroad that our country intends to withdraw from its leadership in world affairs."[40]

Despite Eisenhower's personal persuasion, the Bricker Amendment was only narrowly defeated in the Senate. More than twenty years later similar proposals followed the arousal of suspicion regarding executive agreements related to the unpopular Vietnam War. The only difference was that whereas in the 1950s their principal advocates were conservative Republicans, in the late 1960s and early 1970s they were liberal Democrats. Thus Senator Claiborne Pell of Rhode Island avowed that the Bricker Amendment, "if put up today . . . would be voted overwhelmingly by all of us."[41]

Some might have predicted that Eisenhower, after a lifetime of military service, would surround himself with military types. However, Eisenhower dealt with the military at arm's length. He sought their advice, but he readily rejected it when he did not concur. Thus Radford, the most influential of the military in the 1950s, could in no way convince Eisenhower to intervene with force in Vietnam. Moreover, although the Truman and Eisenhower years were characterized by the perils of the Cold War, in neither administration did the military play an influential policy role. Both Presidents recognized that the service chiefs and their subordinates were woefully apart in their points of view. They both recognized that the decisionmaking system camouflaged, to an extent, these basic disagreements on policy, procurement, research, and strategy. Eisenhower, the old soldier, finally personally sat down to write our present Defense Department organization because no one else would or could. He recognized in the service chiefs ostensible agreement on budgetary goals: the old army game of "you scratch my back and I'll scratch yours." They got less support from him for their budget requests than they did from any of his successors. And he ended up in his Farewell Address warning his fellow countrymen against undue influences of a military-industrial complex. But to deal with the military firmly and forthrightly was not to derogate their professional military role, as both the President and the Congress recognized in the 1950s. The very wise Senator Richard B. Russell, who has recently been described as "one of the most underestimated men in American political history,"[42] declared in 1953, "God help the American people if Congress starts legislating military strategy."[43]

Both Truman and Eisenhower earned the respect, if not the complete approbation, of the Congress in their conduct of national security policy. When Prime Minister Clement Attlee hurriedly came to Washington in December 1950 in one of the darker moments of the Korean War, Senator Richard Nixon and twenty-nine of his colleagues wanted not only a full report of the conversations between the President and the Prime Minister but also an assurance that the two heads of state would refrain from entering upon any agreements or understandings. Secretary of State Dean Acheson (as Nixon would himself later do as President) dismissed such demands as "plainly an infringement of the constitutional prerogatives of the President to conduct negotiations...."[44]

A part of the effectiveness of Truman and Eisenhower in dealing with the Congress was their establishment of legislative liaison with Capitol Hill. The first such step came in 1949, following the Hoover Commission report, when Truman appointed two aides to handle Congressional relations and designated his appointment secretary, Matthew J. Connelly, to head the team. In turn Eisenhower named a team of eight, skillfully headed by General Wilton B. Persons, Bryce N. Harlow, and Gerald D. Morgan.[45] Further, albeit belatedly, Eisenhower created the first White House scientific adviser (a post, to the distress of the scientific community, discontinued in 1973 by President Nixon).

Truman's and Eisenhower's effectiveness was further enhanced by good press relations. In Truman's case, there was a healthy give and take. Indeed, the press on occasion backed off from its traditional protagonist role with Truman to help him extricate his foot from his mouth. Eisenhower's press relations were further enhanced by the ablest of American Presidential press secretaries, James C. Hagerty.[46]

Finally, Truman and Eisenhower owed much of their success to their fundamental understanding of the relationship of national security policy to the body politic, to domestic concerns, and to the economic climate and social needs. Some critics have suggested that their defense budgets reflected the residue after these other concerns were taken care of. This is unfair. But they were both men of judgment and political skills who recognized the differing points of view of civilian and military leaders in regard to the national budget. Moreover, both Truman and Eisenhower recognized that national strength included a healthy economy, domestic tranquillity, popular endorsement, and a sense of moral purpose and national will. Only in such a climate can the chief diplomat and the Commander in Chief effectively operate.

Although their styles of operation were considerably different, both men recognized the relationships of policy machinery to policymakers. As Senator Henry M. Jackson observed near the end of the second Eisenhower administration, "Good national security policy requires both good policy makers and good policy machinery. One cannot be divorced from the other." He recognized that "policy machinery should be adaptable to the style and work habits of individual planners and decision makers."[47]

The difference in style in the post–World War II Presidents' approach to national security policy is especially revealed by their utilization of the National Security Council. As former Under Secretary of State William J. Casey observed, "Each President used this security instrument according to his style and background."[48] So it is that each President has sought to mold the organization and the procedures of his staff to meet the needs as he has seen them; so it is each has selected his top people. As Lee C. White, former Assistant Special Counsel to President Kennedy and Special Counsel to President Johnson, expressed it ". . . the President. . . [is] entitled to have the guys that he is most comfortable with and can rely upon."[49] Quite understandably, Truman and Eisenhower each approached and utilized this instrument of national security policy differently, in accordance with his own background and experience. Truman, protective of the prerogatives of his office, first approached the Council with some distrust. Prior to the outbreak of the Korean War he relied upon ad hoc meetings of advisers. Only after United States entry into the "police action" did he accept the Council as his principal deliberative instrument on national security matters. By contrast, from a lifetime experience in staff work, Eisenhower prior to taking office painstakingly structured the Council to give him the broadest policy areas of study for his decisionmaking.

The nation's entire national security apparatus; the instruments for information gathering and dispensing and decisionmaking, the Central Intelligence Agency, the United States Information Agency, and the National Security Council; the Department of Defense; and the worldwide system of alliances and of military assistance—all were essentially products of the Truman and Eisenhower administrations. Policy and organization are closely related. It is not always clear which is cause and which is effect. But a better understanding of both can be achieved by an examination of the resolution of structural policy during this period. Accordingly, this volume traces the raison d'être of the National Security Act of 1947; the Security Act Amendments of 1949; Reorganization Plan No. 6, 1953; and the Defense Department Reorganization Act of 1958. Particular attention is given to the National Security Council, the central body.

Many concerned citizens, as well as elite advocates of Presidential supremacy (rather than Presidential primacy) in national security policy, picture the Congress as disorganized, fumbling, inept, and obtuse in its handling of national security policy matters. These views have been given credibility by some of the responses to the excesses of the Nixon administration. There was, for example, little wisdom in a 1973 enactment, written in anger, requiring the Department of State, the United States Information Agency, the Agency for International Development, and the Arms Control Disarmament Agency to furnish Congress with requested information within thirty-five days on threat of cutting off their funds. There is even the question of constitutionality of the War Powers Act of the same year.

These were responses by a frustrated Congress, in contrast with a Congress working constructively in the basic national security legislation of the 1947–1958 period, or in such statesmanlike enunciations as the 1948 Vandenberg Resolution. Moreover, during those years the Congress saw to it that its own organizational changes complemented those in the executive branch. Thus, for example, the Armed Services committees of the House and the Senate were established after the creation of the National Military Establishment (the forerunner of the Department of Defense) by the 1947 National Security Act. And thus it should be.

What is also true, despite the direst warnings to the contrary, is that these enactments have brought *no* military takeover; the awesome man on horseback has not appeared, nor has the military come to dominate the formulation of defense policy and strategy. On the contrary, all these acts are based upon the premise of civilian control. Even the several structural changes in the military establishment reflected not so much military influences as it did the tug between their civilian bosses, the service secretaries with the Secretary of Defense. As this volume indicates, civilian control was exercised firmly when intense interservice rivalry erupted in such episodes as the 1949 B-36 controversy, the so-called admirals' revolt (see Chapter 6). Nevertheless, particularly in the late 1940s and the early 1950s it was fashionable to write about what Harold Laswell termed "the garrison state." One writer termed it "more threatening than *praetorianism* or *caesarism*. . . ."[50] Other writers made the dire prediction that the National Security Act of 1947 meant the end of free scientific inquiry and cast doubt upon "whether a free and competitive economic system could survive the governmental controls dictated by vast military spending."[51] It is today obvious that such fears and warnings had no basis in fact.

The Truman-Eisenhower legacy includes more than merely organization. It also involves strategy and weaponry. As the very terms Truman Doctrine and Eisenhower Doctrine indicate, both made fundamental doctrinal contributions. Containment, counterforce, limited war, the New Look, stretch-out, brinkmanship, even massive retaliation— all are indicative of the seminal environment for strategy in a new nuclear age. NSC-68 in the Truman administration had been suggestive of global responses in the Cold War. But as Jerome A. Kahan of the Policy Planning Staff of the Department of State has pointed out, the present-day "basic features of the U.S.-Soviet strategic relationship originated during the Eisenhower administration." Much current military hardware, ranging from the long-range jet bomber to the intercontinental ballistic missile (ICBM) to the submarine-launched ballistic missile (SLBM), was designed during the 1950s. Moreover, as Kahan, a former Brookings senior fellow notes, it was during the eight Eisenhower years that "strategic doctrines reflecting a growing awareness of the new technologies for defense, deterrence and diplomacy" first began "to shape America's security policies."[52]

The foregoing, then, are some of the considerations which prompted this study as basic to our understanding of present and future national security policy and organization and the roles and relationships of the Congress and the Presidency. The dramatis personae of this study include: (1) the leaders of the Truman, Eisenhower, Kennedy, Johnson, Nixon, Ford, and Carter administrations, including the politically appointed department heads and their senior staffs as well as the White House staffs; (2) the career service personnel, often termed "the bureaucracy," including the military and civil servants and the members of the Foreign Service; and (3) the Congress, including the committee members of the Senate Foreign Relations, House Foreign Affairs (now International Relations), Commission on Security and Cooperation in Europe, Senate and House Armed Services, House and Senate Defense Appropriation and Military Construction subcommittees, the Joint Committees on Atomic Energy and Defense Production, and the Senate and House Select Committees on Intelligence.

Inevitably, the human equation enters into these relationships, with honest differences of opinion and certain built-in preconceptions. Although in every administration there are tendencies to reduce the external or public evidences of differences in the executive branch, they were bound to surface in the Truman administration, with such a feisty personality as the President himself. This interplay then occupies many of the early chapters, with such strong personalities as Jimmy Byrnes, James Forrestal, and Douglas MacArthur exhibiting some pyrotechnics before and after being fired. After the Truman presidency, as the chapters on Eisenhower indicate, an outward semblance of relative administrative unity emerged.

The key executive departments in this study are the two principal executive departments involved in national security policy: State and Defense. The tragic figure of the first Secretary of Defense, Forrestal, inevitably looms larger than that of his successors, extending from Johnson, Marshall, and Lovett to Brown. Acheson emerges as the dominant adviser of the last three Truman years. These policy-formative years cannot be understood without a relatively full examination of the Korean War in its military as well as its political features. Commencing with the first Executive Secretary of the National Security Council, Sidney W. Souers, 1947–50, followed by James S. Lay, Jr., 1950–53, this volume notes the key security aides. Eisenhower created the position of Special Assistant for National Security Affairs. Commencing with Kissinger in 1969, the title has been Assistant for National Security Affairs. Thus, from St. Louis insurance executive Rear Admiral Souers to Columbia University Professor Zbigniew Brzezinski thirty years later, there is direct lineage.

Since this is a study of the interplay of ideas and of differing as well as complementary views, two Senators, for different reasons, Vandenberg and Taft, are on stage in the

Truman years. Senator Lyndon B. Johnson played a significant role in the Eisenhower period, and Senator J. William
Fulbright in the Kennedy, Johnson, and Nixon years.

This book examines structure as well as persons, and thus
organizational questions arise. For example, should the Secretary of State, the Secretary of Defense, or the Assistant to
the President for National Security Affairs be charged with
more or less responsibility? Should there be, as Milton
Eisenhower, Nelson Rockefeller, and others have suggested,
"super Cabinet" posts for domestic and national security
affairs? Should this include a "super Secretary of State" with
subordinate secretaries under him for diplomacy, foreign
economic matters, and information? Should the United
States Information Agency be continued as such? Suggestive
answers to these and other organizational issues emerge
from a study of the experience of Truman, Eisenhower,
Kennedy, Johnson, Nixon, and Ford.

Tentative answers also emerge regarding Congressional
organization. Some suggest that the inability of Congress to
make strategic decisions is not so much a technology gap—
the ability to get the facts, especially regarding sophisticated
hardware—as it is an inability to achieve political consensus.
Such was exemplified in 1949 when the House of Representatives insisted on appropriating funds for a 70 Group Air
Force, despite Senate objections, and President Truman impounded the funds. Although the House Appropriations
Committee and the House Armed Services Committee
vigorously denounced the President, and a junior Congressman, Richard M. Nixon, was particularly outspoken in
such denunciation, the Congress was divided against itself.
Despite occasional expressions to the contrary, Congress has
largely come to accept executive control of force levels and
size of the military establishment. Congress' role, as far as
the armed services are concerned, has become more that of
the investigator, as with the B-70 bomber in the 1960s or B-1
bomber in the 1970s. The former they rejected, and the latter
they tentatively accepted. Members of Congress have also
become special advocates, such as Senator Jackson, who
championed the Polaris submarine.[53]

While the Congress continues in general to accept or indeed reinforce executive recommendations on force levels (as in Europe), it has increasingly in the 1970s refused to endorse the recommended levels of military equipment assistance. It was so recalcitrant about Turkey in 1975 that it cut off all military equipment assistance. Further, in the 1970s Congress has sought to inject itself into foreign policy decisionmaking, with regard to both covert and overt operations, as in Angola.

As a means of increasing its roles, the Congress has been playing a catch-up game with the executive office of the President in the size of its own bureaucracy. The real benchmark year for increase was 1970, when both the President and the Congress were finding it fashionable to study their organization. While at the White House the Ash Council was recommending the creation of the Domestic Council and the overhaul of the Office of Budget to form the Office of Management and Budget, the Congress that year had its own Legislative Reorganization Act, with a primary purpose of beefing up its professional staff. Whereas the executive office of the President had more than 1,500 permanent staff positions by 1965, the combined total of the Congressional committee staffs was just over 1,000. In the ensuing decade the staff of the executive office of the President increased 30 percent, while the Congressional committees staff increased 100 percent; thus each totaled about 2,000 staff members.[54] Almost all of the White House growth had occurred before 1970. Indeed, by 1976 President Ford had reduced the immediate White House staff from approximately 600 to approximately 450.

Most of the Congressional growth was in 1970–1975. Two of the most significant acts of the enlarged Congressional bureaucracy were those of 1974 by which the Congress increased its own appropriations and spending authority vis-à-vis the Presidency: the Congressional Budget Act and the Impoundment Control Act.[55] The days of Presidential impoundment of funds against the wishes of the Congress seemed at an end. Yet the President's own Constitutional weapon, the veto, remained effective.

The War Powers Act of 1973 and the budgetary and impoundment acts of 1974 are hallmarks in an historic

Congressional-Presidential "struggle," as Edward S. Corwin termed it, "for the privilege of directing American foreign policy."[56] In the process the clear sense of purpose of the Truman-Eisenhower-Kennedy years has become diffused and beclouded by what Henry Kissinger termed "the growing tendency of Congress to legislate in detail the day-to-day or week-to-week conduct of our foreign affairs."[57] Whereas the process was vexing for Secretary of State Kissinger, some of the ground had been trodden before. Indeed, one can almost hear the reechoing of the Hamilton-Jefferson argument in the first years of the Republic—except that in those years the nation had not suffered the increasing Presidential excesses in foreign affairs of the 1960s and 1970s. Ironically, the tragedies of the protracted Vietnam War, Watergate, and reaction to excesses by the Nixon administration brought the issue full cycle to the point where President Ford, going to the opposite extreme, expressed doubts as to his emergency Commander in Chief functions. For the first time the late Senator Russell's 1953 warning of the consequences of a Congress seeking to legislate national strategy had become a reality. The new Congressional Budget Office was even proposing the redeployment of NATO ground forces.

The congressional-executive balance must be restored, and, in part, through the genius of the Constitution itself. "As for Congress against the president, it must be concluded," wrote Harvey C. Mansfield, Sr., "that Congress has not yet managed even by working full time to organize a dependable method—short of impeachment—of transcending the constitutional separation of powers."[58]

II
****

COMMANDER IN CHIEF AND CHIEF DIPLOMAT: FROM WASHINGTON TO FRANKLIN D. ROOSEVELT

> Energy in the Executive is a leading character in the definition of good government.   ALEXANDER HAMILTON

Introduction

No other office created by the framers of the Constitution has created so much recent concern and such disparate views as has that of Commander in Chief. Many scholars have decried the so-called imperial Presidency. President Ford, however, believed that in the early 1970s the Congress had emasculated the office of Commander in Chief to a dangerous degree and had superimposed itself into the executive branch foreign policy operational roles. While campaigning in 1976 in the New Hampshire primary, he asserted, "Our forefathers knew you could not have 535 commanders in chief and secretaries of state...."[1]

Since leaving office, Ford has detailed his position, based upon six cases of his own Presidency in which he found it well nigh impossible to carry out the dictates of the War Powers Act of 1973 regarding consultation with the Congress. He noted such specific crises as the evacuation of the American airbase at Da Nang, Vietnam; the rescue of the *Mayagüez* crew; and the evacuation of the Americans in the Lebanon civil war. When the roof caved in in Vietnam in the

early spring of 1975, Congress was off on Easter recess, and
Ford noted that "not one of the key bipartisan leaders were
in Washington." He located two in Mexico, three were in
Greece, one was in the Middle East, one was in Europe and
two were in the People's Republic of China. The rest, he
recalled, "we found in 12 widely scattered states of the
union."[2] When the evacuation of Americans in Lebanon
began on June 18, 1976, Congress had adjourned for the day,
and the White House found it difficult to notify Congressional members in accordance with the War Powers Act.
Indeed, Ford later confided that "one member of Congress
had an unlisted number which his press secretary refused to
divulge,"and with another the best the White House could
do was leave a note on his cottage door at the beach.

Because of such experiences, Ford asked President Carter
and the 95th Congress to reconsider the War Powers Act. He
contends that "when a crisis breaks, it is impossible to draw
the Congress into the decision-making process in an effective way." He concludes that not only domestic policy as a
whole but also the foreign policy "general outlines can and
should be advanced in the calm deliberation and spirited
debates . . ." which he recalled from his own days as a Congressman. But he insists, "There is absolutely no way
American foreign policy can be conducted or military operations commanded by 535 members of Congress even if they
all happen to be on Capitol Hill when they are needed."[3]

"What is past is prologue." Historically, Congress was
concerned over Presidential conduct of foreign policy, and
recent Congressional concern erupted in the spring of 1970,
following the so-called Cambodian incursion. President
Nixon defended this foray into the Viet Cong and North
Vietnamese sanctuary area on the grounds that the Commander in Chief must protect American troops. Nonetheless
it triggered the Congressional debates that culminated in the
War Powers Act. During the course of those debates, Secretary of State William P. Rogers testified in June 1971: " . . .
to circumscribe the President's ability to act in emergency
situations—or even to appear to weaken it—would run the
grave risk of miscalculation by a potential enemy regarding
the ability of the United States to act in a crisis."[4]

Arthur M. Schlesinger, Jr., does not share Ford's and Rogers's concern with recent restrictions on the Presidential role in foreign policy. According to Schlesinger these were but actions "to rein in the runaway Presidency."[5] He asserts that the Constitutional framers and those who prior to 1945 have molded the Presidential office had a limited view of Commander in Chief authority. He believes that excessive Presidential zeal began particularly with President Truman and his successors, with "the growing militarization of American life under both the realities and the delusions of the Cold War. . . ." Schlesinger contends that the Commander in Chief "office through most American history had a strictly technical connotation: it meant no more than the topmost officer in the armed forces."[6]

The Conceptions of Madison, Jay, and Hamilton

Since the views of certain illustrious scholars so contrast with those of Ford and Rogers, it may well be asked: What were the conceptions of the Constitutional framers and of those who formulated policy in the early years of the Republic? The views of Madison, Hamilton, and Jay, as set forth not only in *The Federalist* but also in their subsequent actions, are especially illuminating.

James Madison pointed out in *Federalist* No. 45 that "the powers delegated by the proposed Constitution to the Federal Government, are . . . principally on external objects, as war, peace, negociation and foreign commerce. . . ."[7] The effective conduct of such matters required the creation of a strong chief executive. The Constitutional framers had one person in mind for that office, George Washington, and to a considerable extent they modeled the position to fit the man.

The doctrine of separation of powers enunciated in the Constitution largely stems from Montesquieu. However, neither Montesquieu nor the Constitutional framers proposed a rigid separation of powers. Madison, in *Federalist* No. 47, made clear that they rather envisioned a *sharing* of powers, that "the legislative, executive, and judiciary departments are by no means totally separate and distinct from each other."[8] This sharing between the Congress and the Presidency was intended to produce cooperation, not impasse.

John Jay, who had been frustrated by his post as Secretary of Foreign Affairs under the Articles of Confederation, argued in his own five *Federalist* essays for adoption of the Constitution largely because of the needs for strong national security policy: ". . . nations in general will make war," the veteran diplomat wrote, "whenever they have a prospect of getting anything by it. . . ." Accordingly, Jay concluded, the United States must have "the best possible state of defense. . . ." All the armed forces, Jay contended, must be under the "Chief Magistrate." He asked: "Who shall command the allied armies; and from which of them shall he receive his orders? Who shall settle the terms of Peace?"[9] To Jay, the Commander in Chief provision of the Constitution was fundamental. Further, he argued for the adoption of the Constitution, since by it the President "will be able to manage the business of intelligence in such manner as prudence may suggest."[10]

Alexander Hamilton was more than the chief instigator of the Constitutional Convention and the most persuasive advocate for the Constitution's adoption. During the Washington and John Adams administrations he also became the chief architect of both specific plans in the area of national security and the organization for placing them in operation. In the world of realpolitik, Hamilton's maxim was that the United States must "be prepared for war while cultivating peace. . . ."[11]

Hamilton is generally pictured as being unappreciative of the attributes of a democratic society. Yet he clearly grasped the implications of the democratic condition in the formulation of foreign policy. He recognized "the support of public opinion" as being "more essential to our government than to any other" and estimated that such support in utilizing the diplomatic instrument of last resort, military force, would not be forthcoming unless it was demonstrably "resulting from necessity. . . ." Writing long before intervention in Vietnam or Angola would be considered, he speculated that intervention in a particular conflict "is a thing about which the best and ablest men of this country are far from being agreed."¹²

In his "Pacificus" letters, defending Washington's authority to issue the Neutrality Proclamation in the war between Britain and France (despite an alliance with the latter), Hamilton most significantly developed the concept of "executive power." The framers of the Constitution, according to Hamilton, had granted the President *full* authority in foreign relations except when the Constitution provided otherwise, unlike the specifically enumerated powers of the Congress. By Hamilton's thesis, when the Constitution indicates a role for the Congress and a role for the President, as in treatymaking, "a *concurrent* authority" is specified. However, since the *initiation* of treaties resides with the President, and the Constitution gives the Senate a role only in *confirming* treaties, it is left entirely to the President to determine whether treaties should "be continued or suspended." Within his conception of executive power, Hamilton also argued, since the Constitution charged the President to "take care that the laws be faithfully executed," that "he who is to execute the laws must first judge for himself of their meaning."¹³ Further, according to Hamilton, the President is the tribune of the people, a contention Andrew Jackson and both Theodore and Franklin Roosevelt were to espouse in their interpretation of executive power. By Hamilton's conception, it was the President who expressed the national will and view: "Kings and Princes speak of their own dispositions," he wrote. "The Magistrates of Republics of the dispositions of their Nations."¹⁴

Hamilton's philosophical views were reinforced by the fact, as Louis Henkin has expressed it, that "the President was always in session; Congress was not. . . ." Although President Ford found it difficult to reach members of Congress to consult with them, that difficulty was the more compounded in Washington's day sans telephones and jet aircraft. And so Hamilton's view of "executive power" took hold. Cautiously Henkin adds, "That view has not been authoritatively accepted by the Court, but neither has it been rejected."¹⁵ In fact, the 1936 landmark *Curtiss-Wright* decision of the Supreme Court did recognize the conduct of foreign policy as an *executive* function, much as Secretary of State Jefferson, in 1790, had asserted.

Shortly after Jefferson resigned as Secretary of State, in protest of Hamilton's so-called pro-British policies in particular and his broad-ranging activities in national security policy in general, Hamilton launched the executive agreement, which gave the President a new foreign policy instrument. He posited that the Constitution did not specify that treaties were the exclusive and sole instrument for entering upon agreements between nations. In *Federalist* No. 69, in 1788, he portrayed treatymaking as carefully circumscribed, but in the 1796 "Camillus" letters Hamilton asserted that in the Constitutional Convention it had been "understood by all" that the Constitution would provide "the most ample latitude" to include all kinds of "species of Convention usual among nations."[16] Such "species" would include executive agreements. With assuagement he added that such agreements should be entered upon only by persons carefully screened by "the *highest security*" measures to make certain that they are the persons "best qualified,"[17] lest, with "most ample latitude" for utilizing instruments other than treaties, "there would be no security at home, no respectability abroad."[18]

By such generous interpretations of the Constitution, Hamilton never found Presidential authority lacking for a wide range of programs. Thus, as a part of his Treasury Department apparatus, he created, with Congressional approval in 1790, the "revenue marine," the forerunner of the Coast Guard. Subsequently he made initiatives to the President and the Congress for "the *gradual* and successive creation" of a Navy and Navy Department separate from and coequal with the Army and War Department. "Our experience has confirmed," he wrote Washington in 1796, "that the most equitable and successive neutrality is not sufficient to exempt a state from the depredations of other nations at war with each other...."[19] Two years later the Navy Department came into being (nine years after the War Department).

To Hamilton, the design of such military preparedness was peace, not war: "The true inference is that we ought not

lightly to seek or provoke a resort to arms; . . . in the differences between us and other nations, we ought carefully to
avoid measures which tend to widen the breach. . . ."[20]

Presidential Initiative in Foreign Policy

In 1917, shortly after the United States entered World War I,
Edward S. Corwin of Princeton University observed: "Presidential initiative in the formulation of our foreign policy is a
familiar fact."[21] While the roles of Commander in Chief and
chief diplomat are indivisible, most Presidents have had
strong counselors, ranging from Hamilton to Kissinger.
Washington had his Hamilton in the Neutrality Proclamation
of 1793. James Monroe had his John Quincy Adams in the
Monroe Doctrine of 1823, which is often termed a second
declaration of independence. The Monroe Doctrine prohib-
ited the Old World from interfering with the new Latin
American republics; it was made meaningful by the cordial
support of the then number one superpower, Great Britain,
which John Quincy Adams, as Secretary of State, full well
appreciated.

In general, during the nineteenth century, the Congress
was far more bellicose than the President; in 1812 it was the
"War Hawks" in Congress, not President Madison, who
demanded war with Britain. In 1898 the Congress, not the
President, demanded war with Spain. During the critical
period of the American Civil War, when France sought to
impose a protectorate in Mexico under Archduke Maximilian,
the Lincoln administration exercised far more diplomatic
restraint than the Congress. While agreeing in sentiment
to a unanimous Congressional declaration deploring "events
now transpiring in the Republic of Mexico," Secretary of
State William H. Seward noted in diplomatic instructions to
the United States envoy in France that "this is a practical and
purely Executive question. . . ."[22] The United States Congress, upon learning of the message, was in an uproar.
Overwhelmingly they passed a resolution "that Congress
has a constitutional right to an authoritative voice in declaring and prescribing the foreign policy of the United

States. . . ."[23] While the Congress fumed, the Lincoln administration bided its time until the Civil War was won. Thereafter, in the Andrew Johnson administration, Secretary of State Seward issued a virtual ultimatum which brought the withdrawal of French troops from Mexico in 1866–1867 and the toppling of the Maximilian regime. The same Secretary of State took the initiative in the purchase of Alaska from Russia, though the Congress grumbled about paying the Russians $7,200,000 for "Seward's Folly" or "Seward's Ice-Box," as it was derisively termed.

Seward's successor as Secretary of State, Hamilton Fish, serving during both Grant administrations, took the initiative in the settling of the *Alabama* and other claims against Great Britain arising out of Britain's tilting toward the South during the Civil War. In contrast, the bellicose chairman of the Senate Foreign Relations Committee, Charles Sumner, and his colleagues demanded the cession of Canada to the United States and the withdrawal of the British flag from the Western Hemisphere.

Most twentieth-century Presidents have been more assertive than the Congress in the enunciation of foreign policy. William McKinley, who dispatched 5,000 American troops to China in 1900 without Congressional authorization to help quell the Boxer Rebellion, cheerfully followed with the Boxer Protocol of 1900, providing indemnities and exacting guarantees.

Theodore Roosevelt was the first activist President in the United States' new role as a world power. Thrust into the position at age forty-two, following the assassination of McKinley in 1901, in his own words, he made the Presidency "a bully pulpit." He conceived of the United States as exerting a balance of power in European affairs among Britain and France and Germany and her allies. He played an active role through his emissaries in the Algeciras Conference of 1906 ending the Moroccan crisis. In essence this signalized the end of isolation from the affairs of Europe and the beginnings of a close association with Great Britain in world affairs, a policy to have profound effect during the ensuing seven decades.

Although he won the Nobel Peace Prize in 1906 for his

efforts in both Europe and the Far East, including ending the Russo-Japanese War, Theodore Roosevelt also practiced the doctrine of force majeure. While his slogan "Speak softly and carry a big stick" had first been coined to describe his approach to the New York Republican machine, it came to epitomize his diplomacy.[24] As Commander in Chief in 1903 he dispatched the cruiser *Nashville* to ensure the success of the Panama revolution. In 1907–1908 he sent the battle fleet around the world, terming it "the most important service I rendered to peace."[25] Roosevelt also skillfully utilized this demonstration, aimed at Japan, to demand four new battleships. Later, after he got two, he confided, "I knew I would not get two and have those two hurried up unless I made a violent fight for four." He told Speaker of the House Joseph Cannon: "I am acting with a view to the emergencies that . . . may arise within the next decade or two."[26]

Roosevelt had a nagging feeling that Japan would one day attack Hawaii. He sent the affable William Howard Taft, as he was to send his able Secretaries of State John Hay and Elihu Root, to be his emissary on Far Eastern affairs. Taft entered into the tacit understanding, with Roosevelt's concurrence, under which Japan took over the direction of Korean foreign affairs in 1905, while Root entered upon an agreement three years later that recognized Japanese primacy in Manchuria. Such executive agreements, openly or secretly arrived at, caused little stir in the Congress.

In a letter to Taft, whom Roosevelt virtually selected to be his successor as President, the youngest and most aggressive of American Presidents confided:

> You know as well as I do that it is for the enormous interest of this Government to strengthen and give independence to the Executive in dealing with foreign powers, for a legislative body, because of its very good qualities in domestic matters, is not well fitted for shaping foreign policy on occasions when instant action is demanded. Therefore, the important thing to do is for a President who is willing to accept responsibility to establish precedents which successors may follow even if they are unwilling to take the initiative themselves.[27]

Roosevelt based his views, in part, on the powers Lincoln had exercised as Commander in Chief and in the "shall take care" and "executive power" clauses of the Constitution. Taft shared these views, defending Lincoln's Emancipation Proclamation as "an act of the Commander-in-Chief justified by military necessity to weaken the enemies of the Nation and suppress their rebellion." Taft, who became Chief Justice of the United States after serving as President, also believed that Lincoln's suspension of the writ of habeas corpus was "well founded." He contended that "Lincoln always pointed out the sources of authority which in his opinion justified his acts, and there was always a strong ground for maintaining the view which he took."[28]

Taft could dispute as firmly (though not as vociferously) as Roosevelt what he believed was Congressional encroachment on Presidential authority. The differences, if any, between Taft and Roosevelt on Presidential power did not surface until after 1912. In fact, the differences were not in Presidential power per se, but rather in the sources of that authority. Taft, like Lincoln, legalistically found authority in the Constitution, whereas Roosevelt, always in a hurry, invoked a "stewardship" principle: he considered himself as the tribune of the people, serving the higher laws of morality and justice. Ironically, it was Taft's adherence to Constitutional principle that contributed to his loss of public confidence. Although he sought to emulate Roosevelt's role as a world mediator, he did not have the same bold aggressiveness, and he deferred, perhaps excessively, to Secretary of State Philander C. Knox. His failure to gain Senatorial support in arbitration treaties with Britain and France and the unpopularity of his nonintervention policies in Mexico were not due to an inferior knowledge of the Presidential role as chief diplomat and Commander in Chief, but rather, as his empathetic biographer, Donald F. Anderson acknowledges, "his deficient understanding of the relationship between public opinion, national power, and diplomacy."[29]

Taft's successor, Wilson, fell victim to the same failing. Two years before Wilson's League of Nations proposal was defeated by the United States Senate, Corwin warned "that the ultimate viability of an executive policy in this field [foreign policy] will depend upon the backing of public opinion as reflected in Congress, or in the Senate. . . ."[30] A much abler President than McKinley, Wilson was nevertheless a poor politician. McKinley had named three Senators as members of the peace commission ending the Spanish-American War. Wilson, who took no Senators with him to the Paris Peace Conference after World War I, failed to flatter the Senate's sense of *amour-propre* in foreign relations. Although he was warmly greeted by the European people, French Premier Georges Clemenceau said skeptically, "God gave us His Ten Commandments and we broke them. Wilson gave us his Fourteen Points—we shall see."[31] Wilson, who had suffered a mild stroke, seemed to have lost his capacity to maneuver. When Herbert Hoover and British economist John Maynard Keynes convinced British Prime Minister David Lloyd George, Italian Premier Vittorio Orlando, and Clemenceau to make revisions in the peace treaty favoring Wilson's position, the American President failed to grasp the opportunity. This prompted Keynes to quip that "Lloyd George, having bamboozled Wilson could not unbamboozle him."[32] Hoover, a member of the United States delegation, took a kinder view. He found Wilson "too great a man" to participate in European policical intrigue.[33]

Returning home with his covenant of the League of Nations, Wilson was adamant in opposing Senate revisionists. Taking his case to the American people, in an exhaustive journey he suffered a paralytic stroke from which he never fully recovered. Steadfastly loyal to Wilson's memory, Herbert Hoover's final assessment in 1958 was that not since Wilson "has any man risen to the political and spiritual height that came to him."[34]

The lofty height of Wilson's idealism was followed by the pragmatic mediocrity of Warren G. Harding and Calvin Coolidge. They were, however, well served in the international arena by able Secretaries of State, Charles Evans Hughes and Frank B. Kellogg, and by their vigorous Secretary of Commerce, Herbert Hoover. Hughes skillfully presided over the plenary sessions of the Nine Power Washington Conference of 1921–1922. As early as 1916, under Wilson, the United States had vowed to build a navy second to none. By 1921 this goal was in sight although Britannia still ruled the waves. Looming on the horizon was the rapid buildup of Japan. Moreover, the Anglo-Japanese Alliance was troublesome to the United States. Hughes achieved the abrogation of that alliance. Further, he achieved parity between the United States and Great Britain in capital ship tonnage and an inferior position for Japan, in a ratio of 3 to 5 in capital ship tonnage as compared to the other two superpowers. The United States Senate accepted Hughes's successes in the most negative terms: "no commitment to use armed force, no alliance, no obligation to join any defense."[35] By the treaty the United States surrendered the right to improve its fortifications in the Pacific west of Hawaii, but as William V. Pratt has observed, "If the United States erred in limiting its navy and forgoing the building of bases, if by the two means combined it conceded supremacy to Japan in the waters bordering Asia, the fault was that of Congress and public opinion, not of the diplomats at Washington."[36]

"Silent Cal" Coolidge was a more ardent Commander in Chief than many would give him credit for. He was disturbed to note the continual British and Japanese buildup in other than capital ships. Thus, while supporting the Kellogg-Briand Pact, which "renounced war as an instrument of national policy," he urged Congressional authorization for fifteen 10,000-ton cruisers, a bill he signed into law in February 1929, just after the Pact went into effect.

In the fall of 1929, "on a log by the Rapidan," Hoover's rural retreat in Virginia, the new President and the new British Prime Minister, Ramsay MacDonald, reached an understanding ending Anglo-American naval rivalries. The ensuing London Naval Conference of 1930, which extended the provisions of the Washington Conference regarding capital ships ratios among the United States, Great Britain, and Japan, and added limitations on cruisers, destroyers, and submarines, was the last successful attempt to limit the size of superpower navies by international agreement.

A year later, with Japanese aggression commencing in Manchuria, the steps toward World War II were set in motion. In 1934 Japan announced that the limitations of both the Washington and the London conferences would terminate by December 31, 1936. Thereafter the strenuous Japanese naval buildup caused Britain, France, and the United States in 1938 to belatedly invoke the escalator clause of their own 1936 naval treaty limitations.

Although the path to Pearl Harbor now appears to have been marked by futility, neither Hoover nor Franklin Roosevelt took a passive view toward the expanding Japanese aggression. Hoover viewed the 1931 Japanese incident in Manchuria as "rank aggression," but he differed with Secretary of State Henry L. Stimson on the course of responsive action. Stimson favored immediate economic sanctions on Japan, which was especially vulnerable to cut-offs of oil and scrap iron. Hoover wanted the British to join in the sanctions, which he considered an act approaching war, but a new British government refused to do so. The President consulted his military chiefs, General Douglas MacArthur and Admiral William V. Pratt, and received the restoration of funds that had been cut from naval appropriations. In December 1931 he proposed his nonrecognition doctrine, generally termed the Stimson Doctrine, refusing to recognize Manchuko, the new Japanese puppet regime in Manchuria. Not until late January 1932, after the Japanese bombing of Shanghai, did Britain join in the nonrecognition doctrine. Again the American President acted with greater firmness than his European counterparts. As Commander in Chief he sent American ships and troops to Shanghai and directed the strengthening of the Hawaiian and Philippine bases. Further, as Commander in Chief in 1932 he moved the battleship fleet to the Pacific. As Hoover wrote about these command decisions, "There was no bluffing about this."[37]

Finally on March 11, 1932, the Assembly of the League adopted the Hoover-Stimson doctrine of nonrecognition. Japan then withdrew from China but not from Manchuria. The League's subsequent Lytton Commission report, in which General Frank McCoy represented the United States, was followed by Japan's giving notice of its withdrawal from the League.

Before leaving office, Hoover in January 1933 asked Congressional authority to employ an arms embargo against such foreign states as the President might designate. The House authorized his proposal, but the Senate added such qualifications that no such act was passed. When the First Neutrality Act was passed in 1935, it had an entirely different thrust. An isolationist measure, it cut off arms delivery to all belligerents, the attacked as well as the attacker. It may be noted that, as related to Japan, Roosevelt continued Hoover's policies of nonrecognition, keeping a strong battleship fleet in the Pacific, and accepting nonvoting membership in the League's Advisory Committee on the Far East.

While Japanese militarists were seizing control of their government and embarking upon aggressive adventurism, two leading European powers, Germany and Italy, were undergoing similar change. Hitler became German Chancellor in January 1933, and by October of that year he had taken Germany out of both the General Disarmament Conference, which had convened the year before in Geneva, and the League of Nations. In March 1935, in violation of the Treaty of Versailles, the Führer announced that Germany was resuming compulsory military service. By the following spring Mussolini had invaded Ethiopia, driving a wedge between Italy and her former allies, England and France. Hitler, at the same time, repudiated the entire Treaty of Versailles and reoccupied the Rhineland with 200,000 troops.

Despite such aggressive acts, Americans turned inward; isolationist sentiment was rampant. Indeed, the aggressors were calculating on American nonintervention. In April 1935 United States Ambassador to Germany William E. Dodd warned regarding German opinion: "Since American intervention will not be repeated the Third Reich will at a strategic moment seize the [Polish] Corridor or Austria and if war follows, win what was lost in 1918. . . ."[38]

Despite such warnings, Roosevelt, inhibited by public opinion, was helpless to act until after war began in Europe. On September 1, 1939, assured of Russian neutrality, Hitler attacked Poland; two days later Great Britain and France declared war on Nazi Germany; World War II had begun. Two months later the American arms embargo was repealed. On June 10, 1940, Mussolini led Italy into the war on France. That day Roosevelt promised aid to "the opponents of force." Twelve days thereafter France capitulated. Belated beginnings of United States rearmament followed, including the destroyer-base deal with Britain, the Lend-Lease Act of March 11, 1941, and the beginnings of joint American-British military planning. In August 1941, Prime Minister Churchill and President Roosevelt met in Newfoundland and forged the Atlantic Charter, a statement of eight principles for world peace. Chiefly penned by Churchill, it was couched in the ideals of Wilson's Fourteen Points.

By the fall of 1941, Roosevelt clearly wanted to join the war against Germany. Yet as late as November 5, 1941, after the sinking of a number of American ships engaged in "neutrality patrols" on sea lanes as far as Iceland, two-thirds of Americans were still opposed to a declaration of war.[39] Any such declaration would not be caused by Hitler, who wanted no interference from the United States until after Russia and Britain were crushed. It took the Japanese attack at Pearl Harbor on December 7, 1941, to finally bring the American Congress the following day to a declaration of war against Japan. Acting upon their commitment to Japan, Germany and Italy declared war on the United States, and the American Congress responded with declarations against these two nations.

Some maintain that Roosevelt provoked the Japanese attack on the United States in order to bring the United States fully into the European war. There is little evidence for such a thesis. Actually, it was the last minute assurances from Germany to Japan (which Roosevelt could hardly have been aware of) that Germany would join in a war against the United States that emboldened Japan to proceed with the audacious Pearl Harbor attack. A more legitimate criticism of the American Commander in Chief was the lack of precautionary measures. Admiral James O. Richardson had been relieved of command at Pearl Harbor in February of 1941 after his outspoken protest of the vulnerability of the base.

In defense of Roosevelt's position, there were political considerations in his decision to keep the fleet at Pearl Harbor. Both President Hoover and Secretary Stimson had attributed the Japanese backdown at Shanghai and the Japanese withdrawal from central China in 1932 to the advance positioning of the Pacific fleet—i.e., moving it from the West Coast to Pearl Harbor. However, whereas the

Hoover action in 1932 did not place the fleet in jeopardy, since naval aerial warfare was then only in its infancy, by 1941, with the development of the aircraft carrier, there was a clear and present danger. The simple fact is that with Japanese concentrations in Formosa (threatening the Philippines), with convoys heading for Malaya, and with other forces gathering in the Carolines pointing toward the Netherland Indies, apparently no one believed the Japanese might at the same time be planning a sneak attack on Pearl Harbor, and no one saw Admiral Chuichi Nagumo's task force moving down through the North Pacific.

Once the war fully came, Roosevelt proved himself the consummate Commander in Chief. He envisioned an alliance on a grand and glorious scale. He took the lead in the January 1, 1942, Declaration by United Nations—twenty-six in all, which by war's end numbered forty-six. The signatories affirmed the principles of the Atlantic Charter, pledged full support to the war effort, and promised not to make a separate peace with any of the enemies. As Dexter Perkins observed, by one stroke of the pen Roosevelt "virtually contracted an alliance, and this without the consent of any legislative body, and indeed almost without a voice raised in criticism."[40]

In both World War I and World War II, the Congress willingly followed the President as Commander in Chief, but Roosevelt was far more assertive than Wilson of his independence from the Congress. Louis Koenig notes that "Franklin Roosevelt is really the innovator of modern Presidential war making."[41] In fact, his independence as Commander in Chief far transcended that of any President before or since. Harry Bailey points to Roosevelt's September 7, 1942, message to Congress as the pinnacle of pointed threats to govern without Congress. Roosevelt told the Congress that unless they set aside certain portions of the Emergency Price Control Act he would do so himself. "I cannot tell what powers may have to be exercised to win this war," he declared. "When the war is won, the powers under which I act automatically revert to the people to whom they belong."[42]

Commenting on this sweeping declaration, Edwin S. Corwin wrote, "The implication seemed to be that the President owed the transcendent power he was claiming to some peculiar relationship between himself and the people." Corwin, who in his later years became highly critical of Roosevelt, found in this doctrine "a strong family resemblance to the leadership principle against which this war was supposedly being fought."[43] In that particular instance, Congress averted a showdown by complying with Roosevelt's rather vigorous request.

The Supreme Court upheld a number of Roosevelt's command decisions, some of which appeared to set aside civil rights. As Commander in Chief, he was upheld in having appointed a military commission to try German saboteurs in 1942, as well as in his designating "military areas" for persons of Japanese ancestry in 1942. Not until after the war did the Supreme Court declare Roosevelt's wartime suspension of the writ of habeas corpus in Hawaii unlawful (see Chapter Ten).

Most historians and political scientists rank Franklin Roosevelt with Washington and Lincoln as the nation's three greatest Presidents. All three have been rated especially high because of their roles as Commander in Chief. Theodore Roosevelt would also have to receive high points among America's most vigorous Commanders in Chief. The two Roosevelts, however, unlike Washington and Lincoln, never seemed to be bothered by Constitutional scruples in their "stewardship" concepts, their belief in the tribune of the people appealing to a higher law. FDR carried it beyond Theodore Roosevelt, however, when as Commander in Chief he appeared willing to assume the legislative process.

In brief, as this survey reveals, the so-called Imperial President is not a recent phenomenon. Beginning with Washington, Commanders in Chief have asserted their prerogatives in national security policy. Moreover, although on occasion they skirted Constitutional issues and bypassed the Congress, in general the principle of Presidential primacy was arrived at in concert with the Congress itself.

As Abraham D. Sofaer recently pointed out, "scholars have commonly assumed" that Presidential primacy in national security policy was a development of the Cold War period of the post–World War II era. In fact, as Sofaer makes clear, "this assumption is far from accurate." Indeed, as his study, commissioned by the American Bar Association, noted, the basic relationships betweeen the Congress and the Presidency in national security policy had in principle been arrived at during the two Washington administrations. "In sum," as Sofaer observed, "the broad outlines of the presidency as we know it today were drawn during Washington's administration." Nor was this due alone to the genius of Washington and Hamilton. Those principles had also been arrived at by debate in the Congress itself "on foreign affairs and military issues calling for highly sensitive judgments. . . ."[44] It is those accumulated judgments, not the excesses of Richard Nixon, which the Congress of the mid-1970s was setting aside.

III

****

TRUMAN AND CONTAINMENT OF COMMUNISM, 1945–1950

> The presidency of the United States carries with it a responsibility so personal as to be without parallel.... No one can make decisions for him.   HARRY S TRUMAN

Historical Perspective

Former President Truman wrote in his memoirs: "To be President of the United States is to be lonely, very lonely at times of great decision."[1] Similarly describing the Presidential decisionmaking process, Adolf A. Berle, Jr., close adviser to President F. D. Roosevelt, stated that a momentous Presidential decision often was based upon the meeting of "a tired man [the President] on one side of the desk and a trusted friend on the other."[2]

Decisionmaking in F. D. Roosevelt's four administrations was highly personal and informal. It had often resulted in what Gordon Gray has described as the "yo-yo" process, a decision based upon who saw the President last. Such an objective observer and nonpolitical servant as John J. McCloy found Roosevelt both inconsistent and superficial.[3] McCloy later realized that Roosevelt, in his last year in office, suffered mental as well as physical deterioration because of his stroke.[4] It was this weakened Roosevelt who had gone to Yalta in the Crimea in February 1945 for meetings with Churchill and Stalin. Perceiving men as "manipulable,"[5] he believed he could handle Stalin, though there is some evidence he had doubts and misgivings by the time the Yalta Conference was concluded. Two months later, on April 12, at Warm Springs, Georgia, the haggard President, as his wife Eleanor expressed it, "slept away." Only thereafter did Truman learn of the many military and political decisions the dying Roosevelt had made at Yalta.

Such experiences convinced many persons that in the area of national security policy a more formalized advisory system was necessary. The result was the establishment of the National Security Council in 1947. Termed "Forrestal's revenge," since Secretary of the Navy Forrestal had advanced the proposal for the NSC as a counter to Truman's armed forces unification program, the NSC must, at best, be described as advisory. In no way does it eliminate the awesome, lonely Presidential decision. All of this responsibility stems from a few phrases in the Constitution. In the area of national security affairs, Article II, Section 2 (1), states, in part: "The President shall be commander in chief. . . ," and Article II, Section 3, states, in part, that "he shall take care that the laws be faithfully executed, and shall commission all the officers of the United States." Further, by the Constitution, two qualified national security powers are noted in Article II, Section 2 (2): "with the advice and consent of the Senate," he makes treaties and appoints "ambassadors, other public ministers and consuls . . . and all other officers of the United States. . . ."

Lincoln, who made the most effective and sweeping use of these national security powers, exercised his authority as Commander in Chief on the rationale that, in a state of rebellion, he must see to it "that the laws be faithfully executed. . . ." In his quest for effective military leadership he not only commissioned officers but he also relieved (most notably George B. McClellan) and appointed new field commanders (most notably Grant). In doing so he showed but scant deference to the wishes of the Congress. The Congress appointed its own Joint Committee on the Conduct of the War, which reported: "Folly, folly, folly reigns supreme. The President is a weak man." Lincoln rejoined, charging that "this improvised vigilant committee . . . is a marplot, and its greatest purpose seems to be to hamper my action and obstruct the military operations."[6]

It is not clear whether the authors of the Constitution had in mind the complete domination of national security affairs which Lincoln exercised and which has become inherent in the modern Presidency. In *The Federalist*, Hamilton contended with regard to the Commander in Chief role, "In this respect his authority would be nominally the same with that of the king of Great Britain, but in substance much inferior to it."[7] In the same essay, Hamilton concluded, with regard to the overall authority of the President, that "it would be difficult to determine whether that magistrate would in the aggregate possess more or less power than the Governor of New York."[8]

It is clear that Hamilton was setting forth this view to allay the fears of his fellow Americans, lest the Constitution re-create a tyrannical magistrate with the title of President. His own views of the Presidency were more accurately set forth in his next essay, when he declared, "Energy in the Executive is a leading character in the definition of good government. It is essential to the protection of the community against foreign attacks. . . ."[9] President Nixon, in his own assertion of authority with regard to national security policy, was to make this Hamiltonian observation a favorite quotation.[10]

Indeed, the modern Presidency, with its concept of broad sweeping powers, especially in the national security and foreign policy areas, has been described as "neo Hamiltonian." As Louis W. Koenig has observed, the Hamiltonian concept, set forth in a remarkable series of reports written during the last two decades of the eighteenth century, "looked towards the transformation of this nation from an agricultural society—very simple, very defenseless—very rapidly into what Hamilton like to call a mixed economy, and one therefore of manufacture and commerce and also with a respectable capacity for national security."[11]

In marked contrast to the Hamiltonian concept or "model," with a dominant executive, is the Madisonian, with a dominant legislative branch. Of very recent date—since the Nixon downfall in 1974—the Madisonian concept has been reasserting itself.

Hamilton, the principal architect of national security policy, never found Presidential authority lacking for a broad-ranging program in the first twelve years of the new federal government under the Constitution. He made initiatives to the Congress to establish service academies and "in case of invasion" to enact a draft from among "all persons from eighteen to forty-five inclusively. . . ."[12] Moreover, a century and three-quarters before the CIA came into being, Hamilton insisted that "it is essential the Executive should have . . . secret service money." Such use of funds would not be subject to the review of Congress, though Hamilton opined that "if the measure cannot be carried without it, the expenditure may be with the approbation of three members of each House of Congress."[13]

Before 1800, Hamilton had set forth most of the principles of national security policy leadership of the modern Presidency. In most instances he found the authority in the Commander in Chief role. In all of this Washington had expressed either a concurring or, indeed, in part, an initiating view.[14] It is interesting to note that when Washington died, Hamilton referred not to the passing of our first President but rather to "the death of our beloved Commander-in-Chief. . . ."[15]

More than six decades were to pass before another President was so fully to assert the Commander in Chief role. President James Buchanan questioned his own authority to put down rebellion at the South. Lincoln, however, by the broadest views of his authority as Commander in Chief, even went so far as to suspend the writ of habeas corpus. No President since has taken such a broad view of that authority, although twentieth-century Presidents, commencing with Theodore Roosevelt and Wilson, have, in general, taken a rigorous view of such authority. The one modern President who perhaps most closely approached the Lincoln Commander in Chief concept considered himself a special student of the Civil War period. He was Harry S Truman.

Truman's Inheritance

"Mr. President . . . ," reporters addressed Harry S Truman a few moments after he had taken the oath of office.

"I wish you didn't have to call me that," Truman responded.[16] This was doubtless Truman's sincere view during his first months in the Presidency. Indeed, although in the organizational area he made early contributions in the national security sphere, his first twenty months in office were at times lamentably nonassertive and at others bellicose. This was especially so in the national foreign policy area in the face of Soviet aggressive expanionism. However, as he gained confidence in his position and began his program response to Communist aggression in early 1947, he warmed up to his position. Indeed, he was soon able to boast to White House visitors, "I make American foreign policy."[17]

Truman prided himself on his ability to make decisions. Commentators and historians are often prone to express amazement that a former field artillery captain of World War I, whose only post–high school education had been brief attendance at a local law school, would make such difficult command decisions. This ignores his self-study of history as well as his continuing military education as he rose to the rank of full colonel in the Army Reserve. It also ignores the much respected position he had earned in World War II as chairman of the Senate Committee to Investigate the Defense Program. This success as a wartime investigator had given him a claim to supplant Henry Wallace as FDR's 1944 running mate.

Despite Truman's pride in his decisionmaking ability, four of his Presidential command decisions bear further scrutiny. They are: dropping the two atomic bombs on Japan (1945); the incremental entry into the Korean War (1950); firing MacArthur (1951); and seizing the steel mills (1952). Almost defensively, with an eye to history, Truman wrote in his *Memoirs* regarding his decisionmaking process:

> By nature not being given to making snap judgments or easy decisions, I required all available facts and information before coming to a decision. But once a decision was made, I did not worry about it afterward. I had trained myself to look back into history for precedents, because instinctively I sought perspective in the span of history for decisions I had to make.[18]

In this self-analysis on decisionmaking, Truman concluded, "Most of the problems a President has to face have their roots in the past."[19] Because he lacked familiarity with that past and because he had had complete confidence in FDR, Truman was befuddled in his first months as President. He had not been a party to any of the wartime conferences of the allied powers.

At Tehran in 1943, Stalin had dissuaded Roosevelt from accepting Churchill's advice to invade the Balkans, thus leaving that area for the Soviet's postwar occupation. The decisionmaking at Yalta is especially subject to criticism. The Joint Chiefs of Staff had refused to accept the optimistic estimates of the field commanders regarding the imminence of victory over both Germany and Japan, and Roosevelt accepted the JCS position. Moreover, in the European war he retreated from the natural geographic boundary line between East and West occupation, the Elbe River. Although the river did not change its course, immediate postwar political boundaries placed it in the middle of East Germany. Writing in 1947, Eisenhower declared: "I always felt that the Western Allies would probably have secured an agreement to occupy more of Germany than we actually did. I believe that if our political heads had been as convinced as we were at SHAEF of the certainty of early victory in the West they would have insisted, at Yalta, upon the line of the Elbe as the natural geographic line dividing the eastern and western occupation areas."[20]

To Roosevelt's defense it must be said that the dramatic allied breakthrough across the Rhine came a few weeks after (March 1945) rather than before the Yalta Conference. In this breakthrough, which had invited a clear path to Berlin, the Western allies might also have taken Prague and occupied Czechoslovakia, thereby precluding the future tragic course of that nation. Eisenhower shared Roosevelt's concern that the advancing East and West allied armies be kept apart and was content to stop at the Elbe, where they awaited the Soviet troops. As a soldier, he believed that the settlement of the boundaries was a political matter which would not be affected by the disposition of the respective allied troops at war's end.

The German zones that were to be occupied after the German surrender had been drawn by the European Advisory Commission, established by the Soviets, Great Britain, and the United States. The Commission had granted, for occupation purposes, approximately 40 percent of pre-1937 Germany to the Soviets. More significantly, Berlin would be far within that zone, more than 100 miles east of the western allied (British) nearest point. Although the U.S. State Department had expressed concern, there was no reserved corridor from the West for access to Berlin, which would be jointly occupied. Admiral W. D. Leahy later recalled that free access to Berlin "did not seem important at the time. I do not believe any of us... ," he added, "thought that three years later a state of virtual armed truce would exist in Berlin with the Russians enforcing a land blockade...."[21]

The end of the war in Europe had come with surprising rapidity, and on May 8, 1945, Prime Minister Churchill and President Truman had proclaimed VE (Victory in Europe) Day. In early June an Allied Control Committee, consisting of General Eisenhower and Marshals Bernard Montgomery and Georgi Zhukov, had begun functioning in Berlin.

Roosevelt had believed at Yalta that it was imperative, once the war in Europe was over, to have the Soviets establish a second front against Japan. On the basis of outmoded reports, the JCS had concluded on January 23 that Russian assistance in the war against Japan was necessary. Army and Navy intelligence reports portraying Japan as near collapse had been ignored. An Air Force report, with the same conclusion, was actually urgently sent to Yalta, but to no effect. Among the Joint Chiefs it was General George C. Marshall who was especially insistent that Soviet aid was necessary in the war against Japan. Leahy believed it unnecessary, and Admiral Ernest J. King thought that the price Roosevelt was willing to pay was too high.[22] Roosevelt had agreed not only to restoration of Russian losses incurred in the Russo-Japanese War in 1904 but also to the cession of the northern Japanese islands (the Kurils) to the Soviet Union.

At Yalta the principles for a United Nations Charter (enunciated at the Dumbarton Oaks Conference in the fall of 1944) were agreed to; it was further agreed at Yalta to convene the United Nations Charter Conference on April 25 in San Francisco. The UN had been FDR's fondest hope. Upon his return from Yalta he had told the Congress: "The Crimean Conference . . . spells the end of the system of unilateral action and exclusive alliances and spheres of influence and balances of power. . . ."[23]

Roosevelt, in these last days, did have the abundant good sense to include bipartisan Senatorial representation in the American delegation. Hence both Tom Connally and Arthur Vandenberg participated in the San Francisco United Nations Conference. To satisfy the United States Senate as well as the Soviets, some kind of Security Council veto had seemed inescapable. But the Soviet demand that the veto extend to cutting off discussion should have been recognized as a portent of future intransigence. Only because of a personal appeal to Stalin, by Harry Hopkins and Ambassador Averell Harriman in Moscow, did the Russians relent from their gag rule. By June 26 the charter had been completed and President Truman came to address the concluding session at the San Francisco Opera House. There he expressed "the hope for a world of free countries . . . which will work and cooperate in a friendly civilized community of nations."[24]

Truman's baptism of dealings with the Soviets came in the final wartime conference of the Big Three, July 17 to August 2, 1945. The very location, Potsdam, near the ruins of Berlin in the Russian zone, was significant. Already there had been violations of the Yalta agreement regarding "free and unfettered elections" in Poland and "free elections" in Hungary, Rumania, and Bulgaria. Despite the assertion that self-government would be restored in Soviet-occupied countries, Communist regimes had been imposed by force in all these countries. Churchill, who had unsuccessfully urged Truman to send the victorious Eisenhower command on to take Berlin, wanted at least some occupational bargaining power at Potsdam. Accordingly, he urged retention of the Elbe River line, the point at which the U.S. and British forces had awaited the arrival of the Soviet forces. He further urged Truman to come to Britain for discussion before proceeding to Potsdam. Truman declined both suggestions. He stated that he wished to avoid the impression of "ganging up" against the Soviets and contended that to postpone withdrawal of the United States–British troops "would harm our relations with the Soviets." Seventeen days before Truman came into Potsdam with his new Secretary of State, James F. Byrnes, the troops were withdrawn. "This struck a knell in my breast," Churchill wrote. "But I had no choice but to submit."[25]

At Potsdam, Churchill and his Foreign Minister, Eden, represented a position which war-weary Britain, beset with domestic ills, desired to forget. Midway in the Potsdam talks, he and Eden were repudiated at the polls and replaced by Clement Attlee as Prime Minister and Ernest Bevin as Foreign Minister.

There was superficial agreement at Potsdam on such matters as peace treaties with the lesser axis powers and the demilitarization of Germany and four-power (including France) German and Austrian occupation. On August 9, seven days following the end of the Potsdam Conference, Truman assured the American people in a radio address from the White House: " . . . it was easy for me to get along in mutual understanding and friendship with Generalissimo Stalin. . . . Strong foundations of good will and cooperation," he further assured them, "had been laid by President Roosevelt."[26]

Ending World War II

Truman not only lacked prior dealings with the Soviets and shared Roosevelt's hope that wartime allies might become peacetime allies, but he actually believed, because of the expressed anti-Russian views of Churchill and Eden, that the principal United States postwar role involving the Soviets would be as an arbiter in British-Russian disputes.[27] What Truman did, unwittingly and despite the Churchill-Eden warnings, was to throw away some of the United States' strongest Potsdam bargaining points.

At Potsdam, Truman gave the final go-ahead in what many consider to have been his most controversial command decision, to drop the first atomic bomb on Japan "after about August 3" and a *second* bomb "as soon as made ready."[28] If Truman is to be faulted here for a command decision, it is more clearly for the second than the first bomb. The first, codenamed Little Boy, on August 6 killed an estimated 70,000 Japanese at Hiroshima; the second, Fat Man, three days later killed 40,000 at Nagasaki. Horrible as these statistics are (and at least as many additional Japanese were wounded), they cannot be viewed as isolated incidents in a total war. (The massive fire bombings, for example, of Dresden and Tokyo had produced more casualties, though by hundreds of aircraft and thousands of bombs rather than one.) Unless Japan could be brought to surrender earlier, an invasion of Kyushu was targeted for November 1, with an estimated 31,000 allied casualties the first month.

The question is whether the first and the second atomic blasts over Japan were necessary to bring the war to a close. The weapon was a Truman inheritance from Roosevelt, who had commenced the Manhattan Project to beat the Germans in developing an atomic bomb. Roosevelt had, characteristically, not divulged how he had intended to use the bomb. The question of the use of the bomb is also related to the surrender terms that were being exacted and the temperament of the new Commander in Chief.

Barton J. Bernstein of Stanford University, who has studied the bomb-dropping command decision in considerable depth, states that Truman was "anxious, unsure, overwhelmed," as he assumed the Presidential office.[29] In his VE Day proclamation Truman had called for the "unconditional surrender" of the Japanese armed forces. A month later the Japanese were making overtures to the Russians to negotiate terms of surrender to the allies. The United States, having broken the Japanese code, was aware of these overtures; it was also aware that the Russians, having secured enormous promises as a reward for entering the war, were eager to participate in the final kill and would have nothing to do with the Japanese peace feelers.

Secretary of War Henry L. Stimson, who, as Hoover's Secretary of State had had considerable experience with the Japanese, believed that the surrender terms should be qualified to permit the retention of the constitutional monarchy, as did the former U.S. ambassador to Japan, Joseph C. Grew, serving as Under Secretary of State. However, Secretary of State James F. Byrnes and Roosevelt's former Secretary of State, Cordell Hull, talked the befuddled President Truman out of accepting this condition. Thus the declaration on the Japanese surrender had omitted this provision regarding the Emperor, deemed so important by the Japanese people.

The early August sequence of events is significant. In his August 6 announcement of the dropping of the first atomic bomb on Japan, Truman promised that it would be followed by a "rain of ruin" of future aerial attacks. Two days later Emperor Hirohito expressed his "wish that the war be ended as soon as possible on the basis of the Potsdam Declaration." Both Foreign Minister Shigenori Togo and Premier Kantaro Suzuki accepted this position, though three military members of the Big Six (the Supreme Council for the Direction of the War) held out for additional terms.

Early in the morning of August 9, the Russians invaded both Manchuria and Korea and met but token resistance. While the Big Six were debating, at 11:02 A.M. the bomb fell on Nagasaki. The following day the Emperor cast the deciding vote and the offer to surrender was transmitted via Switzerland. It accepted the Potsdam Declaration, but with the understanding that the Emperor be retained. Here was the basic omission of the Potsdam Declaration, which Secretary Byrnes now accepted with the provision that the Emperor's authority would be subject to the supervision of the commander of the occupation forces. Truman named Douglas MacArthur for that post. Ironically, this was to set in motion the beginnings of a collision course climaxed nearly six years later in another of Truman's most controversial decisions, the MacArthur dismissal.

Truman proclaimed the Japanese peace on August 14. On September 2, with MacArthur presiding, the terms of the surrender were signed in Tokyo Bay, aboard the battleship bearing the name of Truman's home state, Missouri. The ship's flag was the one that had been flying over the Capitol at Washington Sunday morning, December 7, 1941, the day of the Pearl Harbor attack. MacArthur, wearing an open-necked shirt and no medals, was in marked contrast to the Japanese party, who wore formal morning clothes and silk hats. They were led by Mamoru Shigemitsu, the Foreign Minister of the hastily formed new Japanese peace government. In his remarks on the occasion of this last act of World War II, MacArthur eased the tensions by his expressed hope "that from this solemn occasion a better world shall emerge. . . ."[30]

The gnawing questions remain today: (1) Should the Potsdam Declaration have accepted the Stimson-Grew recommendations for conditional surrender? (2) Were the first and second atomic bombs necessary? Writing at the time of the August 1945 capitulation, David Lawrence, editor of the *U.S. News*, observed: "The surrender of Japan had been inevitable for weeks. It has come now as anticipated." In this searching editorial, Lawrence inquired whether instead of dropping the bomb on Japan, a warning of its destructive capacity might have been made, "to persuade the Japanese militarists to release their people and surrender?"[31]

Recently it has been revealed that in a meeting of President Truman with the Joint Chiefs of Staff and the secretaries of the armed services, one voice had been raised against dropping the bomb on Japan. John J. McCloy, Assistant Secretary of War, had asked whether a warning of the possible use of the atomic bomb, or a demonstration bombing, might not achieve the desired effect on an already defeated Japan. Regrettably his position inspired no support.[32] Secretary of War Stimson, who perhaps best grasped the full historical, humanitarian, and political implications of the bomb, found one other person opposed to its use, Eisenhower. At Potsdam, Eisenhower "expressed the hope that we would never have to use such a thing against any enemy. . . ."[33] Moreover, Eisenhower expressed his belief that "the Japanese were ready to surrender and it wasn't necessary to hit them with that awful thing."[34] MacArthur, the Supreme Commander of Allied Forces in the Pacific, was simply informed that the weapon would be used. Later he stated that from a military point of view it was completely unnecessary.[35]

At most, the first and second bombs, combined with the Soviet declaration of war (which Truman had sought to preclude since VE Day), had speeded up the Japanese decision process by a few days. More days would have been saved by conditioning the Potsdam Declaration as Grew and Stimson had proposed regarding the retention of the Emperor. Perhaps Truman's observation on receiving word of the dropping of the first bomb, while aboard ship heading home from Potsdam, best sums up his decision. He exclaimed, "This is the greatest thing in history."[36]

Truman and the Origins of the Cold War

Truman's near-greatness as a President has its basis principally in those courageous decisions between 1947 and 1950 when he counterattacked Stalin's aggressive Soviet policies. Some fault him for waiting until early 1947. His relative restraint until then should be emphasized in light of the amazing pronouncements of certain recent revisionist historians who have asserted that the United States, not the Soviets, originated the Cold War. It has also been suggested that if Roosevelt had lived, the Cold War might have been averted and the spirit of accord at Yalta might have carried forward to the post–World War II era. This is extremely doubtful. One of Roosevelt's final communications to Stalin was a lengthy indictment of Russia for violation of the Yalta protocol regarding free elections in Poland, Bulgaria, and Rumania.[37] Stalin had no more trust in Roosevelt than he did in his successor. In Roosevelt's last days Stalin charged him with seeking separate negotiations with the Germans.[38] On his first full day in office, April 13, Truman received from Secretary of State Edward R. Stettinius, Jr., a briefing declaring that "since the Yalta Conference the Soviet Government has taken a firm and uncompromising position on nearly every major question that has arisen in our relations."[39]

The simple fact was that with victory in sight, Stalin was determined to secure governments under Soviet domination in eastern and central Europe. Although in Rumania only 10 percent of the population was Communist, the Soviets had, before Roosevelt's death, already taken over that country. This then was the situation confronting Truman the day he took office. Within a few days, like his predecessor, he was protesting the violation of the Yalta Declaration. A Soviet puppet regime was being established in Austria, and Truman protested this violation of "the spirit of the Yalta declaration on liberated Europe. . . ."[40]

The most difficult issue for both Churchill and Truman was Stalin's refusal to recognize either the Polish government in exile in London or a mixed government with its representatives along with the Soviets' representative. The defense of Poland had brought France and Britain into war against Germany, and Germany's then ally, Russia, had joined in the attack on Poland. Now with the Polish liberation, leaders of the Polish underground who had been enticed to visit Moscow had there been thrown into prison. During the first days of the Truman Presidency, Churchill and Truman jointly protested these events by a communication to Stalin on April 18. Stalin's reply of April 24 made clear that the Soviets could not comprehend why a free and independent Poland could have such meaning for Britain and America. "The question on Poland," Stalin contended, "has the same meaning for the security of the Soviet Union as the question on Belgium and Greece for the security of Great Britain."[41]

Truman, who came to the conclusion that "the Russians were always suspicious of everything and everybody," endeavored to allay those suspicions through two special friends of the Soviet Union. Thus, in late May 1945 he sent Ambassador Joseph E. Davies to confer with Churchill and Harry Hopkins to meet with Stalin, along with the American ambassador to Moscow, Averell Harriman. On May 27 Hopkins reported: "Stalin listened with the utmost attention to our description of the present state of American public opinion and gave us the impression that he also was disturbed at the drift of events. . . ."[42] One student of this period, William L. Neumann, has termed the week-long conversations between Hopkins and Stalin as "the fullest, frankest, and possibly the friendliest Russo-American exchange to take place before the Cold War mood settled down over both capitals."[43] For the time being, Poland was removed from an element of controversy by the admission of Stanislaw Mikolajczyk and some other non-Communist leaders to the

Provisional Government of National Unity, which the United States and the United Kingdom proceeded to recognize. However, in rigged elections, by 1947 the non-Communists were ousted.

Some revisionist historians picture Stimson, Kennan, Leahy, and Marshall as cautioning moderation, while Truman was listening instead to get-tough advice from Forrestal and Harriman. As a part of this scenario they picture Truman as going to Potsdam in 1945 and using the atomic bomb as a club to get his own way.[44] Indeed they suggest that the Hopkins mission to Moscow was a delaying tactic until Truman's ace card, the bomb, was ready.[45] Thus, they assert that "from Potsdam on, the bomb was the constant factor in the American approach to the Soviet Union."[46] To an extent, that statement was true, but Stimson, a most wise counselor to Presidents, realized that an early accommodation must be reached. He wrote Truman on September 11, 1945, ". . . I consider the problem of our satisfactory relations with Russia as not merely connected with but as virtually dominated by the problem of the atomic bomb." He cautioned that "having this weapon rather ostentatiously on our hip, their suspicions and their distrust of our purposes and motives will increase."[47]

Recognizing Stimson's counsel, Truman declared that "the decisions I had to make and the policies I would recommend to Congress on the use and control of atomic energy could well influence the future course of civilization. This," he noted in retrospect, "was to be the beginning of the period of hope and many trials."[48]

Truman was not, however, prepared to accept Stimson's proposal for a joint British–Russian–United States agreement on the control of the bomb. Instead in 1946 he took before the United Nations the Baruch Plan, which would provide international control of atomic energy and inspection and licensing authority. The Soviets took the position that the essential first step in international atomic energy control was the elimination of the American stockpile of atomic bombs. This caused Truman to write Baruch on July 10, 1946: "We should not under any circumstances throw away our gun until we are sure the rest of the world can't arm against us."[49] Although the United Nations Commission accepted the American Plan, the report was blocked from further consideration in the Security Council by the Soviet veto.

In addition to atomic energy control, the other five major areas of contention between the Soviets and the United States during the Truman period were the axis peace treaties, quadripartite government in Austria and Germany, the Soviet satellites, the Middle East, and the Far East.

Soviet ambitions in the Middle East, as in eastern and central Europe, were in part a carryover of Czarist Russia's aims in those areas. Thus, for example, earlier unrealized Russian ambitions for control of the Dardanelles, the strait between the Sea of Marmara and the Aegean, would be a cause of pressure on Turkey. But there was the added ingredient in the Middle East, as elsewhere, of international Communism, the attempt to establish governments espousing the Communist doctrine.

The first postwar move in the Middle East came in oil-rich and strategically important Iran. It had been at the Iranian capital, Tehran, that Roosevelt, Churchill, and Stalin had met in November and December 1943 and agreed to the Normandy invasion. Through Iran the United States had furnished the Soviets with 52,000 jeeps, 400,000 trucks, and 7,000 tanks, the rolling stock for the Red Army's invasion of Germany from the east. At the London Conference of Foreign Ministers in September 1945 it had been agreed that all foreign troops would be withdrawn from Iran by March 2, 1946. Although the Americans and British complied, the Soviets did not, thus posing a threat to the control of Iran's oil reserves as well as flanking neighboring Turkey. Only after the most blunt message from Truman to Stalin did Moscow announce on March 24 that Soviet troops would withdraw from Iran.

In the midst of the Iranian crisis, following the Soviet takeovers in eastern and central Europe, Truman in March 1946 journeyed to Fulton, Missouri, with former British Prime Minister Winston Churchill. There, on the campus of little Westminster College, Churchill warned that an "iron curtain" had been lowered across Europe from the Adriatic to the Baltic. At the time most Americans viewed the pronouncement with considerable skepticism, though Stalin responded like an enraged wounded bull. Stalin compared Churchill and his American "friends" to Hitler and termed the now famous address "a call to war with the Soviet Union. . . ."[50] He defended Soviet takeovers in eastern and central Europe as protective.

Within three weeks after Churchill's Fulton speech, Stalin mounted an almost hysterical effort to keep Western ideas from permeating Russia and her satellites. This included a rejection of the World Bank and the International Monetary Fund and the announcement of a Five-Year Plan for economic self-sufficiency.

Although Stalin had withdrawn from Iran, in July 1946 pressure was renewed on Turkey to share control of the Dardanelles. Truman, with the recommendations of Under Secretary of State Dean Acheson and the service secretaries and service chiefs, adopted a firm posture of Turkish support, as did the British and French. For the time being the Soviets backed down.

Meanwhile, Secretary of State Byrnes was making an heroic attempt to settle the Austrian and German questions. Although the Potsdam Conference had exempted Austria from reparations, the Soviets holding of Vienna and the most productive agricultural and industrial districts were drawing off the nation's resources. The Austrians retaliated by electing an overwhelmingly anti-Communist Parliament in November 1945. The Russians were not about to agree to a treaty settlement to end occupation.

Germany, like Austria, had been divided into four administrative zones, the Russians taking the east, the British the northwest, the French the west, and the United States the south. As such, the Russians got the agriculture, the British and French the industry, and the United States the scenery. Berlin was to be administered jointly by the four powers, and from the Potsdam Conference an Allied Control Conference had been established. The first weeks of joint administration were marked by cordiality. Eisenhower, the American representative, was invited to Moscow. Truman returned the courtesy, inviting Zhukov to the United States, but Zhukov was not permitted to come. John Eisenhower, who accompanied his father to Russia, suggested years later: "Maybe, with the honeymoon at an end—and with Stalin becoming increasingly jealous of Zhukov's popularity—Zhukov had become too much a symbol of U.S.-U.S.S.R. friendship."[51] Even before Eisenhower returned to the United States at the end of 1945 to become Army Chief of Staff, succeeding Marshall, the conflict at higher levels had come to be felt in Berlin.

At Potsdam, Eisenhower had recommended to Byrnes, that the State Department rather than the military handle administration. While at first accepting the recommendation, Byrnes, on the basis of cost and manpower, recommended continuing the military.[52] Eisenhower's successor on the Four Power Control Council, General Lucius Clay, found the Council in constant deadlock. The Russians repudiated the principle that Germany should be treated as one economic unit. Soon an economic union of the British and American zones developed.

In this climate Secretary Byrnes came to Stuttgart, where in a speech on September 6, 1946, he proposed a Germany reunited not only economically but politically. The United States, he offered, would sign a twenty-five- or even a forty-year four-power pact to keep Germany disarmed. The Soviets rejected the proposal. Clearly, the iron curtain Churchill had portrayed had descended over Europe.

Just as an iron curtain had lowered across Europe, a bamboo curtain was about to come down in Asia. With the end of World War II, Chinese Communists under Mao Tse-tung resumed a struggle for control of China. President Roosevelt's personal representative in China, Patrick J. Hurley, had in late November 1945 attacked the Truman foreign policy at a National Press Club talk and submitted a letter of resignation. According to Truman, Hurley "would have been out, with or without that letter."[53] In December 1945, Truman sent Marshall, who had just retired as Army Chief of Staff, to be Hurley's successor. Truman instructed Marshall to make clear to Chiang "that China disunited could not expect American help."[54] As the fighting between the Nationalists and the Communists continued, Truman, on August 10, 1946, criticized Chiang for "failing to comprehend the liberal trend of the times. . . ."[55] Although Chiang's forces had the upper hand in the fighting throughout 1946, Marshall, unable to bring Chiang and Mao to an understanding, asked at year's end to be recalled. There was no love lost on Marshall's part for Chiang, and his feelings were reflected in the estimate of the situation he reported to Truman. In his *Memoirs* Truman wrote, "There is no doubt in my mind that if Chiang Kai-shek had been only a little more conciliatory an understanding could have been reached."[56] The end of the Marshall mission was followed by the virtual end of American military aid for the Nationalists, and Chiang's military fortunes waned until his final withdrawal in 1949 to Formosa. Although Marshall's entire career had been in the armed forces, Truman believed Marshall had been the right man for the China mission "because he was deeply steeped in democracy. . . ."[57] As for Chiang, Truman concluded, he "would not heed the advice of one of the greatest military strategists in history [Marshall] and lost to the Communists."[58]

In this struggle the Soviets had not played a passive role, having made Manchuria the base of Chinese Communist operation and supplied Mao's forces with arms. The controversy continues to this day as to whether with American advisers and arms Chiang might have successfully resisted Mao in 1947 and beyond, as he had in 1946. Certainly by 1949 the situation was irretrievable short of the massive armed intervention of the United States, something which American public opinion would never have tolerated.

Truman named Marshall to succeed Byrnes as Secretary of State in early 1947. Byrnes, the second of Truman's four Secretaries of State, became one of his political critics. One of Marshall's first missions as Secretary, in March 1947, was to go to Moscow for a Conference of Foreign Ministers on German unification. The meeting ended in such total disagreement as to become a benchmark for future Soviet-American relations. If one accepts the position that Tehran and Yalta had been sincere expressions toward understanding, then, as Julius W. Pratt has noted, Marshall's return from Moscow "marked the end of the road."[59] Shortly thereafter, the anonymously written "Mr. X" (George Kennan) article

warning that the Soviets must be "contained" appeared in
Foreign Affairs. It signalized the so-called policy of containment which was to characterize the balance of the first and
the second Truman administrations. It also signaled the institutionalization of the Cold War.

If one were to pinpoint when an American get-tough policy was determined, it might be dated from a handwritten
letter which Truman handed Secretary of State Byrnes on
January 5, 1946. Truman had been nettled by Byrnes's handling of the December 1945 foreign ministers' conference. He
reiterated his dissatisfaction with the chain of events going
back to the Soviet occupation of Latvia, Estonia and
Lithuania, Poland, Bulgaria, and Rumania. He noted the
Soviet pressures on Iran and Turkey. He concluded, "I do
not think we should play compromise any longer. . . . I'm
tired of babying the Soviets."[60] If revisionist historians want
a date, an act, or a word for the Cold War, this blunt Truman
memorandum is it. But it ignores the massive provocation
and reverses cause and effect.

Containment and Collective Security, 1947–1950

Harry S Truman—not George Kennan, George Marshall, or
Dean Acheson—was the author of the policy of containment.
And yet, in a very real sense, it was a response to events in
the eastern Mediterranean, events which inspired the Truman Doctrine in 1947.

Nature abhors a vacuum. In 1946–1947, Britain, which
from the end of the Napoleonic War had been the dominant
power in the eastern Mediterranean, was signaling urgently
that it wanted, it needed, out. Either the United States or the
Soviet Union would step in. If both, a confrontation was in
the making.

Simultaneous with the Chinese civil war, a civil war was
going on in Greece. Britain, which had helped Greece
achieve its independence in the early nineteenth century,
had historically come to its aid. It did so again in the immediate post–World War II period. Indeed, between 1945
and 1947, British troops kept the Greek peninsula from fall-

ing to the Communists, who were receiving aid supplied through Albania, Bulgaria, and Yugoslavia. Now, in early 1947, as in Palestine, a postwar impoverished Britain felt an imperative need in Greece to withdraw its troops. Hence it sent a distress signal to Washington. Britain, which had also been helping Turkey withstand Soviet pressures for control of the Dardanelles and the western end of the Black Sea, also noted that is was time for Washington to do more to help the Turks.

Thus, while the foreign ministers were wrangling in Moscow, Truman on March 12, 1947, went before the Congress to ask for $400 million in aid to Greece and Turkey. The request marked the beginning of a new policy of containment of Communism in Europe. In his address, which came to be termed the Truman Doctrine, Truman told the joint session of Congress, in candor: "Britain finds itself under the necessity of reducing or liquidating its commitments in several parts of the world, including Greece . . . [and] Turkey." The much heralded Truman Doctrine was thus dictated partly by the necessity to replace Britain in the strategic areas of Greece and Turkey. But it went beyond this to a declaration for "helping free and independent nations to maintain their freedom. . . ." Truman asserted that "it must be the policy of the United States to support free peoples who are resisting attempted subjugation by armed minorities or by outside pressures." He made clear that the United States would "assist free peoples to work out their own destinies in their own way." Truman recounted the "violations of the Yalta agreement," noting the forced Communist domination of Poland, Rumania, Bulgaria, and other nations. He called for "immediate and resolute action," including military advisers and technical assistance as well as money, and recognized that "this is a serious course upon which we embark."[61]

Two months later, signing the Greek and Turkish aid programs into law, Truman noted the "overwhelming" support of the 80th Congress as "proof that the United States earnestly desires peace and is willing to make a vigorous effort to help create conditions of peace." He then proceeded to amplify the Truman Doctrine, noting that "the conditions of peace include, among other things, the ability of nations to

maintain order and independence, and to support themselves economically."[62]

The aid to Greece, including a military mission led by
General James A. Van Fleet, came at the eleventh hour. The
Greek Communists, with aid supplied through Greece's
northern neighbors, Albania, Bulgaria, and Yugoslavia, had
nearly toppled the Greek anti-Communist government. (The
strengthening of Turkish forces was to provide an unexpected dividend a few years later, when, in Korea, the Turkish forces proved to be among the most effective against the
Communists.)

On the heels of the Truman Doctrine came the Marshall
Plan, enunciated at the Harvard commencement by Secretary of State Marshall on June 5, 1947. The prologue to
that address, outlining the concept, had been delivered by
Under Secretary Acheson at Cleveland on May 8 (a speech
which Truman had hoped to give himself). The Marshall
proposal was not entirely original. The call to rebuild a prostrate Europe economically marked a reorganization and augmentation of the aid programs the United States was already
financing, especially the United Nations Relief and Rehabilitation Administration. Again Truman succinctly got to
the heart of the matter. In doing so, he indicated considerable skill in rallying popular support. At a time when the
United States might have entered upon a neoisolationism
reminiscent of the 1920s, he asserted that "the people of the
United States recognize, as do the people of the European
nations, that the earliest practicable achievement of economic health and consequent political stability in Europe, is
of utmost importance for the peace and well-being of the
world."[63]

Marshall's proposal had made no distinction between Communist and non-Communist Europe. The Soviet response to
the Marshall Plan proposal was the Warsaw Conference of
September 1947, at which nine east European states resolved
to defeat "American imperialism." Though tempted, the nations in the Soviet orbit declined to participate. The Soviets,
not only by their denunciation of the Marshall Plan but by
their denial of the right of their satellites to participate and by
the simultaneous establishment of the Communist Informa-

tion Bureau (Cominform), further institutionalized the Cold War.

The other sixteen nations of Europe (excluding Spain, which was not invited, and Germany, which did not, as yet, have a government) formed a Committee of European Economic Cooperation.

These European nations accepted the Marshall economic aid proposal with alacrity, but it was the February 24, 1948, Communist seizure of Czechoslovakia which spurred the administration and Congress to speed up massive economic aid for Europe. The takeover of a democratic, liberal, modern, and prosperous Czechoslovakia by a militant minority caused a shock wave also to American diplomatic and military planners. It was coupled with a classified message from General Clay, the American military governor in Berlin, suggesting the possible imminence of war. All of this came when the United States armed forces, which had numbered 13 million at the end of World War II, had shrunk to 1,374,000. Gloomily Marshall told an NSC meeting, "We are playing with fire while we have nothing with which to put it out."[64] It came at a time when the harried Secretary of Defense, Forrestal, was taking the warring service chiefs to Key West to try to get an agreement on missions.[65]

In such a climate Truman on March 17 went before the Congress to personally deliver a forceful message which was broadcast nationally. He asserted, ". . . one nation has not only refused to cooperate in the establishment of a just and honorable peace, but—even worse—has actively sought to prevent it." He further charged, "One nation . . . has persistently obstructed the work of the United Nations by constant abuse of the veto," and declared, "Since the close of hostilities, the Soviet Union and its agents have destroyed the independence and democratic character of a whole series of nations in Eastern and Central Europe." Avowing, "There are times in world history when it is far wiser to act than to hesitate," Truman asked the Congress to "speedily complete its action on the European recovery program." He further asked for "temporary re-enactment of selective service legislation" and for universal military training.[66]

The Congress completed the Economic Cooperation Act of

1948 within a fortnight. (Selective service was reestablished in June 1948, but universal military training was defeated.) On April 3 the Economic Cooperation Administration was created, with Paul G. Hoffman as its administrator. Communist-inspired strikes in France and Italy did not deter those countries from accepting Marshall Plan aid. In the next three years the European Recovery Program (the Marshall Plan), which cost the United States $10,250,000,000, contributed to amazing European economic growth, far exceeding prewar levels, and also contributed to non-European areas. It was Truman's retrospective estimate "that without the Marshall Plan it would have been difficult for western Europe to remain free from the tyranny of Communism."[67]

The Marshall Plan had been designed for countries with advanced economies devastated by the war. Truman recognized that this provided no answer to the Communist threat in lesser-developed countries such as India, Indonesia, and many Latin American nations. Thus in his January 20, 1949, Inaugural Address, his fourth point, which created the term "Point Four Program," recommended technical assistance. It was launched in 1950 with a modest $35 million appropriation.

The following year, 1951, the Mutual Security Agency replaced the European Cooperation Administration as American aid to Europe shifted from economic to military. The fall of Czechoslovakia had stirred the Benelux countries, France, and Great Britain to a fifty-year treaty of economic, social, and cultural collaboration as well as mutual self-defense. This, then, was the basis for the North Atlantic Treaty Organization which Truman encouraged on March 17, 1948, in an address to the Congress. Article 51 of the UN Charter had legalized "collective self-defense" by UN member groups. This had been the principle for the Rio Pact of September 2, 1947, the first regional collective security pact. That the United States had been a signatory was pointed up in the crucial Vandenberg Resolution of June 11, 1948, for Senate support for NATO.

It was the first United States alliance with any European power since that with the French in 1778, and raw Soviet

force had inspired the action as much as Truman's and Vandenberg's statesmanlike views. In an effort to squeeze the
Western Allies out of Berlin, on June 24, 1948, the Soviets
had begun the blockade of the 110-mile land corridor to the
western zones. Neither Truman nor the British Cabinet hesitated to initiate a combined airlift of necessities, including
even coal, to keep the western sectors of the beleaguered city
alive. Although Russia issued threats, none of her planes
attacked the round-the-clock transports, and the blockade
was lifted in May 1949. Truman's command decision, accepting the Soviet challenge, had paid off. As he assessed it,
"The Berlin blockade was a move to test our capacity and will
to resist. This action and the previous attempts to take over
Greece and Turkey were part of a Russian plan to probe for
soft spots in the Western Allies' positions all round their own
perimeter."[68]

In the midst of the Berlin blockade, the NATO alliance was
signed April 4, 1949, by twelve North Atlantic and western
European nations: the United States, Canada, Iceland, the
United Kingdom, France, Belgium, the Netherlands,
Luxembourg, Denmark, Norway, Italy, and Portugal. To
these were added Greece and Turkey three years later. (Finally, in 1954 West Germany became a member.)

Bipartisan Foreign Policy, 1947–1950

During the years 1947–1950, when so much of security organization and policy was being enacted, Truman worked
well with Congress, Republicans as well as Democrats. In
1946, for the first time since 1930, the Republicans had
gained control of both houses of Congress. In the face of the
Soviet threat, Arthur H. Vandenberg, the Republican leader
of national security policy in the Senate, provided early leadership in forging bipartisan foreign policy[69] and maintaining
good relations with the President. When Truman presented
him with the Collier Congressional Award in the spring of
1946, Vandenberg graciously observed, "I wouldn't be here
at this spot today if you hadn't left the Senate because you

would be here instead of me." With characteristic candor the President responded, "That is awfully nice of you to say, but I have my doubts on that."[70]

Whereas during the immediate postwar period Truman had problems in working effectively with a number of his national security advisers, including Byrnes as Secretary of State and Forrestal and Johnson at Defense, he was most fortunate in his relationship with Vandenberg. Despite their cordial working relationship, however, Truman and Vandenberg had differing views on the meaning of bipartisanship. Vandenberg believed it should include early consultation in the shaping of policy. Thus, in 1946, he protested lack of consultation on China policy. To this proposal Truman abruptly responded in his December 18, 1946, news conference, asserting, ". . . the President is responsible for the foreign policy of the United States, and when it becomes the duty of the Senate to become involved, they will be informed and the matter will be discussed with them."[71]

Vandenberg, however, worked toward *joint* formulation of policy. NATO became an example of shared initiative, as did support for the Marshall Plan. Indeed, authorship of the European Recovery Act was shared with the Republican leadership of the House and Senate. In his *Memoirs* Truman generously recorded: "Credit is due to Republican Senator Arthur H. Vandenberg and to Republican Representative Charles A. Eaton, the chairmen, respectively, of the Senate Committee on Foreign Relations and the Committee on Foreign Affairs of the House of Representatives. In a Congress dedicated to tax reduction and the pruning of governmental expenditures," Truman added, "they championed this program in a truly bi-partisan manner."[72]

However, ever on guard against invasion of Presidential prerogatives, Truman continued to view the Presidency as the initiating source of policy and as the branch of government that defined the issues and set forth alternative possible courses of action. "Bi-partisanship in foreign policy," Truman declared, "means simply that the President can repose confidence in the members of the other party and that in turn the leaders of that party have confidence in the President's conduct of foreign affairs." He added, "There were occasions when Senator Vandenberg disagreed with my policies, but he never attempted to sabotage them."[73] On a more positive note, Truman recognized Vandenberg's indispensable role in getting foreign policy programs, including many emanating from the State Department, through the Senate. As Truman put it, Vandenberg "knew how to get results."[74]

Vandenberg emphasized that bipartisanship did *not* preclude debate on foreign policy issues. As he expressed it, in October 1948, on the eve of the Presidential election, bipartisanship "means we attempt to hammer out the greatest possible means of agreement so we can speak to the world, not as 'Republicans' or 'Democrats' but as undivided Americans."[75]

With little room for criticism in the national security area, Truman castigated the Republican-controlled 80th Congress as the "worst in history" regarding domestic policy issues. To the surprise of the Chicago *Tribune* and others, Truman did win the November 1948 Presidential election. His Republican opponent, Dewey, reflected a similar anti-Communist foreign policy stand. To Robert A. Divine, "the election of 1948 marked the institutionalization of the Cold War...." Thereafter, Divine and certain other historians and political scientists reviewing the period contend that it made little difference whether there was a Democrat or a Republican label, since "Wall Street bankers and corporation lawyers such as Robert Lovett, James Forrestal, Averell Harriman, and John Foster Dulles continued to manage the bipartisan policy."[76]

After the 1948 election Senator Robert A. Taft became increasingly critical of bipartisan foreign policy. Even earlier, when he supported aid to Greece and Turkey with some reluctance, he had complained that the President was serving up a fait accompli to the Senate, with no opportunity for Congressional consideration. Taft believed strongly that the President must share with the Congress the responsibility for the *shaping* of foreign policy. Even Vandenberg, who became critically ill in 1950 and died the following year, became concerned in his last days with Truman's extensive utilization of the Commander in Chief authority. Although Vandenberg had supported, and in large part had made possible, American participation in NATO, the subsequent mutual defense assistance program disturbed him—because of its cost, but also because it was "almost unbelievable in its grant of unlimited power to the Chief Executive."[77]

Whatever Vandenberg's reservations, Truman must be given high marks for his own incisive role in the formulation of national security policy and for the inauguration of the collective security system through a system of alliances and mutual defense assistance programs complementing the Vandenberg principles. On June 11, 1948, the Vandenberg Resolution had overwhelmingly passed the Senate; it declared that the United States should, among other measures for the promotion of peace, associate itself "by constitutional process, with such regional and other collective arrangements as are based on continuous and effective self-help and mutual aid, and as affect its national security."[78]

Truman had served as Vice President only eighty-two days when, with Roosevelt's death, the Presidency was thrust upon him. He did a remarkable job. He countered Communist aggression and led the nation in a new role of world leadership. Out of the land of the morning calm, in June 1950, the principles of collective security for which he stood were to receive their supreme test as the Cold War suddenly became a Hot War.

IV

****

TRUMAN AS COMMANDER IN CHIEF

> There are a great many different factors that go into the making of a command decision, but in the end there has to be just one decision—or there is no command.
>
> HARRY S TRUMAN

The Man and the Function

The command decision principle set forth in the above quotation, Truman declared, was a lesson he had learned while serving in France in World War I.[1] Nearing his sixty-first birthday when he became President, Truman hardly cut the figure of a commander: standing only 5 feet 8 inches tall, slightly paunchy at some 170 pounds, genial and jaunty, sporting a bow tie, gray hair parted on the left side and combed back, he had a large nose, and a nasal voice with a Midwest twang. He had friendly hazel eyes and wore thick glasses which the chief usher at the White House recalled, "magnified his eyes enormously, giving him a peering, owlish gaze."[2] His shoulders were square, he moved quickly, and he walked briskly, his favorite exercise being the regulation army step of 30 inches, at 120 steps to the minute.[3]

Though it was usually kept in check, Truman had a temper and could use earthy language. At first hesitant, he rapidly became sure of himself and, following his unexpected 1948 election victory, increasingly cocky. With no hesitancy he fired those who did not express his will. Indeed, during the course of his incumbency he fired more department heads than any other President. By July 1945 all the Roosevelt

Cabinet members were gone except Henry Wallace at Commerce, Harold L. Ickes at Interior, Forrestal at the Navy, and Stimson at the War Department. Truman had great respect for senior statesman Stimson, but little for Ickes and Wallace. By early 1946, he had found Ickes "too big for his breeches" and had fired him.[4] He fired Wallace that fall for his public criticisms of the President's "get tough with the Russians" foreign policy.[5] A year later he fired Byrnes, his own first appointee, as Secretary of State.[6] By the fall of 1950 Truman had fired his first two Secretaries of Defense, Forrestal and Louis Johnson. By then, and for the balance of his second administration, Truman, at long last, had the men he wanted at State and Defense, Acheson, Marshall, and Lovett. Yet these last two and one-half years were to be the most difficult in the Truman Presidency. It was not for lack of able help. He described Marshall, Acheson, and Lovett as "outstanding leaders and remarkably capable organizers."[7] Yet he took pride in always making the difficult decision himself. He believed this an inherent responsibility in the office he occupied.

Truman later wrote that "of all the President's functions that of Commander in Chief has grown the most in importance and in its demands upon the incumbent."[8] Observing this growth and these demands, Supreme Court Justice Robert H. Jackson, who had been FDR's Attorney General, in 1948 termed the Commander in Chief clause of the Constitution as "the most dangerous one to free government in the whole catalogue of powers."[9] Clinton Rossiter, describing Presidential powers in like vein, concluded that those the President exercised as Commander in Chief were "the most basic, spectacular, and injurious to private rights. . . ."[10]

Truman had admired FDR's sweeping exercise of the Commander in Chief role, and he determined in no way to diminish Presidential powers.

Truman and National Security Organization

With the rapid demobilization after World War II, the nation was in urgent need both for a new national security organization and for definition of missions for the armed forces. There were blurred, duplicating, and overlapping missions, especially with regard to air, and no strategic force responsible for delivery of the new atomic weapon. For two years after World War II, while the Cold War was building up and the Soviets were enveloping nation after nation, the United States had no unified national defense organization. Moreover, the only retaliatory weapon of the demobilized nation, the atomic bomb, became shrouded in the new civilian-controlled Atomic Energy Commission. Two perilous years were to transpire before some semblance of unified organization emerged, including a Strategic Air Command, for delivery of the ultimate weapon. During those two years American military power, as a persuasive diplomatic instrument, was virtually in limbo. Truman's primary concern regarding the armed services and national security policy "seemed to lay a greater emphasis on eliminating waste in procurement, ending duplication of effort and materiel," and adopting strategy to the budget than creating a strong posture for free world leadership.[11]

Nonetheless, Truman had a remarkably early and clear grasp of the need to create a unified defense establishment and a central intelligence organization. He had perhaps a lesser understanding of the necessity of a top policy planning organization, such as subsequently evolved in the National Security Council. In August 1944, as the Democratic candidate for the Vice Presidency, Senator Truman became an early advocate of a single defense department, integrating the Army and Navy, with a unified general staff controlling strategy and tactics. By his conception, the necessity for compromises among the chiefs of independent departments would be eliminated. However, with all of the parochial service interests, and rivalries, his concept of one uniform and one service chief was clearly unacceptable, especially to the Navy.[12]

Defense organization and related Commander in Chief responsibilities were those aspects of the Presidency for which Truman by training and experience was best equipped. As a National Guard officer in World War I and as an Army Reserve officer between the wars, as a member of the Senate

Appropriations and Military Affairs Committees, and then as chairman of the Special Committee to Investigate the National Defense Program, Truman prided himself in having studied every plan since World War I for improving military organization. Thus he declared: "One of the strongest convictions which I brought to the office of President was that the antiquated defense setup of the United States had to be reorganized quickly as a step toward insuring our safety and preserving world peace."[13] Paralleling his reorganization concept was Truman's championing of Marshall's and the Army's cause of universal military training.

Truman's initiatives for defense organization—including his December 19, 1945, message to Congress, essentially supporting the unification bill of Senator Lister Hill of Alabama—is detailed in the next chapter. Suffice it to say here that Truman supported a concept for a single Department of National Defense, headed by a civilian as secretary, with clearly subordinated assistant secretaries for the Navy, Army, and a new coequal Air Force. The Navy, unalterably opposed to a concept subordinating the services, held up passage of legislation for more than a year before a compromise unification bill gained acceptability.

Truman appreciated the disaster of delay in organization as well as in policy and the relationship of one to the other. Thus, on June 15, 1946, he succinctly set forth his view that "one of the most important problems confronting our country today is the establishment of a definite military policy." He emphasized that "in the solution of this problem, I consider it vital that we have a unified armed force for our national defense."[14] Passage of the watered-down compromise measure did not come until July 25, 1947. With the impetus of Forrestal and the support of Taft, this landmark National Security Act of 1947 included a National Security Council and a National Security Resources Board. Judge Robert P. Patterson, the last Secretary of War, wisely declined the invitation to become the first Secretary of Defense. The creator of this weak post, James V. Forrestal, accepted the impossible position, seeking to coordinate the entrenched fiefdoms of Army, Navy, and Air, and on September 17, 1947, was sworn into office. In March 1949 a worn and distraught Forrestal resigned,and he took his own life shortly thereafter. His successor, Louis A. Johnson, soon found the Navy in virtual full revolt.[15] Out of this tragedy and rancor, on August 10, 1949, Truman signed into law the National Security Act Amendment of 1949, giving fuller authority to the Secretary of Defense.

In the two-volume memoirs of his Presidency, Truman took particular pride in his Commander in Chief role. However, he devoted little more than half a page to the turbulent and tragic period of intense interservice rivalry described in the ensuing two chapters. Moreover, he made no reference to Forrestal's tragic end. He did conclude, "To me, the passage of the National Security Act [1947] and its strengthening amendment [1949] represented one of the outstanding achievements of my administration."[16] Such was correct, perhaps more than he realized. Though it was to take the personally written amendment of his successor in 1958 to bring the United States to its present national security organization, the basic act of 1947, far more than the National Defense Act of 1920 which it succeeded, did look forward rather than back. Both acts came two years after a world war. But the first sought to codify the World War I organization, strategy, and experience. The second, especially with its National Security Council and its National Security Resources Board and its Research and Development Board, looked to the awesome and bewildering present and future. The act, despite its inadequacies, represented an endeavor to coordinate the economic, military, political, and psychological power of the United States and direct those enormous energies to the fulfillment of its new responsibilities for free-world leadership.

Like Alexander Hamilton a century and a half before, Truman recognized the need for a central intelligence authority. Again, however, as with defense unification, there was resistance. In this instance it was from existing information-collecting and investigatory organizations, including Army, Navy, Federal Bureau of Investigation, State Department, and Office of Strategic Services. On January 22, 1946, Truman resolutely set forth his directive on coordination of foreign intelligence activities: he formed a Central Intelligence

Group under a director of Central Intelligence "to assure the most effective accomplishment of the intelligence mission related to the national security."[17]

The following year this Central Intelligence Group was redesignated as the Central Intelligence Agency as a part of the National Security Act of 1947, which authorized the foreign and internal intelligence activities of the CIA. On the same day he signed that act, July 26, 1947, Truman, by executive order, set forth the functions of the Army, the Navy, and the new coequal Air Force. In doing so, Truman made clear that he was exercising his Constitutional authority in a dual capacity, as "President of the United States and Commander in Chief of the Armed Forces of the United States."[18]

Israel

As President, as Commander in Chief, Truman found three areas of special concern: the Middle East, western Europe, and the Far East. The question of the partition of Palestine, to make possible a Jewish homeland, became both an American and a British goal.

The British, in the Balfour Declaration of 1917, had promised a Jewish homeland. Thousands of Jews in the 1920s and 1930s emigrated to Palestine, which, by the Treaty of Versailles, Britain had governed under a mandate from the League of Nations. But the oil-rich Arab nations' increasing opposition to Jewish settlement in Palestine posed a dilemma challenging the wisdom of a Solomon. After Yalta, although he was ill, President Roosevelt met with King Farouk of Egypt and Ibn Saud of Saudi Arabia to indicate his appreciation of the importance of Arab good will. At the same time, he and his successors, and Republican aspirants alike, had no desire to alienate 5 million Jewish-American voters. As Truman with humor and insight expressed it, "I surely wish God Almighty would give the Children of Israel an Isaiah, the Christians a St. Paul, and the sons of Ishmael a peep at the Golden Rule."[19]

After incidences of mounting violence, climaxed by the bombing of the King David Hotel in Jerusalem, the discouraged British tossed the issue of the future of Palestine into the lap of the United Nations, announcing they would surrender their mandate on May 15, 1948. In the United Nations there was a rare instance of Soviet and United States collaboration. They pushed through the General Assembly on November 29, 1947, a resolution for partition of Palestine, by which there would be an Arab state and a Jewish state; Jerusalem, containing the holy places of three great religions, would be under international administration.

Immediately the Arab delegates marched out of the Assembly and announced they would not be bound by this decision. At midnight on May 14, 1948, the birth of Israel was proclaimed. Reminiscent of Theodore Roosevelt's speed in recognizing Panama in 1903, within eleven minutes Truman announced recognition of Israel. The President's action cut off a United Nations move for a temporary trusteeship.

Full-scale war, which immediately erupted between Israel and its Arab neighbors, was finally ended by the armistice agreement negotiated by Ralph Bunche in behalf of the United Nations. The armistice lines gave Israel considerable additional territory, and Israel refused to allow 880,000 Arab refugees to return to their Palestine homes. Although the Arabs had ample land to absorb all the refugees, they, in turn, refused to do so, since it would be tantamount to recognizing Israel's actions. And so, in 1948, the impasse was reached which has since nettled the world. The first severe crack in the Arab strategy of nonrecognition of Israel came in 1975 with the Egyptian-Israeli signing of a three-year peace accord. Such signing was tantamount, for the first time on the part of an Arab state, to recognition of Israel as a sovereign state.

Italy, Yugoslavia, and Germany

The principal goal of Soviet post–World War II policy was the removal of American influence and the withdrawal of United States forces from the Eurasian continent. A second goal was the prevention of the reemergence of a strong western Europe. A third was the prevention of the reemergence of strength in the former Axis powers, Germany, Italy, and Japan.

Ironically, Communist expansionism led directly to the defeat of these three Soviet goals. In Italy, where the Communists were the largest single party, the crucial test was the April 1948 elections. However, the Pope threatened Italian Communists with excommunication. Italian-Americans joined in the struggle, writing to relatives back home about the evils of Communism. The virtues of the European Recovery Plan were well advertised, with the admonition that a Communist Italy would get no ERP help. Britain, France, and the United States came out with well-timed promises for Italian control of the Adriatic seaport city and Free Territory of Trieste, which was then contested with Yugoslavia. In making these overtures in a letter of April 14, 1948, to the Italian ambassador to the United States, Signor Alberto Tarchiani, Truman expressed "the friendship and good will which the American people feel toward the people of Italy."[20] The result of all these efforts was a resounding Communist defeat at the polls and the election of the de Gasperi government. Not until June 1976 did the Communists severely challenge the Christian-Democrats.

Trieste, which was finally divided between Italy and Yugoslavia through a 1956 UN settlement, had been a cause of strained relations between Yugoslavia and the United States. Then in the spring of 1948 these relations relaxed with the rupture between Tito and "those Trotskyite deviationists in Moscow."[21] The Communist guerrillas in Greece were defeated in 1949 when Yugoslavia stopped providing them with a sanctuary. Truman always considered Yugoslavia, like Berlin and Iran, a strategically critical area.

In Germany the 1945 repulse of the Russian effort to strip the industrial-rich Ruhr, the 1946 economic merging of the British and American zones, and the 1947 formation of "trizonia" with the reluctant addition of the French zone were followed by the 1948 election of the West German Constituent Assembly. The German Federal Republic, comprising the three western zones, was inaugurated at Bonn in September 1949. West Germany, recognized as a bastion against Communist expansion, was soon made eligible for Marshall Plan aid and given a voice in the control of the Ruhr, although its full sovereignty and rearming remained some years down the road (1954).

The Far East

America had high expectations and ideals for East Asia after World War II. These had been presaged by the goals for Philippine independence, announced in 1934 and concluded as promised on July 4, 1946. Other nations, it was hoped, would follow this example, but with the menace of Communist imperialism on one hand and the Soviets themselves on the other posing as champions of anticolonialism, it became a sticky and a tricky wicket. What would happen if France, Holland, and Britain vacated their South Asian colonies?

Another part of the American dream, a strong, democratic China, had already been partially betrayed at Yalta when the Soviets were promised a privileged position in Manchuria. The enlargement of that Communist base until it enveloped all of mainland China has been noted.

At the Cairo Conference in November 1943 Churchill, Roosevelt, and Chiang promised Japanese-occupied Korea freedom and "independence," in due course. The steps and missteps resulting in the Korean War, briefly noted in the next section of this chapter, are detailed in Chapter 7.

Aside from the Philippines, the one area in which the United States could take pride in the success of its postwar policies was Japan. Japan escaped the frustration of postwar Austria and Germany of quadripartite reconstruction. Despite Soviet protests, the Supreme Commander for the Allied Powers took his orders from Washington. The man bearing that title, Douglas MacArthur, had long served in the Philippines during its steps toward independence. His regal bearing and majestic language were highly appealing to a people who had enjoyed Emperor worship. The autocratic MacArthur gathered about him such scholars as Dr. Kenneth

W. Colegrove of Northwestern University; working with the Japanese, they drafted a democratic constitution for Japan, which was put into effect May 3, 1947.

The outbreak of the Korean War in June 1950, far more than Chiang's withdrawal from mainland China to Formosa six months before, stiffened American resistance to Communism in East Asia. Moreover, it now became vital to make Japan the foundation and pivotal area for an anti-Communist counterforce in East Asia. Japan would then play a role parallel to that of America's other principal enemy of World War II, Germany, which would become the central force against Communism in Europe.

A peace treaty with Japan was considered relatively early while none had yet been achieved with Germany partly because Japan escaped political and occupational division, but there was more to it than that. As Alfred de Grazia and Thomas H. Stevenson expressed it, "under occupation, it [Japan] was administered at the direction of one person—General MacArthur."[22] As early as March 1947, MacArthur had recommended a Japanese peace treaty. In July of that year, Truman and Secretary of State Marshall announced their intentions to call an international conference to begin work on such a document. However, those efforts were completely frustrated by the Soviets. Now, with the Korean War making the task imperative, Truman's new Secretary of State, Dean Acheson, called upon John Foster Dulles to undertake the delicate task. He was to seek peace terms as fully acceptable as possible to Japan and to the United Nations.

Dulles showed amazing determination and stamina in these negotiations, which required considerable groundwork; fifty-four nations were called to the peace conference. In a year of arduous labor, Dulles traveled 125,000 miles. As a partial prelude, to quiet the concerns of the Philippines, New Zealand, and Australia, each of which had memories of Japanese aggression, a security treaty was signed with each of those countries (jointly with the latter two).

Thereafter, representatives of Japan and fifty-one other nations convened in San Francisco on September 4, 1951 (India, Burma, and Yugoslavia declined to come). Again Dulles and his State Department colleagues showed considerable skill in the drafting of the "Peace of Reconciliation." For example, disputes were avoided by Japan's relinquishing Formosa, Sakhalin, and the Kurils, without seeking to define their future disposition. Moreover, tacit acceptance was given Japan to rearm, by recognition of the right of self-defense of a sovereign state. Wisely, neither Nationalist China (Formosa) nor Communist (mainland) China was invited to participate.

Despite the opposition of Russia and its satellites, Poland and Czechoslovakia, on September 8, Japan and forty-eight other nations signed the peace treaty. A United States–Japan Security Treaty signed at the same time gave United States armed forces the right to remain in Japan "to contribute to the maintenance of international peace and security in the Far East and to the security of Japan."[23]

Curiously, in his *Memoirs,* Truman made only passing reference to these landmark treaties and *no* reference to Dulles's role therein. Perhaps most revealing of Truman's real feelings was the observation of Dean Acheson in his own reminiscences. Having proposed Dulles for this both delicate and herculean task, somewhat ruefully Acheson noted, "In later years he [Truman] used to charge me for having made Foster Dulles Secretary of State...."[24]

Entry into the Korean War

The Korean War, the strategy of which is analyzed in Chapter 7, involved three of Truman's most famous command decisions. The first was the decision to commit United States armed forces; the second was the dismissal of the United Nations commander; the third was the seizure of the steel mills.

On Sunday morning, June 25, 1950 (Saturday afternoon, June 24, United States time), North Korean troops trained and equipped by the Soviet Union invaded South Korea in heavy force. Immediately (Saturday evening) Acheson advised Truman, who was at his Independence, Missouri, home. Truman flew back the following afternoon to

Washington. In the interim Acheson had also alerted the UN Security Council, which that Sunday afternoon, by a vote of 9–0, with Yugoslavia abstaining, passed a resolution terming the North Korean action a "breach of peace" and demanding the aggressor's withdrawal beyond the 38th parallel. It called upon all members of the UN "to render every assistance to the United Nations in the execution of this resolution and to refrain from giving assistance to the North Korean authorities."[25] The resolution was passed without veto only because the Soviets had since January been boycotting the UN for its refusal to seat Red China.

Truman, who had never been enthusiastic about the National Security Council, did not convene that body. Instead, he had dinner that Sunday evening with his principal military advisers: Secretary of State Acheson and Secretary of Defense Johnson (who had been constantly feuding with each other), the service secretaries and the Joint Chiefs of Staff, Under Secretary of State James Webb, Assistant Secretaries of State John Hickerson and Dean Rusk, and Ambassador Philip Jessup. Following dinner Truman invited their counsel for a course of action.

There was general agreement that General MacArthur, as the U.S. theater commander, should augment military supplies to Korea above those already being provided under the Military Assistance Program and that the U.S. Air Force should protect Kimpo airport while United States dependents were being evacuated; further, that the Seventh Fleet should be ordered to proceed from the Philippines north to prevent any attack from China on Formosa or vice versa. (This action, ensuring Red China from attack by Nationalist China, appalled both Eisenhower and MacArthur.)

Truman directed all those present (including Acheson and Johnson, who were meeting the following day with the appropriation committees) to make no comment to the Congress on Korea. He had not made up his mind whether or not to report to the Congress.[26]

On June 27, three days after the North Korean attack, Truman for the *first* time met with Congressional leaders on the Korean situation. Asked if the United States intended to defend South Korea, he said yes, and that such action was in response to the United Nations Security Council resolution. (Actually the second Security Council resolution, again drafted by the United States, calling for UN members to "furnish such assistance to the Republic of Korea as may be necessary to repel the armed attack and to restore international peace and security in the area," was being debated at the UN at the very time that Truman was making his announcement. Again in the absence of the Soviets, it was passed. (Yugoslavia dissented, and Egypt and India abstained).[27] That same day, with the military situation in Korea rapidly deteriorating, Truman ordered American air and sea forces "to give the Korean Government troops cover and support."[28] Not until the *seventh* day of the war—following, as Acheson described it, MacArthur's "hazardous expedition to the front," where the South Korean retreat had turned into a rout—did Truman commit United States ground forces. *Following* the commitment, Truman met with another Congressional delegation, advised them of his action, and found general support.[29]

Several questions arise concerning both political and military decisions in these seven days and the days immediately following. First, there was Truman's almost leisurely return to Washington, with the first planning session twenty-four hours after he had been called. Acheson, faithful to the President, indicated in his memoirs that he had advised Truman to wait until the following day to fly back.[30] Truman may be forgiven for loss of memory, yet he recorded years later, ". . . we were on our way back in less than an hour. In fact we left in such a hurry that two of my aides were left behind."[31]

On the political side, Truman declined to accept Acheson's suggestion to address a joint session of the Congress, even though Acheson contended that the address should be in the nature of a report rather than a request for authority, since he believed the President was acting within his Constitutional authority as Commander in Chief of the armed forces.[32] Senator Vandenberg was deeply troubled; he, too, believed that the President had the authority as Commander in Chief, but he perceived that Truman's action had set the Presidency and the Congress on an inevitable collision course. From the moment the President had taken the oath of office to "preserve, protect, and defend the Constitution," he was serving as the Commander in Chief of the armed forces. On the other hand, the declaration of war and the appropriations for the armed forces were, by the Constitution, the authority and responsibility of the Congress. Vandenberg, who had wholeheartedly supported Truman's foreign policy initiatives—and, indeed, made many of them possible—regretfully concluded: "The President's great mistake was in not bringing his Korean decision to the immediate attention of Congress...."[33]

Though supporting Truman's decision, Senator Taft doubted its legal authority and proposed a joint Congressional resolution. Acheson had little patience with such views, asserting, "We are in a position in the world today where the argument as to who has the power to do this, that, or the other thing, is not exactly what is called for from Americans in this very critical hour."[34]

Like Acheson, the historian Arthur M. Schlesinger, Jr., admired Truman's sense of passing on to his successors his "sacred trust unimpaired," as Truman himself was wont to express it. Yet twenty-three years later, as Schlesinger assessed it, "By insisting that the presidential prerogative alone sufficed to meet the requirements of the Constitution, Truman did a good deal more than pass his sacred trust unimpaired. He dramatically and dangerously enlarged the power of future Presidents to take the nation into major war."[35]

Criticism is warranted on the military as much as on the political side. Although Truman is generally regarded as having acted swiftly and decisively in intervening, the action (in contrast to Lincoln's immediate response to the firing on Fort Sumter) was arrived at incrementally over a period of a week. The President's first meeting with his foreign affairs and military advisers came twenty-four hours after he had been notified of the attack, and the commitment of ground forces came on the edge of complete disaster—on the seventh day, when the South Korean defense had almost completely crumbled. The South Koreans, though fighting bravely with small arms supplied by the United States, were no match for Soviet-supplied heavy artillery and tanks. John

Eisenhower recalled both his father's support for United States intervention in Korea and his being "alarmed" concerning the delay in full military commitment, while the situation was badly deteriorating.[36]

A review of the means of arrival at this command decision, as with so many of the command decisions of the Truman period (commencing with the dropping of the atomic bombs in the last stages of World War II), reveals not so much a thorough examination as simply a sense that something had to be done. Truman said of the June 25 meeting with his advisers that there was "complete, almost unspoken acceptance on the part of everyone that whatever had to be done to meet this aggression had to be done." Revealingly, he added: "This was the test of all the talk of the last five years of collective security."[37]

Both Acheson and the President believed that the entry into the Korean War was Truman's most significant decision. According to Acheson, ". . . when the Russians, to their great surprise, found that they had started something which the United States met absolutely squarely and hit with utmost vigor, I think they stopped, looked, and listened. And the whole history of the world has since changed."[38] Truman largely credited what was done to Acheson, who treasured Truman's memo of July 19, 1950: "Your initiative in calling the Security Council of the U.N. . . . and notifying me was the key to what followed afterwards. Had you not acted promptly in that direction we would have had to go into Korea alone." (Actually the United States came in virtually alone, as Chapter 7 indicates, though it should be noted that at the same time the British were fighting the Communists in Malaysia and the French were similarly engaged in Vietnam.) Truman added: "The meeting Sunday night . . . was the result of your action Saturday night and the results afterwards showed you are a great Secretary of State and a diplomat."[39]

The United States entry into the Korean War, albeit incrementally arrived at and without benefit of Congressional action, came as a surprise to the North Koreans and their Soviet sponsors. They had both taken at face value the apparently overriding public concerns in the United States for economy in the armed forces, and Acheson and others had made public statements indicating that Korea was not a part of the United States "defense line" in Asia. Moreover, the Soviets' absence from the UN Security Council suggested that they had not contemplated a U.S.-UN response to the go-ahead they had given their client state.[40]

The United States action came as a surprise to the Soviets, the North Koreans, and also the Chinese, but it came as an even greater surprise to the American people. In previous history, the United States had debated as to whether we should get involved or stay out of conflict, and the result, as Walter Millis points out, had been in each instance something of a "national crusade"[41] (though a not very popular one in the War of 1812 and the Mexican War). The American people were not prepared mentally or emotionally for the Korean War. War aims were not clearly defined, and the nation never became united in wholehearted, purposeful support. Like Madison and Polk, and unlike Lincoln, McKinley, Wilson, and Franklin Roosevelt, President Truman did not inspire the nation with a sense of purpose in this war effort.

Conduct of the War

Time waited for no man in the swift-moving scenario that characterized the first weeks of the Korean War. The curtain-raising North Korean artillery barrage was followed within two hours by penetration of the 38th parallel.[42] Seoul fell on the third day. American ground troops, first committed on the seventh day, were on this battle line four days later.[43]

Truman, until July 6, made little use of the National Security Council; thereafter he convened it weekly. (Of the fifty-seven meetings of the NSC held in the three years prior to that time, Truman, ever jealous of his prerogatives, attended only twelve.)[44] At the July 6 meeting, General Omar Bradley, chairman of the Joint Chiefs of Staff, responded to the questions of Vice President Alben Barkley. Bradley described the courageous rearguard action[45] taken by 25,000

South Korean (ROK) troops and 10,000 Americans of the 24th Division, mostly young recruits with no previous battle experience, against the North Koreans, whose largely experienced troops had served in the Soviet World War II forces and with the Chinese Communists. They outnumbered the Americans and the South Koreans three to one, and they were spearheaded by a brigade of 120 T34 Soviet medium tanks. Further, the Americans and their ROK allies lacked adequate antitank weapons.[46] Bradley's report of July 6, then, was a far cry from Truman's first estimate of the situation, in which he had called for a "police action" to stop a "bunch of bandits."[47]

The high tide of the North Korean invasion was achieved by early August, when the port of Pusan, at the northern tip of the Korean Peninsula, was the only remaining allied island in a vast Communist sea. With a "stand or die" order, the South Korean and American forces of Lieutenant General Walton H. Walker, MacArthur's field commander, held a thin line, the Pusan perimeter. During the next month, although the North Koreans mustered thirteen infantry divisions and an armored division against that line, they dissipated their forces by probing attacks rather than a massed effort. Close air support and a tight naval blockade aided in Walker's masterful defense, and the reinforcements, including a British infantry brigade, entered the Pusan port.[48]

Even in the darkest early hours of the war, MacArthur had conceived his plans for counterattack and victory, exploiting control of sea and air and, by amphibious forces, striking behind the enemy's ground forces. On July 7 he advised the JCS of his plans, which two months later they reluctantly accepted. Because of the amazing Inchon landing of September 15, which caught the enemy completely by surprise, by October 1 all of South Korea had been retaken. Perhaps 30,000 out of 400,000 North Koreans escaped (without baggage) across the 38th parallel.

Even Acheson admitted that MacArthur had kept his promise when he had avowed, "We shall land at Inchon, and I shall crush them."[49] This is the same Acheson who had indicated that the United States intervention had been made "solely for the purpose of restoring the Republic of Korea to its status prior to the invasion from the North."[50] If such be the case, this then had been accomplished within three months, since the North Koreans had been pushed back above the 38th parallel. The truth is that Truman, Acheson, the Joint Chiefs, and Marshall (who replaced Johnson as Secretary of Defense in September), their appetites whetted by victory, were eager for more. Moreover, Truman further appreciated the prospective vindication at the polls in the forthcoming fall Congressional elections.

Thus, while MacArthur "halted the UN advance to receive further instructions,"[51] both Truman and the UN urged him on. The UN General Assembly in early October voted that "all appropriate steps be taken to ensure conditions of stability throughout Korea."[52]

The instructions from the Joint Chiefs to MacArthur on September 27 were, as one student recognized, "a study in bureaucratic canniness, an effort to push off on him responsibilities that Washington should have faced."[53] Marshall, in an "eyes only" cable, added, "We want you to feel unhampered tactically and strategically to proceed north of the 38th parallel."[54]

Following this crushing defeat of the North Korean forces, in early October Chou En-lai, Peking's foreign minister, vowed that his fellow countrymen would never "supinely tolerate seeing their neighbors being savagely invaded by imperialists."[55] Truman, despite the Chinese threat, approved an "amplification" of the late September directive to MacArthur to press on. This directive, sent to MacArthur on October 9, is significant because it makes clear the President's full awareness of possible Chinese intervention, and it authorized MacArthur to counter such intervention: "Hereafter in the event of open or covert employment anywhere in Korea of major Chinese Communist units . . . , you should continue the action as long as, *in your judgment, action by forces now under your control offers a reasonable chance of success.*" The directive added ". . . you will obtain authorization from Washington prior to taking any military action *against objectives in Chinese territory.*"[56] The Joint Chiefs, Marshall, and Truman were now clearly indicating a likelihood of

Chinese entry into the war; in such an event MacArthur should retaliate with the forces under his command and should be considering "objectives" for punitive action in China itself.

This, then, was the climate in which Truman asked MacArthur to come to Wake Island on Sunday morning, October 15, for a most unusual meeting. Truman approached the meeting with distinct preconceptions about MacArthur. Inadvertently he had surrounded himself with MacArthur haters and detractors. Averell Harriman had been seeking MacArthur's removal at least as early as 1948.[57] Acheson declined the President's invitation to join him for the Wake Island conference, later writing that he had told the President, "While General MacArthur had many of the attributes of a foreign sovereign, . . . and was quite as difficult as any, it did not seem wise to recognize him as one."[58]

With such views from his closest advisers, it was little wonder that Truman wrote with some surprise that "our conversation was very friendly—I might say much more so than I had expected."[59] MacArthur expressed his personal regret for having given the Veterans of Foreign Wars a statement on Formosa in late August in which he called for "aggressive, resolute and dynamic leadership," decried "appeasement," and asserted the fallacy of the proposition "that if we defend Formosa we alienate continental Asia."[60] At the President's direction, MacArthur had withdrawn that statement. Nonetheless Truman had at the time been so furious as to contemplate relieving him and replacing him with Bradley. Now supposedly all was forgiven in the moment of victory.

At the Wake Island conference MacArthur noted the possibility of "Chinese Communist ground and Russian air" intervention, but neither he nor the President expressed concern.[61] In his report to the nation following his return, Truman on October 17 avoided any reference to such intervention; rather, he emphasized that his talk with MacArthur indicated "complete unity in the aims and conduct of our foreign policy." The President predicted that the forces under MacArthur's command would "soon restore peace to the whole of Korea." He added, "It is fortunate for the world that we had the right man for this purpose—a man who is a very great soldier—General Douglas MacArthur."[62]

The aftermath of the Wake Island conference is detailed in Chapter 7, but Truman's role as Commander in Chief should be discussed here. With the full concurrence of the Joint Chiefs of Staff and of the Departments of State and Defense, the Commander in Chief had determined to take the risk of liberating North Korea. Clearly too little heed had been given to the warnings over the Peking radio and through the Indian delegation at the United Nations General Assembly that the People's Republic of China would not tolerate the elimination of the Korean People's Republic.

In the Wake Island meeting of October 15, the only additional instructions the Commander in Chief had given MacArthur were that if the Chinese did indeed appear in force he should proceed only if he was reasonably sure of victory. Four days later Pyongyang, the North Korean capital, was taken, and on October 24 MacArthur ordered his forces to proceed to the northern border, i.e., the Yalu River, separating North Korea from Manchuria. The following day the United Nations Command found for the first time that they were being opposed by Chinese troops. MacArthur estimated the Chinese force at not more than 50,000 and was confident that the Air Force could destroy the bridges over the Yalu, precluding sizable Chinese entry. A month later, however, 300,000 well-disciplined Chinese combat troops were in Korea, having crossed over in cover of darkness and evaded aerial detection. Thus on November 28 MacArthur directed an orderly withdrawal.

Clearly MacArthur had had faulty intelligence, but the blame cannot rest solely with the theater commander. Truman, Acheson, Marshall, and the Joint Chiefs all knew that the Chinese had armies across the Yalu in Manchuria. Where was their own intelligence apparatus? Force estimates in foreign lands were not the sole responsibility of the theater commander.

Moreover, the Chinese Communists no longer feared American air attacks on their Manchurian supply lines. On October 9 American jets had strafed a Soviet airfield near

Vladivostok. The United States apology and assurance that it would not happen again had been reinforced at the Wake Island conference a few days later. As Stephen E. Ambrose has observed, "The Truman-MacArthur meeting at Wake Island . . . accomplished its main purpose, for the Air Force thereafter confined its activities to the Korean peninsula."[63]

Yet, when MacArthur's forces were confronted by the much larger Chinese force, his response on November 28, requesting reinforcements and terming it "an entirely new war" which raised "considerations beyond the sphere of decision by the theater commander,"[64] was far more mild than that of the Commander in Chief. Two days later an agitated Truman declared at a press conference, "We will take whatever steps are necessary to meet the military situation." Then, in response to the question, "Will that include every weapon that we have?" the President rocked the world when he grimly added, "That includes every weapon that we have."[65] Truman's ever-faithful press secretary, Charles Ross, issued a supplementary statement which vainly sought to calm those both at home and abroad who envisioned Truman's again unleashing the atomic bomb. Ironically, the same day Truman wrote on his own calendar: "General Mac, as usual has been shooting off his mouth."[66]

Horrified, British Prime Minister Clement Attlee rushed to the United States to see if Truman (not MacArthur) had lost his mind, and Charlie Ross died of a heart attack.[67] Truman presented to Attlee his own domino theory: "The problem we are facing is part of a pattern. After Korea, it would be Indochina, then Hong Kong, then Malaya."[68] Attlee failed in his endeavor to get Acheson and Truman to negotiate peace with the Chinese. But, as Dr. Ambrose observed of this early December conference with the worried British Prime Minister, "Attlee had accomplished something, for Truman stopped talking about the atomic bomb in his press conferences. . . ."[69]

Truman accomplished something in addition: a greatly augmented defense budget for NATO as a sequel to his declaration on December 16 of the existence of a national emergency.[70] The declaration was highly significant in itself. It connoted the necessity for Presidential action in the economic as well as the military sphere—in dealing, for example, with labor and industry. Having sought no Congressional declaration of war, the President, with Marshall's recommendation, now used this instrument to justify his expansion of the war effort.[71]

In issuing his declaration, Truman was aware of similar actions Roosevelt had taken in 1939, two years prior to America's declaration of war in World War II. Roosevelt's declarations of 1939 and 1941 were in part superseded by Congressional action, but in 1947 there was no similar Congressional action on the Truman declaration. Thus, Truman's enlargement of Presidential authority remained in effect until its 1976 termination.[72]

Harold C. Relyea, who has made considerable study of emergency powers, has suggested that Truman, by this declaration, made it "a work of art rather than a legal description. . . ."[73] Before taking this action, Truman met with both the National Security Council and Congressional leaders. In the NSC meeting, Marshall emphasized the importance of strongly "launching the NATO armed forces and that our entire international situation depended on strengthening western Europe." Although the clear immediate emergency was in Korea—where MacArthur, outnumbered, was seeking to counter the Chinese onslaught—Marshall carried the day with Truman with his concept for western European priorities. According to Truman, Marshall cautioned that "we could not rush into measures for Korea and the Pacific that would cause such Russian reactions that our European allies would be scared away."[74]

In the meeting with Congressional leaders, Taft voiced opposition to the proposal for a declaration of national emergency "without knowing the details of what is involved. . . ."[75] Moreover, Taft believed that Marshall, who emphasized Europe rather than Asia, had the priorities reversed. (Taft had earlier opposed Marshall's 1947 confirmation as Secretary of State because he believed Marshall reaffirmed "the tragic policy of this administration in encouraging Chinese communism which brought on the Korean war.")[76]

Taft's priorities vis-à-vis Europe and Asia became a matter

of concern for General Eisenhower, who had retired from the Army in 1948, and accepted the presidency of Columbia University, then, in late December 1950, taken a leave of absence from the university to become the first NATO commander. Returning to the United States in late January 1951 to report to the President and, informally, to the Congress on the progress of NATO, Eisenhower learned of Taft's reservations regarding sending troops to Europe.

By this time Eisenhower was being pressured by both Democrats and Republicans to be a Presidential candidate. But he and his wife, Mamie, had just purchased their very own first home, a farm at Gettysburg, Pennsylvania, and Eisenhower appreciated Taft's ambitions for the Presidency. He wrote out an unequivocal statement that he was removing himself from possible candidacy and, armed with it, met with Taft, one of only thirteen Senators who had voted against the NATO Pact in the first place. Coming from that meeting, with no unqualified support for NATO, Eisenhower destroyed the statement before returning to Paris.[77]

Ironically, then, as in World War II, Eisenhower and Marshall were joined together in urging priorities for Europe, and MacArthur with his beleaguered forces found himself with Marshall and the Joint Chiefs in the same posture which had confronted him in World War II. Believing that the real threat was the Soviet Union, not China, and the crucial area was Europe, not Asia, Secretary of Defense Marshall and the Joint Chiefs recommended to the President the immediate dispatch of several divisions to Europe—for the new NATO commander, General Eisenhower, rather than to MacArthur's command. In this desperate hour in the winter of 1950–1951, the secondary-priorities scenario MacArthur had experienced in 1942–1945 was replayed. When Truman on December 19, without prior consultation with Congress, announced his plans to commit 100,000 and ultimately 300,000 troops to Europe, it started the great debate of 1951 on foreign policy and confirmed Taft's suspicions. Taft rose in the Senate, just as Republican Congressman Frederic R. Coudert, Jr., had in the House, to demand a reexamination of American foreign policy.

Acheson disdainfully responded to Taft that a "re-examinist might be a farmer that goes out every morning and pulls up all his crops to see how they have done during the night."[78] Taft questioned Presidential authority to deploy troops without Congressional authority. At the time, Arthur M. Schlesinger, Jr., found such a view "demonstrably irresponsible," but twenty years later he applauded it.[79] An advocate of both air and naval power, Taft argued, as he wrote in 1951 to John Foster Dulles, that "a large land force is of dubious value. . . . The defense of this country as well as the deterring of Russia rests far more on an all powerful air force."[80] He further argued for more aid for MacArthur. Instead Eisenhower got his divisions for Europe.

While MacArthur's forces were withdrawing from North Korea before numerically overwhelming forces, the media were terming the orderly withdrawal America's worst military disaster. Margaret Truman, in her affectionate biography about her father, wrote that "this panic was unnecessary." She pointed out that the casualties were actually "less than 5 per cent of the UN army," though she maintained that "the skill of his field commanders" kept MacArthur from a complete debacle.[81] The Cassandras in the Pentagon, the JCS, were, as Truman termed it, seeking "ways to withdraw from Korea 'with honor.'. . ."[82] Major General Matthew Ridgway was asking the question they wanted to hear: "You can relieve any commander who won't obey orders, can't you?"[83] They gave Ridgway a third star and sent him to Korea as MacArthur's field commander when General Walton Walker was killed in a jeep accident. Though an outstanding combat soldier, cutting a resolute figure with crossed hand grenades on his chest, Ridgway was also a skilled politician, appreciative of the dictates of Marshall and the Joint Chiefs. With a reassuring "All right, Mat, it's yours," MacArthur gave his new field commander wholehearted support that was not entirely reciprocated.

At MacArthur's direction, Ridgway launched the counterattack in February which again retook Seoul, and by mid-March he had the UN forces again moving north of the 38th parallel. Having again dramatically reversed the fortunes of war, MacArthur was now no longer needed, although Marshall still "advised caution" in any moves to fire him.[84] Marshall, a Virginia Military Institute alumnus who had been a colonel in World War I and who had never had a combat command, full well realized MacArthur's unique position: a West Point graduate with the highest academic record in the history of the Academy, MacArthur in World War I had received the nation's highest decoration for conspicuous bravery, and he was the only World War I general on active duty in World War II. Marshall also realized the chink in MacArthur's armor, his personal ego, his sense of the dramatic, his histrionics.

MacArthur on one side and Acheson, Bradley, Harriman, Marshall, and Truman on the other had honest differences of opinion as to the real enemy in this instance. The President and his advisers viewed China as a Soviet client state, while MacArthur believed China was central in any plans for Communist domination of Asia. History was to prove MacArthur right; through Chinese intervention and support, Communist hegemony over North Korea was maintained and was achieved in Southeast Asia during the next twenty-five years. In 1951 the Communist regime in mainland China, little more than a year in being and not yet solidified, might have been toppled. Against this was the posed threat of Soviet military response, World War III, if military operations were directed against mainland China. Would Russia seek to come to China's rescue?

MacArthur and Truman also differed in their concepts of containment. Although Truman and his advisers had for a time in Korea gone beyond containment to hopes for a unified Korea, this had been a fleeting instance. The status quo ante bellum was now fully agreeable. To MacArthur containment of Communism was comparable to containment of cancer; his prognosis was elimination of the source, which, as far as Asia was concerned, he believed was China.

Somewhat condescendingly, Truman said MacArthur had been out in Asia too long (sixteen years). Perhaps he was right, and perhaps containment and prolongation of the Cold War, which triumphed with MacArthur's dismissal, was right. Historians may long argue whether MacArthur or Truman and his advisers were strategically correct, but they cannot argue about Truman's acting within his authority as Commander in Chief.

Although neither the Chinese nor the Soviets had given any inkling of a desire for a negotiated peace, the UN had indicated its own desire in the dark days of January. In March, with MacArthur back above the 38th parallel and prepared to march northward, Truman was ready to negotiate. Believing there was no solution in a stalemate and no strategy in "accordian warfare"—marching up and down the Korean Peninsula—MacArthur had already fired a warning salvo across his Commander in Chief's bridge by his March 7 protest to the JCS against a "military stalemate."[85] Such a statement was not for public consumption. But on March 17 he defied an order of the previous December which forbade public statements on the war without prior approval: he lamented "abnormal military inhibitions" and pointed to the need for "vital decisions. . . ."[86] Then, with characteristic dramatics, on March 24 he reissued an invitation to the Chinese field commander to surrender under threat of "an expansion of our military operations to its [mainland China's] coastal areas and interior bases. . . ." Such action, MacArthur warned, "would doom Red China to the risk of imminent military collapse."[87]

Truman interpreted this as "an open defiance of my orders as President and as Commander in Chief."[88] MacArthur later stated that he found nothing extraordinary in his own statement, that commanders in the field had since time immemorial issued statements to the enemy commander. He avowed that "the notice I put out was merely that which every commander at any time can put out. . . ."[89] Marshall, however, later testified, ". . . it created a very serious situation with our allies. . . . It created . . . a loss of confidence in the leadership of the government."[90]

If Truman needed any further evidence with which to hang his outspoken commander, one of MacArthur's staunchest supporters, Congressman Joseph W. Martin, the Republican minority leader of the House, unwittingly provided it on April 5, when the Congress, unhappy with the conduct of the war and looking for their own whipping boy (which they believed they had in Acheson), proposed its own inquiry. That day in the Senate, Homer Ferguson of Michigan proposed that a Congressional committee should go to Tokyo to confer with MacArthur.[91] The penultimate note that day was Martin's reading to the House, without MacArthur's authorization, the "no substitute for victory" letter.

Truman, who from vast experience was an authority on firing those who disagreed, characteristically emphasized in retrospect that he had made his decision several days before and independent of Martin's April 5 act. The facts do not so indicate, except that there was general sentiment among Truman's closest advisers to fire MacArthur when the time was right. It was that now. The deed was done on April 6, when the Joint Chiefs at last had the courage, with Truman's invitation, to recommend MacArthur's removal. As Acheson recorded, "They [Joint Chiefs] proposed and the President accepted Lieutenant General Matthew Ridgway [as MacArthur's successor] which delighted both Harriman and me."[92] As if to wash his hands of his role in the deed, Acheson recorded in his reminiscences eighteen years later, "As one looks back in calmness, it seems impossible to over estimate the damage that General MacArthur's willful insubordination and incredibly bad judgment did to the United States in the world and to the Truman Administration."[93]

In his order relieving MacArthur, Truman wrote, "I deeply regret that it becomes my duty as President and Commander in Chief of the United States military forces to replace you as Supreme Commander, Allied Powers; Commander in Chief, United Nations Command; Commander in Chief, Far East; and Commanding General, U.S. Army Far East."[94] (Although he was exercising his powers as Commander in Chief in relieving MacArthur as United States commander, he needed no authority from the United Nations to relieve him as UN commander, since the United States acted as the executive agent in United Nations military matters in Korea.) In his accompanying statement Truman declared that MacArthur "is unable to give his wholehearted support to the policies of the United States Government and of the United Nations in matters pertaining to his official duties."[95] When Cabell Phillips of the *New York Times* asked the President if it took much courage to fire the aquiline-faced, corncob-pipe-smoking American hero, Truman retorted, "Courage didn't have anything to do with it. General MacArthur was insubordinate and I fired him. That's all there was to it."[96]

There was fury in the land not only over the firing of the old soldier but also the clumsy handling of the affair; it was in the press before MacArthur was notified. Truman hastily called a 1:00 A.M. press conference on April 11, when advised that the story had leaked.[97] Nonetheless, even such Presidential critics as Taft agreed that Truman "had every right" to remove MacArthur.[98] Eisenhower agreed, although years later he stated that had he been in MacArthur's shoes, commanding under such military and political constraints, he would have forced the issue earlier.[99]

The elemental fact was that Truman, who a few months before was threatening to unleash the atom bomb on China, until he had been constrained by Attlee, was now ready, willing, and eager to negotiate a peace. Explaining his actions to the American people on April 11, he declared, "We are trying to prevent a third world war." And he contended, "We are ready at any time to negotiate for a restoration of peace in the area."[100] The only problem was that the enemy, assured by MacArthur's ouster that the United States would fight only a most limited war, confined to Korea, was in no hurry to negotiate.

At the same time Truman told the American people that the attack on Korea was part of a greater Communist plan for conquering all of Asia.[101] In this, he shared MacArthur's sentiment, although their solutions differed. Truman gave encouragement to Assistant Secretary of State Dean Rusk's view that Chiang rather than Mao "more authentically represented the views of the great body of the people of China." Rusk, a favorite of the China lobby, suggested that if the Chinese people rose up against the Communist "tyranny," Americans would help. Responding to these visionary views, Walter Lippmann sardonically wrote, "Regimes do not negotiate about their survival. . . . These issues can be settled only by total victory."[102]

MacArthur came home to the greatest hero welcome in

American history. On April 19, addressing a joint session of the Congress (viewed by a record 60 million Americans on television), with moving oratory he declared: "Why, my soldiers asked of me, surrender military advantages to an enemy in the Field? [Pause] I could not answer."[103] But in the weeks of combined Senate Armed Forces and Foreign Relations hearings which continued through May and June, people began to ask whether the overthrow of Communist regimes in mainland China and North Korea, were, indeed, worth the risk.

MacArthur was challenging the entire philosophy of containment, not merely in Asia, but worldwide. In the MacArthur hearings, however, administration witnesses again argued persuasively that containment was the only possible course of action. By this time the emotionalism of the MacArthur dismissal had subsided, and with the Truman victory the continuing course of the protracted Cold War conflict was reaffirmed.

With the removal of MacArthur, an elated Acheson could write that "the White House, the State Department, the Pentagon, and the Supreme Command in Tokyo found themselves united on political objectives, strategy, and tactics for the first time since the war had started."[104] But the American people never did come to an understanding of those objectives.

Ten days after the MacArthur dismissal, the Chinese launched another offensive. When it failed, the Soviets put out peace feelers and the armistice negotiations began on July 8. But, as detailed in Chapter 7, not until nearly two years after armistice negotiations began and five months after Truman left office was the armistice agreed upon and the fighting ended.

Ironically, during this same period the seeds for future United States involvement in Southeast Asia were sown. The month before the outbreak of the Korean War, Acheson announced the beginning of military aid to Vietnam, Laos, and Cambodia to encourage "genuine nationalism." Although the aid for the next decade was to be largely monetary and technical, some historians date the arrival of the

Military Assistance Advisory Group in August 1950 as "the real beginning of United States involvement in the cold war in Indo-China."[105]

The Final Truman Years, 1951–1953

The final Truman years were marred by a virtual hysteria regarding Communist influence in government, rampant inflation, influence peddling by persons uncomfortably close to the President, and corruption in the Bureau of Internal Revenue and the Reconstruction Finance Corporation. Newspapers headlined the influence peddlers, who supposedly passed out favors for returns, including deep freezers and mink coats. Taken together, these were manifestations of what came to be termed "the mess" in Washington.

The Korean War seemed to have settled into a costly stalemate, and the MacArthur dismissal and the seizure of the steel mills caused Truman's support, according to the pollsters, to fall to the lowest level in the history of the American Presidency. When Truman's name was overwhelmingly rejected in the New Hampshire primary, the President discreetly announced that he was not a candidate for reelection. Adlai Stevenson, governor of Illinois, would get the unhappy nod. The only question for the Republicans was whether it would be Taft or Eisenhower. The President, the Commander in Chief, was furious when he discovered that Eisenhower was a Republican and was prepared to come home from NATO to Columbia in 1952 en route to the Republican convention.

For the first time since 1928 the Republicans sniffed the sweet scent of victory in the coming Presidential election. Yet, like that ill-fated Republican candidate of 1928, Hoover, it was not all Truman's fault. He was, in part, the victim of a near-hysteria climate in internal security matters. As President, as Commander in Chief, he was responsible for internal as well as external security. Soviet aggression and the worldwide Communist conspiracy had caused Truman in 1946 to order "a sweeping study of the government's loyalty procedures." This had led to the establishment of a Loyalty

Review Board. Loyalty probes during the next several years had led to the dismissal of 384 government employees or, as Truman termed it, "nine one thousandths of one per cent of all those checked."[106]

Simultaneous with the administration's security investigations was the work of the House Un-American Activities Committee, established in January 1945. By its reckless accusations the Committee had registered a low degree of respect, until the Hiss case came along in 1948.

Alger Hiss, the State Department's deputy director of the Office of Special Political Affairs, had been a major planner at the Yalta and San Francisco conferences. Repentant former Communist Whittaker Chambers, a senior editor of *Time* magazine, shocked the nation by terming Hiss a member of the "underground organization of the United States Communist Party." Inviting a libel suit, which Hiss had threatened, Chambers repeated his accusation on the *Meet the Press* radio program. In a subsequent civil action Hiss was convicted of perjury and sentenced to five years in a federal penitentiary. Such action would not have been damaging to the President had he not termed the inquiries of the House Un-American Activities Committee, which had secured Chambers's testimony, a " 'red herring' to keep from doing what they ought to do."[107] Since Truman repeated and repeated this charge in an August 5, 1948, press interview, the 1950 Hiss conviction came back to haunt him. Richard M. Nixon, a young Congressman from California, fanned the flames, terming the Hiss case "the most treasonable conspiracy in American history."[108] The junior Senator from Wisconsin, Joseph R. McCarthy, made it a platform of a four-year campaign of vituperation against Truman and Eisenhower as well as Marshall and Acheson. Regrettably, there were some elements of truth in McCarthy's vicious and wild accusations.

Among others, Judith Coplon, a young political analyst in the Department of Justice, was convicted of espionage (later reversed on a legal technicality). More shocking were the atom spy convictions which disclosed how the Soviets had gained British and American nuclear knowledge. The national response was the McCarran Internal Security Act, which Truman vetoed as injurious to individual rights, only to see it overridden in 1951 by overwhelming Congressional majorities in a buildup of the atmosphere of hysteria. In 1952 Congress overrode his veto of the McCarran-Walter Act, which sought to strike at Communism by various immigration exclusion provisions. Although again standing up for individual rights, Truman had clearly lost the confidence of the Congress and the American people.

Capping the debacle was the Kefauver investigation into corruption in government, including the Reconstruction Finance Corporation. Evidence of skulduggery in high places removed any remnant of credibility in the waning months of the Truman administration. When Truman protested there was no "evidence of illegal influence in the RFC," Democratic Senator Fulbright responded that the President was "setting a low level if our only goal for official conduct is that it be legal instead of illegal."[109]

Of all of his command decisions, Truman was faulted most for the MacArthur dismissal. Actually, it was the decision for which he was least to blame. More in question was his order at war's end to drop the two atomic bombs on Japan without consultation with the Supreme Allied Commander, whom he rightfully dismissed five years later for insubordination.

To Truman's credit, it should further be stated that he never hesitated, no matter now unpopular the action, to exercise his Presidential and Commander in Chief authority. He did so in the period April 3–June 2, 1952, by his seizure of the steel mills to prevent their threatened shutdown in a labor-management wage dispute. Truman might have averted or at least postponed the strike by an 80-day "cooling-off period" through action under the Taft-Hartley Act authority. It did not provide the authority for seizure. More important, he detested everything about Taft-Hartley, enacted over his veto in 1947.[110] Truman did believe that his action was more directly related to national defense during the Korean War through the Defense Production Act of 1950. This act had been designed to curb inflation and keep defense production from being interrupted.[111] Charles E. Wilson, the former chairman of the General Electric Company, whom Truman had appointed director of Defense Mobilization, resigned when the quarrelsome President charged him with proposing a settlement too favorable to the steel industry. As Truman quipped, "I . . . put him straight."[112]

In another of his inept press conferences, Truman sought to justify his seizure action. Although Truman prided himself as a student of history, his references to Jefferson, Tyler, Polk, Lincoln, and Roosevelt were termed by Arthur Schlesinger, Jr., "a somewhat garbled historical excursion. . . ."[113] But his fullest ineptness was revealed in response to the question as to where he drew the line about what he would seize—how about newspapers and radio stations? "Under similar circumstances the President of the United States has to act for whatever is for the best interest of the country," the President retorted. "That's the answer."[114] In defense of the President, it must be said that he had invited Congressional action before asking acceptance of the Wage Stabilization Board's proposed settlement.

The steel owners immediately sued to get their property back. In the district court the assistant district attorney argued in Trumanesque terms for inherent Presidential power, limited only by impeachment, to save the country from any catastrophe. Judge Daniel A. Pine rejected this thesis. In the appeal before the Supreme Court the government attorneys took a somewhat more modest view, pointing to the severity of the national emergency and "the aggregate of his constitutional powers" as President and Commander in Chief.[115] By a 6 to 3 vote (eight weeks after the seizure) in the case of *Youngstown Sheet and Tube Company* v. *Charles Sawyer*, the Supreme Court declared Truman's action unconstitutional.

Although neither the majority nor the minority made the President's authority as Commander in Chief the central issue, Justice Hugo Black did opine that "we cannot with faithfulness to our constitutional system hold that the Commander in Chief . . . has the ultimate power as such to take possession of private property in order to keep labor disputes from stopping production."[116] Justice Robert H. Jackson, who had been FDR's Attorney General, disputed the view that the Commander in Chief of the Army and Navy was "Commander in Chief of the country, its industries and its inhabitants." Somewhat erroneously, Jackson declared that the President's powers as Commander in Chief were to be "measured by the command functions usual to the topmost officer of the army and navy." Jackson admonished: "No penance would ever expiate the sin against free government of holding that a President can escape control of executive powers by law through assuming his military role."

In what might be termed obiter dictum thrown in to admonish the President for his conduct of foreign policy, especially in Korea, without Congressional concurrence, Jackson avowed, "No doctrine that the Court could promulgate would seem to me more alarming than that a President whose conduct of foreign affairs is so largely uncontrolled, and often even is unknown, can vastly enlarge his mastery over the internal affairs of the country by his own commitment of the Nation's armed forces to some foreign venture."[117]

And so the President, as Commander in Chief, received a stinging rebuke from the highest court in the land. However, when the owners got their mills back, the workers struck. After nearly two months of negotiations the owners accepted most of the workers' original demands. Had the rebuke set back Presidential control of American foreign policy? The answer is no. As Justice Jackson expressed it, "I have no illusion that any decision by this Court can keep power in the hands of Congress if it is not wise and timely in meeting its problems."[118]

After the illness and death of Vandenberg, despite the protests of Taft, Coudert, and a few others, the President reigned supreme in foreign policy. From June 1950 onward, initiative and power clearly passed to the President, his Secretary of State, and his Secretary of Defense. The Korean police action, chiefly authored by Acheson, stands as the demarcation point or watershed of power. Acheson declared on that occasion, "Not only has the President the authority to use the Armed Forces in carrying out the broad foreign policy of the United States and in implementing treaties, but it is equally clear that this authority may not be interfered with by the Congress in the exercise of power which it has under the Constitution."[119]

The MacArthur hearings might have posed a Congressional challenge to Presidential authority, but the administration headed off all such efforts. Despite Republican protests, the hearings, in marked contrast to those of Watergate two decades later, were closed to the media and the public—even though the star witness was then the nation's most idolized figure. Although MacArthur during a three-day period was on the stand twenty-one hours and ten minutes, there were no klieg lights, no television cameras, no public quotations. The administration and the Democratic majority in Congress rejected all such requests for public focus on the grounds that the material was classified. As Merle Miller, Truman's sympathetic biographer, expressed it, ". . . only what was supposedly non classified was released each day."[120]

On the other hand, Truman never hesitated to release highly classified documents when it seemed to further his own political purposes. Thus on November 2, 1952, two days before the Presidential election, in a desperate effort to counter Eisenhower's position on the Korean War, Truman released selected top-secret documents.[121]

In the light of such fancy footwork of a seasoned politician, the pious plea for an open Presidency voiced by President Truman in his final (324th) press conference on January 15, 1953, has a somewhat hollow ring. Nonetheless, to his credit, he then avowed that ". . . it is important for our democratic system of government that every medium of communication between the citizens and their Government, particularly the President, be kept open as far as possible."[122]

Along the Campaign Trail

Truman, in his final six months in office, focused his efforts on ending the Korean War and securing the election of a Democratic successor as President. The two concerns became interrelated, and his actions in both areas revealed his best and his worst.

Years later Truman was to ridicule the Republicans for the Twenty-second Amendment. Without it, he said, they could have readily elected Eisenhower to a third term. But "the damn thing,"[123] as Truman termed it, didn't apply to himself, only to his successors. And it had been the disastrous results of the New Hampshire primary that inspired his March 29, 1952, statement, "I shall not be a candidate for reelection."[124] Along the campaign trail he was to state, "I could have run again...."[125] This was technically true, since he could have secured the Democratic nomination despite his loss of popularity and his approaching sixty-ninth birthday. After his own first choice, Chief Justice Fred Vinson, "firmly declined on the basis of his physical condition," Truman picked Governor Adlai Stevenson of Illinois as his successor.[126] The Republicans, in Chicago on July 7, nominated Eisenhower rather than Taft. Two weeks later in the same Windy City, an exasperated Truman finally secured Stevenson's acceptance of the nomination.

During the final six weeks before the election, Truman hit the campaign trail more vigorously than the two candidates combined. In doing so, he released his invective against the general he had named as both Army Chief of Staff and NATO Commander. Veteran correspondent Arthur Krock, chief of the *New York Times* Washington bureau, termed the President's "protracted assault on the personal integrity of General Eisenhower... without parallel for a man in Mr. Truman's position."[127] Nor did Truman relent his position after the election. When invited by reporters to do so in the good humor of his final Presidential press conference, Truman said, "Those campaign speeches speak for themselves."[128]

In many of Truman's campaign speeches he defended his foreign policy actions as President and Commander in Chief. Eisenhower's criticisms of conduct of foreign policy, especially in the Korean War, particularly nettled the President. Beginning with a speech in Cincinnati on September 22 and culminating in one in Detroit on October 24, Eisenhower charged Truman and Acheson with "appalling and disastrous mismanagement of foreign affairs" and "bungling into Korea." Although for some students of public affairs this "raised... serious doubts" about Eisenhower's "understanding of these complex diplomatic problems,"[129] thereafter Truman was on the defensive. With Acheson's counsel he issued two statements on the background of American force withdrawal from the Korean Peninsula in 1949.[130] Ever smarting from his own Press Club pronouncement of early 1950, which to many had invited the North Korean adventure, Acheson prompted Truman to this faulty logic of involving Eisenhower as well as MacArthur in the 1949 troop withdrawal. Little time was expended on MacArthur, although Truman did suggest that ". . . if we had followed the advice of some of our generals, we would probably be involved in a much greater conflict in the Far East." Truman asserted, "One general almost got us into a much bigger war—against China and Russia—and I had to remove him." [131] But Eisenhower, not MacArthur, was now the principal target, and Truman suggested, ". . . he had suffered more than most from soft delusions about Soviet intentions."[132]

What really outraged the Commander in Chief was that one of his own generals suggested that he could find a means of ending the Korean War. If Ridgway and Mark Clark—and, yes, Eisenhower's classmates Bradley and Van Fleet and his former superior, Marshall—could not, how then could Eisenhower? Terming him a demagogue and charging him with undermining the morale of the fighting forces in Korea, the feisty President was also angered by Eisenhower's failure to denounce Marshall's critics. By his silence on that subject, Eisenhower had, Truman declared, "endorsed a . . . reign of terror by slander."[133] "Finding out what manner of man he is has been to me . . . a most sad experience," the President asserted. "It has been to me, as it was to the students of his university, 'the great disenchantment.'"[134] Years later, Truman also sought to tear down Eisenhower's military reputation, terming him "very weak as a field commander."[135] During the campaign he still insisted he had "every confidence in him as a military man." It was rather "as President and politician, he wouldn't know what to do. . . ."[136] Moreover, "by attacking our efforts in Korea and calling them a blunder," the Commander in Chief asserted, Eisenhower "has raised questions that strike a blow at the morale of the free nations fighting there."[137]

During the campaign, when not speaking from personal

anger and pique, Truman gave some of his best statements on his foreign policy. "The only sure defense of this country, the only sure path to peace," he declared on October 17, "is the policy of firm resistance to communism which we have been following—a policy of avoiding another great war on the one hand and of avoiding appeasement on the other...." In this, as in several of his addresses, he liked to refer to the Presidency as "the most powerful office that has ever existed in the history of the world." When he mentioned rulers such as Louis XIV and Napoleon, he almost seemed to suggest that they did not hold a candle to the man from Independence. Despite his own outbursts, even his threat to drop the bomb, he seriously insisted, "You must have a man in that office who has a level head...."[138]

Perhaps better than at any previous time, Truman during the campaign expressed his views as to why we were fighting in Korea. He endeavored to relate it to each community he visited, saying that the action was so that we would not have to fight in Cedar Rapids, Waterloo, Wichita, or wherever he was speaking. This did *not* come through convincingly. But when he came to the home town of the late Senator Arthur F. Vandenberg (and of a young Congressman, Gerald R. Ford), he ably interpreted the meaning of American foreign policy. At Grand Rapids, Michigan, on October 30, 1952, Truman declared, "Despite his tragic and untimely death last year, Arthur Vandenberg is still a great figure of importance in this campaign." The President then recalled the efforts at the end of World War II "to work with all our war time allies to build a lasting peace. But," he charged, "the Kremlin started its cold war against the free world." He recalled how Vandenberg had stood with him in rallying "strong resistance to the threat from Moscow." Citing the Greek-Turkish aid program, NATO, and other efforts to build "strong friends and allies," he termed Vandenberg "a tower of strength, a leader and a counselor at every step of this great enterprise."

At Grand Rapids, Truman also asserted: "Korea marks the greatest test, the most important landmark in all that we have done to hold and counter Soviet imperialism." He recalled our earlier failure to challenge "Hitler's march into

Austria and Japanese aggression in Manchuria," and
suggested that equal "will or courage" at that time might
have precluded World War II.[139]

In his election eve broadcast of November 3, the President
amplified his view that his administration had countered
"the conspiracy of godless communism. Our efforts have
given all men hope for peace and freedom." He found this
"one of our greatest achievements as a Nation." A basic
faith, a religious conviction, had helped Truman make many
tough decisions, but a sense of divine purpose had rarely
entered into his public utterances. "I believe," the President
concluded, "that God intended for this Nation to lead the
way to peace for all men, and that we are going ahead to lead
it to peace obedient to His will."[140]

In a very real sense, it was the record of Truman's administration that the voters rejected. National prosperity, despite
inflation, and the Democratic assertion that the people
"never had it so good" made but little impression. "Communism, corruption, and Korea" became a devastating slogan. So was "It's time for a change." More telling even than
"the mess in Washington" was an unpopular war. Just as an
earlier President had been labeled with "Mr. Madison's
war," this had become "Truman's war." Terming it a
"stalemate," Eisenhower at Detroit on October 24 promised
not only to make "a personal trip to Korea" but also to "concentrate on the job of ending the Korean War . . . until that
job is honorably done. . . ."[141] As one writer later reflected,
"For all practical purposes, the contest ended that night."[142]

On November 4 Eisenhower won in thirty-nine of forty-
eight states. It was the consensus of most Americans, as the
New York Times expressed it, that his "personal and intellectual integrity" would provide the "effective and . . .
forthright leadership" the nation needed.[143]

Truman: An Assessment

In 1951, with considerable clairvoyance, Arthur Meier
Schlesinger, Sr., estimated: "The Truman administration
will probably be longest remembered for what it did in inter-

national affairs."[144] And so it has proven. When Professor
Schlesinger conducted a poll less than ten years after Tru-
man left office, historians and political scientists placed Tru-
man right after Theodore Roosevelt among the "Near Great"
Presidents. The same 1962 poll of "75 experts" placed
Eisenhower at the bottom end of the "Average" Presidents,
just one above the only President ever impeached, Andrew
Johnson.[145]

In these and subsequent polls Truman received especially
high marks as an "activist" President. He inherited the Presidency after less than three months as Vice President, and
few other Presidents have ever been confronted with such a
complexity of domestic and foreign issues; few were forced
by circumstances to make so many awesome command decisions. Hesitancy and indecision were not parts of Truman's
character, nor were misgivings about decisions that were
made. Even Taft admitted, "He has the quality of decision
which is a good thing in an executive."[146] Like but few other
Presidents, Truman came to relish every moment in office. If
one were to seek to further define the Truman character by
comparing him with the President he was least like, Buchanan would have got the nod. On the eve of the Civil War,
as the South began to secede from the Union, Buchanan
as President, as Commander in Chief, was filled with indecision. Truman found Buchanan "just like the fella that followed me into the White House. He couldn't make a decision
to save his soul in hell."[147]

Truman's changing attitude toward Eisenhower was
partly caused by an intense partisanship toward a political
opponent; similarly, his friendship for Herbert Hoover involved partisanship. He believed FDR had treated the only
living former President badly. One of his first acts upon becoming President was to get the Congress to rename the
great dam in Arizona that Hoover had planned. In those
early years it had been the Hoover Dam project, only to be
dedicated by FDR as the "Boulder Dam." Truman's action
was the beginning of a close personal friendship with
Hoover in which both men judiciously avoided the subject of
politics. In 1946 he named Hoover as his personal emissary
to take charge of the war on famine and poverty in thirty-

eight nations. Truman's abiding affection for Hoover contrasted with his disdain for the Kennedys. "The whole Kennedy family, as nearly as I can make out," he asserted in his now famous 1961–1962 interviews, "about all they're interested in is getting the power."[148]

Some political scientists point out that Truman had the first institutionalized Presidency. Although he revered the office, had a certain sense of history, and came to accept an orderly process for decisionmaking, he found advisory bodies thrust upon him by the critics of his predecessor, who were taken aback by FDR's informal, offhanded, indeed, disorganized method of decisionmaking. Hoover, to combat the depression, had increased the professional staff from two to nine;[149] Truman, in support of an institutionalized Presidency, increased his policy staff from sixty to two hundred.[150]

The intellectual elite had first viewed Truman as the little unsuccessful haberdasher from Missouri, whose only post–high school formal education had been two years of evening study at the Kansas City School of Law. To their amazement, they found Truman a student of both history and music. He was also competent in governmental organization: Truman evaluated, with constructive recommendations, each of the reports issued during the 1947–1949 period by the Hoover Commission, even though it had been established by the detested 80th Congress.

Truman's efforts in domestic policy, in the light of demanding foreign policy concerns, were doomed to defeat almost from the start. No other twentieth-century President had attempted to simultaneously forge major domestic and foreign policy programs during times of peril. Wilson's New Freedom reforms came to an end before America's involvement in World War I. No New Deal enactments were accomplished after 1938. Johnson achieved his Great Society legislation before getting bogged down in Vietnam. Truman's failures in a particular area of foreign policy, Marshall's mission to China, aroused in some quarters a deep distrust, coloring attitudes toward domestic policy. Even before the Marshall mission the honeymoon with Taft and other conservative Republicans abruptly terminated when they discovered that Truman intended to keep faith with the New

Deal. In this opposition they were joined by southern Democrats. Thus Truman's efforts for legislation in such fields as
civil rights, minimum wages, and health insurance, as well
as the defense-related universal military training, all failed
passage.

Even so sympathetic a biographer as Cabell Phillips admitted that Truman's "gains on the domestic front, in the end,
were modest. . . ."[151] Aside from the Atomic Energy Act
(1946), the Council of Economic Advisers (1946), the National Security Act (1947) and its 1949 amendment, and other
Hoover Commission–related organizational changes, including the elevation of the Bureau of the Budget and the Housing Act of 1949, there is little to report. Ironically, the Housing
Act had been chiefly sponsored by Truman's Republican
nemesis, Taft, and it was, indeed, "the high water-mark of
Truman's Fair Deal."[152] Perhaps Truman's chief legislative-
related claim to fame was that he vetoed more bills (250)
than any other two-term President. Eisenhower exercised
the veto 181 times and was never overridden on substantive
issues, but Truman was again and again overridden, even
though, except for two years, he enjoyed a majority in Congress in his own party, whereas Eisenhower's party controlled the Congress only two of his eight years in office.

After the 1945–1948 domestic legislative failures, Truman
focused his attention almost exclusively on foreign policy
issues, and his 1949 Presidential Inaugural Address was the
first in American history devoted completely to the foreign
policy area.[153] Nonetheless, he remained a courageous liberal
spirit to the last. Deploring such legislation as the McCarran
Act of 1951 with its Subversive Activities Board, Truman
compared it to the Alien and Sedition Acts of 1798, which, he
said, "didn't work either."[154]

Thoroughgoing liberal that he was, Truman's views on the
CIA are confusing and perhaps even contradictory. It was
almost as though he had a professional view and a public
view. Truman was proud that he had helped to form the
CIA. Emphasizing the CIA's essential advisory role in Presidential decisionmaking, the President in a November 21,
1952, news conference avowed that the CIA "has worked
very successfully. We have an intelligence information ser-

vice now that I think is not inferior to any in the world."[155] Nearly twenty years later, the aged former President assured a professional audience at the Army Command and General Staff School, during the Nixon Presidency, that the CIA "is going very well." Yet in recordings made in 1961–1962 for public broadcast, Truman charged Eisenhower with letting the CIA get "out of hand. . . . The people have got a right to know what those birds are up to," the peppery elder statesman added. "And if I was back in the White House people would know."[156]

As President, as Commander in Chief, Truman especially respected the nation's civil servants and its armed services and was concerned about public confidence in both. In his Farewell Address he deplored "recent reckless attacks" on the civil servants.[157] In his final Presidential press conference he charged that "to weaken public confidence" in the armed services and their leaders "by destructive criticism is reprehensible." With appealing modesty, intermixed with pride, he recalled how he had "served in the Armed Forces during World War I, not with any high command. . . ." Out of such experience and his Senatorial investigatory role in World War II, he said, "I understand what the difficulties are and the things that the men have to go through with who are responsible for the operation of the military part of our Government." Earnestly he concluded, "I am hoping that this statement will have some effect."[158]

Truman's primary concern during his final weeks in office was that the new administration would continue what he believed had been a courageous foreign policy. "The new administration and the new Congress will face extremely difficult problems, particularly in the field of foreign affairs," he stated the day following the election. "The proper solution of those problems may determine whether we shall have a third world war—and, indeed, whether we shall survive as a free and democratic Nation."[159]

Truman had an abiding faith in the nation's survival and eventual victory in its ordeal with Communist imperialism. He fervently believed that "in the long view the strength of our free society, and our ideals will prevail over a system that has respect for neither God nor man."[160] Perceiving sources of moral and spiritual strength in our churches and synagogues, he concluded that "the only hope of mankind for enduring peace lies in the realm of the spiritual."[161] He further believed that the President, especially in times of crisis, must provide moral leadership for the nation.

Although Truman insisted that the decision to release the atomic bomb over Japan never troubled him, it was yet on his mind in his Farewell Address, when he said, "I made that decision in the conviction that it would save hundreds of thousands of lives—Japanese as well as Americans."[162] Acheson, who did not participate in this, one of Truman's first momentous command decisions, has suggested that during those first months Truman's decision process "was hasty as though pushed out by the pressure of responsibility, and—perhaps also—by concern that deliberateness might seem indecisiveness."[163]

But if Truman's first major command decision was arrived at without due consideration, assuredly his firing of MacArthur nearly six years later came after canny deliberation. It is interesting to speculate what the Truman-MacArthur relationship might have been without Acheson, Harriman, and Marshall. At Wake, Truman, who had brought along a five-pound box of candy for Mrs. MacArthur, was pleasantly surprised with the rapport he found with his senior general. (It was years later that Truman propounded the myth that, at Wake, MacArthur kept him waiting.) His own first reaction with the Chinese entry into the war was to support MacArthur to the hilt, even with the A-bomb, but his advisers together with Prime Minister Attlee, prevailed.

No matter how difficult or unpopular the decision, Truman never sought to evade it. As he said in his Farewell Address, "The greatest part of the President's job is to make decisions. . . . The President—whoever he is—has to decide." With those famous words he concluded, "He can't pass the buck to anybody."[164]

What did he consider his most difficult, most important decision? It was clearly the decision to enter the Korean War.[165] History was to bear this out. A nation which, as Hamilton had pointed out in *The Federalist*, had from its beginning distrusted large military establishments and had held back from giving the Commander in Chief vast strategic authority, was to find no other choice after 1950. During the five preceding years, Truman had again and again been called upon to stand up against Communist aggression, but as far as having the armed forces to back it up was concerned, it had been mostly "bluff."[166] Korea, then, and the attendant state of national emergency gave Truman the go-ahead for a crash program to build up the armed services, including the garrisoning of NATO. He now denied all past American tradition, with more than just words. He even denied what FDR had counseled for post–World War II military responsibilities, that we "should not get roped into accepting any European sphere of influence."[167]

True, we had come along reluctantly. Later the United States liked to take credit for founding NATO, but in fact Vandenberg's 1948 enabling resolution followed European initiatives, and as early as 1945 Anthony Eden had urged "regional arrangements complementary to those of the Soviet in Eastern Europe." As Eden assessed the situation in 1951: "If the democratic nations of the West had formed regional associations without delay, the balance with the communist East might have been struck years ago, and under more favorable conditions. The Soviet Union," Eden concluded, "wasted no time."[168]

But now inaction was past. Whereas the Defense budget had stood at $13.3 billion on the eve of Korea, Truman immediately asked for $57.6 billion; the Senate by an amazing 70 to 0 upped this to $59.5 billion; the House approved $56.1 billion by 342 to 2, and the conferences compromised on $56.9 billion. Korea was, indeed, the watershed, and no future President, as long as the Soviets continued to pose a threat, would recommend returning to America's traditional stringent "peacetime" military budgets. Nor would the Congress deny thereafter provision for the "common defense."[169]

Asked in his final Presidential press conference, "If you had to do it over again, would you call it police action in Korea?" Truman responded, without hesitation: "I sure would." Asked whether he was right in not seeking a Congressional declaration of war, he responded, "Let history decide that."[170]

With the exception of Lincoln and FDR, no other President ever took such a strong view of the Commander in Chief role of the President as did Truman. Perhaps his strongest statements on that role, setting forth his thesis of the authority of the President and Commander in Chief in a nuclear age, were made at the time of his seizure of the steel mills. "We live in an age when hostilities begin without polite exchanges of diplomatic notes," he warned. "There are no longer sharp distinctions between combatants and non-combatants, between military targets and the sanctuary of the civilian areas. Nor can we separate the economic facts from the problems of defense and security."[171]

No one could quarrel with the President as the modern state girds itself against the possible onslaught of nuclear warfare. The only question is whether the security of the nation was being periled by hard-headed steel owners and workers. The majority of the Court obviously thought not. The Congress should have acted, not the President. Nonetheless, it was the defense of his own action of seizing the steel mills, in the midst of the Korean War, that prompted Truman to sum up his view of Presidential authority in national security affairs:

> In this day and age the defense of the nation means more than building an army, navy, and air force. It is a job for the entire resources of the nation. The President, who is Commander in Chief and who represents the interest of all the people, must [be] able to act at all times to meet any sudden threat to the nation's security.[172]

In setting forth these views of the modern President and Commander in Chief, Truman, while pronouncing truths, was, in a sense, fencing with windmills: neither the Congress nor the Court had denied his authority to enter the Korean War. Labor disputes might come and go, Congress might pass a War Powers Act, but only one person could act in an all-out national emergency. That person, as Truman expressed it in those last days in the Presidency, occupied "an office that is without parallel in the history of the world."[173] As Clinton Rossiter expressed it, "We have placed a shocking amount of military power in the President's keeping, but where else, we may ask, could it possibly have been placed?"[174]

How well had he occupied it? The person who worked most closely with him in national security policy decisions, Dean Acheson, had a unique vantage for evaluation. The two men were studies in contrast. Acheson, the son of an Episcopal bishop, was educated at Groton and Yale and Harvard Law School; Truman, the son of a Missouri farmer, was schooled at Independence High and a few evening law courses. One was an aristocrat, the other a commoner; one large, fierce, and imposing; the other small, at times seemingly reticent and retiring. Yet there was "never any doubt as to which was the boss." Having served as Under Secretary of State during the secretaryship of the peripatetic Jimmy Byrnes (who had been on his world travels half his time in office), Acheson had learned, amid Truman's temper tantrums, the importance of keeping the President informed at all times. As Under Secretary, commencing in August 1945, more than anyone else Acheson had encouraged Truman's get-tough-with-the-Russians attitude in the Iranian and Turkish episodes. (Indeed in the Bosporus Straits crisis it had been Acheson who got Truman to send the *Missouri* to Istanbul. Unprepared as we were in 1946, he had even proposed war with the Russians if they did not give up their demands on Turkey.)[175]

A part of the Truman evaluation is his own estimate of his lieutenant. Truman made a fair assessment when he wrote Acheson at the conclusion of his administration, "You have been my good right hand.... Certainly no man has been more responsible than you for pulling together the people of the free world, and strengthening their will and their determination to be strong and free." Truman generously recognized Acheson as the officer successful in building up NATO and establishing a military assistance program. Moreover, the homespun President concluded with the words of praise that the aristocratic Acheson yearned for: "I would place you among the very greatest of the Secretaries of State this country has had."[176] This Trumanesque hyperbole bears qualification with regard to Asian policy: much as Acheson sought to label MacArthur with inviting Chinese intervention in Korea, Acheson's own insensitivity to Chinese concerns, together with the go-ahead for the MacArthur advance north of the 38th parallel, actually inspired Chinese intervention in the Korean War, just as his earlier Press Club talk had invited the original North Korean southward excursion. Rightly or wrongly, he laid the foundations for American involvement in Vietnam. In brief, Acheson and Truman must share both the successes in Europe and the frustrations in Asia.

Acheson, according to his reminiscences, liked Truman more than he did his fellow aristocrat Roosevelt, who he believed was an ineffective administrator. He perceived that Truman, like Roosevelt, seldom admitted his own mistakes but, unlike Roosevelt, learned by them. Ignoring the mistakes of 1945–1946, including the China mission, in which he played no role, Acheson found a "heroic mold"[177] in the sweep of events from the enunciation of the Truman Doctrine through the European Recovery Plan, NATO, and the Korean intervention.

However, Acheson, who abhorred Roosevelt's lack of orderliness, was somewhat carried away by his own rhetoric in describing Truman's "passion for orderly procedure...." Terming the National Security Council as the instrument through which Truman introduced due deliberation "into executive administration,"[178] Acheson ignored Truman's reluctance in utilizing the NSC. Nor did Truman effectively utilize his Cabinet in decisionmaking. As Harold Gosnell and Thomas E. Cronin have pointed out, Truman had a penchant for mustering "ad hoc groups" for advice,[179] just as he did in reaching his decision for Korean intervention. It remained for Eisenhower, who had a penchant for administrative orderliness, to seek to organize the NSC and the Cabinet as effective instruments for decision. Acheson concluded his evaluation with an incontrovertible view: "In the last analysis Mr. Truman's methods reflected the basic integrity of his own character."[180]

Acheson emerged as the President's principal professional

adviser on national security policy, but an assessment should not ignore the inner family circle. Bess, Harry, and Margaret Truman were appropriately termed the "Three Musketeers" by the White House staff. Not only was Truman devoted to his family; he also sought their counsel. Bess, "The Boss," as Harry Truman called her, was, as J. B. West observed, "keenly intelligent, well-educated, politically experienced. . . ." West, who served every First Lady from Eleanor Roosevelt through Pat Nixon, further observed Bess Truman's well-grounded, unique counseller role: "Although it went unsuspected by nearly everybody in government," West confided years later, "Bess Truman entered into nearly every decision the President made."[181]

His childhood sweetheart, his lifelong mate, Bess did much for Harry (she insisted it had taken a lifetime to get him to say "manure"). She encouraged his avid reading, especially of history—though his readings of the "greats" of history gave him a somewhat simplistic view of how others had acted, and how accordingly he should act in different times and circumstances.

After starting hesitantly, Truman came to relish making decisions so much that many believed he was making too many. What, in his own final words from the White House, did he perceive as his legacy? He believed that he had brought the United States to the role of world leadership which it should have assumed immediately following World War I.[182] In his Farewell Address he mused, "I suppose that history will remember my term in office as the years when the cold war began to overshadow our lives." He recollected, "I have had hardly a day in office that has not been dominated by this all-embracing struggle. . . ." Recounting his years of crises, he concluded with a reference to Korea: "So a decision was reached—the decision I believe was the most important in my time as President of the United States."[183]

The following day Dwight D. Eisenhower called at the White House. Only Harry Truman could fail to understand, after all he had said about the President-elect, why Eisenhower was scarcely conversant as they rode together to the inaugural.

Truman was neither a popular nor an inspiring President.

Yet his Presidency had indelible characteristics of greatness: courage, energy, integrity, tenacity. Those who recollected the cockiness of the man who said, "I make foreign policy," might recall the earlier statement of his credo: "As President of the United States, I am guided by a simple formula: to do in all cases, from day to day, without regard to narrow political considerations, what seems to me to be best for the welfare of all of our people."[184]

V

****

JAMES V. FORRESTAL AND THE NATIONAL SECURITY ACT OF 1947

> If we falter in our leadership, we may endanger the peace of the world—and we shall surely endanger the welfare of our own Nation.
> HARRY S TRUMAN, addressing a joint session of the Congress, March 12, 1947

When Gerald R. Ford became President of the United States, he placed pictures of Truman, Washington, and Lincoln in the Oval Office. All three had been strong Commanders in Chief. Truman, as Vice President, had little opportunity to participate in national security policy, but after Roosevelt's death he unhesitatingly assumed the Commander in Chief role, especially in his decision to use the ultimate weapon, the atomic bomb, to end the war in Japan.

As the Soviet Union revealed its hostile intentions after World War II, Truman enunciated a doctrine to contain Communist aggression. On March 12, 1947, he asked the Congress for military appropriations to help save Greece and Turkey from Communist domination. In June of that year Secretary of State George C. Marshall proposed a war "against hunger, poverty, desperation, and chaos," which became the European Recovery Plan (ERP). During the next four years Congress appropriated about $17 billion for factories, machine tools, transportation facilities, housing, dams, and farm machinery. This contributed most significantly to western Europe's recovery. By 1952 those war-ravaged countries had far surpassed their prewar production figures.

By 1948, the Soviets, less successfully, had countered with a plan for their eastern European satellites: Czechoslovakia, Poland, Hungary, Rumania, Bulgaria, Albania, Yugoslavia, and the Russian zones of Germany and Austria. (Although Finland was nominally independent, its internal foreign policy was also dominated by the Soviets.)

Most threatening was the German situation. Americans were now regretting that, despite military capabilities, Roosevelt had allowed Stalin to take eastern Germany, including Berlin. Eastern Germany had become a Soviet satellite, but Berlin had been divided into Soviet and U.S., British, and French zones. The western zones could be reached only by a 110-mile corridor crossing Soviet-controlled East Germany. As discussed in Chapter 3, in 1948 the Soviets cut off land and water routes to the western zones of Berlin, and British and Americans flew round-the-clock airlifts to the city until the blockade ended. The Berlin airlift was clearly a Western victory.

Truman, along with many leaders of western Europe, believed in the interdependence of nations and adherence to the principles of collective security as set forth in 1945 in the charter of the United Nations. He agreed with British Foreign Secretary Anthony Eden that "the purpose of collective endeavor is not only to win wars but to prevent them."[1] In January 1949 the Council of Europe had been created "to achieve greater unity." The North Atlantic Treaty Organization (NATO) was created three months later, and the United States was a signator. With the exception of the Rio Pact, not since the Franco-American Alliance of 1778 had been terminated by the Convention of 1800 had the United States been a member of a peacetime alliance. Soviet aggression had created this reversal of a 149-year American policy.

ERP and NATO formed two legs of the Truman anti-Communist program. The third, enacted in 1950, was the Mutual Defense Assistance Program, by which arms were shipped to the NATO allies.

While concerned with strengthening the free world, Truman also wanted to build a united security establishment at home. Moreover, he was concerned about interservice rivalries and desired more effective relationships among the departments and agencies contributing to national security policy. There was nothing entirely new in the discordant voices seeking to influence policy in the post–World War II era. Disunity and rivalry are as old as man himself. The experience of the United States in its War for Independence had pointed to the need for a strong Commander in Chief. This the founding fathers sought to provide in the Constitution.

National security organization in the first Washington administration began in seeming unity in 1789, with a Department of State and a War Department. Even then, however, there were strong differing views. The first Secretary of State, Thomas Jefferson, resigned near the end of 1793, partially in protest to the foreign policy of Secretary of the Treasury Alexander Hamilton, who was, in essence, Washington's principal national security adviser. Hamilton was also the principal author of Washington's September 1796 Farewell Address, which counseled: "... always to keep ourselves, by suitable establishment, on a respectably defensive posture. . . ."[2]

The requirement of national security, including an undeclared naval war with France, dictated the establishment in 1798 of a separate Department of the Navy. And so the two departments, War and Navy, soon went their separate ways. In the midst of the Civil War, Lincoln's strong Secretary of War, Edwin S. Stanton, sought to place the Navy under the Army. But that diary-keeping Navy Secretary, Gideon Welles, resisted with Lincoln's cordial support, even though Lincoln's own previous service identification had been Army—as a militia captain in the Black Hawk War.

Perhaps the pre–World War I War and Navy Department relationships were most eloquently described when President Wilson's Secretary of War, Lindley Garrison, responded to Navy Secretary Josephus Daniels's communication about cooperation: "Joe, I don't care a damn about the Navy, and [don't you] care a damn about the Army." Far from being unity-minded, Garrison concluded: "You run your machine, and I will run mine."[3]

During World War I, but before the United States entered

the war, the 1916 National Defense Act established a National Defense Council of five members as a move toward mobilization. The Secretary of State was *not* included.

The seeds of unification and the evolvement of an integrated national security organization were sown in the experience and the aftermath of World War I, principally on the part of the aviators led by Brigadier General William (Billy) Mitchell. He was specifically court-martialed because he released a statement to the press accusing the Navy and Army high commands of "incompetency, criminal negligence, and almost treasonable administration of our national defense." Although Douglas A. MacArthur had, as a member of the court-martial hearing, supported Mitchell, he was no advocate of a separate Air Force or of a unified defense establishment. In 1925 Dwight W. Morrow had headed President Coolidge's board on civil and military aviation, which had reaffirmed retaining autonomous Army and Navy military departments, each with its own air arm. MacArthur supported the Morrow Board position and reiterated this view in response to a 1932 Congressional inquiry while he was then serving as Army Chief of Staff.

In vain, the American aviators pointed to the British post–World War I example, with its coequal Royal Air Force (including naval aviation) in a unified military establishment. There was no Congressional effort between 1932 and the end of World War II to achieve the Army aviators' goals of a separate Air Force within a united defense establishment.

However, the exigencies of World War II created a semiautonomous Army Air Forces, and its chief, General H. H. Arnold, was a member of the Joint Chiefs of Staff, who first met on February 9, 1942. They continued to operate throughout the war without so much as "a chit or a memorandum from the President."[4] And they cordially bypassed the Secretaries of both the Army and the Navy.

Four salient aspects of the thrust toward military service unification in the pre-1947 period were: (1) the 1920s quest of the aviators; (2) the failure of interservice coordination at Pearl Harbor; (3) Army and Navy wartime duplications and inefficiencies; and (4) the successes of the World War II unified commands.

In 1944, in the midst of the war, Secretary of the Navy James V. Forrestal appeared before the House Select Committee on the subject of unification. He then testified that it would not work because no one was capable "of sitting on top of all that. . . ."[5]

The story of the origins of the National Security Act of 1947 has been well documented,[6] but I will reiterate it briefly. In the fall of 1945, following the end of World War II, the Collins-Hill (or the War Department Plan) and the Forrestal-Eberstadt (or Navy Plan) were proposed. Both plans made distinct contributions. The Collins-Hill Plans (named for Lieutenant General J. Lawton Collins and Senator Lister Hill) called for a Secretary of the Armed Forces, an Under Secretary, and assistant secretaries for "coordination of scientific research and development" and the supervision of "procurement and industrial mobilization, legislative affairs, and public information." In the hierarchical structure there would be no Joint Chiefs of Staff and no service secretaries, but there would be a military Chief of Staff and three service branches, including a coequal Air Force.

The Forrestal-Eberstadt Plan made a distinction between policy planning and operations. As envisioned by Navy Secretary Forrestal in 1944, at the apex of policy planning there would be a national security council. Other high-level planning bodies would include a national resources planning board, Joint Chiefs of Staff, and a military munitions board. Unlike the Army Plan, there would be no Secretary of the Armed Forces (Secretary of Defense), and no coequal separate Air Force. When the proposal was more fully defined the following year by Ferdinand Eberstadt, the feature of an Air Force separate from the Army and coequal with the Army and the Navy was reluctantly added, with the understanding that the Navy would continue its own air arm.[7]

Since Forrestal was to emerge as the central figure in national defense policy, a fuller understanding of his view is important. Moreover, since Eberstadt was to become the principal author both of the National Security Act of 1947 and of its significant 1949 amendment, his views warrant further examination. Forrestal and Eberstadt had been friends since college days. Both had gone to Princeton (although Forrestal never graduated). Two years Forrestal's senior, Eberstadt, a member of the class of 1913, graduated from Columbia Law School in 1917. He served in France in World War I in the field artillery, while Forrestal was a lieutenant in the U.S. Naval Air Service. After the war, both worked for the prestigious Wall Street banking firm of Dillon, Read and Company. Eberstadt moved on to head his own firm of investment bankers, while Forrestal rose to become president of Dillon, Read (1938) before becoming Under Secretary of the Navy in 1940, the year following the outbreak of hostilities in World War II in Europe.

During the war, Forrestal was impressed by Eberstadt's work on the War Production Board and the Army and Navy Munitions Board. Both men believed that national security policy and organization should transcend the armed forces. Forrestal had participated in the State-War-Navy Coordinating Committee (SWNCC, or "Swink," as it was colloquially called), since its founding in 1944 through the initiative of War Department Secretary Henry L. Stimson, an early advocate of armed forces unification.

Stimson, who served from 1929 to 1933 as President Hoover's Secretary of State, appreciated, as did few other Americans in the early 1940s, the vital relationship between political and military matters which SWNCC represented. Stimson was a colonel in the American Expeditionary Forces in World War I, and he had served as Secretary of War to both Taft and Roosevelt. He thus had a unique perspective of the vital importance of total mobilization of the nation's resources in wartime. He shared these views with Forrestal, who succeeded to the post of Secretary of the Navy following the death of Frank Knox in 1944.

Stimson contributed much to Forrestal's emerging view for a coordinating council or a national security council at the apex of a national security organization, as well as a national security resources board as a significant part of any postwar national security organization. As Forrestal expressed it in 1945: "The question of national security is not merely a question of the Army and Navy. . . . We have to take into account our whole potential for war. . . ," including "our mines, industry, manpower, research and all the activities that go into normal civilian life. . . . I think," he concluded, "the State Department is also part of the team."[8]

The War Department under the venerable Stimson had then shared these views, as it was to do so under his successor, Robert P. Patterson, who moved up from Under Secretary after Stimson's retirement in September 1945. The War Department, including the Army Air Forces, differed from the Navy on the question of unification of the armed forces. The idea of an emerging coequal Air Force, encompassing naval aviation, conjured up nightmares, and, if the Navy Department lost autonomy with a superimposed defense department, even naval control of the Marine Corps might be threatened.

The Navy Department lost a great friend with the death of President Roosevelt. The new President, Truman, whose military experience had been in the Army, gave immediate support to the War Department unification plans.[9] Perceiving in the War Department's plan the best hope to overcome Navy intransigence about giving up naval aviation, the Army Air Forces leaders backed the Collins-Hill proposal.[10]

Six days after Truman became President, Forrestal found himself confronted with a Presidential proposal for a "single department of defense." Forrestal invited the President to "reread the Morrow Board Report"[11] of 1925. But he realized he must now have a full response to the Army Plan; hence he called on Eberstadt to prepare such a report, 250 "close packed pages" to be completed by September 25.[12] The Forrestal-Eberstadt proposals would counter the creation of a Secretary of Defense with a coordinating National Security Council.

Despite the persuasive qualities of Eberstadt's report, President Truman stuck to his support of the Army Plan for a Cabinet Secretary in charge of a new Department of National Defense. In his message to Congress of December 19, 1945, he included an "advisory body" composed of the Chief of Staff and the three service commanders.[13] Firmly facing naval resistance, Truman asserted he would appoint "the hardest, meanest so and so" he could find to become his new Secretary of National Defense.[14]

To rally support for his position as well as to provide counsel, the President, on March 28, 1946, created a National Defense Council, including the five-star heroes of World War II. There is no record that he ever assembled this body.[15] By April 1946, the Senate's Military Affairs Committee had introduced a bill reflecting the President's message. It gave considerable concessions to the Navy's position by including service secretaries (though without Cabinet rank) and a National Security Council.[16]

Seeking support for his own position on organization, as well as attempting to assess Soviet intentions in the erupting Cold War, Forrestal in March 1946 conferred with Winston Churchill. "I talked with him [Churchill] at some length about unification," Forrestal confided in his diary March 10, 1946. "I said that I greatly feared the attempt that was now being made to consolidate the civilian Departments of War and Navy under one administrative head." Churchill felt very strongly that there should, indeed, be only a single "Minister of Defense." Nonetheless, Forrestal found comfort in the fact that Churchill "agreed with me that he should perform a staff and coordinating function rather than an administrative function."[17]

The well-organized Navy position was gathering strength. Even Truman was prepared to make further concessions despite his predilections for the Army position. On May 13, Truman convened a meeting at the White House with Secretaries Forrestal and Patterson, the Chief of Staff to the Commander in Chief of the Army and the Navy, Fleet Admiral William D. Leahy, and the service chiefs and senior staff. A major issue was the single chief-of-staff concept, which had been a feature of the Collins Plan and had been espoused in the President's December 19 unification message. (Truman's proposal, like the Collins Plan, had additionally included "U.S. Chiefs of Staff" to make recommendations on military policy, strategy, and the budget, but with no operational control.)[18] Moreover, in the Army's and the President's concept, this single Chief of Staff superseded the armed forces in the chain of command to the Secretary of the Armed Forces.

At this meeting with the President, Admiral Leahy spoke

persuasively against the single chief-of-staff concept and advocated the joint chiefs proposed by Forrestal and Eberstadt.
Truman thereupon announced he was dropping the single
chief of staff in favor of the joint chiefs proposal. Leahy also
helped secure Forrestal's much-sought guarantees for naval
aviation.[19]

Still, the President had not given up his advocacy of subordinated service departments headed by assistant secretaries, and fears remained that the Marine Corps might be
taken over by the Army. The Army's strategy of unification
appeared, at least in part, inspired to make certain that the
ground Army did not suffer neglect by comparison with the
more glamorous Air Force and Navy.

Forrestal, unlike his admirals and generals, sought a middle ground combining the economics and experiences of
coordination without relinquishing Navy autonomy.[20] He
secured Patterson's concurrence on many elements of
Eberstadt's report, including a Council for Common Defense
(National Security Council), a National Security Resources
Board, a Central Intelligence Agency, and a Military Munitions Board. Forrestal continued to balk at the Army's concept of a Secretary of National Defense with broad administrative authority over the military department.[21] He continued to oppose those aspects of the Senate Military Affairs
Committee's bill (the Thomas bill, named for Senator Elbert
D. Thomas of Utah) which reduced the status of the service
secretaries. By such a bill, he told the President, they would
have "neither responsibility nor power."[22]

Air Force opposition and publicity were abhorrent to Forrestal, as was the Army's Assistant Secretary for Air, W.
Stuart Symington. The Navy Secretary in March 1946 recorded in his diary, with some satisfaction, that the President said "that the Air Force had no discipline."[23]

By June 1946, Forrestal could tell the President that "a very
long road had been travelled toward reconciling the conflicting views of the Army and the Navy...."[24] Yet it was also
clear that the further compromising would have to be on the
part of the Army. Forrestal openly suggested, as an alternative, that he resign.[25]

By such continuing pressure, but not until January 16,

1947, Forrestal secured final agreement from Patterson. The Army capitulated to the Navy proposal for limited authority for the Secretary of National Defense over the services. In this victory Forrestal had planted the seeds of his own subsequent demise.[26]

What then emerged was a Secretary of Defense, which Truman and the Army had championed, but one with limited authority. On the other hand, Forrestal's coordinating feature, the National Security Council, also secured Presidential concurrence. Truman referred to it as "Forrestal's revenge."[27] Just as Forrestal had viewed with suspicion a diminution of Navy autonomy, so Truman viewed any proposed body which might subvert Presidential authority. Although the proposed National Security Council was to be advisory to the President, Truman looked at it with a somewhat jaundiced view.

The final passage of the National Security Act involved a new political dimension. For the first time since 1930, the Republicans had in the November 1946 elections gained control of the Congress. The GOP policy chairman, Senator Robert Taft, emerged as a principal final architect, along with Senator Arthur H. Vandenberg. On December 12, 1946, Taft met with Forrestal to discuss "the organization form of the Armed Forces." Their conversation even ranged to the "guided missiles" of the future. Forrestal wrote: "I told him [Taft] that the development of the Air arm was probably the most uncertain of all in modern war, that the phrase 'guided missile' was a misnomer because the missiles were not guided and it looked like a long time before they would be." Forrestal concluded, "When they [guided missiles] were fully developed it would be a question then whether the airplane became a guided missile or the guided missile an airplane." He did add, looking toward final resolution of the National Security Act, "Senator Taft said he would be here continuously from now on. . . ."[28]

After two years of debate and study, the National Security Act was enacted by the 80th Congress. One of the features Taft pressed on Truman was the coordinating National Security Council. On July 26, President Truman signed into law the National Security Act of 1947. It created three levels or categories of defense organization. At the apex would be the national security machinery: the National Security Council and the National Security Resources Board.

The next level, the "National Military Establishment," was designed to provide "more effective, efficient and economical administration" and to "eliminate unnecessary duplication." It encompassed two levels. The first, headed by the Secretary of Defense, consisted of four committees: Joint Chiefs of Staff, War Council, Munitions Board, and Research and Development Board. The second level consisted of the three departments, Army, Navy, and Air, and the specified and unified field commands. By the 1947 statute the Army, Navy, and the new coequal Air Force were all executive departments. The secretary of each service would be a member of the President's Cabinet and a member of the National Security Council.

These departments were charged with the training, supply, administration, and support of their respective forces for land, sea, and air operations. Specific provision was made within the Department of the Navy for the Marine Corps as well as naval aviation, which was to "include land-based naval aviation, air transport essential for naval operations, all air weapons and air techniques involved in the operations and activities of the United States Navy. . . ."

The National Security Act also created the Central Intelligence Agency, which served in an advisory capacity in the newly created National Security Council. This was an outgrowth of the wartime Office of Strategic Services and the National Intelligence Authority that had succeeded it at the war's end.

The War Council, consisting of the service secretaries and their chiefs, with the Secretary of Defense as chairman, was to advise the Secretary "on broad armed forces policy matters." It has since been renamed the Armed Forces Policy Council.

The Joint Chiefs of Staff would consist of the Chief of Staff to the Commander in Chief (Admiral Leahy's position, subsequently abolished and replaced by a chairman) and the Chief of Staff, Army, Chief of Naval Operations, and Chief of Staff, Air Force. They were to be the principal military advisers to the President and the Secretary of Defense. Concern for a too powerful general staff limited this joint staff membership to one hundred officers. The act specifically guarded against a single chief of staff or an overall armed forces general staff—a principle maintained in all its subsequent amendments.[29]

Of equal significance to the steps toward unification of the armed forces achieved by the National Security Act of 1947 was the statutory recognition that national security policy required joining political, economic, and industrial, as well as military, power. As Richard E. Neustadt has observed, "Through both world wars our Presidents grappled experimentally with an emergency-created need to 'integrate' foreign and military policies; the National Security Act now takes that need for granted as a constant of our times."[30]

The National Defense Council of 1916 was vastly different from the National Security Council created by the 1947 Act. In the 1916 Act, the Secretary of State had not been included. In the 1947 Act, he was a permanent member along with the Secretaries of Defense, Army, Navy, and Air Force and the chairman of the National Security Resources Board.

The National Security Resources Board, another feature of the Act taken from the Eberstadt Report, further pointed up the philosophy of mobilization of the nation's total resources. Its chairman was of Cabinet rank, and its other members included the Secretaries of State, Treasury, Defense, Interior, Agriculture, Commerce, and Labor, whose mission was to advise the President on the coordination of military, civilian, and industrial mobilization.[31] Through the experience of the Korean War it was to evolve by 1953 into a part of a new Office of Defense Mobilization.

The National Security Act of 1947 was a compromise measure. The Air Force achieved its basic goal in unification, coequality with the Army and Navy as an executive department, although it fell short of its ultimate aspiration, to include marine and naval aviation. The Navy, in turn, suffered less than it feared. It opposed the Army's giving up its air arm, but concluded that was the Army's business. Although it had retained naval aviation, it sensed the Air Force as a rival in future definitions of missions and goals.

The National Military Establishment was essentially what Forrestal had hoped for. It was *not* a Department of Defense, as Army Secretary Patterson, who yielded to Forrestal on most issues, recognized. Patterson declined Truman's invitation to serve in the Cabinet as the first Secretary of Defense, choosing instead to retire from government service (purportedly in order to earn more money). Forrestal was then offered the post and accepted. New York attorney Kenneth E. Royall was named as Secretary of the Army; the Navy Under Secretary, John L. Sullivan, was moved up to Secretary; and the former Assistant Secretary of War for Air, W. Stuart Symington, was named the first Secretary of the Air Force.

Forrestal's good-natured response on July 29, 1947, to Symington's congratulations was almost foreboding: "If I don't do this job well, I certainly can't blame lack of support—although, as you observed this morning, honeymoons are soon over and roses are soon followed by bricks."[32]

The honeymoon was, indeed, of short duration, as both Forrestal and Symington soon discovered. Forrestal quickly recognized that the halfway house he had engineered was not fully operable. Earlier, in 1944, he had testified that unification would not work because the job was too big. Now he saw it in another light. In June 1946, when he had threatened to resign as Secretary of the Navy, he had seen as the central issue "whether or not a law could be written which would clearly leave the Secretary of the Navy power to run his own department without kibitzing from above and while at the same time giving the Secretary of National Defense the global authority to make decisions on broad issues."[33]

Forrestal believed he had secured an act which would meet those criteria. Now, would the prohibition against "kibitzing from above" also apply to the Air Force? It was a matter far larger than the clash of personal wills or of interservice rivalries. The first Secretary of Defense was deeply concerned about the events of the Cold War and the continuing decline of American military strength in the face of Soviet aggression.

Forrestal had to defend the Truman austerity defense budget at a time when he believed the several Cold War crises of 1947–1948 dictated more support. Reading the *Forrestal Diaries,* one is struck with the Secretary's anguish over the rapidly deteriorating international situation, including the 1946–1948 threat to Greece and Turkey, the Czechoslovakian coup of 1948, and the 1948 Berlin blockade.

Robert Cutler, Boston lawyer-banker and adviser to the President and Cabinet members on national security affairs, left a graphic picture of Secretary Forrestal during this period: "He was living every day of 1948 in a Cold War crisis. Although he took regular exercise for health, the exercise seemed—like his work—less relaxation than escape."[34] Physically, Forrestal was small and wiry, with a nose flattened from a boxing incident. His mouth, "a straight unyielding line," characteristically gripped a briar pipe. He had what Cutler termed "the aggressive look somewhat belied by a quiet voice."[35] Forrestal believed, and in this even included the President, that but "few Americans understood the spreading danger of Communist power...."[36]

Unfortunately, this period of international tension coincided with efforts to make the National Military Establishment operable, to further define service missions and weapon systems, and to end interservice squabbling over the parceling out of severely constricted military budgets. Forrestal thought the service secretaries (notably Symington) were presiding over their own independent duchies or fiefdoms. Few persons could appreciate what went into the introductory statement in Forrestal's first (and only) *Report of the Secretary of Defense,* in which he declared that "the 12 month period that ended on September 17, 1948 marked the first year since 1798, that all armed forces have been part of a single military establishment."[37]

Any Cabinet officer presiding for the first time in a century and a half over the several services was bound to have his hands full. Although some have since contended that the Act gave Forrestal the authority to *direct,* he, as its principal author, had conceived a *coordinating* role for the Secretary. He further believed that his mission was to adjudicate and conciliate, and he moved toward this in two 1948 confer-

ences with the Joint Chiefs of Staff on service missions and
roles. He met with them at Key West (March 12–14) and at
Newport (August 20–22), taking the view that "the nerve
center of unification lies in the Joint Chiefs of Staff"[38] and
seeking through them to resolve roles and mission con-
troversies.

The Chiefs came to Key West in the midst of a quarrel over
the allocation of air power, which focused primarily on the
long-range bomber and the flush-deck supercarrier. Forrestal
asserted: "The problem can be stated very simply: What is to
be the use, and who is to be the user of air power?"[39] The
Key West "agreement" sought to define the primary
functions of the Army, Navy, Marine Corps, and Air Force.
Obviously, areas overlapped: for example, antisubmarine
warfare was decided to be a primary function of the Navy
and a collateral function of the Air Force.

For an appreciation of the emotion-packed feelings at the
meeting, one must understand the arguments that had preceded. The Air Force, for example, was still smarting from an
inquiry by Vice Admiral Arthur W. Radford, who in December 1946 asked "what foundation there was for the Air
Force to believe that there was a place in the war of the future
for a strategic air force."[40]

From such a protracted, acrid climate there presumably
emerged from the Key West conference agreement that: (1)
"strategic air warfare" should be the responsibility of the Air
Force; (2) the Navy should have sufficient air for its mission;
and (3) both the Navy and the Air Force should help the
ground forces (which had been passive witnesses to the
feud). The Key West agreement gave the Joint Chiefs "general direction of all combat operations" and designated "one
of their members as their executive agent" for unified and
specified commands. But this command authority concept
for the JCS was to undergo considerable debate until its resolution by the 1958 amendment to the National Security Act.

On the eve of the Key West conference, Forrestal had told
the reporters that if the Chiefs were unable to decide, "I shall
have to make my own decisions."[41] A brave assertion, it was
not to be followed in fact. The services disagreed on what
had been agreed upon from the minute the Chiefs left the

conference table.⁴² Cutler recalls that Forrestal came back deeply troubled after his "three days of controversy with the Service Chiefs at Key West." By this point, "an inner turmoil of worry occasionally seeped out through his apparent calm." He was beginning to reach the conclusion that "it was *his* fault that the Secretary of Defense lacked sufficient power to compel unified policies and cohesion among the Services."⁴³

The Newport Conference, which ostensibly met to refine the Key West "decisions," found little more to agree upon. It postponed the decision on control and direction of atomic operations, obligated the Air Force to recognize a naval strategic bombing capability, and established a weapons evaluation group. But there was disagreement as to whom it should report—the Joint Chiefs or the Research and Development Board.⁴⁴

The Key West and Newport conferences were hailed as resolving differences, but Forrestal distrusted budget planning for fiscal year 1949. Both Symington and Air Force Chief of Staff Carl Spaatz, with considerable Congressional support, argued for a 70 Group Air Force. While not opposed to this goal, Forrestal stood for what he termed a "balanced military establishment." Funds were not available to achieve both the Air Force goal and the needed Army and Navy–Marine Corps modernization. Forrestal called upon his friends Cutler, Karl Bendetsen, and Eberstadt to try to secure Air Force compromise, but to no avail. As a result, relationships between Forrestal and Symington had so deteriorated by April 1948 that Forrestal contemplated going to the President to demand Symington's resignation. Forrestal confided to Cutler, "I can't *make* Stu obey me. . . . If I can't persuade him . . . I shall have come out a failure."⁴⁵

Forrestal, indeed, could not "persuade" Symington, who went to the Congress for support for a supplement in the budget in behalf of the 70 Group Air Force goal. The President took the view that the national economy could not support a budget for the National Military Establishment in excess of $15.5 billion for the fiscal year ending June 30, 1949, and of $15 billion for the following fiscal year. Despite such a ceiling, the Congress did pass a supplementary bill authorizing an additional $822 million for the Air Force in support of its 70 Group goal. Thereupon, Truman on May 30, 1948, announced that the funds would "not be spent." As the editor of the *Forrestal Diaries*, Walter Millis, expressed it, "This was the President's rather original solution for the dilemma ... [of] reopening all the issues of strategy and Service rivalry which Forrestal had striven so hard to adjust."[46]

First-term Congressman Richard M. Nixon did not so view it. He denounced the President for impounding funds (as he was to somewhat ruefully recall as President Nixon a quarter-century later). Symington, in what Gladwin Hill of the *New York Times* termed a "gloves off talk before five hundred aviation engineers" in Los Angeles in mid-July,[47] aroused Forrestal to write him on July 18 decrying "official disobedience and personal disloyalty...."[48] The same day he called on the President, telling him he would have "to ask for Mr. Symington's resignation unless he could provide a satisfactory explanation for his conduct in Los Angeles."[49] Yet the next day he was dining "in seeming amicability" with Symington, Sullivan, and Royall, seeking to get at the root causes of disagreement.[50]

If Forrestal was looking for an opportunity for major overhaul of his authority through the National Security Act, that opportunity had now arrived. The First Hoover Commission on governmental reorganization had been established in 1947 by the 80th Congress. Quite appropriately, the Task Force on National Security Organization was headed by Forrestal's old friend, Eberstadt. The Task Force had begun its investigations in June 1948, in the midst of the Forrestal-Symington controversy. It is not surprising that the recommendations of the Task Force, which became the basis for the 1949 amendment to the National Security Act, followed Forrestal's recommendations quite closely.

Now Forrestal had a very real sense of ambivalence. Desiring to make a success of what he had authored, he avowed in a memorandum for the Eberstadt Committee on July 22, 1948, that "the departments should retain autonomy, and with that, prestige, not merely in order to increase the position and prestige of the individual secretaries, but ... to spread the burden of the work which would fall upon this office. . . ."⁵¹

By October, however, his own further experience and Eberstadt's counsel had convinced him that he had created an impossible dichotomy. The service secretaries' authority must be decreased and his own increased.⁵²

A deeply disturbed Secretary Forrestal, in September 1948, wrote his first and only report as Secretary of Defense regarding interservice rivalries. "I have been quite frank in outlining the foundations of the controversy between the Air Force and the Naval Air Arm," he stated, "because I think the country should have a background against which to measure the argument on both sides."⁵³ Forrestal, while acknowledging the vital importance "of the strategic air arm," was concerned that the Air Force budget did not reflect the importance of tactical air "capable of close cooperation with ground troops."

One must conclude that Forrestal, caught up in an interservice rivalry between the Navy and the Air Force, sincerely strove to support the Air Force position as much as he did that of his old Navy colleagues. Yet he satisfied neither. He found the Navy "tightly organized" and the Air Force "dispersed and diffused," and wisely oberved that "the time may come when both the carrier and the long-range bomber are obsolete weapons, but that time has not come." And he wearily concluded: "Balancing the demands of these two aspects of air power, and seeing to it that adequate, but not unnecessary, funds are allocated to each, is one of the most difficult tasks of the Secretary of Defense."⁵⁴

Forrestal also despaired at budgetary support in the Cold War. He saw George F. Kennan's cable of February 1946 from Moscow, regarding the Soviet threat, go unheeded. He espoused the position Kennan took in an anonymous article in *Foreign Affairs* in July 1947, advocating "a policy of firm containment." He witnessed the formation that year of the Department of State's new Policy Planning Staff. State seemed alerted to the threat and better organized to plan to meet it than his own department.⁵⁵ Moreover, he viewed the outcome of the 1948 budget hearings "as both a personal defeat and conclusive evidence that the nation lacked the leadership and stamina necessary for victory in the Cold War."[56]

Doggedly, in October 1948, Forrestal set forth his views for strengthening the National Military Establishment. He would have it converted into a single executive department, reducing the Departments of the Army, Navy and Air Force from executive departments to military departments (as envisioned in the 1945 Army proposals). The secretaries of these three military departments would no longer be members of the National Security Council. There would be an Under Secretary of Defense (also as envisioned in the 1945 Army proposals). There would be a chairman of the Joint Chiefs of Staff, and the position of the Chief of Staff to the President serving as a member of the Joint Chiefs would be eliminated. The size of the Joint Staff would be enlarged. The authority of the Secretary would be strengthened by eliminating the word "general" in describing the Secretary's "direction, authority, and control" and also with regard to "policies and programs." The last urgent organizational recommendation of the weary Secretary, made to the President on December 3, 1948, and on February 4, 1949, to Senator Millard E. Tydings, chairman of the Senate Armed Services Committee, was for the immediate "creation of the post of Under Secretary of Defense."[57]

Forrestal never lived to see these changes made. He felt an urgent need for help, and, on January 21, 1949, he secured the services of General Dwight D. Eisenhower, then the president of Columbia University, as his principal military adviser. Eisenhower later wrote compassionately about Forrestal's feeling of "acute need for help. . . ." He ascribed it to Forrestal's "inborn honesty and his very great desire to serve the country well." As Eisenhower explained, Forrestal "would listen carefully to presentations even where he was certain that these were partisan and prejudiced. . . ." Eisenhower perceived, as did others, including the President, that in those last months, Forrestal's "ability to see truth on both sides of a bitter question led him to turmoil, out of which it was difficult to form a clear-cut decision in which he could personally have real confidence."[58]

In the fall of 1948, it appeared that Truman would not be

reelected, and Forrestal talked of resigning. However, with Truman's surprise reelection he renewed interest in staying on. But events and his own health conspired against him. More than the others, his old Navy Department colleagues resisted the proposed organizational changes. At the very time that some were criticizing Forrestal for lack of forceful decision, on January 13, 1949, Senator Harry P. Cain charged Forrestal with seeking "dictatorial powers" and with "conspiring with the administration to throw the country into war without even notifying the Congress."[59]

The President had had enough of the interservice rivalry as voiced in the media, and he recognized Forrestal's deep fatigue. He suggested that Forrestal resign and be replaced by Louis A. Johnson, a West Virginia banker and lawyer. Johnson's ebullience and effusiveness were in marked contrast to the quiet, reserved Forrestal. The former national commander of the American Legion and former chairman of the Democratic National Finance Committee, Johnson had the reputation of a skilled politician.[60]

Forrestal intended to step down about the first of June, but found it a "shattering experience" when asked by the President on March 1 to resign at the end of that month. A personal sense of inadequacy, at least partially born of fatigue, seemed to overwhelm him.[61]

On March 28, Johnson was sworn in as Secretary of Defense, after which the President pinned on Forrestal the Distinguished Service Medal. That evening Forrestal spoke most graciously at a dinner honoring Johnson. The next morning there was another rare act of recognition, a special meeting of the House Armed Services Committee in Forrestal's honor. Then Forrestal left for Hobe Sound, Florida, to see his old friend, Robert A. Lovett, former Under Secretary of State.

In nervous exhaustion, Forrestal was flown back to Washington the evening of April 2 and admitted to the Naval Hospital at Bethesda, Maryland. He seemed to respond to treatment; his depression lessened and he gained weight. On the night of May 21–22 he copied the sorrowful translation of Sophocles' "Chorus from Ajax":

> Worn by the waste of time—comfortless, nameless, hopeless save
> In the dark prospect of the yawning grave. . . .

At three o'clock in the morning he fell to his death from an unguarded sixteenth-story window.[62] There was truth in the official Pentagon statement that his breakdown had been "directly the result of excessive working during the war and post war years."[63] But it was more than this. As Walter Lippmann wrote a few days later, "He was exhausted—not so much by the long hours that he worked as by his realization that he would never have a chance to repair his mistakes and achieve what he had been appointed to achieve."[64]

The National Security Act of 1947 made the greatest changes in the organization of the armed forces since Washington had taken command of the Continental Army in 1775. But the specifications for the job of Secretary of Defense, authored by Forrestal, had come home to mock him. As he concluded, the job "combined too much coordination with too little control, and too much responsibility with too little power."[65]

Hoover, who is credited with being an architect of the modern Presidency, had, it may be recalled, two assistants, a number which he doubled to four. Forrestal, the architect of the Office of the Secretary of Defense, had only three civilian special assistants. In addition to the Joint Chiefs of Staff, the Munitions Board, and the Research and Development Board, Forrestal had only the War Council, which advised him on both military and civilian affairs.[66] Already, however, before the 1949 amendment to the National Security Act came into being, Forrestal in his last weeks in office, commencing with the public relations staffs, reduced the functions of the service secretaries, thus beginning the process of consolidation at the Department of Defense level, a process which has since continued.[67]

On August 22, exactly three months after Forrestal's death, President Truman signed into law the organizational changes which Forrestal had recommended and his friend Eberstadt had enlarged. If the President believed that a change of Secretary of Defense would reduce interservice rivalry and decrease controversy in the press, by that time the opposite had occurred. Louis Johnson, the astute politician, found himself embroiled in the B-36 and carrier controversy, with a full-scale revolt of the admirals on his hands.

It is difficult to assess Forrestal's brief tenure as the first Secretary of Defense. His friends saw more evidence of his accomplishment from his seven years in the Navy Department than his one and one-half years in his final post. John C. Ries notes: "The final irony of Forrestal's career was that the administrative difficulties he experienced as Secretary of Defense were due in no small measure to his own influence in shaping the 1947 legislation creating the position."[68] Such students of administration are inclined to agree that the 1947 Act was wrongly based upon "negotiations among service representatives rather than on decisions by independent authority in the Office of the Secretary of Defense."[69]

But there are those who believe that the 1947 legislation had, indeed, given adequate authority. They contend that Forrestal simply had not exercised it. Perhaps, as Ries suggests, "the vision that interpreted the act was less than the vision which created it." Ries goes so far as to conclude that "the Secretary of Defense decided to abdicate his role in the policy process."[70]

The military editor of the *New York Times*, Hanson Baldwin, an old friend of Forrestal and of the Navy, took a differing view. He blamed the problems of unification on the service secretaries, particularly Symington, who went over the head of the Secretary of Defense as well as the President.[71] The fact is that Symington stayed on as the first, and a most vigorous, Secretary of the Air Force until 1950 and did have strong support from Congress as well as the President. Even Symington's critic, Robert Cutler, who found him "too ambitious to work in tandem with the other Services," readily admitted that "America has cause to be grateful to Symington for what he did when it was needed, to build up the nation's air strength."[72]

Perhaps the most objective, statesmanlike view will look beyond the intense Navy–Air Force interservice rivalry, beyond the parochialism and the personalities involved, to the problem facing Forrestal and the other senior participants. Here was the first attempt toward unification; it was simultaneous with the birth of a vigorous new sister service. It all came about at the time of a new phenomenon in American history, the Cold War. It was then "the profound and awful nature of the problems faced" that brought both the tragic end of Forrestal's distinguished career and the imperative need to amend the National Security Act of 1947.

Forrestal's concepts were ahead of his time, concepts which were to be achievable by Eisenhower's authorship of the 1958 amendments to the National Security Act. Forrestal envisioned for the Secretary of Defense leadership in budgetary, legislative, procurement, research and development, military planning, reserve forces, and public relations matters. He had made a beginning in centralizing those responsibilities. Moreover, despite austerity budgets, he began the rebuilding and modernization of the force structures.[73]

The days of improvization in national defense had at last come to an end. In a severely bipolarized world Forrestal recognized the necessity for rallying the nation's total resources—material, manpower, military, economic, social, moral, and spiritual.

George C. Marshall, as Secretary of State from January 1947 through January 1949, worked closely with Forrestal in the implementation of the Truman Doctrine for the containment of Communism and the shoring up of non-Communist countries. Marshall, in September 1950, became the third Secretary of Defense, fulfilling along with his successors the promise of Forrestal's vision. It was not a vision confined to the Pentagon. Appearing before the Committee on Foreign Relations of the Senate in 1948 Forrestal had declared:

> France had its Maginot line... and ancient Rome had her legionnaires, but none of them gave real security.... In our own case the security of our nation has to be viewed not merely in the light of our military strength but in the light of the restoration of balance throughout the world.[74]

Thus Forrestal pointed the way to national security policy a quarter-century later, as pronounced by a Secretary of

State who, when Forrestal spoke, was a Harvard undergraduate. Forrestal was possessed of a rare mind of
statesmanlike qualities. To grapple with the issues of the then
new Cold War, with nuclear weapons as a deterrent for the
first time, required greater mastery than the issues of conventional warfare. Recently, when the Chaplain of the
United States Senate, Dr. Edward L. R. Elson, was asked
who he considered the three best minds in the executive
branch during the past thirty years, he named Forrestal as
one of them without hesitation.[75]

****

THE ADMIRALS' REVOLT AND THE 1949 AMENDMENTS

All hell broke loose.   JOHN MILTON

Introduction

The fifteen-month period from the resignation of Forrestal as the first Secretary of Defense until the outbreak of the Korean War in June 1950 was characterized by constant inter-service feuding. It featured the dismissal of the Chief of Naval Operations and the eventual resignations of all three service secretaries. The focal struggle was between the Navy and the Air Force in the continuing internecine warfare over respective air missions and weapons. Fought during a period of budgetary retrenchment, it culminated at fever pitch in the so-called revolt of the admirals and the reorganization of the military establishment.

Meanwhile, the Soviets vigorously expanded their armed forces. Probes and sorties in the Cold War continued. The February 1948 coup resulting in Communist control in Czechoslovakia had been compensated, in part, by the break later that year in the seemingly solid Communist bloc. Under its own Communist dictator, Tito, Yugoslavia had, by the summer of 1948, openly asserted independence from Moscow in foreign policy. By necessity Tito sought friendlier relations with the West.

But Soviet pressure on Germany continued. Not until the spring of 1949 was the Berlin blockade lifted. By the fall of that year there were clearly two Germanies, the German

Federal Republic in the West and the so-called German Democratic Republic in the East.

The answer to Communist aggression was sought in collective security, which had been presaged by the Rio Pact of September 2, 1947, prescribing hemispheric collective security. In Brussels in March 1948, Great Britain, France, and the Benelux countries formed a treaty of collective self-defense. But to be truly meaningful, such a document needed the participation of the United States, an act urged by President Truman in an address to the Congress on March 17. However, the crucial action, paving the way for the United States' entry into an Atlantic Alliance, was the Vandenberg Resolution of June 11, 1948, wherein the Senate recommended United States participation in "such regional and other collective arrangements" as have as their basis the proposition of "effective self-help" and "as affect its [United States] national security."[1]

This, then, was the prelude to the North Atlantic Treaty signed by twelve nations on April 4, 1949 (and in 1952 by Greece and Turkey).[2]

While by 1949 containment of Communism was being achieved in Europe, it was not in Asia. The 1946 Marshall mission had not brought an end to civil war in China. The following summer General Albert C. Wedemeyer was sent by President Truman on an investigation tour. Wedemeyer recommended an advisory United States task force of 10,000 officers and other qualified persons, but the idea was rejected. Chiang Kai-shek was left to his own devices, and by the end of 1949 the retreating Nationalist Chinese forces withdrew to Formosa. On the mainland the Communist People's Republic of China, led by Mao Tse-tung and Chou En-lai, was installed.

Meanwhile, on the divided Korean Peninsula, adjacent to the People's Republic of China, north of the 38th parallel (in the post–World War II Russian-occupied zone), a Communist Democratic People's Republic had been created. Moscow rejected a UN proposal for free elections to form a government for all of Korea, but election in the South installed Dr. Syngman Rhee as the first President of the Republic of Korea. Korea's occupation by Japan from 1910 to 1945 was replaced by divided Soviet and American occupation. By the summer of 1949 all Soviet and American forces were withdrawn, and the two Koreas were glowering at each other.

While such ominous external events occurred during 1948–1949, here at home the leaders of America's armed forces were locked in the most bitter interservice rivalry in American military history. It was partially the legacy of the longtime feud between army and naval aviation, but a new dimension had been added. The Navy now viewed with suspicion what it believed was a new alliance between the Army and its offspring, the Air Force, to dominate the new National Military Establishment.

The National Military Establishment organizational structure satisfied no one. Within it were the executive departments of Army, Navy, and Air Force, but it was not itself clearly an executive department, even though its manager, the Secretary of Defense, had Cabinet status. It was created in the first major legislative step toward service unification, and the need for its overhaul was self-evident.

Congressional and Hoover Task Force deliberations, spurred on by the events of the Cold War and the related Forrestal tragedy, were thrown into disarray by the fever pitch of interservice rivalry, characterized by the 1949 "revolt of the admirals" and the related B-36 inquiry.

The Admirals' Revolt: Part One

Back in the 1770s George III had picked the wrong time to be firm, or in his mother's words and with her encouragement, to "be king, George." In 1948 Secretary of Defense Louis Johnson may have picked the wrong time for his own firmness. He was determined *not* to follow Forrestal's tactics of compromise and conciliation. But in his earnest desire to make decisions, he picked the worst possible test case.

In 1947 the Navy Department, faced with Army, Air Force, Congressional, and Presidential plans for unification, dictated the principal organizational terms. Then, with one of their own as the first Secretary of Defense, they felt relatively secure in their posture. Now, however, with the advent of

Johnson and with the retirement in early 1949 of Admiral William Leahy from the post of Chief of Staff to the Commander in Chief, they believed their position of leadership in the formulation and implementation of national security policy and of the operation of the National Military Establishment was being threatened.

Air, rather than ground or capital ship forces, offered the greatest new mission opportunities in an era of budget retrenchment. The Navy's most particular concern was the future of carrier aviation and the need for a new class of superaircraft carriers. The Air Force, with its proposal for the B-36 superbomber, was inevitably on a collision course with the Navy, with its supercarrier proposal.

General Eisenhower, having early in 1949 been named the principal military adviser to the President and to the Secretary of Defense, had, in essence, succeeded Admiral Leahy as the unofficial chairman of the Joint Chiefs of Staff. In the light of budget restraints, Eisenhower recommended the cancellation of the supercarrier, the U.S.S. *United States,* on which construction had just begun. This giant flush-deck carrier had been envisioned by Vice-Admiral Marc A. Mitscher as early as 1945. In May 1948 Secretary of Defense Forrestal had approved its construction. Then, early in 1949, the Joint Chiefs, 2 to 1, voted for cancellation.

Secretary of Defense Johnson, with President Truman's approval, on April 23, 1949, ordered work stopped on the construction of the U.S.S. *United States.* This action, coming less than a month after Johnson had succeeded Forrestal, was immediately followed by the resignation of Secretary of the Navy Sullivan. Now a full-scale "revolt of the admirals" was on.[3]

Naval concern was underscored by the circumstances. While on the one hand the administration had *consistently* refused to carry out the Air Force's prime target, the 70 Group Force, and the Congress had *repeatedly* refused to enact the Army's principal program goal, universal military training, the Navy had had no such experience. Both the administration and the Congress had approved the Navy's prime target, the supercarrier. Now suddenly and without warning their support had been withdrawn.

Not limiting their appeal to the Secretary of Defense, the frustrated Navy Department set off a series of media salvos. Soon an anonymous letter began circulating in Washington, charging both Johnson's and Symington's complicity in letting the contract for the Air Force's new superbomber, the B-36, to Floyd Odlum, head of the Atlas Corporation, which controlled Consolidated Vultee Aircraft Corporation. The letter charged that the contract had been given Odlum in exchange for a $6 million political contribution through the Democratic National Finance Committee. The letter further criticized the efficacy of the B-36 as a military weapon.

Representative James E. Van Zandt, a captain in the Naval Reserve, displayed the letter on the House floor, and on May 25 a resolution was introduced directing a full-scale investigation of the alleged wrongdoing and an evaluation of the B-36 as a strategic weapon.[4] The ensuing hearings before the House Armed Services Committee in August not only disproved the accusations but also uncovered the fact that the letter had actually been written by Cedric R. Worth, a special assistant to the Under Secretary of the Navy.[5] Both Johnson and Symington were absolved from the political bribery charges. Amid the anger and the frustration, many overlooked the fact that it was Forrestal, not Johnson, who had made the decision to go ahead with the B-36.[6]

The Air Force had not been devoid of its own self-serving public relations initiatives. They exploited to the full a series of four pro-Air Force articles which appeared in the *Reader's Digest* in the period January–April 1949. Moreover, a vigorous interchange of correspondence between Symington and Eberstadt was leaked to the press by the Air Force.[7]

In the spring of 1949 members of the Hoover Task Force, headed by Eberstadt, completed their report. Although their focus was organizational changes, they also expressed their aversion to the political and public relations pressures of the warring services. Led by pro-Navy Eberstadt, the Hoover Task Force cited their displeasure at the Air Force tactics in securing Congressional and public support for the 70 Group goal. They asserted that this was "a case of a service program making national policy rather than national policy being implemented by a service program." They charged: "The mili-

tary have picked up the ball of national policy and are starting down the field with it."[8]

On June 17, 1949, Air Force Secretary Symington took
umbrage with this view. He insisted that "these criticisms
are contrary to the facts . . . and to Air Force policy. . . ." He
set forth three Air Force goals:

> 1. Air supremacy for the United States and other demo-
> cratic nations of the world.
> 2. Adequate air power at minimum cost to the American
> taxpayer and at minimum sacrifice of our individual liberties.
> 3. Real unification, both within the national military estab-
> lishment and within the framework of the entire integrated
> national security program.

Symington concluded, regarding the third point, that
"without this unification the other two objectives cannot be
achieved."[9] With obvious reference to the Navy's anti-B-36
program, Symington asserted that the Air Force views regarding strategic bombers were "being misinterpreted, misquoted, and distorted completely out of perspective." He
insisted that the new Chief of Staff of the Air Force, General
Hoyt S. Vandenberg, nephew of the Senator, clearly stood
for "the highest degree of team work among the three services." Emphasizing interdependence of all three services
and a balanced concept such as presented by General
Eisenhower, Symington insisted that "each service should
specialize in developing forces for certain specific functions."[10]

The 1949 Amendment

The heated Eberstadt-Symington interchange reduced the
effectiveness of the Eberstadt task force report. Although
it came to parallel many of Forrestal's final recommendations on organization, members of the Congress turned increasingly to the Forrestal views. As a principal author of the
1947 Act, Eberstadt had contended that the Secretary of Defense already had adequate authority.

In the task force report, however, Eberstadt did go along
with the Forrestal recommendations, which were now joined

by those of Johnson, for strengthening the Secretary's position and reducing that of the service departments.[11] Johnson, echoing Forrestal's final sentiment about the possible danger of too much authority being lodged with the Secretary of Defense, assured the Senate Armed Services Committee that "that proposed here is not a dangerous form of power."[12]

Forrestal had urgently requested an Under Secretary, and the task force endorsed this idea. The House Armed Services Committee, headed by veteran Representative Carl Vinson of Georgia, who had earlier headed the Naval Affairs Committee, gave its support, and the position of Under Secretary of Defense was created in April 1949. By these amendments the position would be upgraded and redesignated as Deputy Secretary of Defense. The committee observed that at the time the 1947 legislation had been written "it could not be foreseen that the duties of the Secretary would be of such magnitude and diversity as to require an additional statutory official." The committee added that the Deputy Secretary should rank higher than the service secretaries, so that he might be an effective alter ego to the Secretary.[13]

The House Armed Forces Committee got stalled in amending the National Security Act by July 1949. Its members became so concerned in the B-36 controversy that they supplanted reorganization hearings with those of the warring Navy admirals and Air Force generals. Moreover, opinion within the committee was so divided regarding both the Air Force–Navy controversy and the reconstitution of the National Military Establishment that the possibility arose that no amendment would be enacted that year.

Truman was disgusted by the lack of progress in amending the National Security Act in the House of Representatives of the 81st Congress (in which the Democrats had been swept back into control as a part of Truman's Presidential surprise victory). On July 18, 1949, the President submitted to the Congress his Reorganization Plan No. 8, based upon the Hoover (Eberstadt) Task Force, as the basis for amendment. In the interim, however, the Senate Armed Services Committee, headed by Senator Millard E. Tydings of Maryland, had brought in a bill based on the fourteen points left as a legacy by Forrestal. These had included removal of the word "general" in describing the Secretary of Defense's "authority, direction, and control" and transforming the National Military Establishment into the Department of Defense, making it clearly an executive department.

By July there was both a Senate bill (named for Tydings) and the President's Reorganization Plan. Now, goaded by the President's proposal, the Congress took a course of action for which there was rare precedence. They bypassed the House Armed Services Committee, which was enmeshed in the B-36 controversy. Then a Conference Committee proposed a double measure which became the basis of the enacted legislation: they rejected Eberstadt's Reorganization Plan No. 8, and essentially accepted the Senate measure based on Forrestal's fourteen points. The legislation also provided for a Deputy Secretary of Defense and three assistant secretaries; a chairman of the Joint Chiefs of Staff; an increase in the size of the Joint Staff; and the removal of the service secretaries from the National Security Council. The service departments were transformed into military departments; thus the service secretaries were removed from the Cabinet and the "reserved powers" concept of their authority was eliminated.

The 1949 amendments to the National Security Act authorized the military departments to make recommendations to the Congress and to the President, after informing the Secretary of Defense. (Quite obviously, this was the last thing President Truman wanted, having had more than his quota of service secretaries and senior military personnel seeking to bend his ear to their particular points of view. By contrast, the Congress relished keeping these lines of communication open.) Some students of public administration have deemed this feature self-defeating of one of the basic reasons for amending the National Security Act, that is, eliminating end-runs or going over the head of the Congress and of the President.[14]

Because of his distressing experience of rancor with the Joint Chiefs, Forrestal had recommended transferring a number of JCS functions to the Office of the Secretary of Defense. The Chiefs' vigorous protest before the Senate

Armed Services Committee regarding any such reduction of their role resulted in the failure of enactment of this recommendation.

Forrestal had been willing either to have one of the three chiefs named as chairman *or* a fourth person added for that purpose. The Congress concluded with the Hoover Task Force, which proposed *only* the addition of a fourth person as chairman.

A rather meaningless prohibition was included in the enactment; it stated that the chairman "shall not exercise military command...." This was primarily to assuage Congressional and popular concerns regarding the "man on horseback" threat; there had been no suggestion by either Forrestal or Eberstadt that the chairman would be commanding or voting. The Joint Chiefs have never acted by majority vote: split decisions have always been referred to the Secretary of Defense for decision.

In the final analysis, in creating the chairmanship, the Congress envisioned precisely what Forrestal had suggested: the chairman was to be the "person to whom the President and the Secretary of Defense look to see to it that matters with which the Joint Chiefs should deal are handled in a way that will provide the best military assistance to the President."[15] Actually, the chairman was to become the spokesman for the Joint Chiefs: he, and only he, has usually had personal contact with the Secretary of Defense, the National Security Council, and the President.

The 1949 amendments authorized increasing the size of the Joint Staff from 100 to 210. One of the three assistant secretaries of defense authorized by the act was, as suggested by Eberstadt, named comptroller. Since Forrestal had had three assistants, this merely meant giving them titles, but it marked the beginning of what was to become an increasing number of assistant secretaries.

The comptroller feature was at the heart of the first Hoover Commission. It was part of a new Title IV enacted by the 1949 amendments for the "Promotion of Economy and Efficiency through Establishment of Uniform Budgetary and Fiscal Procedures and Organization." Title IV of the amendments also provided for a comptroller for each of the three

military departments. For the first time there were to be uniform budgetary and fiscal procedures throughout the defense establishment. The concept of a "performance budget"
was also emphasized. Quite significantly, the 1949 amendments introduced another concept from private industry by
authorizing the creation of working capital and management
funds.

Finally, the National Security Act amendments of 1949,
while eliminating the service secretaries from the President's
National Security Council, did add the Vice President as a
statutory member, along with the Secretary of State and the
Secretary of Defense (the chairman of the Joint Chiefs and
the director of the Central Intelligence Agency thereafter
served as the NSC's chief advisers).[16]

The 1949 amendments to the National Security Act were
approved in the Senate by voice vote and passed by the
House, 356 to 7. They were thereafter signed into law by
President Truman on August 22, 1947, during a lull in the
B-36 controversy, when Congress was not in session.[17]

It remained to be seen whether anyone would be happy
with the changes. Former Secretary of War Patterson, to
whom President Truman had initially offered the post as first
Secretary of Defense, declared that the 1949 amendments
"cleared away the clouds."[18] This reaction was understandable, since Patterson had had distinct reservations about the
1947 Act.

Secretary Johnson was temporarily encouraged by the
terms of the Act, but his three demoted service secretaries
were not. Always a gentleman, Gordon Gray, the new Secretary of the Army, had enjoyed Cabinet and NSC status
only since June 1949, when he succeeded Secretary Royall.
Twenty-two years later, Gray recalled, "I am one of the two
living persons who has been kicked off the National Security
Council." He politely credited it "perhaps to reduce military
influence," adding that he shared this dubious honor with
Stuart Symington.[19]

The able Gordon Gray resigned as Secretary of the Army a
few months later and became president of his alma mater,
the University of North Carolina. He returned to
Washington in 1955 and served in significant national secu-

rity policy assignments during the last six years of the Eisenhower administrations.

Symington was no happier than Gray, and he resigned at almost the same time, ostensibly in protest of budgetary constraints. But he stayed on the Washington scene, serving for a year as chairman of the National Security and Resources Board and then as administrator of the Reconstruction Finance Corporation before his election in 1952 to the United States Senate. By 1960 he was to advocate eliminating entirely the positions of service secretaries.[20]

The Joint Chiefs of Staff were also unhappy. The service secretaries had been supplanted by the assistant secretaries of defense, but the Chiefs' new chairman was the primary military adviser to the Secretary of Defense. The first chairman (1949–1953), Omar N. Bradley, was a respected five-star soldier; he did little to ease a difficult situation.

The Admirals' Revolt: Part Two

A particular thorn in General Bradley's side was Admiral Arthur W. Radford, Commander in Chief Pacific and Commander U.S. Pacific Fleet. Eisenhower, as Army Chief of Staff during the 1947 unification discussions, had declared he would not attend another Joint Chiefs session "if [Admiral Chester W.] Nimitz brings along that so-and-so Radford."[21] Yet Radford's strong parochial views for naval air had helped earn him promotion in 1949 from three- to four-star rank. Radford's truculency—he called the B-36 bomber "a billion-dollar blunder"—aroused Bradley to term him one of the Navy's "fancy Dans who won't hit the line with all they have on every play unless they can call the signals."[22]

Unlike their rival sister service, the Navy did not have such a clear-cut goal as the 70 Group Air Force. After World War II, the Soviets built up their ground and air forces, which by 1949 considerably exceeded those of the United States. Such was not the case with naval forces: in 1949 the power and size of United States ships so outstripped those of any other nation that one Air Force general referred to our "five ocean navy to fight a no-ocean opponent. . . ."[23] Realizing this ironic vulnerability, admirals such as Radford perceived the Navy's future growth in aviation, including *land* targets.

In September 1949, while Congress was still in recess, the Navy Department released correspondence between senior naval officers (including Chief of Naval Operations Louis Denfeld and Radford) and the new Secretary of the Navy, Francis P. Matthews, deploring the "emasculating" of the Navy and the resulting low state of naval morale.[24] In a subsequent naval inquiry, naval Captain John G. Crommelin, Jr., admitted that he had released the letters, insisting that he had done so "in the interest of national security." Secretary Matthews suspended him.[25]

Critics of the 1949 amendments have decried their making the Secretary of Defense "an administrative manager" instead of an "agent of Presidential control" as envisioned in the National Security Act of 1947.[26] Whatever the amendment made him, Secretary Johnson had his hands full when the Congress came back into session in September. On October 5, 1949, under the chairmanship of Carl Vinson, the House Armed Services Committee, as a second part of its B-36 inquiry, began hearings on the "National Defense Program—Unification and Strategy."[27]

For this second round of the "admirals' revolt," the Navy flew its highest-ranking flag officers into Washington from throughout the world. They voiced disapproval of the B-36 and affirmation of carrier aviation, but they also stressed that they had been made into a subordinate service. They were still smarting because construction of the supercarrier *United States* had been stopped only two weeks after her keel had been laid. Since she had been designed for naval plans to carry atomic bombs, it appeared that the Air Force with its A-bomb-carrying B-36 had won the war for nuclear air weapons. The Navy was desperate to find its own "mousetrap," as carrier admiral J. J. Clark expressed it. In candor he added, "This is how we can justify going to Congress for funds to maintain this 'mousetrap.'"[28]

In looking back on the 1947–1949 unification steps, the Navy admirals now perceived their worst fears being realized. They recalled Admiral Ernest J. King's dire warning in 1945: "Sea power will not be accorded adequate recognition because the organization contemplated would permit reduction of sea power by individuals who are not thoroughly familiar with its potentialities."[29]

The admirals insisted that their views on national strategy were not being given careful consideration. They felt themselves outnumbered by the Army and Air Force generals, who were acting in concert, and they also thought the Secretary of Defense and the President were siding against them.

Some of the admirals' contentions were highly subjective, and their methods of pleading their case became, on occasion, subject to question. On October 3, 1949, copies of letters from Admiral Denfeld, Vice Admiral Gerald F. Bogan, and Admiral Radford were distributed to reporters. Letters addressed to Navy Secretary Matthews endorsed charges by naval aviator Captain John G. Crommelin, who asserted that the Army and Air Force were seeking to emasculate naval aviation. Bogan wrote that "the morale of the Navy is lower today than at any time since I entered the commissioned ranks in 1916." Denfeld cautioned that "a navy stripped of its offensive powers means a nation stripped of its offensive power."[30]

The following day the Navy launched an inquiry to ascertain how the letters had been made public. Captain Crommelin, who momentarily became something of a naval hero, took the blame for the release to the press. He said he did it to bring the full light of Congressional inquiry. The upshot of this and other aspects of the "admirals' revolt" was the removal of Admiral Denfeld as Chief of Naval Operations by Secretary Matthews, with President Truman's approval. Crommelin, too, was forced to retire. Bogan, then Commander Air Force Atlantic Fleet, lost his job, but Radford, who had denounced the B-36 program as wasteful and the plane itself as obsolete, escaped back to his Pacific command with all four stars intact. Others did not fare so well. Admiral Richard L. Conolly, then commanding American Naval Forces in Europe, who had flown to Washington to join in the foray, lost a star and was sent to the presidency of the Naval War College to complete his career. Conolly's subordinate, Vice Admiral Forrest P. Sherman, then commanding the Sixth Fleet, wisely stayed out of the controversy. He was promoted over the heads of the "revolting admirals" as the new Chief of Naval Operations.

Such precipitous action quelled the revolt but not the feelings of mistrust and misunderstanding. Sherman proved a wise choice as the new Chief of Naval Operations. With the understanding support of President Truman and Secretary of Defense Johnson, prestige was regained and the go-ahead was given for a new carrier. As Admiral J. J. Clark later assessed it, the late September 1949 "orientation cruise" for the military chiefs "demonstrated the effectiveness of naval aviation much better than Crommelin's utterances had."[31]

On March 1, 1950, The House Armed Services Committee, under Carl Vinson, concluded a 33-point report arising out of its B-36 inquiry. Point 17 indicated that the ultimate solution to interservice rivalry was education, particularly interservice education, with an armed forces mix in all the service schools. The committee concluded that "a much greater concentration of effort is needed in this field." Related to this was point 19, on "joint training centers," which they also conceived as a step toward better understanding. Similarly, point 21 recommended "an augmentation of interservice war games."[32]

In the committee's view, the Joint Chiefs of Staff organization had not ensured "at all times adequate consideration of the views of all services." It recommended that the chairmanship of the Joint Chiefs be rotated every two years among the services and that the Commandant of the Marine Corps be added as a member—a strategic move in a naval victory. (Even General Eisenhower proposed that the Marine Corps be amalgamated into the Army.)[33] In a compromise measure enacted in 1952, the Commandant of the Marine Corps was granted coequal membership on the JCS in all matters affecting the Corps.[34] The chairmanship rotation procedure, however, has never been accomplished.

In its March 1, 1950, report, the House Armed Services Committee concluded that it firmly supported unification but emphasized that the concepts and goals required further "definition." In seeking to define unification and end the interservice bickering, they suggested what unification was and was not. They did not find the avenue through operational control of the armed forces by the Joint Chiefs of Staff. Further admonishing the Chiefs, they suggested that unification did not mean the imposition of the views of two of them on a third. On the constructive, positive side, they perceived that unification should comprise a comprehensive and thoroughly integrated national security program; they envisioned the retention of three military departments, separately administered but with overall strategic planning and direction and unified field commands. In brief, they foresaw much of the organization and philosophy of today. And they pledged their continuing support for the goal of a united land, sea, and air force team.[35]

In a sense the B-36 controversy, the "revolt of the admirals," had been a victory for the Secretary of Defense and the Air Force.[36] Secretary of Defense Johnson had been exonerated of false charges, just as Air Force Secretary Symington had been. The B-36 production continued; the supercarrier construction did not resume, though a new carrier was soon projected. In disdain of the committee's report, one of the admirals, J. J. Clark, wrote in retrospect, "As the Korean war came along, it demonstrated the Navy's position in the defense of the country, far better than any Congressional inquiry."[37]

The assignment to the Air Force of strategic bombing as a *primary* mission remained unscathed. Navy's strategic bombing remained only a *corollary* mission. Yet in a larger sense the controversy had been a victory for no one. Paul Y. Hammond, who has studied the episode in greatest depth, concluded that "the primary accomplishment was a demonstration to both the Navy and the Air Force that Congress could not be fooled by either. . . ."[38] Secretary of Defense Johnson came through much bruised and mauled. As a result he was on his way out in a situation not entirely of his own making. An economy-minded Congress and President mandated a defense budget reduction for fiscal 1950 to $14 billion as compared to the supposed austerity budget of fiscal 1949 of $15.5 billion. Such severe budgetary constrictions had, as Admiral Clark put it, prompted the Navy to seek its own "mousetrap." All of these circumstances, with the stoppage of construction on the supercarrier as the final straw, had produced the short-lived revolt of that branch of the service which had had the greatest misgiving about unification and the creation of the separate Air Force.

The alarm sounding in the night, only partially noted amid all this rancor, was the Soviet Union's first nuclear detonation. While the Air Force and Navy were squabbling over who should carry nuclear weapons, President Truman on September 23, 1949, announced that the United States no longer had exclusive control of this awesome source of power. Equally as ominous as this mushrooming cloud was the announcement two weeks before of the failure of the United Nations Commission in Korea to settle the dispute between the Republic of Korea and the militant North Korean regime. Although the Commission reported "military posturing" on both sides of the 38th parallel and warned of the distinct possibility of "barbarous civil war," it gained but scant attention.[39]

VII

****

THE KOREAN WAR AND NATIONAL STRATEGY, 1950–1953

There is no substitute for victory.

Douglas MacArthur

Strategy Planning, 1947–1950

The eleven-year period 1950–1961 witnessed first a limited war of unprecedented cost in both lives and material, then a rejection for a time of a limited war strategy, and finally its reacceptance following the 1960 Presidential election. Thus the stage was set, despite the bitter lessons of the Korean War, for the most protracted and costly of limited wars that was to mark the decade of the 1960s.

The concept of limited war was advanced in the late 1940s as a rational alternative to total war for the new nuclear age.[1] Credit for the advancement of the concept does not rest with the Joint Chiefs of Staff or with the armed services they represented; the division of functions of the Key West agreement had disappeared in the storm of the admirals' revolt. Limited warfare instead had its birth through the then new Policy Planning Staff of the Department of State. It arose, in part, out of the views of George F. Kennan, who directed that staff. By 1949 limited war was a part of his conception and that of the Department of State, but it had, as yet, no comparable role in the strategic planning of the Joint Chiefs of Staff.

The Joint Chiefs rejected the concept of limited warfare partially because of lack of funding.[2] They had emerged from the B-36 controversy on the horns of a strategic dilemma. The quarrel had in large measure been whether Navy planes as well as the B-36 should deliver A-bombs. In the winter of 1949–1950, with the Truman–Louis Johnson–Omar Bradley austerity defense budget, military policy focused on only two contingencies, a possible Soviet attack either on the United States or on Europe. Military policy did not consider possible Soviet moves into other areas (including the Korean Peninsula) or subversion or guerrilla warfare.[3]

Both limited and total war may be viewed as force levels beyond diplomacy in a policy of containment. The shoring up of the free world against further Communist incursions had been at the heart of the 1947 Truman Doctrine. That year, the then new National Security Council sought to define instruments of containment. Through the leadership of the Department of State, containment continued to be an NSC concern. The Secretary of State was recognized as the "first among equals" among Cabinet officers serving on the NSC.[4] (Until the Vice President was added in 1949, the Secretary of State, in the absence of the President, chaired NSC meetings. Moreover, during the Truman and Eisenhower administrations three-fourths of the papers considered by the NSC originated in the Department of State.)[5]

However, until the Korean War, President Truman reluctantly continued to view the NSC as the nation's top security-planning instrument. The most important document of such policy, NSC 68, was produced in the spring of 1950 on the eve of the Korean War. It was not the work of the NSC or of its working committee, the Senior Staff, but rather that of a State-Defense study group. NSC 68 sought further to answer the arresting question as to whether a democracy could only respond to aggression or whether it could arm as a means of deterrence.[6]

NSC 68 was written in a climate of peril. In August 1949 the Soviets had made their first nuclear explosion. A few months later the Communists had completed the conquest of mainland China, forcing Chiang Kai-shek and his forces to evacuate to Taiwan. In view of the gravity of the world situation, NSC 68 recommended an immediate buildup of our armed forces and modernization of the force structure. Looking back on NSC 68 two years after its completion, President Truman declared:

> It seemed clear, as a result of this study, that the United States and all other free nations were faced with a great and growing danger. It seemed clear that we could meet the danger only by mobilizing our strength—and the strength of our allies—to check and deter aggression.
>
> This meant a great military effort in time of peace. It meant doubling or tripling the budget, increasing taxes heavily, and imposing various kinds of economic controls. It meant a great change in our peacetime way of doing things.[7]

President Truman's retrospective observations seem to suggest that in advance of the Korean War he was prepared to recommend legislation authorizing massive increases in our armed forces. The fact is that the NSC 68 recommendations were largely academic until June 25, when the North Korean attack brought the urgency sharply home.

Truman, MacArthur, and the Korean War, 1950–1952

As early as 1957, Henry A. Kissinger observed that "the Korean War revealed that our almost exclusive concern with all-out war and with the most destructive type of strategy had obscured the most likely security problem: the attempt by the Soviet leaders to upset the strategic balance, not at one blow, but piecemeal."[8]

Many myths and misconceptions have arisen regarding the "Hermit Kingdom," or the "Land of the Morning Calm," as Korea has been called. It is a land neither calm nor in the morning of its youth, though it did seek to become something of a hermit before Japan occupied it by force beginning in 1905. With the collapse of the Japanese war machine at the end of World War I, the State Department recommended that all Japanese forces in Korea surrender to the U.S. forces. Though sound in principle, it seemed at the time both difficult and unnecessary. The Soviets had entered the war against Japan in the last weeks of that struggle. Stalin needed no encouragement to accept President Truman's cabled suggestion that the Soviets occupy Korea north of the 38th parallel. To Truman's consternation (and that of Colonel Dean Rusk, who had recommended the action), "the Russians ... began at once to treat the 38th Parallel as a permanent dividing line."[9]

If Truman and Dean Rusk must jointly bear the responsibility for creating the 38th parallel, Secretary of State Acheson should not be given the sole credit for advising the Soviets that Korea was not within the U.S. defense perimeter. Acheson, who succeeded Marshall at State early in 1949, indeed stated at the National Press Club on January 12, 1950, that Korea was not within the U.S. defense perimeter. But such had been a determination by the Joint Chiefs of Staff, not the State Department. (General of the Army Douglas MacArthur, U.S. Far East Commander, had on March 2, 1949, described that perimeter in terms similar to those Acheson used.)[10] But Acheson hardly presented a picture of strong deterrence to aggression when he declared in his National Press Club speech, "Should such an attack occur ... the initial reliance must be on the people attacked to resist it and then upon the commitment of the entire civilized world under the Charter of the United Nations. ..." Soviet Foreign Minister Andrei Vyshinsky was far from impressed. He perceived that the South Koreans had no pledge of defense from the United States and had received but little United States military and economic aid.

By the spring of 1950, then, with the Soviets' miscalculating America's determination to resist aggression, Korea was ripe for trouble. As Carl Berger has observed, "the fountainhead of Korea's tragedy, like that of ancient Palestine or modern Poland, has been her geographic emplacement."[11] A rocky peninsula of only 85,000 square miles, extending from the Manchurian mainland southward toward Japan, it is surrounded by larger, more powerful neighbors, China, Russia, and Japan. Often overrun, Korea's people had known neither democracy nor security. Their greatest hope in 1945–1947, following the exchange of Soviet and American for Japanese occupation, seemed to be in rallying about their patriarchal freedom fighter, Syngman Rhee. This the Soviets sought to counter by encouraging Kim Il Sung, a guerrilla leader who had fought with them in Manchuria against the Japanese, to form the nucleus of a North Korean government.

The Soviets, who opposed American proposals of August 1947 for national elections leading toward a united independent Korea, countered the following month with a proposal that all occupation troops be withdrawn by early 1948. The Joint Chiefs of Staff, on September 25, 1947, also recommended withdrawal of the 45,000 U.S. troops stationed in Korea. The only difference between the JCS and the Soviet position was the precipitate nature of the Russian proposal. The JCS did have the benefit of the recent mission of Lieutenant General Albert C. Wedemeyer, who had recommended that "so long as Soviet troops remain in occupation of North Korea, the United States must maintain troops in South Korea."[12]

While withdrawal was being considered, the United States, with the Soviets protesting, carried its case for free elections to the United Nations. John Foster Dulles presented the American position to the General Assembly. Despite Communist disruptive effort, with UN supervision the first free election in Korean history was successfully held on May 10, 1948, in South Korea. The National Assembly, elected by a great outpouring of voters, in turn elected Syngman Rhee as President of the Republic of Korea on July 20. The Soviets countered with the proclamation of the Democratic People's Republic of Korea under Kim Il Sung.

Following these political actions, the withdrawal of foreign troops from North and South, which had been delayed until that point, proceeded. Both Soviets and Americans were supplying and training Korean troops in their formerly occupied areas. The Soviets were building up a large "People's Army" with heavier equipment, while President Truman was experiencing difficulty in securing Congressional support for substantial military aid to the Republic of Korea. By June 29, 1949, all U.S. armed forces had been withdrawn from Korea, with the exception of a 500-member advisory group which was helping train a 65,000-member Korean army.[13] However, the troops were only lightly armed, since there was fear in certain American policy circles that a heavily armed South Korea might not resist the temptation to invade the North.[14]

By the end of June 1949, for the first time in a half-century, Korea was not under the occupation of foreign troops. Instead Koreans, North and South, were preparing to have a go at each other. From June 1949 to June 1950, from his Far East Command Headquarters in Tokyo, General MacArthur sent to Washington "constant intelligence reports of increasing urgency" regarding "a possible North Korean thrust." According to MacArthur, "But little impression was made against the general apathy and the inspired 'agrarian reform' propaganda."[15]

After a June 19, 1950, visit to Korea, John Foster Dulles sent the following cablegram to Secretary of State Acheson: "Believe that if it appears the South Koreans cannot themselves contain or repulse the attack, United States forces should be used even though this risks Russian counter moves." Dulles concluded: "To sit by while Korea is overrun by unprovoked armed attack would start a world war."[16]

Encouraged by the Chinese Communist victory over Chiang, by the United States arms retrenchment, and by U.S. failure to make clear its determination to come to the direct aid of South Korea in the event of an attack, the Soviets gave the word to Kim Il Sung's puppet government to launch an attack. The lightly armed South Korean constabulary force of 100,000 was no match for the heavily armed 200,000-man Soviet-trained North Korean army, which was equipped with tanks, heavy artillery, and fighter aircraft.

In the absence of the Soviets (who were boycotting the United Nations Security Council for its membership of Taiwan rather than Red China), the Council in an emergency session on Sunday afternoon, June 25, called upon UN member nations to "render every assistance" to South Korea. President Truman interpreted this as authorizing military assistance.[17] After consultation with the Secretaries of State, Defense, and the armed services and the Joint Chiefs of Staff, the President directed General MacArthur to utilize the Air Force and Navy to help evacuate Americans from Korea, to keep the Inchon and Kimpo-Seoul areas from falling, and to isolate Formosa from mainland China. There was still vague hope that the Communists would heed the Security Council resolution and withdraw.[18]

After another meeting the following evening, Truman approved use of American naval and air forces to repel the invasion, limiting the forces to action south of the 38th parallel. By this point the South Korean capital city of Seoul was already occupied by the swift-moving North Korean forces. There seemed nothing to stop them from marching to Pusan, at the south end of the peninsula. MacArthur, who surveyed the scene, including the burning fourteenth-century city of Seoul along the Han River, cabled the Joint Chiefs "for its full utilization of the Army-Navy-Air team in this shattered area. . . ."[19] His request to use ground forces led to a third meeting of the President and his advisers on June 29. Thus the United States moved incrementally into the war, without Congressional action.

MacArthur accomplished the removal of two thousand American and United Nations personnel without loss of life. On July 7, by Security Council resolution, the United Nations Unified Command was formed, and the following day Truman named MacArthur as the first UN Unified Commander. In the interim, American ground forces had made their first contact with the enemy on July 5. So began, against overwhelming odds, what has been termed "the most successful improvisation in the history of warfare."[20] For a time, with thirteen divisions in the field, the North Koreans seemed invincible in their southward march. As MacArthur cryptically put it: "The Cassandras of the world gloomily speculated on a vast Asiatic Dunkirk." But with orders "to stand or die," the beachhead of American and South Korean forces under Major General Walton Walker held at Pusan.[21]

In late August, General J. Lawton Collins and Admiral Forrest Sherman flew to Tokyo. They came not so much to consult MacArthur as to dissuade him from his proposal for an amphibious operation. The decisive mid-September Inchon landings followed. Within the next two weeks MacArthur's bold strategy "had broken the back of the Communist armies. . . ."[22]

An elated and optimistic General Assembly on October 7 approved MacArthur's advancing north of the 38th parallel.[23] The first and only meeting between Truman and MacArthur then occurred at Wake Island on October 15. Truman seemed disappointed that MacArthur could greet him with "his shirt . . . unbuttoned, and . . . wearing a cap that had . . . seen a good deal of use."[24] At this private meeting, which lasted only an hour and thirty-six minutes, the possibility of Chinese intervention was discussed. MacArthur recalled advising that if America had airpower capable of destroying Chinese supply lines "north as well as south of the Yalu," the Chinese would not risk an invasion.[25] Truman's memoirs merely state that "he . . . informed me that the Chinese Communists would not attack."[26]

Four days later, on October 19, Pyonyang, the North Korean capital, was captured. A week thereafter, the first United Nations force reached the Manchurian border. By month's end Premier Kim's North Korean army, 135,000 of which had been taken prisoners, had been almost completely destroyed.

The surprising destruction of the North Korean army brought a Mao-Stalin plan for Chinese intervention. In late October, Chinese "volunteers" had begun filtering in. In early November, Chinese men and material began pouring across the Yalu bridges from Manchuria. In a message of November 6 to the Joint Chiefs, MacArthur declared that "the only way to stop this reinforcement of the enemy is the destruction of the bridges by air attack. . . ."[27] Authorization, at first denied lest Manchurian air space be violated, was modified to the impossible authorization to bomb only the "Korean end of the Yalu bridges." MacArthur later charged that the order was "the most indefensible and ill-conceived decision ever forced on a field commander in our nation's history."[28]

Truman later defended his position in restricting MacArthur's air operations on the grounds that it might result in "a general war." Moreover, Truman, as he recollected, shared the view of "our British allies and many statesmen of Europe" that Europe, not Asia, "was the most important target for world Communism's attack." Truman termed the Chinese action in Korea "a gigantic booby trap." He insisted, "I had no intention of allowing our attention to be diverted from the unchanging aims and designs of Soviet policy," which he believed to be the dominance of Europe.[29]

MacArthur wrote his Chief of Staff, General Doyle Hickey, that the restrictions placed on operations against the Chinese "foreshadows a future tragic situation in the Far East. . . ." In protest of the constraints on his military operations, MacArthur drafted a statement of resignation. Hickey dissuaded MacArthur from submitting it.[30]

MacArthur's early November pessimism had by mid-November turned to optimism as his Chief of Intelligence, Major General Charles Willoughby, misestimated the Chinese force in Korea as 100,000 "volunteers" rather than the 300,000 seasoned troops of Lin Piao's Fourth Field Army and Chen Yi's Third.[31] MacArthur's land forces of about 200,000 included, besides the South Korean and U.S. forces, a British brigade, a Turkish brigade, and a battalion each from Canada, the Netherlands, the Philippines, and Thailand. These were then a truly United Nations force of the Eighth Army on the west under Lieutenant General Walker and the X Corps on the East under Lieutenant General Edward Almond, MacArthur's former Chief of Staff. Unfortunately, a corridor of about 50 miles lay between them.

MacArthur's critics have since termed his drive to the Yalu rash and ill-conceived. Eisenhower, twenty years later, wrote that he believed MacArthur right in seeking "to complete the destruction of the North Korean force." The gross error was the underestimation of the size and character of Chinese forces who had crossed the bridges under cover of darkness and hidden out during daylight hours. As Eisenhower assessed the matter:

> If the Chinese Communists were present in large numbers, they represented a definite threat to the United Nations forces, which were then badly extended both in depth and frontage as their forward units pursued the beaten enemy. Immediate concentration for battle would become vitally necessary. But if the reports were untrue, then the opportu-

nity still remained to destroy the last vestiges of the enemy's strength by vigorously continuing the attack in both corners of Korea.[32]

In mid-November hopes were running high for complete and final victory by Christmas, to be followed by what the United Nations General Assembly in an October resolution described as "a unified, independent, and democratic Government in a sovereign state of Korea."[33]

Actually, with the severe North Korean winter closing in and the prospect of a mounting Chinese force by spring, there was no alternative to this "final" offensive. This ill-fated "end-the-war" offensive, personally launched by MacArthur on November 24 in zero weather, was countered by Chinese Communist Commander Lin Piao on the twenty-seventh with overwhelming forces. Lin Piao later wrote, "I would never have made the attack and risked my men and reputation if I had not been assured that Washington would restrain General MacArthur from taking adequate retaliatory measures against my lines of supply and communication."[34]

So "an entirely new war," as MacArthur termed it, had erupted. The Eighth Army made a successful withdrawal to the 38th parallel, and the X Corps Army and Marine veterans of the Inchon victory advanced to the rear, to withdraw by sea to Pusan. Although the press played up the withdrawal as a rout accompanied by heavy losses, it was neither. Total Eighth Army and X Corps casualties in the Yalu operation, killed, wounded, and missing, numbered approximately 13,000, about one-fifth those at Okinawa.[35] By the end of December 1950 the Communist armies, without a major battle, had recovered North Korea.[36]

President Truman termed the successful evacuation of the 105,000 men of the X Corps, together with 91,000 Korean refugees, "the best Christmas present I've ever had,"[37] but *Time* magazine termed the withdrawal "the worst defeat the United States ever suffered," and *Newsweek* predicted that United Nations forces in Korea required "a new Dunkerque to save them from being lost in a new Bataan."[38]

Withdrawal from North Korea was a sobering aftermath to

the heady wine of the Inchon landings and the drive north-ward. Containment was again in vogue, the focus was on Europe, and only a conservative minority, represented by Senator Robert Taft, favored more aggressive Asiatic policies. MacArthur's December 30 proposal to expand the war against China by naval blockade, air and naval bom-bardment, and entry of Formosan troops was accordingly rejected.[39]

On December 23 the Eighth Army commander, General Walker, was killed in a jeep accident. He was succeeded by the resolute, hawk-nosed Lieutenant General Matthew Ridgway. The military situation continued to deteriorate. On January 7, Seoul was recaptured by the Communists. A pes-simistic exchange between MacArthur and the Joint Chiefs of Staff during this period predicted, in the light of military and political constraints, possible complete withdrawal from the Korean Peninsula, or at best a holding operation in the Pusan area.[40]

After a December 4–7 conference between Truman and British Prime Minister Clement Attlee, on December 14 the United Nations General Assembly voted to seek an armis-tice. Premier Chou En-lai responded that the only terms would be complete United Nations withdrawal, American withdrawal from Formosa, end of Western rearmament, and recognition of the Red Chinese government.

Finding these terms completely unacceptable, Truman and Acheson yet hoped that the Eighth Army, with limited objec-tives, could produce a better climate for negotiations. The X Corps forces were placed in the Eighth Army, with a single field command, in hopes of making a more effective instru-ment.

By the end of January the Eighth Army, having stabilized its position approximately 70 miles below the 38th parallel, was ready to resume the offensive. MacArthur told reporters at Ridgway's headquarters, "There has been a lot of loose talk about the Chinese driving us into the sea, just as in the early days there was a lot of nonsense about the North Ko-reans driving us into the sea."[41] Now the situation had re-versed from that of late November at the Yalu. By mid-February MacArthur observed of the enemy: "He is finding it an entirely different problem fighting 350 miles from his base than when he had sanctuary in his immediate rear."[42]

MIG air superiority dissolved when the American F-86 saberjets arrived. Seoul was retaken for the second time on March 15; of an original population of 1,500,000, only 200,000, chiefly women and children and old men, remained to greet the second United Nations liberation of the city. With these reverses, Lin Piao was relieved of command.

By late March, despite UN misgivings, Ridgway had advanced 6 to 8 miles beyond the 38th parallel. MacArthur proposed a meeting with the commander of the badly mauled Chinese troops to discuss disengagement. While Truman was trying to negotiate a settlement with the Chinese through the United Nations, MacArthur on March 24 warned the enemy in a public statement that the United Nations might "depart from its tolerant efforts to contain the war to the area of Korea. . . ." He predicted that action against China's "coastal areas and interior bases," accompanied by the severe losses being suffered in Korea, "would doom Red China to the risk of imminent military collapse." MacArthur later termed this only a "routine communique. . . ."[43]

It may have been "routine" to MacArthur, but it shook Washington and the capitals of Europe. Truman wrote, "By this act MacArthur left me no choice—I could no longer tolerate his insubordination." However, the President took no immediate action other than to order the Joint Chiefs of Staff to silence MacArthur. This they did, adding that "the President has also directed that in the event Communist military leaders request an armistice in the field, you report that fact to the JCS for instructions."[44]

The gag on MacArthur came too late. His views had found many friends in the Congress, one of whom was the minority leader of the House, Joseph Martin, who invited MacArthur's views on the war. On March 20, MacArthur replied, and on April 5, without consulting MacArthur, Martin read the letter on the floor of the House of Representatives. The letter's stirring peroration, "There is no substitute for victory,"[45] culminated in Truman's 1:00 A.M. press conference on April 11, 1951, announcing MacArthur's removal.[46]

A fight for Truman's Presidential life followed. His impeachment was discussed, and public opinion polls gave him the lowest vote of confidence ever recorded for a President. After a hero's welcome home, in an address before both houses of the Congress on April 19, 1951, MacArthur called for "new decisions in the diplomatic sphere to promote the realistic adjustments of military strategy."[47]

Although MacArthur concluded his address by implying he would "just fade away," he did not. He later stated that limited war had introduced "a new concept into military operations—the concept of appeasements, the concept that when you use force, you can limit that force." He predicted that such a strategy in Korea could result only in stalemate.

In the subsequent Congressional inquiry into national strategy and conduct of the war, Truman's position was supported by General Bradley and General Marshall (who had succeeded Louis Johnson as Secretary of Defense in September 1950). MacArthur's supporters included Admiral Sherman, General Spaatz, and General Wedemeyer.

Speaking for the Joint Chiefs of Staff, Bradley declared that MacArthur's "strategy would involve us in the wrong war, at the wrong place, at the wrong time, and with the wrong enemy."[48] Secretary Marshall charged that MacArthur would "have us accept the risk of involvement not only in an extension of the war with Red China, but in an all-out war with the Soviet Union." Although Marshall had never been a field commander, he explained to the Senate committee that "this fundamental divergence arises from the inherent difference between the position of the field commander, whose mission is limited to a particular area . . . and the position of the Joint Chiefs of Staff, the Secretary of Defense and the President, who are responsible for the total security of the United States. . . ."[49]

In assessing this great debate six years later, Henry Kissinger concluded: "In the face of the inhibitions produced by our strategic doctrine, we tended to be more aware of our risks than of our opportunities. . . . We thought we could not afford to win in Korea, despite our strategic superiority, because Russia could not afford to lose."[50]

With MacArthur's departure came the two-year stalemate

in the Korean War. As Dr. Kissinger pointed out, Communist China was unable to commit more to the conflict. We were unwilling to do so.[51] Armistice negotiations got under way, following a June 23, 1951, Soviet proposal for a cease-fire. Hundreds of sessions between military representatives of the UN Command and the Red Koreans were to follow for nearly two years at Panmunjon, near the 38th parallel. During this protracted period, fierce fighting continued in the hilly and mountainous terrain of central Korea. The air forces as well as artillery constantly pounded the area; the Chinese and North Koreans, suffering heavy losses, lived like moles in caves.

MacArthur noted in 1964 that "approximately three-fifths of our casualties took place during the indecisive aftermath which followed my recall." He added that the strategic decisions of 1951 "reversed United States military doctrine of a century and a half from the attack to the defense, although the history of warfare shows that the latter never attained more than an indecisive stalemate."[52]

MacArthur never contested the President's authority, as Commander in Chief, to relieve a military commander (although Truman believed this principle was at stake). As MacArthur expressed it, "The supremacy of the civil over the military is fundamental to the American system of government. . . ."[53] In Ridgway, MacArthur's replacement, Truman found an able commander willing to accept the political decisions which dictated the limited warfare strategy. In turn, Ridgway found his own worthy successor as Eighth Army commander in James A. Van Fleet, who had just returned from a successful effort in somewhat similar terrain, Greece, in helping shore up defenses against Communism.

Dwight D. Eisenhower, Van Fleet's classmate at West Point, had not become involved in the controversy. After serving as the first NATO commander, he returned to New York in 1952 and was succeeded by General Ridgway as the Supreme Allied Commander in Europe. In the spring of 1952, General Mark W. Clark became the third United Nations commander. Like Ridgway, Clark recognized that his mission was not victory but stalemate. As he later expressed it, "Since it was not our government's policy to seek a military decision, the next best thing was to make the stalemate more expensive for the Communists than for us. . . ."[54]

The increasingly unpopular war in Korea ground on. President Truman announced that he would not run again for President in 1952, and, that summer both major parties sought in their approaching Presidential nominations the person who might untie "the Korean knot."

Eisenhower and the Korean War, 1952–1953

In the Wake Island conference, MacArthur said to Truman, "If you have any general running against you, his name will be Eisenhower, not MacArthur." Truman allegedly responded, "Why, if he should become President his Administration would make Grant's look like a model of perfection."[55]

Nonetheless, the Democrats as well as the Republicans made overtures to the apolitical, popular military leader turned educator. In the ensuing campaign, Eisenhower's acceptance of the Republican nomination discomfited Truman more than it did the Democratic standard-bearer, Adlai Stevenson. Eisenhower promised, if elected, to journey to Korea as a step in bringing the war to a close. Truman later castigated Eisenhower's statement, terming it a "piece of demagoguery."[56] More than three years later, he continued to be nettled, writing: "I will never understand, how a responsible military man, fully familiar with the extreme delicacy of our negotiations to end hostilities, could use this tragedy for political purposes."[57]

True to his promise, Eisenhower, following his election, journeyed to Korea. Landing on December 2, he conferred with President Rhee, who had proved increasingly adamant in demands for a unified Korea. He consulted not only with Generals Clark and Van Fleet and allied commanders but also with "privates in the ranks." There was general agreement that if the armistice, long pending, could not soon be consummated, "our only recourse would eventually be to mount an all-out attack."[58]

By December 14 Eisenhower was back at the residence of

the president of Columbia University, where MacArthur advised him "that if we were to go over to a major offensive . . . to keep the attack from becoming overly costly, it was clear that we would have to use atomic weapons." Almost grimly Eisenhower announced: "We face an enemy whom we cannot hope to impress by words . . . but only by deeds—executed under circumstances of our choosing."[59] Nevertheless, Eisenhower, a master at influencing others, was not averse to words, if they would help.

Accordingly, with the further benefit of C. D. Jackson, publisher of *Life,* and James C. Hagerty, whom Eisenhower selected to become Presidential press secretary, he began, even before his inauguration, to engage the Red Chinese and the Soviets in psychological warfare. He adroitly requested permission to publish an exchange of views which he had invited from MacArthur.[60] MacArthur had found the use of the Seventh Fleet to isolate Formosa from mainland China particularly repugnant. Eisenhower shared this view; in his February 2, 1953, State of the Union message he announced he was "issuing instructions that the Seventh Fleet no longer be employed to shield Communist China." As a result, the Chinese Communists redeployed some of their troops opposite Formosa. The psychological import of this action was doubtless even more significant. Although India's Prime Minister Jawaharlal Nehru believed it would intensify "the fear psychosis of the world," many persons began to realize that Eisenhower was far more skillful than "the amateur politician he professed himself to be."[61]

Eisenhower also handled the "insubordination" of a field commander, James Van Fleet, with considerable tact. Influenced by Syngman Rhee, Van Fleet told reporters he could mount a successful campaign to end the war. He was probably correct. At this point, United Nations forces had risen to 768,000. Communist troops exceeded a million men—three-fourths of them were Chinese—but they lacked the UN firepower, were badly mauled, and were overextended. In anger at a junior MacArthur, Clark relieved Van Fleet of command, but Eisenhower saw to it that Van Fleet received his high praise upon his retirement. On February 11, 1953, Van Fleet was succeeded by Lieutenant General Maxwell Taylor.

Eisenhower empathized with both MacArthur and Van Fleet. MacArthur had proposed a summit meeting between his former aide and Stalin,[62] a possibility eliminated with Stalin's death on March 5, 1953. Stalin's death doubtless helped end the impasse. His error in having launched the Korean invasion was clear to others in the Kremlin, but his infallibility could not be challenged while he lived. His immediate successor, Georgi Malenkov, did not share Stalin's appetite for foreign aggrandizement. Moreover, Mao Tsetung, considerably senior to Malenkov in the Communist ideological world, could not be expected to waste his treasury for the new Soviet leader.

With the climate so improved, Eisenhower's psychology of persuasion continued. He recalled, "One possibility was to let the Communist authorities understand that, in the absence of satisfactory progress, we intended to move decisively without inhibition in our use of weapons, and would no longer be responsible for confining hostilities to the Korean Peninsula. . . ."[63]

Eisenhower and Hagerty, like Truman, perceived that the Indian government might be able to get their message to the Soviets and the Red Chinese. During the fall of 1952 the U.S. ambassador to India, Chester Bowles, had suggested to Indian diplomats that unless a solution could be found the war might have to be extended.[64] Following Bowles's suggestion the Indians, on December 3, 1952, introduced to the UN General Assembly a cease-fire proposal that was adopted by fifty-four nations, though initially rejected by Moscow and Peking. It sought a solution for the thorny issue of exchange of prisoners.

Many Chinese and North Korean prisoners had no wish to return to their masters, who were insisting on complete repatriation. General Mark Clark proposed humane considerations, which might not require repatriation, for the sick and the wounded. Chou En-lai, on March 30, following his return from Stalin's funeral (where he doubtless argued for the war's end), agreed to Clark's proposal. Thus Operation "Little Switch" was carried out for the sick and wounded; it involved 684 UN personnel and 6,670 Communists.

Eisenhower combined support for these compassionate proposals with, as Hagerty expressed it, "word through the

Indian Government to North Korea, to Peking, and to Moscow" of stern military measures (there was the long-range threat of atomic weapons). Immediately, there was to be relentless change in the air war. As Hagerty put it, "If they did not settle the war, there would be no imaginary line across the Yalu River. There would instead be hot pursuit of their planes regardless of where they came from."[65]

The effectiveness of Eisenhower's assertions involved both his personal credibility and the force with which to back them up. As Eisenhower expressed it, and the Communists understood, "There is no such thing as a little force—don't ever use it. If you have to use force, use it in overwhelming superiority and get it over fast."[66]

Hagerty later explained, "Mr. Eisenhower came into office, following service as Supreme Commander in Europe in World War II and Supreme Commander NATO, with a resulting personal knowledge and acquaintanceship with the leaders of Europe and most of the leaders of the rest of the world." Hagerty concluded, "I have always thought that the Russians had a great deal of respect for him."[67]

That "respect" combined with nuclear and air and naval superiority paid off. Hagerty noted, "They [the Soviets] happened to believe him, and they [the North Korean puppets] sat down to talk."[68]

Despite President Rhee's misgivings, talks got under way at Panmunjon on April 27 between the United Nations and North Korean military representatives. When President Rhee, to the consternation of General Clark, released 25,000 non-Communist North Koreans rather than have them returned to the Communists, negotiations were broken off. In a masterpiece of understatement, General Clark wrote Kim Il Sung on June 29: "The United Nations agrees, of course, that the escape of about 25,000 captured personnel of the Korean People's Army is a serious incident and unfortunately has not been conducive to the early armistice for which both sides have been earnestly striving."[69]

On July 8, the Communists agreed to proceed. In the interim great pressure was put on Rhee to secure his concurrence. The Department of State dispatched one of its most skillful persuaders, Walter S. Robertson, Assistant Secretary for East Asian and Pacific Affairs, to confer with the combative Rhee. Eisenhower wrote strongly to Rhee, assert-ing, "Unless you are prepared immediately and unequivo-cally to accept the authority of the UN Command to conduct the present hostilities and bring them to a close, it will be necessary to effect another arrangement."[70]

Perhaps even more persuasive were the Communist mili-tary blows. Avoiding contact with U.S. troops, the Chinese Communists launched a series of attacks on five ROK di-visions. The offensive was apparently also aimed at gaining real estate for the bargaining table. It was the cause of the ultimate frustration for both the Americans and the South Koreans. American forces, in order presumably to expedite the armistice negotiations, had been ordered to take a strictly defensive position. The Communist attack had finally exhausted itself after advancing 15 miles on the one-third of the front then being held by the South Koreans, who literally begged to counterattack. According to a senior American consultant, Harold Wendell Lady, Rhee and his senior staff reported to the United Nations Command: "The Com-munists are now exhausted—out of food and ammunition. If you will supply us with ammunition and gasoline [which the UN Command had in good supply] we will counterattack and drive them to the Yalu River with no other help from you."[71]

As recounted by Dr. Lady:

> The Commander of the UN forces [Mark Clark] called a meeting of his staff to discuss the ROK request. A canvass of the American Military Advisers assigned to ROK Army units confirmed the correctness of the ROK estimate of the situa-tion. The staff advocated resupplying the ROK Army. The UN Commander argued against this on military grounds, but was unable to convince anyone. Finally, he said: "It doesn't really matter what the military considerations are. Rhee gets no ammunition. I have my orders."[72]

So it was, as Lady relates, that the final battle of the war "was hailed world-wide as an impressive Communist victory."[73] Following this episode, Rhee again took the posi-tion that if need be he would fight on alone until all Korea was liberated. Clark, however, on July 12 had already wrung from Rhee a promise to go along with the UN conciliatory position. Clark had done so only by giving assurances of a military security pact with the United States, long-term economic aid, and a buildup of the Republic of Korea army. With continued firmness, Eisenhower, although the Communist offensive had died out by July 20, authorized moving two additional army divisions and an additional Marine division to Korea on July 23. By this point he doubted if an effective armistice could be accomplished. The following day, July 24, he wrote in "near exasperation" in a memorandum: "There has been so much backing and filling, indecision, doubt and frustration engendered by both Rhee and the Communists that I am doubtful that an armistice even if achieved will have any great meaning."[74]

Three days later, at 10:00 A.M. on July 27, the armistice was signed in eighteen copies in the tarpaper "peace pagoda" at Panmunjon. Neither Kim Il Sung nor Clark participated, and their representatives exchanged no words. Twelve hours later the fighting ceased, and the Korean War, or "police action," as Truman had termed it, was ended, with provision for the exchange of prisoners scheduled to follow.

Sixteen United Nations had fought to contain Communist aggression. An estimated 1,820,000 military had been killed or wounded, of which 1,420,000 were Communists, including 900,000 Chinese. The United Nations had sustained the loss of 150,000 dead and 250,000 wounded. The South Koreans suffered most, and 33,629 Americans had died, with 103,284 wounded. No other United Nation suffered a loss of more than 1,000 dead.[75]

It had been an expensive "police action." Only time would make manifest its accomplishment. Eisenhower and Secretary of State John Foster Dulles made succinctly clear what a breach of the armistice would mean. A joint statement prepared by the sixteen United Nations allies the same day the truce was signed declared that "the consequences of such a breach of the armistice would be so grave that in all probability it would not be possible to confine hostilities within the frontiers of Korea."[76]

Eisenhower wrote on armistice eve: "We have won an armistice on a single battlefield—not peace in the world."[77]

PART TWO

FROM EISENHOWER TO CARTER

I am intrigued with, but not convinced by, the argument that the Congress ought to resolve all its troubles by just delegating all its powers to the executive branch.

SENATOR RICHARD B. RUSSELL

VIII

****

BUILDING PEACE

> We cannot afford the luxury of ignorance; it costs too
> much.   MILTON S. EISENHOWER

Introduction

The Korean War, 1950–1953, may be termed Checkmate II for
Soviet expansionism, with Checkmate I comprising the Berlin airlift of 1948–1949 and the formation of NATO (1949).

The Soviet's first nuclear detonation (1949), ending United
States exclusivity in the nuclear club, ushered in a new aspect of the Cold War and a search for a new national security
policy. In an age of unprecedented technological advance,
that search was to be conducted, especially until 1958, in a
continuing severe interservice rivalry.

As no longer one but now two power blocs developed
nuclear capability, the alternatives to mutual self-destruction would have to be researched. In the United
States, long-range missile research got under way belatedly;
the first arm of American security would be the retaliatory
force of the long-range nuclear-bomb-carrying Strategic Air
Command. It had so emerged from the "admirals' revolt."

But the debate now involved a larger issue than who
should be the nuclear carrier. Earnest men were questioning
the adequacy of our national security policies. In the debates of the 1948–1953 period, tempers rose and careers were
abruptly altered. Chief of Naval Operations Denfeld was removed, Secretary of Defense Forrestal suffered a breakdown,
and his successor, Secretary Johnson, resigned. Generals
MacArthur and Van Fleet were relieved of command.

In the United States public debates on defense and foreign policy—or national security issues, as they were increasingly termed—usually followed rather than preceded policy. Withdrawal of United States air and ground combat forces from Europe in 1946 tempted Stalin too strongly, and he made the central and eastern European states Soviet satellites. The counter-policy of containment of Communism, the Truman Doctrine, was enunciated in 1947, and Stalin took Czechoslovakia the next year.

Public debates during the 1946–1952 period ranged over the virtues of: (1) negotiations and concessions; (2) isolationism, or rather restriction of concerns to the Western hemisphere and the surrounding oceans; (3) showdown. Of the three alternatives, the United States government, in general, followed the first course, with tentative probes in the third, as in the Berlin airlift, Greece, and Korea. Among the advocates of the second policy course were former President Herbert Hoover, and, of the third, Douglas MacArthur.

The professional service schools could scarcely take a detached view in the national security policy debate. The heat and cold of rancor seemed to be producing fog rather than a clear view for the future. The courageous, outspoken commander of the Air War College, Major General Orvil A. Anderson, was suspended for his too vigorous public advocacy of a more dynamic foreign policy.[1] The president of the Naval War College, Vice Admiral Richard L. Conolly, who had lost his fourth star as a sequel of the admirals' revolt, was receptive subsequently to an offer to retire to the presidency of a then small, unaccredited institution, Long Island University.

A searching, unsettling question remained with the ending of the Korean War. Would the United States for the first time in peacetime maintain an adequate defense posture? A related question in the protracted Cold War was: How could a free society defend itself against a totalitarian society without losing certain of its freedoms? Would we become a garrison state? What should be the responsibilities of American youth? General George C. Marshall, among others, had advocated universal military training for young Americans. The proposal was defeated in the Congress and instead a "peacetime" draft, first enacted in 1940, was re-enacted a decade later.

For the time being, the Korean War ended arms retrenchment. The Army got new tanks and other heavy weapons. The Navy acquired the *Forrestal* class of heavy carriers, and the Air Force was given the B-52 jet bomber.

But as the Korean War became the *bête noire* in the last year of the Truman administration, so also did the armaments program. Congressional cuts in the defense budget during the fiscal year ending June 30, 1953, before the truce was secured, totaled $4.3 billion. The largest dollar cut in the defense budget for any year since 1946, it meant a "stretching out," deferring the attainment of goals in both the U.S. and NATO force structures. President-elect Eisenhower, who had campaigned for "security with solvency," offered no prospect for budgetary increases.

The United States was not alone in cutting defense programs. Despite the clear aggression of the Soviet Union in Korea and its overwhelming numerical superiority in Europe, vis-à-vis NATO, free-world taxpayers were guarding their pocketbooks.

With a substantial unified military force in Europe and with lessening of tensions by 1953, western Europeans looked toward a period of economic unity and growth. Japan, too, with American assurance of defense, concentrated on its own economic and social programs. The 1953–1961 period was to produce unprecedented economic growth both in western Europe and in Japan.

To a lesser extent, the Communist world also concentrated on domestic programs. With the Korean War ended, the first Chinese Communist Five-Year Plan emerged. Even the Soviet Union seemed to look inward after the death of Stalin. While coveting influence in the emerging new nations, such as Burma, Indonesia, India, Pakistan, and the African states, as well as in such strategic areas as the Middle East and Southeast Asia, the Soviets needed time to evolve their moves in these areas.

The climate of opinion in the United States and the countries of its allies made the role of military planners difficult. The system of alliances and new technological advances

moved across traditional structures, and the term "infrastruc-
ture" arose to complement "stretch-out." If funds were
not available for raising force levels, refinements could at
least be made in the organization and deployment of U.S.
and allied forces. Service rivalries would focus on
technologies and mission assignments.

Even if there had not been service budgetary limitations,
NATO planners would have shared the concern of planners
in the Joint Chiefs of Staff and the National Security Council.
Some believed that the answer to Soviet superiority in force
size and conventional weaponry was the "deterrence" and
the "retaliatory" capability of the U.S. Strategic Air Force,
combining present bombers with projected intermediate and
eventual long-range missiles. Others, at home and abroad,
became proponents of relatively small, finely honed,
mechanized tactical forces, teaming ground and air units,
and including tactical "nukes" (atomic weapons), which were
beginning to come off the production line.

Defense Department Reorganization (1953)

Into the midst of these debates in a period of unprecedented
technological advance and new weaponry came the first
twentieth-century President who had been a professional
soldier. Eisenhower brought immense prestige and popularity to America's defense posture. While immediately
strengthening the NSC advisory structure, he made clear
that he would serve as his own principal adviser on American military policy. He designated his new Secretary of
State, John Foster Dulles, as his principal adviser on foreign
policy. With his penchant for clear lines of organization and
communication, on June 1, 1953, he stated that "other officials of the executive branch will work with and through the
Secretary of State on matters of foreign policy."[2] From his
November 1952 election until his January 1953 inaugural, in
addition to his trip to Korea, he took steps to name a new
national security policy team, with the encouragement of
Senator Taft. Moreover, he pondered what he considered

necessary changes in the organizational structure for such policy.

Eisenhower named the blunt-spoken chairman of General Motors, Charles E. Wilson, as his Secretary of Defense. Wilson got off to a rather shaky start with an often misquoted statement that what was good for the corporation he had headed was "good for the country."[3]

The terms of all the incumbent members of the Joint Chiefs were to expire in 1953. As chairman of the Joint Chiefs of Staff Eisenhower named Admiral Radford to succeed General Bradley. To Taft and other Republican leaders this augured an end of what they considered an inordinate emphasis on Europe in defense posture. General Ridgway succeeded General Collins as Army Chief; General Nathan F. Twining succeeded the seriously ill General Vandenberg as Air Force Chief, and Admiral Robert B. Carney was named to succeed Admiral William M. Fechteler as Chief of Naval Operations.

Robert A. Lovett, General Marshall's successor as Secretary of Defense, had sought to arrest the continuing downgrading of the role of the service secretaries, which had followed the 1949 Reorganization Act. As Deputy Secretary of Defense in 1950–1951 and then as Secretary of Defense through the remainder of the Truman administration, Lovett had witnessed the wartime upgrading of the role of the Joint Chiefs of Staff. He had further witnessed their continuing inability to reach agreement on such issues as individual military service roles. He had recognized that many of these issues, such as force levels and proprietorship of nuclear weapons, involved political considerations as much as military issues. Since the 1949 amendments to the National Security Act, the service secretaries had been almost completely isolated from high-level policy. Lovett proposed further reorganization to balance the roles of service secretaries and chiefs.

In keeping with Lovett's views, as well as his own regarding the strengthening of civilian lines of control, Eisenhower directed Secretary Wilson to form a study committee. Headed by Nelson A. Rockefeller, the committee included

Lovett and Omar Bradley; the President's brother, Dr. Mil-
ton S. Eisenhower, then president of Pennsylvania State
University; David Sarnoff, chairman of Radio Corporation of
America; Dr. Vannevar Bush of the Carnegie Institution; and
Dr. Arthur S. Flemming, director of the Office of Defense
Mobilization. Serving as military advisers were Generals
Marshall and Spaatz and Admiral Nimitz. Their reports
would be one in an overall series on government reorganiza-
tion of the Second Hoover Commission.

As the Rockefeller Committee approached the issues of
reorganization, President Eisenhower shared Lovett's hope
of reviving the role of the service secretaries. He described
them as the "principal agents for the management and direction of the entire defense enterprise."[4] However, to Rockefeller this did not mean that they should participate in
policy formulation[5] but only in policy execution.

The resulting Reorganization Plan Number Six of 1953, as
it was named, further strengthened the role of the Secretary
of Defense, in this instance at the expense of the JCS as well
as the service secretaries. Lovett could attest to what every
Secretary of Defense beginning with Forrestal had experienced: lack of authority, lack of clear, coherent military advice, and lack of control over the quarreling services.

By April 30, 1953, the committee's report was submitted to
Congress. As had been the case in 1949, the result was
another major amendment to the National Security Act of
1947. Overall goals as enunciated by Eisenhower to the Congress included the elimination of waste and duplication, as
well as "three basic objectives: (1) to strengthen civilian control by establishing clearer lines of responsibility; (2) to improve administrative procedure in the Department of Defense by eliminating unwieldy boards and committees and
substituting instead responsible executive officials; (3) to
provide a mechanism for better strategic planning."[6]

To carry out these objectives, the Eisenhower-Rockefeller
Plan would abolish the Munitions Board, the Research and
Development Board, and other staff agencies and replace
them with six additional Assistant Secretaries of Defense
(plus the General Counsel who was elevated to that rank).

There would be ten assistant secretaries, including the General Counsel. The chairman of the Joint Chiefs of Staff was to be given additional administrative responsibility so that the individual chiefs might focus on their roles as military advisers and planners. For the same purpose, and to enhance the role of the service secretaries, separate and apart from Reorganization Plan Number Six there was to be a revision of the Key West agreement of 1948 regarding the chain of command for unified commands: unified commands were to be channeled through the service secretaries, not the service chiefs.

A plan which subordinated the Joint Chiefs of Staff and reenhanced the service secretaries was bound to arouse resentment and opposition. However, the prestige of President Eisenhower carried the day. When testifying before the House Committee on Government Operations, Admiral Leahy declared:

> He [the President] has been a good soldier, and he has been in it all his life. When people ask me whether I object to this or not, I say, "How can I object to it if the President approves it?" He has more experience in wars than I have had. He is recognized as an expert. So if he wants it why not let him have it?[7]

Reorganization Plan Number Six went into effect on June 30, 1953. It strengthened the authority of the Secretary of Defense, but actually it neither diminished the Joint Chiefs nor enhanced the service secretaries. For the Joint Chiefs, it meant that their chairman had become their spokesman. For the service secretaries, it confirmed their virtual demise as policymakers. Inexorable forces continued the process of centralization at the Office of the Secretary of Defense (OSD) level. As an apologist, the General Counsel of the Department of Defense (DOD), who had been the former legal counsel of the Rockefeller Committee, wrote eight months after the enactment:

> The Secretaries of the Military departments have not been submerged. They are not subject to orders from the Assistant

198 From Eisenhower to Carter

Secretaries of Defense. They do not have to go through the Assistant Secretaries to reach the Secretary of Defense. The channels of communication are just as simple and direct as the lines of authority. . . .

The additional Assistant Secretaries have facilitated the delegation of operating authority to the Secretaries of the military department. The Assistant Secretaries of Defense are not operators or commanders. . . .[8]

It simply did not work out that way. Moreover, the clearest indication that the service secretaries had not been restored to policy positions was the fact that no consideration had been given to returning them to membership on the National Security Council. The services were increasingly to become administrative subdivisions of the Defense Department. With the continuing service rivalries, Eisenhower lost all interest in restoring the service secretaries' prestige.

A continuing and nagging anxiety to the friends of the individual armed forces was the possible elimination of the three armed services in favor of one uniformed service. From time to time, as service rivalries continued, Eisenhower would suggest, somewhat in exasperation, one uniform for all the armed services. Consummate politician that he was, he appreciated both the proud heritage of each and the healthfulness of a degree of competition, and his remarks were meant only as a spur to greater unity.

Further centralization at the OSD level did aid in one avowed goal of the President and the Rockefeller Committee: the reduction in personnel. Between January 1, 1953, and June 30, 1954, a reduction of 16 percent was accomplished in OSD personnel.[9]

In his triple-program goals of economy, efficiency, and technological advance, Eisenhower worked effectively with the Congress. In only two of his eight years in office did the Republicans control the Congress, and that was by the slimmest of margins. To strengthen the communications with Capitol Hill he enlarged the Congressional liaison office. Heading this office was Major General Wilton B. (Jerry) Persons, ably assisted by Bryce W. Harlow, formerly staff director of the House Armed Services Committee.[10]

NSC and Economy

Eisenhower considered the structuring of the National Security Council and identifying its role in shaping policy more fundamental than the refinement of the Defense Department organization. Even before his inaugural, on January 12–13, 1953, he had convened a two-day session with his future Cabinet members which was largely devoted to an examination of the role of the National Security Council and of its relationship to the Cabinet.[11] "Forrestal's revenge," reluctantly accepted by Truman, became the central planning instrument for national security affairs throughout the eight Eisenhower years. Moreover, from the outset he broadened the concept of the NSC role. Economic affairs, budget and fiscal policy, were wedded to security matters.

If Eisenhower needed any justification for relating economy and security, it had been supplied by a report submitted to the NSC the last day of the Truman administration. This report, NSC-141, calling for substantial military budgetary increases, had been prepared with the cordial support of Acheson, Lovett, and W. Averell Harriman, director of the Mutual Security Agency.[12] As if to present the new President with their own optimum expectations, the outgoing Joint Chiefs had also specified an expanded program which over a five-year period would have resulted in a budget deficit aggregating $44 billion. A consternated Eisenhower desired to "correct this kind of habit."[13] Conservative in his economics, he believed a balanced budget and the elimination of inflation were concomitant ingredients of national strength. He was concerned not only with the budget deficits, which had characterized all but four of the preceding twenty-two years, but also with the steady unchecked mounting inflation of the preceding twelve years. As he expressed it, "between the Scylla of a deep deficit and the Charybdis of an inadequate military budget, we had to make a start without encountering either."[14]

Because of these considerations, Secretary of the Treasury George Humphrey participated in the meetings of the National Security Council after March 23, 1953.[15] Not unlike

Alexander Hamilton, the first Secretary of the Treasury, Humphrey was to play a key role in national security policy. He was to become, along with John Foster Dulles, Radford, and the President, one of the big four in conceiving and promulgating what came to be called the philosophy of the "New Look."[16] They secured a record reduction—nearly $8 billion—of the defense budget, cutting it to $34.5 billion.

Eisenhower also emphasized internal security and psychological factors as elements in national security policy. Hence, (for internal security affairs), Attorney General Herbert Brownell, and (for external security matters), CIA Director Allen Dulles and (for psychological affairs) Special Assistant to the President C. D. Jackson played significant roles in NSC meetings. So also did Joseph Dodge as director of the Bureau of the Budget in 1953–1954. Also usually present at NSC meetings in the Eisenhower period were the director of the newly formed (1953) United States Information Agency, the Special Assistant for Foreign Economic Policy, and the Special Assistant for National Security Affairs and his aide, the Council's Executive Secretary and Deputy Executive Secretary.[17]

Eisenhower's first Special Assistant for National Security Affairs, a new post, was the Boston attorney-banker Brigadier General Robert Cutler. At the President's direction, Cutler prepared a "Report of Recommendations on the National Security Council" which was to establish the NSC operating structure for the next eight years. This included the elevation of the NSC "senior staff" to the NSC Planning Board, with the Special Assistant as the active chairman.[18] Eisenhower further strengthened the procedural side of the NSC by establishing, through directive order, the Operations Coordinating Board. Complementing the Planning Board, it would "ride herd" to make certain programs were implemented.[19] After he left office, Eisenhower concluded that the OCB had "functioned fairly well." However, he had already concluded before completing his tenure in office "that this work could have been done better by a highly competent and trusted official with a small staff of his own, rather than by a committee whose members had to handle the task on a part-time basis."[20]

Building Peace — page 201

Accustomed to orderly staff procedures, Eisenhower introduced NSC staff papers on each country and on issues of strategic concern. He also established committees to monitor the formulation and implementation of policy. In forging policies through the NSC, Eisenhower believed he "could not only tolerate disagreement, but needed it." Both Radford and Foster Dulles were strong-willed, and they clashed on occasion. Eisenhower believed he benefited from both the heat and the light of the exchanges. "Those differences," he recalled, "always involved issues and courses of action and, of course, never became personal."[21]

Eisenhower, who wanted the NSC to become "correlative in importance with the Cabinet," felt more at home presiding in NSC sessions than those of his Cabinet. As Cutler wrote, "President Eisenhower is at home in this kind of operation. The old soldier is accustomed to well-staffed work."[22]

Cutler was succeeded in 1955 by Dillon Reed, a Houston lawyer, as the Special Assistant for National Security Affairs. Cutler returned for a second brief tour in 1957–1958, and Gordon Gray, the former Army Secretary, ably occupied the post in the final three Eisenhower years. Gray contrasted the structural decisionmaking of the Eisenhower years with the rather informal methods of the Roosevelt-Truman years. His recollection of the Roosevelt-Truman administrations was of endless parades of advisers and shifting of decisions according to which one saw the Presidents last—what he called the "yo-yo" form of decisionmaking. In the structured Eisenhower NSC, he concluded, "You don't have this kind of ad hoc piecemeal business of arriving at a decision."[23]

Unlike Truman, who until the Korean War seldom attended NSC sessions, Eisenhower rarely missed one, and the Council convened weekly during his administration.[24] Eisenhower had firm views regarding the Council's composition, despite the several bills in the Congress to add persons as statutory members. He emphatically declared that "if they added persons" he did not desire, his response would be to "create and use his own advisory body in lieu of the statutory Council."[25]

In the examination of issues in the NSC, Eisenhower

tended to avoid planning toward a particular critical year. He viewed the Cold War as a protracted conflict, and he rejected the "crisis year" concept of NSC-68, replacing it with planning, as he termed it, "for the long haul."[26] On May 8, 1953, while Mamie's canary chirped in the background, Eisenhower met with Jackson, Cutler, Allen Dulles, and General Walter Bedell Smith, the Under Secretary of State, to establish a series of task forces to explore long-range policy, ranging from "containment" to "liberation."

By October, with the intervening events of the Korean armistice, the unsuccessful East German uprisings, and the Soviet detonation of the hydrogen bomb, the policy of containment had been reconfirmed but with greater emphasis on air-nuclear forces as a deterrent to any future "proxy insurgencies."[27]

The New Look

Early in 1953 the term "the New Look" was probably more familiar to Mamie than to Ike, since it referred to women's hemlines. Then, on December 14, 1953, Radford used it to describe the administration's military policies. As Eisenhower recalled, the term "probably suggested to many minds a picture of a far more radical change in the composition of our armed forces than was truly the case."[28] It meant overall force reductions, increased reliance on the reserves, and reallocation among five categories of the armed forces: nuclear retaliatory or strike, overseas, sea lanes, air defense, and reserve.

England's Prime Minister Churchill and the British Chiefs of Staff had taken a similar "new look" in 1951.[29] However, the United States' new view had at its heart Radford's assumption that within a broad range of contingencies (including limited warfare), nuclear weapons might be used. On October 30, 1953, Eisenhower approved NSC-162/2, with its planning assumption that nuclear weapons would be used. The implication was that there would be no future large-scale infusion of conventional ground troops in Korea-type situations. The former Korean commander, General Ridgway, now Army Chief of Staff, and Navy Secretary Robert B. Anderson argued unsuccessfully for their conventional forces. Deputy Secretary of Defense Roger Keyes expressed the administration position against "outmoded procedures and weapons."[30] Eisenhower put it more succinctly: "If it works, it's obsolete."[31]

Whereas the NSC-68 program had been rendered academic within a few weeks by the outbreak of the Korean War, the New Look was actually carried into being. Internally, the administration's desires, matching those of the American taxpayers, were to balance the budgets, reduce expenditures, and reduce taxes. Externally, following the death of Stalin and the ending of the Korean War, there was an easing of tensions.

It was a period of Air Force dominance in strategic thinking, reflected in the following increases in the Air Force and decreases in the Army and Navy.[32]

MANPOWER

	December 1953	October 1954	January 1955
Army	1,500,000	1,600,000	1,000,000
Navy/Marines	1,000,000	920,000	870,000
Air Force	950,000	960,000	970,000

BUDGET
(IN BILLIONS OF DOLLARS)

	Fiscal 1954	Fiscal 1955
Army	12.9	8.8
Navy/Marines	11.2	9.7
Air Force	15.6	16.4

In part, the foregoing represented primary focus on long-range nuclear-strike forces. To use Foster Dulles's phrase, from a Council on Foreign Relations speech of January 12, 1954, it meant "massive retaliatory power" capability. The most substantial budget and personnel reductions in the New Look were in ground forces. Overall substantial budgetary reductions made possible a balanced budget, but Air Force costs increased because of the SAC transition from the propeller-driven B-36 to the jet B-47 and B-52 fleets. During the first three years of the Eisenhower administration, both the President and the Congress believed that the United States should have the world's best Air Force. The world climate and the frustrating experience of the costly Korean ground war had so dictated, and the New Look accordingly supported the Air Force in particular.

The New Look was largely an accomplishment of JCS Chairman Radford, who had shed his old parochial views and become the "new Radford." His NSC-162/2 of October 1953, although setting forth a broad range of nuclear contingencies, was obscured by Dulles's "massive retaliation" concept (even though in fact Dulles completely deferred to the professional in military matters and accepted Radford's views). Moreover, Radford also effectively supported his Commander in Chief in the New Look force reduction through what he termed "an informed state of readiness of air reserve forces."[33]

The years of the New Look, 1953–1956, are now viewed with a degree of nostalgia. The New Look not only marked, vis-à-vis the Soviet Union, "the high water mark of relative American military strength in the Cold War," but it had been achieved in a new era of reduced taxes and balanced budgets.[34]

In Pursuit of Peace

The Eisenhower years are also remembered with nostalgia because they were relatively peaceful, although there were ample opportunities for the United States to get involved, in various parts of the world, in engagements which might have ranged in intensity from brush fires to World War III.

The second volume of Eisenhower's Presidential reminiscences is appropriately named *Waging Peace*. He determined to wage peace, despite war hawks in the Congress, despite the China lobby, despite the "brinkmanship" of Secretary of State Dulles, and despite the Chairman of his Joint Chiefs of Staff, Radford, who was especially spoiling for a showdown with Communist China.

Among the areas inviting United States armed intervention were: Southeast Asia, the captive nations of Europe, and the Middle East. Southeast Asia warrants greatest discussion because of the United States' subsequent involvement there in its most protracted war.

SOUTHEAST ASIA. The Korean War was followed by the buildup of a war that had been sputtering in French Indochina since 1946 between the French and their native allies and the Communist Vietminh led by Ho Chi Minh.

With the end of the fighting in Korea, the Chinese Communists could substantially supply Ho Chi Minh's forces. By this time French forces in Vietnam numbered 200,000 and their native allies from the Associated States of Indochina (Laos, Cambodia, and Vietnam) numbered an additional 200,000.

Although he was determined not to get involved in another Korea-like ground action, Eisenhower believed that it might be necessary to strike a decisive blow by airpower at the head of the dragon, China, rather than take desultory action against the tail, Vietnam. But Eisenhower could see no purpose in air strikes in Vietnam, aside from their being beneficial to French morale. If force were to be applied there he believed it must "be decisively effective."[35]

After consulting with Congress, Eisenhower in February 1954 did send 200 technicians to Vietnam to participate until mid-June in support of the French plan for victory, and some B-26 aircraft were turned over to the French. The Navarre Plan for victory envisioned raising another 100,000 Vietnamese forces and another 50,000 volunteer French legionnaires, bringing the total strength on the French side from 400,000 to 550,000. Eisenhower expressed concern that the French had in 1953 established a garrison at Dien Bien Phu, removed from lines of supplies in a hostile area of northern Vietnam, in hopes that they could lure the elusive enemy into an open battle in which superior French firepower could secure a victory. But the enemy, refusing the bait, instead cut off lines of supply. By year's end the French garrison was under attack, by the spring of 1954 under siege.

The protracted war had become increasingly unpopular in France. Regardless of the outcome of the Dien Bien Phu siege, the French Chief of Staff, General Paul Ely, told

Eisenhower, Dulles, and Radford that France was ready for a negotiated peace. Radford, with SAC Commander Curtis LeMay's support, recommended American air strikes (with conventional bombs) to lift the siege. Always more cautious than either Radford or Dulles, Eisenhower was not prepared to give the order without Congressional and allied support. Lyndon Johnson asked, "Where do the British stand?"[36]

On April 4, 1953, Eisenhower wrote Churchill, "I am sure . . . you are following with the deepest interest and anxiety the early reports of the gallant fight by the French at Dien Bien." He warned his old wartime friend that "regardless of the outcome of this particular battle, I fear that the French cannot alone see the thing through. . . ." He concluded with the admonition: "We failed to halt Hirohito, Mussolini and Hitler by not acting in unity and in time. . . ."[37] But the aging Prime Minister, who was about to step down in favor of Anthony Eden, had no desire to intervene. Neither Eisenhower nor the Congress wanted to intervene unless it was as a part of a coalition and unless France, with the avowed intention of independence for its colonies, would continue the struggle. The war-weary French were ready to do the former but not the latter. The fall of the garrison at Dien Bien Phu on May 7, 1953, did not have to signalize the end of the French struggle there. But it did result in the overturn of the French government. The new French government of Pierre Mendès-France, which took office on June 18, promised that by July 20 it would secure a negotiated peace in Vietnam. It did so one day after the deadline.

The terms of the armistice were worked out in Geneva following a number of preliminary meetings: Chou En-lai and Mendès-France met at Bern on June 23, and on June 25, Churchill, Eden, Eisenhower, and Dulles met in Washington. Most reluctantly, Eisenhower agreed to a dividing line between Communist-dominated North Vietnam and an independent South Vietnam. He recognized that if elections had then been held for all of Vietnam, Ho Chi Minh would have been elected head of state. Moreover, the Vietminh apparently agreed to withdraw their forces from Laos and Cambodia. And so after seven and a half years of fighting, in which the French had suffered 150,000 casualties in killed, wounded, or missing, peace presumably had come to Southeast Asia. Supposedly, independent Laos, Cambodia, and South Vietnam would be able to determine their own future destinies.

In the Washington meeting the British agreed in principle to a Southeast Asia Treaty Organization, which Eisenhower had earlier proposed to Churchill. SEATO was signed into being in the Manila Pact of September 8, 1954, by France, Britain, Australia, New Zealand, Thailand, the Philippines, Pakistan, and the United States. Aimed at repelling future Communist aggression, the pact agreed that the signatories would act together in the event of armed attack on any of them.

Quite incorrectly, in 1973 former Air Force Under Secretary Townsend Hoopes wrote: "The absence of a strong conventional capability was an important factor in keeping the Eisenhower administration from a military intervention in Vietnam...."[38] The simple fact is that Eisenhower was steadfast in his determination never to get involved in another Korea-type operation.

THE CAPTIVE NATION UPRISINGS. In the political rhetoric of the 1952 campaign, hawks, both Republican and Democrats, had made vague promises of relief for the captive nation states of central and eastern Europe. The first test of turning such rhetoric into action came in East Germany on June 16, 1953, when riots broke out in East Berlin and spread to Halle, Jena, Leipzig, and other cities. But fists and stones were no match for Russian tanks, and Dulles's moral protests and offers of $15 million worth of free food fell on Soviet Foreign Minister V. M. Molotov's deaf ears.[39]

United States action regarding East Germany could not have greatly encouraged the larger, tragic Hungarian rebellion three years later, which rather had its prelude in the October 20, 1956, uprising in Poland. The rebellion was swiftly put down by Soviet troops imported from East Germany, but as Eisenhower noted, "The Polish unrest spread like a prairie fire."[40]

In Hungary on November 1 the courageous Imre Nagy renounced the Warsaw Pact and appealed to the United Nations. On November 4 the Soviets vetoed an American resolution introduced into the United Nations Security Council which called on Russia to withdraw its troops from Hungary; the Soviets further responded with 200,000 troops and 4,000 tanks, leaving 50,000 Hungarians dead and wounded in the streets of Budapest. Nagy was subsequently executed.

In response to Eisenhower's letter of November 4, Premier Nikolai Bulganin's replied that the situation was an internal matter. Eisenhower, who recognized "that Hungary was, in the circumstances, as inaccessible to us as Tibet," recorded that this "was almost the last provocation that my temper could stand."[41] On December 1 he announced that the United States would welcome Hungarian refugees. Despite its sympathy for the plight of the Hungarians, the United States was not willing to embark on armed intervention which would almost certainly result in World War III.

MIDDLE EAST. Simultaneous with the Polish and Hungarian uprisings, war came to the Middle East. These events, combined with an American Presidential election campaign, caused Eisenhower to quote from John Milton, "All hell broke loose."[42]

On October 29, 1956, Israeli troops attacked Egyptian forces in the Sinai. On receiving word, Eisenhower exploded: "All right, Foster, you tell 'em [Israel] that, godam it, we're going to apply sanctions, we're going to the United Nations, we're going to do everything that there is so we can stop this thing."[43] But the French and British, who had their own designs, vetoed both United States and Soviet cease-fire resolutions. Since the revolutionary Nasser government had seized the Suez Canal Company, which was controlled by Britain and France, both countries had been spoiling for a fight to bring Nasser down. On October 31 their bombing began. On November 2, Dulles entered the hospital with cancer and did not return to State until January. In the interim Eisenhower acted decisively with his old allies and secured a United Nations–supported cease-fire by November 7. This meant the end of the political career of his friend Anthony Eden, who was succeeded by Harold Macmillan as Prime Minister.

With considerable sadness Churchill wrote Eisenhower on November 24. The President replied on November 27, agreeing "that . . . back of the difficulties that the free world is now experiencing lies one principal fact that none of us can afford to forget. The Soviets are the real enemy of the Western World, implacably hostile and seeking our destruction."[44]

Eisenhower later termed the period beginning October 20 with the Polish uprising and ending November 7 with the Middle East cease-fire as "the most crowded and demanding three weeks of my entire Presidency." In the midst of it, the American people went to the polls. On the eve of the election Adlai Stevenson warned that Eisenhower might not, in view of his first-term health record, live through a second term. Governor Stevenson said he "recoiled" at the thought of Richard Nixon as the custodian of the hydrogen bomb.[45] Nonetheless, the American people, while withholding from Eisenhower a Congressional majority, returned him in a landslide.

1958 Defense Reorganization

INTERSERVICE RIVALRY AND SPUTNIK. The Eisenhower experience following the 1953 amendments to the National Security Act led within five years to the final basic overhauling of the Department of Defense. The tortuous course from 1947, at last to be completed, was to become one of the permanent significant accomplishments of the Eisenhower years.

The further major amendment to the National Security Act resulted not merely from the operational experience with the 1953 amendment. It was largely an outcome of service competition, which was directly related to the New Look philosophies and the awesome force of the hydrogen bomb. The bomb had been tested in the Pacific in 1952–1953 as a direct response both to the Soviet's nuclear detonation in 1949 and their hostile intent in the Korean War. Moreover, the New Look, by downgrading conventional forces and upgrading nuclear weapons, envisaged intense service competition for a "piece of the action."

Secretary of Defense Wilson, who had found rivalry between the several divisions of General Motors beneficial, accepted competition as a principle in the armed services. The development of missile technology was the focus of such competition. Prior to Eisenhower's inaugural, virtually nothing had been done in this field. By 1954, in a spirit of intense competition and with limited funds, all three of the services were engaged in research and development for both intermediate-range (1,500 miles) ballistic missiles (IRBMs) and intercontinental ballistic missiles (ICBMs).

Despite, and in part because of, the 1953 amendment, despite also the addition of the Secretary of the Treasury and the director of the Bureau of the Budget to NSC deliberations, Eisenhower found himself increasingly exasperated at his uniformed chiefs. "Each believed," he wrote, "that although the sums allocated to the others were quite sufficient for national safety, the amounts approved for his own particular service were inadequate."[46]

Instead of receiving the detached professional advisory service he had hoped for, Eisenhower was getting static that "tended to neutralize the advisory influence" which the service chiefs "should have enjoyed as a body." Despite his own new appointments, he found himself yearning for chiefs with "breadth of understanding." He confided on August 20, 1956, to his boyhood friend "Swede" Hazlett, "Strangely enough the one man who sees this clearly is a Navy man who at one time was an uncompromising exponent of Naval power and its superiority over any other kind of strength. That is Radford."[47]

Radford did his best to create harmony among the chiefs, predicating it on the grounds of their own enlightened self-interest. As he testified before Symington's Airpower Subcommittee in 1956, "I have often pointed out to the chiefs that the more they disagree, the more power they hand to the chairman."[48] Not all the Chiefs viewed it that way. Army Chief of Staff Taylor, who was unhappy with the reductions in ground forces, found Radford "an able and ruthless partisan, who did his utmost to impose his views upon the chiefs."[49] Nor was Taylor happy with the Army's relationships with the Air Force: "Since 1947, the Army has been dependent upon the Air Force for tactical air support, tactical airlift, and for long range air transport. Throughout this period," he concluded, "the Army had been a dissatisfied customer, feeling that the Air Force has not fully discharged its obligations undertaken at the time of unification."[50]

The Army aroused little support in such criticism of the Air Force during the New Look period. Eisenhower had adroitly appealed to both the "security conscious" and the "solvency conscious," to both the isolationist and the internationalist. His reductions in defense spending had been joined not merely with "a bigger bang for a buck" Air Force, as Army adherents called it, but also with a system of alliances and mutual defense commitments. While public and Congressional opinion allied with him, he remained unhappy with the posture of his old Army associates.

Taylor and his Army colleagues, while displeased with the reduction in conventional ground forces, perceived in the New Look a new Army opportunity: ballistic missiles. Accordingly, at the Redstone Arsenal in Huntsville, Alabama, they quietly undertook the development of a brilliant, capable research team, headed by Dr. Wernher von Braun and including other German scientists who had developed the V-1 and V-2 "buzz bombs" in World War II. They had the able administrative leadership of Major General John B. Medaris, and in 1955 Lieutenant General James Gavin back in Washington as the new Assistant Chief for Research and Development.

The Air Force ballistic missile program, which found its early impetus in the February 1953 report of the Strategic Missile Evaluation Group headed by Hungarian-born scientist Dr. John von Neumann, was carried forward through the efforts of California industrialist Trevor Gardner, who served as Assistant Secretary of the Air Force for Research and Development in the 1953–1955 period. He in turn picked German-born Air Force Major General Bernard A. Schriever to lead the Air Force effort. As he wrote, he perceived in young Schriever an officer "unconventional enough to find new methods of operation, to short circuit official red tape

and circumvent bureaucratic meddling, and to break
through the barriers that stood in the way of the successful
completion of the missile program."[51]

The Navy, with the appointment of Admiral Arleigh P.
Burke as Chief of Naval Operations in August 1955, served
notice of its own (albeit belated) interest in the ballistic missile field. Secretary Wilson designated naval interest as a
joint Army-Navy program. Having achieved success in pit-
ting Buick against Oldsmobile, Wilson now proceeded to pit
Army versus Air Force. The Navy, apparently having
learned its lesson in the 1949 "admirals' revolt," stayed out
of the Army–Air Force feud over Nike-Talos and Thor-
Jupiter missiles. As Admiral Radford quaintly expressed it,
"You might say we had a small sweet voice singing lightly on
one side and two anvil choruses going on the other."[52]

By the fall of 1955 both the Air Force and the Army were
giving highest priority to both IRBM and ICBM programs.
The case for such priorities had been considerably
strengthened by the February 1955 report of the Technological Capabilities Panel of distinguished scientists that the
NSC had created in the fall of 1954 at Eisenhower's direction.
Chaired by Dr. James R. Killian, president of Massachusetts
Institute of Technology, the panel's report warned that unless the United States stepped up its missile programs, its
strategic superiority would be seriously threatened by the
Soviets by the early 1960s.[53]

The Army–Air Force feuding continued amid such warnings, and Eisenhower became increasingly concerned. Wilson tried unsuccessfully at Quantico, Virginia, in July 1956 to
get the Joint Chiefs of Staff to modify the Key West and
Newport agreements on roles and missions, which had
made no reference to missiles. Following the 1949 dictum of
Secretary of the Army Gordon Gray that each of the services should develop its own missile programs, such programs had grown like Topsy, with little coordination and
practically no limitations. Except for the fact that each of the
services had promising programs, Eisenhower would have
envisioned a super agency like the Manhattan project, for
missile development.

The Army inevitably was the one to suffer constraints.

Admiral Burke joined General Twining in isolating General Taylor's position on IRBMs, and Eisenhower and Secretary of Defense Wilson had come to the conclusion that in longer-range missiles the Army was intruding into Air Force and Navy fields. Moreover, they affirmed the position that troop lifts and tactical air support should remain Air Force missions.

The Army could begrudgingly accept restrictions about its aviation, but it had paralleled Air Force efforts and tasted success in developing missiles, and elimination from a heady competitive race was bitter. Wilson indicated that the Army, in its jurisdiction over tactical ballistic missiles, was to be limited to those with ranges not to exceed 200 miles. Although Generals Gavin and Medaris remained cool-headed, Colonel John C. Nickerson publicly asserted the superiority of the Army's ICBM, Jupiter, over the Air Force's Thor and charged Wilson with partisanship and favoritism in contractual matters. In his resulting court-martial Nickerson was suspended from rank for one year with forfeiture of $100 per month for fifteen months.

The 1955 Killian Report had been a spur to the missile program. Two years later, an even more compelling report emerged: the Gaither Report, named for H. Rowan Gaither, the chairman of the board of the Ford Foundation. Others on the blue-ribbon panel appointed in April 1957 included Lovett, John J. McCloy, then chairman of the board of the Chase Manhattan Bank, and Frank Stanton, president of CBS. The highly classified Gaither Report predicted that by late 1959 the Soviets would be capable of launching one hundred ICBMs against the United States.[54]

While the Eisenhower administration was aware of this threat and strenuously engaged in stepping up its missile program, the world was electrified on October 4, 1957, by the Soviet launching of the first man-made satellite, Sputnik (Russian for "traveling companion"). The 184-pound satellite caused, as Eisenhower expressed it, "a wave of apprehension throughout the Free World."[55] Criticisms against the administration were led by Democratic Senators Henry Jackson and Symington. Eisenhower responded to the partisan attack by pointing out that in 1947 and again in 1950

President Truman had impounded funds the Congress had appropriated for Air Force missile development. Defending Eisenhower's position, Wernher von Braun testified, "Our present dilemma is not due to the fact that we are not working hard enough now, but that we did not work hard enough during the first six to ten years after the war."[56]

Following Sputnik, both Vice President Richard M. Nixon and Senate Majority Leader Lyndon Baines Johnson urged public release of the Gaither Report (with classified matters deleted). Eisenhower, despite the pressures put upon him, refused to do so because, as he explained, "Throughout our history the President has withheld confidential advisory opinions."[57]

Eisenhower did go on radio and television to make two post-Sputnik addresses. In the first, on November 7, he announced the creation of the new post of Special Assistant to the President for Science and Technology. He emphasized the importance of a scientific adviser in the modern Presidency and proposed scientific committees for both NATO and SEATO. He also declared, "The world had not forgotten the Soviet military invasions of such countries as Finland and Poland, their support of the war in Korea, or their use of force in their ruthless suppression of Hungarian freedom."[58] Though recognizing that "no defensive system today can possibly be airtight in preventing all breakthrough of planes and weapons," Eisenhower assured his audience that an effective United States–Canadian defense shield (the North American Air Defense Command had been established in September 1957), as well as strong retaliatory nuclear forces, had been built.

Six days later, after identifying "the retaliatory nuclear power of our Strategic Air Command and our Navy" as "a principal deterrent to war," Eisenhower noted the importance of a dispersal program for the Strategic Air Command. Nevertheless, he warned against "any misguided attempt to eliminate conventional forces and rely solely upon retaliation. Such a course," he concluded, "would be completely self-defeating."

Pointing to military assistance agreements with forty-two nations, he observed that we could not personally maintain garrisons worldwide "to prevent the outflow of Communism," and he stressed the essential soundness of the joint security programs.

A significant aspect of Eisenhower's address was his emphasis on scientific education for the future of the nation's security: "When a Russian graduates from high school he has had five years of physics, four years of chemistry, one year of astronomy, five years of biology, ten years of mathematics through trigonometry and five years of a foreign language."[59] As a sequel to this address, the administration introduced its National Defense Education Bill, which established a massive student loan and grant program, a graduate fellowship program, and grants for public school instruction in science, mathematics, and languages. This legislation, which Eisenhower signed into law on September 2, spurred education at all levels, from elementary through postdoctoral. By 1975 some 40,000 persons had received PhD degrees with assistance from the National Defense Education Act.

On January 31, 1958, three and one-half months after Sputnik, the United States launched its first orbiting earth satellite, the Army's Explorer I, followed by the Navy's Vanguard on March 17, and Explorer III on March 26. A week later, Eisenhower requested the Congress to establish a National Aeronautics and Space Agency (NASA). All aeronautics and space activities, except those determined by the President as being associated with national defense, would be controlled by this civilian agency. On August 8 Dr. T. Keith Glennan, president of Case Institute in Cleveland, became the first administrator of the new agency.

In December 1958, NASA launched its first communications satellite, rebroadcasting Eisenhower's Christmas message from space. On April 9, 1959, the names of the first seven astronauts were announced. They began training for Project Mercury, which would put man into orbit and bring him safely back.

Sputnik and the Gaither Report advanced the reorganization of the Department of Defense, but they also hastened two other most important legislative enactments, the National Defense Education Act and the creation of NASA.

If the interservice rivalries had made principally clear the need for an overhauling of the defense establishment, so also had the need for more effective long-range planning and command execution been made obvious. In response to questioning by James Reston of the *New York Times*, Eisenhower, in a May 15, 1957, news conference, had deplored that each of the services sought "guided missiles of all kinds" and, more important, that "war plans are not clear enough in fixing responsibility."[60]

THE 1958 DEFENSE REORGANIZATION ACT. Five days after Sputnik, a dynamic new Secretary of Defense, Neil H. McElroy, on leave from the presidency of Proctor and Gamble, was sworn into office. His first and largest task, with Nelson Rockefeller, who had continued to serve since 1953 as chairman of the Advisory Committee on Government Reorganization, was a thoroughgoing reorganization of the Department of Defense. Serving with them were Radford, Bradley, Twining, Alfred Gruenther (who had just retired as NATO Commander), former Deputy Secretary of Defense William C. Foster, and Lovett.[61]

In his January 9, 1958, State of the Union Message Eisenhower described as the "imperative... first need... to assure ourselves that military organization facilitates rather than hinders the functions of the military establishment in maintaining the security of the nation...."[62] In the "revolutionary" technical advance he found challenges "reminiscent of those attending the advent of the airplane half a century ago." Many of these defied traditional identification to a particular branch of service; many had inspired "jurisdictional disputes" and "mistaken zeal" which, he asserted, "America wants stopped."

Eisenhower emphasized the importance of "strategic planning and control," which he believed had to be done "under unified direction." He also emphasized full coordination in the development, production, and use of new weaponry. And he underscored the importance of real rather than superficial "civilian authority" over the military. As a prerequisite, he urged not only "clear organization" but also

"decisive central direction" and "unstinted cooperation. . . ."[63]

With these principles in mind, Eisenhower, accompanied
by Staff Secretary General Andrew Goodpaster and Bryce
Harlow, on January 25 went to the Pentagon to meet with
McElroy, Deputy Defense Secretary Donald A. Quarles, the
Joint Chiefs, and members of the Advisory Committee. He
found civilians and military alike seeking to defend the
status quo. In other areas persuasive advisers could dissuade
Eisenhower, but with the military, where he felt most at
home, he would not be deterred from completely overhauling what he viewed as a "fragmented organization," which
by its very nature fostered "rivalries and divisive influences. . . ."

From a professional view, Eisenhower particularly desired
to make the Joint Chiefs of Staff more effective "as a corporate body." To achieve that end, he advised a better-
integrated Joint Staff and the abolition of the Joint Staff
committee system. "The Joint Chief system, as it now
exists," he declared, "is too complicated to work in warfare
when minutes will be as precious as months have been in the
past."[64] So that the vice chiefs might focus on their
functions, Eisenhower proposed legislative revisions upgrading their posts; he would also give the chairman of the
JCS the right to vote along with the other members.

Reacting to these principles, which would strengthen the
"central direction" of the Secretary of Defense and con-
versely seemed to threaten the prerogatives of the individual
services, the Chiefs and service secretaries found ready allies
on Capitol Hill even before Eisenhower brought in his specific proposals.[65] Senator Richard B. Russell of Georgia, who
viewed Eisenhower's initiative as a challenge to the prerogatives of the Congress, declared, ". . . I am intrigued with, but
not convinced by, the argument that the Congress ought to
resolve all its troubles by just delegating all its powers to the
executive branch. . . ."[66]

Carl Vinson went further in the House than his fellow
Georgian, Russell, in the Senate when he brought in a
"Reorganization Bill" even before Eisenhower revealed the

details of his own proposal. Vinson's specific target was the Secretary of Defense rather than the President. "It was never intended and is not now intended," he asserted, "that the office of the Secretary of Defense would become a fourth department within the Department of Defense, delving into operational details on a daily basis."[67]

Vinson proposed limiting the size of the staff of the Secretary of Defense while reasserting the role of the service secretaries. He wanted to reinstall the service secretaries as members of the National Security Council, thus restoring them to their position before the 1949 fall from grace. Eisenhower found Vinson's proposal "meaningless unless its sole purpose was to raise the 'prestige' of service Secretaries." This concerned him long afterward. In 1965 he concluded, "Even to this day I become alarmed by the many misconceptions about the National Security Council."[68]

Vinson sought to retain the chain of command through the service secretaries. Eisenhower considered this system "cumbersome and unreliable in time of peace and not usable in time of war." Although his motives were at the time misconstrued, he was seeking neither to eliminate nor to consolidate the service departments but rather to have them perform what he believed they should be doing: administrative, logistical, and training functions.[69] Eisenhower therefore proposed the elimination of the 1947 National Security Act's provision that the military departments be "separately administered," as well as the system set up in 1953 of having one of the services serve as the "executive agent" for a particular unified command. There would henceforth be a direct command channel from the Secretary of Defense through the Joint Chiefs of Staff, as an operational command post, to the unified (which would include joint and specified) commands. By Eisenhower's proposal the Joint Chiefs would serve as a unit in assisting the Secretary of Defense in controlling all of these new unified commands.

Vinson charged that this part of Eisenhower's proposal smacked of a "Prussian style general staff."[70] Many members of the Congress also opposed placing legislative liaison and public affairs funds under the control of the Secretary of Defense rather than the military departments. Still others charged favoritism toward the Air Force in the office of the Secretary of Defense. Eisenhower was usually highly persuasive, but in a breakfast meeting on March 28 with Vinson and other leaders of the House Armed Services Committee, he found them adamant against his proposals. In particular they were insistent on keeping the service secretaries in the chain of command.

It was clear that Eisenhower, in the field of his own greatest professional competence, had a severe battle on his hands. He must make his special message to the Congress most persuasive, which he did on April 3. He must in this instance also appeal over the heads of the Congress for public support; with the effective coordination of James Hagerty, he did so in a series of press conferences and in an address on April 17 to the American Society of Newspaper Editors.

In his message to the Congress, Eisenhower began with the proposition that "separate ground, sea and air warfare is gone forever," and that "strategic and tactical planning must be completely unified...."[71] He then proceeded with a masterful historical analysis of the development of the defense establishment: in the 1947 reorganization, "lessons were lost, tradition won. The three service departments were but loosely joined." Tracing the 1949 and 1953 amendments, he noted that "each such step... has prompted opponents to predict dire results." He warned that "we must free ourselves of emotional attachment to revise systems of an era that is no more." Then he cogently set forth his organizational structure, including "truly unified commands" which would "be established at my direction."

For "military research," Eisenhower proposed a significant new post: a Director of Defense Research and Engineering, replacing the Assistant Secretary of Defense for Research and Engineering, would be senior to the Assistant Secretaries of Defense and would "help stop the service rivalries."

Eisenhower concluded with a proposal to subordinate the authority of the service secretaries over budget and procurement matters to that of the Secretary of Defense. The end product of all these changes, he believed, would be better planning and decision making, greater effectiveness in science and technology, and elimination of "organizational defects which have encouraged harmful service rivalries."[72]

Secretary of the Navy Thomas Gates and Admiral Arleigh Burke had warned the President about the possible "emotionalism" his proposals would cause "among officers at lower levels in the Navy."[73] To head off any possible repetition of the admirals' revolt, or of the Nickerson incident, Eisenhower, in his April 16 news conference, gave the assurance: "If a man has a duty to give his convictions, he should do so freely, and there is certainly no thought ever, of reprisal of any kind."[74] The following day, in an address to the American Society of Newspaper Editors and the International Press Institute, Eisenhower emphasized "American strength . . . " as "inseparable from the waging of peace," a theme he hoped would characterize his years in the Presidency.

Eisenhower and his press secretary, Jim Hagerty, came to the editors amid a well-organized national propaganda effort against the defense reorganization. As in 1947 and 1949, it was particularly led by Navy advocates. Eisenhower recalled, without specifically identifying the Navy League by name, that "one of the service (civilian) 'Leagues' . . . [was] stirring up so much trouble that some of my friends in the organization threatened to resign."[75] Focusing on these critics, he avowed, "these sources often resist military change far more vigorously than the services themselves."[76]

Placing all his prestige on the line to secure support for his Defense Reorganization Bill, Eisenhower, in addressing the editors, recounted the progress of five years:

> In Korea and Vietnam, the wars are ended. In Formosa—Guatemala—Iran—the Communist threats are blocked. In Trieste, the age-old struggle is resolved. Austria is liberated, the Red Army withdrawn. Germany—at least West Germany—is once again sovereign and today reinforces European unity. "Atoms for peace," so meaningful to mankind, is at last under way. The stature of the United Nations is appreciably raised; free world nations are more united in collective defense. And slowly but significantly the Iron Curtain has started to lift. Behind it the personal security and intellectual freedom of oppressed peoples gradually increase. . . .

Yet he recognized the continued threats:

> Communist imperialism persists in striving to master the world. Germany remains divided. Eastern European nations remain enslaved. Turmoil and bitterness plague North Indonesia, the Middle East, and parts of North Africa. France, our historic ally, has major difficulties. New weapons of fantastic power appall the world. Humanity now threatens its own existence. Dependable disarmament remains but a hope. . . .[77]

Eisenhower reminded the editors, and through them the American people, of the lessons he and others had learned in World War II and the postwar period regarding both national security policy and organization, concluding with the central focus, "our strategic plan," whose one fundamental prerequisite for success was unity. He found "the sum total of unification" which "is lacking in our defenses today" to be the proposition "that the directing head, the Secretary of Defense–Joint Chiefs of Staff mechanism, has sufficient authority over supporting activities to assure execution of the basic plans."

This then was at the heart of the Eisenhower reorganization proposal: (1) strengthening the role of "the top strategic planners," the Joint Chiefs of Staff; (2) clearing the lines of military command; (3) establishing unified commands; (4) providing centralized research and development and integrating new weapons; (5) defining the authority of the Secretary of Defense, particularly regarding appropriations, without "depriving Congress of the power of the purse."

Full well aware of the entrenched opposition of the Congress, Eisenhower emphasized that his conclusions were based upon "all the years since 1911 when I entered military service. . . ." He gave assurance, which he could not have three months before, "that the convictions of senior civil and military leaders in all parts of the Defense Department closely parallel my own." He assured the American people, through the editors, that, contrary to the warnings of Congressional opposition voices, "each service will remain intact" and there would be no "Prussian general staff," no "czar" Secretary of Defense, no usurping of Congressional authority. Instead there would be "clear-cut civilian responsibility, unified strategic planning and direction, and completely unified combat commands." The further dividends, he asserted, would "be a stop to unworthy and sometimes costly bickering . . . a stop to inefficiency and needless duplications. . . ."

Skillfully Eisenhower concluded on his twin themes: "safety and solvency." On this foundation, with the media united behind him, he put the matter squarely before the Congress. "The Congress willing," he concluded, "we shall have maximum strength, with minimum cost, in our national defense."[78]

Not content to rest his case only with the media, Eisenhower, with Hagerty's and Harlow's encouragement, took what was for him another unprecedented step: he wrote to hundreds of friends throughout the nation, asking them to convey their views to their friends as well as to the Congress. The nation became flooded with such letters. One business leader alone wrote 20,000 support letters. Cries of "going over the heads of Congress" went up. Eisenhower found this "most welcome," since it indicated he was getting results. He found two special allies in Missouri: Clarence Cannon, chairman of the House Appropriations Committee, and former President Truman. He also found one special ally in Massachusetts: Representative John McCormack.[79]

Nonetheless, on May 22 the House Armed Services Committee presented a bill recommending continuation of the service secretaries in the chain of command. To Eisenhower's consternation, with the service secretaries as the cause célèbre and the more basic issues lost sight of, the bill was rammed through the House on June 11. But by that point his own campaign for support was picking up adherents, and he found members of the Senate more amenable to his position and more reasoned in their criticisms. For example, in the Senate hearings, Senator Henry Jackson, who in his five years in the Senate had already established special expertise in national security affairs, challenged the necessity to create the post of Director of Defense Research and Engineering to replace the Assistant Secretary for Research and Development. The more general opposition was to the downgrading of the service secretaries, what Secretary

McElroy in the House Committee on Armed Services Hearings termed "sand in the gear box,"[80] and to the general transfer of their authority and lines of communication to the office of the Secretary of Defense. This McElroy justified in terms of placing "authority... [at] the levels where most of the decisions must be made." Although critics countered that the Secretary of Defense could not perform all the functions already assigned, the testimony in favor of his enlarged functions and of clarifying his authority over the military departments carried the day.[81]

Basically, the final version of the bill from the Senate and House conferees emerged to Eisenhower's satisfaction with two exceptions. In what he termed "legalized insubordination," the service secretaries and the military chiefs were given the right to bypass the Secretary of Defense in going directly to the Congress with "any recommendations relating to the Department of Defense that they might deem proper." Eisenhower accepted this assertiveness philosophically, citing the view of an earlier soldier-President, Ulysses S. Grant, "I cannot make the Comptroller General change his mind, but I can get a new Comptroller General." His other objection, though he deemed it less important, was that the Congress was given sixty days in which to veto the transfer, abolition, merger, or reassignments of a "major combatant function." This would be accomplished by the passage of a disapproving resolution in either house. Further, it gave any member of the Joint Chiefs the right to define "any such major function." Despite this provision, the Secretary of Defense had the authority to assign both the development and the operational use of any new weapons system to any military department, and the President during an emergency could transfer a major combatant function without awaiting Congressional approval.[82]

In brief, the word "separate" had been retained to head off any possible unification of the services, a check or veto had been placed on altering service roles and missions, and direct access of the service secretaries and the chiefs to the Congress had been retained. But in their concern for the preservation of the separate services and their secretaries and Chiefs, Congressional defenders of the status quo had in essence won an engagement and lost the war. The locus of power in the Department had clearly and finally been shifted to the Secretary of Defense. Subject to the foregoing technical limitations, the Secretary of Defense clearly had achieved the power to abolish, consolidate, reassign, and transfer functions for the purpose of increased effectiveness. Not only could he now assign combat forces to a unified or specified command, but he could also consolidate and assign service and support activities that were common to more than one service.[83]

The Joint Staff, with their new service role for the Joint Chiefs in unified commands, was authorized an increase in size from 210 to 400; moreover, the bill, according to Eisenhower's desires, made possible the replacement of the Joint Staff committees with a unified staff system developed around seven directorates. The bill gave the chairman of the Joint Chiefs the responsibility for selecting the staff director. They in essence not only continued their role as principal military advisers but also became the heads of a national military command post. The bill eliminated the word "command" from the statutory duties of the Chiefs. In turn, they were relieved from the day-to-day operations of their respective services by the upgrading of the Vice Chiefs.

More significantly, the bill gave the President, acting through the Secretary of Defense, the authority to establish and control "unified or specified combatant commands for . . . military missions," and to determine the forces which the Army, the Navy, and the Air Force would assign to these commands; those units would be under the control of the Joint Chiefs of Staff through the commands of the unified and specified forces. (Initially there were eight of these, two unified and six specified: Alaskan Command, Atlantic Command, Caribbean Command, Continental Air Defense Command, Eastern Atlantic and Mediterranean Command, European Command, Pacific Command, and Strategic Air Command.)

After all the controversy, then, the service secretaries were never again seriously considered for membership on the National Security Council. The 1949 loss was irretrievable; whereas the secretaries had formerly been responsible for

ERRATUM

page 224, ninth line from bottom should read:
six unified and two specified

the "conduct" of military operations, they were now specifically eliminated from the lines of command. Their functions became, "under the direction, authority, and control of the Secretary of Defense," the "organization, training, and equipment" of the forces in their departments. The use made of these forces became completely beyond their discretion (being determined by the President, to the Secretary of Defense, through the Joint Chiefs of Staff).

The bill also established the post of Director of Defense Research and Engineering, making him in essence, after the Secretary and the Deputy Secretary, the third most powerful member of the department, in recognition of the imperative role of science and technology in national security.

On August 6, 1958, President Eisenhower signed the Defense Reorganization Bill into law. Coming thirteen years after the end of World War II, eleven years after the halfway Defense Establishment of the 1947 National Security Act, it reflected the accumulated experience of many, but principally of President Eisenhower himself and his tenacity of purpose in seeing it through. As a sequel, nearly two hundred of the three hundred Joint Department of Defense committees were abolished.[84]

Since intelligence communications and functions were still being performed by the three military departments, the Defense Communications Agency was added in the spring of 1960 and the Defense Intelligence Agency and Defense Supply Agency were added in the fall of 1961; they were natural outgrowths of more centralized authority. Moreover, since not all combat-ready forces were under the unified and specified commands, the United States Strike Command was created in October 1961; as a new unified command, it completed the transfer of all combat-ready forces not already assigned. Thus, today the Secretary of Defense can instantly communicate directly with the unified and specified commands throughout the world through the Pentagon's National Military Command Center.

In the 1947 concept, the office of the Secretary of Defense was engaged only in policy formulation, but by the 1958 legislation it could and did become both a key national security policy formulator and an effective centralized operating agency. No longer, as had been the case after the 1953 amendment, was power diffused and hard to determine: it lay clearly with the Secretary—a far cry from the role the first incumbent, Forrestal, had initially accepted.

In bringing these organizational and operational functions to fruition, Eisenhower characteristically gave full credit to his staff and to McElroy, who served as Secretary of Defense until December 1959 and was succeeded by Navy Secretary Thomas Gates. It was to remain for Gates's successor, Robert S. McNamara, to bring this authority to fullest fruition during the Kennedy administration. Radford had been succeeded by Nathan F. Twining as chairman of the Joint Chiefs of Staff in August 1957. He effectively implemented the new JCS roles and was succeeded two years later (for reasons of health) by Lyman L. Lemnitzer.

The Act of 1958 stands as the hallmark of today's national defense organization. It was largely a personal accomplishment of President Eisenhower, both in its authorship and in its enactment. There were those thereafter who would view the individual armed services as medieval trappings of another age.[85] Eisenhower was not among them. He personally cherished their finest traditions, and he envisioned a larger purpose for them. As he expressed it in the peroration of his remarks in support of the 1958 legislation, their "purpose is peace—a just peace—and the advancement of human well-being at home and throughout the world." He exhorted his fellow Americans to "hold fast in our struggle for lasting peace" and concluded on the hopeful note that "the strength that endures rests with those who live in freedon."[86]

IX
****

THE FINAL EISENHOWER YEARS

> Concessions to despotism lead inevitably to a "point of no return...."
>
> JOHN FOSTER DULLES

Organizing the Presidency

The last two years of Eisenhower's second administration were increasingly characterized by his own personal, vigorous leadership. With the possible exception of Secretary of State Dulles, Assistant to the President Sherman Adams, the former governor of New Hampshire, exercised the greatest influence over the first Eisenhower administration and the first two years of the second. Not even Wilson's Colonel House or Roosevelt's Harry Hopkins had exercised such authority as this chief of the White House staff.

Any person who exercises great authority is bound to make enemies. A relatively small series of incidents, the acceptance of gifts from a Boston manufacturer, led to Adams's downfall. Although the Democratic-controlled House Committee on Legislative Oversight found Adams guiltless of any wrongdoing (a view shared by Eisenhower), the pre-1958 election fervor over his having accepted such gifts as a vicuña overcoat from Bernard Goldfine had led to Adams's resignation that fall.

John Foster Dulles was by then critically ill. He resigned on April 15, 1959, and died six weeks later. These two resignations coincided with Eisenhower's triumph over his own severe illnesses, including his 1955 heart attack, his 1956 intes-

tinal operation, and his 1957 "slight cerebral stroke."
Eisenhower's self-confidence as a leader increased. Dulles's
successor, Christian Herter, and Adams's, Major General
Wilton B. Persons, able team members, did not try to assume
the leadership roles of their predecessors, nor were they invited to.

Nelson Rockefeller, having completed his important advisory role with the 1958 Defense Reorganization Act, returned
to New York State, where he was elected governor in the fall
of 1958 in the only notable Republican victory. Since he had
served as a member of the Advisory Committee on Government Organization, his counsel was sought by the Congress
on reorganizing the Presidency itself. Testifying before the
Senate Committee on Government Operations in 1960, Rockefeller asserted that "few realize the tremendous load the
President carries. . . ." His solution included a "First Secretary of the Government," who would act "at the prime
ministerial level . . . in the area of national security and foreign affairs," and an "Executive Assistant to the President,"
who would head the "Office of Executive Management."[1]
But Eisenhower and the Congress did not accept the prime
ministerial concept for foreign policy and national security
affairs. Indeed, in his last two years in office, Eisenhower
had become his own prime minister.

Dr. Milton Eisenhower was perhaps his brother's closest
personal adviser throughout both administrations. Serving
as president of Kansas State University from 1945 to 1950,
then as president of Pennsylvania State University until
1956, and thereafter as president of Johns Hopkins University, he was one of the nation's most respected educators.
Moreover, he had performed meritorious service with every
President commencing with Coolidge (and was to do so with
subsequent Presidents). Like Rockefeller, Milton Eisenhower
envisioned two supra-Cabinet posts; the one, Executive Vice
President for International Affairs, paralleled Rockefeller's
"First Secretary of the Government."[2]

Summing up his own views based upon a lifetime of public service, Milton Eisenhower concluded on March 11, 1975:
"Changes are needed, especially time-consuming trivia
should be removed from the President's desk, and he very

much needs at least two supra-cabinet positions to help him with his larger duties, a change which will, in my judgment, restore the dignity and value of the department heads who constitute the Cabinet."[3]

Former President Hoover suggested the post of Administrative Vice President to relieve the President of a myriad of details. Eisenhower liked the concept but not the title. He favored instead a "Secretary for Business Management." Like Milton and Rockefeller, he came to favor an overall coordinator for foreign affairs, which Eisenhower termed "Secretary for International Coordination." At first Dulles had been taken aback by the concept, but he came to support it, recognizing the President's persuasive argument that "a modern Secretary of State must be out of the country on vital missions much of the time."[4] No Secretary of State before Dulles had ever traveled abroad so much, and none did subsequently until Kissinger.

The need for these two supra-Cabinet posts seemed as apparent to Eisenhower as it did to his brother and many other students of governmental organization. A master of organization, Eisenhower nonetheless believed "that organization and procedures, save where they are rigidly fixed by law, should conform to each President's experience, desires, and methods of work."[5] Accordingly, since he was about to leave office, Eisenhower did not press for these changes.

Strategic Policy: The Eisenhower Doctrine in Operation

Henry Kissinger, who had worked with Rockefeller in the defense reorganization proposals, was back at Harvard as associate director of the Center for International Affairs, and, like Rockefeller in the area of organization, was agreeable to offer counsel in the area of strategic doctrine. In the fall of 1958 he was warning of the risks in President Eisenhower's one-year suspension of nuclear weapons tests and also in his invitation to the Soviet Union to negotiate a permanent ban on testing nuclear weapons. Kissinger, noting the

Soviets' preponderance of conventional weapons, declared that "nothing now stands in the way of Soviet domination of Eurasia save the Soviet reluctance to pay the price of a nuclear war."[6] Eisenhower was not nearly as concerned as the young professor, nor was he impressed with the nation's recent advocacy of the virtues of a doctrine of limited warfare.

By the time of the Kennedy Presidency, limited warfare was in vogue and Kissinger was its qualified advocate. He did not, in 1961, find it "a substitute for constructive policy," but he did believe it offered "the possibility—not the certainty of avoiding catastrophe."[7] Eisenhower never warmed up to this concept. "In my opinion," he wrote, "this kind of solution was the product of timidity—a solution that began by seeing danger behind every tree or bush."[8]

Eisenhower's increasing personal assertiveness was demonstrated in two significant strategic successes in 1958: the landing in Lebanon and the defense of the Republic of China's offshore islands of Quemoy and Matsu.

Both actions may be viewed as affirmations of the Eisenhower Doctrine of helping nations preserve their political and territorial integrity from Communist encroachment. On January 5, 1957, Eisenhower had asked the Congress for authority to call upon American armed forces "to secure and protect the territorial integrity and political independence of such nations requesting such aid against armed aggression from any nation controlled by International Communism." In particular, Eisenhower recognized the strategic importance of the oil-rich Middle East, which he viewed as the "bridge of three continents."

President Camille Chamoun of Lebanon asked for such assistance in the summer of 1958 when Communist-inspired rebels sought to overthrow his government. Eisenhower immediately gave a bipartisan briefing to twenty-two Congressional leaders. He found Senator William Fulbright "most skeptical of all" that the revolution was Communist-inspired.[9] Eisenhower exhibited considerable skill in personally directing not only the Sixth Fleet operations and Marine landings but also the increased alert of the Strategic Air Command. As he put it, "I felt this knowledge would be desirable, showing readiness and determination. . . ."[10] Since the oil fields of Kuwait were also threatened, he instructed JCS Chairman Twining "to be prepared to employ, subject to my personal approval, whatever means become necessary to prevent unfriendly forces from moving into" that area.[11] During this tense period he sought and received the strong support of both living former Presidents, Hoover and Truman. They recognized with him the high stakes involved and the possibilities of a worldwide conflagration resulting from the unstable Middle East and viewed with concern the posture of Nikita S. Khrushchev, who had succeeded Bulganin as the Soviet Premier on March 27, 1958.

When the government of King Hussein in Jordan was threatened as Lebanon had been, Eisenhower invited British aerial landings, after a 2:30 A.M. telephone conversation between Foster Dulles and Israel's Prime Minister, Ben-Gurion, who agreed to British overflights.

Khrushchev railed and ranted at these joint British-American actions. Eisenhower, however, ignored Khrushchev's proposal for a joint USSR, U.S., British, French, and Indian conference to settle the Middle East differences. Instead, in October, only after order had been restored in Lebanon and King Hussein's government had been saved in Jordan, Eisenhower ordered U.S. troop withdrawals and went before the UN General Assembly to justify the actions he had taken.

In retrospect he observed that the Korean experience and these Middle East Communist probes had convinced him that "if 'small wars' were to break out in several places in the world simultaneously, then we would not fight on the enemy's terms and be limited to his choice of weapons. We would," he concluded, "hold the Kremlin—or Peking responsible for their actions and would act accordingly." Eisenhower emphasized that "these facts were not secret; they were well advertised. The Communists had come to be aware of our attitude and there was reason to think that they respected it."[12]

Peking's bombardment of the offshore islands of Quemoy and Matsu was simultaneous with the Soviet Middle Eastern pressures. Eisenhower recognized the joint Moscow-Peking orchestration, but would not be dissuaded. Hence, while the Sixth Fleet operated in the Mediterranean in support of Lebanon, the Seventh Fleet was resupplying Quemoy and Matsu, where 100,000, or one-third, of Chiang's ground forces were pinned down by heavy Communist bombardment. The resupply operation began on September 7. Peking announced on October 5 that it would cease bombardment if the U.S. would cease its escort operations. Eisenhower observed, "The fire stopped and United States vessels went back to normal patrolling of the Strait, ready to resume convoying if necessary."[13] Later the Communists announced they would bombard only on odd days if the U.S. would limit its resupplying to even days. This inspired Ike to refer to the "Gilbert and Sullivan war."[14]

National Security and the Economy

Eisenhower had always insisted that a healthy economy was fundamental to national security. He was concerned with trade imbalances, a phenomenon in the American experience which first appeared in 1957 and has continued in most years to the present. Trade imbalances resulted in part from the flow of capital abroad for investment purposes, from large expenditures abroad by American tourists, and, to a small extent, from foreign aid (small because most foreign aid was in goods, not money). Eisenhower also was concerned with the outflow of dollars resulting from the military establishment abroad. A large part of the monetary outflow was directly attributable to the maintenance of military personnel overseas as well as their dependents. This principally involved NATO, whose 14,000 civilian employees and 310,000 military personnel, plus 235,000 wives and children, were costing $14 billion (increased to $17 billion by 1973) in Europe. Eisenhower realized the necessity for the maintenance of these troops. The real problem was that the dollars they received in Europe were largely spent in Europe.

With only partial success he had been insisting that our allies should carry a fuller share of the costs, especially in

NATO, which he considered our most important alliance. By 1960 only West Germany, among the NATO allies, was filling monetary and troop quotas. Eisenhower was unalterably opposed to the retaliatory tactics of the troop withdrawals which some Congressmen were urging. The psychological effect would be deleterious worldwide; it would signal to friend and foe a weakening of our posture. After consulting the NSC and the NATO commander, what he did, by executive order, was to reduce foreign military purchases and bring the dependents home. He reasoned that this would not only cut the outflow of dollars but would focus the attention of military personnel on their primary job. Why should military personnel have their families in Europe when, for example, they could not in Korea or Southeast Asia? However, one of President Kennedy's first acts was to be the revocation of the Eisenhower order to call dependents home.

As a member of the Senate Foreign Relations Committee, John F. Kennedy had joined the committee's chairman, Fulbright, and other members, including Hubert Humphrey, in advocating more economic and social assistance for smaller and so-called Third World countries, by comparison with military aid for United States allies.[15] Eisenhower was dubious about the special privileges being sought in the community of nations for Third World developing nations. He wanted to help them develop a healthy system of private capitalism, but he resisted paying for their socialism. As far as sums spent in our own defense budget, he agreed that "we would like to see these outlays shifted to the economic benefit of our own Nation and our friends abroad striving for economic progress." But in view of Communist aggression and Communist force levels,he found it "rudimentary good sense for the peoples of the free nations to create and maintain deterrent military strength." He countered to Fulbright, Humphrey, and Kennedy that "it is not in our nature to wish to spend our substance on weapons" and that the $1.6 billion he was seeking in 1960 for military assistance to our allies "will buy more security than far greater expenditures for our own forces."[16] As was the experience with Truman and every President since, Eisenhower was under pressure by the Congress to reduce these military assistance funds. However, his personal prestige made his defense more successful than was the case of other Presidents.

He was equally effective in dealing with the economy at home. Working closely with his chief economic advisers, Arthur F. Burns, Gabriel Hauge, and Raymond J. Saulnier, he insisted on firm fiscal restraint. During the 1958 business downturn, he successfully resisted Congressional proposals for tax reductions and rebates. The following year, when stoppage of Polaris missile construction was threatened, his concern for the national security caused him to invoke the Taft-Hartley Act in the nationwide steel strike. His negotiators, Labor Secretary James P. Mitchell and Vice President Nixon, secured a noninflationary settlement.

By the end of his second administration economic upturn had resumed. As the President wrote in his final economic report, the basis for future growth had been laid by "the enlargement and improvement of our productive capacity and in policies that have brought the forces of inflation under control."[17] That record, according to Dr. Saulnier, might have "continued indefinitely if inflationary distortions had not been allowed to develop in 1964–65."[18]

Latin American and Far Eastern Policies

During his last two years of office, Eisenhower determined to enlist his personal prestige and respect worldwide in the cause of peace. Hence, he embarked upon unprecedented travel abroad for a peacetime President. In December 1959 Eisenhower made an eleven-nation tour and was warmly received in Italy, Turkey, Pakistan, Afghanistan, India, Iran, Greece, Tunisia, France, Spain, and Morocco.

But there were other areas he was determined to visit before leaving office, places where the greeting might not be so cordial. These included Latin America, the Far East, and ultimately the Soviet Union.

As in so many areas, Ike received sound counsel on Latin American affairs from brother Milton, who, while continuing to serve as president of Pennsylvania State University, had served additionally since 1953 as special ambassador and the President's personal representative on Latin American affairs. Relations with Latin America did not ostensibly improve until near the end of the second Eisenhower administration. A Communist-controlled government in Guatemala had been ousted with American aid in 1954, but in Cuba by 1959 Fidel Castro had taken over and, as Vice President Nixon had suspected, with Communist support.

The good-will tour of Vice President and Mrs. Nixon to Latin America in 1958 had revealed great hostility to "Yankee imperialism." Latin Americans did admire the Nixons for their personal courage, especially when their lives were threatened by an angry mob in Venezuela.

At this point, with Milton's counsel, Eisenhower determined to take several constructive steps regarding Latin American relations. First, he secured Congressional approval to expand the lending authority of the Export-Import Bank, which did about half its business with Latin America. Then he championed the Inter-American Development Bank, established in 1959 in a twenty-one-nation agreement. Although the bank had long been sought by the Latin American nations, the United States had opposed such a move until the Eisenhower period.

Likewise contrary to past policy, Eisenhower launched a regional economic association concept—a common market—for Latin America. A third precedent-shattering move involved commodity stabilization agreements to prevent catastrophic price swings in coffee and other basic commodities.[19]

Despite these economic advances, antagonism to so-called Yankee imperialism persisted. Ike then decided in early 1960 to embark on his own good-will mission. On Washington's birthday he began a 15,000-mile journey which took him to Puerto Rico, Brazil, Argentina, Chile, and Uraguay. The Eisenhower grin was magical to the Latins screaming "Viva EEKE," though he found a bit disconcerting one sign proclaiming: "We like Ike; we like Fidel too."[20]

This journey was followed by the historic Act of Bogotá. Enacted September 13, 1960, by the Organization of American States (Cuba dissenting), it launched a massive program for inter-American cooperative social reform programs. Eisenhower's successor, John F. Kennedy, called the program "Alliance for Progress," and thus it is often forgotten that its basic legislation was enacted five months before the end of Eisenhower's second administration. As Kennedy's Secretary of State, Dean Rusk, wrote many years later, Milton Eisenhower had organized the program.[21]

Completion of Alliances

As the first Supreme Allied Commander, Eisenhower had in 1950–1952 participated in the organization of NATO; then in 1954, as President, he had strengthened that alliance by leading efforts to bring West Germany into it; the same year, in association with Churchill, Eisenhower had led in the formation of SEATO as a second major regional alliance system. The Baghdad Pact (1955) had been followed four years later by the formation of a third major regional alliance, the Central Treaty Organization (Iran, Pakistan, Turkey, and United Kingdom), which the United States cordially supported. Moreover, each of the three regional members, Iran, Pakistan, and Turkey, concluded bilateral alliances with the United States. Earlier bilateral arrangements had been made with both South Korea and Taiwan. Thus, with one major exception, before the end of the first Eisenhower administration there were United States alliances with every area facing on the Sino-Soviet land mass.

That one exception was Japan. With American aid, Japan had emerged from the ashes of defeat, at the end of World War II, as the third-largest industrial power a decade later. In December 1960, Japanese Prime Minister Nobusuke Kishi, whom Eisenhower described as "a brave opponent of Communism," joined Eisenhower in signing a United States–Japan mutual defense pact.[22] To sign a treaty was one thing; to get it ratified by the Japanese House of Representatives and invite Eisenhower to Japan was another. Kishi was determined to acquire ratification before Eisenhower's scheduled June 19 arrival. The Communists effectively rallied pacifists, socialists, and neutralists, especially among the students and labor unions. Street riots accompanied sitdown tactics in the House.

It was clear that the Communists' high stakes were Germany and Japan.[23] Kishi had to suggest Eisenhower's "postponement" of his journey, but the treaty was ratified. President Ford, fifteen years later, was to describe it as "the cornerstone of stability in the vast reaches of Asia and the Pacific."[24]

In June 1960, Eisenhower flew to the Philippines, Taiwan, Okinawa, and Korea. It was his first return to the Philippines since his service there as a major and lieutenant colonel on MacArthur's staff a quarter-century before. And it was his first journey to Korea since his mission to help end the war there in the weeks before his first inaugural. He received a warm homecoming in Taiwan, whose independence he had championed, and in Okinawa, where his popularity with American servicemen remained as high as ever.

Soviet Relations

While Eisenhower, from the beginning of his first administration, recognized the Soviets as the principal threat to world peace, he was always prepared for rapprochement.

THE GENEVA SUMMIT. There had been a glimmer of hope in 1953 with the death of Stalin and the end of the Korean War. Churchill had then proposed a summit conference, but Eden, his Foreign Minister, had opposed it. Eisenhower looked for some specific evidence of a thaw before going to the summit. It came early in 1955 with the Soviet acceptance of the Austrian peace treaty. Although Austria had to pay the Soviets a large indemnity and refrain from joining any alliances, the treaty marked a Soviet reversal in central Europe, as Austria gained its freedom and independence.[25]

In the spring of 1955 Churchill stepped down for the last time as Prime Minister. Eden, who replaced him, withdrew his opposition to a summit. Edgar Fauré, the French Prime Minister, likewise favored it. So in the summer of 1955

Eisenhower had agreed to his first Presidential summit meeting with the Soviets to convene in Geneva, Switzerland, in July with the Soviet, French, and British heads of state and foreign ministers.

N. A. Bulganin headed the Soviet delegation. Eisenhower's press secretary, Jim Hagerty, who accompanied Eisenhower and Dulles to Geneva, wrote later that "the Russians had a great deal of respect" for Eisenhower and that at Geneva there was "not necessarily agreement, but a mutual respect."[26] Certainly the Soviet military respected the former World War II and NATO Supreme Allied Commander. At Geneva Eisenhower advanced his "Open Skies" proposal for mutual aerial inspection. But the euphoria of the summit was diminished in the subsequent foreign ministers' conference that fall, where the Soviets were intransigent on both the German question and disarmament. Moreover, "Open Skies" never found Soviet acceptability despite its enthusiastic adoption by the General Assembly of the United Nations. Tangible results of the "Spirit of Geneva" did include, however, the inauguration of certain scientific, commercial, and cultural exchanges.[27]

ATOMS FOR PEACE.   Another advance stemmed from Eisenhower's 1953 "atoms for peace" proposal, which recommended turning over to a United Nations agency fissionable material that would be used "to serve the needs rather than the fears of mankind." The Soviets first rejected the proposal, but after Geneva they agreed to join the International Atomic Energy Agency. Ironically, in the United States twenty years later concern was being expressed that nations, ranging from Israel to Korea, might be utilizing atomic energy for other than peaceful purposes. Such critics, including many who espoused Third World development, traced "the wrong turning" to the 1953 liberal policy on sharing nuclear energy. On balance, however, clearly the Eisenhower policy of "atoms for peace," one of which he was most proud, was a boon for mankind.

THE MIDDLE EAST.   When Stalin died, the Soviets began efforts to penetrate the Middle East, and after 1955, Egypt became a client state for arms. This action contributed to the United States' withdrawal the following year from the Aswan Dam project. Eisenhower, the master politician, considered John Foster Dulles's handling of the matter "abrupt," but he did accept Dulles's contention that Egypt had provoked response by "its flirtations with the Soviet Union. . . ."[28] Following this United States action, Nasser nationalized the Suez Canal, which had been operated by a largely British-owned Canal Company. Eisenhower repeatedly sought to dissuade Eden from retaliatory action "contemplating the use of military force . . . ,"[29] and assured Egypt that "the United States remains deeply interested in the welfare of the Egyptian people and the development of the Nile."[30]

The cease-fire Eisenhower secured in the Israeli-British-French confrontation with Egypt that fall was followed by the enunciation of the Eisenhower Doctrine early in 1957 and its application in Lebanon the following year. Britain conducted a simultaneous operation in Jordan—a clear indication, despite the 1956 experience, of continuing British presence in association with the United States. Moreover, Eisenhower continued to strengthen the Sixth Fleet in the Mediterranean and regional alliance arrangements. Indications of complete United States dominance in the Middle East at the end of the Eisenhower period were the development of SAC bases in Saudi Arabia, Libya, and Morocco and the installation in Turkey of Jupiter ballistic missiles targeted on the Soviet Union.[31] In brief, Soviet Middle Eastern designs had been checkmated despite their increased presence and pressures.

GERMANY. Although problems in the Middle East loomed large, the Berlin and German questions continued to overshadow them. As a military commander in World War II, Eisenhower was aware of the political decisions for the occupation zones in Germany, and he wrote in his wartime memoirs: "This future division of Germany did not influence our military plans for the final conquest of the country." Berlin would be in the Russian zone by political agreement; which force got there first was irrelevant.[32]

As President, Eisenhower insisted that these political decisions for occupation zones, which made Berlin an isolated island in East Germany, had been temporary wartime provisions. But, as with the temporary demarcation of Korea at the 38th parallel, the Soviets seized such proposals to their own advantage. Understandably, Eisenhower asked later, "How did we ever accept a situation in which our only feasible response to an attack on a thirteen thousand man garrison surrouded by numerous Communist divisions would likely mean the initiation of World War III?"[33]

KHRUSHCHEV AND THE ABORTED SUMMIT. Even at Geneva, three years before Khrushchev supplanted Bulganin, Hagerty "assumed Khrushchev was the real head."[34] He soon proved both a ruthless antagonist and a flamboyant salesman. Launching a war of nerves, on November 10, 1958, Khrushchev announced his intention to sign a "peace treaty" with East Germany. After May 1959 the three Western powers in Berlin would have to negotiate their status with a government none of them recognized. But the day for turning over access (May 27) came and went without incident. The four foreign ministers concerned were at the time all en route to Dulles's funeral. Firmness and the memories of the success in combating the 1948 blockade had prevailed.

While standing firm on Berlin, Eisenhower emphasized his willingness to go anywhere to discuss means of relaxing tensions. He liked former President Hoover's suggestion: the new Premier should be told that, if he desired, he could be remembered in history as the great peacemaker. In 1959, Khrushchev was invited to visit the United States. The actual invitation was extended by Vice President Nixon, with whom Khrushchev had engaged in a heated televised debate in an American kitchen at a Moscow trade fair in July 1959. The joint announcement of August 4, 1959, in the Soviet Union and the United States indicated the purpose "to be the better understanding between the U.S.A. and the USSR, and promote the cause of peace."[35]

During his visit, Khrushchev boasted of Soviet space and atomic energy feats as "a victory for the entire socialist camp," adding with an attempt at humor that "the Soviet emblem, as an old resident of the moon, will welcome your emblem."[36] In a wide-ranging journey that included an Iowa farm, Khrushchev offered advice to many. He found the Eisenhower farm in Gettysburg, Pennsylvania, "rather small," its soil not very good. "But," he ingratiatingly added, "the President says he wants to work to improve the land and thereby leave behind a good memory of himself."[37] Before his departure, Khrushchev retracted his threat to turn over the Soviet sector of Berlin to the East Germans. But he told a nationwide American television audience that "the position of the U.S. President is more difficult than mine"—because, he asserted, "the forces obstructing better relations between our countries and a relaxation of international tension are still influential in the United States of America."[39]

Eisenhower did not savor such comments from his guest. Nonetheless, the American press came to refer to "the spirit of Camp David" because of the good will generated by the talks at the President's Maryland mountain retreat. Eisenhower avowed later that this "was a term that I never used or deemed valid."[39]

Eisenhower sent Vice President Nixon to see Khrushchev off at the airport. The Premier, between his earlier conversations with Nixon in Moscow and his American visit, concluded that Nixon was an uncompromising foe. Upon his return, Khrushchev told a Moscow audience that he found Eisenhower cooperative, but that Nixon was not. "One would think," Khrushchev asserted, that "he [Nixon] was afraid of the atmosphere really turning warmer, of the cold war really ending."[40]

To prepare for one final try at the summit, Eisenhower met with Macmillan, de Gaulle, and Adenauer in Paris in December 1959. The prospects for reaching an agreement with the Soviets on Berlin and Germany were not good. There is reason to believe that the Soviets wanted to preclude a negotiated settlement. Despite the political talk in the United States about a "missile gap," the Soviets were aware that the gap was actually in the United States' favor. NATO had been greatly strengthened, and the United States and Canada had developed an effective early warning system against air attack. Moreover, with its system of alliances encircling the Soviet-Sino land mass worldwide, the United States clearly would be negotiating from strength.

The out the Soviets were seeking came with their May 5, 1960, announcement that they had shot down an American high-altitude U-2 reconnaissance plane some 1,200 miles inside Russia. Eisenhower declined to apologize. Khrushchev refused to meet with him and withdrew an invitation to visit the Soviet Union. Regrettably, Eisenhower concluded that "from the breakup of the Paris meeting in May 1960 to the end of my administration, the Soviets indulged in an intensified campaign of vituperation and false charges."[41]

Summary

ALLIANCES.   Despite the frustration of the aborted second summit with the Soviets, Eisenhower could look back over a successful eight years of waging peace and strengthening the free world. An effective system of alliances was an asset. In addition to strengthening NATO by the addition of West Germany, Eisenhower had been the principal architect of SEATO, of the bilateral arrangements with CENTO members, Turkey, Pakistan, and Iran, and of the strengthened mutual security arrangements with Taiwan, Japan, and Korea. Moreover, by inaugurating in Latin America what came to be termed the Alliance for Progress, he had greatly strengthened the 1947 Rio Pact of mutual assistance between the United States and the Latin American nations.

These alliances, which were forged in the Truman and Eisenhower administrations, remain fundamental today in our national security policy. They are vital links to the non-Communist world.

DETERRENCE.   The Eisenhower deterrence-oriented military policy emphasized a nuclear umbrella for the United States and its allies, substantial economic and military aid, and the allies' handling of low-intensity conflicts. The United States was to perform the principal air and sea roles, though in close association with allied air and sea forces.

After Korea, ground forces had been decreased and

strategic and tactical aid increased. With NATO, Eisenhower had supported a concept of limited general-purpose ground forces deployed well forward, providing a potential trip-wire function for nuclear response led by the Strategic Air Command. In terms of manpower augmentation, emphasis had been placed on the reserves. Among weapon systems, airpower dominated.

RECOMMENDATIONS TO KENNEDY. Eisenhower, when he met with President-elect Kennedy at the White House on December 6, 1960, emphasized the vital importance of the National Security Council, describing it as "the most important weekly meeting of the government."[42] Despite this, the NSC, until after the debacle of the Bay of Pigs, was to become virtually inoperative. Ambassador Robert D. Murphy later observed: "I've often wondered what his innermost thought was when President Kennedy . . . decided to suspend and abandon the Security Council for the time being. Perhaps that was a wise move at the time; I never thought it was."[43]

Eisenhower was also concerned that Kennedy, on the recommendations of Senator Symington, would undertake a further "streamlining" of the defense establishment. Accordingly he related to Kennedy how "the present organization and the improved functioning of the establishment had, during the past eight years, been brought about by patient study and long and drawn out negotiations with the Congress and the Armed Services."[44] The Eisenhower effort, including his personally written 1958 Defense Reorganization Act, remains a legacy.

SOUTHEAST ASIA. A major concern of the final weeks of the second Eisenhower administration was Southeast Asia, where with Russian airlift support a North Vietnamese and Communist Pathet Lao attack on Laos was under way. Eisenhower wrote three years later, "Despite its remoteness, we were determined to preserve the independence of Laos against a takeover backed by its neighbors to the North— Communist China and North Vietnam." He then added his famous domino thesis. "For the fall of Laos to Com-

munism," Eisenhower warned, "would mean the subsequent fall—like a tumbling row of dominoes—of its still
free neighbors, Cambodia and South Vietnam, and, in all
probability, Thailand and Burma. Such a chain of events
would open the way to Communist seizure of all Southeast
Asia."[45]

In a meeting with the new chairman of the Joint Chiefs of
Staff, General Lyman L. Lemnitzer, on January 2, 1961,
Eisenhower concluded, "If we ever have to resort to force,
there's just one thing to do: clear up the problem completely."[46] Two and one-half weeks later, after attending the
inaugural of his successor, John F. Kennedy, Eisenhower
retired with Mamie to their Gettysburg farm.

EVALUATION.   Three major polls by historians and political scientists have sought to evaluate the effectiveness of
American Presidents. The first of these was conducted by
Arthur M. Schlesinger, Sr., in 1948 with responses from
fifty-five "experts" and the second in 1962 with responses
from seventy-five "experts." The third was conducted in
1968 by the Organization of American Historians. The first,
of course, did not include Truman and Eisenhower because
of the date of the poll. The second included both and placed
Truman in the "Near Great" category and Eisenhower in the
next to the bottom rung of "Average." Like the 1962 poll,
the 1968 poll also gave Eisenhower low marks.[47] In the
personal-psychological evaluations of James David Barber,
of Duke University, Franklin D. Roosevelt has emerged as
number one among twentieth-century Presidents.[48]

Senior historians, looking at the record of accomplishment, are now beginning a drastically upward revision of the
Eisenhower Presidency. In 1974 a nationally televised CBS
program, "Greatness in the American Presidency," found
Eisenhower to be the most underrated of our Presidents. It
further recognized that Eisenhower, who institutionalized
Congressional liaison "was most effective in his relationships with that body."[49] Curtis P. Nettels of Cornell University, who has consistently ranked F. D. Roosevelt in that
number-one category, wrote on May 5, 1975: "My opinion is
that Dwight Eisenhower and Franklin Roosevelt are the two

foremost Presidents of this century."[50] Nettels, the author of a number of works related to the American Presidency, offered these eleven points in arriving at his decision:

1. The ending of the Korean War on favorable terms.
2. The maintaining of peace 1953–1961.
3. Keeping the country on an even keel economically—a high rate of employment without injurious inflation.
4. Refusing to become involved in the French war in Indochina, rejecting the doctrine that the President may lawfully involve the country in a war in a foreign country without a declaration of war by Congress.
5. Upholding a high standard of honesty and integrity in the financial affairs and administration of the Government.
6. Ending the extreme tension with respect to the Soviet Union by establishing personal relations with its authorities.
7. Supporting the United Nations in the cause of preventing war aimed at Egypt.
8. Enforcing federal laws in protecting the civil rights and liberties of minority groups.
9. Maintaining the national defenses without excessive outlays for armaments or exciting a militaristic spirit.
10. Dealing with people as individuals and on the whole in a humane and honorable manner.
11. Giving citizens a sense of personal security by maintaining freedom of speech and the press and by avoiding the methods of a police state.[51]

Eisenhower never lived to see this revaluation. In a personal letter to Jim Hagerty, October 18, 1966, he confided his distress at the low marks his administration had received from persons who "equate an individual's strength of dedication with oratorical bombast; determination, with public repetition of a catchy phrase; achievement, with the exaggerated use of the vertical pronoun. . . . To them record means little. Manner and method are vital."[52]

With no view of its ever being published, Eisenhower listed in this letter the twenty-three principal accomplishments of "a team effort." As Hagerty later observed, "It is quite interesting that he did not refer to *my* administrations."[53] Eisenhower's points ranged from the "first civil rights laws in 80 years" and "desegregation in Washington

D.C. and the Armed Forces without laws" to "slowing up, and practical elimination of inflation" and "fighting for responsible fiscal and financial policies throughout eight years." He noted Alaskan and Hawaiian statehood, the St. Lawrence Seaway, the massive interstate highway system, the establishment of the Department of HEW (he might have added NASA and the Federal Aviation Administration), "intelligent application of federal aid to education" and substantial extension of old age insurance, and "the largest reduction of taxes to this time."

In the area of national security Eisenhower offered these ten points:

> End of Korean War (thereafter no American killed in combat);
> Prevention of Communist efforts to dominate Iran, Guatemala, Lebanon, Formosa, and South Vietnam;
> Reorganization of the Department of Defense;
> Initiation of a space program which successfully orbited within three years, after starting from scratch;
> Initiating a strong ballistic missile program;
> Conceiving and building the Polaris program, with ships operating at sea, within a single administration;
> Preservation for the first time in American history, of adequate military establishment after the cessation of war;
> Goodwill journeys to more than a score of nations in Europe, Asia, South Pacific, and the Pacific;
> Initiation of plans for social progress in Latin America after obtaining necessary authorization from the Congress;
> "Atoms for Peace" proposal.

Eisenhower concluded in his letter to Hagerty that "all of this was done with the Congress controlled by the opposition party for six years, the other two having only a nominal Republican majority."[54] It is notable that Eisenhower worked effectively with the Democratic as well as the Republican party. He might have added that he exercised his veto 181 times and was overriden only twice, and then on minor porkbarrel bills. History records Andrew Jackson as having made most effective use of the veto. In fact, Jackson exercised the veto only twelve times. Eisenhower most skillfully utilized his veto to secure support for his programs.

George E. Reedy, Jr., who throughout those eight years served as the assistant to Senate Majority Leader Lyndon Baines Johnson, said of Eisenhower a decade later: "I had, what I now realize was a somewhat naive idea that this man was a 'push-over.' We believed that we were the master politicians—that Eisenhower did not really know what he was doing and that we were the geniuses that were guiding the developments." Reedy, subsequently Johnson's press secretary and now dean of journalism at Marquette University, concluded, "Lord, it is funny how different things look a few years later. I really believe today that he was a master politician. . . ."[55]

But he was more than a masterful politician. Eisenhower was a keenly interested student of history. In his presidency of Columbia University he especially enjoyed participating with Professor Robert Livingston Schuyler and the graduate students in the historiography course in discussion on the great historians and historical methods. He also exchanged views on history and political science with other members of the History and Political Science Departments, including Harry J. Carman, John A. Krout and Allan Nevins, and his successor, Grayson Kirk.

In 1968, shortly before his death, he proposed a Center for the Study of the Presidency. In his memorandum on this subject he observed: "The serious student of this phase of our Nation's history must . . . read widely—across the entire spectrum of opinion—if he is to obtain a reasonably accurate picture of an individual's capacities, qualities and character." Eisenhower emphasized: "There must be gained, also, an appreciation in each case of the responsibilities carried, the mutually conflicting considerations prevailing, and the tensions of the particular time, if we are to achieve confidence in the opinions we form about any Chief Executive."[56]

Essentially he had devoted his life not to waging war but rather to waging peace. He had reluctantly come to the conclusion that we must make a marked break with our past peacetime experience of complete demobilization. We must "sustain security forces fully adequate to counter any hostile move against us."[57] In his State of the Union Message of January 9, 1959, he expanded upon this doctrine. "We cannot," he declared, "build peace through desire alone. Moreover, we have learned the bitter lesson that international agreements, historically considered by us as sacred, are regarded in Communist-doctrine and in practice to be mere scraps of paper. . . . Yet," he told his fellow citizens, "step by step we must strengthen the institutions of peace—a peace that rests upon justice—a peace that depends upon a deep knowledge and clear understanding by all peoples of the cause and consequence of possible failure in this greatest purpose."[58]

In this search for peace he struck a spiritual note and also emphasized qualities of friendship and freedom. Thus in Manila on June 16, 1960, he avowed that "the free world must increase its strength—in military defenses, in economic growth, in spiritual dedication."[59] So also in Taipei, two days later, he referred to "our friendship, tested in war and in peace. . . ."[60] And in Seoul the following day he saluted the Koreans "who have so amply proven their love of liberty. . . ."[61] Both here at home and overseas he underscored building understanding. Thus he told the American community in Seoul, "We want to live as confident people. And if we are going to live as confident people, we must live as cooperative people."[62]

Many of these observations were spontaneous. Eisenhower was often the butt of jokes about mixing up his syntax; nonetheless, he characteristically spoke with a quiet unassuming eloquence and good humor and the spark of a new idea. He also spoke in candor, as when he told the Koreans that theirs was the challenge to build "a free press and responsible expression of popular will. . . ."[63]

For all of this, for his candor, courage, and integrity, he was perhaps America's most respected modern ambassador. And so he is remembered in the nations of Europe, the Middle East, South Asia, Africa, the Americas, and the Far East. He was more then than merely our most traveled President. He saw his greatest crusade in having rallied our "military, economic, political, and moral strength to prevent war and to build a solid structure of peace."[64]

In his final State of the Union Message, he noted the continuing areas of special concern: Berlin, the Middle East,

Cuba, and Southeast Asia. These remain areas of special concern for the President and the Secretary of State today. On May 21, 1975, Secretary Kissinger referred to Berlin as the "acid test" in any policies of détente with the Soviet Union.[65] President Carter has spoken similarly.

Eisenhower ended his final Presidential message on a prayerful note for the strength and peace of the nation and the moral purpose of the people.[66] It harked back to the "little prayer" he had written the morning of his first inaugural:

> Especially we pray that our concern shall be for all the people, regardless of station, race or calling. May cooperation be permitted and be the mutual aim of those who, under the concept of our Constitution, hold to differing political beliefs—so that all may work for the good of our beloved country and for Thy glory.   Amen.[67]

EISENHOWER IN RETROSPECT. The Truman and Eisenhower Presidencies are studies in contrast, as are the personalities of the two men. Nonetheless, both spent their formative years in the rural Great Plains area, little more than 100 miles apart; both were schooled in homespun qualities of frugality, honesty, virtue; and both had long identifications with the military. Although, as indicated, early evaluations of Truman ranked him high among the near-great Presidents and placed Eisenhower low among the mediocre, inevitably there will be a revision of these rankings—not so much in a possible slightly downward revision on Truman as in a remarkable upward reevaluation of Eisenhower. Students of public affairs and of history are already beginning to make that reassessment.

John J. McCloy, who served under Truman in charge of the occupation of Germany, a position parallel to that of MacArthur, recently emphasized the imperative upgrading of Eisenhower.[68] McCloy was also closely associated with both Eisenhower and Roosevelt and found them a study in contrast, Eisenhower arriving at decisions through careful painstaking organized staff studies, Roosevelt through personal assessments, feelings, and hunches. McCloy, though he found Roosevelt inconsistent and superficial in his decision processes, admired his political and rhetorical mastery. He observed that Roosevelt simply could not organize his ideas in an essay or a speech. However, if that speech were written by someone else, Roosevelt could deliver it with a charm and persuasion rarely matched. By contrast, as McCloy has pointed out, Eisenhower had great powers of exposition. He could place his own ideas on paper with brilliance, charm, cogency, clarity, depth, and succinctness. Yet when he came to read those words aloud or otherwise orally discourse, he stumbled over his own syntax. Such contrasting delivery contributed directly to Roosevelt's high marks and Eisenhower's low.[69]

His verbal lapses were a failing Eisenhower shared with one of our greatest Presidents, Washington. The parallels between Washington and Eisenhower are more basic than that. Nettels recently set forth the following seven points spanning the lifetime of both men:

1. Each was born in a rural setting and grew up in a countryside environment.
2. At the end of the period of youth, each entered upon military activities.
3. During the stage of young manhood each was engaged in public service.
4. Each served as the chief commander of a large army in a successful war that had great significance in world history and that served a good cause.
5. During a postwar period of six or seven years, each was active in various forms of public service.
6. Each served eight years as President, receiving widespread popular support in presidential elections.
7. After retirement from the Presidency, each one continued to take an active part in public affairs.[70]

Truman did not recognize these similarities, though he admitted that Adlai Stevenson had "a handicap of waging political battles against a military man who was also a war hero." Truman further conceded that "the incoming President was, or should have been, acquainted with the world situation."[71]

Truman was most apprehensive about the new Eisenhower administration's conduct of national security.

"The proper solution of those problems," he warned in a postelection public statement, "may determine whether we shall have a third world war—and, indeed, whether we shall survive as a free and democratic nation."[72] In the midst of the campaign, Truman had offered to provide Eisenhower a series of classified briefings on national security affairs. Though accepting CIA weekly reports, Eisenhower had declined the briefings. This angered Truman, who charged "that you have allowed a bunch of screwballs to come between us."[73] After the election Eisenhower did accept Truman's invitation for a meeting. Somewhat gratuitously Truman completed the memoirs of his own Presidency by observing: "Up to this meeting in the White House, General Eisenhower had not grasped the immense job ahead of him."[74]

Eisenhower's own words and deeds bespoke a fuller grasp both of the enormity of the job and of his understanding of it than Truman would credit him with. Eisenhower had already filled many other posts requiring great stature, ranging from Supreme Allied Commander in the largest military operation in history, to the presidency of Columbia, one of the great universities in the world, to the first NATO commander. He full well recognized the gravity of the situation. As he expressed it in the first weeks of his first administration: "Today the hope of free men remains stubborn and brave, but it is sternly disciplined by experience." Then from firsthand experience he recounted "what happened to the vain hope of 1945."[75] Eisenhower early challenged the Soviets and the People's Republic of China to join the free world in waging peace. He noted that such a peace "can be fortified, not by weapons of war but by wheat and by cotton, by milk and by wool, by meat and by timber and by rice."[76]

The Presidency is, in part, a matter of personal style. Roosevelt and Truman in large measure conducted affairs, both foreign and domestic, on an informal personal basis, thus creating the impression that they were "activist" Presidents. With his experience and belief in staff organization, Eisenhower determined to reactivate the Cabinet and structure the National Security Council. Working through these bodies, he gained the erroneous reputation of being a passive, nonactivist President. Eisenhower, both instinctively and by experience in dealing with people, determined that the wisest course was to "build up" and encourage the initiative of others. Moreover, he believed more in the power of persuasion than of directives and ultimatums. As such he was masterful in his relations not only with his staff but also with the Democratic-controlled Congress.

But a President seeking concurrence does not come through as the activist firing off directives. Moreover, Eisenhower realized that following twenty years of social revolution and war, the nation both needed and yearned for a period of calm, consolidation, efficiency, and understanding. Because of the special affection with which he was held by the American people and the skillful manner in which he was portrayed by his "Man Friday," Jim Hagerty, the controversial matters focused on others. In the area of foreign policy it was Eisenhower, *not* Dulles, at the helm. However, when there was a furor regarding refusal to give aid to Egypt for the Aswan Dam or stopping British-French-Israeli aggression against Egypt, the press targeted Dulles rather than Eisenhower.

For this admixture of seemingly calm persuasion rather than bombastic direction, for a recognition of the need for consolidation while moving ahead, for this mixture of affection and quiet strength, Eisenhower did not earn the sobriquet of the activist President. Yet an examination of his public papers and personal letters, his personal reminiscences, and the record of his two administrations reveal his mastery of command.

President Eisenhower's April 30, 1953, special message to the Congress regarding the reorganization of the Department of Defense is exemplary of both his concerns and his philosophy. He began this message, only three months after having taken office, with the statement that "the defense of our country . . . has been of primary concern to me all the years of my adult life. . . ." He identified himself "as a former soldier who had experienced modern war at first-hand, and now, as President and Commander in Chief. . . ." While pointing up the need for improving the Department of Defense organization, he emphasized that "we are not . . . a warlike people. Our historic goal is peace. . . ." Deploring the

Soviet policy "neither of total war not total peace," he asserted our desire to regain the initiative in foreign policy.[77]

His attempts were not entirely successful. His best hopes for a change of basic Soviet policy following Stalin's death earlier that year were not borne out by Stalin's eventual successor, Khrushchev. Indeed, Khrushchev scored something of a diplomatic and propagandistic triumph over Eisenhower is his 1959 visit to the United States and was highly insulting to the President the following year in calling off the summit conference on the pretext of the U-2 incident. Moreover, Eisenhower was frustrated at his inability to aid the captive nations in their uprisings against their Soviet masters.

Yet Eisenhower did achieve what he set forth as basic national security principles in this early 1953 message: military security with economic solvency. During his two administrations, inflation was virtually brought to a halt, and a system of alliances and bases was completed, encircling the Soviets and their satellites. Ironically, Cuba, at our own doorstep, with the 1960 Castro takeover was the only additional nation to enter the Communist camp during the two Eisenhower administrations.

It is understandable that Eisenhower related far more effectively to the armed services than Truman in his command decisions. When he relieved Van Fleet in Korea, for much the same reasons Truman had relieved MacArthur, he did it with far more adroitness. Confronted, as Truman had been, with the most severe interservice rivalries, again Eisenhower was far more masterful. Although during both Eisenhower administrations there were sharp reductions in the Army and the Navy vis-à-vis the Air Force, they were in no instance attendant with such episodes as the "admirals' revolt." Eisenhower simply made clear that interservice public squabbles must cease, and if they did not, he would recommend one uniformed armed service. With the exception of the intense Army-Air Force missile competition, they ceased.

Eisenhower's conduct of the 1953 and 1958 Defense Department reorganizations was much better handled than the 1947 and 1949 Truman efforts. Such might well be expected in the light of Eisenhower's professional expertise, but again it was also a matter of skill in handling people. And when Secretary of Defense Wilson virtually put his foot in his mouth early in the first Eisenhower administration with his "what is good for General Motors" statement, Eisenhower quieted the furor and inspired Wilson to years of constructive governmental service.

In many of these instances the aid of the most masterful of Presidential press secretaries, James Hagerty, was helpful. Many of his press conferences focused on national security affairs, but the President avoided controversy. Early in his first year in office Eisenhower had suggested that the Key West agreement on mission roles should be reviewed. Perhaps more than anything else, the rancor regarding this so-called agreement had broken Secretary Forrestal. At Eisenhower's April 30 press conference, following his message to Congress on defense policies, Mrs. May Craig inquired: "Mr. President, if you open up the Key West agreement, will you open up also the roles and mission assignments made there?" To this the President replied: "Well, I must tell you, Mrs. Craig, I am not going back into some of those things. I have got other things that occupy my time."[78]

Eisenhower approached security subjects with considerably more humility than his predecessor. He candidly told the press, "I don't believe any of us are smart enough to lay out a blueprint for a perfect organization."[79] Eisenhower recognized "team work" as indispensable to national security organization. He made clear at the outset that under his personal direction the Secretary of State was to be the "channel of authority within the executive branch in foreign policy."[80] It would have been unconscionable to Eisenhower (as to Dulles) that the Special Assistant for National Security Affairs, who served as the executive officer in vitalizing the NSC, could in any way come between the President and the Secretary of State. Eisenhower made the Secretary of State, the Secretary of Defense, and the Secretary of the Treasury a triumvirate to review national security plans and operations on the premise that diplomatic, military, and economic affairs were necessarily related.

Eisenhower believed that American foreign policy goals could not be achieved by unilateral action; they required common goals and teamwork. He recognized that he was not "a particularly patient man"— he often had a "sense of frustration" when allies balked or seemingly did not carry their full share of the burden—but he emphasized that "only patience, only determination, only optimism, and only a very deep faith can carry America forward."[81] Accordingly, he noted the necessity for compromise, but as Hagerty observed, "He had mastered the art of compromise, of achieving the common good without the surrender of principle and integrity."[82]

Eisenhower, like Lincoln, was perhaps at his best in his expression of the American ideal. He often liked to quote Lincoln on the purpose of government "of, by, and for the People." At the same time he emphasized, "We are a republic, not a democracy."[83] Like Lincoln, Eisenhower could make a moving appeal for America as man's best hope for freedom. Like John F. Kennedy, he could call upon young Americans to serve mankind. It was most appropriate that as he neared his retirement and looked toward the farm in Gettysburg, he visited the college there and spoke of "the true meaning of mutual security," of "helping one another build a strong prosperous world community," of applying "God-given talents toward creating an ever-growing measure of man's humanity to man. But this," the old soldier concluded, much as he had told the students at Columbia when he had come there as their university president more than a decade before, "will only come out of the hard intellectual effort of disciplined minds."[84]

Eisenhower, a soldier devoted to peace, warned in his valedictory of the dangers of an industrial-military complex; however, the one basic thing he had failed to achieve was Soviet and United States mutual disarmament. He had to leave a legacy, for the first time in our peacetime history, of military strength—such strength that when the Cuban missile confrontation came a year after his retirement, there was no question that the Soviets must be the ones to back down. Yet in his last days in office Eisenhower spoke of the need "to help the less developed nations" and reconfirmed his aspiration for world disarmament. He concluded with the hope "that the nations of East and West will find dependable, self-guaranteeing methods to reduce the vast and essentially wasteful expenditures for armaments, so that part of the savings may be used in a comprehensive and effective effort for world improvement."[85]

That fervent Eisenhower wish remains mankind's best hope.

FAREWELL. By contrast with the personalized Presidency of Franklin D. Roosevelt, his successor has been credited with institutionalizing the office. The Council of Economic Advisers and the National Security Council are noted as examples. In truth, both were thrust on the reluctant President Truman by the "do-nothing" 80th Congress, in protest to FDR's freewheeling operations.

As Edward S. Corwin accurately pointed out, "The 'Institutionalized Presidency' is the contribution of Congress and of recent Presidents, but particularly of President Eisenhower. . . ."[86] Pictured as spending much of his time at the Burning Tree golf course in suburban Maryland, Eisenhower actually worked much harder at the job than he is given credit for, but he did make the job seem easier than any other modern President. He organized the executive office of the Presidency around four functional bodies. One of them, the Operations Coordinating Board, he created to make certain that national security policy programs were carried through. The others were the Office of Budget, the Cabinet, and the National Security Council.

Roosevelt and Truman, who had able persons in their Cabinets, preferred to deal with them on an informal basis. Eisenhower rather considered his Cabinet members administrators of their respective executive departments; he felt that they could be both advisers of the highest order and formulators of policy. Accordingly Eisenhower, taking literally that portion of Article II, Section 2, of the Constitution indicating that the President "may require the opinion in writing of the principal officer in each of the Executive departments. . . ," created a staff secretary for the Cabinet and working agendas for their meetings. Similarly, he established a Secretariat for the National Security Council. The Cabinet, the National Security Council, and the Operations

Coordinating Board became interdependent organizations in the institutionalized Eisenhower Presidency.[87]

Eisenhower's young successor dismantled most of this institutionalized Presidency machinery, and with his boundless energy, for a thousand days he created the image of the activist President that most students of the office find exciting. Such personal attention to myriad details scores high points on activist Presidency scales created by psychologist-political scientists, but it provides little measure or means of running the world's toughest managerial job. As Milton Eisenhower recently concluded in a personal letter to me, "The American people must understand that the burdens of the Presidency are such that no man, no matter how young, vigorous, and intelligent, can possibly redeem them."[88]

Historians and political scientists have been prone to brand Eisenhower a conservative. However, as one discerning student has noted, "To doctrinaire liberals he was a hidebound conservative; to conservatives, a dangerous liberal."[89] At one point, John Birchers even called him a Communist. He has, however, been generally regarded as more conservative than his brother Milton, who, as president of three major universities, won the respect of liberal faculty members. Milton recently confided that ". . . I, if I differed with my brother at all, was more conservative than he on economic and fiscal policy. We never differed," Milton concluded, "on matters of human values and human welfare."[90]

When human rights were being denied, Eisenhower could be an activist, even calling upon his authority as Commander in Chief. Indeed, his sending troops to Little Rock, Arkansas, to compel admission of Negro students aroused Senator Richard Russell of Georgia to accuse him of Hitler stormtrooper methods. Pointing out the difference to the revered Senator, Eisenhower wrote that "in one case military power was used to further the ambitions and purposes of a ruthless dictator, in the other to preserve the institutions of free government."[91]

Again and again Eisenhower never hesitated to consider political expedience in his command decisions. His political advisers in the weeks before the 1956 Presidential elections counseled the necessity of securing the support of the Jewish population and Jewish media leaders. Nonetheless, the week before the election, he exercised the full force of his office to stop the Israeli-English-French attack on Egypt. "We'll do what we think is right regardless of how it affects the election," Eisenhower informed John Foster Dulles. "If they don't want me, let them get someone else."[92] Eisenhower, who personally telephoned 10 Downing Street several times to dissuade the British, also realized that his own unconditional action was ending the career of the British Prime Minister, his friend Anthony Eden. But he went before the nation on television on October 31, 1956, to avow: "There can be no peace—without law. And there can be no law—," he added, alluding to the fact that Egypt was then seeking aid from Russia, "if we were to invoke one code of international conduct for those who oppose us—and another for our friends."[93] At the same time Eisenhower coolly ignored the Soviet invitation to join in stopping the Anglo-French-Israeli invasion. By Ike's estimate Soviet physical intervention in Egypt, in the presence of NATO-CENTO forces, had about as much likelihood as U.S. intervention in Hungary.

Eisenhower likewise maintained his composure when many Americans a year later pushed the panic button over Sputnik and the Gaither Report, which predicted that by 1959 the Soviets might hit the United States with a hundred ICBMs. He could not tell the American people the sources of his own intelligence that there were radar bases around the Soviet periphery as well as high-altitude U-2 flights which he had directed since 1956. When one of the spy planes was shot down in 1960, Eisenhower, to the horror of diplomats both at home and abroad, readily admitted his personal responsibility for the operation. According to the Gallup poll his sustained eight years of overwhelming confidence with the American people actually rose after his announcement.[94]

By contrast, then, with his predecessor Eisenhower completed his Presidency with strong popular support—even though the Twenty-second Amendment had made him a lame-duck President ineligible for reelection. At seventy, he was the oldest person to have held the office, but without the Constitutional restraint he would have easily been reelected.

Americans agreed that history must record him as either a good or a great President. Clearly he had been our most effective post–World War II President and Commander in Chief. They further believed with him that "the only answer to a regime that wages total cold war is to wage total peace."[95]

This he had done, and not merely as an institutional President. Although he was no more completely at ease with the professional politicians in Washington than he had been with some of the faculty at Columbia, he reached the hearts and minds of peoples in the democratic world to a degree matched in the twentieth century only by Churchill and Franklin Roosevelt. More even than they, he did so in terms of moral and spiritual purpose. In a press conference in 1953 he declared that the "true posture of defense is composed of three factors—spiritual, military, and economic."[96] It was more than an institutional act to have the Pledge of Allegiance a year later changed to include "under God" after the words "one Nation." He related peace to social justice at home and abroad, and in his final Presidential press conference he confided that "the big disappointment . . . was that we could not in these years get to the place where we could say it now looks as if permanent peace with justice is now in sight."[97]

Disarmament remained his steadfast goal. Dealing with the Soviets with integrity and necessarily from strength meant, while maintaining fiscal responsibility, continuing a powerful military establishment. Hence in his Farewell Address to the American people, he warned that "in the councils of government we must guard against the acquisition of unwarranted influence, whether sought or unsought, by the military-industrial complex." The old soldier concluded in these last days in Presidential office that "only an alert and knowledgeable citizenry" could guarantee that "security and liberty may prosper together."[98]

X
****

DEMOCRACY'S DILEMMA

> ... it is especially in the conduct of their foreign relations that democracies appear... decidedly inferior to other governments.... JAMES R. SCHLESINGER,
> quoting Alexis de Tocqueville

Tocqueville's Challenge

Writing in his *Democracy in America* in 1835, that most astute observer Alexis de Tocqueville expressed concern whether the United States could develop and implement an effective foreign policy. "Upon this point," he concluded, "its adversaries as well as its friends must suspend their judgment." Tocqueville pointed out that "almost all the nations that have exercised a powerful influence upon the destinies of the world, by conceiving, following out, and executing vast designs, from the Romans to the English, have been governed by autocratic institutions."[1]

Although Tocqueville was not certain that the United States would be successful in its foreign policy, he did predict, at a time when neither the United States nor Russia was a first-rate power, that "each of them seems marked out by the will of Heaven to sway the destinies of half the globe."[2]

When, on November 10, 1975, James R. Schlesinger stepped down as Secretary of Defense, he quoted from Tocqueville: "... it is especially in the conduct of their foreign relations that democracies appear... decidedly inferior to other governments...." Terming it "Tocqueville's challenge," Dr. Schlesinger concluded, "Let us be sure it is not an epitaph."[3]

What happened to Schlesinger, aside from his personality differences with President Ford and Secretary of State Kissinger, points up one of democracy's failings. Neither the people nor the politicians want to be told, especially in the area of defense policy, that they are becoming second best. When there are only two super powers, second means last. No administration, no Congress, wants to be accused of having made the United States secondary. John F. Kennedy won a closely contested Presidential election in 1960 by making the charge that American defense was inadequate. Only after the election did the so-called missile gap vanish. Both Kennedy and Khrushchev appreciated that it had been a myth when in October 1962 they had their Cuban missile crisis confrontation.

That crisis pointed up another democratic frailty in foreign policy: with so many voices, the intentions of a democracy such as the United States can be misread. The Berlin-Rome-Tokyo axis miscalculated those intentions in the prelude to World War II; Stalin did in giving the North Koreans the go-ahead to invade South Korea; and Khrushchev did when he placed missiles in Cuba.

Aleksandr I. Solzhenitsyn, like Tocqueville, has recognized in the area of foreign policy another democratic weakness: idealism. Indeed, even czarist Russian foreign policy was hampered by idealism. But the Soviets never lose sight of national self-interest. Idealism is no match for cunning and guile. Thus, as Solzhenitsyn has pointed out, in the crucial period at the end of World War II, "Stalin, who had always easily outplayed Roosevelt, outplayed Churchill, too."[4]

Tocqueville recognized another democratic frailty, affirmed by America's travail in the mid-1970s: a democracy like the United States "cannot combine its measures with secrecy or await their consequences with patience." So it was, as the *New York Times* editorially observed, that the Congressional investigations of the intelligence community were characterized by "a counterproductive rash of leaked reports and premature disclosures."[5]

Since, despite these weaknesses of commission and omission, the United States and a few other societies of shared democratic values were still around in the final quarter of the twentieth century, there must have been a genius and a saving grace. The genius has been in brains, faith, and resolution; and the grace, as Tocqueville expressed it, in democracy's ability to "repair its errors."

Before suggesting the repair for the error of our ways, I might note that Congressman Fisher Ames, Alexander Hamilton's contemporary and staunch supporter, found another saving grace in democracy. Comparing autocratic states to swift-sailing vessels which are prone to sink on reefs and shoals, Ames perceived that democracy is like a raft; those on board are likely to get their feet wet, but they are not likely to sink.

On occasion Americans have taken comfort in our "muddling through." But, as Herman Kahn points out, ". . . given the pace of technology and the catastrophe-prone way in which problems come up today, particularly in the military and foreign policy fields, it just does not seem credible that muddling through will be a satisfactory approach to the future."[6]

Were Tocqueville to return for America's two-hundredth birthday, he might well conclude that we are "muddling through" rather than being the architects of an effective foreign policy. The fact is that no modern state took on such a large role of leadership as did the United States in the post-World War II era. Whatever may be America's future overseas role, upon which the Vietnam War cast a pall of doubt, history must record a facing up to the severe trials of leadership. As William G. Carleton, professor of history at the University of Florida, expressed it, "It has never been easy, whether in Roman days or American days to lead the world, but the direct and blunt Roman ways of knocking provincial heads together and building an empire was in some respects less difficult than the complicated task America had of leading a world of nationalism, democracy, self-determination, and ideological conflict."[7]

Perhaps that task was best borne in the Truman years, with the building and rebuilding of other democratic societies, and in the Eisenhower years, when the Korean

War was ended and the Soviets were contained and encircled by a system of alliances.

Kennedy possibly went too far when he promised in his 1961 inaugural to "pay any price, bear any burden, meet any hardship, support any friend, oppose any foe to assure the survival and the success of liberty." Less than three years later, the brave young President was gone. When his successor got bogged down in the ground war in Asia that Eisenhower had warned against, the liberal elitists who had helped write the Kennedy inaugural deserted their new Commander in Chief in droves. They had scorned the Eisenhower Presidency, which shared responsibility with the Congress. Now they found the Kennedy-Johnson model of the assertive executive imperial in character. Suddenly 535 Congressmen were engaged in making foreign policy on which they could not agree.

As a nation, we have been undergoing a period of travail. Gone is the consensus which characterized American foreign policy in the twenty-five-year period 1940–1965. Gone is America's unchallenged position of primacy among world powers. Our relative power and our relative influence have diminished in a world which is not so clearly bipolarized and in which our own voice is blurred. Détente, a search for accommodation, has replaced the protagonist lines of the Cold War.

Although debate as to who lost Vietnam or who lost China is useless, the lessons of history should not be forgotten. Nations cannot successfully conduct wars without a national will, a sense of purpose. Several years before the withdrawal of American combat forces in Vietnam, it was manifestly clear that the United States wanted out. As early as 1967, Leonid I. Brezhnev, as Secretary of the Communist party, correctly predicted the victory of "the patriots of Vietnam relying on varied aid from the socialist countries. . . ." He further predicted "a most profound undermining of U.S. prestige throughout the world."[8] In the 1970s, in his summit meetings with Presidents Nixon and Ford, Brezhnev doubtless sought the confirmation of his 1967 predictions.

Nixon, from the day he took office as President, began the

orderly withdrawal of American combat forces from Vietnam. It is ironical that he, more than President Johnson, felt the full fury of the Congress and the American people in the conduct of the war. Albeit the ironies of history, the fact remains that with the greatest difficulty a now discredited President extricated us from the most protracted and divisive war and inaugurated new relationships with both the Soviet Union and the People's Republic of China. Today, the People's Republic and the Soviets, the Third World, and old allies all wait to see whether we have the determination, the integrity, the moral leadership, the economic and military leadership, for the tough decisions ahead.

The Congress and the Presidency: Reforms

Part of our current business is the restoration of the effective working relationship on foreign policy between the Congress and the Presidency that Roosevelt, Truman, and Eisenhower achieved. This presupposes a return to a degree of equilibrium between the executive and the legislative. Prudently, not unwittingly, the founding fathers created shared responsibilities in foreign policy. They had read the Baron de Montesquieu's *Spirit of the Laws* (1748) and had found with him the genius of "political liberty" in checks and balances. Like him, they recognized that when that equilibrium was thrown out of kilter there could be tyranny from either the executive or the legislative.[9] The founding fathers created a representative republic, not a democracy. Nonetheless, they were to learn early of the fundamental importance of public opinion and a degree of consensus about certain principles of policy. To achieve consensus today, we should seek the resolution rather than the stifling of the debate. No purpose was served in 1976 when an angry Kissinger and a hostile Congress exchanged charges and countercharges.

The years of rubber stamping in the Senate's "advice and consent" role were over. Revelations of conflicts of interests and influence peddling ended automatic appointment or reappointment to executive positions; intelligence abuses, poor communications, the cloud of secrecy—all contributed to the impasse on both domestic and foreign policy. Kissinger correctly wanted to separate Presidential-Congressional supervision of foreign policy, from the day-by-day conduct of foreign policy, but his difficulty was his refusal to recognize a Congressional role in policy formulation. His ideal was a unified voice, what he termed "a strong national government which can act with assurance and speak with confidence on behalf of all Americans... ,"[10] although he could not comprehend how to bring it about. Cultural origins made him and his equally brilliant State Department Counselor, Helmut Sonnenfeldt, pessimistic regarding the democratic process. As early as 1971, Sonnenfeldt had expressed particular concern about "many of our young people and a large segment of our intellectual community," concluding that "the psychological underpinning for American involvement in the world has become very complex and very difficult."[11]

In vain, Kissinger warned in 1976 that our "domestic decisions" posed greater danger than our overseas adversaries.[12] In 1968, President Johnson, in a final futile attempt toward consensus, had declined to run again for the Presidency, the kind of an act of self-abnegation which, Sonnenfeldt observed, "does not obviously enhance the power of the Presidency."[13]

What are the continuing concerns that stand between the Presidency and the Congress and preclude consensus? Despite the curbs on the Presidency in foreign affairs that the Congress enacted during the 1972–1975 period, a distrust, an uneasiness, remains. As long as it does, effectiveness in foreign policy formulation and execution will be weakened.

Basically, and with some justification, the Congress believes it has been bamboozled. It had heard so much about secrecy and dispatch that again and again it has acquiesced to the Presidency in crisis situations. The Congress, which built an effective bipartisanship with the President from 1947 to 1950 never quite got over the Acheson-Truman handling of the dispatch of armed forces to Korea and to NATO in 1950–1951 without meaningful Congressional consultation. Eisenhower reassured the Congress, seeking again and again, as in Taiwan and Lebanon in 1958, Congressional action jointly with the Presidency. But the old bamboozlement came back increasingly in the mid-1960s. Subsequent events in Southeast Asia made members of the Congress feel that they "had been had" by the August 1964 Tonkin Gulf Resolution.

Clearly, the Congress wants to play its full role intelligently. It is angry that it does not, despite its expanded staff. Many Democratic and Republican Congressional leaders, including the chairman of the Republican Conference, Congressman John B. Anderson, therefore advocate for the Congress a Foreign Policy Research and Analysis Institute. This would be designed, with computer technology, to gear up the Congress in times of national emergencies in order to respond to the Presidency "with complementary speed and efficiency." (This is the same Congressman Anderson who views an ill-equipped frustrated Congress portending "executive emasculation.")[14] As far as the speed and dispatch are concerned, one may well conclude with Marian D. Irish of American University, that there has not been "a single instance in the history of American foreign policy where the national interests were better served by speed and secrecy than by debate and deliberation."[15]

Aside from a general uneasiness in responding to crisis situations, the Congress continues to have four basic areas of distrust regarding its relationships with the Presidency in national security affairs. All four of these relate to the President's roles as Commander in Chief and chief diplomat. In all four the Congress in the 1970s has conducted investigations and/or attempted legislative responses: (1) executive agreements; (2) war powers; (3) intelligence gathering; and (4) declarations of a state of emergency.

EXECUTIVE AGREEMENTS.   Since the 1953 defeat of the Bricker Amendment, there has been no serious attempt to eliminate all executive agreements without Congressional approval, although the June 1969 sense-of-the-Senate National Commitments Resolution declared that a national commitment results only from concurrent action of the Congress and the Presidency. Specifically the resolution was aimed at military assistance (armed forces or financial). But a sense-of-the-Senate resolution is in no way legally binding on the President. Recognizing the inherent weaknesses of the National Commitment Resolution, the Symington sub-committee of the Senate Foreign Relations Committee, in its final report in 1971 (U.S. Security Agreements and Commitments Abroad), did recommend that executive agreements must be ratified by the Congress. Further, harking back to Truman's 1951 action in deploying troops to Europe, the Symington committee recommended prior Congressional approval for all overseas troop deployments. Again, this was only a recommendation.

The following year Senator Clifford Case secured legislation making it mandatory that all executive agreements be transmitted to the Congress within sixty days (or, if classified, be routed to the Senate Foreign Relations or House Foreign Affairs Committee). Nonetheless, respected students of the Presidency were still suggesting in the mid-1970s that the most urgently needed reform in the area of national security policy was a curb on executive agreements. In 1975 Thomas E. Cronin concluded that "the worst features of U.S. foreign policy and diplomacy since World War II have arisen out of the concepts of executive agreement." Although President Ford, Kissinger, and Secretary of Defense Donald Rumsfeld might not have agreed with his contention, Cronin charged that "the Senate, which once played a vital part in foreign policy matters, today serves largely as an echo of the Pentagon and the White House."[16]

While Cronin's brilliance and persuasiveness are indisputable, the validity of this conclusion is highly questionable. The only period in which the Pentagon and the White House exercised joint dominance of American foreign policy was during the tenure of Robert S. McNamara, under President Kennedy and particularly President Johnson. As a White House Fellow, Cronin had observed the Johnson-McNamara team making policy in Southeast Asia, but at no other time in our history—and most certainly not in 1975 when Cronin was so writing—has this alleged White House–Department of Defense dominance of foreign policy obtained. What did follow, after McNamara and Clark Clifford, was a restoration by Nixon's Secretary of Defense, Melvin Laird, of a strategy role to the Joint Chiefs of Staff. However, under Nixon, both the Secretary of State and the Secretary of Defense lost their roles in policy formulation by placing it in the hands of the Assistant to the President for National Security Affairs (Kissinger) at the White House itself. Inevitably this became intolerable to Secretary of State William P. Rogers, as it did subsequently to Secretary of Defense Schlesinger. President Ford's elimination of Kissinger's role in 1975, with the appointment of Lieutenant General Brent Scowcroft as Assistant to the President for National Security Affairs, marked the denouement of this policy concentration at the White House. President Ford had returned to the multiple sources of advice which characterized the Truman and Eisenhower Presidencies by contrast with the Johnson and Nixon Presidencies.

Cronin, like Arthur M. Schlesinger, Jr., had also found particularly awesome and dangerous "the wide discretionary powers inherent in his [the President's] prerogative as commander-in-chief."[17] Granting the validity of this statement historically, and potentially in the future, certainly such "discretionary powers" had been curbed in 1975 when Cronin was writing of legislation and the climate of opinion. Again, this is an experience of two scholars whose firsthand observations in the White House were during the Kennedy-Johnson years. Schlesinger, who had participated in both the Bay of Pigs fiasco and the Cuban missile crisis, found the latter "superbly handled,"except "one of its legacies," he attested, "was the imperial conception of the Presidency that brought the republic so low in Vietnam."[18] An additional legacy, which Schlesinger failed to note, was the determination of the Soviets never again, from an inferior military posture, to have a humiliating confrontation with the United States. They would never forget those fateful days in October 1962 when, under threat of an air strike on Cuba, which could escalate to a nuclear war, the Soviets withdrew their missiles. According to Secretary McNamara, the United States had "faced . . . the possibility of launching nuclear weapons" had the Soviets not complied. Indeed, McNamara asserted that "Khrushchev knew . . . that he faced the full military power of the United States, including its nuclear weapons.... That," McNamara concluded, "is the reason, and the only reason, why he withdrew those weapons."[19] Parenthetically it may be noted that had the United States, instead of issuing an ultimatum, offered to withdraw missiles from Turkey, which were already approved for deactivation, the danger of nuclear war might have been reduced (as it turned out, such an offer became a last-minute addition to the deal, anyway).

Despite Cronin-Schlesinger concerns about discretionary powers, the President, as Commander in Chief, is not a power unto himself. The Congress can withhold appropriations, and it has. It so ended military operations in Cambodia in 1973. The Congress can, and has on numerous occasions, reduced the number of American armed forces stationed abroad. The Congress can, as it did in the Cooper-Case-Church amendment prohibiting future ground operations in Cambodia, bar specific kinds of action. Its investigations do have a profound effect on policy and organization. Moreover, the professional military, not unlike the civilian bureaucracy, has its own means to "resist, delay, and amend." The Courts, as noted below, have imposed few restrictions on the Commander in Chief's role, but—and this is too often forgotten—the electorate may vote a Commander in Chief out. Truman appreciated this in 1952, as did Johnson in 1968, when each declined to run again following public loss of confidence in their roles as Commander in Chief.

WAR POWERS. A principal concern of both the Congress and scholars is the "discretionary powers" of the President as Commander in Chief—most notably, but not exclusively, in warmaking. Historically there have been three doctrines for Presidential action in waging war: (1) self-defense; (2) protection of American lives and property; and (3) hot pursuit. (President Eisenhower, by threatening the use of the third, speeded up an armistice in the Korean War.) Congress, by its 1973 War Powers Act, authorized the Commander in Chief to initiate military action abroad, in the absence of a declaration of war, provided only that he advise Congress, in writing, within forty-eight hours following his action. Such combat military operations with United States armed forces must

be ended within sixty days unless Congress has authorized
the action. The President may extend such an operation for
thirty days in order to permit safe withdrawal if he has so
certified this as his intent. *But,* and constitutionally this is
most important, at any time within the sixty- or ninety-day
period that the Congress so decides by joint resolution, it can
order the withdrawal of such forces. Further, such action
cannot be subject to a Presidential veto. Hence Congress can
seemingly countervene the Constitutional and historical role
of the President as Commander in Chief.

The War Powers Act was introduced by Republican
Senator Jacob K. Javits of New York in 1971 in order to combat what he considered to have been the excesses of the
President as Commander in Chief in the Indochina war.[20]
But it was not enacted until 1973, when the Nixon administration was mortally wounded by Watergate. Hence it
passed over the Presidential veto. As Louis W. Koenig, one
of our most respected students of the Presidency, observes,
the War Powers Act "is unlikely to be accepted with
equanimity in future, more normal Presidencies."[21] It could
be interpreted as actually inviting Presidential military action, without an expression of cause, subject only to time
limitations. Moreover, the probability of Congressional intervention would be highly unlikely in the midst of dangerous combat. In the only new combat operation since the
passage of the War Powers Act, the *Mayagüez* incident, President Ford did fulfill the requirement of a written report to
the Congress within forty-eight hours. Yet, Arthur Schlesinger, Jr., wrote that " . . . the President, without Congressional
authorization or even consultation, started a small war
against the new Cambodian Government. . . ."[22]

INTELLIGENCE GATHERING. More lacking in wisdom
than the well-intentioned War Powers Act of the 93rd Congress have been a series of actions in 1974–1976 by the 94th
Congress which have been described by William E. Griffith,
professor at Massachusetts Institute of Technology, as
"headstrong."[23] These included: severely reducing military
supplies to South Vietnam; cutting off aid to Turkey; and
turning an inquiry regarding the intelligence community into

a public spectacle. Robert Novak and other critics of excessive Congressional intervention in foreign policy have attributed to the first, in part, the fall of South Vietnam; to the second, the possible permanent impairment of our relationship with our strategically important Turkish ally; and to the third, the permanent impairment of our intelligence community.[24]

Not a single American life was saved by denying arms to South Vietnam, since all United States combat forces had long since been withdrawn. The net result of reducing aid to Turkey was our being ousted from approximately twenty bases there, including four highly sensitive electronic stations monitoring Soviet missile tests and military communications. Although by October 1975 Congress had partially lifted the embargo, the United States was left with but one base in Turkey; the ostensible purpose of the Congressional action, aid to Greek Cypriots, had in no way been accomplished. (In like manner Congressional pressure on the Soviets, through the Jackson-Vanik amendment to the Trade Act of 1974, far from helping Jewish émigrés, hurt them: The amendment made the liberalizing of the trade agreements with the Soviet Union conditional upon their liberalizing of Jewish immigration; the angry Soviets responded by reducing the number of émigrés from 35,000 in 1973 to 13,000 in 1975 and by taking its lucrative trade elsewhere.[25]

The intelligence community has undoubtedly committed excesses, but the recent compromising of sensitive sources of information has hardly been justified. As Elliot L. Richardson observed in January 1976, we still live in a time of "adversary relationships," in which it is vital to "find out what the other side is doing." He could not comprehend how any "responsible person" could willfully seek to dismantle that capability.[26] (It may be noted that this is the same soft-spoken Elliot Richardson who as Secretary of Defense in 1973, when Congress cut off funds for air operations in Cambodia, said such funds would be secured by reducing other areas of defense appropriations. Such action, Richardson argued, directly supported the Commander in Chief's protection of American troops during the period of their withdrawal.)

In his 1976 State of the Union Address, President Ford, with obvious reference to the Congressional investigations, asserted that "it is time to go beyond sensationalism and insure an effective, responsible, and responsive intelligence community." He warned that "the crippling of our foreign intelligence services increases the danger of American involvement in direct armed conflict." The President concluded that making charades of our intelligence community inquiries not only encourages "our adversaries" to enter upon "new adventures" but also, by undermining our monitoring ability, reduces our own options "to influence events short of military action. . . ."[27] It is this reduction of options which especially concerns old foreign policy hands, who perceive the Soviets, at the same time, increasing their own covert operations. Henry Kissinger viewed such operations as "the gray area between foreign policy and overt conflict."[28]

DECLARATIONS OF A STATE OF EMERGENCY.   Of all the four principal areas of Congressional concern—executive agreements, war powers, intelligence, and declaration of emergency—the least heralded is the last. Yet more than the others it has challenged civil liberties and property rights. The removal of thousands of Americans of Japanese ancestry from their West Coast homes in World War II, the denial of the writ of habeas corpus in Hawaii in World War II, and the steel mills seizure in the Korean War are all suggestive of emergency powers.

Too many Americans forget that the Korean War declaration of emergency, for example, was still operative in 1976. In the United States' bicentennial year, four Presidentially proclaimed states of national emergency were still in effect: the March 6, 1933, declaration of Roosevelt on the banking crisis; Truman's December 16, 1950, declaration; the March 23, 1970, Nixon declaration calling upon the Ready Reserve and National Guard to help move mail during the postal strike; and Nixon's August 15, 1971, declaration to control the balance-of-payments flow. With little fanfare, the 93rd Congress formed a Special Committee on the Termination of National Emergency of the United States Senate. It cataloged

470 federal provisions, operative through declarations of emergencies, which truly gave the President, as Congressman Anderson describes, "awesome discretionary powers."[29] Review of those provisions and proposed legislation to reset the balance between the Congress and the President were among the least publicized and most significant efforts of the Congress, which not only sought means to terminate these declarations but would additionally "recommend ways in which the United States can meet future emergency situations with speed and effectiveness but without relinquishing of congressional oversight and control."[30]

Congressional reform in the area of declaration of national emergency is most essential. This source of power, so often called upon by heads of state in the past half-century, caused Clinton Rossiter to coin the term "Constitutional Dictatorship." How the Congress overreacted in this instance is noted in the Epilogue. Executive agreements, war powers, declarations of emergency, and intelligence, while worthy of continuing concern, do not so readily lend themselves to legislative reform. They represent abuses in a period of excessive Presidential power and its aftermath of decline.

During the eight Eisenhower years there was a conscious effort to restore equilibrium between the Congress and the Presidency, but the period 1932–1965 witnessed the most sustained period of Presidential omnipotence in American history. With the Vietnam War, liberal scholars and many media representatives, in an age of instant communications, became most unyielding opponents of executive power: they urged the counterexcesses of Congressional reform. The result has been an unhealthy climate of mutual suspicion and distrust between the Congress and the Presidency, causing Senator Charles Mathias, Jr., to conclude concerning the 94th Congress, "If George Washington asked this Congress for a single platoon, he'd be suspect up here."[31]

The Courts and the Presidency

If the Congress to date has had dubious success in its efforts to check the President as chief diplomat and Commander in

Chief, what of the Courts? With the exception of the Supreme Court ruling on the Truman seizure of the steel mills, the Court has been ineffectual in challenging the Commander in Chief role of the modern Presidency. In 1801, Chief Justice Marshall, in *Talbot* v. *Seeman*, found the authorizing of both general and limited war to be vested solely in the Congress.[32] Yet experience in his friend John Adams's naval war against the French had already proven otherwise. As his son John Quincy Adams looked back on the first half-century of the Presidency, he saw clearly that, by a series of Presidentially initiated military (and naval) actions, albeit mostly defensive in character, the Presidents had exercised "the power of involving the nation in war, even without consulting Congress. . . ."[33]

In a 5-to-4 decision, the Supreme Court in 1861 upheld Lincoln's war powers, those acts in the first twelve weeks of the Civil War prior to the convening of Congress (on July 4) in special session. The dissenting judges, to no avail, insisted that "Congress alone can determine whether war exists or should be declared."[34] Lincoln defended his most provocative war powers act, the suspension of the writ of habeas corpus, on the exception stated in the Constitution (Article I, Section 9): "In cases of rebellion or invasion the public safety may require it." True, the Constitution had failed to note who was to do the suspending. The Congress, in the Habeas Corpus Act of 1863, affirmed Lincoln's actions of the two preceding years. Not until after the ending of the grave emergency, and after Lincoln's death, did the Supreme Court in *Ex parte Milligan,* in 1866, declare that the Constitution worked "equally in war and in peace." Only then did they dismiss Lincoln's doctrine of necessity.[35]

As Louis Koenig has pointed out, "despite the potential restrictiveness of the Milligan doctrine," the Court in both World War I and World War II "proved tolerant" of the President's Commander in Chief powers.[36] Thus the Court upheld Roosevelt, as Commander in Chief, in having appointed a military commission in 1942 to try German saboteurs. Members of the German armed services, dressed as civilians, they had been put ashore from a German submarine off Long Island. The following year, in *Hirabayashi* v.

United States and again in 1944 in *Korematsu* v. *United States,* the Court upheld Roosevelt's sweeping 1942 action as Commander in Chief in designating "military areas," thereby removing 112,000 persons of Japanese ancestry, many of whom were American citizens, from the West Coast. Not until after the war did the Court, in 1946, in *Duncan* v. *Kahanamoku, Sheriff,* declare Roosevelt's wartime suspension of the writ of habeas corpus in Hawaii unlawful. Further, during the war (indeed even before the December 8, 1941, declaration of war), Roosevelt had, as Commander in Chief, seized control of certain American aircraft plants, shipyards, and a railroad threatened with stoppages.

In brief, despite the *Milligan* doctrine, as Clinton Rossiter observed, "There do, indeed, seem to be two Constitutions—one for peace, the other for war."[37] In a very real sense there are also, as Aaron Wildavsky expressed it, two Presidencies, one for domestic affairs, the other for foreign affairs.[38] The President, in the 1939–1965 period, was relatively uninhibited in foreign affairs. Indeed, although public pressure mounted on the Presidency in foreign affairs after 1965, with the increasing unpopularity of the Vietnam War, it was not until after the 1968 election that severe Congressional constraints were imposed. The Court was a passive witness to these events.

The Courts have, as Rossiter expressed it, been "one of the least reliable restraints on presidential activity."[39] What remains unanswered, at this writing, is whether Congressional excesses with regard to the President as Commander in Chief, such as the War Powers Act, will find any more "reliable restraints" on the part of the Courts.

Communications and Consensus

If Congressional legislation and court decisions have not allayed concerns regarding Presidential actions in the area of national security policy, where, indeed, is relief to be found? And, equally important, how is consensus on policy to supersede devisiveness? Adolf Berle, while maintaining in 1971 that recent Presidents had acted in this area within their

Constitutional authority, did suggest that improved communications would help get to the heart of the problem. Thus he wrote, "The change I would like to see made lies not in the fact of Presidential powers but in the conduct of the President's dialogue as it is progressively exercised."[40]

Berle believed in our Presidential system. He did not concur with those who would overhaul it in favor of the British parliamentary system. Yet he did recognize that the kind of dialogue enjoyed between the British Cabinet and Parliament was helpful. He thus proposed a somewhat similar dialogue, though not with the whole Congress. He suggested periodic meetings of the President, or his formally appointed representative, with the House Committee on Foreign Affairs (renamed International Relations) and the Senate Committee on Foreign Relations.

Others have recently taken Berle's suggestion a step further. The Foreign Affairs and Foreign Relations committees never did represent the total Congressional concern in national security policy. Today at least fourteen separate Congressional committees are involved. William E. Griffith has proposed the formation of a Joint Committee on National Security, consisting of leaders of the Congress and key committee chairmen,[41] which would work with the President to achieve consensus. Essential to this is the restoration of the principles of bipartisanship in foreign policy, which operated so effectively in the 1940–1950 and the 1953–1961 periods.

The breakdown of bipartisan support in the 1950–1952 period cost the Truman administration dearly. The Truman-Acheson team may or may not have accomplished more than the Eisenhower-Dulles team, but both Eisenhower and Dulles, by contrast with Truman and Acheson, worked effectively with the Congress. Acheson appeared before the Senate Foreign Relations Committee only when summoned, whereas Dulles constantly sought the Committee's views and appeared before them forty-eight times over a six-year period.[42]

Rapport between the Congress and the Presidency is essential for effective policy. The Dulles-Eisenhower approach of seeking Congressional participation in policy formation, as in Taiwan and Lebanon, is a prime example. It contrasts with the Acheson-Truman approach of asking endorsement of a *fait accompli,* as in Korea and NATO troop commitments. Presidents and Secretaries of State should not conduct foreign policy for the sake of popularity polls, but they cannot conduct effective foreign policy without Congressional *and* popular support. The two are essentially interrelated: Congress will not fly long in the face of public opinion, but neither will public opinion long support a President's constant wrangling with the Congress. The wisdom of Berle's observations is supported by the polls, which indicated that fewer than one-third of the American people approved of the conduct of foreign policy during the last two years of the Truman period, whereas more than two-thirds approved during the last two years of the Eisenhower period.

Congress has repeatedly suggested that more effective communication is essential, and much of its more worthy recent legislative efforts have been toward that end. Thus the Case Act of 1972 (proposed as early as 1970) sought to establish a means by which the Congress (or, in the instances of classified matters, appropriate committees) would be informed of the contents of executive agreements. Here was a modest proposal, indeed. So also the initial procedure in the War Powers Act is the Presidential *informing* of the Congress. Legislation the same year requiring certain government agencies (State, USIA, AID, and the Arms Control Disarmament Agency) to supply the Congress with information, on threat of cutting off these organizations' funds, was angrily ill-conceived. Such measures of duress are bound to be counterproductive.

Again and again, with compelling earnestness, members of the Congress and their staff have indicated that being kept informed is the heart of the issue. Illustrative of this is the assessment of the staff director of the Senate Special Committee on the Termination of the National Emergency. William G. Miller, who also ably headed the staff for the Church committee on intelligence investigations, voiced one principal concern from both of these inquiries: that the Presidency must do more in advising the Congress in the national security and foreign policy areas. This omission, Miller concludes, "to say nothing of availability to public scrutiny . . . is clearly a great danger."[43]

This "availability to public scrutiny" to which Miller refers is, then, a basic dilemma of a democracy in its conduct of foreign policy. In our open and pluralistic society, it is necessary to secretly conduct many aspects of foreign policy. The Cuban missile crisis is again a case in point. "If our deliberations had been publicized," wrote Robert Kennedy in defense of their secrecy, ". . . the course we ultimately would have taken would have been quite different and filled with far greater risk."[44] Democracy's dilemma is compounded by the vital relationship in such a society between public opinion and national security policy. How do we defend the covert operations of our intelligence community? We must do so on the basic moral principles of self-preservation of a nation devoted to the protection of democratic values.

The dilemma is heightened by the relatively complex decisionmaking process in a democracy such as the United States, where a full reckoning and consideration must be made with opposition views, as compared to an autocracy like the Soviet Union, where, in a monolithic structure, decisions emerge as a single view no matter how sinister the consequences. (This is not to say that there are no disputed views within the Politburo; witness the eventual dismissal of Premier Nikita Khrushchev, who had lost face in his concessions to Eisenhower in Berlin in 1959 and in 1962 to Kennedy in the Cuban missile crisis.)

All these considerations—the necessity for openness in basic policy and secrecy in many operations, the complexity in decisionmaking—point to the basic necessity to secure a degree of consensus based on understanding. The Presidency, which Theodore Roosevelt liked to refer to as a "bully pulpit," is central to such consensus. Richard Neustadt, in his classis work *Presidential Power,* has suggested that the basic Presidential power is the "power to persuade." The two Roosevelts and Eisenhower were perhaps our most effective twentieth-century Presidents because they were the best persuaders. As Neustadt says, the President must convince the Congress "that what the White House wants of them is what they ought to do for their sake and on their authority."[45] President Truman recognized this even if he was not always artful in carrying it out. "The principal power that the President has," he lamented, "is to bring people in and try to persuade them to do what they ought to do without persuasion."[46]

Two of the most valuable subcommittees the Senate has ever had on the subject of national security policy were headed by Senator Henry M. Jackson in the 1959–1965 period. They made perhaps the wisest recommendations to date on the President's persuasive role, the division of labor between the Congress and the Presidency in national security policy, and the machinery for the formulation and conduct of policy. In 1959, when Eisenhower was still President, the Jackson Subcommittee on National Policy Machinery emphasized the paramount Presidential role in both the formulation and the implementation of policy. The Committee members, including Hubert Humphrey, Edmund Muskie, Jacob Javits, and Karl Mundt, *then* declared: "By law and practice the President has the pivotal role in matters of national security policy. He is responsible for the conduct of foreign affairs; he is Commander in Chief; he makes the great decisions on the budget." Lauding Eisenhower's creation of the position of scientific adviser, they noted that "increasingly his choices involve complex scientific and technological questions. . . ." In summing up, they observed, "The interpretation of national policy—domestic, foreign, and military—must take place first of all in the President's mind." They wisely concluded, then, with an appreciation for our democratic processes, that "the consensus needed to support National policy depends largely upon his [the President's] powers of leadership and persuasion. . . ."[47]

Perhaps a better word in this instance than "consensus," which connotes agreement, is "understanding." A very wise former Secretary of State, Elihu Root, wrote in 1922 that in the conduct of foreign policy in a democracy there is one essential ingredient, "one inevitable condition" for success: the people "must acquire a knowledge of the fundamental and essential facts and principles. . . . Without such knowledge," Root emphasized, "there can be no intelligent discussion and consideration of foreign policy." Root, like Stimson, had been a Secretary of War as well as a Secretary of State, which may have contributed to the breadth of view of both on national security policy. Root first had been McKinley's and Theodore Roosevelt's Secretary of War before serving as Roosevelt's Secretary of State. Looking back on a lifetime of experience in advising Presidents on national security affairs, he concluded that when there is a lack of communications, a lack of understanding, among the Presidency, the Congress, and the people, "misrepresentation will have a clear field and ignorance and error will make wild work with foreign relations."[48]

Forty-eight years later, Adolf Berle, nearing the end of a lifetime of advising Presidents, testified that "if measures are needed, they should be directed toward better and more accurate information for the American public, accuracy that American public opinion will function more continuously and more responsibly as it deals with the day to day decisions a President must make. . . ."[49] Berle further believed that better public understanding of the decisionmaking process would increase mutual respect, toleration, and compassion.

Today there is a healthy concern on the part of the body politic, the American people, for a better understanding of the issues involved in national security policy and the machinery or means for its conduct. Although the American people may not have the expertise to judge the means, they have, with the communications of Jefferson, Lincoln, Roosevelt, Truman, and Eisenhower, grasped the fundamental principles. In both the colonial and their national experience, Americans have further proved that, given the facts, they have been able to determine the ends, the goals, of policy. As James Bryce, examining democracy in both Britian and America, concluded, "History shows that [the people] do this as wisely as monarchs or oligarchies, or the small groups to whom, in democratic countries, the conduct of foreign relations has been left, and that they have evinced more respect for moral principles."[50] Peoples and their leaders in nondemocratic societies may not fully grasp this last point. Nonetheless recent American history has so reconfirmed.

XI

****

FROM COLD WAR TO DÉTENTE: THE SEARCH FOR A NATIONAL STRATEGY

> Our task is to devise a national strategy. . . .
> SENATOR JOHN F. KENNEDY

The "Open" Presidency

As the United States approached its bicentennial, there was seeming apathy and weariness in the land. The immediate causes were quite clear: the traumatic experiences of Vietnam and Watergate. But a searching inquiry of cause of the malaise has to go beyond those two manifestations. In at least one of the bicentennial examinations of American institutions two troublesome questions emerged, each with a disturbing consequent question: (1) From what characteristics of the modern Presidential office could a Watergate be spawned? Can it happen again? (2) How could the most powerful nation in the world have become bogged down in Vietnam? Is there the possibility of a recurrence of this kind of operation?[1]

Questions regarding cover-ups at home, such as Watergate, and operations overseas, such as Vietnam, do not at first seem related. And yet they are. Both are, in part, by-products of a "closed" as compared to an "open" Presidency.

Avowals are made that never again will the United States get involved in a Vietnam-type operation, that the United

States had learned its lesson. We cannot be so sure. How could the nation so rapidly have forgotten the lessons of Korea? How did the American conscience dismiss the warnings of both President Eisenhower and General MacArthur that the United States must never again fight a land war on the Asian continent?

Although a policy of arms aid and military advisers for Southeast Asia was initiated by Truman and Acheson in 1950, the urgent French plea for armed intervention in 1954 was turned down by Eisenhower. It was not for lack of solicitude. Indeed, with the 1954 departure of the French, supposedly ending the eight-year Indochina War, the United States had initiated the Southeast Asia Collective Defense Treaty (SEATO), signed that same year by the United States and seven other nations, pledging to protect South Vietnam and other nations in that area. Southeast Asia had been one of Eisenhower's major concerns in his last days in office, when, with Russian airlift support, a North Vietnamese and Laotian Communist (Pathet Lao) insurgency in Laos was under way. Eisenhower's final counsel on the subject of Southeast Asia had been to the new Chairman of the Joint Chiefs of Staff, General Lyman L. Lemnitzer, on January 2, 1961: "If we ever have to resort to force, there's just one thing to do: clear up the problem completely."[2] Amplifying on this Ambassador Robert D. Murphy recalled, "What... Eisenhower said [is] that you *don't* win wars by hesitation. You don't do it by nibbling or piecemeal."[3]

Despite such counsel, the United States during the next eight years got deeper and deeper into the Vietnamese quagmire, reaching a peak force of 541,500 in March 1969, but with no national will to achieve a military decision. Never in its history had the nation fought a war so devoid of overall strategy and effective planning. The focus was rather on domestic policies and the Great Society legislative program. Louis Koenig, who has studied crisis management and Presidential command decisions in depth, observed that "the development of the Vietnam decisions suggest a kind of sliding operation being developed rather incrementally." Dr. Koenig concluded that "because of the absorption then in the domestic legislative program... decisions related to

Vietnam"⁴ were relegated to "second class citizenship." Helmut Sonnenfeldt corroborated this view. "Vietnam," he assessed, "is a case where piecemeal decisions were made when perhaps more basic decisions should have been made in earlier years."⁵

The incremental sliding operation, as Koenig aptly terms it, had certain demarcation points: the 1950 Truman initiative in dispatching equipment and advisers to the French; the 1955 action of Eisenhower in sending advisers to train South Vietnam's army; the first two Americans (advisers) killed in action in 1959 in guerrilla attack; the 1961 arrival of armed helicopters with U.S. crews authorized by President Kennedy to aid in combat operations; the 1964 retaliatory bombing of North Vietnam ordered by President Johnson in response to the Gulf of Tonkin attack; and the 1965 first U.S. ground forces combat operation ordered by President Johnson.

Clearly, despite all of the nation's resources and its machinery for decisionmaking, there was no comprehensive plan for waging and winning a war in Southeast Asia. More tragically, Lyndon B. Johnson, the Commander in Chief, amid all the modern means of communication, found himself cut off from the American people. This insulation of the Presidency, which Johnson's press secretary, George Reedy, described so eloquently, contributed directly to the American people's loss of confidence in the conduct of the war. Reedy concluded that "the rising tide of opposition . . . came more from the fact that the people thought they had been sold a bill of goods than it did from actual considered judgment towards the war itself."⁶

Johnson was a masterful parlimentarian in his role as Senate Majority Leader during the Eisenhower administration. Always seeking consensus, he could muster the vote that Eisenhower needed. As Commander in Chief, Johnson unfortunately approached the Vietnam War in the same fashion. He got the votes, overwhelming, in the Southeast Asia (Tonkin Gulf) resolution of August 1964. Drafted several months before it was served up in an emotional moment to leaders of Congress, it followed an attack on American destroyers off the coast of North Vietnam (in the Gulf of Tonkin) by North Vietnamese torpedo boats. In convening the Congressional leaders, Johnson skillfully recalled Taft's admonition when Truman had failed to consult the Congress before entering the Korean War.

In the Tonkin Gulf Resolution, the House, by a unanimous vote, and the Senate, with only two nays, avowed that Congress "approves and supports the determination of the President, as Commander in Chief, to take all necessary measures to repel any armed attack against the forces of the United States and to prevent further aggression."[7] In this and subsequent actions on the war, Reedy recalls, if a member of Congress or of the National Security Council posed an objection to Johnson's views, it was "almost apologetic."[8] Only as the war continued, with little progress and mounting casualties, did both the Congress and the people began to feel that "they had been sold a bill of goods."[9] Nixon, as Johnson's successor, disavowed the Gulf of Tonkin Resolution, and in January 1971 it was revoked by the Congress. Thereafter, the President's sole authority for military action in Southeast Asia was that of the Commander in Chief protecting American lives. Thus Nixon rationalized the April 30–June 30, 1970 incursion into the Cambodian sanctuaries for the purpose of defending "the security of our American men."[10]

As Reedy points out, the entire atmosphere of consultation and decisionmaking in 1954 regarding the French in Vietnam was completely different from that ten years later which culminated in the Gulf of Tonkin Resolution. In the 1954 relief of Dien Bien Phu, as in the 1958 defense of Quemoy and Matsu and the landing in Lebanon, President Eisenhower had invited the most thorough discussion and debate. What disturbed Reedy in the Johnson Presidency was the almost complete absence of debate. Reedy recently recalled how "in 1954 when we were being pushed by Admiral Arthur W. Radford, then Chairman of the Joint Chiefs of Staff, and the then Vice President Nixon to go into Vietnam to the aid of the French at Dien Bien Phu, Eisenhower asked Lyndon Johnson to sound out the sentiments of Senate Democrats for reactions." What Johnson did on that occasion, at Eisenhower's urging, he was unable to do as President; he never asked for a frank exchange of views on a controversial foreign policy issue. Reedy, who witnessed the genuine debate which followed, recalled how the chairman of the Senate Foreign Relations Committee, Senator Walter F. George, "said that we would lose face if we did not go into Dien Bien Phu. By contrast," Reedy related, "Senator Robert S. Kerr of Oklahoma, a big rugged oilman with a fist like a ham slammed it on the table and allowed that he was more concerned about losing another part of his anatomy if we did go in. At the end of the debate," Reedy concluded, ". . . we had a really good human view of the thing."[11]

This episode points up the completely contrasting decisionmaking process of the Eisenhower and the Johnson Presidencies. Through the structure of the National Security Council, Eisenhower encouraged divergence of views, from which he could make his command decisions. NSC decisionmaking and decision-implementing structures were largely dismantled at the beginning of the Kennedy administration. The NSC never returned to being a vigorous deliberative body during the Johnson years. As George Reedy recalled, everything "was very gentle," with the overwhelming weight of unified opinion expressed by the President, the Secretaries of State and Defense (Rusk and McNamara), and the Special Assistant for National Security Affairs (Walt Rostow). The protesting voice of Under Secretary of State George Ball went unheeded.[12] Recognizing these characteristics of the "closed" Johnson Presidency, Nixon promised in his inaugural an "open Presidency." Although he restored much of the deliberative quality of the NSC, his very own introverted personality, as well as the designs of his personal staff, made this professed effort a failure. He himself was to be caught up in the closed Presidency in the tragedy of Watergate and its cover-up. George Reedy recognized all these dangerous tendencies more than two years before Watergate. On April 5, 1970, he noted "that one of Mr. Nixon's biggest mistakes was enlarging the White House staff. Believe me, any White House assistant with any sensitivity could get out and write a novel about the court of Paleologus in Byzantium; all he would have to do would be to get out and look up a few Greek names." Speaking from personal observation and experience of the Johnson years, Reedy continued, "Now you can take it as virtually certain that the more dedicated, progressive, creative, innovative men you crowd into the place, the more jockeying you are going to have. . . ." Reedy concluded with the prophetic warning that "there will be more people trying to envelope the central man [Nixon] in the kind of blanket that he doesn't need."[13]

From Truman through Nixon: The Foundations of National Strategy

THE 1950s: THE DECADE OF STRATEGIC LITERATURE. In 1958, Robert Strausz-Hupé inquired, "What must be the strategic doctrine of the United States?" Answering his own question, Professor (subsequently Ambassador) Strausz-Hupé concluded, ". . . it must be the defense of the Continental United States against an all-out attack, the maintenance of the balance of power in Europe and the Far East, and the capability of using the appropriate means in order to maintain that balance of power."[14]

Former Secretary of State Henry Kissinger would doubtless agree with those three strategy goals, as did a younger Professor Kissinger in the 1950s. That was the remarkable decade of writing on national strategy by a group of talented writers, of which Professors Kissinger and Strausz-Hupé were representative, although their views were contrasting and divergent. Strausz-Hupé, identified with the "protracted conflict," represented those with a grim conception of implacable foes. Kissinger, by contrast, while mounting a strong defense posture and advocating instruments for securing a balance of power, held out hope for accommodation. Détente, a policy of reaching accommodation with the Soviets, had been a part of the British strategic literature as early as 1954. A number of Americans, including Kissinger, were also writing on this subject before the end of the second Eisenhower administration. But it never became a part of the conception of either Strausz-Hupé or his colleague Colonel (since Ambassador) William Kintner.

Other brilliant strategic writers of the era included Bernard Brodie, who had pioneered in 1946 with his volume *The Absolute Weapon: Atomic Power and World Order,* setting forth strategy still pertinent today; Roger Hilsman, who in the mid-1950s was helping coin the terms "counterforce" and "countervalue"; William W. Kaufmann, whose *Military Policy and National Security* appeared in 1956; and Robert E. Osgood, whose volume *Limited War: The Challenge to American Strategy* appeared in 1957, the same year as Kissinger's *Nuclear Weapons and Foreign Policy.* Army Chief of Staff Maxwell Taylor should not be forgotten for such essays as "The Strategy of Sword and Shield" (1958), advocating mobile strategic forces for limited war. The following year Oskar Morgenstern's *The Question of National Defense* suggested that it was in the best interest of both the United States and the Soviet Union to have sea-based (relatively invulnerable) missiles in order to ensure the continuation of the nuclear stalemate.

Nor in assessing this decade can the writings on strategic policy of the Secretary of State John Foster Dulles be overlooked. The decade was rounded out with Maxwell Taylor's highly influential *Uncertain Trumpet* (1960), published after Taylor's resignation as Army Chief of Staff. It was to catapult him into a leading strategy role in the Kennedy administration and mark the beginning of the decline of the Air Force share of the defense budget. The same year Herman Kahn's *On Thermonuclear War* appeared. Also in 1960, Kissinger's *The Necessity for Choice* prescribed (as had Dulles, Eisenhower, and Radford) tactical nuclear weapons in limited war.

Taken together, such works and others produced the most prolific literature on national security policy that has come forth in any decade in American history, and comparatively little new doctrine has since been added. With the exception of the doctrines of indirect strategy and revolutionary war, which were coming from the pens of the French during this same period, based partly on their Vietnam and Algeria experiences, most of the still-current doctrine on deterrence, counterforce, countervalue, multipolarity, massive retaliation, flexible (or selective) response, finite (minimum) deterrence, nuclear superiority or overkill, limited war, and second strike forces had all been written by Americans in the decade of the 1950s. As Michael Howard has assessed it, "Together they have done what Clausewitz and Mahan did in the last century during times of no less bewildering political and technological change; they have laid down clear principles to guide the men who have to make decisions."[15] Many of these writers of the 1950s became practitioners of the 1960s and the 1970s.

THE TRUMAN ERA.   If such "clear principles" were enunciated, why the confusion, the obfuscation, that has at times characterized policy? There are three basic reasons: the difficulty of comprehending and defining a strategy for the nuclear age; the shifting balances of power; and the multiple interests in our pluralistic democratic society.

When the first atomic device was tested at Alamogordo, New Mexico, on July 16, 1945, Stalin, at the Potsdam Conference at the time, had no comprehension of the meaning of the "superbomb." He learned a few weeks later, when bombs fell on Hiroshima and Nagasaki. Within a year, it was clear that the Soviets would not be content with a second place in nuclear weaponry. That same year, 1946, Bernard Brodie wrote with a vision regarding the future purposes of military power: "Thus far the chief purpose of our military establishment has been to win wars. From now on its chief purpose must be to avert them."[16] With the dawn of the nuclear age, deterrence necessarily became a principal purpose of the armed forces; however, no philosophy of deterrence was enunciated until the Eisenhower administration.

The earliest responses of the Truman administration to Soviet post–World War II expansion in 1945–1947 had been anger and dismay. Dismantling of American armed forces, which had followed every war, in this instance left no credible deterrent—other than the bomb itself. Then, as in our past history, with the 1947 enunciation of the Truman Doctrine, a doctrine of containment evolved. The Monroe Doctrine of 1823, opposing European intervention or further colonization in the Western Hemisphere, had been in keeping with this American containment philosophy. In it President Monroe (and his Secretary of State, John Quincy Adams) had stated, in keeping with American experience: "It is only when our rights are involved or seriously menaced that we resent injuries or make preparation for our defense." Theodore Roosevelt, in 1904, expanded the Monroe Doctrine, which was limited by geography to the New World, when he justified United States intervention.

As Curtis P. Nettels has pointed out, there was essentially nothing new in the Truman Doctrine, except in its worldwide geographical and timeless scope. Other early examples of seeking to resist or contain a hostile force by actions short of war had included: (1) the ten years of colonial efforts to contain the British Parliament, preceding the American revolution; (2) the seven years of Republican opposition to the spread of slavery in the territories, following the passage of the Kansas-Nebraska Act in 1854, preceding the Civil War; (3) Wilson's efforts, 1914–1917, to maintain freedom of the high seas, prior to American entry into World War I; and (4) Roosevelt's efforts, 1937–1941, to arrest Nazi expansionism.

Noting that all these examples of containment had been followed by war, Nettels pessimistically viewed Truman's address of March 12, 1947, announcing the Truman Doctrine of seeking to arrest the spread of Communism. Nettels was one of the few persons at the time who recognized the doctrine to be boundless in time and space in its efforts to prevent the subjugation of free peoples "by armed minorities or outside pressures." In the spring of 1947, Nettels asked his Cornell classes: "Who would give assurance that there would ever be an end to 'attempted subjugation by armed minorities'?" As a result he found himself castigated in the Cornell *Daily Sun*. At most, he was seeking to draw lessons from history. He concluded that "the doctrine of containment is an American innovation ... a by-product of American democracy," in keeping with American traditions "to assert, by peaceful public acts and utterances, their opposition to a hostile force...."[17] While appreciating the moral provocation, he predicted it would lead to such armed conflicts as followed in Korea and Vietnam.

Nettels recognized in 1947 that while the Truman Doctrine was inspired by a request to the Congress for aid to Greece and Turkey, it seemed to offer help in any place at any time to peoples subjugated to "outside pressures." Such a sweeping doctrine paralleled Kennedy's inaugural promise to "support any friend, oppose any foe to assure the survival and the success of liberty."

George Kennan's 1947 "Mr. X" article and the Truman Doctrine were our earliest post–World War II foreign policy statements. Both suggested the responsive policy of containment. Neither was clearly enunciated. Seeking to analyze "the sources of Soviet conduct," Kennan suggested in his anonymously written *Foreign Affairs* article that Soviet goals after 1945 included getting control of the industrial-rich Ruhr area of Western Germany and getting the United States entirely out of the Eurasian continent. A specific Kennan objective in this influential article was to raise the hopes and confidence of western Europe. In this he was successful. However, Kennan has spent years explaining what he did not mean, and today his own emphasis is more on moral and spiritual than military rearmament.

John Lewis Gaddis rightly noted that both the Truman Doctrine and the Kennan "Mr. X" article "are excellent examples of the obfuscating potential of imprecise prose."[18] The first comprehensive official post–World War II national strategy statement, NSC-68, had scarcely been digested by President Truman and Secretary Acheson before the outbreak of the Korean War, which, along with simultaneous Soviet pressures on western Europe, dictated American rearmament far more than NSC-68. These events came to preoccupy Truman's able national security advisers, Acheson, Marshall, and Lovett, through the end of his administration.

THE EISENHOWER ERA.   In 1950 John Foster Dulles, serving only as a consultant to Secretary Acheson, had the time in his *War or Peace* volume to reflect philosophically on the development of an American policy. While the United States was endeavoring to rebuild its military forces, Dulles reminded the American people that strength could not be equated merely with military power, that we must make more effective use of our "unchallenged economic power

and intangibles, such as moral judgment and world opinion, which determine what men do and the intensity with
which they do it."[19] The Korean War, Dulles contended, had
resulted from our failure to make clear both our concern for
the security of the Korean Peninsula and our determination
to resist aggression. According to the Dulles thesis, the
Communists opportunistically step in whenever American
will is lacking.

Eisenhower was so impressed with Dulles's views and
with his success in helping to secure the Japanese Peace
Treaty that he invited the stern Presbyterian to be his Secretary of State. For the six remaining years of Dulles's life,
he and Eisenhower made an effective, perceptive, politically
astute team. Dulles's relationship with his President was, as
veteran diplomat Robert D. Murphy observed, "one of the
closest... which a Secretary of State has ever received." It
was always clear that the ultimate decision rested with
Eisenhower, but "in the development of policy," Eisenhower
and Dulles, as Murphy pointed out, always had broad "consultation."[20] Whereas during the Johnson Presidency second-
and third-level officers, particularly in the Departments of
State and Defense, were cut off from policy inputs,[21] Eisenhower indicated his desire for consultation by creating the
post of Staff Secretary; it was first occupied by Brigadier
General Paul T. Carroll. He was succeeded upon his death in
1954 by Colonel Andrew J. Goodpaster, who in 1950 had received his PhD degree in political science from Princeton University.

The Eisenhower team developed the so-called New Look
policies, seeking to plan not just on a crash basis, but for "the
long haul." Dulles described these policies in a January 12,
1954, speech before the Council on Foreign Relations. He
began with acknowledgment "that many of the preceding
foreign policies were good," but he noted that most of them
had been responsive, "mostly emergency action, imposed
on us by our enemies." He then emphasized the need for
long-range planning. Recalling Lenin's prediction that
anti-Communist forces would build "beyond their strength,
so that they come to practical bankruptcy," Dulles insisted
on the need for "a maximum deterrent at a bearable cost"

and "more basic security at less cost"[22]—which, in good-humored military parlance, was termed "more bang for the buck."

Dulles was following the NSC recommendation which Eisenhower had accepted "to depend primarily upon a great capacity to retaliate, instantly, by means and at places of our choosing." Eisenhower had concluded that local ground forces alone could not contain the massive Communist ground forces. Nuclear weapons, controlled and supplied by the United States, would be part of the offsetting factor. But there must also be an umbrella of long-range nuclear weapons on air, sea, and land—what Dulles, not Eisenhower, termed "massive retaliating power."[23] So was born, in Dulles's January 1954 speech, what was thereafter always termed the Dulles policy of "massive retaliation." His conclusion, ignored by his critics, was: "If we can deter such aggression as would mean general war, and that is our confident resolve, then we can let time and fundamentals work for us."[24]

Eisenhower, less rhetorically, emphasized that his own "first guidepost was... to make certain always that our strength was equal to the most strenuous demands that could be made upon it."[25] Essential in his strategy were "strong and binding alliances." He appreciated what Truman and Senator Vandenberg had jointly accomplished in helping give birth to NATO, which he had helped implement as its first military commander. During his Presidency, in addition to strengthening NATO by encouraging the addition of West Germany, he made other regional alliances and bilateral mutual security arrangements. All these steps, he felt, forged "a linking of trust and strength that would prevent the step-by-step deterioration of the world."[26] What he termed the "Sino-Soviet complex" was, by this system of alliances, virtually encircled.

Central in the New Look was reinforcement of the Strategic Air Command (SAC). Many took a dim view of the Army's reduced size and budget, and they were the more frustrated as the Army lost out to SAC control of the intercontinental ballistic missile (ICBM). The Navy, also faced with reductions, found a new dimension in the submarine-launched ballistic missile (SLBM). Before the end of Eisenhower's second administration, almost all present weapon and reconnaissance systems (including satellites as replacements for the U-2) were being developed.

An effective political as well as strategic policy evolved during the Eisenhower years with Democratic control of the Congress. As Herbert S. Parmet has expressed it, "For all Eisenhower's platitudes and public displays of innocence and for all Dulles' blend of righteousness and bellicosity, they were in basic agreement about the political requirements of their mission."[27] Dulles was not particularly innovative, and his rhetoric exceeded his accomplishment, but his policy was far more prudent than the term "brinkmanship," with which he has been associated, implies. More important, Eisenhower himself, though often deeply frustrated, especially with America's inability to offer more to the captive nations, always avoided a head-on confrontation with both the Soviets and the People's Republic of China. Again and again the Soviets were permitted to pull back from their excessive demands. Moreover, as in the forced Anglo-French-Israeli withdrawal following their 1956 attack on Egypt, firmness was indicated toward American friends.

THE KENNEDY-JOHNSON ERA. Eisenhower's deterrence-oriented military policies emphasized a nuclear umbrella for the United States and its allies and substantial economic and military aid to the allies with their handling of low-intensity conflicts. However, strategists, commencing with Bernard Brodie in November 1954, were advocating American forces for such conflicts[28] and criticizing Eisenhower's strategic policies. President Kennedy invited Robert S. McNamara to put this all together in keeping with Kennedy's "support any friend, oppose any foe" concept. As Stephen Ambrose expressed it in 1971, "Kennedy promised to get the country moving again. Where to, no one knew precisely. . . . Fundamentally," Ambrose pointed out, "Eisenhower had rejected the idea that there could be a military solution to Cold War problems. . . . He had accepted limitations on America's role. Kennedy did not." Ambrose concluded, "Kennedy and his aides were especially interested in restoring the prestige and primacy of the Presidency, which they felt had fallen under Eisenhower."[29]

Just before receiving the Democratic nomination, Senator Kennedy had declared: "Our task is to devise a national strategy...." He contended that "as a substitute for policy, Mr. Eisenhower has tried smiling at the Russians; our State Department has tried frowning at them; and Mr. Nixon has tried both." Candidate Kennedy promised he would not have a national strategy predicated upon "eleventh-hour responses to Soviet-created crises, but a comprehensive set of carefully prepared long-term policies designed to increase the strength of the non-Communist world." Contending that a missile gap had developed, he said his first priority was to "make invulnerable a nuclear power second to none...." Next, he would have the United States "regain the ability to intervene effectively and swiftly in any limited war anywhere in the world...." His third point was that "we must rebuild NATO."[30] Throughout his thousand days in office Kennedy insisted on the importance of a strong military posture. In his Inaugural Address on January 20, 1961, he declared that "only where our arms are sufficient beyond doubt can we be certain beyond doubt that they will never be employed."[31] This continued to be a principal theme, with special emphasis on conventional ground forces. In his third State of the Union Message on January 14, 1963, he counseled, "This Country... continues to require the best defense in the world...."[32]

As the Kennedy-Johnson Secretary of Defense for eight years, the longest anyone has held that post, Robert McNamara exhibited great energies and resourcefulness. Although he perceived the immediate role of the Department of Defense policies "in association with other Government policies" to be the containment of Communism, he also perceived as "the long range objective... the spread of freedom throughout the world."[33]

McNamara was correct in his 1963 projection "that in the decade of the 1960's the decisive struggle" would be in "the kind of war which is now going on in South Vietnam."[34] Having surrounded himself with a civilian group of so-called Whiz Kids, McNamara subordinated the advisory role of the

Joint Chiefs of Staff. He and Kennedy found Congress far
more accommodating than America's allies. All kinds of
"limited war" forces were created, headed by the Kennedy-
sponsored elite Green Berets. A new Strike Command was
established, with forces which could be transported at a
moment's notice to all parts of the world. During the
Kennedy-Johnson years manpower in the armed services increased by a million. By contrast military assistance declined,
and the United States came increasingly to bear the burden
of nonnuclear as well as potential nuclear conflict throughout the world.

A part of the goal was to build an invulnerable "second
strike force," another force of such proportions as to be able
to fight a major war in Europe and one in Asia at the same
time, plus a good-sized brush war thrown in to boot: two
and a half wars at once, the military called it; by contrast,
Eisenhower wanted to avoid one and a half. Such were the
aspirations of the Kennedy administration, and academic
strategists, more than the professional military, were invited
to propose strategy. Michael Howard observed that the
McNamara strategy had "a logical coherence—almost an
elegance—which may have commanded rather more admiration among academics than it did in world affairs."[35]

France, along with other countries, choked on the assumption that the United States was not dealing with its peers but
rather as *the* leader of the free world. President Charles de
Gaulle asserted, "In politics and strategy, as in economics,
monopoly naturally appears to him who enjoys it as the best
possible system."[36] In protest, de Gaulle invited the United
States and her NATO allies to leave France in 1963. Granted
the difficulties inherent in de Gaulle's personality, clearly
this would not have occurred during the Eisenhower Presidency. Eisenhower could have written books on the tact required to handle a de Gaulle or a Montgomery, but this was
not Kennedy's stock in trade. As Ambassador L. Dean
Brown expressed it, what emerged was "a basic misunderstanding on our part, a thought that France, as a smaller
country would automatically accept as valid our belief that
the United States is omniscient in political, economic, and
military policy." Laconically, Ambassador Brown, a most

able career foreign service officer, concluded, "It never worked."[37] Four years after de Gaulle served notice, the NATO departures from France and relocations were completed.

France remained a member of the North Atlantic Council, but the Council itself moved from Paris to Brussels in October 1967, a half-year after the relocation of the military headquarters from Paris to Belgium. The United States European Command Headquarters likewise left France, going to Stuttgart, Germany. Although France has maintained a liaison with the thirteen-member NATO Military Committee (made up of all NATO members except France and Iceland) and retained certain forces in Germany, the alliance and its strategic posture was weakened.

Not having learned a lesson with the French experience, the United States forced its new "flexible response" doctrine on the NATO Council in 1967, as a final repudiation of the "massive retaliation" doctrine. Although the Germans, unlike the French four years before, did not walk out of the NATO Military Committee, the sturdy burghers did not buy this "spectrum of deterrence" concept of building their forces to fight a "conventional war." They had been through that twice in the twentieth century and lost. Other NATO members admitted they also found comfort in the old-fashioned "massive retaliation" deterrence.

NATO public relations officers made "flexibility in response" sound good: its "aim," they rationalized, "was to increase . . . options and to be able to counter aggression at any level by an appropriate choice of responses, leaving the enemy in doubt as to which response would be selected."[38] A 1976 assessment of NATO strength vis-à-vis the Warsaw Pact by the chairman of NATO's Military Committee, Sir Peter Hill-Norton, recognized the "considerable imbalance" in ground forces, considering the "reinforcement capabilities" of Soviet forces west of the Volga—this despite the U.S. "massive airlift capability. . . ." NATO air and sea forces remain superior, but Sir Peter concluded that unless there is an augmentation of NATO's ground-force conventional defense "an early resort to nuclear weapons will become the only option in terms of deterrence."[39]

The Europeans are not alone in pointing to what may become mandatory "early resort to nuclear weapons." Ironically, by the time limited or conventional war doctrine had been imposed upon NATO, such early advocates as Bernard Brodie were swinging back toward the Eisenhower-Dulles nuclear retaliation concept.[40] Increasingly unhappy with the credibility of United States deterrence, NATO planners were turning toward détente and mutual and balanced force reductions (MBFR) with the Warsaw Pact forces. The Harmel Report of December 1967, based on a year-long study initiated at the suggestion of the Belgian Foreign Minister, declared, "The way to peace and stability in Europe rests in particular on the use of the alliance constructively in the interest of détente."[41] The NATO Council's MBFR Declaration, which followed in June 1968, suggested "a balanced reduction of forces, particularly in the Central part of Europe."[42] Not until 1970 did the United States (through the NSC) begin its own MBFR studies as a sort of spin-off of the multiple Kissinger-initiated studies during the first hundred days of the Nixon administration.

The Kennedy-Johnson strategic policies did not seriously rock the boat at home. The boat rocking was caused by the waves of Southeast Asia policies. Kennedy defenders insist he would not have got us involved in Vietnam. But he did. When Eisenhower stepped down in January 1961, there were a few hundred American advisers in Vietnam. By November 1963 there were 15,000 American troops in Vietnam and a large buildup of men and equipment was under way. The augmentation had been accompanied by the most optimistic announcements. In June 1962, Secretary of Defense McNamara had reported: "Every quantitative measurement we have shows we're winning this war,"[43] and Secretary of State Dean Rusk, in March 1963, gave the assurance that the war had "turned an important corner" and would soon be over.[44] In his final press conference, President Kennedy asserted that "to withdraw ... would mean a collapse not only of South Vietnam but Southeast Asia. So we are going to stay there."[45]

Impatient with Diem policies in land reform and strategic hamlets, the Kennedy administration withdrew support for

President Ngo Dinh Diem and Ngo Dinh Nhu, his powerful brother. Both were killed by the Vietnamese just three weeks before Kennedy's assassination. Kennedy died while still a Cold War warrior. After the Cuban missile confrontation, he had sought better relations with the USSR. In his eloquent "Strategy for Peace" commencement address at American University, June 10, 1963, he gave assurance that "the United States will never start a war." That message was clearly directed to the Soviets. "But," he added, "we shall also do our part to build a world of peace where the weak are safe and the strong are just. . . . Confident and unafraid," he concluded, "we labor on—not toward a strategy of annihilation but toward a strategy of peace."[46] He earnestly believed we were so doing in Vietnam, where at the time of his death his Green Berets and others of the 15,000 Americans already there were serving as instructors, not yet directly engaged in combat.

In Vietnam, as in his domestic programs, Lyndon B. Johnson sought to adhere to the policies of his predecessor. Kennedy's buildup of American conventional forces enabled Johnson to accelerate efforts in Vietnam without declaring a national emergency or calling up the reserves.

In the 1964 election the Republican candidate, Senator Barry Goldwater, an Air Force Reserve major general, declared that, if elected, he would direct the Joint Chiefs of Staff to take whatever measures were necessary, including use of nuclear weapons, to win the war. Posing as the man of peace, Johnson effectively asked the American people whose finger they wanted on the nuclear trigger, and he portrayed Goldwater as threatening to bomb North Vietnam back into the Stone Age. Ho Chi Minh nonetheless apparently believed Goldwater: before the election, he put out feelers to negotiate a settlement, which "only showed that he misunderstood the Americans as completely as they misunderstood the Vietnamese."[47] At that point neither Johnson nor the ARVN (Army Republic of Vietnam) was prepared to negotiate.

As the war deepened, critics within the Johnson administration, including the Kennedy liberals, found a scapegoat in Secretary Rusk, who adhered to his view that the Vietcong and North Vietnam were, like the North Koreans, clients of the Chinese Communists. Under Secretary of the Air Force Hoopes wrote deridingly of Rusk, "In his always articulate, sometimes eloquent formulations, Asia seemed to be Europe, China was either Stalinist Russia or Hitler Germany, and SEATO was either NATO or the Grand Alliance of World War II."[48] Although Johnson had inherited Rusk, he stood by him and concurred in his grand conception of containment of Communism and the theme that another Munich must be prevented. Thus he linked the doves with Chamberlain and himself with Churchill. Fulbright, who could not buy this conception of ground warfare against North Vietnam, momentarily departed from the political posture of the former Rhodes scholar and quipped: "We go ahead treating this little piss-ant country as though we were up against Russia and China put together."[49]

Limited as American objectives had been in Korea, they were even more limited in Vietnam. Unlike in North Korea, there never was an attempt to conquer the "piss ant." While an amphibious landing reminiscent of Inchon could have been carried out in North Vietnam, it was never seriously considered. Just as the fear in the Korean War had been the possible intervention of the Soviets, the fear in Vietnam was the potential armed intervention of the Chinese. Thus the United States military action against North Vietnam was limited to sporadic bombing raids, a so-called ouch campaign— if the North Vietnamese said "ouch" often enough they might sit down at the bargaining table.

During the Kennedy-Johnson years the most influential military advice came from Maxwell Taylor. Eisenhower had been his own military adviser, but Kennedy installed Taylor in the White House. Taylor next served as chairman of the Joint Chiefs of Staff and ambassador in South Vietnam. He returned to the White House as a Johnson consultant, and in 1967 he reached the brilliant conclusion that we should pull out of Vietnam, proclaiming we had won the war. Johnson did not buy that.

Political considerations finally got to Johnson where military ones did not. And this was doubtless because the American people had lost confidence in their Commander in

Chief. Vietnam was the first American war daily refought on the television screen. Since it was based on the strategy of containment, the American people could not perceive any linear advance on the enemy. Ironically, it was the Nixon-ordered May 8, 1972, mining of the Haiphong harbor and the concentrated bombing of the Haiphong–Hanoi area which finally did get peace negotiations under way. (The mining of the Haiphong Harbor, discussed for years, had never been carried out because of concern for the Soviet reaction; thus Soviet supplies for the war had continued to enter the harbor unmolested. Such had been the limited war strategies of the Vietnam War, reminiscent of those of the Korean War.)

What were the lessons gained from the Vietnam War? Hanson Baldwin, the dean of military analysts, was basically critical of the doctrine of "gradualism," the gradual raising of the force level. In 1960–1961, Eisenhower advised hitting hard "to clear up the problem completely," and Baldwin, by 1968, had decided that overwhelming forces, including tactical nuclear weapons, should be applied in future interventions.

Walter Lippmann, the dean of newspaper commentators, became so depressed by the Vietnam experience that he ruled out all future small-state interventions, maintaining that they paralleled the inability of elephants to swat mosquitoes.[50] In this instance the elephant clearly could have done it had it had the will to do so, but it did not. Nor was there a unified command. Indeed, the Americans, Vietnamese, and Koreans all fought independently. Although the Republic of Korea forces developed into a splendid fighting machine (and supplied the 50,000 most effective troops in South Vietnam), the ARVN never effectively responded to American training. Unlike the Koreans, they had no sense of what they were fighting for. Their morale was always low and their desertion rate the highest of any fighting force in the world. Inevitably, in the face of a direct assault, which finally came in March–April 1975, just two years after the Americans (and the Koreans) were out, they were doomed to defeat. The attack was launched on March 10, and on April 30 the South Vietnamese government unconditionally surrendered.

True, under Congressional and popular criticism we had failed to adhere to the truce accord agreement to replenish the Vietnamese equipment losses. Even more significantly, we had further impaired their morale by making clear we would not help. However, even though the American attitude invited the North Vietnamese to launch their counterattack, the outcome from limited aid would have been merely a prolongation of the inevitable defeat.

The United States should have learned much from the costly Vietnam War. Overcautious gradualism had led to the escalation of manpower rather than of technology. Moreover, in what was viewed basically as a ground operation, effective use had not been made of sea and air power until the final weeks preceding the cease-fire. All of the past American experience of the importance of unified command was ignored, and the maze of Vietnamese bureaucracy was never sorted out. The Vietnam War should further have taught Americans that while in emergency situations there is no substitute for Presidential action, neither is there a substitute for Congressional acts of declaration in protracted military engagements.

NIXON DOCTRINE. Richard Nixon was unusually well equipped to be President, especially in national security affairs. His six years of World War II service as a naval officer were followed by four years in the lower and upper houses of Congress before he became Eisenhower's running mate in 1952. During the Eisenhower Presidency he was active in the affairs of the NSC and was sent to capitals throughout the world. His narrow defeat in the 1960 Presidential election gave him eight more years for worldwide travel, contemplation, and law practice. Upon his election in the fall of 1968, Nixon realized the necessity for extricating the United States from the war in Vietnam and the need for new approaches to American foreign policy.

Factors other than Vietnam made it clear that the time had come for a change of national strategy. As Helmut Sonnenfeldt expressed it, "The key issue Nixon had to confront was ... the change in the power balance and power structure. . . ."[51] America's nuclear superiority had ended in the mid-1960s, and bipolarity had ceased as new power blocks, China, Japan, and western Europe, emerged to compete with the Soviet Union and the United States. The urgency for a new national strategy had been intensified by inflation and mounting trade imbalances, civil strife, and campus turbulence.

Much of the so-called Nixon Doctrine emerged in the quite unlikely setting of a press conference on the island of Guam in the summer of 1969. Its significance should not be underestimated. Richard A. Ware has quite correctly termed it "an historic change in American foreign policy . . . telling the world that we . . . are no longer going to be the policeman of the world."[52] The Nixon Doctrine, then, emphasized greater self-reliance on the part of America's friends, to be coupled with increased foreign aid. Korean- and Vietnam-type interventions would have to be eschewed. Any threatened nation must of itself accept the "primary responsibility of providing the manpower for its defense."[53] The President told the Congress that "a clear lesson of the 1960's is that deterrence against local aggression, or against subversion supported outside a country's borders cannot be achieved without a strong contribution by the threatened country itself."[54] Allies would have to play more than a token part when the United States proffered aid. Negotiation was to replace confrontation. Strength, partnership, and negotiation thus became the three terms to describe the Nixon Doctrine. And in Pentagonese, "massive retaliation," which had become "flexible response," now became "realistic deterrence."

It now appears quite ironic that Nixon took office with the recognition of the importance of communicating more effectively with the people. He established the new post of Director of Communications for the executive branch, separate from the press secretary, and later added still another special assistant to communicate to the American people on foreign policy and national strategy. He shared the view of his Director of Communications, veteran newspaper editor Herbert G. Klein, that "when the President loses the confidence of the people, he loses a good deal of the power he has to lead the people."[55] Nixon's failure was therefore not a lack of recognition of the importance of effective communications for vital public support for American foreign policy. His failure was rather in himself, in his personal withdrawal from doing the communicating—even though he inaugurated informative annual State of the World Addresses to the Congress. His first term press relations were good.

Nixon had three principal national security advisers: William P. Rogers, as Secretary of State; Melvin R. Laird, as Secretary of Defense; and Kissinger, as Assistant for National Security Affairs and Secretary of State. He was well acquainted with the first two but not with Kissinger. Laird had served in the Congress with Nixon, and Rogers had been with him in the Eisenhower Cabinet, as Attorney General. Kissinger in four years outmaneuvered both, but not beyond the first Nixon administration. In the remaining year and a half of the second Nixon term and the first year of the Ford administration, Kissinger occupied without precedence the two posts of Assistant to the President for National Security Affairs and Secretary of State, but his manipulative tendency and basic distrust of the democratic process diminished his effectiveness.

Nixon restored the National Security Council to the central deliberative position which he had witnessed during the Eisenhower years.[56] Immediately upon assuming the Presidency, he called upon the NSC staff under Kissinger's direction "to clarify our view of where we want to be in the next three to five years."[57] In essence he invited Kissinger to develop a series of national strategy proposals. In the next hundred days a torrent of NSC papers flowed forth, and the rate in the Nixon administration abated only slightly. The size of the permanent NSC staff more than doubled that of the pre-Nixon era, when the NSC became a command and control post for foreign policy. In 1969 the SALT studies originated from the NSC, and it also made the studies on China and Soviet policies. The dramatic breakthroughs, especially on China policy, and the break in the deadlock of the SALT talks with the Soviets in May 1971 caused Harrison E. Salisbury of the *New York Times* to observe, "For the first time since President Nixon proclaimed in his inaugural address that we would now move from the era of confrontation to the era of negotiations, it seemed that this indeed was the case."[58]

Nixon's efforts in foreign policy were fulfilled in his February 1972 visit to the People's Republic of China; the May 1972 summit meeting with Brezhnev in Moscow, at which limits in the ABM system and an interim strategic offensive weapons limitation were agreed upon; and the January 27, 1973, signing by his representatives in Paris of "The Agreement on Ending the War and Restoring Peace in Vietnam." Thereafter, with the revelations of Watergate, Nixon was increasingly preoccupied in domestic controversy, culminating in his August 1974 resignation. Nonetheless he continued to act resolutely in the foreign policy area. Under stress, he acted firmly and precisely in his command decisions during the Arab-Israeli October 1973 war, declaring a worldwide "defense condition three" alert (including nuclear forces) in the related confrontation with the Soviets, as well as taking steps to bring an in-place cease-fire. Thereafter his journey to the Middle East, especially his talks with President Anwar el-Sadat in Egypt, during his last troubled months in office, encouraged stability in the Middle East. All of this won the admiration of other concerned major powers. As Peter L. Sargent and Jack H. Harris concluded in their discerning study, "American performance in the Middle East, in particular, was impressive to the Chinese."[59]

At the same time it must be said that the 1973 oil embargo of the Organization of Petroleum Exporting Countries (OPEC) was a destabilizing force. Further, it pointed to additional power alignments (beyond the U.S., USSR, western Europe, China, and Japan) as these oil-rich nations exerted pressures on the industrial giants.

After the heights of his sweeping electoral victory in 1972, the final revelations of the Watergate cover-ups in the summer of 1974 caused Nixon to leave office completely discredited. His apparent desperate effort to involve the CIA and the FBI in the cover-up appears highly reprehensible. Apart from his alleged wrongdoing, he became ideologically targeted from both the left and the right. Détente with the Soviets, friendship with the Chinese Communists, and falling behind in the arms race made him anathema to the extreme rightists. They found nothing to cheer about in his statement: "In this Administration," for the first time in more than twenty years, "we have been able... to spend more on domestic social programs than on defense."[60] Nor would such statements, coming from him, ever warm the cockles of the heart of the liberal left, who would never forgive him for having unseated Helen Gahagan Douglas in the Senate and getting Alger Hiss locked up.

Certainly the climate had changed in America. When Nixon had come on stage in January 1969, asking Americans to lower their voices, they were shouting at one another. Now they were shouting at him. Only with the passage of time could history properly assess the Nixon national security policies. At least one seasoned observer has found in them "perhaps the first major change since the days of Woodrow Wilson"[61]—an interesting comparison, since Nixon always professed a particular admiration for the World War I President. However, Wilson's crusade to "make the world safe for democracy," had its antithesis in the Nixon Doctrine.

There were some quaint reminders of the Nixon détente efforts in 1975–1976. For example, the joint Soviet–United States space journey in 1975 was a symbol of the "spirit of Moscow" agreed upon in 1972. Nixon himself was too much of a realist to confuse détente with peace. "We do not mistake climate for substance," he reported to the Congress on May 3, 1973.[62] Yet, for a broken man, an invitation back to the People's Republic of China four years after his historic journey there must have had meaning. And American tourists in Alexandria and Cairo, Egypt, where he had visited just weeks before his resignation, were surprised a year later to still see his picture publicly displayed with that of President Anwar el-Sadat. What these people did not fully grasp was that the office of President, created by the founding fathers with George Washington in mind, was also equated with the basic values of honesty and integrity which the first and succeeding Presidents had come to symbolize.

The Presidential Role in Present and Future Strategies

The world in which President Ford and his fellow Americans lived in America's bicentennial year was vastly different from that which had confronted President Truman and his fellow Americans in 1946. Although Harry Truman would probably not agree, his foreign policy problems were far less complex than those of 1976. After Truman, the issues in a bipolarized world focused on national survival, and the body of doctrine that developed contained four fundamental words which were all responsive in character: containment, counterforce, countervalue, and counterinsurgency; all were born of the Cold War. So also were the strategic doctrines of massive retaliation and flexible response.

Both counterinsurgency and flexible response were exemplified by United States involvement in Vietnam from 1963 to the cease-fire ten years later; counterinsurgency is responsive to insurgency, and like it is a political-military strategy. Aside from the age-old concepts of limited and global war, none of these doctrines provided systematic differentiated functions, as McNamara and Taylor sought to in their concepts of gradualism and flexible response. In his *Uncertain Trumpet*, Taylor had boldly rejected the Eisenhower strategic doctrines out of hand, proclaiming that "the United States will prepare itself to respond anywhere, anytime, with weapons and forces appropriate to the situations. Thus," Taylor optimistically concluded, "we would restore to warfare its historic justification as a means to create a better world upon the successful conclusion of hostilities."[63]

This had all been very hopeful in 1960, but nine years later—after the Vietnam experience and after the Soviets overtook the United States in the strategic arms race—Nixon and Laird prescribed a less glamorous doctrine, one which the Ford administration continued to advocate. Simply termed "strategic sufficiency," it sought to halt the arms race. It pragmatically prescribed "the maintenance of forces adequate to prevent us and our allies from being coerced."[64]

In 1955, while the United States was ahead of the Soviets in the arms race, Winston Churchill predicted that we were all approaching the time when "safety will be the sturdy child of terror, and survival the twin brother of annihilation."[65] That time had not been reached in August of 1949 when the Soviets detonated their first atomic bomb, four years after the Americans; nor in 1953 when they detonated their first hydrogen bomb, only nine months later than the Americans; nor in 1962 at the time of the Cuban missile crisis, when American superiority clearly remained. But by the end of the decade of the 1960s, what had been a one-sided nuclear deterrence had, indeed, become a nuclear stalemate. Today, both sides possess an "overkill" capacity, a technological revolution's response to an ideological conflict. Should one side or the other achieve a technological breakthrough, temporarily destroying this balance of terror, the temptations of a preemptive strike could loom large. Hence success in the SALT talks is imperative.

What, if any, comfort does the United States find in the array of strategic nuclear doctrine in the interim? Although such doctrine as counterforce and countervalue is presumably responsive to another's initiative, no American President in the nuclear age has unequivocally under all circumstances ruled out a preemptive first strike. This most awesome of Presidential command decisions might be enlightened by the experiences of Truman and Eisenhower. Both recognized a moral purpose in the containment of Communism. Both believed, like Lincoln, in Henry Clay's statement that if our system of government "is to be preserved, it must be by the practice of virtue. . . ."[66] Both had served under Franklin Roosevelt and recalled his statement that "the presidency is not merely an administrative office. It is a place of moral leadership."[67] Truman, the World War I artillery captain, later Army Reserve colonel, had as President seemingly fewer moral qualms in his command decisions that his successor, the former five-star Supreme Allied Commander. To Truman, even dropping the atom bomb on Japanese cities was morally justifiable to preclude further loss of life in World War II. There are those who have inquired, perhaps unfairly, whether he would have had more difficulty in making the decision had the bombs been targeted over Occidental rather than Oriental cities.[68]

By contrast, in 1954, after the Soviets had entered the previously exclusively American atomic club, Eisenhower publicly ruled out preemptive or preventive atomic strikes on the Soviets on moral considerations. "But," as Jerome Kahan of the Brookings Institution points out, "practical considerations undoubtedly influenced the decision as well—a U.S. counterforce strike could not be assured of completely eliminating the USSR's capability to retaliate with nuclear weapons."[69]

President Kennedy, in his first budget message in 1961, also insisted, "Our arms will never be used to strike the first blow in any attack...." Yet, as one of the nation's most discerning students of strategy, Major General Robert N. Ginsburgh, inquires: "Does our policy of not striking the 'first blow in any attack' mean that we would never 'strike first' with nuclear weapons as a response to successful enemy conventional attacks?"[70] Indeed, Secretary of Defense James Schlesinger, who in 1974 later reopened the issue and the debate on strategic doctrine, has suggested that not even Eisenhower had absolutely ruled out a preemptive first strike. "Counterforce," as viewed by Schlesinger and others, assumed the superiority of American technology; it envisioned targeting nuclear warheads on selected and escalating military targets, and only as a last resort on civilian targets. By contrast, "mutual assured destruction" aimed at civilian targets. Both counterforce and countervalue have as their premise, as Churchill had predicted, two nuclear superpowers preventing war with each other by a balance of terror. Present targeting doctrine is far more sophisticated than the counterforce policy which Secretary of Defense McNamara outlined in 1962. This is due primarily to advances of technology that permit greater selectivity in targeting. Yet the support for such doctrine, as Joseph Cernik realistically concluded, is dependent upon "political support...."[71]

"Countervalue" reads almost like something out of *Dr. Strangelove*. As the editors of the *Strategic Review* have described it, countervalue poses "specious arguments as to how many undefended civilians either side can incinerate...." Actually this is "a preoccupation of our defense intellectuals not shared by our adversary and incomprehensible to military men of either side."[72]

At the time of its bicentennial, America, while having fewer long-range ballistic missiles than the Soviets, presumably still had a technological lead in its guidance systems and its multiple independently targetable reentry vehicles. Moreover, its cruise missile development (a descendent of the buzz bomb of World War II) indicated a more significant American technological advance. Ironically, this heritage of Schlesinger's service as Secretary of Defense made the imperatives of SALT and détente more persuasive to the Soviets than even Kissinger's diplomacy.

Seeking better understanding with the Soviets and the furtherance of SALT, President Ford, in his first months in office, journeyed to Vladivostok for a summit meeting with Brezhnev in November 1974. This was a significant sequel to the October 1972 treaty accords with the Soviets (based on Nixon's May 1972 visit to Moscow), which had frozen for five years the overall number of ballistic missile launchers for both the Soviet Union and the United States. The Vladivostok accord placed numerical limitations of 2,400 on the strategic systems and heavy bombers of both countries. The establishment of this point of parity was designed to head off, at least numerically, another arms race.

Still, President Ford and Kissinger had difficulty in convincing the American people that they had not been taken in by Soviets and, indeed, in explaining the meaning of détente. Ford, very much a realist, dropped the word "détente" during the 1976 Presidential primary contests. As Helmut Sonnenfeldt expressed it, "détente" recognized that the Soviets were a superpower; it suggested accommodation to achieve relaxation of tensions.[73] That it further means negotiating from a position of strength was underscored by President Ford's 1976 State of the Union Address, in which he asked the Congress for "an essential increase" in the defense budget.[74] It was becoming increasingly clear at America's two-hundredth birthday that the American people were moving again toward a strong defense posture, and the Congress was giving support to the President's measures.

Détente, to date, has been a mixed blessing. One can agree

with the conclusion of the BDM Corporation that "the danger of inter-continental nuclear war has lessened." But one must also conclude, as BDM notes, that it provides the Soviets with a climate for continued opportunism, "secure in the knowledge that for the West détente is something greater than an expedient tactic."[75] To the President and the people, "negotiation from strength" seemed a better term.

Six months into the Carter administration, it could be perceived that détente, which had been nourished by the Nixon-Kissinger style of diplomacy, was proving at best a fragile instrument. Western Europe, today concerned with the Carter diplomatic style, had welcomed the Nixon-Ford-Brezhnev agreements. For example, the antiballistic missile treaty had given greater credibility to the relatively modest British and French nuclear forces which could target on the Soviet Union. Likewise Western Europe had welcomed the lessening of Soviet presssures on Berlin, Greece, and Turkey. Yet the reduction of the very pressures which had inspired the beginning of a European Defense Community in the 1948 Brussels Pact, the year *preceding* NATO, meant that Western Europe, which had survived the perilous, virtually defenseless era of 1945–51, never did come to contribute its full share to its own defense.

A part of American strategy should then be the encouragement of a true European defense community. Two-hundred seventy million Western Europeans, with their far superior economic resources, should not feel inferior to 250 million Russians. The key is whether the West, and especially Western Europe, has the *will* to invest even one-half of what the Soviets do in terms of the percent of GNP devoted to military expenditures.

XII

****

COMMAND DECISION, CONTINUITY, AND CRISIS MANAGEMENT

> We are still the keystone in the arch of freedom.
> JOHN F. KENNEDY, *November 22, 1963*
>
> Only in those instances in which the Senate can be sure of a complete command of all the essential information prerequisite to an intelligent decision, should it take the terrific chance of muddying the international waters by some sort of premature and ill-advised expression of its advice to the Executive.   ARTHUR H. VANDENBERG, *1948*
>
> When peace or war is at issue, the President cannot leave the decision to others without forfeiting the responsibility of his office.   HERBERT FEIS, *1970*

Continuity

From the Declaration of the founders of the Nation, who pledged "our lives, our fortunes, and our sacred honor," to President Carter's definition of a foreign policy that will "make you proud to be an American," there is a continuity of idealism. So also from the time Washington took the oath of office of President through Carter's having done so there is a continuity of principles of leadership. Immediately after the Constitution's adoption, in urging Washington's candidacy for the Presidency, Hamilton emphasized, "It is of little purpose to have introduced a system,

if the weightiest influence is not given to its firm establishment in the outset."[1]

By the end of the first Washington administration, aided
by both Hamilton and Jefferson, Washington had established Presidential primacy in national security policy. This
then has been no Cold War aberration or conceit. It is only
that the nuclear age has underscored the principle of command decision, again and again confirmed in crisis management.

Kennedy

Many of the most persuasive critics of the so-called imperial
Presidency were witness to the most crucial command decision of the nuclear age, the Kennedy execution of the Cuban
missile crisis. In his quest for the Presidential nomination
Kennedy contended, "Our task is to devise a national
strategy." He promised he would not have a strategy predicated upon "eleventh hour responses to Soviet created
crises. . . ."[2] Ironically, of the Kennedy thousand days, the
most masterful thirteen were "eleventh hour responses."
The Kennedy of the October 1962 missile crisis had grown
considerably beyond the Kennedy of June 1961, who, in his
meeting with Khrushchev in Vienna, had given the wily
Soviet Prime Minister the impression of a muted schoolboy.

Concerning that Vienna meeting, diplomat-scholar
George Kennan observed that Kennedy "had not acquitted
himself well on that occasion. . ." and that "it definitely mis-
led Khrushchev."[3] This, then, taken with the pressures on
Khrushchev by his own military elite, prompted Khrushchev
to direct the placement of Soviet missiles in Cuba. Much in
the tradition of Cato the Elder, who repeatedly warned in the
ancient Roman Senate that "Carthage must be destroyed,"
Senator Kenneth B. Keating finally alerted the Kennedy administration to the menace only 90 miles from the Florida
coast.

In the ensuing thirteen critical days of Soviet–United
States confrontation, as James T. Crown has pointed out,
"the missile crisis set a far reaching precedent of turning the

White House into a battle command post. . . .''[4] Former Under Secretary of State U. Alexis Johnson amplified that fact, based upon his own participation: "I remember Admiral Anderson and other admirals of the Navy were not at all pleased at having their destroyers controlled from the White House. However, it was only by such fine selective and detailed control that we were able to bring about the result that we did." Johnson concluded, "I am convinced that any other control could have resulted in the situation getting quickly out of hand, not because of lack of confidence on the part of anybody, but simply because the President is at the only point at which all aspects of a situation like that can be seen and the point from which all aspects must have control."[5]

United States demands that the missiles be removed was countered by a Soviet threat on beleaguered West Berlin. Kennedy kept his cool, asserting in a telecast on October 22, 1962: "Any hostile move anywhere in the world against the safety and freedom of people to whom we are committed— including in particular the brave people of West Berlin—will be met by whatever action is needed."[6] "Whatever action," as in Truman's pronouncement after the Chinese entry into the Korean War, was regarded as including "going nuclear." In a communication four days later, Khrushchev offered to remove the missiles if the United States did likewise with its missile emplacement in Turkey. Standing tough, Kennedy refused to do so, thereby earning the criticism of doveish critics. However, Kennedy was so conciliatory as to promise, beyond the Cuban missile crisis, to review the whole issue of NATO and Warsaw Pact forces and, indeed, general disarmament.

Throughout the thirteen days, aided by his brother Robert, the President, receiving multiple advice from his immediate staff and from the Defense and State departments, was clearly in command of the situation. Proffered strategies ranged from air strikes to a blockade. As Bobby Kennedy said of the President, "It was now up to one single man. No committee was going to make this decision."[7] As Commander in Chief he ordered a blockade of any ships equipping or supplying the missile installations. In the face of such persuasion, despite the invasion on October 28 of the Soviet airspace by an American reconnaissance plane, Khrushchev that day directed the dismantling and withdrawal of the missiles.

Secretary of State Rusk avowed, "We looked into the mouth of the cannon; the Russians flinched."[8] "Perhaps it was not quite so simple as that," British Prime Minister Harold Macmillan estimated. "Nevertheless, the President's will prevailed. . . . He was ready to carry the burden of responsibility himself."[9]

This shining hour was followed by Kennedy's efforts at rapprochement with the Soviets, including the establishment of the "hot line" for Soviet–United States dialogue and the nuclear test ban treaty, both signaling the beginnings of détente.

The new national strategy which Kennedy had promised, "a comprehensive set of carefully prepared long term policies designed to increase the strength of the non-Communist world,"[10] brought forth the Peace Corps, through which volunteers served in projects ranging from agriculture to education to medicine in the Third World; also the Alliance for Progress, building upon Eisenhower's Latin American programs. Limited war and graduated response comprised the new Kennedy military strategy. The second-youngest Commander in Chief created all kinds of limited war forces, headed by his personally sponsored elite, the Green Berets. A new Strike Command was created, with forces which could be transported to all parts of the world at a moment's notice to put out fires.

Kennedy first involved the Americans more directly in combat operations in Vietnam, commencing in December 1961 with U.S. crews flying armed helicopters. (It was not, however, until June 1965 that Johnson directed the first U.S. combat ground operations.) Although the Cuban missile crisis under Kennedy represented the upper reaches in the employment of force and Vietnam under Johnson the lower, both were consonant with the gradual response theories advanced by General Maxwell Taylor and, among others, Harvard professor Henry Kissinger. Since 1954 Kissinger had headed a study group mandated to "explore all factors in making and implementing foreign policy in the nuclear age."

By 1957 he was writing of "a twentieth century equivalent of 'showing the flag.'"[11] McGeorge Bundy, then Harvard dean of the arts and sciences faculty (he became Kennedy's Special Assistant for National Security Affairs in 1961 and was to continue in that post under Johnson until 1966) was much impressed by this work of his former student.

Despite the brilliance of Camelot, the President's relationships with the Congress so deteriorated during his last year in office as to create a legislative stalemate. Surveying this in October 1963, Walter Lippmann wrote, "This is one of those moments when there is reason to wonder whether the Congressional system as it now operates is not a grave danger to the Republic."[12] Such was the political climate when President Kennedy the following month journeyed to Texas to seek to rebuild his political support. As George Reedy observed, "President Kennedy... was definitely losing his political force at the time he made his tragic trip to Dallas. ..."[13] On the day the brave, inspiring President was struck down, he was holding the torch of freedom high. That fateful morning, November 22, 1963, he avowed, "We are still the keystone in the arch of freedom, and I think we will continue to do as we have in the past, our duty."[14]

It was and is poignantly difficult to assess the martyred President. He had a magnetism coupled with a rapierlike wit. When a reporter once asked him whether McGeorge Bundy and the National Security Council staff were not getting a bit too powerful, he responded, "I shall continue to exercise some *residual* function."[15] In fact, although he had with Bundy created his own cadre of security advisers at the White House, he had dismantled the Eisenhower NSC structure. As former Under Secretary of State Casey observed, Kennedy as a Senator had been accustomed to "a small free-rolling staff."[16] This had been his style, as it was to become that of his successor, Lyndon Johnson, who was likewise inspired by Senatorial experience. By training, experience, and instinct, Eisenhower had a much stronger administrative sense of command than either of them.

Such seasoned observers as General Lucius Clay and Alexis Johnson recognized Kennedy's administrative difficulties.[17] Nonetheless, Kennedy, particularly in the thirteen days of the Cuban missile crisis, best exemplified to Alexis Johnson the vital importance of the Presidential command decision: "In the world of nuclear weapons today," Johnson concluded, "the President of the United States has control of virtually unlimited power, and correspondingly having unlimited power, he requires virtually unlimited control. The day that a commander in the field could be given a mission and permitted to go off to carry out the mission only with broad guidance is gone. The world is entirely too dangerous for that."[18]

Johnson

Former Presidents have provided valuable bridges in times of crisis. It is perhaps useless to speculate whether Richard Nixon would have conducted himself differently if there had been a living former President in whom he might have confided and received counsel at the time he first was confronted with the Watergate break-in. Certainly Eisenhower, who sent his own Chief of Staff, Adams, packing over a vicuña coat, would have counseled a different course of action than that which Nixon pursued. Eisenhower was available when Lyndon Johnson, following the Kennedy assassination, was confronted for the first time with Presidential responsibilities. At Johnson's request, the day after the assassination, Eisenhower drove down from Gettysburg to meet with the new President. After this meeting, at Johnson's further request, Eisenhower prepared a confidential memorandum setting forth principles and policies for action and suggesting persons who would be helpful. The former President reminded the new President, "You are sworn to defend the Constitution and execute the laws. In doing so you will follow the instincts, principles and convictions that have become part of you during many years of public service."[19]

Johnson as President and Commander in Chief did follow those "instincts, principles and convictions" which had served him so well as Senate Majority Leader in working with President Eisenhower. But as President he lacked the ability of a Roosevelt or an Eisenhower to make of the Presidency a "bully pulpit" or a "crusade." Still, if he had not bogged down in the swamps around the Mekong, he might have been viewed as a remarkable President and Commander in Chief. He sought consciously to carry through the Kennedy programs at home and overseas. In domestic policy he pledged in his first address before a joint session of Congress on November 27, 1963: "This nation will keep its commitments from South Vietnam to West Berlin."[20] He also sought to carry forward the Kennedy beginnings in détente. As Senate Majority Leader he had supported Eisenhower's 1955 "open skies" proposal to ensure meaningful inspection of disarmament agreements. He also sought what he termed "building bridges" to eastern Europe through trade, travel, and humanitarian aid.

Johnson sought to restore policymaking primacy to the Department of State through the formation of the Senior Interdepartmental Group (SIG), which consisted of the Deputy Secretary of Defense, the administrator of AID, the director of CIA, the chairman of the Joint Chiefs of Staff, the director of the USIA, and the Special Assistant for International Security Affairs. With State's Under Secretary as chairman of SIG, it was anticipated that State would be restored to primacy in national security policy. However, policy increasingly gravitated about the President and his White House staff, a tendency which was even more characteristic of the succeeding administration. Johnson was increasingly occupied in his Commander in Chief role. As a result, the Department of Defense's International Security Agency, which Kennedy had fostered as a "little State Department," continued to exert considerable influence. However, the National Security Council as such under Johnson, as under Kennedy and Truman, never played the full institutional role it had under Eisenhower.

Just as Eisenhower's efforts for a final summit with the Soviets were aborted by the U-2 incident, Johnson's for a final summit were negated by the 1968 invasion of Czechoslovakia. Yet he did complete the Nuclear Nonproliferation Treaty with the Soviets, although its Senate confirmation in March 1969 would be credited to the Nixon administration.

Also, at Glassboro and beyond, Johnson laid the foundations for the SALT talks which were finally to get under way in Helsinki in November 1969. Johnson was deeply troubled that he had not secured an armistice in Vietnam or a lessening of tensions in the Middle East, which had erupted in the swift Israeli victory of the Seven-Day War of 1967. So also he was remorseful that he had not slowed down the nuclear arms race. Yet, as he concluded, "Five years and more of crisis, of meetings and memos, of agonizing decisions and midnight phone calls, had taught me that the work of peace is an endless struggle to tip the balance in the right direction."[21]

Johnson's last futile command decision, the bombing pause in Vietnam, was greeted with contempt by the implacable North Vietnamese enemy. Secretary of State Rusk correctly analyzed: "It boils down to a question of will." Rusk added, "I realize that I am branded as a 'hawk' and that this has been an embarrassment to the administration in some quarters. But looking at all of our experiences in the management of crisis in the past three decades, I cannot for the life of me see how we can achieve any peace unless some elementary notions of reciprocity, fairness, and equity are maintained."[22]

Nixon

And so it remained for Nixon, with his command decisions—mining the harbor at Haiphong and the December 1972 bombing attacks on North Vietnamese military targets, plus overtures to the People's Republic of China—to bring the January 27, 1973, signing by his representatives in Paris of "The Agreement on Ending the War and Returning Peace to Vietnam." This was followed by the summer 1973 Brezhnev-Nixon final summit visit. Crisis management was much on the mind of the troubled President. He reached an agreement with Brezhnev for "urgent consultations" should relations between the Soviets and the United States or between one and another country "appear to involve the risk of nuclear conflict."[23]

Shortly thereafter, when the Egyptian-Israeli so-called Yom Kippur War erupted in October 1973, in the light of the threatening intervention of the Soviets, a United States command decision was swiftly exercised, placing the nation's armed forces on alert. By that time rumors were spread that the President, emeshed in Watergate inquiries, was not clearly in command. This was vigorously denied by both Admiral Thomas S. Moorer, chairman of the Joint Chiefs of Staff, and Secretary of Defense James R. Schlesinger. Although Schlesinger asserted that Nixon was "in command at all times. . . ," a student of crisis management, Louis Koenig, has suggested that "a remote President cannot fulfill his Commander in Chief role in a nuclear age."[24] Rumors were even floated during Nixon's last days in office in August 1974 that Secretary of Defense Schlesinger and Chairman of the Joint Chiefs of Staff Brown had conferred on steps to be taken should the Commander in Chief pull an irrational act. Such rumors have been unequivocally denied by both men.[25]

Although disgraced by Watergate, Nixon exhibited strength in making command decisions. While the Congress had forced the War Powers Act upon the wounded President, the Courts, for their part, had refused to interpose. In Congresswoman Elizabeth Holtzman's 1973 effort on that subject (on the war in Cambodia), which went all the way to the Supreme Court, only two justices perceived a possible case.[26] This underscored Archibald Cox's conclusion that "the task of formulating a workable principle for delimiting the President's power to engage in military activities overseas is far from easy."[27]

Who is to decide the constitutionality of such operations? The Court has never accepted an invitation to do so. However, Justice William H. Rehnquist of the Supreme Court, who learned much of his law under Justice Jackson, did, while serving as Assistant Attorney General, term Nixon's Cambodian incursion a "valid exercise of his constitutional authority as Commander in Chief. . . . The President's authority to do what he did," Rehnquist concluded, "must be conceded by those who read Executive authority narrowly."[28]

Ford

For an understanding of President Ford's views as Commander in Chief it is well to recall the conceptions of his mentor, Senator Arthur Vandenberg, regarding the Congressional role in national security policy. Vandenberg viewed the Congressional role as at best consultative and jointly formulative with the Presidency on major policy issues. There should be no Congressional interference in Presidential command decisions, and Congressional advice should be given sparingly in strategic matters. Indeed, as Vandenberg expressed it in 1948, ". . . only in those instances in which the Senate can be sure of a complete command of all the essential information prerequisite to an intelligent decision, should it take the terrific chance of muddying the international waters by some sort of premature and ill-advised expression of its advice to the Executive."[29]

Ford also shared his mentor's concern as to how the Congress could perform even an intelligent consultative role in crisis management. As Vandenberg lamented, "The trouble is that these 'crises' never reach Congress until they have developed to a point where Congressional discretion is pathetically restricted."[30] Vandenberg's answer, like Congressman John B. Anderson's a quarter-century later, was to gear up the Congress with better information gathering for a more intelligent consultative role. This had also been the view of Senator Fulbright as late as 1967, as he surveyed what he termed "an entire era of crises in which decisions have been required again and again, decisions of a kind that the Congress is ill-equipped to make. . . ."[31]

Although as a junior Congressman Ford had been witness to the 1951 foreign policy debate regarding the Commander in Chief's conduct of the Korean War and his movement of troops to NATO without Congressional consultation, for the next fifteen years he had witnessed considerable Congressional consensus with the Presidency on foreign policy, including that in Southeast Asia. He recalled how in 1955, for example, the SEATO treaty had been approved by the Senate 82 to 1 and how the Gulf of Tonkin Resolution in 1964 had been passed in the Senate 88 to 2 and in the House 414 to

0. By the latter the Congress had avowed that it "approves and supports the determination of the President as Commander in Chief, to take all necessary measures to repel any armed attack against the forces of the United States and to prevent further aggression."[32] But by 1967, as the frustrating Vietnam War deepened, Ford recalled, "Our national unity was shattered, and with it the essential foreign policy coordination between President and Congress."[33] And so the move culminating in the War Powers Resolution of 1973 got under way. Ford, who was in a small minority that opposed the resolution, held with Senator George Aiken of Vermont that it was "largely a political effort . . . , an attempt to amend the Constitution by Congressional resolution."[34] He also held with former Under Secretary of State George Ball, who perceived the resolution as a means of trying to do what the constitutional framers "felt they were not wise enough to do."[35]

As President, Ford was particularly troubled as to how to make meaningful the War Powers Resolution's mandate of Presidential consultation with the Congress in times of crisis. He inquired, "Can the President satisfy the law by having breakfast with three or four or a dozen leaders he decides are the key people?"[36] He was also troubled by the implication of continuing consultation during the execution of policy. How can command decisions be shared in fast-moving operations?

Ford contended that "when the President as Commander in Chief undertakes . . . military operations . . . ," he should "take the Congress into his confidence in order to receive its advice and, if possible, ensure its support." But he found this kind of consultation vastly different "from the detailed information and time limits imposed by the War Powers Resolution." He believed the crisis management role of the President was succinctly clear: "as Commander in Chief and Chairman of the National Security Council . . . to concentrate on resolving the crisis as expeditiously and as successfully as possible."[37]

In accordance with the War Powers Resolution, Ford consulted and reported to the Congress in six crisis situations during his Presidency: the evacuation of United States citizens and refugees from Da Nang, Phnom Penh, and Saigon in the spring of 1975, the rescue of *Mayagüez* in May of 1975, and the two evacuation operations in Lebanon in June 1976. He did not, in candor, believe that the War Powers Resolution was applicable to these kinds of operations, and he found some Congressional sentiment agreeing with him. He recognized that a President in a more urgent crisis situation could by his failure to consult and report open himself up to impeachment. But, he mused, in a swiftly moving scenario, if the President waited for Congressional consultation "the consequences to the Nation" might be irreparable.[38]

The Congress might well ponder whether Truman could have taken the incisive action he did to salvage South Korea in the first weeks of the Korean War if he had had to operate through the War Powers Resolution. Could Kennedy have successfully consummated the Cuban missile crisis if he had been inhibited in his Commander in Chief role by the War Powers Resolution? Such ill-conceived measures as the Jackson-Vanik Amendment to the Trade Act of 1972 and Congressional restrictions on military assistance to Turkey point to the wisdom of Vandenberg's warning about "muddying the international waters." If such a climate is to continue, as Eugene Rostow has observed, it "would tend to convert every crisis of foreign policy into a crisis of will, of pride and of precedence between Congress and the President."[39]

The decade 1966–1976 has then witnessed the partnership of the Congress and the Presidency in foreign policy formulation replaced by a relationship of conflict, distrust, and suspicion. On that foundation the Congress has sought to erect a new and permanent legalistic structure by such measures as the War Powers Resolution, the National Emergencies Act, and the Impoundment Control Act. Within this climate the Presidency has sought means to circumvent legislation. In the case of the Impoundment Act, so seasoned a hand as Ford contested the legislation by sending back to the Congress a barrage of proposed budget recisions and deferrals. Such maneuvering and mutual suspicion leads, as Ford pointed out, to division at home and danger abroad. Ford believed that both the National Emergencies

Act, with its provision for Congressional termination of Presidential declarations by a concurrent resolution, and the War Powers Resolution were unconstitutional encroachments on Presidential authority.

An imperative and a crucial opportunity for the Congress and the Presidency is to restore a working partnership in the building of a new American foreign policy. In this there must be recognition of Presidential responsibility in crisis management, in which the ultimate decision must reside with the President. In such decisionmaking there is through the NSC machinery provision for advisory inputs. There is also the counselor role of the Congress. There is the vital sense of public opinion. But in the system conceived by the framers of the Constitution and set in motion by the first Washington administration, command decision is inherent in the Commander in Chief office. There has been continuity in the exercise of this principle from Washington and Lincoln to the present. As Herbert Feis expressed it, "When peace or war is at issue, the President cannot leave the decision to others without forfeiting the responsibility of his office."[40]

From the Eberstadt report of 1945 through the Jackson Subcommittee of 1960 and the Murphy [Robert D.] Commission of 1975 (Commission on the Organization of the Government for the Conduct of Foreign Policy) there has been a continuum of concern for the organization of the instruments and institutions for national security policy formulation and implementation. Beyond structure, however, there are other basic ingredients for coherent policy formulation and implementation. These are public debate, followed by consensus and disciplined diplomacy, conducted with a necessary degree of confidentiality. Bipartisanship of the best sense will foster and respect these ingredients.

XIII
****

CHANGE OF COMMAND

> Great men are not chosen Presidents, firstly because great men are rare in politics; secondly because the method of choice does not bring them to the top; thirdly, because they are not, in quiet times, absolutely needed.
> JAMES BRYCE, *The American Commonwealth*

> In presenting the State of the Union to the Congress and to the American people, I have a special obligation as Commander in Chief to report on our national defense.
> PRESIDENT FORD, *January 12, 1977*

> ... we will continue to speak out against violations of human rights wherever they occur and whoever the victim. We do so not for short-run political advantage, but because it is right. At the same time, we have indicated that we will stand prepared to seek with the Soviet Union cooperative solutions to the problems that face us all. PRESIDENT CARTER *to Henry Hall Wilson, March 12, 1977*

> We have learned in recent years that these decisions cannot be made by one man. CONGRESSMAN SAMUEL S. STRATTON, *May 23, 1977*

The New Congress and the New President

The Twentieth Amendment to the United States Constitution, adopted in 1933, would have pleased the ancient Romans. In moving from March to January the completion and beginning of a Congress and a Presidency, it gave recognition to Janus, who presided over endings and beginnings. The month named for Janus is, then, in four-year intervals, a special time for looking back and looking ahead. There is more a looking ahead, as John F. Kennedy expressed it in his New Frontier: "the frontier of the 1960's—a frontier of unknown opportunities and perils—a frontier of unfulfilled hopes and threats."[1] Tragically, Kennedy did not have the opportunity for a retrospective view. His successor, Lyndon Johnson, did, and shortly before his death he confided to Eugene V. Rostow how Congress had deserted him over the Vietnam War. "I knew that if I wanted Congress with me at the crash-landing, they had to be with me at the take-off," Johnson ruefully recalled regarding the Gulf of Tonkin Resolution. "But I forgot about the availability of parachutes."[2] As Sterling Professor of Law and Public Affairs at Yale, Rostow insisted that as regards the Vietnam War, "the alleged usurpation of Congress' war power by the President is a myth. . . . Then, having created the myth," Dr. Rostow diagnosed, "Congress passed the War Powers Resolution to cure the imaginary disease."[3]

It was the Nixon Presidency which witnessed the enactment of the War Powers Resolution, despite the cautioning of former Under Secretary of State George Ball that it "represents an attempt to do what the Founding Fathers felt they were not wise enough to do."[4] President Ford, who insisted that the Resolution was unconstitutional, was defeated in the closely contested 1976 Presidential election. And so in January 1977 both a new Congress and a new President took up their duties.

The new Congress, the 95th, had more changes in its leadership than any other Congress convening in the twentieth century. New leadership provides new opportunity for approaches to both policy and organization. On the other hand, it may mean the loss of perspective. Thus the longtime chairman of the House Armed Services Committee, Congressman F. Edward Hébert, who retired at the end of the 94th Congress, lamented,"Do you realize that with the House sworn in in January there is over a thousand years of experience missing?"[5]

With a new Speaker of the House, Thomas P. O'Neill, Jr., and a new Senate Majority Leader, Robert C. Byrd, together with so many new committee chairmen, there was a renewed challenge for responsible leadership. This was particularly so with the greatly expanded Congressional staff. As Robert N. Ginsburgh recently warned, "There is the danger that Congress may be creating a swollen bureaucracy which has a life of its own."[6] By its sheer numbers, by its varied constituencies, the Congress is not equipped to assume the operational role in foreign policy, nor can it perform the Commander in Chief role of crisis management. Aside from its basic role in policy formulation, the Congress can play an especially vital and urgently needed role, as Ginsburgh recently testified, "in educating the public and helping to develop a broad national consensus on issues of national security and foreign policy."[7] Not since the Eisenhower-Kennedy years has that consensus existed.

Achieving that understanding is then also the challenge to the new President, the thirty-ninth, James Earl Carter, Jr. He is the first President since Eisenhower who was not a part of the Washington political scene prior to taking office. He is also the first southern governor since Andrew Johnson of Tennessee to occupy the White House; neither had any previous Congressional experience. Aside from Eisenhower, the best President to date drawn from the professional military, Carter is the only President in the twentieth century to have graduated from one of the service academies (Annapolis, 1947). He thus shares a unique perspective for the office of Commander in Chief and a unique experience for the office of President. His seven years of commissioned service in the United States Navy, where he had the tutelage of Vice Admiral Hyman Rickover, were followed by very down-to-earth experience as a farmer and small businessman prior to his election to the Georgia governorship.

To understand Carter's roots one must appreciate what it meant to be governor of Georgia. Of all fifty states it was the one in which gubernatorial authority was greatest, in which there was the least concern for the legislature's position on public policy.[8] Completing that four-year term (from which one is not eligible for reelection in a successive term), Carter entered upon an arduous, unprecedented three-year quest for the Presidency.

As Carter took office on January 20, 1977, it was the first inaugural since Lyndon Johnson in 1965 in which the leadership of the new Congress and the new President were both from the same political party. This poses both new responsibilities and new opportunities, accompanied by not a few hazards, especially in regard to foreign policy. The fact that the new President is from the same political party as the majority in the Congress is no guarantor of harmony. Having increasingly asserted itself in foreign policy in the past decade, Congress is not about to acquiesce in that area. Within a week after the inaugural Senate Majority Leader Byrd, complaining that his opinion had not been sought, admonished that "it's in the President's best interest that the leadership be consulted. It's a process of learning."⁹ Speaker of the House O'Neill, according to a member of his staff, "just loves that Jimmy Carter, but he says that we're going to have to keep an eye on all those Georgians."¹⁰

Carter, unlike the two Roosevelts, Wilson, Kennedy, and Johnson, did not promise a torrent of activity in his first hundred days. The Roosevelts and Lyndon Johnson in their first hundred days besieged the Congress with a myriad of bills. In his inaugural Carter made no such pledge, and he has kept his promise.

Whereas Carter enjoyed immense popularity with the American people and with the leaders of other industrial democracies at the end of his first hundred days, he was clearly having problems on Capitol Hill. Republican campaign bumper stickers proclaiming that the nation "ain't no peanut farm" had been ineffective. Now, however, although the visible signs had not appeared, Congress was making clear that Washington "ain't Atlanta."¹¹

An early augury that Carter would have difficulty on Capitol Hill was Congressional opposition to his nominee for director of the Central Intelligence Agency. When members of the Senate Select Intelligence Committee made clear that they opposed the nomination of Theodore C. Sorensen, they were not conspiring against a liberal. Some, quite unfairly, may have believed Sorensen arrogant; some were troubled by his having been a conscientious objector to combat duty in the armed services; others disliked his handling of classified documents in writing a Kennedy biography. Sorensen, an able attorney who brilliantly served President

Kennedy as both a foreign and a domestic policy aide, actually might have won appointment to almost any other post in the Carter administration. But Congress, having completed its own inquiries a year before in the operations of the intelligence community, was now the more concerned to determine the meaning of the startling Soviet arms buildup. They had come to the conclusion that "intelligence is in the literal sense, the gut sense, a deadly serious business."[12] Although, in view of the opposition, Sorensen withdrew his name, such Senate opposition to a nominee of Cabinet rank by a President-elect was without precedent.

Even with the Sorensen nomination dropped, the more hawkish Democrats complained about "a party of mush and meekness" and revived their Coalition for a Democratic Majority.[13] Nonetheless, the credentials of most of the Carter staff in the national security policy area were impressive: Cyrus R. Vance as Secretary of State; Harold Brown as Secretary of Defense; Zbigniew Brzezinski as Assistant to the President for National Security Affairs; James R. Schlesinger as energy administrator with Cabinet rank; Stansfield Turner as director of the Central Intelligence Agency; Paul C. Warnke as director of the Arms Control and Disarmament Agency and negotiator with the Soviets on arms limitations; Elliot L. Richardson as ambassador at large as related to law of the sea issues; Gerard C. Smith as ambassador at large as related to nuclear issues; and former Defense Secretary Clark M. Clifford as special representative of the Secretary of State on the Cyprus situation. All of the foregoing were veteran students of national security affairs.

New perspectives on social concern in Third World relationships were to be contributed by W. Michael Blumenthal as Secretary of the Treasury and Andrew Young at the United Nations. However, within a fortnight Andrew Young had expressed views on Angola, Rhodesia, and Vietnam which in all three instances brought denials by State Department spokesmen. Throughout the first hundred days and beyond Young was to remain unpredictable in his public utterances and in his disavowals of State Department briefings prior to his African and South American "fact-finding" missions. Moreover, Warnke's views on possible unilateral disarmament, albeit exaggerated by Senators Henry Jackson, Sam Nunn, and Strom Thurmond, presaged a heating up of the national security debate. It would be asked why, for example, there was not a place for a more hawkish Paul Nitze in the Carter administration to balance the congenial Warnke's views.

Who would emerge as Carter's principal foreign policy spokesman? In the 1940s and 1950s the Secretary of State (especially Acheson and Dulles) had been the dominant adviser. In the 1960s and the early 1970s the tilt had been either to the Secretary of Defense (McNamara) or the Special Assistant to the President for National Security Affairs (McGeorge Bundy, Walt W. Rostow, and especially Henry Kissinger, who was the first to have the pejorative appellation "Special" dropped from his title). Past experience would clearly indicate that a dominating personality in an inferior post can outshine the incumbent in even the most senior Cabinet post of Secretary of State. Such was the case with able but less aggressive persons such as Dean Rusk and William Rogers.

Zbigniew Brzezinski, given the geography of his proximity to the Oval Office, may, indeed, dominate the able Cyrus Vance and the brilliant Harold Brown, both more reserved in personality than the ebullient new Assistant to the President for National Security Affairs. By January 15, five days before the Carter Inaugural, Brzezinski had already announced that he would restructure the National Security Council, reducing from six to two the NSC committee structure. Both organizationally and in terms of staff, the vestiges of the Kissinger-Scowcroft period of 1969–1977 would be gone within a week.

From Truman to Carter: the NSC

Each President has utilized the National Security Council according to his own dictates. Truman always dealt with the NSC at arm's length, preferring ad hoc informal advisers.

From the outset, Eisenhower broadened the concept of the NSC role. Economic affairs and budget and fiscal policy were wedded to security matters. He created the NSC Planning Board and, for implementation, the Operations Coordinating Board. He introduced the NSC staff papers on each country and on issues of strategic concern. In forging policies through the NSC, Eisenhower (popular opinion to the contrary) believed that he "could not only tolerate disagreement but needed it."[14] Out of this climate came American strategic doctrine. Under Eisenhower, as Jerome A. Kahan has pointed out, "strategic doctrines reflecting a growing awareness of the new technologies for defense, deterrence and diplomacy" first began "to shape America's security policies."[15]

Kennedy, as Commander in Chief, attracted outstanding academicians, including both McGeorge and William Bundy, Richard Neustadt, and Arthur M. Schlesinger, Jr. After the fiasco of the Bay of Pigs, much of the NSC machinery which had been dismantled early in the Kennedy administration was restored. However, the Commander in Chief role swelled in the Kennedy Presidency by virtue of a diplomacy of force. Institutionally, the Department of Defense, as compared to the Department of State, made the dominant policy inputs. The energetic President, who took pride in his capacity for rapid reading, constantly involved himself in the details of decisionmaking. However, as George T. Sulzner of the University of Massachusetts concluded, Kennedy's "attempt to maintain direct control over decisions met with only mixed success."[16]

Kennedy's successor, President Johnson, with Joseph A. Califano, Jr., as his deputy, achieved great success in domestic policy formulation. But Johnson was not suited by temperament to institutionalize national security policy formulation. As Dr. Sulzner expressed it, "The 'Johnson treatment' which was so effective in creating domestic agreements was not readily adaptable to international relations."[17] The National Security Council under Johnson, as under Kennedy and Truman, never played the full institutional role it had under Eisenhower. Instead, there was the "Tuesday Luncheon Group"—Dean Rusk at State, McNamara at Defense,

Richard Helms of the CIA, General Earl Wheeler, chairman of the Joint Chiefs of Staff, and Walt W. Rostow, the Special Assistant for National Security Affairs. McNamara was the dominant member. He convinced the President that he had so fine-tuned the Kennedy doctrine of flexible response as to bring the enemy to the conference table. They would apply varieties of "squeezes" and "fast full squeeze" and "progressive squeeze and talk." Johnson suffered a loss of support from the bureaucracy and the politicians. However, contrary to George Reedy's view that the President retreated into isolation and was cut off from differing points of view, his military aide, Robert N. Ginsburgh, believed that the Commander in Chief was listening to *"too many different* voices and that he was seeking to compromise fundamentally irreconcilable points of view. And," General Ginsburgh concluded, "it is a specially difficult way to try and fight a war."[18] Nonetheless, Johnson stoically stuck to the end to his early (November 26, 1963) statement of objectives on Vietnam, to help "the people, and Government of that country to win their contest against the externally directed and supported Communist conspiracy."[19]

There are those who are impatient with the transition time between administrations. Nixon and Carter both used that time well in working out their organization for national security policy formulation. Nixon, basing his decision largely on what he had learned from the Eisenhower administration, restored the National Security Council's essential role in decisionmaking. Eisenhower was the first President to designate his Special Assistant for National Security as being responsible for long-range planning. However, Nixon went much further. He made Henry Kissinger, his energetic Assistant for National Security Affairs, his principal deputy in foreign policy rather than relying on his Secretary of State, William P. Rogers. It became then, as Ernest S. Griffith of American University has pointed out, "the first White House dominant system in foreign policy in our history."[20]

The President authorized Kissinger to double to 120 the size of the permanent NSC staff. He also gave Kissinger the go-ahead to serve as chairman of a series of policy committees, including the Senior Review Group, the Washington Special Action Group (for crisis management), the Defense Policy Review Committee, the Verification Panel (for SALT studies), the "40 Committee" (for covert CIA operations), and the NSC Intelligence Committee. Essentially, the same men served on each of these six committees: Kissinger, the Under Secretary of State, the Deputy Secretary of Defense, the chairman of the Joint Chiefs of Staff, and the director of the CIA. Under Nixon's direction, the President invited the NSC staff "to clarify our view of where we want to be in the next three to five years."[21] In Nixon's and Kissinger's first hundred days in office a torrent of NSC papers followed, and their rate only slightly abated throughout the five and one-half years of the Nixon administration. The NSC became a sort of command and control post for foreign policy. It was there in 1969 that the SALT studies originated. It was also there that the studies on China and Soviet policy were made. However, Nixon recently emphasized that the origins of the new relationships with China were of his own origination. As he put it, "I do not know when Dr. Kissinger may have conceived of the possibility of an initiative toward China. I do know that I conceived it before I ever met him."[22] The concentration of policy inputs at the White House reached its zenith in 1971–1973 with one man for the first time in history serving both as Assistant to the President for National Security Affairs and as Secretary of State. Recently Nixon confided, "I'd gone through the Rogers-Kissinger feud for four years, and I didn't want to buy another feud with another Secretary of State, and that's why I finally gave Henry both hats, which I would not have done could we have found some individual who would be Henry's equal."[23]

When President Ford relieved Kissinger of his former position and appointed Brent Scowcroft as Assistant to the President for National Security Affairs, it was clearly a step in the right direction. Neither an Eisenhower nor a John Foster Dulles would have countenanced a staff assistant with all the authority in national security policy tendered Kissinger. But Secretary of State Rogers accepted these facts of life. Quite surprisingly, Nixon, in contrast to Kennedy, did not endeavor to involve himself in the details of decisionmaking. He did, however, in company with his famous yellow pad, reserve to himself the finalization of decisions. Although the Nixon NSC is generally regarded as the most structured, this, according to Brent Scowcroft, was "only in terms of numbers of subsidiary organizations. In the formal sense," Scowcroft recently opined, "it was not as structured an operation as the Eisenhower NSC." There are those who have termed the NSC as Nixon's "validating body." Scowcroft disputes this view. "There is no doubt that President Nixon made the decisions, nor that Kissinger's views generally prevailed," Scowcroft assessed in retrospect. But he insisted, "That did not in any way prevent vigorous debate or differences of opinion in NSC meetings."[24] Although President Carter thought these "numbers of subsidiary organizations" were too many, the Nixon-Ford NSC was innovative and productive in policy. Moreover, after Kissinger was relieved of his NSC role, under Scowcroft the NSC organization and operations had become far less dominated by one person. No longer did one person chair the six committees. No longer was a self-styled lone ranger directing the operations.

In the Carter NSC there is simply a Committee on Policy Review and a Committee on Special Coordination.[25] Appellations would also change. In place of the Kissinger-Scowcroft National Security Study Memorandum, the final product served up to President Carter is called a Presidential Review Memorandum; Carter decisions are called Presidential Directives instead of the National Security Decision Memoranda of the Nixon and Ford administrations.[26] The very term "Presidential Directive" is indicative of the conviction of Annapolis graduate Carter that his command decisions as President and as Commander in Chief are indivisible. However, in Scowcroft's estimation, "At least thus far, the reorganization of the NSC in the new administration is purely cosmetic. Reduction of the number of committees from six to two has no substantive significance," Scowcroft observed, "since the membership was virtually identical on all committees and the principle of different chairmen for different committees was established under my administra-

tion. The change from NSDM to PDM is likewise cosmetic,"
Scowcroft added, "since every NSDM was, and was
explicitly so stated, a Presidential directive."[27]

The Managerial Presidency

As a person and as a symbol, President Carter enjoyed great
popularity at the end of his first one hundred days in office.
Following his first economic summit meeting with the heads
of the other six industrial democracies and the fifteen-
member NATO gathering in May 1977, the *Times* of London
proclaimed, "For the first time since President Kennedy
died, the Western world can feel it has a leader—and one
who can both arouse the enthusiasm of peoples and inspire
the confidence of statesmen."[28] Indeed, the French appeared
to like him more than Kennedy who, rather than referring to
America's peer group, had proclaimed America's leadership.
They liked the way Carter listened. French President Giscard
d'Éstaing described Carter, after their meeting, as a person
of "great simplicity and modesty, low keyed, who accepts
the advice and even criticism of others."[29] These favorable
working relationships with allied heads of state may be the
most valuable asset gained by a new President at his first
summit. However, amid such plaudits for Carter, James Reston observed that "the test of those high altitude meetings
is what the great men do when they descend into the political valley back home." Reston recalled, "Roosevelt at Yalta,
Truman at Potsdam, Eisenhower at Geneva, Nixon at Shanghai, Ford at Vladivostok all produced comforting and even
heroic communiques; but their backswing was better than
their follow through."[30] Sensing Carter's increasing problems with the Congress, one of his summit colleagues
avowed "that a political man must be ready to take on the
party and force things through when necessary."[31]

A further test of leadership is how the President works
with his own senior staff. Whether, as some predict, he will
reduce them to technicians remains to be seen. The new key
national security members, Vance, Brown, and Brzezinski,
are no strangers to one another. Brown and Brzezinski

served together in the privately supported Trilateral Commission for strengthening relations among western Europe, the United States, and Japan. It was through this Commission that Carter, when he was the Georgia governor, met them. Vance and Brzezinski were previously associated through the New York–based Council on Foreign Relations. Nonetheless, keeping such advisers in balance and reaching out for other sources of counsel will be a challenge for President Carter.

No matter what his personal predilections, the new President, like all his predecessors since 1940, will find foreign policy matters occupying at least two-thirds of his time. In the area of foreign policy he will be well advised, despite the ability of these immediate national security advisers, to encourage, in a well-structured setting, what Alexander L. George has described as "well prepared advocates making the best case for alternative options."[32] A word of caution may well be given, however, regarding multiple advocacy. Lyndon Johnson as President tried the approach of Lyndon Johnson as parliamentarian, of pleasing everyone. He ended up pleasing no one. Today, domestic matters are increasingly related to foreign policy (in the case of energy), I. M. Destler points out, "the effective integration of domestic political and foreign policy advice becomes a matter of some urgency."[33] The central purview should continue through the National Security Council. However, just as President Ford invited intelligence estimates drawn from the private sector to supplement those of the government's intelligence community in evaluating the Soviet arms buildup, President Carter may well encourage competent "outside" alternate counsel.

Except during a concentrated period of crisis command decisions, as in the Cuban missile crisis or, to a lesser extent, the *Mayagüez* incident, a President simply cannot filter out other issues demanding his attention. As Richard Rose has expressed it, "a President cannot govern indefinitely in a crisis state." Nor can he "concentrate upon a single policy area, even one as complex as national security,"[34] as domestic concerns also press upon him.

A new President, a new Commander in Chief, should

quickly establish a good working relationship with his principal military advisers, the Joint Chiefs of Staff. Lamentably,
Commanders in Chief have often neglected to do so until
after a crisis situation is upon them. There was a communications gap between President Kennedy and the Chiefs not
only at the time of the abortive Bay of Pigs invasion but even
at the time of the Cuban missile crisis. Not until 1966 did
President Johnson bring the chairman of the JCS and the
director of the CIA into his Tuesday luncheon group, where
the key operational decisions were being made on the
Vietnam War. President Ford, however, established an early
close relationship with his Chiefs, which contributed notably
to the success of the *Mayagüez* operation.

The modern President, especially in his role as the Commander in Chief in a nuclear age, must have finely honed
managerial skills. In 1922, Arthur M. Schlesinger, Sr., when
he sought to define "the illusive quality of greatness" in
American Presidents, made no reference to managerial
ability, but by 1974, Peter Drucker could state, "The President... is first of all a manager."[35] Indeed, as chief executive officer of the world's largest corporation, the federal
executive department, his (or someday hers) is the number
one managerial post. The President is chief of state, ceremo-
nial chief, chief initiator and executor of public policy, chief
defender of the Constitution, Commander in Chief of the
nation's armed forces, chief diplomat, chief exemplar of the
moral and spiritual tone of the nation, leader of his political
party, and sole authoritative spokesman of his administration both at home and abroad—a position demanding of the
most exacting organizational skills and management. The
Commander in Chief has the awesome responsibility for national security in this nuclear age. He alone makes the decision "to press the button," to employ nuclear weapons. As
James C. Hagerty observed, "He has to be a man of great
wisdom and great patience to bear that burden."[36]

Staffing and Organizing the Presidency

All Presidents in the nuclear age have shown considerable
care in the selection of their Secretary of State and their

Secretary of Defense. Their choice of domestic counterparts more frequently involves political considerations; even the selection of the Vice President, who is only a heartbeat away from assuming full Presidential responsibilities, is generally a political decision.

Truman is the classic case of a Vice President cut off from national security policy considerations. Ambassador Robert D. Murphy, who has served as a foreign policy adviser for Presidents since Franklin Roosevelt, recounted how completely uninformed Vice President Truman was:

> Shortly after Mr. Roosevelt's death, I happened to be at the Potsdam Conference with Mr. Truman. I discovered that he actually hadn't been informed of the vast bulk of the foreign policy decisions that were in progress. Nor did he really know the President's planning for the future. Thus when Mr. Roosevelt died on the eve of the conference, it was extremely difficult for the new President who had nothing to do with it before.[37]

Truman was thus catapulted into the final days of World War II and the first days of the Cold War. Indeed, at the Potsdam Conference with Stalin and Churchill, Truman had a simplistic, albeit refreshing, view of world affairs. At the conference, Ambassador Murphy recalled, Truman asked Secretary of State James F. Byrnes, "Jimmy, do you realize we've been here ten whole days? God, you can settle anything in ten days!"[38]

One of the reforms sought in the 1949 National Security Act Amendment was to ensure the involvement of the Vice President in foreign affairs. Accordingly, he was added as a statutory member of the National Security Council. President Carter has clearly sought to involve Vice President Walter F. Mondale, sending him a week after the inaugural to visit not only European capitals but also NATO headquarters and such symbolic sites of concern as Berlin.

As President-elect, Carter made it clear that he did not consider the Secretary of State a second President for foreign affairs. In his selection of Vance, he sought to tap proven, sound experience. The qualifications which Professor Samuel Huntington set forth in 1957 for Secretary of Defense are equally appropriate for Secretary of State:

> First, he should be a man of experience, possessing some
> familiarity with the problems with which he will be
> dealing. . . . Second, the Secretary should be a man of respect,
> commanding the admiration of informed public opinion. . . .
> Third, he should be a man of dedication, acting and thinking
> purely in terms of the needs of the office. . . . Finally, the
> Secretary must be a man of policy. His greatest needs are
> breadth, wisdom, insight, and, above all, judgment. He is
> neither operator, administrator, nor commander. But he is
> policy maker.[39]

Both Vance and Brown appear to eminently fulfill Professor Huntington's qualifications. As the late Peter Lisagor, the dean of Washington correspondents, concluded in his final column, "It's good to know that there are Cy Vances available and that Jimmy Carter has the good judgment to seek them out."[40] The same could be said for Brown. Both were veterans of the Pentagon of the Kennedy-Johnson years, Brown being perhaps the brightest of all of the so-called Whiz Kids of the McNamara era. Their experience should serve them well, for State and Defense bureaucrats have been past masters of constricting and subverting Presidential and Commander in Chief authority through negotiating such instruments as military assistance agreements, contingency plans, and operational directives. (For example, during the Cuban missile crisis President Kennedy had directed that provocative intelligence against the Soviets be halted; yet at the height of the crisis a U-2 entered Soviet air space.)[41]

Far more than Brzezinski with the NSC, where the changes are largely cosmetic, Brown with the Department of Defense proposes sweeping organizational changes. He would replace the present structure, wherein ten assistant secretaries of defense and eleven directors of offices report to the Secretary of Defense, with undersecretaries for resources, for policy, and for evaluation.[42] This would be the first major overhaul of the department organization since President Eisenhower personally wrote the 1958 Defense Reorganization Act. Eisenhower would applaud Brown's desire to reduce the number of persons reporting to the Secretary, which has more than doubled in the intervening nineteen years. At the same time, the principles which

Eisenhower achieved would be retained: (1) strengthening the role of "the top strategic planners," the Joint Chiefs of Staff; (2) clearing the lines of military command; (3) establishing unified commands; (4) providing centralized research and developments and integrating new weapons; (5) defining the authority of the Secretary of Defense, particularly regarding appropriations, without "depriving Congress of the power of the purse."[43] However, unlike Brzezinski's proposals for the NSC reorganization, Brown's for the Department of Defense will require legislative approval. It may be noted that similar changes were being proposed in the Ford administration. Indeed, they were in the final stages of staffing under the then Deputy Secretary of Defense, William Clements, when the Ford administration terminated.

One Carter campaign pledge, to cut defense spending, was also an early concern of Secretary Brown. During the campaign Carter declared that "without endangering the defense of our nation or commitments to our allies, we can reduce present defense expenditures by about $5 billion to $7 billion annually."[44] The new President early made clear that this would not be done at the expense of NATO—that, indeed, support might even be increased for NATO, accompanied, it was to be hoped, with increases by other financially strong members. Nor would Carter, a former naval nuclear engineer, recommend to Brown, a former director of Defense Research and Engineering, reductions in research and developments. In the long-range view, some personnel savings might be achieved in the Defense Department. An all-volunteer Army was proving extremely costly; some civilian personnel and domestic base reductions might also be made along with savings from purchasing and maintenance standardizations. But with fiscal 1977 one-third over on the day Carter took office, the best immediate prospect for reductions was simply to slow down the rate of weapon delivery. This would be nothing new. Eisenhower had called it "stretch-out." As Dr. Brown appreciated, other cost cuts would not come easy, what with inflation, weapon sophistication, the need to maintain both the strategic nuclear balance and strengthen conventional forces, and bureaucratic intransigence.

President Carter appears to suffer somewhat from the hand-.

icaps of President Kennedy, who insisted upon personal involvement in every area of the decisionmaking process, and of President Nixon, whose distrust of both the bureaucracy and his peers negated his own best efforts through his Domestic Council to restore the Cabinet to its full advisory and executive potential. Return to Cabinet government would not come easy; it would mean reducing the size and influence of both the Presidential staff and the Executive Office of the President, a creation of Franklin Roosevelt during the New Deal years of the 1930s. As the depression deepened, Hoover doubled his assistants from two to four and increased his total staff to thirty-seven. It was to continuously grow through the Nixon years. Even though President Ford made some reductions below the level he inherited, what with the panoply of boards, commissions, and special groups, the White House staff and the Executive Office of the President today number more than five thousand.

Every President has his own style of conducting business, but organizational changes are normally more marked when the incoming administration's party is different from that of the outgoing. The opportunity to move away from an overdependence on staff to a greater reliance on Cabinet existed at the beginning of 1977. Some significant beginnings had been made by Ford, whose able Cabinet had increased access to the President. Indeed, Ford advocated both a strong Cabinet and a strong staff. Senator Henry Jackson, who has probably studied national security organization more thoroughly over a longer period of time than any other member of the Senate, long ago reached the conclusion that a strong chief executive can command and should have *both* a strong Cabinet and a strong staff. Thus, he wrote, quoting from "A Staff Report of the Subcommittee on National Policy Machinery":

> In the American system, there is no satisfactory alternative to primary reliance on the great departments, and their vast resources of experience and talent, as instruments for policy development and execution. At the same time, there is no satisfactory substitute for the budgetary process and the staff work of Presidential aides in pulling departmental programs together into a truly Presidential program, prodding the de-

partments when necessary and checking on their performances.[45]

Although this Jackson report, dated January 28, 1961, was
for President Kennedy eight days after his inaugural, it could
perhaps have well been written for President Carter eight
days after his inaugural. However, if written in 1977 its reference to "the budgetary process" would have to be qualified. Since the passage of the 1974 Budget Reform Act, the
budget office of Congress has become increasingly involved
not merely in "checking on . . . performances," a role Jackson
envisaged for the Presidential budget office, but even in
evaluating military strategy. Thus in 1976 the Congressional
budget office released a report critical of the Presidential
handling of the *Mayagüez* incident and another critical of
NATO strategy. Senator Russell's warning of the 1950s
about the dangers of Congress attempting to legislate
strategy might well be pondered today.

In concluding these considerations for the new Congress
and the new President, one might well reiterate the principle
on Presidential appointments enunciated by Lee C. White,
former Assistant Special Counsel to President Kennedy and
Special Counsel to President Johnson: ". . . the President . . .
is entitled to have the guys he is most comfortable with and
can rely upon."[46] In similar spirit the Congress, the President, and his principal advisers might reflect upon a principle regarding organizational structure for decisionmaking.
Helmut Sonnenfeldt, for years a principal adviser in the area
of national security policy, has written: "Every President inherits something from his predecessor as far as machinery is
concerned. Of course," Sonnenfeldt noted, "he inherits a
great deal as far as his policies and options are concerned.
But it is not likely that the particular machinery is going to
reappear in its present form in the case of . . . [a President's]
successor."[47] Brzezinski's and Carter's actions in restructur-
ing the National Security Council already confirm that prediction.

Certain members of the Congress and the press would like
to legislate somewhat permanent organizational machinery
(and constraints) for Presidential decisionmaking, but as

Sonnenfeldt put it, Presidential "responsibilities... are obviously so enormous that if he constantly finds himself fighting his own machinery and his own system because of rigidities this is going to be utterly debilitating and will detract from his ability to focus on the real issues."[48] Another veteran senior adviser on national security policy, Richard F. Pederson, agreed wholeheartedly with Sonnenfeldt, his successor, "that the system of establishing foreign policy has to be a system which is in accord with the desires, the interests, and the way of working of the President."[49]

A Climate for Decisionmaking

"A President need not try to make his mark by the number of things that he does, like someone seeking entry to the *Guinness Book of Records*,"[50] observed Richard Rose. Greatness does not consist in the number of decisions made but rather in the wisdom of those decisions. Helmut Sonnenfeldt adds, "He becomes truly a great President only after he has succeeded in enforcing those decisions."[51]

Presidents do need machinery for sifting out priorities. Walter N. Thayer, while serving as a member of the President's Advisory Council on Executive Organization, cautioned in April 1970, "... the Bob Haldemans, the John Ehrlichmans, the Sherman Adams, the Joe Califanos, of all the Administrations, are just simply swamped and overwhelmed by the priority problems of the moment. They are," Thayer, the former editor of the New York *Herald Tribune*, concluded, "addressing themselves to the one or two percent of the problems that take 99 percent of the President's time, of their time, because those are the key issues... be it Vietnam, Middle East, or Washington."[52]

Viewing both the political and the strategic consequences of Truman's decision on Korea and Johnson's decision on Vietnam, Louis W. Koenig, who has studied crisis management extensively, has inquired: Are there "ways to reduce as much as possible the risks, the hazards to the President, in these final hours or days after the presentations have been made when he may act without the full benefit of this machinery?"[53] Eisenhower, who proved to be a consummate politician as well as one of the ablest Commanders in Chief, found the safety valve for his command decisions in Congressional as well as Cabinet and NSC debates. His cautious approach to command decisions caused former President Truman to caustically compare him to President Buchanan, who had hesitated to act as Commander in Chief on the eve of the Civil War.

But Buchanan doubted his Constitutional authority to act in 1860–1861, whereas Eisenhower never doubted his authority as Commander in Chief: before making his command decisions, he simply wanted the counsel of both the Congress and America's closest allies. He sought the advice of the Congressional majority (Democratic) party as well as that of the Republicans. Eisenhower also consulted his old English friends Churchill and Eden in 1954 when he was considering intervention in Vietnam. They were unenthusiastic about the venture, so despite the eloquent arguments of Vice President Richard M. Nixon and Chairman of the Joint Chiefs of Staff Arthur W. Radford, Eisenhower declined the French invitation to send combat troops to Vietnam. In China (Taiwan) and the Middle East as well, Eisenhower dexterously involved the Congress in decisionmaking. The Eisenhower Doctrine which thus evolved, enunciated in a special message to the Congress of January 5, 1957, supported the sovereignty of all Middle Eastern nations against "international communism." As one scholar observed, the Eisenhower Doctrine was "a necessary and constructive step . . . in the development of an American policy for the Middle East, . . . the Administration wisely chose a method which would associate the Congress with the President in a solemn declaration of national intent."[54] So skillfully did Eisenhower involve the Congress that Senator Fulbright lamented that "we snoop and pry" and Speaker Sam Rayburn avowed, "he would have no criticism from me."[55]

Neither the Truman Doctrine on aid to Greece and Turkey nor the Nixon Doctrine on lowering America's profile as the world's policeman was formulated with the care for Congressional considerations that Eisenhower's was. President Carter will be well advised to seek in advance Congressional views for what one day may be termed the Carter Doctrine. As the *New York Times* observed editorially ten days after Mr. Carter took office, he "will have to observe more than the forms of consultation if he is to prevail on substance."[56]

The salient note of Carter's inaugural address, which was couched in moral precepts, emphasized reductions in nuclear arms. Six months into the Carter administration, however, this did not seem so readily obtainable, nor did a Geneva peace settlement for the Middle East. From the President's meeting with Egypt's President Sadat, Jordan's King Hussein, Saudi Arabia's Prince Fahd, Syria's President Hafiz al-Asad, and Israel's new Premier Menachem Begin came euphoric Carter statements. However, Secretary of State Vance had no illusions of immediate success in his August 1977 journey to the Middle East.

After six months, the President's promised reorganization programs being drawn by OMB for fall Congressional consideration appeared on schedule. However, with his pledges to reform the bureaucracy, Carter should not be dismayed by intransigence. Nor should hopes of organizational remedies be raised too high.

The current national security organization has evolved considerably since its foundations in the National Security Act of 1947. The tragic end of the first Secretary of Defense, Forrestal, and the extreme interservice rivalries epitomized by the "admirals' revolt" of 1949 were among the severe object lessons along the way. Today the machinery does work, but as Helmut Sonnenfeldt concluded, " . . . machinery itself is not the answer for this very crucial problem: the implementation of the Presidential will."[57] Moreover, the best of machinery can by its very efficiency stifle rather than encourage innovation and can in no way ensure wisdom. The spirit of innovation and the wisdom of judgment rest finally on the character of the President himself. As Richard Neustadt has expressed it, "presidential power is the power to persuade." To this may be added that the ultimate source of Presidential power is public opinion itself. President Carter recognizes this in reinstituting President Franklin D. Roosevelt's fireside chats. Let us hope that what James Reston observed in 1961 remains true today: "The

President is one man who can get the attention of the American people. They will listen to him . . . ," Reston concluded, as to "what he thinks is necessary for the safety of the Republic. . . ."[58]

Strategic Balance

As the Carter administration began, the Congress, indeed the American people, were readying for a national debate as to where the United States stood vis-à-vis the Soviets and what should be done about it. What of the Cold War and of détente? How did the Soviets and the United States get into their present positions?

President Carter seeks the reduction and eventual elimination of nuclear weapons, as well as the control of nuclear proliferation so that other nations offered nuclear technology for peaceful purposes will not turn it into weaponry. This has been the hope and the policy of every nuclear-age American President. The world of today is a far cry from that of July 16, 1945, when the first atom bomb exploded and the Soviets began feverish efforts to develop their own nuclear device. Eisenhower, as Army Chief of Staff, warned as early as June 14, 1946: "We must move, by steps, toward international control of atomic energy if we are to avoid an atomic war." He added that "equally adequate control of other weapons of mass destruction" must be found.[59] However, the Soviets rejected the Baruch Plan and other early arms reduction proposals which were submitted to the United Nations. Thanks to espionage, the Soviets rapidly unlocked the nuclear riddle and on September 29, 1949, produced their own first atomic explosion. The Marxist-Leninist doctrine of expansionist Communism and the United States containment philosophy appeared to put the two nuclear powers on a collision course.

The rise of two nuclear superpowers was an aftermath of the destruction in World War II of the old Berlin-Rome-Tokyo power axis. Moreover, the defeat of Germany, Italy, and Japan in World War II was accompanied by the decline of Britain and France. The old power blocs were swept away. By 1947 the Soviets were dominant in eastern and central

Europe and threatening Greece and Turkey. Then came the beginnings of an American response: the Truman Doctrine, the Marshall Plan, the Berlin airlift, and NATO.

As Anthony Eden noted at the time of NATO's formation, Britain had been in the business of "mutual and reciprocal" alliances at least since the Anglo-Portuguese alliance of 1373, which declared "they shall henceforth reciprocally be friends to friends and enemies to enemies, and shall assist, maintain and uphold each other mutually by sea and by land. . . ."[60] Air was the only new dimension to this ancient treaty, as far as the British and the Portuguese were concerned. Still, as every American schoolboy knows, Americans have been well counseled against "entangling alliances." It was a bold departure in American foreign policy to become a NATO member, and it was achieved by bipartisan Congressional support.

Simultaneous with the formation of NATO came NSC-68, the first American post–World War II comprehensive statement of national security policy. Drafted by Dean Acheson, and signed by President Truman on April 12, 1950, the document stated: "It is quite clear from the Soviet theory and practice that the Kremlin seeks to bring the free world under its dimensions by the methods of the cold war."[61] While the document called for substantial enlargement in the United States defense budget, the Korean War which erupted a few weeks later, rather than NSC-68, led to the restoration of American military might, which had been dismantled after World War II.

The economic resurgence of Japan and West Germany in the 1950s and their entry into the system of alliances which encircled the Soviets before the end of the first Eisenhower administration had given the United States and its allies by 1956 a sense of security lacking during the previous decade. The strategy of the period was characterized by the Dulles phrase "massive retaliation," based upon overwhelming United States nuclear strength. The following year, with the launching of Sputnik, the first orbiting satellite, and the leaking of the Gaither Report with its intelligence estimates, this sense of security vanished and was replaced by the specter of

Soviet missiles raining down upon American cities and the spawning of the missile-gap myth.

Now the United States demanded a new national strategy, under which it would respond anywhere, at any time, with weapons and forces of its choosing. The justification was the creation of a better world. After positioning the Soviet Union and the United States on the brink of a nuclear holocaust in confrontations over Cuba and Berlin, Khrushchev and Kennedy in 1963 initiated the policies of détente. A direct communications link, the "hot line," was established between Moscow and Washington, who joined Great Britain in entering upon a nuclear test ban treaty. Eisenhower had commenced negotiations eight years earlier on such a treaty, but credit for its consummation must go to President Kennedy, whose address at American University on June 10, 1963, inspired the Soviets to sign the treaty six weeks later. (Today 114 nations are signatories to this prohibition of nuclear explosions in the atmosphere, underwater, or in outer space.)

Simultaneous with these declarations of détente, which Khrushchev termed "mutual coexistence," the Soviets determined never again to be forced to back down as they did in the Cuban missile crisis. Hence they began a massive arms buildup which, within a decade, brought them to parity with the United States in both conventional and nuclear weapons. How near dead wrong were United States estimates of that buildup is indicated by Secretary of Defense McNamara's 1965 assertion that "the Soviet rate of expansion today is not such as to allow them to equal, much less exceed our own force.... The Soviets have decided," McNamara announced, "that they have lost the quantitative race, and they are not seeking to engage us in that contest.... There is no indication that the Soviets are seeking to develop a strategic nuclear force as large as ours."[62]

So deluded, the United States turned its back on the Soviet buildup and dissipated its own military energies in Vietnam. This strategy of the 1960s was followed by the Nixon Doctrine of the 1970s. In seeking today to extricate the good from the bad in the Nixon heritage, we must, in the spirit of Lincoln, now "disenthral ourselves." Ernest S. Griffith and Louis W. Koenig are two of the few Presidential scholars since Watergate to recognize the constructive foreign policies associated with Nixon's name. Dr. Griffith had the courage to refer to "... the really great foreign policy achievements of Nixon's first term."[63] And Dr. Koenig recognized that the Nixon Doctrine did "diminish the likely use of awesome military power."[64]

The Nixon Doctrine recognized the arrival of a coequal superpower, and it emphasized a new willingness to negotiate with the Soviet Union. Thus, President Nixon, while seeking to extricate the United States from the swamps around the Mekong, had to create a new military balance. It partially included renewal of détente with the Soviets, lowering the profile of America's role as policeman of the world, and an invitation to allies to engage in more self-help. The Nixon Doctrine related moral principle and the national interest. Foreign aid and negotiation became essential diplomatic instruments, transcending confrontation and show of force; friendly overtures were made toward the Soviet's archenemy, the People's Republic of China. In the first of a series of unprecedented annual reports to the Congress on American foreign policy, Nixon announced: "No nation need be our permanent enemy."[65] In keeping with that expression Nixon journeyed to the People's Republic of China February 21–28, 1972, to the Soviet Union three months later, and two years thereafter to Egypt, restoring diplomatic relations with that most populous Arab nation just before his resignation.

On September 3, 1971, in the Four-Power agreement on Berlin, the Soviets guaranteed there would be no future interference in civilian traffic between West Berlin and West Germany. As Nixon expressed it, the prospects for détente could be radically improved if the tensions surrounding Berlin—a focus of perennial crisis since 1948—were alleviated. The agreement on access to Berlin, faithfully carried out, has indeed proved what Nixon, with characteristic hyperbole, termed at the time "a milestone achievement."[66] Despite the vigorous opposition of the Soviet Union, Kissinger visited West Berlin on May 21, 1975, addressed the city assembly, and emphasized that "only if Berlin flourishes will détente flourish; only if you are secure will Europe be secure."[67] Vice President Mondale expressed a similar sentiment in his own visit there in January 1977. Nonetheless, West Berlin, an island in a Communist sea, is not prospering. Though still the most populous West German city (2,047,948), increasingly it is becoming a city with an aging population. Several hundred thousand West Germans have moved out. The younger generation cannot remember the Berlin airlift as the 1948 symbol of resistance to Soviet aggression. The Berlin Wall, created in 1961 to prevent East Germans from fleeing to the West, remains as foreboding as ever. Although the *Ostpolitik* drive of former Chancellor Willy Brandt has been muted by the Helmut Schmidt government with its emphasis on strengthening relations with the Western allies, that could change again. A future German Federal Republic government may not deem West Berlin worth the drain on the treasury, and thus this Western symbol in the Soviet satellites could one day fall without a fight. To forestall that possibility, a communiqué was issued on May 9, 1977, by French President Giscard d'Éstaing, British Prime Minister James Callaghan, West German Chancellor Helmut Schmidt, and President Carter, emphasizing that strict adherence to the existing agreement on Berlin was "indispensable to the continued improvements of the situation and essential to the strengthening of détente, the maintenance of security and the development of cooperation throughout Europe."[68]

The first United States–Soviet dialogue on strategic arms limitations, SALT I, achieved in 1972, was an even more significant landmark than the 1971 Berlin agreement. Moreover, it marked the first time since the inception of the Cold War that an agreement was reached with the Soviets separate and apart from America's European partners. In 1967, President Lyndon Johnson proposed limitations on both antiballistic missile systems (ABMs) and ICBMs in his communications and in his historic meeting at Glassboro, New Jersey, with Aleksei N. Kosygin, who succeeded Khrushchev as Prime Minister in 1964. In essence, Nixon and Kissinger's initiatives, commencing in 1969 with the Secretary General of the Communist party, Leonid Brezhnev, marked a renewal of Johnson's efforts. In May 1972 Nixon and Brezhnev signed two agreements in Moscow. The one, a Treaty on the Limitation of Anti-Ballistic Missile Systems, permitted each side to protect its capital (Moscow and Washington) plus one other site (the United States selected the Grand Forks, North Dakota, missile site). Each side was also limited to two hundred antimissile missiles. The treaty is of indefinite duration.

The other 1972 SALT agreement was an interim measure, of five years' duration, that would expire on October 3, 1977. It placed limitations on the number of launchers for international ballistic missiles carrying nuclear warheads—that is, for silos on land and tubes on missile-bearing submarines. According to this SALT I interim agreement, the Soviets would be permitted 2,358 land- and sea-based launchers and the United States 1,710. This included for the Soviets 1,408 land-based launchers and for the United States 1,000. The reasoning in the lesser number for the United States was its lead in Multiple Independently Targeted Reentry Vehicles (MIRV). SALT I limited the United States to no more than 44 modern ballistic missile submarines with a total of 710 SLBMs and permitted the Soviets to have 62 modern ballistic submarines with 950 SLBMs. Just as the Soviet ICBM numerical superiority was offset by United States MIRVs, so also the Soviet submarine superiority was offset by the more sophisticated United States bomber fleet. (Bombers were added to the aggregate of delivery systems two years later in the Vladivostok Accord.)

Although an extensive literature has been written in analysis of SALT, [69] there is little agreement as to which side achieved the better position in SALT I. This much can be said: (1) The United States representatives then and now found the Soviets the most intransigent negotiators; (2) both sides gave up portions of their antiballistic missile systems, thereby in essence settling for a mutual assured destruction stand-off; technically in this respect the United States gave up more because its ABM system was more sophisticated; (3) the Soviets accepted numerical ceilings on ICBM and SLBM deployment; here critics of Nixon and Kissinger point out that the Soviets, who feverishly built after 1965, when they were far behind the United States, had by 1972 achieved far greater total throw-weight capacity as well as numerical superiority in launchers and were only too happy to have these superior positions frozen.[70]

Contrary to the prevalent view, both Scowcroft and Sonnenfeldt assert that the Soviets gave up more than the United States. Scowcroft contends that "while we did give up what probably would have been a technologically more advanced ABM system, the Soviets stopped an active program of adding to their offensive nuclear inventory whereas we gave up no program at all."[71] In brief, prior to SALT I we had already stopped building land-based launchers, while the Soviets had not. Sonnenfeldt finds sacrifice on the part of the Soviets as related to withdrawal of ABM systems. "For the defensive minded Russians," he asserts, "it was not an insignificant psychological step that, in the interest of greater stability, this vulnerability was to be sanctioned by a treaty with its principal competitors."[72]

Kissinger, in one of his euphoric moments, is alleged to have claimed that SALT "cracked the code" of Soviet strategic thinking. "While," Scowcroft commented, "I cannot deny that he may have made the statement," he never found Kissinger advancing such a claim for SALT. The Soviets having achieved equilibrium, instead continued their old tactics of exploitation, including use of client state troops. Walter Millis had recognized this many years before, when he forecast in 1956:

> Assuming that a substantial military equilibrium had been established on the major plans of grand strategy, this simply frees the Soviet Union to proceed in great areas of the world by those piecemeal tactics of disruption, subversion, propagandist and economic pressures backed by the existence of Soviet military power.[73]

Perhaps most significantly, SALT I began a dialogue, although not one involving an interface with Western doctrine. The simple fact is, as Millis noted more than twenty years ago, the Soviets continue to utilize military muscle to exploit political advantage and to intimidate other nations. In November 1974 Communist Party Secretary General

Brezhnev and President Ford, in the Vladivostok Accord, placed ceilings on aggregate strategic forces, including bombers, and reaffirmed the desire of achieving SALT II before the termination of SALT I. Brezhnev proved himself a more reasoned and less volatile negotiator than Eisenhower and Nixon found Khrushchev—or as Nixon recently put it, "a much safer man to have sitting there with his finger on the button."[74]

On Ford's last day in office, Brezhnev remarked, "Of particular importance were the accords we achieved at Vladivostok regarding a long term agreement on strategic arms limitations."[75] Such pleasantries must be measured against the lip service paid to the Helsinki Accords, which specified "general and complete disarmament." Since that August 1975 signing, Soviet arms buildup on all levels (other than the SALT numerical missile launcher and submarine limitations) has continued at a record pace, with more and more powerful missiles coming off assembly lines. Moreover, the subsequent talks in Vienna for Warsaw Pact and NATO forces have made no progress, nor has the perennial Geneva international disarmament conference.

The Carter administration has approached SALT II with two proposals. The first of these would stick with the Vladivostok limits of 2,400 strategic nuclear delivery vehicles. Of that number, 1,320 could be MIRVS. The proposal deters all issues relating to the controversial mobile ICBMs, the Soviet Backfire bomber, and the cruise missile. The proposal does, however, ask for agreement on some of the details not reached at Vladivostok, including MIRV verification. The second, and the preferred, option of the Carter administration would reduce the aggregate number of authorized nuclear delivery vehicles (aircraft, ICBMs, and submarines) from the Vladivostok limit of 2,400 down to 1,800 to 2,000. The limit on the total number of MIRVed launchers would be reduced from 1,320 to 1,100 or 1,200. MIRVed ICBMs, which were not limited at Vladivostok, would be restricted to no more than 550. Finally, the number of Soviet modern, large ballistic missiles, which is now in the low 300s, would be restricted to 150. The United States would continue its own ban on any equivalent missiles.

Since there is no symmetry in the differing Soviet and United States missile systems, the proposed reductions would not affect the two sides in precisely the same manner: the Soviets would give up some of their SS-18 superheavy missiles, which the United States does not have, and the United States would accept a reduction in MIRVed missiles, where it enjoys a numerical and technical superiority.

When these proposals were presented by Secretary of State Vance on March 30, 1977, in Moscow, they were seemingly summarily rejected. Why? First, the Soviets doubtless wanted to probe the best possible deal with the new American President and his representatives. Second, they had, indeed, been miffed both by Carter's human rights pronouncement (even though they join in disclaiming linkage) and by the prior public announcement of the American proposals. As students of strategic arms limitations appreciate, each side equips itself with so-called bargaining chips.[76] On the United States side this includes the amazingly accurate and relatively cheap cruise missile and the Mark 12-A greatly improved warhead system. The Soviets, understandably, would prefer that neither of those systems be placed in operation. Indeed, they contend, erroneously, that the cruise missile was among the weapons limited by the Vladivostok Accord. Looming on the developmental horizon is the MARV, a maneuverable reentry vehicle. In brief, the Soviets are worried about American technology. But then the Americans are concerned about the Soviets' heavy SS-18 missile, which is why the preferred Carter option calls for their reduction. To this the Soviets resound like a wounded bear.

It appears quite clear that in order to achieve a SALT II accord both sides will go for the option retaining the Vladivostok levels and excluding both the cruise missile and the Backfire bomber from the strategic limitations list; by a separate protocol some limitation may be made deferring or eliminating the deployment of the sea-based missile and restricting the range of the land-based cruise missile and the Backfire bomber. In the interim, while the negotiations continue, Americans remain as much in the dark regarding the relative strength of the two sides as they did a generation ago about the alleged missile gap. According to Major General George J. Keegan, Jr., who retired January 1, 1977, from service as Chief of Air Force Intelligence, the Soviets have already "achieved military superiority over the United States." Chairman Brown countered this with a JCS report. He acknowledged that Soviet long-range missiles could propel heavier nuclear warheads with more detonating power than those of the United States, but he asserted that "the United States has a substantial lead over the Soviet Union in bomber payload, missile accuracy, survivability and numbers of warheads [MIRVs] and bombers."[77]

With that assurance, the new Commander in Chief signaled his Secretary of Defense to slow down development of the sea-based cruise missile. The Chiefs and Carter's old Navy shipmates would not be pleased. As early as 1971 Admiral Rickover had envisioned the sea-based cruise missile as vital "to deny the enemy full use of the seas for whatever purpose he might choose...."[78]

With such a concession, SALT II seemed achievable in 1977, including a statement of goals for Salt III. The Chiefs shared General Keegan's misgivings regarding Soviet intentions, as evidenced by the extensive buildup of Soviet civil defense, but they agreed with the Commander in Chief that the United States "is moving in the correct direction" militarily and diplomatically vis-à-vis the Soviet Union.[79]

The Soviets, through Georgi A. Arbatov, director of the Institute of U.S.A. and Canada Studies, have insisted that the specter of a "Soviet threat" is a figment of the imagination of American military, intelligence, and industrial communities, who fear "that the new Administration will really take the road of easing tensions and curbing the arms race." Arbatov, writing in the Communist newspaper *Pravda,* expressed special concern with the "militarist right-wing forces" which might obstruct SALT II, and he sought particularly to counter American concern over the Soviet civil defense buildup. "All the means and methods of civil defense have been known for a long time," he assuaged, "and they give no sort of key to victory in a nuclear war. If it were otherwise, American military specialists would probably have preferred to spend tens of billions of dollars not on a new bomber [B-1], the Trident [submarine] program or aircraft carriers, but on underground shelters and stores."[80]

Arbatov's arguments ignore the facts: Soviet defense expenditures as a whole exceed those of the United States by about one-third, ($120 billion versus $90 billion in 1976),[81] and even more ominously, Soviet research and development expenditures are estimated to exceed those of the United States by as much as 90 percent. Further, they have grain stored in hardened underground silos to feed the entire Russian population for one year; they estimate they could survive a nuclear exchange with a loss of "only" 7 million to 11 million persons (half the losses they sustained in World War II).[82] By contrast to these civil defense preparations with a disciplined population, Americans have indicated apathy for civil defense measures. Still, Arbatov's arguments must cheer a segment of the American Congress, represented by Thomas Downey of New York, Robert Leggett of California, and Robert Carr of Michigan. These members of the House Armed Services Committee have written President Carter and Dr. Brzezinski to disclaim CIA estimates "as an attempt to present military capability falsely and in the worst possible light, in order to scare the American people into raising defense expenditures."[83] Such persons are critical of NIE 11/8, the National Intelligence Estimate of the strategic capabilities and intentions of the Soviet Union, described by John W. Finney of the *New York Times* as "probably the most important document to be placed before President Carter in his first days in office. . . ."[84] NIE 11/8, the basic document for planning the President's defense budget, was prepared for Nixon and Ford, as recommended by the President's Foreign Intelligence Advisory Board. Such veteran students of national security affairs as Robert D. Murphy, Gordon Gray, and William J. Casey proposed a Team A, with representatives from the defense community, and a Team B, headed by Dr. Richard E. Pipes, professor of Russian history at Harvard. Critics of Team B have termed it "acknowledged hardliners on the soviet Union" and charged the team with using the tactics of the 1958 Gaither Report, that is, leaking their conclusions. The Gaither Report was embarrassing to President Eisenhower, who denied the validity of the "missile gap myth" it helped spawn, but it spurred the redoubling of America's then pioneering missile programs. President Ford was quite upset by the way the Team B report was exploited.[85] President Carter has discontinued the President's Foreign Intelligence Advisory Board.

Lieutenant General Daniel O. Graham, former chief of the Defense Intelligence Agency, has offered the following answer to the question "Who's ahead in the U.S.-Soviet Military Balance?"

> By most standards of measuring military forces, the Soviets have surpassed or are surpassing us—despite the "spirit of détente" and the ongoing Strategic Arms Limitation Talks (SALT). In the last decade the Soviets have gone from 224 intercontinental ballistic missiles to more than 1600. In sea-launched ballistic missiles they've gone from 29 to around 800, in nuclear warheads, from 390 to around 3500.
>
> America has fallen from being 600 *ahead* in ICBM's to about 600 *behind*; from 16 nuclear missile submarines *ahead* to 13 *behind*; from 2900 tactical aircraft *ahead* to more than 350 *behind*. The Soviets have more major surface ships then we; they have 168 ground divisions compared to our 19; their 34,500 tanks dwarf our 9000. And more ominous than the sheer numbers is the sheer speed with which the build-up occurred.[86]

Such statistics should be qualified: whereas the Soviets have more missiles, the United States has more warheads; the Soviets have more ships, but the tonnage of American ships exceeds the Soviet, as do the number of aircraft carriers. Whereas the Soviet ground forces outnumber those of the United States, two to one, and their divisions several times more, the size of each of the Soviet divisions and their firepower are less than each of those of the United States. Nonetheless, the statistics are far from comforting, and the direction in which they are headed will indeed create a severe imbalance another decade hence if the situation is not reversed. Further, if it is not reversed, the United States doctrine of credible deterrence will no longer be applicable.

The Center for the Study of the Presidency posed these considerations to Chairman Brown of the Joint Chiefs of Staff in 1976. "As of today," he responded, "our strategic nuclear forces retain a substantial, credible capability to deter an all-out nuclear attack. Neither we nor the U.S.S.R. can launch a disabling first strike, hence we have stability." However, longer-range tendencies, which cannot be reversed overnight, concern Brown. His two major concerns are: "First our submarine and bomber forces are aging, while the Soviets are improving both their antisubmarine warfare capability and their defense against bombers. Second, if the Soviets should continue their current strategic programs—even within the constraints of SALT—they could pose a significant threat to our Minuteman force within a decade."[87] (He and President Carter are concerned about the Soviets' heavy SS-18 missiles.)

Voices of gloom picture Warsaw Pact forces poised at the Elbe ready to race to the Rhine should "the balloon go up" (the old SHAPE parlance for the outbreak of war), but NATO forces have come a long way since the perilous beginnings a quarter-century ago. Brown is more optimistic than most other experts regarding NATO conventional forces. "Today," Brown asserts, "we do not need to rely on the early use of tactical nuclear weapons following an attack. . . ."[88] Further, he believes that after initial "serious shipping losses," NATO naval forces "could control the North Atlantic sea lanes to Europe," as could the Pacific fleet as far as Alaska and Hawaii, but *not* beyond, "because of a shortage of surface warships." Brown warns that "this situation will become more serious as the Soviets increase their nuclear attack submarine force."[89]

As the senior military adviser to the President, Brown knows that his assessment of the long-range Soviet threat is not universally shared. "Should Congress wish to decrease Defense spending, he pragmatically observed, "it in effect must accept a greater degree of risk than found reasonably acceptable by the Joint Chiefs of Staff, the Secretary of Defense [then Donald Rumsfeld], the National Security Council, and the President."[90] Before leaving office, Ford, as Commander in Chief, appointed Brown to another two-year term as chairman of the Joint Chiefs of Staff. Now there is a new Congress, a new Secretary of Defense, and a new President. Certainly no one can disagree with Chairman Brown's conclusion that, in the final analysis, "National security policy is... dependent upon our country's role and goals as determined by those institutions of our government which reflect the will of the people."[91]

Does the United States have a strategic doctrine, a national strategy, for SALT II and beyond? One of the most seasoned students of national strategy, Colin S. Gray, charges that "the Emperor has no clothes for a new era."[92] Dr. Gray finds that American strategic doctrine regarding the Soviet Union fails to recognize the basic "conceptual, decisional, political and economic" differences between the two nations.[93] It is later than we think. Americans have too long lulled themselves with such terms as "parity," "stability," and "deterrence." There must be something better than the doctrine of mutual assured destruction that McNamara promulgated in the 1960s, simultaneous with his assurance of American strategic superiority. Moreover, we need to go beyond an exchange of pleasantries in an examination of Soviet behavior, intentions, strengths, and weaknesses. We need to determine the bases for détente. Nixon himself was such a realist as to conclude that "the mere atmosphere of détente ... is insufficient—not only because this is not durable, but also because it is difficult to evaluate measures proposed in the name of so vague an objective."[94]

We should determine the meaning of the so-called Helsinki accords, the 1975 Conference on Security and Cooperation in Europe, which emanated not from the West but from a Warsaw Pact proposal. The Soviets—concerned about the borders established in central Europe by force in the decade of the 1940s, fearful that troops of their own satellites would oppose them in the event of a war with the West, wary of China, whose neighboring armed border extended several thousand miles—had much to gain from ending the Cold War with the West. Relaxation of tensions could mean the deterioration of NATO, as President Ford recognized in his May 29–30, 1975, meeting with the other allied heads of state in Brussels. When the meeting had initially been planned in the wake of the fall of South Vietnam, there had been considerable despondency in European capitals. Then came the *Mayagüez* incident, which caused the *Times* of London to conclude that President Ford "has shown that he can make decisions and take actions."[95] The Milan newspaper *Corrier-della Sera* added: "Mr. Ford has done much toward restoring American credibility."[96] President Ford, after his defeat by Governor Carter in a closely contested election, sent Secretary Kissinger to Brussels with President-elect Carter's reassuring message: "I am convinced that NATO's mission and the North Atlantic alliance are no less important today than when NATO was originally established."[97]

Ford's record defense budget requests for fiscal 1977, which included funds for the B-1 and the cruise missile, placed high priority on alliances and military assistance, emphasizing "a basis of shared values, even as we stand up with determination for what we believe."[98] But he could not convince Congress to join him in countering Cuban intervention in Angola, even though, commencing in the summer of 1975, more than twenty briefings were given Congressional committees.[99] With Cuban troops and Russian arms the MPLA gained control in the Angolan civil war by February 1976. It marked the first successful Communist takeover on the African continent, and it was on the strategic west coast. The new ambassador to the UN, Andrew Young, stated within the first two weeks of the Carter administration that the presence of Cuban troops in Africa had brought "a certain stability and order"; this brought a blunt disavowal from a spokesman for Cyrus Vance, the new Secretary of State.[100] However, those who know the former Georgia Congressman (the only black member to vote for Gerald Ford's confirmation as Vice President and the only one to support Ford's pardon of Nixon) find a strategy in Young's startling observation. As one astute reporter observed, Young believes "he can find common ground in almost any conflict with almost any adversary,"[101] but in his African fact-finding journey of February 1977 Young was disturbed to find that black insurgent forces in tragically divided Rhodesia were trained and supplied by the Soviets.

It is well to recollect *pre*-détente Soviet failures: Berlin blockade, South Korea, South Vietnam, and missiles in Cuba; and *post*-détente Soviet successes: conquest of South Vietnam, Cambodia, Laos, and Angola. Far from reflecting a diminution of Communist aggression, détente has witnessed its furtherance. Here is the count of the spreading net of Communist control in three decades:

Albania 1946	East Germany 1949
Bulgaria 1946	Hungary 1949
Yugoslavia 1946	North Vietnam 1954
Poland 1947	Cuba 1959
Rumania 1947	Cambodia 1975
Czechoslovakia 1948	South Vietnam 1975
North Korea 1948	Laos 1975
China 1949	Angola 1976

In assessing such advances, it may be noted that at the end of World War II only 7 percent of the world's population and 18 percent of the world's land area were under Communist rule. Today more than 1.4 billion people—35 percent of the world's population—and more than one-fourth of the world's land area are controlled by Communist governments.

Cuba and Angola are the only Communist regions not on the Eurasian land mass. Would Rhodesia be next? In Europe, though the Soviets have drawn close in Italy and Portugal, they have not been able to implant Communist government in any areas beyond those occupied by their armed forces at the end of World War II. They have not given up their design, however, and at least one astute observer, W. Howard Chase, perceives a long-range Soviet design to build a system of alliances, bases, and naval power "to encircle China and ultimately the U.S., almost the way the USSR felt that the foreign policy of John Foster Dulles was to create a military encirclement of Russia."[102] While the United States was making significant withdrawals from overseas commitments, Soviet buildup of alliance and aid-mission personnel was generally successful in the so-called period of détente, 1972–1976. Although South Vietnam involved the largest withdrawals, American reductions of armed forces for three other longtime Asiatic allies were significant: South Korea, Taiwan, and Thailand. The 1976–1977 revelations of overly zealous South Korean lobbying with members of the U.S. Congress, combined with reports of repression of critics of the Park Chung Hee regime, pressured the Carter administration to fulfill a campaign promise to eliminate or at least further reduce American military presence in South Korea. However, the Korean Peninsula, with its proximity to China, Japan, and the Soviet Union, is strategically important. Prospective American withdrawal caused such concern to Japan that President Carter assured its principal Asiatic ally of full consultation before any such action is taken. Moreover, withdrawal would force President Park to turn South Korea into a virtual garrison state in order to withstand Kim Il Sung's North Korean forces, poised only 30 miles north of Seoul.

Nonetheless, Carter as Commander in Chief avowed that he would redeem his campaign pledge to accomplish the withdrawal within four to five years. The blow would presumably be softened by continuing arms aid to South Korea and strategic positioning of the Seventh Fleet and the Far East Air Forces, including its 7,100 airmen, who would remain in Korea. Even so, Major General John K. Singlaub, the third-ranking U.S. general in South Korea, lamented in an attributable statement to a Washington *Post* reporter that "if we withdraw our ground forces on the schedule suggested it will lead to war."[103] Reading this in the *Post,* the angered Commander in Chief ordered the fifty-five-year-old officer to report to him at the White House. There, in the company of Secretary of Defense Brown, Carter directed that Singlaub be reassigned outside the Korean command. Afterward Secretary Brown stated that since Singlaub's statements were "inconsistent with announced national security policy" it would have been "difficult for him to carry out" his Korean duties.[104] Brown indicated that members of the armed services have ample opportunity to express their views within command channels in the decisionmaking process; however, if they desire to make public utterances contrary to policy they should resign before doing so. Editorially, the *New York Times,* which has been critical of the President's handling of domestic issues ("Is the Presidency still all that much like being Governor of Georgia?")[105] supported his dismissing the general: ". . . nothing short of a tough and public reaction by the President could have so established his authority." This is particularly timely, according to the *Times,* "as he undertakes a whole series of policy reviews that will challenge assumptions of the military commands." The *New York Times* concluded that ". . . direct challenge of a President's announced military policy is simply unacceptable. The price of democracy is obedience within bureaucracy and above all in the military."[106]

There must be something about the climate on the Korean Peninsula which gets the military into trouble. Both MacArthur and Van Fleet were relieved during the Korean War for public utterances contrary to the Commander in Chief's policies. Carter's critics as well as his supporters agreed that he was consciously emulating Truman in his action. The two-star general called on the carpet in the Oval Office could see on the Presidential desk the Truman sign: "The buck stops here," and he could gaze at the Truman bust. But he might well wonder whether his remark to a reporter in which he said he shared the concern of the South Koreans about another possible invasion by the North Koreans put him in a league with the legendary MacArthur, who had threatened to destroy the Chinese war machine. Nonetheless, like MacArthur, he would have his day with the Congress—albeit only a Congressional subcommittee. The chairman of that subcommittee, Congressman Samuel S. Stratton, a Democrat from New York, told the House, "We have learned in recent years that these decisions cannot be made by one man."[107] In essence, this was the Congressional rejoinder to President Ford's conclusion that there can be only one Commander in Chief. It was ironical that it was made by a Democratic Congressman pointing at a new Democratic President. It underscored the depth of the issues on Congressional-Presidential roles in national security policy.

Despite assertions that the future of Taiwan is now an internal Chinese affair, the fate of a longtime ally cannot be taken lightly. Nor need United States support for an independent Taiwan blur the bases for détente with the People's Republic of China, to whom the friendship of the United States, to counter the enmity of the Soviet Union, is more important than the annexation of Taiwan. The People's Republic, internally torn since the deaths of Chou En-lai and

Mao Tse-tung and plagued by earthquakes and poverty, has no high priority on combining the two Chinas.

The Communists, who have exploited the term "interference," do not like to be reminded that Soviet interference in China provided the Japanese arms seized in Manchuria used by the Chinese Communists to defeat the Chinese Nationalists. It was Chinese Communist interference by one million troops in Korea which turned that war from a Communist disaster into a stalemate. Continued United States presence in Taiwan, even if it is a token force, as well as a continuing major American presence in Korea, means much to Asians and all anti-Communists who saw the United States lose face in Southeast Asia. Although the political environment in Southeast Asia necessitated the withdrawal of United States forces in Thailand, the Thai government has made abundantly clear its continuing desire to maintain its alliance with the United States. So also have the Philippines: President Ferdinand Marcos has clearly indicated that he will negotiate with the new Carter administration on renewal of historic relationships and that he wants continued United States presence as an antidote to potential Communist expansion in the Western Pacific region.

With all the great and lesser powers wanting to meet the Carter foreign policy team, an orgy of travel was predictable: to the European allies and Japan, Panama (re a new canal treaty) and Latin America, Africa, and the Middle East, as well as the Soviet Union and the People's Republic of China.

To achieve his inaugural goal, "the elimination of all nuclear weapons from this earth," Carter must deal with powers lesser than the Soviet Union. Although one hundred nations are signatories to the nonproliferation treaty, under which the nuclear powers agree not to transfer nuclear weapons or control over them to nonnuclear powers, several important potential weapons states have not signed the treaty (including Argentina, Brazil, Israel, Saudi Arabia), as well as some which have exploded nuclear devices (such as France, People's Republic of China, and India). With six nations today in the nuclear weapons club, it is a nightmare to contemplate a potential sixteen or more which might convert fissionable material to weapons. President Ford, on October 28, 1976, announced measures to be imposed against any country that endeavors to buy reprocessing equipment or materials that could lead to nuclear weapons capability.

President Carter has asserted that even stronger reprisals should be found. By way of example, he stopped the development of plutonium reprocessing in the United States. In his first summit with the heads of six other industrial democracies he was less than successful, however, in securing prohibitions against the spread of breeder reactors and plutonium technology. Particularly troublesome is West Germany's promise to sell Brazilians $2.7 billion in nuclear technology. The most Carter got from the London summit was an agreement for a preliminary and long-term study. Pointing up the importance of these issues, Carter nominated Gerard C. Smith as ambassador at large to serve as his nuclear negotiator. Smith, a veteran of twenty-seven years' experience in arms control, is like Carter's other recently appointed ambassador at large, Elliot Richardson, a Republican, pointing up the President's bipartisan approach to national security policy issues.

Amid the political campaign rhetoric in the United States in the fall of 1976 regarding military assistance, it was forgotten that the dramatic reductions had already been made, and the beginning of the end of the Military Assistance Advisory Groups, which had served throughout the world since the Truman-Eisenhower period, was at hand. The MAAGs that existed in forty-four countries in July 1946 were rapidly being phased out by the end of 1976. As testimony of Congressional dominance in an area previously directed by the Commander in Chief, commencing in mid-1977 only those MAAG units specifically authorized by the Congress would be continued.

The largest single region for military assistance in 1976, the Middle East, received approximately 70 percent of total U.S. arms aid. This indicated its critical importance as well as the volatile character of the region. The Ford administration did much to defuse the volatility. As 1977 began, there was both increased opportunity and greater urgency for an Arab-Israeli peace conference. The brief United Nations Conference in Geneva in 1973 after the Yom Kippur War had come to naught. Unless such a conference could be convened again and could this time achieve a settlement, war was again predictable. On the other hand, both President Sadat and Prime Minister Rabin looked to the United States for terms of settlement. Sadat's convictions were reexpressed in his November 1975 address to the American Congress and by his having repudiated Egypt's treaty arrangements with the Soviets. Equally impressive of earnest intent was Israel's pulling back in the Sinai and giving up in the Gulf of Suez, "its single oil resource,"as Rabin expressed it to the American Congress in January 1976, "in the hope that it will move us some steps closer to peace."[108]

Secretary of State Cyrus Vance, on his first major peace initiative, visited the Middle East in February 1977. He did so in a climate far improved over that which obtained the year before. The end of the civil war in Lebanon and of the threat of another oil embargo so testified. After twenty-nine years of perilous existence as a nation Israel glimpsed light at the end of the tunnel. Arab opinion was divided between the moderates favoring settlement with Israel (Egypt, Saudi Arabia, Jordan, and Syria) and the rejectionists (Libya, Iraq, and some radical Palestinians). But even to the moderates a settlement would call for return of the territories seized in the June 1967 War: the remainder of Sinai to Egypt, the Golan Heights to Syria, and the former Jordanian West Bank along with the Gaza Strip to the Palestinians. The Israelis would, however, stand firm for full control of Jerusalem. For Egypt, as for Israel, the realization that economic stability was dependent upon political stability was an added incentive to settlement. It was clear, two and one-half years after the announcement of the "open door" in Egypt, that the hoped-for flow of foreign capital would not come until there was genuine peace and stability in the Middle East.[109]

The auguries were hopeful until the scandal-ridden Labor party was defeated in the May 1977 parliamentary elections in Israel. Menachem Begin, the sixty-three-year-old leader of the Likud (Unity) coalition, would be the new Premier. NSC scenarios had not conceived of this outcome. "No, no," Zbigniew Brzezinski responded incredulously when alerted that the Labor government was out. "That's wrong."[110] Superhawk Begin had long avowed that Israel would never give up the West Bank and Gaza, the areas President Carter doubtless had in mind in his public statements that there must be a Palestinian homeland, as well as a secure Israel, if there is to be peace in the Middle East. These unexpected events made the May 24–25, 1977, visit to the White House of Crown Prince Fahd of Saudi Arabia the more meaningful, since Saudi Arabia would be seeking a moderate Arab position and the United States would seek equal moderation on the part of Israel. Hence in the conference with Prince Fahd, President Carter noted both "tremendous challenge" and "tremendous opportunities."[111] At the same time the Likud representatives in Israel were promising a moderate position on the West Bank and the Gaza Strip "so long as there are negotiations with the aim of achieving peace between us and the Arabs."[112] By August "negotiations" seemed stalled.

Even more compelling in human terms, though strategically not as demanding, is the goal of majority rule in South Africa. This Carter goal extends beyond the Kissinger position. Belatedly, in his final year as Secretary of State, Kissinger espoused majority rule in Rhodesia and Namibia (South West Africa). But Kissinger was not prepared to move on South Africa, itself. There, with 18 million blacks and only 4.3 million whites, Prime Minister John Vorster remains firmly committed to apartheid—racial segregation, with "separate development" for blacks which would include quasi-independent tribal homelands within South Africa. As unrest deepens, whites are leaving South Africa at a rate in excess of 1,500 every month.

Carter has assigned both Vice President Mondale and UN Ambassador Young to carry his human rights message to South Africa. In May 1977, Mondale held sessions extending nearly nine hours with Vorster in Vienna; the Prime Minister described them as "tough." In what appeared to be a shifting away from a historic friendship, Mondale warned that the South Africans should "not rely on any illusions that the U.S. will in the end intervene to save South Africa." To the argument that the South African government was keeping the region free of Communism, Mondale rejoined, "We

believe that perpetuating an unjust system is the surest incentive to increase Soviet interference and even racial
war."[113] Vorster has reluctantly agreed to press Rhodesian
Prime Minister Ian Smith to accept a British-inspired agreement for an independent Zimbabwe (the African nationalist
name for Rhodesia). Vorster has also reluctantly accepted
the general propositions that Namibia, the UN trust territory
that South Africa has administered since 1920, should become an independent state.

For his part, Young participated in the ninety-two-nation
UN conference on Rhodesia convened in May 1977 in
Mozambique. However, he irritated some of the delegates by
comparing southern Africa to the American South and by
advocating gradualism in the move toward majority rule.
Robert Mugabe, a leader of Rhodesia's militant Patriotic
Front, found Young's speech "hollow" and representing "no
change" in U.S. policy.[114] He was wrong. Carter, with his
human rights espousal, was providing leadership for
change.

The new UN ambassador's even larger portfolio will be the
Third World in general. His able predecessors, Patrick
Moynihan and William Scranton, only slightly stayed the
consolidation of the Third World into an antagonistic radical
bloc. Theirs were not the first of the United States' efforts.
President Truman, immediately following World War II,
dispatched former President Hoover to organize relief and
rehabilitation efforts, and every President since had made a
conscious effort to aid nations plagued by famine, disease,
and short life expectancy.

Today there are more than a hundred aligned and un-
aligned developing countries (including mainland China and
India), and they comprise nearly two-thirds of the world's
population. An estimated 800 million of their people suffer
from malnutrition. Eighty-five percent have no regular access
to health services, and in some countries 95 percent can
neither read nor write. The Third World, a strange admixture, ranges from black African states, to the Middle East
nations (except Israel), to such Communist states as Cuba,
Vietnam, and North Korea. Some—Mexico, Peru, Pakistan,
and Iran—are aligned with the United States but increas-

ingly show loyalties to the Third World. Indeed, between
Canadian and Mexican overtures to the Third World, the
United States finds its dilemma compounded by its friends
and neighbors.

Various parts of the industrialized First World (the United
States and its allies) and the industrialized Second World
(the Soviet bloc) are today cut off from some part of the Third
World. Where assistance can be given, United States government and voluntary efforts are today joined through the
Agency for International Development (92 out of 400 private
voluntary organizations serving overseas are registered with
AID's Advisory Committee on Voluntary Foreign Aid). Andrew Young may well point to these good works as well as to
United States efforts channeled through the United Nations
and such groups as the International Monetary Fund and the
World Bank. However, the day of indiscriminate membership in myriad international organizations appears over. The
Senate Government Operations Committee, while admitting
that some such groups provided "an important opportunity
to work with the third world . . . ," has concluded that many
"are organizations to which the United States belongs without any clear idea why." According to Senator Abraham A.
Ribicoff, Senate Government Operations Committee chairman, the United States contributed more than $1 billion to
international organizations in 1975. Ribicoff recommended
dropping membership in sixty-five such organizations.[115]

In 1976 industrial countries provided some $14 billion of
conventional aid to developing countries. This included $4.3
billion from the United States, part of which was distributed
through multilateral institutions. Carter asked the American
Congress to increase this amount by 30 percent. Moreover,
on May 30, 1977, addressing the concluding ministerial meeting of the Conference on International Economic Cooperation and Development, in Paris, Secretary of State Vance
pledged $375 million support toward the $1 billion action
program initiated by the European Economic Community for
the poorest countries. He also urged the continuation of a
body such as the Conference for so-called north-south continuing dialogue. The Conference on International Economic
Cooperation and Development, which President Ford

helped create, was in session for eighteen months, and nineteen developing nations and sixteen industrial countries participated in it. The United States has also agreed to help create a common fund to stockpile global commodities to moderate price fluctuations. Moreover, Carter and Vance have perceived in the Conference a means of restraining the OPEC nations from further major oil price increases, which impinge severely upon the Third World developing economies.

Beyond this conference there is the challenge, as a part of national strategy, to define a more effective approach to the Third World, with its twin problems of hunger and overpopulation. A part of this strategy is channeled through the Department of State Coordinator of Population Problems. The incumbent, Marshall Green, the former Assistant Secretary of State for East Asian and Pacific Affairs, finds particular hope in the increasing awareness of Asian women that population must be controlled. Nonetheless he portrays the world as sitting on a self-destruct time bomb in failing to come "to grips with the population explosion. It has dilly dallied until the problem has now reached the point where a horrendous spectacle of human misery threatens to unfold."[116]

The United States, with fewer and fewer farmers producing more food, fortunately continues to have food surpluses for combating famine. At times this gets caught up in the distinction between feeding friend and foe—should the Third World or the Soviet Union (which pays more) receive United States grain surpluses? Ambassador Young can tell the UN an inspirational story about American handouts, but Ambassador Green adds a word of caution: constant parceling out of food can diminish the local population's determination to improve its own agriculture; this improvement must be the long-range imperative.[117]

America's economic and security imperatives must not be lost sight of amid its humanitarian concerns. Not only oil, but other strategic raw materials such as bauxite and iron, come from the Third World. Indeed, today the Third World is involved in one-third of the United States total foreign trade. Secretary Kissinger left President Carter a challenge to statesmanship in bettering relationships with both Second and Third Worlds when he warned in 1976: "A world of hostile blocs is a world of tension and disorder."[118] President Carter has accepted this challenge with statesmanlike vision. As he expressed in on May 22, 1977, in a major foreign policy address at Notre Dame University: "We will cooperate more closely with the newly influential countries in Latin America, Africa, and Asia. We need their friendship and cooperation in a common effort as the structure of world power changes. More than 100 years ago, Abraham Lincoln said that our nation could not exist half slave and half free. We know," President Carter concluded, "that a peaceful world cannot long exist one-third rich and two-thirds hungry."[119]

How can the Third World best be helped? Many Third World countries point to the 1974 United Nations General Assembly Declaration on Economic Rights and Duties. This appears to provide a kind of fuzzy transfer of the concept of individual human rights into national rights. As Robert Moss, editor of *Foreign Report,* the weekly newsletter of the *Economist* of London, has observed, "national wealth is something that is earned by the capacities of the country's people and the policies of its Government; it is not something that is just shipped around."[120] Recognizing this, President Carter points out that "in the long run, expanded and equitable trade will best help developing countries to help themselves."[121] This truth is borne out by the experience of the five market-oriented Third World countries which in 1976 led in growth of exports: South Korea, 68 percent; Taiwan, 51 percent; Chile, 29 percent; Thailand, 27 percent; and Argentina, 21 percent. Ironically, these are nations which have been singled out in the West for criticism on the human rights issue. However, the Third World as a whole has not enjoyed high marks for human rights, and as Robert Moss has observed of these free-enterprise-oriented countries, "they are neither more nor less repressive than the third world norm."[122] Nor have the countries demanding Western handouts enjoyed any success with industrial democracy.[123] With inspiring idealism President Carter calls for "the Western Democracies, the OPEC nations, and the developed Communist countries" to "cooperate through existing international institutions in providing more effective aid."[124] The only problem with this is that the "developed Communist countries" have no inclination to so "cooperate." Their revolution is economically based on the disparity between the haves and the have-nots. Hence they sit on the sidelines denouncing the "colonialists." Thus they ignore United Nations aid requests, even though, for example, East Germany's per capita income has surpassed that of Britain. Likewise, oil-rich Arabs disregard these requests, and the conscious-stricken West laments a condition not of its making. Moreover, although there is scant comfort in this fact, amid Third World poverty, illiteracy, and disease, the true facts are *not* that the Third World gets poorer while the West gets richer. They *both* get richer, and the Third World real per capita income has doubled in the past twenty years.[125]

As President Carter perseveres in his efforts in behalf of the Third World, in the splendid Truman tradition, he might well slow down his Condorcet-like optimism regarding the perfectibility of mankind. Reprehensible as may be the regimes in Argentina and Uruguay, the United States cannot disassociate itself from these governments, which like Brazil, Iran, and South Korea, are on our side, as opposed to our strategic opponents, the Soviet Union. Indeed, it is not in those countries, but rather with the Soviet Union and its satellites, that President Carter's human rights pronouncements will have their most telling effect. As Henry Hall Wilson, former Administrative Assistant to Presidents Kennedy and Johnson, wrote to President Carter in February 1977, "The uneasiness of the Soviet leaders about their tiny minority of dissidents is eloquent testimony to their awareness of this problem. This is like smoke coming through the cracks under the door."[126]

Taken with the enunciation of the human rights principles in the 1975 Conference on Security and Cooperation in Europe, Carter's initiatives on human rights build on the principles of Wilson's Fourteen Points, and on the Churchill-Roosevelt Atlantic Charter, emphasizing the self-determination of peoples. This powerfully counters the Brezhnev Doctrine of 1968, which justified the use of force to protect (as in Czechoslovakia) Communist regimes. The human rights to which Carter refers are basically those set forth in the Universal Declaration of Human Rights adopted by the United Nations in 1948, and those rights have long been reflected in United States legislation. For example, the United States Foreign Assistance Act reads: "A principal goal of the foreign policy of the United States is to promote the increased observance of internationally recognized human rights by all countries." The Statue of Liberty, which beckons endless refugees to American shores, had special meaning in America's bicentennial year, when 31,000 refugees (many from Vietnam) were accepted for permanent resettlement in the United States.

In an address on April 30, 1977, at the University of Georgia's Law School, Secretary Vance succinctly set forth the rights to which the Carter administration is referring:

> First there is the right to be free from governmental violation of the integrity of the person. . . . Second, there is the right to the fulfillment of such vital needs as food, shelter, health care, and education. . . . Third, there is the right to enjoy civil and political liberties. . . .[127]

While no other President ever gave such repetitive public utterance to human rights in his first hundred days in office, the principles enunciated are in keeping with American roots. As Secretary Vance pointed out, "Our encouragement and inspiration to other nations and other peoples have never been limited to the power of our military or the bounty of our economy. They have been lifted up by the message of our Revolution, the message of individual human freedom."[128]

Although beyond the hundred days there was a lowering of voices on human rights, the President continues to pledge "to speak out." By May 1977 a Carter Doctrine was emerging. His basic foreign policy commitments were in the tradition of all of his post–World War II predecessors, with emphasis on NATO as a first line of defense and on the sanctity of the guarantees on Berlin. NATO's own vision and concern have increasingly become worldwide rather than just a regional alliance. Even Carter's withdrawal of forces from overseas areas other than NATO was a process that had been going on at least since the beginning of the Nixon administration and was in keeping with the Nixon Doctrine. The pledges to Israel have historic continuity: other Presidents recognized that in exchange for security guarantees Israel might be forced to withdraw, with slight modification, to its borders prior to the 1967 war. Others also realized the necessity for a solution of the Palestine refugees problem through a West Bank homeland. While working both with the other industrial democracies and with the Third World was in keeping with these traditions, Carter proposed an increase in Third World support. Moreover, his disarmament goals are in keeping with each of his predecessors, as is his concern for sale of arms. His predecessors took the pragmatic view that if the United States did not sell arms, the other industrial democracies and the Soviets would both fill the vacuum. On May 19, 1977, the White House avowed: "The United States will henceforth... [make] arms transfers... only in instances where it can be clearly demonstrated that the transfer contributes to our national security."[129] This was the very same view as that of all of his predecessors. Even Carter's human rights aspirations had been shared, if not as fully vocalized, by his predecessors. What he had said was that he could do it better.

But there was also a change in substance which transcended style. It showed most clearly when he spoke out on human rights. The only sticky wicket was how to match the national interest with a denunciation of undemocratic regimes of friend and foe alike, how to cut off aid to some undemocratic friends and not others in the light of strategic considerations. Nonetheless the message was striking home throughout the world. Within NATO itself, democracy appeared increasingly strong, and in eastern Europe the message was happily finding a responsive chord in the hearts of individuals if not of governments. Kissinger might feel that actions speak louder than words. Still, there was a message Carter was enunciating, a style in which policy was being determined, which did have a democratic meaning. Here then was the Carter Doctrine emerging: as he expressed it, "a foreign policy that is democratic, that is based upon our fundamental values and that uses power and influence for human purposes."[130]

It was a profound change. Whereas Kissinger scorned moralizing and expressed concern about the future of democracy, Carter perceived democracy's hope. As the London *Times* expressed it: "The starting point for this [Carter's] policy is an optimism about the intrinsic strength of democracy which has been unfashionable for some time. This is a stirring vision."[131] However, the French, Germans, and Japanese, concerned by the frailties of détente, were not finding the vision quite so stirring.

Carter, an energetic President and Commander in Chief, was in a hurry his first seven months in office. He placed himself at the vital center of issues ranging from human rights, SALT, and weapons systems to arms transfers, law of the sea, and nuclear proliferation. He confronted the problems of strategic areas ranging from Berlin, Cyprus, Greece, Turkey, and the Middle East to southern Africa, China, Taiwan, Korea, and Panama. He was finding there was no ready solution in many of these areas and issues.

Increasingly, as he approached the dilemmas of the projected Korean troop withdrawal, of the Panama Canal treaties, of relations with China and Taiwan, and of disarray in NATO's southern flank (Greece and Turkey), the necessities for bipartisan approach, for debate followed by consensus, were becoming more self-evident. The productive bipartisan results from Truman and the 80th Congress thirty years before may well be recalled: European Recovery Plan, NATO, the National Security Council, Council of Economic Advisers, a unified defense establishment, and the CIA were a part of their legacy. With all the decisions now pending, the 95th Congress, like the 80th, again has the opportunity for statemanship.

Now Carter has been turning to the art and meaning of command decision: persuasion. In candor, he told Kissinger after these first seven months: "We've got obviously just an absolute continuum of what you and he [Ford] started that we are trying to proceed with."[132]

XIV
****

EPILOGUE

> The transaction of business with foreign nations is executive altogether.   Thomas Jefferson
>
> For some decades our purposes abroad have been the establishment of universal peace with justice, free choice for all peoples, rising levels of human well-being, and the development and maintenance of frank, friendly, and mutually helpful contacts with all nations willing to work for parallel objectives. The broad programs of the United States used toward these ends have been forged over a period of time, but once initiated they have changed little.   Dwight D. Eisenhower

We the People

From Washington to Carter, the United States has traversed frontiers from the Appalachians to Mars. In the beginning the American people and the Congress voiced concern over the President's leadership in foreign affairs and national security policy. His assumption of the Commander in Chief role aroused especial anxiety. Patrick Henry, warning, ". . . the army will salute him monarch," granted that George Washington would not abuse "dicatorial powers," but, he inquired, "Shall we find a set of American Presidents of such a breed?"[1]

Nearly two centuries later, Patrick Henry's concerns were reechoed when Anthony Lewis, in a special bicentennial issue of the *New York Times Magazine*, noted that "the most dangerous aspect of the concentration of power in Washington and the White House is that labeled national security." Lewis recounted how the events of the nuclear era since the end of World War II, the superpower confrontation between the Soviet Union and the United States, had "led Congress to vest enormous discretion in the Presidency," with "profoundly anti-constitutional results."[2] Writing in a similar vein, Donald L. Robinson asserted that the restoration of "consitutional government" and the end of an "autocratic... Commander in Chief" will not come "until the nation adopts a new approach to its role in world affairs."[3]

It was the Vietnam War which inspired the most prejudicial views of Commander in Chief authority. The "anti-constitutional results" to which Lewis especially referred were Commander in Chief actions in that protracted conflict. Unpopular as that war was, it should not confuse views of Presidential power. Adolf A. Berle observed of the Kennedy, Johnson, and Nixon actions in Southeast Asia, "The rumpus kicked up was not because the Presidents in question misused their powers. It was because they used their powers legitimately to act and achieve objectives that their critics did not want."[4] Or, as former Secretary of Defense Clark Clifford put it more succinctly, one's views of Presidential authority in such national security issues really depended upon "whose ox was being gored."[5]

In his bicentennial essay Lewis partially blamed the Supreme Court for Presidential usurpation in national security affairs. With the notable exception of the Court's rebuff to Truman in his seizure of the steel mills during the Korean War, Lewis is correct about the Court's reluctance "to play their usual role as guardian against abuse of authority when military matters are involved."[6] Clinton Rossiter reached the same conclusion twenty years before when he stated that the Court "is clearly one of the least reliable restraints on presidential activity."[7] However, it is not so much a matter of reliability as it is a reluctance on the part of the Court in terms of national crisis to rock the boat. Only after wars had ended did the Court rebuke the actions of the late President Lincoln and President Franklin D. Roosevelt for having set aside the writ of habeas corpus.

In essence, we have witnessed two Constitutions, one for war and one for peace, recognizing the basic right of national survival in time of national crisis. These facts of American

political existence were recognized long ago, when Lord
Bryce observed, "In quiet times the power of the President is
not great.... In troublesome times it is otherwise, for immense responsibility is then thrown on one who is both the
commander-in-chief and the head of the civil executive...
who becomes a sort of dictator."[8] Although the term "dictator" is repugnant to the American tradition, it accurately
describes the wartime posture of both Lincoln and Franklin
Roosevelt, and, indeed, as Patrick Henry noted, that of
Washington himself.

Such facts and observations should not lessen protest
against unnecessary usurpation under the guise of national
security. Jeffersonian editors goaded the thin-skinned John
Adams, in the midst of the undeclared naval war with France,
to respond with the suppressive Alien and Sedition Acts,
which caused Madison to observe to Jefferson, "Perhaps
it is a universal truth that the loss of liberty at home is
to be charged to provisions against danger, real or pretended from abroad."[9] The result was not simply the political triumph of the Jeffersonians; it was the death knell of the
Federalists, who, aside from such unwise acts, had for the
first dozen years under the Constitution provided perhaps
the most exemplary executive administration of our national
experience.

Certainly the Courts cannot be the sole, or necessarily the
primary, guardian against Commander in Chief usurpation.
Public opinion, not the Courts, brought President Adams to
heel. We may well conclude with Michael A. Genovese,
"The Court can be one check upon presidential power, but it
cannot be the primary check...."[10] The people themselves
must also act through public opinion, which in the area of
foreign affairs is nowhere more sensitive than in the United
States, and, in the check and balance system through "a
responsible Congress..."[11] of their choosing.

At the beginning of a new administration, it is most appropriate to inquire whether too much or too little authority
had been given the American Presidency and/or the Congress by the framers of the Constitution and whether one or
the other had taken unto itself powers beyond the framers'
design. In the years between 1776 and 1787, the national

experience pointed up the need for a stronger executive, especially with regard to national security policy. Nearly two centuries later President Ford read his history correctly when he asserted that "the framers of our Constitution knew from hard experience" that the "direction" of foreign policy must be a Presidential "responsibility."[12] However, as Edward S. Corwin expressed it, the admixture of shared responsibility between the Presidency and the Congress which the framers created "left for events to resolve" whether the Congress or the Presidency would "have the decisive and final voice. . . ."[13]

This question was on Washington's mind when he asked the opinion of his Secretary of State, Thomas Jefferson, who responded, "The transaction of business with foreign nations is *executive altogether.* It belongs, then, to the head of that department," Jefferson opined, "except as to such portions of it as are especially submitted to the Senate." Indeed, Jefferson went so far as to assert that "the Senate is not supposed, by the Constitution, to be acquainted with the concerns of the executive departments. *It was not intended,*" Jefferson emphatically concluded, "that these should be communicated to them."[14] John Quincy Adams was to take a similar view when he became Secretary of State.

Jefferson's political differences with Hamilton became so extreme that he resigned as Secretary of State; for the remainder of the Washington and the John Adams administrations, he sided with the anti-Federalist (Republican) members of the Congress. In 1795, Presidential authority in foreign affairs was severely tested in a wrangle over the implementation of the Jay Treaty. The Jefferson forces in the House of Representatives not only refused to appropriate funds for the implementation of the treaty, but also passed a bill granting the House the right to reconsider all treaties even after Senate confirmation and to supervise all foreign policy actions of the chief executive. An outraged President Washington asserted that their action had brought "a constitutional crisis of greater magnitude than may ever again occur." In a strongly worded message to the Congress, the irate father of his country told members of the House that, except in the case of impeachment, they had no right to

examine Presidential documents. He further advised the
House that treaties ratified by the Senate were law binding
upon the House. The House received the Washington message in an uproar, and went into a Committee of the Whole
to map their response. Washington's prestige was to no
avail; it was finally an inspiring address by Congressman
Fisher Ames which ended the Constitutional crisis.[15]

President Jefferson seldom hesitated to assert his primacy
over foreign affairs; in 1801 he even dispatched a naval force
on a punitive expedition against Tripoli. However, as he
pridefully reported to Congress, after the American expedition captured "one of the Tripolitan cruisers . . . after a heavy
slaughter of her men, without the loss of a single one on our
part," his constitutional scruples so bothered him, since the
Congress had not declared war, that "the vessel, being dis-
abled from committing further hostilities was liberated with
its crew."[16] Jefferson's hesitancy aroused Hamilton to make
his famous observation that "when a foreign nation declares,
or openly and avowedly makes war upon the United States,
they are then by the very fact *already at war,* and any declaration on the part of Congress is nugatory; it is at least unnecessary."[17] Two years thereafter, in negotiating the largest
real-estate deal in American history, the Louisiana Purchase,
Jefferson exhibited fewer constitutional scruples.

From the beginnings of the twentieth century, as America
emerged as a world power, aside from the short-lived Congressional triumph over Wilson at the end of World War I,
Presidents held primacy in foreign policy until the last years
of the Nixon Presidency. James L. Sundquist of the Brookings Institution declared, "Viewed in the perspective of history, the changes in the executive-legislative power balance
wrought by a single Congress—the 93rd—are truly momentous."[18] Indicative of this radically shifted balance of authority since 1972 are the limitations on executive agreements;
the War Powers Resolution; the budgetary curbs on the impoundment of appropriation (which every President since
Jefferson had engaged in); the Congressional curbs on covert
foreign policy operations (subject since 1974 to the review of
six Congressional committees); Congressional revocation of
Presidential declarations of national emergency; the disarray

of executive privilege, which every President commencing with Washington had invoked during periods of sensitive negotiations with other heads of state or their representatives; the curbs on security assistance (subjecting any specific arms transaction over $25 million to any specific country to possible Congressional veto); and the undue Congresssional pressures on State, Defense, and USIA to supply Congress with information on threat of cutting off funds for noncompliance.

Even if we accept the premise that by 1970 the balance of authority in foreign policy had swung too far away from Congressional oversight (largely by Congressional abdication of responsibility), the fact remains that no other democratic society has so emasculated the role of the chief of state in foreign policy in the decade of the 1970s as has the United States. Speaking to his own frustration on this subject, Secretary of State Kissinger protested in the fall of 1975, "There is no parliament in the world that has the access to policy-making that the Congress of the United States has—not in Britain, not in France, not in any of the democracies."[19]

Kissinger might be forgiven for subjectivity in his observation, since he spent more of his time appearing before multiple Congressional committees than he did conducting foreign policy. Nonetheless, his view is corroborated by the observations of more objective students of comparative government. As Corey T. Oliver, Ferdinand Wakeman Hubbell Professor of Law at the University of Pennsylvania, expressed it in 1976, ". . . the American chief of state increasingly finds himself cut down well below his peers in the world system as to powers related to foreign affairs operations that even in other democratic societies are exclusive to the chiefs of state there."[20] Writing following the challenges to time-honored executive privilege and in the wake of leaks of security matters, Oliver added, "I know of no other governments in the world in which the legislative branch claims, as Congress seems to be claiming today, that the executive departments are not privileged to keep internal communications to themselves and that state secrets must be revealed to legislative assemblies."[21]

Oliver's concern complemented that of *New York Times*

veteran observer C. L. Sulzberger, who also concluded in 1976 that in the area of foreign affairs "the Presidency has been weakened to such a degree that the Chief Executive cannot operate with the full authority allotted to him by the Constitution."[22] David E. Rosenbaum, also of the *New York Times*, similarly observed near the year's end, "By the time the 94th Congress adjourned [in October 1976], there were many in and out of Government who thought that the pendulum had perhaps swung too far, that Congress had begun to encroach on the prerogatives of the executive."[23]

A review of the events of 1972–1976 must confirm the views of Oliver, Sulzberger, and Rosenbaum. Although Congress could act negatively in establishing restraints on the executive branch and in countering Presidential initiatives in such areas as Vietnam, Cyprus, and Angola, and in such matters as trade with the Soviet Union (unwisely coupled with Jewish emigration), nonetheless whenever Congress positively sought to formulate foreign policy, it failed. As Rosenbaum concluded, "They simply cannot act decisively in the absence of Presidential leadership over clear national consensus. . . ."[24]

These truths should be self-evident: (1) Congress is *not* equipped to *conduct* foreign policy, to legislate national strategy, or to command the armed forces; but (2) Congress must *share* with the President in the *formulation* of national security policy. A decade ago, Aaron Wildavsky quite wisely forecast, "In foreign affairs we may be approaching the stage where knowledge is power."[25] In keeping with this view, Congressman John B. Anderson, the liberal chairman of the Republican Conference, has proposed some ideas that would foster Congressional partnership with the Presidency in policymaking and decisionmaking, even of a crisis character. Anderson would have the Congress geared up with a sophisticated "Foreign Policy Research and Analysis Institute," patterned after the Rand Corporation, so that it could, as a deliberative body, respond to the Presidency "with complimentary speed and efficiency."[26] Anderson agrees with Norman C. Thomas of the University of Cincinnati that conflict between the Presidency and the Congress, largely an outgrowth of the Vietnam War, continues severely after the cause has been eliminated. Both men believe that the "constitutional conflict now exceeds the bounds that produce merely a creative tension and has assumed the proportion of a malfunction in the democratic process."[27]

Despite Congressional enactments and investigations and the inauguration of a new President, Congressional concerns continue in six specific areas: (1) executive agreements; (2) executive branch withholding of foreign policy information from the Congress; (3) military actions without Congressional authorization; (4) impoundment of funds; (5) covert operations; and (6) declarations of a state of national emergency.

The four Presidentially proclaimed states of national emergency declared between 1933 and 1971, had, as Anderson described them, given Presidents "awesome discretionary powers."[28] The National Emergency Act, which President Ford signed into law in September 1976, terminated these four states of national emergency. Senator Charles Mathias, the principal sponsor of the legislation, termed the signing "a historic act of relinquishing powers of the presidency" and hailed the legislation as a hallmark in "restoring constitutional democracy...." He was referring to the restrictive features of the legislation: it authorized Congress to terminate future Presidential declarations of national emergencies by a concurrent resolution. According to Mathias, the authority which Congress had granted itself would "safeguard Americans against abuse of presidential power." But President Ford took a differing view: he declared this feature of the Act "unconstitutional." He directed Attorney General Edward H. Levi to contest in the federal courts what Ford termed "Congressional encroachment on Presidential authority."[29]

The day of reckoning may well soon be coming on several recent Congressional curbs, not only regarding declarations of national emergencies but also concerning executive agreements and war powers. What are the consequences of negating the actions of the Commander in Chief? This harks back to the Jefferson-Hamilton dispute over the Tripolitan naval action, and as Ernest S. Griffith has wisely observed, "No one has yet successfully defined even what a 'war' is."[30]

We can, however, once the shooting has begun, agree with former President Ford's dictum, "There can be only one Commander in Chief."

The full aftermath of Vietnam and Watergate—especially in the areas of national security policy, and most particularly in the Commander in Chief roles, in which the Congress has sought to curb the Presidency—has not yet been written. The disillusion of Vietnam, the tragedy of Watergate, did not eliminate the need for a strong Presidency. As Louis W. Koenig put it, looking to 1977 and beyond, "... if we're going to make our way in foreign affairs, we will need a Presidency of substantial power."[31] As Congressman Anderson noted, we do not want "to supplant an imperial Presidency with an imperial Congress,"[32] and James J. Kilpatrick observed similarly that whereas the so-called "Imperial Presidency had many bad aspects, ... the shift to Congressional dominance is in many ways worse."[33]

History reveals not only that Congress by itself is ineffectual in making foreign policy, but also that it is no guarantor for peace. It was the "War Hawks" in the Congress, not the reluctant President Madison, who brought on the unnecessary War of 1812 with England. It was the Congress, not President McKinley, who in 1898 insisted on war with Spain. In a nuclear age, command decisions for the awesome power of releasing weapons, after appropriate consultation, is not divisible. What is needed is a Presidency with "prudence, discretion, and restraint...."[34] What is also needed is mutual confidence to replace suspicion between the Presidency and the Congress. That principle was eloquently enunciated in 1826 by Senator J. S. Johnston of Louisiana, when his colleagues expressed suspicions of the motives of President John Quincy Adams's Panama policy. "The President has, at all times, the power to commit the peace of this country, and involve us in hostilities... ," Johnston reminded his colleagues. "To him is confided all intercourse with foreign nations.... But there must be confidence. No Government can exist without it. And this distrust and jealousy of the Executive will destroy all power to do good, and all power to act efficiently."[35]

We therefore need an alert intelligent electorate as well as the responsible executive, legislative, and judicial branches which the constitutional framers envisioned. To them, separation of powers connoted cooperation. Inevitably the balance between the Congress and the Presidency will be restored, and, in part, through the genius of the Constitution itself. The framers of the Constitution, wisely instituted *shared* authority between the Congress and the Presidency, especially in the area of national security policy. It is the American people who must keep that shared responsibility in balance. A more balanced Presidential-Congressional relationship in foreign policy formulation should ensure continued overview of policy. *But* the *execution* of that policy must be securely in the hands of the executive branch.

Many commentators have insisted that the lack of discipline within the two major political parties rules out a restoration of the bipartisan support for foreign policy that worked so effectively in the 1940–1960 era. Nonetheless, the imperatives of a multipolarized world demand the restoration of a bipartisan approach to national security and strategy. An America with its policy spokesmen so united cannot be ignored or misunderstood by either its adversaries or its friends. It must be the kind of bipartisanship which fosters Congressional and public debate, followed by consensus and disciplined diplomacy, including necessary confidentiality. These are ingredients for cohesive policy which was so lacking in Vietnam. America's experience in Vietnam was a case of being damned if it did and damned if it did not: standing tough seemed necessary to counter the long-range threat Communism posed for the American way of life, yet President Johnson's command decision came to be viewed as warmongering. As journalist Ben J. Wattenberg put it, Johnson become condemned "for zealotry in the cause of idealism," and his vain attempts at a bombing pause to wind down the war were not appreciated.

In turn, President Nixon, while ordering the withdrawal of American ground forces in Vietnam, was castigated for entering the enemy's sanctuaries in Cambodia and renewing the bombing in order to bring the North Vietnamese to the conference table. His more momentous decision, attempts to negotiate with both Communist China and the Soviet Union, provoked charges of "zealous over-pragmatism in the name of detente."[36]

Johnson was charged with taking too hard a line on Communism, and Nixon—quite surprisingly, considering his earlier views while Congressman, United States Senator, Vice President, and private citizen—was accused of being too soft. Lord Bryce's observation, made nearly a century ago, still applies: ". . . nowhere is the rule of public opinion so complete as in America. . . ."[37] Out of the dilemma posed by the attitudes toward Johnson and Nixon and others who have been on center stage in this book, one may well ask whether it is possible to draw some conclusions about decisionmaking and the future of American foreign policy.

In this study, I have pictured the President, the Commander in Chief, as central in national security policy formulation and decisionmaking. I have surveyed the historical as well as the contemporary scene. Journalist Clark R. Mollenhoff, a Pulitzer prize winner, stated that there has been too much of "a tendency to regard the nuclear age with its complicated weapon systems as so far removed from the past that there is no point in searching our history for guidance to contemporary problems." I believe, as Mollenhoff does, that, "in fact, there is every reason to reach back and examine our experiences with war and defense for an understanding of the decisions the United States must make. . . ."[38] Therefore, I have examined the national security policy views and the conceptions of the Presidential and Commander in Chief role as portrayed by Washington, the Adamses, Jefferson, Madison, Hamilton, Jackson, Polk, Buchanan, Lincoln, McKinley, and all of the twentieth-century Presidents plus the Congressional leaders of the earlier periods, as well as those of the nuclear era.

I also concur with Professor Neustadt's views that the President's principal power is persuasion, that his principal source of power is public opinion, and that national security policy decisions are inevitably related to domestic politics. There is considerable evidence for John Kenneth Galbraith's conclusion, for example, that "in the Cuban missile crisis

President Kennedy had to balance the danger of blowing up the planet against the risk of political attack at home for appeasing the Communists."[39] My study has also revealed the complicated inputs to foreign policy—not just the Presidency, the Congress, the Cabinet, the National Security Council, the intelligence community, the bureaucracy, and the armed forces, but that continuing manifestation of public opinion, the "we the people," basic to the constitutional principles in providing for "the common defence."

Service Roles and Decisionmaking

I have noted the historical struggle for roles and missions of the armed forces. The competition continues, although it has not erupted as openly as in the early post–World War II period, and it is, in part, beneficial. The fundamental conventional warfare role of the oldest service, the Army, has today almost begrudgingly been recognized. Should the day arrive when nuclear swords are beat into plowshares, the foot soldier, the doughboy, the G.I. Joe, and his Navy counterpart, the Marine, would still be there as the nation's first line of defense. Yet of all the armed services in an era of all-volunteer forces, the Army suffers most.

As the Carter administration began, there were renewed discussions on reinstituting the draft. Beyond this, obligated national service—active, reserve or guard, combatant or noncombatant—is in keeping with the American democratic tradition. Two years of such service between ages eighteen and thirty, ranging from a civilian conservation corps to doctors, dentists, engineers, and lawyers in the armed services, is not too much to expect for every able-bodied American. Presently far too much of the defense budget is spent on enticing persons to serve in the all-volunteer armed services.

As we have seen, the Air Force did best its parent, the Army, in securing control of land-based ICBMs, but it could not preclude the Navy's development of SLBMs. Reaching its paramount influence and support in the Eisenhower years, the Air Force has had to share tactical nuclear delivery with both the Army and the Navy. Few, if any weapons systems have undergone such careful scrutiny as the B-1 bomber. The Air Force Scientific Board, the Defense Systems Acquisition Review Committee, and the Alternatives Review Panel recommended the B-1 go-ahead not only on the basis of Soviet capabilities but also because of the relative costs of other delivery systems and of the time imperatives involved. In making his command decision declining to replace the overaged B-52 with this B-1, the new Commander in Chief was negating public opinion, JCS views, those of his predecessor, and bipartisan Congressional opinion. As Democratic and Republican Congressmen jointly wrote, "There is just no way that a bomber built in the 1950's is going to be able to get near enough to Russian targets in the 1980's to hit them with cruise missiles."[40]

The Navy, after the "admirals' revolt," witnessed the victory of the carrier admirals. The Trident submarine is the successor to Polaris, a weapons system virtually forced upon the Navy by the combined efforts of Senator Henry M. Jackson and President Eisenhower. Jackson recalled, "I was told that this strategic system would just eat away and erode their limited funds.... The result was that Polaris was not pushed hard until Sputnik came along."[41] In the interim the carrier admirals had almost succeeded in terminating the career of the outspoken father of the nuclear submarine, Admiral Rickover (as one of his boys, Jimmy Carter, could recall). The United States must, indeed, have a guardian angel when such basic strategic weapons carriers as the nuclear submarine and the B-1 bomber arrive only after the most protracted debate. This study has suggested that national debate is vital to the American system. Debate should focus not only on foreign policy, on going into such tragic adventures as Vietnam, but also on weapons systems, to head off wrong decisions, as with Carter and the B–I.

This brings us then to the appropriate roles of the military and intelligence communities in decisionmaking. Their inputs—to weapons policy, to military strategy, to national security policy—are indispensable but in that descending order of priorities. Nor in any instance should they be the final arbiters of policy. The investigations of the intelligence community were a sequel to the Congressional Watergate inquiries on secrecy and abuse of power. Watergate focussed on Nixon's excesses, but liberal spirits in Congress were embarrassed to find that many of the clandestine foreign operations which they abhorred dated from the Kennedy administration. Carter has strengthened the overall coordinating role of the CIA director in a new National Intelligence Tasking Center while leaving the Secretary of Defense in charge of that Department's National Security Agency and National Reconnaissance Office. According to former Director of the Defense Intelligence Agency, Graham, "The rise of the anti-establishment syndrome stripped away the tacit restraints which had made the system work."[42] These "tacit restraints" were replaced by the creation of Senate and House committees and by President Ford's establishing what Anthony Marro of the *New York Times* described as "clear lines of accountability for decisions involving covert operations or sensitive intelligence-gathering activities."[43] Ford also warned overzealous reformers that "without effective intelligence capability, the United States stands blindfolded and hobbled."[44]

The *human* equation in intelligence, ranging from the collector to the reporter, the analyst or estimator, the operator, the briefer, the director, the secretary (such as State, Defense, Treasury), and the President himself must be borne in mind in evaluating intelligence information. Views vary, depending on time, place, and circumstances; as Thomas C. Hughes, former director of intelligence and research for the Department of State, charmingly expressed it, "Can we even count on the constancy of the intelligence presented by the same personality as he emerges from the coordinated printed papers into his personal role—as he moves out to the White House situation room, the JCS War Room, the State Department Operations Center; and on to the interagency working lunch, the Georgetown reception, and the foreign embassy for dinner, brandy and cigars?"[45]

Opinion is shaded not only by the work or social setting but also by the level of consideration. As those who have frequented "New State," in Foggy Bottom, can attest, attitudinal levels between the fifth, sixth, and seventh floors vary. From the fifth-floor bureaus, to the sixth-floor regional assistant secretaries, to the seventh-floor counselor, policy planning staff director, under secretaries, deputy secretary, and the Secretary of State is an elevating experience. On any floor or in any bureau there will and should be varying opinions on subjects as diverse as cruise missiles and selling grain to the Russians. However, since the bureaus, the country desks, operate directly on the chiefs of mission, the ambassadors, throughout the world, there is always considerable latitude between the operational level, which often enters upon substantive international agreements, and the expressed views of the chief diplomat, the President. The same obtains at the Pentagon and overseas commands and missions in relation to the Commander in Chief.

In all these processes of decisionmaking, there must be a place for debate and dissent but not for obfuscation and obstruction, the twin tools of the bureaucracy that President Carter, like his predecessors, has avowed to overcome. The military, more prescribed in their channels of communication than the civil servants, find their ultimate protest in resignations. During the "admirals' revolt" a number of naval persons resigned and thereby helped to shift attitudes. During the Eisenhower administration, encouraged by Senator John F. Kennedy, General Maxwell Taylor resigned as Army Chief of Staff. Once the dissenters are in the driver's seat, however, the view looks different. As Clark Mollenhoff observed, "While Kennedy and General Taylor had been loud dissenters against Eisenhower Administration policies they were less than encouraging to dissenters after Kennedy entered the White House...."[46] And thus has it ever been, with degrees of intolerance ranging from the thin-skinned John Adams to the magnanimous Lincoln, who accepted criticism even from his military commanders as long as they defeated the enemy.

It is vital in our democratic society that the right of dissent be preserved. We must safeguard against computerized or, indeed, overinstitutionalized decisionmaking. In the nuclear age scientific knowledge becomes so specialized that, as Sir Isaiah Berlin observed, "the fewer are the persons who know enough... about everything to be in charge."[47] If getting decisions from the computer is one extreme, the other is the yo-yo method to which Gordon Gray referred, in which the

Presidential crony may have as much influence on security policy as the chairman of the Joint Chiefs of Staff or the Senate Foreign Relations Committee. The well-structured decisionmaking of the National Security Council serves the nation well as long as the President encourages adversary reports and dissents.

A healthy legacy of the post-Vietnam era has been a restoration of national confidence in and respect for the military professions. As Chairman Brown of the JCS has pointed out, the military had come to be viewed "as a vast organization with a life and purpose of its own. . . ." He and his fellow Chiefs have performed a valuable service in negating that view. As Brown bluntly puts it, "The United States military establishment has no life of its own. Its existence does not generate its needs. Quite the opposite. The needs of national security generate the requirements for a national defense establishment." Brown and his JCS colleagues have well answered the question as to how the size and character of our armed forces must be determined. There are "three factors: one is the task to be performed; two is the threat to our national security; the last is the degree of risk judged acceptable."[48]

Continuity and Principle

For eight years the dominant adviser on national security policy was Henry Kissinger. Whereas it is too early to fully assess his contributions, his biographers, Marvin and Bernard Kalb, place as most "meaningful. . . the launching of SALT."[49] In this, as in the furtherance of détente, Kissinger created nothing essentially new. The British had advanced the concept of détente at least as early as 1954, as had members of the American intellectual community, including Professor Kissinger, by 1959. So had Nikita Khrushchev, who, following his 1959 visit to the Presidential retreat, referred, as had the American press, to "the spirit of Camp David." Every nuclear-age President has sought both conventional and nuclear disarmament and reduction of tensions with the Soviet Union. Thus, for example, Eisenhower reflected, upon leaving the White House, "One of my major regrets is that . . . I had to admit to little success in making progress in global disarmament or in reducing the bitterness of the East-West struggle."[50]

Presumably Kissinger, along with Nixon and Ford, made some modest progress on both these counts, leaving a legacy of SALT I, the Vladivostok accords, and near-completion of a SALT II agreement, even though there was no progress in conventional force reduction such as had been espoused in the conferences in Geneva and Vienna. President Carter has placed high priority on the early completion of SALT II and on longer-term goals of the reduction of nuclear arms. As he expressed it in his first press conference, February 8, 1977: "The overall balance of mutual restraint, cutting down on the overall dependence on nuclear weapons, is what counts."[51] Carter, like Ford, has pragmatically indicated a willingness to defer action on controversial weapons, the cruise missile and the Backfire bomber, in order to achieve SALT II before the October 1977 expiration of SALT I. Moreover, his longer-range goal, lowering nuclear levels on both sides, complements the views of his predecessors, who from Truman through Ford all expressed the hope for the eventual elimination of nuclear armaments.

Continuity of principles of national goals and purpose must also be transmitted from one administration to another. From President Wilson's Fourteen Points of 1919 to the present, there has been a continuity of expression toward international amity. As Eisenhower put it, "For some decades our purposes abroad have been the establishment of universal peace with justice, free choice for all peoples, rising levels of human well-being, and the development and maintenance of frank, friendly, and mutually helpful contacts with all nations willing to work for parallel objectives." Eisenhower noted that "the broad programs of the United States used toward these ends have been forged over a period of time, but once initiated they have changed little."[52] Thus there is essentially nothing new in the statement of principles of national purpose and strategy which Ford transmitted to Carter. It was, however, well articulated by Kissinger:

To maintain our national strength and national purpose;

To revitalize continuously our bond to allies who share our traditions, values, and interests;

To reduce the perils of nuclear war;

To build a rational relationship with potential adversaries;

To help resolve regional conflicts that imperil global peace;

To resolve the crucial economic issues before us, in the context of a new era of global economic cooperation among all nations, industrial and developing, producers and consumers, east and west, north and south.[53]

Contrast such goals and objectives with those enunciated by the Soviets. The congeniality of Khrushchev and Brezhnev has perhaps blinded a few wishful-thinking American policymakers to incontrovertible facts. There have been changes in Soviet tactics but not strategy. Lulls followed the power struggle after Stalin's death in 1953, after the Cuban missile crisis of 1962, and after the brutal 1968 application of the Brezhnev Doctrine by the suppression of Czechoslovakian unrest. But just as there was no governmental repudiation of Hitler's *Mein Kampf* until after the fall of the Third Reich, there has been no denial of Lenin's 1917 revolutionary statement: "Only after we overthrow, completely defeat and appropriate the bourgeoisie in the entire world... will wars become impossible."[54] Lest the Russian people be confused by the Brezhnev-Nixon Moscow Summit Conference of May 1972, the Moscow military district commander announced immediately thereafter: "The soldiers of our Moscow District are well aware that the nature of imperialism has not changed and the danger of war has not disappeared and that our foreign policy is implemented under the conditions of a fierce struggle in the international arena...."[55]

As such an astute observer as George W. Ball points out, when Brezhnev visited the United States in 1973 he was all sweetness and light. Upon his return to Moscow, however, he assured a visiting delegation of North Vietnamese that the Soviets had never renounced "our class privileges or the interests of the revolutionary struggles for national and social liberation."[56] Ball, who served as Under Secretary of State with Dean Rusk and President Johnson until his resignation in protest of their obdurate stand on the Vietnam War, quite surprisingly found Kissinger too conciliatory to the Soviets. Kissinger contended that détente was a realistic recognition that the Soviets had arrived at "true superpower status," that "in the past the emergence of a country into superpower status, such as, for example, imperial Germany vis-à-vis Great Britain, has generally led to war." Accordingly Kissinger emphasized the importance of "conscious restraint by both sides."[57]

Carter and Vance, while seeking arms accords, have bluntly criticized the Soviets on human rights. Actually, it was not Vance or Carter, but rather the State Department bureaucracy, which only ten days after the Carter inauguration issued a statement warning the Soviets not to silence Nobel Prize-winning physicist Andrei D. Sakharov. This, in turn, caused President Carter to assert that "this should have been said by myself," or Secretary Vance. The President added, "We're not going to back down on the human rights issue."[58] A week later, Carter, in his first Presidential press conference, asserted, "Secretary Kissinger thought that . . . if you mention human rights . . . you might endanger the SALT talks. I don't feel that way."[59] Perhaps he has.

The Ford administration strategy in these issues was well summed up in its last weeks by Secretary of the Treasury William E. Simon, when he concluded, "that if we want to make progress on . . . issues such as SALT, we must be careful not to . . . harm the political atmosphere. . . . The process of détente remains fragile."[60] Between human rights and arms accords, the whole issue of détente is warming up into a national debate. Pro-détente writers, such as Norman Cousins, contend, "All that detente means is that the leaders of both countries recognize that their peoples are in the same boat. . . ."[61] Others, like Aleksandr Solzhenitsyn, insist that the Soviets have not renounced "war . . . as an instrument for achieving a goal" but have simply been diverted from it by United States nuclear strength.[62]

United States and Soviet Strategies and Strengths

Since his election, aside from what may become a lowering of voices on human rights on the eve of SALT II, Carter has

progressively toughened his defense posture. His record defense budget is less than $3 billion below the Ford recom-
mendations, and this to be achieved by weapons stretch-out,
in procurement.[63] For this strong defense posture, he has the
support of Senate Majority Leader Robert C. Byrd, who will
bring the weight of Congressional approval to Carter's firm
stand. It will also be appreciated by Chairman Brown of the
Joint Chiefs of Staff, who perceives that the United States
armed forces have a role "in deterring adventurism by the
Soviets in areas important to our interests." Brown also con-
ceives of a strong military posture "providing the necessary
incentives for the Soviets to pursue policies of political cooperation and arms limitation with the United States."[64] The
strategy for such a posture is identified by the Chiefs in three
interrelated elements: (1) collective security; (2) credible deterrence; and (3) flexible response.

What are the Soviets' strengths and weaknesses? So much
has been written of their numerical and arms strength that
their economic, social, and psychological weaknesses have
virtually been ignored. Russia's almost paranoid inferior feeling toward the West is accompanied by fervent patriotism,
but prowess in arms, success in athletic games, and boasts
that "we shall bury you" are scant compensation for a
gnawing suspicion and sense of inferiority. On the other
hand, the Soviets occupy what geopoliticians call the "heart-
land" of the "world island," advantages suggested in the
nineteenth century by Sir Halford John Mackinder.

By contrast, the United States is geographically an island
power, with basically the same relationships to the land
masses of Europe and Africa as Britain had in her
nineteenth-century period of hegemony through economic
strength and seapower. Airpower, seapower, and alliances
are thus necessary concomitants of American power. Today,
this is recognized increasingly not just by the United States
but also by its NATO allies. As the Supreme Allied Commander, Atlantic, Admiral Isaac C. Kidd, Jr., expressed it,
"Alliance interests are being threatened outside as well as
within NATO boundaries. . . ."[65] The United States must
either maintain its positions in Europe and Asia or forever
abandon them. In an American island-based strategy, sea

lanes to Adak, the Azores, Bahrain (Persian Gulf), Diego Garcia (Indian Ocean), Crete, Guam, Guantanamo, Hawaii, Iceland, Okinawa, and the Philippines are vital. The Soviets have contiguity, proximity, and interior lines of communication in their continental land mass. In the event of war in Europe, then, their supply lines and their reserve forces would be closer to the area of conflict than those of the United States. Further, with an area more than twice the size of the United States, they have far greater dispersion of the industrial and population centers in the event of aerial war. In 1801, Jefferson made comforting reference to the United States disposition, "kindly separated by nature and a wide ocean from the exterminating havoc of one quarter of the globe." This no longer obtains.

Moreover, despite miscalculations, as in Korea, Berlin, the Cuban missile crisis, and Egypt, the Soviets have developed an effective doctrine of indirect strategy, since direct confrontation with the West is eclipsed by the nuclear stalemate. This strategy, involving such client states as Cuba, North Korea, and North Vietnam, includes subversion, crisis management, and negotiation. Soviet strategy combines economic, political, and military instruments while indirectly as well as directly influencing other nations. The Communist ideology of building proletarian internationalism has been far more effective than was Nazism as an exportable idea. Geography and ideology have combined to the Soviets' advantage as well as disadvantage. Communist revolution has effectively joined nationalism in Asia, in North Korea, mainland China, and the former French colonies in southeast Asia. Recognizing the island position of the Philippines in this hostile environment, President Ferdinand Marcos declares, "It would be impossible to maintain peace in the area without the U.S. being present in the Western Pacific." Marcos deems such "continued American presence in Asia" fundamental "to maintain the military balance."[66]

Statistics reveal both the Soviets' strengths and their weaknesses. Measured in terms of constant 1974 prices, American military expenditures in the NATO countries have decreased substantially since the peak year of 1968, but Warsaw Pact expenditures have considerably increased. The

Soviet weakness begins to appear when military expenditures are measured against the total gross national product: from 11 to 13 percent of the total as compared to 6 percent for the United States (and less than 5 percent for all other NATO nations).[67] Further, the might of the industrial democracies of western Europe and North America (Canada and the United States), which comprise NATO, is such that, with Japan, they produce 65 percent of the world's GNP and engage in 70 percent of the world's trade.

The Soviets' albatross may well be the European satellites, which are held in check solely by military force. With the possible exception of Bulgaria, all have major internal unrest and none is a reliable Soviet ally. In the areas of planning, decisionmaking, and crisis management, any assessment must consider the advantages and disadvantages of the democracies vis-à-vis the Soviets. As Sir Peter Hill-Norton has observed, "NATO is a democratic institution and like all democratic bodies, is bound to be slow in making up its collective mind." Accordingly, "national unanimity in the Council of NATO is . . . an all important prerequisite."[68] On the other hand, decisionmaking for the Soviets is not simple. Helmut Sonnenfeldt, who has studied the Soviets intensively at first hand, concludes:

> It isn't that just five or six or eleven men sit around a table and get the yellow note pad or red note pad out and make their calculations and then reach an agreement either enforced or otherwise, and off they march. . . . The Soviet Government, not to mention the disagreements and back-biting and political maneuvering among the eleven people in the Politburo, is not without its peculiar pressures and countervailing arguments and pullings and hauling.[69]

Khrushchev himself eventually became a victim of these "peculiar pressures," but the fact is that when the Soviets feel their security threatened, as they did in Czechoslovakia in 1968, they do not hesitate to act decisively and overwhelmingly—and, in that instance, to the surprise of NATO intelligence sources.

History indicates that the totalitarians succeed in tactical, short-range matters and the democracies are better in strategic, long-range matters, such as the Marshall Plan, with Congressional participation. Nazi Germany expended considerable energy, as Albert Speer recounts, in bureaucratic in-fighting[70] while it competed with the United States in a race to build the atomic bomb. The United States won. At the same time it is noteworthy that in mounting the Manhattan project, Roosevelt, rather than tapping an established bureaucratic force, such as the War Department, placed the ablest military and civilian managers and scientists in a totally independent agency reporting to him as the Commander in Chief.

In an assessment of national strategy, we should ask ourselves about the lessons learned from the Vietnam ordeal. Henry Kissinger put it bluntly: "... when the United States becomes militarily engaged, it should prevail, and, if it cannot prevail, it should not engage itself." Back of this must be the basic determination "of what the fundamental American interest is."[71] Interests and threats to security are diverse and complex. As Richard F. Rosser has observed, increasingly the fundamental decision must be the "determination of whether or not an international crisis directly threatens the vital interests of the United States."[72] The American people were not convinced that Vietnam was of "vital interest," and therefore a protracted low-level conventional operation with considerable casualties could not be sustained.

The National Will

Samuel P. Huntington has suggested that the United States is not likely to become involved in another Vietnam-type operation because it "came at the end of a cycle of active American concern with foreign affairs...."[73] Although Dr. Huntington may be correct, it may be for the wrong reason: it may be for a lack of "active American concern." William M. Franklin, longtime historian of the Department of State, does not believe we have lost our active concern, but rather our idealism and thereby much of the genius of our national will: "We have more power than ever before, but less prestige." He points out that earlier in our history, "even during periods of American isolation and physical weakness . . . we represented certain standards and certain values which carried tremendous weight. . . ." He concludes that if America can regain this inspiring sense, such as "the idea of social organization represented by the Statue of Liberty," then "less force would be necessary for American leadership to be effective throughout the world."[74]

Henry Kissinger adds one ingredient to Franklin's idealism: pragmatism. He believes "America's success has come from its blend of pragmatism and idealism. Our pragmatic tradition," according to Kissinger, "had helped us confront reality, neither blinded by dogma nor daunted by challenge. Our idealism has given us not only principles to defend, but the conviction and courage to defend them."[75]

During the celebration of the nation's bicentennial, after a long travail of divisiveness and disillusionment, a sense of pride and unity occasionally returned. Sensing this, Ambassador William W. Scranton, in his concluding address before the United Nations General Assembly, described what he termed one "simple emotion: I rejoice. I find an America which is quieter, calmer, more modest, but sounder and more secure." He predicted that the world "will hear a great deal from us about freedom and human rights. . . ."[76]

Americans could hope and pray that Scranton was correct and that the idealism kindled in the bicentennial year will not expire. The motto from Virgil on the Great Seal of the United States, adopted by the Continental Congress during the American Revolution, is suggestive of that rekindling: *Novus Ordo Seclorum:* A New Age Beginning. In that spirit, the *New York Times* declared editorially on July 4, 1976: "What America . . . [today] requires of its leadership most of all is what the American leadership of 1776 had in abundance: courage, imagination, principle and purpose."[77] America does have dynamic, appealing, exportable ideas, including those set forth in the birthright document, the Declaration of Independence. It is not for a lack of moral concern that the ideals and the dynamics of American leadership have receded. It is quite the contrary. Our moral preaching and self-flagellation have made us so guilt-ridden that we are not making fullest utilization of our strengths, faith, innovation, practicality. We have become Prometheus chained. Although few other nations understood why, it is to America's credit that she purged herself of the deceits and excesses of Watergate. Let us hope that it is now behind us. But what Dwight Waldo terms "the propensity of Americans to holistic moral judgment on complicated matters of state" continues. Dr. Waldo, the Albert Schweitzer Professor at Syracuse University, notes that this phenomenon is "often remarked upon by foreign observers."[78] Henry Kissinger put it succinctly, "We must learn to distinguish morality from moralizing."[79] We should be emphasizing the moral imperatives of peace, global cooperation, and nurturing human values rather than moralizing how constantly wrong we are.

So able a student of both foreign and domestic affairs and governmental operations as Elliot L. Richardson, who resigned as Attorney General in recognition of the abuses of Watergate, believes we may have overreacted. He cites, for example, the proposals to establish a permanent special prosecutor separate and apart from the Attorney General. Richardson concludes, ". . . there can be too much of a good thing, and in our zeal to prevent another Watergate we must not discourage good people from participating in government, we must not tie the hands of our public officials. . . ."[80]

This is precisely what we have done in the Vietnam-Watergate syndrome: we have tied the hands of the President and Commander in Chief in the area of foreign policy. Irving Kristol puts it this way: "It's an old story: Reforms aiming to solve today's problems are likely to constitute the problems of tomorrow. Having spent three decades increasing Presidential prerogatives at the expense of 'irresponsible' Congressional government we are now busy curbing the 'imperial Presidency' and restoring power to the Government's other branches." Kristol predicts, "In the years ahead, a great many people are suddenly going to discover that, in the course of curbing the 'imperial presidency,' we have created 'imperial bureaucracy.' And," Kristol concludes, "there are ominous murmurings about an 'imperial judiciary,' which seems to have moved into a power vacuum while no one was looking."[81]

In assessing the strength and weakness in our society in an

era of interdependence, we should also consider our Western allies. Although the American obsession with moralism is not so pronounced in other parts of the West, patriotism throughout the West must be rekindled. Communism makes a constant appeal to national patriotism and finds it a most effective instrument. General Karl von Clausewitz, the German military historian and theorist, writing in the early nineteenth century, is remembered for his emphasis on the importance of the national will and psychological factors in national strength. He also pointed up what he termed the "moral factors in war." (It is noteworthy that Lenin studied Clausewitz's writings while in exile in Switzerland.) Clausewitz's factors—will, patriotism, a sense of moral purpose, an appreciation of freedom—are still pertinent, as is Goethe's observation: "Nur der verdient sich Freiheit wie das Leben, der täglich sie erobern muss"—Only he deserves freedom and life itself who must daily fight for it.

It is au courant in certain elements of western European society to disparage America, its economic system, its concept of freedom, and its domestic and foreign policies. Furthermore, the self-destruct tendencies which President Ford deplored in elements of American society also characterize segments of the population in many NATO allies. They, too, have found their intelligence communities beset by what Ambassador Alexander Böker of West Germany has termed an "almost masochistic campaign."[82] As he points out, a younger generation in the West has no personal recollection of the American role in World War I and World War II or of the American humanitarian efforts after both wars. In so many places in the West today to be anti-Communist is interpreted as being in favor of the Cold War and opposed to détente.

Chairman Khrushchev endeavored to traffic the idea of "the spirit of Camp David," but after the humiliation of the Cuban missile crisis, he exploited what he termed "peaceful coexistence." There is conjecture as to how appealing President Kennedy found this in 1963 in the months before his death. Paul-Henri Spaak, then Secretary General of NATO, termed the Khrushchev ploy as the Soviets' most dangerous and skilled proposal, designed for NATO's atrophy. As Spaak then put it, "We cannot possibly say 'no' to an offer of peaceful co-existence; but if we say 'yes', what effect will this have on our public opinion and on our eventual will to resist?"[83] An anecdotal story went about NATO Headquarters about Western visitors, an Intourist guide to the Moscow Zoo, and the keeper of the lion's cage. "I've spoken to you about our Soviet policy of peaceful coexistence and its marvelous results," the Soviet guide confides to the Western tourists. "Here is the lion living in the same cage with a lamb." The Western tourists are agog. That is, all but *one* who speaks Russian and goes behind the lion's cage and inquires of the keeper: "Look here, this can't be true; how does it work?" And the keeper replies: "It's very simple; every day a new lamb."[84]

The decline in the West's "will to resist" is at the heart of the Soviet strategy. However, in 1977, in view of the continuing Soviet arms buildup, America's NATO allies have assured the new American Commander in Chief of their determination to stand firm and have received assurances of his. Allies who can should do more.

It was already clear from President Carter's first weeks in office that he shared the Truman-Ford views on command decisions. He selected one of the giant Airborne Command Post 747s as his mode of transportation for his first trip home to Georgia after his inauguration, a plane from which he, as Commander in Chief, might direct his response in the event of a nuclear attack. Subsequently, he cruised with his old skipper, Admiral Rickover, on a nuclear submarine. Further symbolizing his dual role as chief diplomat and Commander in Chief is his fifteen-minute intelligence briefing each morning from Zbigniew Brzezinski, his Assistant for National Security Affairs. This is complimented by the memorandum which Secretary Vance dictates each evening to his Assistant, Elva Morgan, for the President.

By the nature of their office, Presidents must make command decisions. As long as there is the courage and sense of moral purpose for these decisions in the West, freedom's bastion will stand. To waver, to falter, in the face of totalitarian bluff breeds disaster. In 1936, Hitler, although he was only beginning to build up the wehrmacht, took the calculated risk of reoccupying the Rhineland. France was then strong enough militarily to have stopped him, and if she had done so, the world would still be debating whether Hitler was a misunderstood nationalist or a maniac bent on world destruction.

Today, the United States, in concert with its allies, can, with the *will*, mount the strength to maintain peace and resist external aggression. The years 1814–1914 have been described as the century of Pax Britannica. History may be able to describe the hundred years commencing with the end of the Vietnam War in 1975 as Pax Americana. As historian-philosopher Russell Kirk concludes, "... the alternative is almost unthinkable."[85] But it will require more than merely maintaining the power balance. It will require agility, courage, decisiveness, perception, vision, and a united will for peace.

The quality of "agility" is included advisedly. Kissinger, after eight years of globe circling, shuttle diplomacy, and mounting Capitol Hill, referred to "the athletic aspect of decision making," the need "to react in very short timeframes that do not permit time for reflection."[86] In such an environment for decisionmaking, there must be a moral compass to offer direction. Strong Presidents, strong Commanders in Chief, strong Congressional leaders—Washington, Lincoln, Webster—have all had an inner faith, a spiritual quality. Webster meant it with religious faith, as well as pride, when he declared, "Thank God I am an American." Eisenhower literally believed, "America is not good because it is great. American is great because it is good." Ford so agreed with this that he quoted it in his own 1976 State of the Union message.[87] He believed "God and man made America what it is."[88] With Carter came "policy from the pulpit."

If religion has been one compass, history and philosophy have provided another. Truman took pride in being a student of both subjects. Dean Acheson, who found his fellow patrician Franklin Roosevelt superficial, found the plebian Truman possessed of "an Aristotelian understanding of power." Acheson and General Marshall agreed that Truman's "greatest quality as President, as a leader, was his ability to decide."[89]

Presidential Initiatives and Restraints

These then are the kinds of leadership qualities that are needed for America's third century. But there will also have to be more restraint than an exuberant, impulsive Theodore Roosevelt, or Truman, or thus far Carter has often exhibited. Yet, as with Theodore Roosevelt, who won the Nobel Peace Prize in 1906 for his role in ending the Russo-Japanese War and in keeping peace in Europe, the truly great Carter accomplishment could be as conciliator. As Louis Koenig has observed of Presidential values, "History... must become more generous in awarding its accolades to Presidents who excel as peace keepers." Such a President, in his capacity as chief diplomat, with respect for humankind, must be "conscious of the potentialities of international negotiation," he must be possessed of empathy, endurance, rectitude; such a President as Commander in Chief will be the "responsible steward" of the awesome military power at his command.[90]

This brings us full circle to the matter of trust on the part of the Congress and the American people so that the President may effectively fulfill his constitutional duties. Presidents do act with an eye on history. Theodore C. Sorensen wrote, "A President knows that his name will be the label for a whole era. Textbooks yet unwritten and schoolchildren yet unborn will hold him responsible for all that happens. His programs, his power, his prestige, his place in history, perhaps his reelection, will all be affected by key decisions."[91] His command decisions, made after all the counsel he can get, must not equivocate, must not temporize.

Following State Department initiatives, President Carter, on February 5, 1977, wrote Andrei Sakharov, "The American people and our government will continue our firm commitment to promote respect for human rights not only in our own country but also abroad."[92] This bold gesture to the leading Soviet dissident caused consternation in many diplomatic circles at home and abroad. Although it was couched in the most general terms, it was written to one whose writings covered the broad spectrum of international politics—Sakharov, for example, had warned, "One might even speculate that the exaggeration of the Chinese menace is one of the elements of the Soviet leadership political game."[93] The members of the Politburo might well be concerned with such an intellect arguing that "the Chinese menace" and other potentially threatening forces were played up to keep the lid on and rally the people in defense of Mother Russia.

Zbigniew Brzezinski termed the Carter letter a "prudential response," written after discussion "with the responsible officials at the NSC and the State Department."[94] Nonetheless, the implications of this command decision bear consideration. The last time we inspired freedom spirits in the mid-1950s, we witnessed the brutal quelling of revolt in East Germany, Poland, and especially Hungary. If we were not prepared to offer succor then, are we now when the strategic balance, unlike then, is no longer clearly in our favor? Still, the Carter letter was an inspiring note, reminiscent of the equally unorthodox pronouncements of a Theodore Roosevelt or a Woodrow Wilson. It was Carter at his best: compassion, faith, human dignity. Yet his continued preachments, ranging from human rights to nuclear proliferation, have caused disenchantment on the part of the political leaders of other industrial democracies and a hardened line on the part of the Soviets. A President seeking to communicate intelligibly with the First, Second, and Third Worlds must combine compassion and faith with restraint in his pronouncements. Vance has implied as much.

A modern President must also have a grasp of the realities of the scientific and technical age. President Carter is uniquely qualified for this by his own naval engineering background and through the scientific expertise of his Secretary of Defense, Harold Brown. Both welcomed the legislation under which President Ford had reestablished the White House Office of Science and Technology; first established by executive order by Franklin Roosevelt in World War II, the office had been reestablished by a Congressional act initiated by Eisenhower after Sputnik.

With his sense of science, history, and philosophy, the President today must have a command of grand strategy and purpose, transcending even the disciplines of international politics, foreign policy, and military strategy. His is the responsibility to preserve and transmit, hence to provide the security for, the values of the American people. He must recognize that domestic tranquility, based on justice and fulfillment of human dignity, is a prerequisite for a nation standing as a peacemaker with other peoples. In speaking out for freedom and human dignity abroad he must also always seek a more perfect freedom at home. While he must adjust and accommodate to the realities of international politics, he cannot accept a double standard for the conduct of friend and foe. Both must be handled with patience and with understanding of cultures, attitudes, and backgrounds that vary from our own. We have been too prone to seek to impose our own standards of conduct and human values on others. Finally, the President's command decisions must consider both economic and psychological factors, the ability and the will to pay and inspire fulfillment.

Strategic Balance and Stability

These then are some of the outlooks, the outreaches, in a world still economically, socially, and politically fragmented while it is bipolarized militarily. Whether we term it Cold War or hot détente, we continue to face an implacable foe whose strategy has followed the strictures set forth by the Chinese sage Sun Tzu 2,500 years ago: "To subdue the enemy without fighting is the acme of skill. Thus, what is of extreme importance in war, is to attack the enemy's strategy. Next best is to disrupt his alliance. The next best is to attack his army."[95]

The Soviets seem to be somewhere between points one and two: attacking strategy and disrupting the NATO alliance. Despite the tremendous Soviet defense expenditures, increasing at an annual rate of 3 percent, there appears, as British Defence Minister Fred Mulley observes, little prospect of NATO increases, "as the defence budgets of the allies

come under increasing pressure from inflation and competing social and economic priorities."[96] Will is the key.

This is not to say that these forces, nuclear and conventional, are presently insignificant. The British presently contribute four nuclear submarines armed with Polaris missiles.
The French, while technically outside the NATO integrated
military organization and the theater nuclear force, are not so
far removed as was suggested by de Gaulle's dramatic stalk-
ing out in the 1950s. Their continuing consultation offers
reasonable assurance, should a nuclear response be required,
of both their SLBMs and IRBMs. The West Germans are our
strongest ally.

The Soviets have a vast arsenal, including second-
generation ICBMs—the SS-16, SS-17, SS-18, and SS-19—
which are being introduced into the inventory at the rate of
200 per year, plus the SS-20 mobile missile, which is listed as
"intermediate range" and thus not applicable to SALT limitations, plus tactical nuclear weapons extending down to
one-tenth-kiloton artillery shells. The time has indeed come
to reassess the geopolitical and military threats facing the
United States and its NATO allies. One of the most sensitive
such problems is the modernization and reorganization of
the tactical nuclear forces. Their present disposition, with
but little concealment, makes them too readily available
Soviet targets. However, their redeployment raises concerns
in certain quarters "that the Soviet Union would interpret
this as preparation for their use and would elect to attack the
tactical nuclear forces first."[97] Weighing this, and considering also the recommendations of the Congressional Budget
Office, President Carter and Secretary of Defense Brown will
probably use the occasion for the introduction of new nuclear weapons (such as the Harpoon submarine missile, the
Maverick air-launched missile, and SRAM, or short-range
attack missile), to make their deployment more secure. They
also recommended the neutron bomb.

Significantly, although principally by weapon procurement stretch-outs, Secretary Brown and President Carter
have effected a $2.75 billion reduction in President Ford's
budget recommendation for the fiscal year ending September 30, 1977, and they have recommended to the Congress some modest ($600 million) increases for the European

theater, again largely for better dispersal, storage, and pre-positioning of arms.

As this study has indicated, the Soviets do not accept the nuclear-stalement premise of mutual assured destruction. Moreover, as William V. Kennedy of the U.S. Army War College has pointed out, their civil defense effort is predicated on making certain, in the event of a showdown, that "they are not the ones who are going to fall apart."[98]

What the United States lacks in numbers and geopolitical space, it must and can make up in scientific and technological advance. The two glaring United States strategic deficiencies are in air defense and civil defense. The strategic TRIAD must also be updated, including replacing the B-52 with the B-1, advancing the nuclear submarine, and introducing the airborne and seaborne cruise missile and the M-X mobile missile. This M-X mobile missile is believed far more advanced than the Soviets' SS-20 and could be used as a SALT "bargaining chip." Secretary Brown's "slow-down" order on its development would provide such a signal while sending the Air Force back to further study its deployment.[99]

In addition to making advances in deployment and weaponry, NATO must mend the cracks in its southern flank caused by the Greek-Turkish imbroglio over Cyprus and compounded by Congressional meddling; hence, the importance of former Defense Secretary Clifford's mission. So also must the Panama Canal issue, extending from the 1903 treaty regarding jurisdiction and sovereignty, be resolved. This has been the mission of Ambassador at Large Ellsworth Bunker, and Sol M. Linowitz. This resolution can be accomplished in a new treaty without compromising United States defense garrisons while returning the canal territory to the jurisdiction of the Republic of Panama.[100] The transit of naval forces and supplies from the Atlantic to the Pacific, while not as fundamental as in earlier history, does make the Canal a continuing vital link. The larger law-of-the-sea issues are the province of Ambassador at Large Elliot Richardson. The overriding mission, peace in the Middle East, is Secretary Vance's own assignment, as is southern Africa for Ambassador to the UN Andrew Young and Vice President Mondale.

The foregoing then are basics not merely for maintaining

the strategic balance but also for building a stabilized world environment. Within that environment, the Soviets, looming militarily strong, are economically, politically, and socially weak. A cap on dissidence in eastern Europe is maintained both by military force and by conceding a degree of bourgeois nationalism in the satellites. Such a society, beset by problems of administration and distribution of consumer goods, is hardly prepared to embark upon a direct path of further conquest. It will instead continue a strategy of intimidation, threats, and use of proxy forces. War between the Soviets and the United States is unlikely to come by a direct attack, but it could come through a series of escalating steps, such as brought the great powers into World War I. We must then seek to lower those possibilities in strategic areas such as the Middle East, where Soviet prestige is today lower than at any time since the end of World War II. An Arab-Israeli peace settlement is now an imperative, to ward off future Soviet meddling. Equally imperative is the continuing American presence on the Korean Peninsula to preclude a North Korean invasion, which would be tantamount to a Communist dagger pointing at Japan. A third potential trouble area, after venerable strongman Tito's death, is Yugoslavia.

These tinderboxes do point up the need to persevere with détente, fragile and unreliable as it has proven. The United States can approach disarmament only with the greatest caution. In his statement before the Senate Foreign Relations Committee, as a prelude to Senate confirmation of his appointment to head the Arms Control and Disarmament Agency, Warnke, to the relief of a number of administration supporters, not only rejected unilateral disarmament but also avowed that "any agreement which is not verifiable is worse than no agreement at all." Editorially, the *Wall Street Journal* suggested a copy of this statement "be engraved in his office door where he will see it first thing every morning."[101]

Long-Range Perspective

The United States in two centuries of national experience has traversed four epochs of foreign policy, of war and peace: (1)

the four perilous decades, 1775–1815, of achieving and confirming nationhood, including the American Revolution, the
naval war with France, the Tripolitan War, and the War of
1812 (two were declared wars; two were not); (2) the century
of world balance of power, presided over by Britain, during
which the United States enjoyed relative security; in the
process of growth, this period was marked by two declared
wars with lesser powers (Mexico and Spain) and numerous
punitive expeditions, Indian wars, and the War between the
States; (3) World War I, followed by isolationism until 1939;
(4) World War II, followed by the Cold War, the Korean War,
the Vietnam War, and the hiatuses of proclaimed détente,
first by Kennedy and Khrushchev through their communications in 1963 and again in June 1973 by Nixon and Brezhnev
during the latter's nine-day visit to the United States.

Presumably détente continues, despite record defense
budgets on both sides and increased sensitivity in human
rights, commencing in 1974–1975 with the denunciations of
the Soviet government by two of their leading intellectuals,
the Pulitzer Prize–winning Solzhenitsyn and the "father" of
the Soviet hydrogen bomb, Sakharov. The United States
Congress got involved in human rights in 1974 through its
unsuccessful efforts to help Jewish émigrés in exchange for
trade concessions; President Ford confronted the Soviets on
human rights through the 1975 Helsinki Pact, which, although guaranteeing the post–World War II European
boundaries, encouraged the peoples of eastern Europe in
their aspirations for rights. It remained for President Carter
to proclaim human rights as a major foreign policy issue,
inspiring the *Tass* commentary on the eve of the June 1977
review of the Helsinki agreements: "James Carter has assumed the role of mentor to the U.S.S.R. and other socialist
countries. . . ." The *Tass* writer charged that the President's
report criticizing the Soviet noncompliance with the human
rights aspects of the Helsinki convention were "compiled by
the enemies of détente."[102]

In *The American Commonwealth,* his masterful work written
in 1888, Lord Bryce, though perceiving lurking dangers in
the United States' future, always returned to "the hopeful-
ness of her people . . . the abounding strength and vitality of

the nation."[103] Pericles in Athens, almost twenty-five centuries ago, in assessing the strength of the Athenians vis-à-
vis the Spartans, extolled Athens's open versus Sparta's
closed society: "We are superior to our enemies in our preparations for war. Our city is open to the world. We are not
always expelling foreigners for fear of their learning or seeing something of military importance. . . ."[104] Shortly thereafter, freedom-loving Athenians were defeated by the disciplined Spartans.

Is history going to repeat itself in the contest between the
Soviets and the United States? It need not. Yet there is ample
cause for concern if the dangerous tendencies set in motion
in 1964 are not reversed. That was the year when
Khrushchev, author with Kennedy of détente, was ousted.
That was the year Brezhnev, Kosygin, and their colleagues
embarked on a purposeful long-range program to overtake
United States military primacy. First, having suffered the
humiliation of the Cuban missile showdown, the Soviets
were determined to build a missile force superior to that of
the United States; second, having been subjected to the
blockade and interception of the United States Navy in the
Cuban missile crisis, they were determined to gain parity
and beyond with United States naval forces; third, having
witnessed the United States' increased involvement in the
Vietnam War, they determined to so back North Vietnam as
to ensure its eventual triumph. Thus in 1967 Brezhnev predicted the victory of "the patriots of Vietnam, relying on
varied aid from the socialist countries. . . ." He further predicted, as a result, "a most profound undermining of U.S.
prestige . . . throughout the world."[105]

By 1968, when the Soviets sought SALT I, they had
achieved missile superiority in numbers and throw weight.
Indicative of Soviet priorities, the May 8, 1972, mining of
Haiphong harbor at Nixon's direction did not preclude Nixon's flying to Moscow a few days later to sign with
Brezhnev the SALT I agreements, including ABM restrictions. By 1975 North Vietnam, which had received 90 percent
of its military supplies from the Soviets, had triumphed. On
the Soviets' third goal, sea power, they had not yet achieved
parity with the United States Navy by 1977, either in total

tonnage or the experience of their naval personnel, but they were well on their way. Only in aircraft carriers was the United States still overwhelmingly ahead. The Soviets' first full-fledged carrier, the 40,000-ton *Kiev* with its 36 YAK vertical takeoff and landing jets, entered the Mediterranean in mid-July 1976; others were being built in the Black Sea; the days when the Mediterranean was clearly an American lake appeared numbered. Moreover, Soviet designs in Africa include naval bases for both the West and East Coasts and control of strategic passages, such as the Gulf of Aden.

Contingency Planning

There were those who believed that the Soviets, with their overwhelming ground forces, could in a surprise attack sweep to the Rhine within forty-eight hours. Could they? Would they? The official Joint Chiefs of Staff response to both questions, at least for the balance of the 1970s, is no. However, a number of respected students of NATO affairs have distinct reservations. These include Philip Goodhart, member of the military committee of the British House of Commons; Senator Sam Nunn, Democrat of Georgia, member of the Armed Services Committee; Lieutenant General James F. Hollingsworth, U.S.A. (ret.); Robert W. Komer, former United States ambassador to Turkey, now serving as senior social science researcher at the Rand Corporation; and General Johannes Steinhoff of West Germany, who recently headed NATO's military committee. None of these experts quarrel with the NATO doctrine of flexible response, that is, meet any type of Soviet attack, conventional or nuclear, with appropriate countermeasures. What they do believe, however, is that the *ability* to respond flexibly simply does not exist. Nunn shares their concern. Steinhoff emphasizes that NATO must stop deploying forces that are *not* combat-ready. He believes that present NATO forces are not trained sufficiently either individually or cooperatively. Both Hollingsworth and Steinhoff urge NATO development of a short-war strategy, to resist a sudden massive Soviet attack, which Soviet training manuals emphasize as the key to victory in western Europe. The scenario which Hollingsworth and Steinhoff fear, which is shared by NATO central front commanders and NATO senior staff, is that the Soviets might launch a "come as you are" invasion. This would be with forces already positioned in East Germany and Czechoslovakia; thus the West would have no prior warning through its aerial observation of reinforcements. Having missed the positioning with the 1968 attack on Czechoslovakia makes the prospect doubly chilling. This, or an unexpected mobilization by Warsaw Pact members, points up the necessity, should "the balloon go up," for rapid and coordinated command decisions by the respective political leaders of the NATO alliance.

Senator Nunn shares the conclusion of the Congressional Budget Office, which has been studying NATO strategy, that the positioning of NATO ground forces and their supply situation are cause for concern. Nunn believes that the Soviet invasion route would follow the classical Lowlands northern route, avoiding the undulating terrain farther south where NATO ground forces are heavily positioned. Moreover, Nunn finds the supply situation of especial concern.

The following areas which should then undergo urgent review are believed critical to the alliance's future credibility:

1. Planning assumptions regarding prior warning time and the duration of a war in Europe;
2. Deployment of forces;
3. Firepower and ammunition stocks;
4. Combat readiness;
5. Air defense as related to the qualitatively improved Soviet tactical air forces;
6. Command, control, and communications capabilities;
7. Reserve reinforcement capabilities;
8. Interoperability and standardization of weapons.

Two decades ago, one of America's most brilliant and outspoken strategic planners, General Thomas S. Power, set forth a principle that is just as valid today: "The strength and position of our strategic forces must always remain such that they can accomplish their mission *under any set of conditions and circumstances. . . ."*[106] The same principle applies to even the smallest tactical unit.

In brief, NATO should be doing more *contingency planning* as well as increasing its combat readiness in the light of both Soviet nuclear improvement and their superior land forces in the European theater. There should be particular contingency planning in the event the Soviets should apply the Brezhnev Doctrine to Yugoslavia. This appears a distinct possibility when Tito, now eighty-five, is gone. Presently nonaligned Yugoslavia is the major missing link in the Warsaw Pact defences. Its strategic location flanking Warsaw Pact forces and on the Adriatic Sea create a nightmare for Warsaw Pact planners. President Carter's preelection disavowal of intervention should the Soviets attack should be viewed as a sincere view of a political candidate subject to review in his new role as Commander in Chief. NATO must and would follow his lead in such contingency planning.

In the interim, in NATO the United States continues its largest sustained overseas deployment of forces as its first line of defense. Recently Secretary of Defense Brown told these forces that "military service is public service in its highest form."[107] With the decline of the antimilitary feeling engendered by the Vietnam experience, more Americans are today inclined to agree with Dr. Brown's assessment.

What is the real meaning of the conventional and nuclear arms reduction talks (SALT and MBFR)? How does the West react to President Carter's avowed goal of eliminating nuclear armament? How did the SALT talks begin? To answer the last question first, it is highly revealing that in 1968, three days after the United States announced it was commencing an ABM system of amazing technical promise, Soviet Foreign Minister Gromyko came forward with his proposal for the initiation of SALT talks (which got under way the following year in Helsinki). It is also highly revealing that the Soviets were more concerned in SALT I for ABM limitations than they were for missile ceilings. The SALT I agreement of 1972 limiting the ABM sites to two for each nation (respective capitals and a missile site) was followed by a protocol further reducing the ABMs to one each. Interestingly, the Soviets picked Moscow and the United States elected Grand Forks, North Dakota (a Minuteman missile site). Simultaneous with all this the Soviets embarked upon a massive civil defense system, expending more than ten times that of the United States in its civil defense program. At the same time they were continuing their arms buildup (including nuclear weapons, even though the Nonproliferation Treaty pledged reduction of nuclear arms). By 1974 their total defense costs had not only outstripped those of the United States, $103 billion versus $85 billion, but also the major portion was going for armaments with only 30 percent in personnel costs versus 60 percent for the United States. Surveying these programs, one may, indeed, inquire regarding Soviet intentions. If the trend continues they might, in the phraseology of the Godfather, "make an offer we can't refuse." *That* is a concern of the West.

Carter Foreign Policies

Aside from the Presidents, the Commanders in Chief, the central figures in this book have been their principal security advisers ranging from Hamilton and Jefferson under Washington to Vance, Brzezinski, Chairman and Secretary Brown under Carter. Of these Presidential deputies, the most tragic was Forrestal, who contributed brilliantly in concepts. As Sonnenfeldt recently recalled, "James Forrestal deeply understood that the attainment of our country's goals requires of Americans a new understanding of the crucial relationship between military power and foreign policy."[108] Forrestal understood the truth Luke set forth two thousand years ago: "When a strong man armed keepeth his palace, his goods are in peace."[109] With this preponderance of strength, through the Johnson years, the United States sought not only to guard its own palace but also to be the world's policeman. However, Nixon, Ford, and Kissinger endeavored, with the arrival of the Soviets to superpower strength, to move from a policy of containment to one of negotiation. Some of those negotiations, such as the Nixon-Brezhnev 1974 Treaty on the Elimination of Underground Nuclear Weapons Tests and the Brezhnev-Ford 1976 Treaty on Peaceful Nuclear Explosions (which for the first time established the principle of on-site inspections) have not yet been ratified by the Senate.

Now clearly Carter seeks to move beyond his predecessors in arms control and nuclear restrictions as well as human rights proclamations. During his campaign for the Presidency he insisted "we must replace balance of power politics with world order politics." He projected that "in the near future . . . issues of war and peace will be more a function of economics and social problems than of the military security problems which have dominated international relations in the world since World War II."[110] An idealist, a moralist, he doubtless meant this. Not believing this attainable in four or eight years, European observers are concerned about what his reaction may be when nuclear disarmament is not so readily obtainable. Will the arms race be exacerbated? Carter, while an idealist, is also a realist. Already by the end of one hundred days in office he had tempered his goal in nuclear armaments for the years of his Presidency to "substantially reducing the level throughout the world."[111] He had also already indicated a determination for massive cutbacks in arms sales to other nations. Critics believe such actions will only enhance the arms research and sales of both America's friends and foes. So also critics of his indefinite suspension of commercial reprocessing of plutonium in the United States or of his embargo on export of such plants, materials, or technologies that would permit uranium enrichment say that this again invites other nations to step in. After his first summit in London, in May 1977, United States' allies in western Europe and Japan remained adamant in their opposition to Carter's desire to outlaw plutonium-fueled nuclear power facilities. Since plutonium or enriched uranium provides the basis for nuclear weapons, international inspection and control must be firmly established. However, as Gordon R. Corey, vice-chairman of Commonwealth Edison, recently expressed it, "The United States will have the best chance to shape such controls if we maintain our nuclear leadership."[112] Accordingly, many American businessmen and some members of Congress argue that the United States should proceed with its domestic breeder reactor, as are

France, West Germany, Great Britain, Japan, and the Soviet Union. All five will also doubtless move into the spent fuel reprocessing and the export of materials and technologies which Carter is embargoing.

The Carter foreign policies are running into opposition in three other areas: the Korean troop withdrawal (to which many members of Congress as well as the military are opposed); the Carter goal for a "homeland" for Palestine refugees, where the hard-lined Likud party may not prove cooperative; and the Cuban normalcy program, embarrassed not only by the continued Cuban troop presence in Angola but more recently, in the spring of 1977, by a military training mission in Ethiopia. Still, the Carter-Vance goal of establishing diplomatic relations with Communist countries like Cuba and Vietnam had a pragmatic principle of advancing our own views as well as hearing theirs.

United States-Soviet Relations and Strategies

At the heart of the problem between the Soviet Union and the United States is their asymmetry. There is simply no moral, intellectual, or spiritual symmetry between the two superpowers. The one is an open pluralistic society, the other a closed monolith. The United States again and again makes its intentions known to the Soviets; they never do theirs. Accordingly, our contingency planning should be for the worst possible case at the same time that we continue to seek an accommodation.

There is then a question of perception: how the Russians see us and how we see them. That search must continue to be covert as well as overt. One of the mistakes of critics of the American intelligence community is to suggest that the CIA and the KGB, the Russian secret police, are one and the same thing. One of our ablest directors of the CIA, Allen Dulles, put the case well, "It is not our intelligence organization which threatens our liberties. The danger is rather that we will not be adequately informed of the perils which face us. . . . The last thing we can afford to do today is to put our intelligence in chains."[113]

President Carter clearly recognizes this principle. At the same time there is understandable concern over his having discontinued the President's Foreign Intelligence Advisory Board. Robert D. Murphy, a former member of that Board, in a half-century of service in the national security area, has left with us another precautionary note regarding the Soviets' tendency to negotiate for propaganda purposes. "During the past years, when they were straining their resources to build military power," Ambassador Murphy noted, "they continually used disarmament discussions as a device to win over neutral opinion."[114] They pose then as the champions for peace. They have also sought to win adherents, particularly in the Third World, by extolling what Edmund Burke one termed "the revolution of rising expectations."[115] In brief, they both raise Third World expectation and blame their poverty on the "imperialists." They do this while enjoying the lowest level of consumer goods of any major industrial state.

In its dealings with the Soviets, the United States has not exploited their weaknesses. The Soviets are not ten feet tall; they have chronic inefficiency in their armed forces, and their bomber as well as their naval forces are clearly inferior to those of the United States. That the Warsaw Pact in 1976 proposed that they and NATO renounce any *initial* nuclear strike emphasizes their dependence on mass rather than technology. The Soviet Union is sorely dependent upon imported wheat to feed its people, and the United States has cheerfully obliged without exacting any concessions. Although grain sales are good for surplus-ridden American farmers, they should also provide trading chips in negotiations ranging from human rights to MBFR and SALT. For the foreseeable future, at least the next six years, the Soviets will continue to have critical grain shortages.

Nor has the United States exploited its superior technology, ranging from computers to guidance systems. Although there are no United States arms sales to the Soviets, there is no guarantee that advanced computers sold to the Soviets will be utilized only in peaceful pursuits. Furthermore, licensing agreements in a host of technologies with other nations do not preclude the transfer of these technologies from thence to the Soviets.

A further exploitable Soviet weakness lies in their economy, their dearth of consumer goods, and their burdensome defense costs. Whereas 13 percent of their GNP now goes into defense, compared to the United States' 6 percent, theirs is moving toward 15 percent and beyond, while the United States percentage has been moving downward. And yet this provides no advantage if it is not exploited in the world marketplace. Nor is the West's relatively low contribution to its own defense a strength.

Clearly we are faced with an implacable foe who seeks to exploit the weaknesses of the West. For too long whenever the United States has developed an advance technology, be it the ABM, the cruise missile, or the 12A warhead, it has been termed "destabilizing." The concession on the ABM, which the Soviets constantly sought from 1968 and achieved in 1972, may one day in retrospect be proven as the United States' most costly strategic error. A similar course in the interest of stabilization, which is another word for mutual assured destruction, must not be followed with the cruise or the 12A. The statement of Jeremy J. Stone, director of the Federation of American Scientists, that "the 12A warhead is eliminating any negotiating maneuver"[116] in the arms talks is exactly the opposite of the facts. Instead, it can counter the Soviet supermissiles which Carter and Vance unsuccessfully sought to reduce in their SALT II proposal, or it can counter the SS-20 mobile missile which the Soviets use as a bargaining chip. For their part, the Soviets have been moving relentlessly toward a first-strike capability. The United States has based its sense of security on the continuing credibility of TRIAD—land, sea, and air based launchers. However, within a decade the Soviets could so advance their submarine warfare capability and their missile technology as to eliminate both the land and sea based United States launchers, leaving, ironically, the manned bomber (deemed outmoded by some a decade ago) as the only surviving delivery system. It would survive, since it would be airborne during a missile exchange. In the face of advancing ABM technology, this makes the B-1 equipped with the cruise missile an imperative responsive weapon system for the 1980s. What would the *supersonic* Soviet backfire bombers and fighters be doing while the *subsonic* B52's or 747's were lumbering into position to release cruise missiles?

Advancing technology on both sides, then, also makes imperative a continuing search for arms control and arms reduction with the Soviets. But it will be accomplished only when they are convinced that they are in an inferior rather than a so-called stabilized posture. Despite United States restraints, they have never relented in the arms race. To give up the cruise, the 12A, and other advanced systems would only permit the Soviets to press home their present land-based missile advantage. The B–1 remains a must.

The Soviets have proven themselves the world's most obdurate negotiators. As John J. McCloy put it, they negotiate from the position: "What is mine is mine, what is yours is negotiable." Yet if *we keep strong,* if we keep the Soviets strategically encircled, it is they, not the West, who may be forced to work out a modus vivendi. Time can then be on our side. With a hostile China on their eastern borders, with restive satellites on their west, with human rights a growing issue, with increasing dissidents both in the Soviet Union and in the satellites, with the average age of their leadership in the Politburo and the military over seventy, with President Nikolai V. Podgorny ousted from the Politburo and Brezhnev taking over the titular head of state position, the Soviet monolith must inevitably soon undergo change. President Ford sensed these stirrings during his 1975 visit to Poland, Yugoslavia, and Rumania. Although President Carter had no plans following his May summit meetings for a further visit to Europe in 1977, it is to be hoped that in 1978 he too might visit those and other central and eastern states, including Yugoslavia and Czechoslovakia, where the Charter 77 statement of intellectual leaders testified to the human rights movement. All of this would, however, have to be weighed against the possibilities of raising false hopes only to be quelled by Soviet arms.

The stirrings are increasing in the satellites. In Poland, Stefan Cardinal Wyszniski has pledged his support for the human rights effort. In a sermon in May 1977 he emphasized that "even the most efficient police action will not guarantee social peace."[117] There is Presidential tradition in the encouragement of these efforts, the tradition of Franklin D. Roosevelt's "four essential freedoms: freedom of speech and expression... freedom of every person to worship in his own way... freedom from want... freedom from fear...." President Kennedy put it well: "Is not peace, in the last analysis, basically a matter of human rights?"[118] However, a negotiating President should speak softly.

Ironically, while freedom is stirring in the Soviet satellites, in the West the Communist party, alleging independence from Moscow and espousing human rights, is growing. How the electorate will sort this out, especially in France and Italy, is a matter of concern, as is the impact on NATO of the growth of the Communist party in the West. Carter ostensibly takes a more relaxed approach to this issue than Kissinger, who continued to warn that "if the United States has a responsibility to encourage political freedom throughout the world, we surely have a duty to leave no doubt about our convictions in an issue that is so central to the future of the Western alliance and therefore to the future of democracy."[119] The effective working together of American private citizens with their kin in Italy and the Catholic Church in opposition to the Communist party thirty years before, when the threat was even greater, may well be recalled. There appears to be little legitimacy to the contention that spread of "Euro-Communism" would have a debilitating effect on the Moscow variety.

All of our post–World War II Presidents, Truman to Carter, have come to the conclusion that the one thing the Soviets respected is strength and the one thing they scorn is weakness. In addressing the North Atlantic Council in London on May 10, 1977, President Carter reaffirmed, "Achieving our political goals depends on a credible defense and deterrent."[120] But America's allies must do more.

The building of a power base for achieving "political goals" is no discovery of the modern Presidency. As Michael P. Riccards observed of the Federalists, who framed the Constitution and launched the new government under Washington and Hamilton's direction, "they wanted not just liberty, but grandeur, not just republican virtue but also world prominence."[121] Hamilton and Washington early perceived that if the United States were to be respected in world affairs it must be powerful as well as just.

Call for Leadership

What has been lacking in the generation since Churchill, de Gaulle, Franklin Roosevelt, Truman, and Eisenhower is leadership with statesmanlike stature, with an understanding of national and international strategies and purpose. Such leadership must not tell the people what they want to hear but rather what they need to know: that these are perilous times requiring greater effort, greater sacrifice, if the future of the West is not to be imperiled. Such leadership cannot define Soviet intentions, but it can and should explain Soviet capabilities. It should rebuild a sense of national will and of the need to make personal sacrifice. There is thus the need again for Churchillian exhortation: "What is the use of living, if it be not to strive for noble causes and make this muddled world a better place for those who will live in it after we are gone."[122] Such leadership is sorely needed today to act with clarity, courage, purpose, and understanding.

Another aspect of leadership is needed: the ability to make the command decision. As Truman put it, "There are a great many factors that go into the making of a command decision, but in the end there has to be just one decision—or there is no command."[123] There is another urgently needed quality of leadership exemplified by Eisenhower: taking the rap rather than passing it off to a subordinate. Just as Eisenhower stepped forward to bear the responsibility for the U-2 incident, the President must bear those command decision reponsibilities. They will test his courage and his character. This recalls the counsel on another covert operation which Arthur Schlesinger, Jr., gave President Kennedy on April 10, 1961. In a secret memorandum just before the Bay of Pigs invasion, Schlesinger counselled "... someone other than the President [should] make the final decision and do so in his absence—someone whose head can be placed on the block if things go terribly wrong."[124] Similar counsel, but to no avail, had been given by Allen Dulles to Eisenhower on the U-2 incident.

Presidents who must make command decisions do not need Cassandras, as the Joint Chiefs of Staff proved to be in their top-secret document, December 3, 1950, advising, after the Chinese entry into the Korean War, that it would be unsound for United States forces to remain on the Korean peninsula with the Chinese and that they should accordingly withdraw to Japan.[125]

Command decisions must rest with the President, who has his duly constituted advisers. Perhaps, however, there is a place in these United States where former Presidents can join in a counselor role, made possible by their own unique experience and perspective. It was in that spirit that former President Ford recently declared, "The new administration—free of the burden of war, unfettered by mistakes of the past—has an historic opportunity to lead America to a new age in foreign policy...."[126] Perhaps Jimmy Carter is just the person to do that, especially with his perception of moral and spiritual purpose. Perhaps he can help find the answer to the basic searching question posed by Alastair Buchan: "Can highly industrialized states sustain or recover a quality in their national life which not only satisfies the new generation but can act as an example or attractive force to other societies?"[127]

While President Carter has completed his review of the NSC organization and is doing so with the Department of Defense, in the longer-range view he might well consider the wisdom of a council on national goals and strategy. Strategy has been fragmented and responsive to external threats: the very terms containment, counterinsurgency, counterforce, and countervalue are all fragmented and responsive. There is a need to equate and interpret the continuing American Revolution with human aspirations worldwide and America's role of leadership. There is a need to develop long-range goals looking toward the end of the century and beyond. There is a need to reexamine the sources of national strength and national will, economic, social, political, moral, spiritual, and military. Such a council on national goals and strategy, including educational inputs from both civilian universities and service schools, might well contribute toward a renewed sense of national purpose and will for the nation as it moves into its third century.

In the interim there is a need to equate the Presidency, the

Commander in Chief, in less imperial and more human terms. The Commander in Chief role is founded in our democratic principle of civilian direction of national security policy. It is not a power unto itself. The framers of the Constitution did provide in the separated and enumerated principles the means for national security without Caesarism.

The Congress has overreacted, perhaps, in at least some of its legislation and mandates during the 1972–1974 period. In part, they were arresting not only what they considered a runaway Nixon Presidency but nearly two centuries of Congressional-Presidential experience in the conduct of national security policy. Presidents, commencing with Washington, engaged in executive agreements; commencing with Jefferson, they impounded funds appropriated by the Congress for defense purposes. The Congressional purse has always been as powerful as the Presidential sword. Indeed, it may be asked whether the War Powers Resolution in reality gave the Congress any new authority. The Congress can, as it has done on numerous occasions, reduce or enlarge the number of American armed forces stationed abroad. The Congress can, as it did in the Cooper-Church Amendment, bar specific kinds of military operations. The Congress can, as it has done, withhold appropriations, thereby ending military operations.

Additionally, Congressional investigations (like the Truman Senate Committee to Investigate the Defense Program) have a profound effect on policy and organization. Moreover, the professional military have their own means to "resist, delay, and amend." Quite wisely, in wartime the Courts have placed but few obstacles to the Commander in Chief role. When, however, a President has assumed the Commander in Chief mantle to enforce actions not clearly demanded by national security, they have not hesitated, as President Truman learned in 1952, to renounce that mantle. Further, and this is too often forgotten, the electorate themselves may vote a Commander in Chief out. Truman appreciated this in 1952, as did Johnson in 1968, when each declined to run again following the loss of confidence in their role as Commander in Chief.

Scholars, at least until 1965, generally equated greatness in the Presidency with energy in the Executive. However, the vigor so characteristic in the Kennedy years turned to rigor with Johnson as the days of war lengthened. And so a dichotomy developed, suggesting a Presidency energetic in domestic policy and not so energetic in foreign policy. Aaron Wildavsky's "two presidencies" then took on special meaning. But long before that appellation was coined, a wise editor and philosopher, Felix Morley, suggested you cannot have it both ways. Writing in 1951, when advocacy of energy in the Commander in Chief found a corollary in hands off at home, Morley pointed out that one "cannot consistently urge that the Administration be untrammeled in its conduct of foreign relations yet subject to strict Constitutional checks and balances in its control over domestic activities."[128] Reversing this, one cannot find consistency in those who would today advocate a President debilitated in foreign policy yet filled with vigor in domestic policy.

As for energy in the Executive, it is well to remember that the Commander in Chief is charged not merely with the conduct of war alone. Even more importantly, his responsibility is the preservation of peace. "Waging peace," as Dwight Eisenhower termed it, requires as much vigor as waging war.

Summing Up

This study has not presented an altogether bright picture. Yet certain hopeful truths should be apparent. Truman and Eisenhower, two old soldiers to whom this volume is dedicated, would applaud a strategy of flexibility, deployability, and readiness; a recognition of components of national security, including economic, moral, and intellectual as well as military elements; some form of obligated national service; weapons modernization; civil defense; and strengthening of alliances—all of these to reaffirm credible deterrence. They would tell us, as Truman expressed it, "In this day and age the defense of the nation means more than building an army, navy, and air force. It is a job for the entire resources of the nation. The President, who is Commander in Chief and who represents the interest of all the people, must [be] able to act at all times to meet any sudden threat to the nation's security."[129] Truman and Eisenhower would again call upon a bipartisan Congressional-Presidential team; they would declare, as Eisenhower expressed it, "The occasion has come to manifest again our national unity in support of freedom and to show our deep respect for the rights and independence of every nation."[130] They would remind us, from their own experience, that "we cannot build peace through desire alone." They could testify " . . . that international agreements, considered by us as sacred, are regarded in Communist doctrine and in practice to be mere scraps of paper. . . ."[131] Nonetheless, they would tell us to persevere: " . . . step by step," Eisenhower concluded, "we must strengthen the institutions of peace—a peace that rests upon justice—a peace that depends upon a deep knowledge and clear understanding by all peoples of the cause and consequence of possible failure in this great purpose."[132]

They would also testify that toward that purpose the President will need all the help he can get. Both Truman and Eisenhower were vexed by the parochialism of the bureaucracy in their own executive departments, as have been each of their successors. But Truman and Eisenhower, like each of their successors, were more concerned with their relations with the Congress. When pressed by the Congress, Truman, though *not* Eisenhower, would go so far as to remind the Senate: " . . . the President is responsible for the foreign policy of the United States, and when it becomes the duty of the Senate to become involved, they will be informed and the matter will be discussed with them."[133] In the absence of formal institutional Congressional support, as would be obtained in a parliamentary system, both Truman and Eisenhower recognized the importance of improving communications with Capitol Hill. Hence, Truman instituted, and Eisenhower enlarged, a Congressional liaison office. They also both noted the lack of an integrating policy party structure within their respective parties. Truman, a Democrat, got his best help in the Senate from Arthur H. Vandenberg, a Republican, while Eisenhower got his from Lyndon Johnson, a Democrat. They both achieved the most in for-

eign policy through bipartisan support. Deploring the deterioration of Presidential-Congressional relationships in the
era of Vietnam and Watergate, they both would conclude
that in reasserting its role in foreign policy, the Congress
went too far, getting into day-by-day operations. They
would both understand President Ford's assertion in his
final State of the Union Message to the Congress: "In these
times crises cannot be managed and wars cannot be waged
by committee. Nor can peace be pursued solely by parliamentary debate."[134]

There have been changes in the international scene and in
national strategy since those challenging days of 1949–1952
when Truman and Eisenhower worked together to help form
NATO. There was then a less complex bipolarized world,
with the Marxist influence directed from Moscow. Marxism,
soon thereafter bifurcated between Moscow and Peking, is
today identifiable also as a force in much of the Third World.
But while today there is no unity in Marxism, neither is there
in the West. Twenty-five years ago there was yet a sense of
unity born of urgent necessity, involving military needs as
well as steps toward economic and even political union in
western Europe. When NATO was being formed, western
Europe and Japan were just recovering from post–World
War II exhaustion. Today, these industrial democracies have
long since graduated from their junior status. Their full
partnership should include a more equitable distribution of
the responsibilities for the defense of the free world. All of
this is the more complicated by the competing domestic demands of the societies which they represent and their dependence for strategic materials on Third World sources
whose political positions and views, extreme left and right,
are often inimical to those of the industrial democracies. The
future course of freedom depends upon the ability of the
industrial democracies to act in concert, economically, politically, militarily. Clearly there is a need for collective security. In terms of both manpower and military resources the
United States and the other industrial democracies cannot go
it alone.

Here in these United States, and in the other industrial
democracies, there must be more than just a capability; there

must be a *resolve*, a *will*. Given the facts by the Congress and the President, given inspiring leadership, the American people can again respond with will and determination. "In the last analysis," Carl Lotus Becker has reminded us, "everything depends upon the possession by the people of that *virtue* . . . which Montesquieu declared to be the fundamental principle, the indispensable guarantee, of the republican form of government."[135] Montesquieu set forth many principles for the framers of the Constitution, which provided "for the common defence. . . ." That, plus the experience in the first years of the Republic, especially the views enunciated by Washington and Hamilton, set the ship of state upon its way. We may well conclude with Richard Rose "that the Federalists, with their realistic acceptance of the fact that men—including Presidents—are not angels, built institutions of governance that, on balance, are better designed to accommodate the multiple and contradictory objectives of the American people today than any institutions that could be designed by an architect of authoritarian or democratic centralism."[136]

To the institutions which they transmitted may be added Washington's counsel in his Farewell Address. Warning "against the mischiefs of foreign Intrigue . . ." and "the Imposters of pretended Patriotism," Washington concluded that in the conduct with other nations, "nothing is more essential than . . . just and amiable feelings towards all . . . ," providing that we take "care always to keep ourselves, by suitable establishments, on a respectably defensive posture. . . ."[137]

Writing in 1960, Associate Professor Henry A. Kissinger lamented the decline in American prestige over the preceding fifteen years. He described the policies of Secretary of State Dulles as "stagnation" and deplored the personal traveling diplomacy of President Eisenhower as suitable for "a state which wishes to demoralize its opponents by confusing all issues."[138] History will determine whether Secretary Kissinger and his colleagues did better and whether hopefully President Carter and his can.

NOTES

Acknowledgments

1. R. Gordon Hoxie, ed., *Frontiers for Freedom* (Denver: University of Denver Press, 1952), p. 25.
2. *Ibid.*, p. 27.
3. Elliot L. Richardson, *Annual Defense Department Report, FY 1974* (Washington, D.C.: U.S. Government Printing Office, 1973).

Author's Preface

1. George B. de Huzar, ed., *National Strategy in an Age of Revolutions* (New York: Frederick A. Praeger, 1959), p. 3.
2. *New York Times,* May 16, 1975.
3. *Ibid.*
4. *Ibid.*
5. Ford, Address Before a Joint Session of the Congress, April 10, 1975, *Department of State Bulletin,* LXXII, 1870 (April 28, 1975), 529.
6. Raymond L. Chambers, "The Executive Power: A Preliminary Study of the Concept and of the Efficacy of Presidential Directives," *Presidential Studies Quarterly,* VII, 1 (Winter, 1977), p. 22.
7. Richard E. Neustadt, *Presidential Power* (New York: John Wiley & Sons, Inc., 1960), pp. 9–10.
8. *Ibid.*, pp. 10, 32.
9. Richard Rose, "The President: A Chief But Not an Executive," *Presidential Studies Quarterly,* VII, 1 (Winter, 1977), p. 9.
10. Transcript of President Ford's State of the Union Message, *New York Times,* Jan. 13, 1977.
11. Rose, "President," p. 17.
12. *New York Times,* Jan. 7, 1977.
13. Hoxie, *Frontiers,* p. 163.
14. Victor Hugo Paltsits, *Washington's Farewell Address* (New York: Arno Press, Inc., 1971), p. 158.

Foreword

1. Eisenhower Press Conference, November 14, 1956.

2. Louis W. Koenig, *The Chief Executive*, 3d ed. (New York: Harcourt, Brace, Jovanovich, Inc., 1975), p. 213.

3. *Ibid.*

I. Congress and the Presidency

1. S. P. Huntington, "Civilian Control and the Constitution," *American Political Science Review*, Sept. 1965.

2. Arthur M. Schlesinger, Jr., *The Imperial Presidency* (Boston: Houghton Mifflin Company, 1973), p. 3.

3. Koenig, *Chief Executive*, p. 215.

4. Schlesinger, *Imperial Presidency*, p. 19.

5. R. Gordon Hoxie, "Who Owns Presidential Papers," *Presidential Studies Quarterly*, V, 1 (Winter 1975), p. 77.

6. *Ibid.*

7. Eisenhower manuscript, in Center for the Study of the Presidency.

8. Koenig, *Chief Executive*, p. 217.

9. Julius W. Pratt, *A History of United States Foreign Policy* (Englewood Cliffs, N.J.: Prentice Hall, 1955), p. 248.

10. Schlesinger, *Imperial Presidency*, p. 41.

11. Norman P. Graebner, "Presidential Power and Foreign Affairs," in Charles W. Dunn, ed., *The Future of the American Presidency* (Morristown, N.J.: General Learning Press, 1975), p. 183.

12. Norman J. Padelford and George A. Lincoln, *International Politics* (New York: The Macmillan Company, 1954), p. 330.

13. Schlesinger, *Imperial Presidency*, pp. 100–103.

14. James MacGregor Burns, *Roosevelt, the Lion and the Fox* (New York: Harcourt, Brace and Company, 1956), p. 255.

15. *Ibid.*, p. 396.

16. Koenig, *Chief Executive*, p. 257.

17. Gar A. Alperovitz, *Atomic Diplomacy: Hiroshima and Potsdam* (New York: Simon and Schuster, 1965), p. 267.

18. *Ibid.*, p. 276.

19. Stephen E. Ambrose, *Rise to Globalism* (Baltimore: Penguin Books, Inc., 1971), p. 134.

20. Alperovitz, *Atomic Diplomacy*, p. 278.

21. Ambrose, *Rise to Globalism*, pp. 137–138.

22. Thomas G. Patterson, "The Search for Meaning: George F. Kennan and American Foreign Policy," in Stanley Bach and George T. Sulzner, *Perspectives on the Presidency* (Lexington, Mass.: D. C. Heath and Company, 1974), pp. 568–575.

23. Samuel P. Huntington, *The Common Defense, Strategic Programs in National Politics* (New York: Columbia University Press, 1961), p. 124.

24. Clinton Rossiter, *The American Presidency*, quoted in Donald L. Robinson, "The President as Commander in Chief," in Bach and Sulzner, *Perspectives*, p. 369.

25. Louis Fisher, "War Powers: A Need for Legislative Reassertion," in

Rexford G. Tugwell and Thomas E. Cronin, eds., *The Presidency Reappraised* (New York: Praeger Publishers, 1974), p. 57.

26. L. Dean Brown, "A New Posture Abroad," *Presidential Studies Quarterly*, V, 4 (Fall 1975), pp. 16-19.

27. John B. Anderson, "A Republican Looks at the Presidency," in Dunn, *Future*, p. 233.

28. R. Gordon Hoxie, *A History of the Faculty of Political Science, Columbia University* (New York: Columbia University Press, 1955), p. 125.

29. Adolf A. Berle, "Power in Foreign Relations," in Tugwell and Cronin, *Presidency*, pp. 75-80.

30. J. W. Fulbright, "The Decline—and Possible Fall—of Constitutional Democracy in America," in Bach and Sulzner, *Perspectives*, pp. 355-357.

31. R. Gordon Hoxie, ed., *The White House: Organization and Operations* (New York: Center for the Study of the Presidency, 1971), p. 97.

32. Arthur M. Schlesinger, Jr., "Congress and the Making of Foreign Policy," in Tugwell and Cronin, *Presidency*, p. 97.

33. *Ibid.*, p. 110.

34. *Ibid.*, p. 100.

35. *Ibid.*, p. 113.

36. *Ibid.*, p. 100.

37. Stephen Hess, in Symposium on the Presidency, University of California at Irvine, January 12, 1976.

38. Schlesinger, "Congress," in Tugwell and Cronin, *Presidency*, p. 99.

39. Herbert S. Parmet, *Eisenhower and the American Crusades* (New York: The Macmillan Company, 1972), pp. 306-311.

40. Henry Bamford Parkes and Vincent P. Carosso, *Recent America, Book Two: Since 1933* (New York: Thomas Y. Crowell Company, 1963), pp. 436-437.

41. Schlesinger, *Imperial Presidency*, p. 312.

42. R. Gordon Hoxie, ed., *The Presidency of the 1970s* (New York: Center for the Study of the Presidency, 1973), p. 11.

43. Huntington, *Common Defense*, p. 135.

44. Schlesinger, "Congress," in Tugwell and Cronin, *Presidency*, p. 99.

45. Maura E. Heaphy, "Executive Legislative Liaison," *Presidential Studies Quarterly*, V, 4 (Fall 1975), pp. 42-46.

46. Donald R. Burkholder, "Caretaker of the Presidential Image," *Presidential Studies Quarterly*, V, 1 (Winter 1975), pp. 35-43.

47. Henry M. Jackson, ed., *The National Security Council*, Jackson Subcommittee Papers on Policy-Making at the Presidential Level (New York: Frederick A. Praeger, 1965), pp. 4-5.

48. Hoxie, *White House*, p. 115.

49. *Ibid.*, pp. 78-79.

50. Louis Smith, *American Democracy and Military Power* (Chicago: University of Chicago Press, 1951), p. 7.

51. William G. Carleton, *The Revolution in American Foreign Policy*, rev. ed. (New York: Random House, 1957), p. 276.

52. Jerome H. Kahan, *Security in the Nuclear Age* (Washington, D.C.: The Brookings Institution, 1975), pp. 26-27.

53. Samuel P. Huntington, "Interservice Competition and the Political Roles of the Armed Services," *American Political Science Review*, LV, 1 (March 1961), 40–52; also Huntington, *Common Defense*, p. 135.

54. Harrison W. Fox, Jr., and Susan Webb Hammond, "The Growth of Congressional Staffs," in Harvey C. Mansfield, Sr., ed., *Congress Against the President*, Proceedings of the Academy of Political Science, XXXII, 1 (New York, 1975), p. 113.

55. Allen Schick, "The Battle of the Budget," in *ibid.*, pp. 61–69.

56. Edward S. Corwin, *The President: Office and Powers, 1787–1957* (New York: New York University Press, 1957), p. 200.

57. *U.S. Department of State Bulletin*, LXXII, 1860 (Feb. 17, 1975), p. 203.

58. Mansfield, *Congress*, p. 19.

II. Commander in Chief and Chief Diplomat

1. *The Economist*, March 6, 1976.

2. Gerald R. Ford in lecture at the University of Kentucky, April 11, 1977, in *New York Times*, April 12, 1977.

3. *Ibid.*

4. *Department of State Bulletin*, LXIV, 1667 (June 7, 1971), p. 732.

5. Schlesinger, *Imperial Presidency*, p. 413.

6. *Ibid.*, p. 188.

7. Jacob E. Cooke, ed., *The Federalist* (Middletown, Conn.: Wesleyan University Press, 1961), p. 313.

8. *Ibid.*, p. 325.

9. *Ibid.*

10. *Ibid.*

11. Harold C. Syrett, ed., *The Papers of Alexander Hamilton, Jan. 1796 – March 1797*, Vol. XX (New York, Columbia University Press, 1974), p. 385.

12. Richard B. Morris, *Alexander Hamilton and the Founding of the Nation* (New York: Dial Press, 1957), p. 381.

13. Harold C. Syrett, ed., *The Papers of Alexander Hamilton, June 1793–Jan. 1794*, Vol. XV (New York: Columbia University Press, 1969), pp. 39–43.

14. *Ibid.*, p. 135.

15. Louis Henkin, "A More Effective System for Foreign Relations: The Constitutional Framework," *Virginia Law Review*, May 1975, p. 754.

16. Syrett, *Hamilton Papers*, XX, p. 22.

17. *Ibid.*, p. 24.

18. *Ibid.*, p. 33.

19. *Ibid.*, pp. 381–385 *passim.*

20. Harold C. Syrett, ed., *The Papers of Alexander Hamilton, August 1794–December 1794*, Vol. XVII (New York: Columbia University Press, 1973), p. 499.

21. Edward S. Corwin, *The President's Control of Foreign Relations* (Princeton, N.J.: Princeton University Press, 1917), p. 126.

22. *Ibid.*, pp. 41–42.

23. *Ibid.*, p. 42.

24. Henry R. Pringle, *Theodore Roosevelt* (New York: Harcourt, Brace and Company, 1931), p. 279.

25. *Ibid.*, p. 409.

26. *Ibid.*

27. Donald F. Anderson, *William Howard Taft* (Ithaca, N.Y.: Cornell University Press, 1973), p. 19.

28. *Ibid.*, pp. 300–301.

29. *Ibid.*, p. 288.

30. Corwin, *President's Control*, p. 126.

31. R. Gordon Hoxie, "Herbert Hoover: Multi-National Man," *Presidential Studies Quarterly*, VII, 1 (Winter 1977), p. 49.

32. Eugene Lyons, *Herbert Hoover: A Biography* (Garden City, N.Y.: Doubleday and Company, Inc., 1964), p. 133.

33. Herbert Hoover, *Memoirs*, Vol. I, *Years of Adventure 1874–1920* (New York: The Macmillan Company, 1951), p. 451.

34. Herbert Hoover, *The Ordeal of Woodrow Wilson* (New York: McGraw-Hill Book Company, Inc., 1958), p. 300.

35. Pratt, *History*, p. 552.

36. *Ibid.*, p. 554.

37. Herbert Hoover, *Memoirs*, Vol. II, *The Cabinet and the Presidency, 1920–1933* (New York: The Macmillan Company, 1952), pp. 11–13.

38. Pratt, *History*, p. 595.

39. *Ibid.*, p. 643.

40. Dexter Perkins, *The American Approach to Foreign Policy* (Cambridge: Harvard University Press, 1952), pp. 138–139.

41. Louis W. Koenig, "The President as Commander in Chief," in Philip C. Dolce and George H. Skaw, eds., *Power and the Presidency* (New York, Charles Scribner's Sons, 1976), p. 191.

42. Harry A. Bailey, Jr., "Controlling the Runaway Presidency," *Public Administration Review*, XXV, 5, Sept./Oct. 1975, p. 548.

43. Corwin, *President*, p. 252.

44. Abraham D. Sofaer, *War, Foreign Affairs and Constitutional Power* (Cambridge: Ballinger Publishing Company, 1976), pp. 74–75, 129.

III. Truman and Containment of Communism

1. Harry S Truman, *Memoirs*, Vol. II, *Years of Trial and Hope* (Garden City, N.Y.: Doubleday & Company, Inc., 1956), p. ix.

2. Adolf S. Berle in First Annual National Student Symposium on the Presidency, Center for the Study of the Presidency, Dec. 2, 1970.

3. John J. McCloy in CBS television interview with Eric Severeid, July 13, 1975.

4. *Ibid.*

5. William L. Neumann, "Roosevelt's Foreign Policy Decisions, 1940–1945," *Modern Age*, XIX, 3 (Summer 1975), p. 273.

6. Koenig, *Chief Executive*, p. 248.

7. *The Federalist,* No. 69, cited in Morris, *Hamilton,* p. 184.

8. *Ibid.,* pp. 184–185.

9. *The Federalist,* No. 70, cited in *ibid.,* p. 185.

10. Letter from Richard M. Nixon to R. Gordon Hoxie, May 2, 1973, Center for the Study of the Presidency.

11. Remarks of Louis W. Koenig at the Sixth Annual National Student Symposium, April 12, 1975, in manuscript collection of Center for the Study of the Presidency.

12. Morris, *Hamilton,* pp. 438–439.

13. Hamilton, "Measures of Defense" (1799), in *ibid.,* p. 441.

14. Curtis P. Nettels, "Alexander Hamilton and the Presidency," *Presidential Studies Quarterly,* V, 1 (Winter 1975), pp. 23–25.

15. Hamilton to General Pinckney, Dec. 1799, cited in Morris, *Hamilton,* pp. 520–521.

16. *Long Island Press,* July 6, 1975, p. 15.

17. Koenig, *Chief Executive,* p. 213.

18. Truman, *Memoirs,* II, 1.

19. *Ibid.*

20. Dwight D. Eisenhower, *Crusade in Europe* (Garden City, N.Y.: Permabooks, 1952), p. 521.

21. W. D. Leahy, *I Was There* (New York: Whittlesey House, 1950), p. 382.

22. Pratt, *History,* p. 690. See also Herbert Feis, *The China Tangle: The American Effort in China from Pearl Harbor to the Marshall Mission* (Princeton: Princeton University Press, 1953), p. 236; also E. M. Zacharias, *Behind Closed Doors: The Secret History of the Cold War* (New York: G. P. Putnam's Sons, 1950), pp. 56–57.

23. Pratt, *History,* p. 698.

24. Harry S Truman, *Public Papers of the Presidents of the United States, 1945* (Washington, D.C.: U.S. Government Printing Office, 1961), p. 143.

25. Pratt, *History,* pp. 712–713.

26. Truman, *Public Papers, 1945,* p. 204.

27. Pratt, *History,* pp. 710–711.

28. Barton J. Bernstein, "Doomsday II," *New York Times Magazine,* July 27, 1975, p. 24.

29. *Ibid.,* p. 21.

30. R. B. Ritkin, "The Surrender Aboard the USS Missouri Thirty Years Ago," *American Legion Magazine,* Aug. 1975, p. 9.

31. David Lawrence, "What Hath Man Wrought," in *U.S. News,* Aug. 17, 1945, editorial page, reprinted in *U.S. News and World Report,* July 21, 1975, pp. 71–72.

32. McCloy, in CBS interview, July 13, 1975.

33. Eisenhower, *Crusade,* p. 488.

34. Alperovitz, *Atomic Diplomacy,* p. 14.

35. *Ibid.,* p. 239.

36. Harry S Truman, *Memoirs,* Vol. I, *Year of Decision* (Garden City, N.Y.: Doubleday, 1955), p. 421.

37. William L. Neumann, *After Victory: Churchill, Roosevelt, Stalin and the Making of Peace* (New York: Harper & Row, 1967), p. 14.

38. Truman, *Memoirs*, I, p. 200.

39. *Ibid.*, p. 15.

40. *Ibid.*, p. 217.

41. *Ibid.*, p. 85.

42. *Ibid.*, p. 262.

43. Neumann, "Roosevelt's Foreign Policy Decisions," p. 165.

44. Alperovitz, *Atomic Diplomacy*, p. 13.

45. *Ibid.*, pp. 270–275.

46. Ambrose, *Rise to Globalism*, p. 127.

47. Alperovitz, *Atomic Diplomacy*, p. 278.

48. Truman, *Memoirs*, II, p. 2.

49. *Ibid.*, p. 11.

50. Ambrose, *Rise to Globalism*, p. 132.

51. John S. D. Eisenhower, *Strictly Personal* (Garden City, N.Y.: Doubleday, 1974), p. 112.

52. Eisenhower, *Crusade*, pp. 486–487.

53. Truman, *Memoirs*, II, p. 66.

54. *Ibid.*, p. 68.

55. *Ibid.*, p. 83.

56. *Ibid.*, p. 90.

57. *Ibid.*

58. *Ibid.*

59. Pratt, *History*, p. 719.

60. Truman, *Memoirs*, I, pp. 551–552.

61. Harry S Truman, *Public Papers of the Presidents, 1947* (Washington, D.C.: U.S. Government Printing Office, 1963), pp. 176–180.

62. *Ibid.*, p. 255.

63. *Ibid.*, p. 439.

64. Walter Millis, *Arms and Men: A Study in American Military History* (New York: G. P. Putnam's Sons, 1956), p. 315.

65. See Chapter 5.

66. Harry S Truman, *Public Papers of the Presidents, 1948* (Washington, D.C.: U.S. Government Printing Office, 1964), pp. 182–186.

67. Truman, *Memoirs*, II, p. 119.

68. *Ibid.*, p. 131.

69. Henry W. Berger, "Bi-Partisanship, Senator Taft and the Truman Administration," *Political Science Quarterly*, XC, 2 (Summer 1975), p. 222.

70. Harry S Truman, *Public Papers of the Presidents of the United States, 1946* (Washington, D.C.: U.S. Government Printing Office, 1962), p. 197.

71. *Ibid.*, p. 507.

72. Truman, *Memoirs*, II, p. 119.

73. Berger, "Bi-Partisanship," pp. 224–225.

74. Truman, *Memoirs*, II, p. 244.

75. Berger, "Bi-Partisanship," p. 223.

76. Cited in *ibid.*, p. 229.

77. *Ibid.*, p. 234.

78. A. H. Vandenberg, Jr., ed., *The Private Papers of Senator Vandenberg* (Boston: Houghton Mifflin Company, 1952), pp. 403–411.

IV. Truman as Commander in Chief

1. Harry S Truman, "The President's Responsibility," *Military Review*, XLII, 9 (Sept. 1962), p. 2.

2. J. B. West, *Upstairs at the White House* (New York: Coward, McCann & Geoghegan, 1973), p. 61.

3. Frank McNaughton and Walter Hehmeyer, *This Man Truman* (New York: Whittlesey House, 1945), p. 123.

4. Truman, *Memoirs*, I, p. 555.

5. *Ibid.*, pp. 555–560.

6. *Ibid.*, pp. 552–553.

7. Truman, "President's Responsibility," p. 4.

8. *Ibid.*

9. Ernest R. May, ed., *The Ultimate Decision: The President as Commander in Chief* (New York: George Braziller, 1960), p. xvi.

10. *Ibid.*, p. 5.

11. *Ibid.*, pp. 184–185.

12. See Chapter 5.

13. Truman, *Memoirs*, II, p. 46.

14. Truman, *Public Papers, 1946*, p. 303.

15. See Chapter 6.

16. Truman, *Memoirs*, II, p. 53.

17. Truman, *Public Papers, 1946*, p. 88.

18. Truman, *Public Papers, 1947*, pp. 359–361.

19. Truman, *Memoirs*, II, p. 157.

20. Truman, *Public Papers, 1948*, pp. 213–214.

21. Robert E. Riegel and David F. Long, *The American Story*, Vol. II (New York: McGraw-Hill Book Company, Inc., 1955), p. 428.

22. Alfred de Grazia and Thomas H. Stevenson, *World Politics: A Study in International Relations* (New York: Barnes and Noble, Inc., 1962), p. 100.

23. Pratt, *History*, pp. 746–748.

24. Dean Acheson, *Present at the Creation: My Years in the State Department* (New York: W. W. Norton & Company, Inc., 1969), p. 432.

25. Pratt, *History*, p. 740.

26. Acheson, *Present*, pp. 402–408.

27. *Ibid.*, pp. 408–409.

28. Pratt, *History*, p. 740.

29. Acheson, *Present*, pp. 412–413.

30. *Ibid.*, p. 404.

31. Merle Miller, *Plain Speaking: An Oral Biography of Harry S Truman* (New York: Berkley Publishing Corp., 1973), p. 273. Obviously Miller or Truman or both were confused. Miller says the President recalled receiv-

ing the call on Saturday evening; he was on his way "in less than an hour," and after a three-hour flight he rushed to the dinner: that leaves twenty hours unaccounted for.

32. *Ibid.*, p. 414.

33. Schlesinger, *Imperial Presidency*, p. 134.

34. *Ibid.*, p. 138.

35. *Ibid.*, p. 135.

36. John Eisenhower, *Strictly Personal*, p. 156.

37. Burt Cochran, *Harry Truman and the Crisis Presidency* (New York: Funk & Wagnalls, 1973), p. 312.

38. Miller, *Plain Speaking*, p. 285.

39. Acheson, *Present*, p. 415.

40. Maurice Matloff, general ed., *American Military History* (Washington, D.C.: Office of the Chief of Military History, United States Army, 1969), p. 545.

41. Millis, *Arms and Men*, pp. 328–329.

42. Truman, *Memoirs*, II, pp. 333–334.

43. The strategy is detailed in Chapter 7, on the Korean War.

44. I. M. Dester, in Conference on Presidential Advising, Princeton University, Oct. 31–Nov. 1, 1975.

45. Truman, *Memoirs*, II, p. 344.

46. Matloff, *American Military History*, pp. 545–550. At the time of the North Korean attack the ROK Army, an ill-equipped constabulary force, numbered 95,000; it was reduced to an effective field force of 25,000 by the end of the second week of the war.

47. Parkes and Carosso, *Recent America*, II, p. 373.

48. Matloff, *American Military History*, pp. 550–553.

49. Acheson, *Present*, p. 448.

50. Cochran, *Truman*, p. 319.

51. De Grazia and Stevenson, *World Politics*, p. 113.

52. *Ibid.*

53. Cochran, *Truman*, p. 319.

54. *Ibid.*

55. Parkes and Carosso, *Recent America*, p. 374.

56. Truman, *Memoirs*, II, p. 362. Italics added.

57. *Ibid.*, p. 447.

58. Acheson, *Present*, p. 456.

59. Truman, *Memoirs*, II, p. 365.

60. *Ibid.*, p. 354.

61. *Ibid.*, p. 365.

62. *Ibid.*, pp. 367–368.

63. Ambrose, *Rise to Globalism*, p. 203.

64. Truman, *Memoirs*, II, p. 384.

65. Harry S Truman, *Public Papers of the President of the United States, 1950* (Washington, D.C.: U.S. Government Printing Office, 1965), pp. 726–727.

66. Margaret Truman, *Harry S Truman* (New York: William Morrow & Company, Inc., 1973), p. 493.

67. *Ibid.,* pp. 498–499.

68. Ambrose, *Rise to Globalism,* p. 207.

69. *Ibid.,* p. 209.

70. Truman, *Public Papers,* pp. 746–747.

71. Truman, *Memoirs,* II, pp. 417–419.

72. Harold C. Relyea, in "A Brief History of Emergency Powers in the United States," prepared for Special Committee on National Emergencies and Delegated Powers, United States Senate (Washington, D.C.: U.S. Government Printing Office, 1974), p. 91.

73. *Ibid.,* p. 87.

74. Truman, *Memoirs,* II, pp. 419–420.

75. *Ibid.,* p. 424.

76. Patterson, *Mr. Republican,* p. 455.

77. Dwight D. Eisenhower, *The White House Years, 1953–1956, Mandate for Change* (Garden City, N.Y.: Doubleday, 1963), pp. 13–14: Milton S. Eisenhower, *The President Is Calling* (Garden City, N.Y.: Doubleday, 1974), pp. 243–245; and John Eisenhower, *Strictly Personal,* p. 157.

78. Patterson, *Mr. Republican,* p. 477.

79. Schlesinger, *Imperial Presidency,* pp. 137–139.

80. Patterson, *Mr. Republican,* p. 477.

81. Margaret Truman, *Truman,* p. 494.

82. Truman, *Memoirs,* II, p. 432.

83. Margaret Truman, *Truman,* p. 492.

84. Truman, *Memoirs,* II, p. 447.

85. Acheson, *Present,* p. 518.

86. Koenig, *Chief Executive,* p. 244.

87. Truman, *Memoirs,* II, p. 441.

88. *Ibid.,* p. 442.

89. Cabell Phillips, *The Truman Presidency* (New York: The Macmillan Company, 1966), p. 339.

90. *Ibid.*

91. Acheson, *Present,* p. 520.

92. *Ibid.,* p. 522.

93. *Ibid.,* p. 526.

94. Harry S Truman, *Public Papers of the President of the United States, 1951* (Washington, D.C.: U.S. Government Printing Office, 1965), p. 222.

95. *Ibid.*

96. Phillips, *Truman Presidency,* p. 350.

97. Truman, *Memoirs,* II, p. 449.

98. Patterson, *Mr. Republican,* p. 488.

99. See Chapter 7, note 30.

100. Truman, *Public Papers, 1951,* pp. 223–226.

101. *Ibid.,* pp. 223–224.

102. Ambrose, *Rise to Globalism,* p. 214.

103. Patterson, *Mr. Republican,* p. 488.

104. Acheson, *Present,* p. 529.

105. Evan T. Luard, ed., *The Cold War: A Reappraisal* (New York: Frederick A. Praeger, 1964), p. 175.

106. Parkes and Carosso, *Recent America,* p. 388.

107. Truman, *Public Papers, 1948,* pp. 432–433.

108. Parkes and Carosso, *Recent America,* p. 390.

109. *Ibid.,* p. 398.

110. Patterson, *Mr. Republican,* p. 361.

111. Truman, *Memoirs,* II, p. 467.

112. *Ibid.,* p. 469.

113. Schlesinger, *Imperial Presidency,* p. 142.

114. *Ibid.,* pp. 142–143.

115. *Ibid.*

116. *Ibid.,* p. 144.

117. *Ibid.,* pp. 144–145.

118. *Ibid.,* p. 150

119. *Ibid.,* p. 138.

120. Miller, *Plain Speaking,* p. 314.

121. Harry S Truman, *Public Papers of the President of the United States, 1952–53* (Washington, D.C.: U.S. Government Printing Office, 1966), p. 1046. These documents were released in an attempt to prove that Eisenhower, while serving as Army Chief of Staff in 1947, participated in a Joint Chiefs of Staff statement that "the United States has little strategic interest in maintaining the present troops and bases in Korea. . . ." Since the withdrawal came two years later, in mid-1949, following the completion of the Soviet withdrawal in December 1948, it seemed to be considerably stretching a point for Truman (and Acheson) to associate Eisenhower in the withdrawal.

122. *Ibid.,* p. 1189.

123. Miller, *Plain Speaking,* pp. 334–335.

124. Truman, *Public Papers, 1952–53,* p. 225.

125. *Ibid.,* p. 1028.

126. Truman, *Memoirs,* II, pp. 490–494.

127. Phillips, *Truman Presidency,* pp. 427–428.

128. Truman, *Public Papers, 1952–53,* p. 1194.

129. Parkes and Carosso, *Recent America,* p. 404.

130. Truman, *Public Papers, 1952–53,* pp. 945, 1046.

131. *Ibid.,* p. 960.

132. *Ibid.,* p. 961.

133. *Ibid.,* p. 858.

134. *Ibid.,* p. 740.

135. Miller, *Plain Speaking,* p. 337.

136. Truman, *Public Papers, 1952–53,* p. 713.

137. *Ibid.,* p. 789.

138. *Ibid.,* pp. 851–852.

139. *Ibid.,* p. 996.

140. *Ibid.,* p. 1047.

141. Parkes and Carosso, *Recent America,* II, p. 405.

142. Parmet, *Eisenhower,* p. 143.

143. Parkes and Carosso, *Recent America,* II, p. 406.

144. Arthur M. Schlesinger, *The Rise of Modern America, 1865–1951* (New York: The Macmillan Company, 1951), p. 471.

145. *New York Times,* July 29, 1962. See also Erwin C. Hargrove, *The Power of the Modern Presidency* (Philadelphia: Temple University Press, 1974), pp. 4–7.

146. Patteson, *Mr. Republican,* p. 302.

147. Miller, *Plain Speaking,* p. 353.

148. *Ibid.,* p. 409.

149. Stephen Hess to R. Gordon Hoxie, Aug. 4, 1977.

150. Hargrove, *Power,* p. 86.

151. Phillips, *Truman Presidency,* p. 401.

152. Patterson, *Mr. Republican,* p. 434.

153. Elmer Plischke, *Conduct of American Diplomacy* (New York: D. Van Nostrand Company, 1950), p. 1n.

154. Miller, *Plain Speaking,* p. 414.

155. Truman, *Public Papers, 1952–53,* p. 1061.

156. Miller, *Plain Speaking,* p. 392.

157. Truman, *Public Papers, 1952–53,* p. 1216.

158. *Ibid.,* p. 1190.

159. *Ibid.,* p. 1048.

160. *Ibid.,* p. 1201.

161. *Ibid.,* p. 1064.

162. *Ibid.,* p. 1198.

163. Acheson, *Present,* p. 731.

164. Truman, *Public Papers, 1952–53,* p. 1197.

165. *Ibid.,* p. 1200.

166. Donald L. Robinson, "The President as Commander in Chief," in Stanley Bach and George T. Sulzner, *Perspectives on the Presidency* (Lexington, Mass.: D. C. Heath and Company, 1974), p. 371.

167. *Ibid.*

168. Hoxie, *Frontiers,* p. 159.

169. Robinson, "President," p. 372.

170. Truman, *Public Papers, 1952–53,* p. 1058.

171. Truman, *Memoirs,* II, pp. 472–478.

172. *Ibid.,* p. 478.

173. Truman, *Public Papers, 1952–53,* p. 1061.

174. Clinton Rossiter, *The American Presidency,* rev. ed. (New York: Harcourt, Brace and World, Inc., 1960), p. 25.

175. Robert H. Ferrell and David McLillan, "Dean Acheson, Architect of a Manageable World Order," in Frank J. Merli and Theodore A. Wilson, eds., *Makers of American Diplomacy* (New York: Charles Scribner's Sons, 1974), p. 532.

176. Truman, *Public Papers, 1952–53,* p. 1203.

177. Acheson, *Present,* p. 731.

178. *Ibid.,* p. 733.

179. Thomas E. Cronin, *The State of the Presidency* (Boston: Little, Brown and Company, 1975), p. 181.

180. Acheson, *Present,* p. 734.
181. West, *Upstairs,* pp. 63–77.
182. Truman, *Public Papers, 1952–53,* p. 1061.
183. *Ibid.,* pp. 1199–1200.
184. Truman, *Public Papers, 1947,* p. 130.

V. James V. Forrestal and the National Security Act of 1947

1. Hoxie, *Frontiers,* pp. 155–156.
2. Paltsits, *Washington's Farewell Address,* p. 156.
3. Demetrios Caraley, *The Politics of Military Unification: A Study of Conflict and the Policy Process* (New York: Columbia University Press, 1966), p. 4.
4. *Ibid.,* p. 17.
5. Arnold A. Rogow, *James Forrestal: A Study of Personality, Politics, and Policy* (New York: The Macmillan Co., 1963), p. 213.
6. See Michael J. Nizolek, "The Origins of the National Security Act of 1947," a senior thesis submitted to the Faculty of the Department of History, Fordham University, May 1972, New York, Center for the Study of the Presidency.
7. *Ibid.,* pp. 27–49; also John C. Ries, *The Management of Defense Organization and Control of the U.S. Armed Forces* (Baltimore: The Johns Hopkins Press, 1964), pp. 9–12.
8. Caraley, *Politics,* p. 59.
9. Nizolek, "Origins," pp. 32–33.
10. *Ibid.,* p. 34.
11. Walter Millis, ed., *The Forrestal Diaries* (New York: Viking Press, 1951), pp. 46–47.
12. *Ibid.,* pp. 64–65.
13. Truman, *Public Papers, 1946,* pp. 546–560.
14. Jonathan Daniels, *The Man of Independence* (Philadelphia: Lippincott, 1950), p. 305.
15. Truman, *Public Papers, 1946,* p. 171; also Nizolek, "Origins," p. 55.
16. Nizolek, "Origins," pp. 54–55.
17. Millis, *Forrestal Diaries,* pp. 144–145.
18. Analytical Digest of Testimony Before the Senate Military Affairs Committee, Oct. 17 to Dec. 17, 1945, and of the President's Message to the Congress, Dec. 19, 1945. Manuscript Collection, Office of Air Force History, Washington, D.C.
19. *Ibid.,* p. 161. The new Commanding General of the Army Air Forces, General Carl Spaatz, and Major General Lewis Norstad, Assistant Chief of the Air Staff, attended this meeting. The Collins Plan had included U.S. Chiefs of Staff.
20. *Ibid.,* pp. 146–147.
21. Nizolek. "Origins," p. 59.
22. Millis, *Forrestal Diaries,* p. 148.
23. *Ibid.,* p. 149.

24. *Ibid.*, p. 169.

25. *Ibid.*, p. 170.

26. *Ibid.*, pp. 229–230; also Nizolek, "Origins," pp. 59–76.

27. Hoxie, *Presidency*, p. 140.

28. Millis, *Forrestal Diaries*, pp. 227–228.

29. National Security Act of 1947 (Public Law 253, 80th Congress, 61 Stat. 495); as amended by Department of Defense Reorganization Act of 1958, Aug. 6, 1958 (72 Stat. 514), 50USC 401. See also *First Report of the Secretary of Defense* (Washington, D.C.: U.S. Government Printing Office, 1948).

30. Richard E. Neustadt, *Presidential Power: The Politics of Leadership* (New York: John Wiley & Sons, Inc., 1960), pp. 5–6.

31. *First Report of the Secretary of Defense*, p. 29.

32. Millis, *Forrestal Diaries*, p. 300.

33. *Ibid.*, p. 169.

34. Robert Cutler, *No Time for Rest* (Boston: Little, Brown, and Co., 1965), pp. 243–244.

35. *Ibid.*, p. 242.

36. *Ibid.*, p. 244.

37. *First Report of the Secretary of Defense*, p. 2.

38. *Ibid.*, p. 9.

39. *Ibid.*

40. Millis, *Forrestal Diaries*, p. 225.

41. Rogow, *Forrestal*, pp. 286–288.

42. Ries, *Management*, p. 126.

43. Cutler, *No Time*, p. 244.

44. Ries, *Management*, p. 126. Also Timothy W. Stanley, *American Defense and National Security* (Washington, D.C.: Public Affairs Press, 1956), pp. 84–89.

45. Cutler, *No Time*, pp. 254–258.

46. Millis, *Forrestal Diaries*, pp. 435–439.

47. *New York Times*, July 18, 1948.

48. Millis, *Forrestal Diaries*, p. 463.

49. *Ibid.*

50. *Ibid.*

51. *Ibid.*, p. 465.

52. *Ibid.*, pp. 497–498.

53. *First Report of the Secretary of Defense*, pp. 10–11.

54. *Ibid.*

55. Paul Y. Hammond, "Super Carriers and B-36 Bombers: Appropriations, Strategy and Politics," in Harold Stein, ed., *American Civil-Military Decisions* (Birmingham, Ala.: University of Alabama Press, 1963), p. 503.

56. Rogow, *Forrestal*, p. 299.

57. *First Report of the Secretary of Defense*, pp. 2–4; also Millis, *Forrestal Diaries*, pp. 497–498, 512, 538, 550.

58. Millis, *Forrestal Diaries*, pp. 547–548.

59. Rogow, *Forrestal*, p. 210.

60. Millis, *Forrestal Diaries,* pp. 544–546.

61. *Ibid.,* pp. 552–553.

62. *Ibid.,* pp. 553–555.

63. Jack Raymond, *Power at the Pentagon* (New York: Harper & Row, Publishers, 1964), p. 279.

64. Cutler, *No Time,* p. 258.

65. Rogow, *Forrestal,* p. 233.

66. Stanley, *American Defense,* p. 46.

67. Hammond, "Super Carriers," pp. 490–495. The Air Force was winning the publicity war over the Navy, which saw its flush-deck supercarrier threatened. This did not bother Forrestal nearly as much as the principle of policy being conceived and carried through the public press. In 1948 he ordered that all controversial articles and speeches be submitted to him for approval prior to publication.

68. Ries, *Management,* p. 146.

69. *Ibid.*

70. *Ibid.*

71. *Ibid.*

72. Cutler, *No Time,* p. 256.

73. *First Report of the Secretary of Defense,* pp. 2–9.

74. Hearings, European Recovery Program, 80th Congress, 2d Session, quoted in Adam Yarmolinsky, *The Military Establishment* (New York: Harper & Row, 1971), p. 117.

75. Edward L. R. Elson, in interview with the author, April 15, 1977. Dr. Elson's other two choices were Sidney Souer, President Truman's first Executive Secretary of the NSC, and Elliot L. Richardson, presently serving as President Carter's Ambassador at Large.

VI. The Admirals' Revolt and the 1949 Amendments

1. Vandenberg, *Private Papers,* pp. 403–411.

2. See Hoxie, *Frontiers,* pp. 189–202.

3. Variously termed the "B-36 controversy" and the "revolt of the admirals," the story is well recounted in Hammond, "Super Carriers," and Ries, *Management.*

4. H. Res. 227 and H. Res. 234, 81st Congress, 1st Session.

5. Harry Hansen, ed., *The World Almanac and Book of Facts for 1950* (New York: New York World Telegram Corp., 1950), pp. 341, 352.

6. Millis, *Forrestal Diaries,* p. 551.

7. Hammond, "Super Carriers," pp. 590–595.

8. Eugene M. Emme, *The Impact of Air Power* (Princeton, N.J.: D. Van Nostrand Company, 1959), p. 627.

9. *Ibid.*

10. *Ibid.,* pp. 631, 633.

11. Ries, *Management,* pp. 129–138.

12. Arthur O. Sulzberger, *The Joint Chiefs of Staff, 1941–54* (Washington, D.C.: U.S. Marine Corps Institute, 1954), p. 71. Forrestal had concluded in his own testimony on the proposed amendments: "After having viewed the problems at close range for the past 18 months, I must admit to you quite frankly that my position on the question has changed. I am now convinced that there are adequate checks and balances inherent in our government structure to prevent misuse of the broad authority which I feel must be vested in the Secretary of Defense." Quoted in *ibid.*

13. Stanley, *American Defense*, p. 90.

14. Hammond, "Super Carriers," pp. 501–502.

15. Ries, *Management*, p. 142.

16. *First Report of the Secretary of Defense*, p. 4; also Ries, *Management*, pp. 129–138, *passim*.

17. PL 216, 81st Congress, 61 *Stat.* 499, 5 U.S.C. Supp. 171.

18. Stanley, *American Defense*, p. 93.

19. Hoxie, *White House*, p. 137.

20. W. Stuart Symington et al., "Reorganization Plan," *Air Force and Space Digest*, Jan. 1961, pp. 38–41.

21. *New York Times*, Aug. 18, 1973.

22. *Ibid.*

23. Major General H. J. Knerr, USAF, quoted in Huntington, *Common Defense*, p. 377.

24. Hansen, *World Almanac*, pp. 341, 352, 360.

25. *Ibid.*, p. 360.

26. Ries, *Management*, p. 145.

27. "Unification and Strategy, a Report of Investigation by the Committee on Armed Services," House of Representatives, House Doc. No. 600, 81st Congress, 2d Session, 1950.

28. J. J. Clark, with Clark S. Reynolds, *Carrier Admiral* (New York: David McKay Company, 1967), p. 252.

29. *Ibid.*, p. 251.

30. Hansen, *World Almanac*, p. 360.

31. Clark, *Carrier Admiral*, p. 263.

32. Hammond, "Super Carriers," p. 550; Stanley, *American Defense*, p. 95.

33. Clark, *Carrier Admiral*, p. 251.

34. P.L. 416, 82d Congress, 2d Session, 1952. The original bill had proposed full JCS membership for the Commandant. The story is recounted in Sulzberger, *Joint Chiefs*, pp. 75–82.

35. Hammond, "Super Carriers," p. 550, Stanley, *American Defense*, p. 95.

36. Ries, *Management*, pp. 114–115.

37. Clark, *Carrier Admiral*, p. 264.

38. Hammond, "Super Carriers," p. 554.

39. Hansen, *World Almanac*, p. 359. Walter C. Langsam, *The World since 1919*, 7th ed. (New York: The Macmillan Company, 1954), p. 718.

VII. *The Korean War and National Strategy*

1. Morton H. Halperin, *Limited War in the Nuclear Age* (New York: John Wiley and Sons, 1963).
2. Hammond, "Super Carriers," p. 503.
3. Henry A. Kissinger, *Nuclear Weapons and Foreign Policy* (New York: Harper & Brothers, 1957), p. 37.
4. Jackson, *National Security Council,* p. 100.
5. Huntington, *Common Defense,* p. 191.
6. Paul Y. Hammond, *Organizing for Defense: The American Military Estab-lishment in the Twentieth Century* (Princeton: Princeton University Press, 1961), p. 255. See also Huntington, *Common Defense,* pp. 48–52. Huntington credits the Policy Planning Staff of the Department of State with a sense of the gravity of the situation. This was shared by Rear Admiral Sidney W. Souers, a St. Louis insurance executive who served (1947–1950) as the first Executive Secretary of the National Security Council. It was Souers who took the initiative in January 1950 in ordering a general strategic reassessment.
7. Quoted in Huntington, *Common Defense,* p. 53.
8. Kissinger, *Nuclear Weapons,* p. 28.
9. Truman, *Memoirs,* II.
10. Kissinger, *Nuclear Weapons,* p. 43.
11. Carl Berger, *The Korean Knot* (Philadelphia: University of Pennsyl-vania Press, 1968), p. 15.
12. Truman, *Memoirs,* II, pp. 323–326.
13. *Ibid.,* p. 329.
14. Douglas MacArthur, *Reminiscences* (New York: McGraw-Hill, 1964), p. 328.
15. *Ibid.,* p. 324.
16. *Ibid.,* p. 328.
17. *Ibid.,* p. 331.
18. Berger, *Korean Knot,* p. 107; also Truman, *Memoirs,* II, pp. 333–336.
19. MacArthur, *Reminiscences,* pp. 332–334.
20. Berger, *Korean Knot,* p. 114.
21. MacArthur, *Reminiscences,* pp. 345–346.
22. Berger, *Korean Knot,* p. 119.
23. Robert Leckie, *Conflict: The History of the Korean War, 1950-53* (New York: G. P. Putnam's Sons, 1962), p. 167.
24. Truman, *Memoirs,* II, p. 365.
25. MacArthur. *Reminiscences,* pp. 360–363.
26. Truman, *Memoirs,* II, p. 365.
27. MacArthur, *Reminiscences,* pp. 368–369.
28. *Ibid.,* pp. 369–373.
29. *Ibid.,* pp. 377–381.
30. MacArthur, *Reminiscences,* pp. 369–370. Years later Eisenhower stated that under the circumstances he would have refused the order

about the bombing constraints on the Yalu bridges, thus forcing a decision on being relieved or supported in his command.

31. Leckie, *Conflict,* pp. 194–195.
32. Eisenhower, *Mandate,* p. 176.
33. *Ibid.,* p. 175.
34. MacArthur, *Reminiscences,* p. 375.
35. *Ibid.,* p. 374.
36. Berger, *Korean Knot,* p. 127.
37. Leckie, *Conflict,* pp. 227–228.
38. *Ibid.,* pp. 231–232.
39. Truman, *Memoirs,* II, pp. 433–436; MacArthur, *Reminiscences,* pp. 378–382; Berger, *Korean Knot,* pp. 131–133.
40. Leckie, *Conflict,* pp. 236–255.
41. MacArthur, *Reminiscences,* p. 383.
42. *Ibid.,* p. 384.
43. *Ibid.,* pp. 387–388.
44. Leckie, *Conflict,* pp. 266–269.
45. *Ibid.,* pp. 269–270.
46. *Ibid.,* pp. 271–274.
47. *Ibid.,* pp. 273–278.
48. *Ibid.*
49. Berger, *Korean Knot,* pp. 138–139.
50. Kissinger, *Nuclear Weapons,* p. 48.
51. *Ibid.,* p. 50.
52. MacArthur, *Reminiscences,* p. 390.
53. Truman, *Memoirs,* II, p. 445; MacArthur, *Reminiscences,* p. 393.
54. Berger, *Korean Knot,* p. 151. Like both his predecessors, Clark, to no avail, recommended that Chinese Nationalist forces enter into the conflict.
55. MacArthur, *Reminiscences,* pp. 362–363.
56. Eisenhower, *Mandate,* p. 96.
57. Truman, *Memoirs,* II, pp. 501–502.
58. Eisenhower, *Mandate,* p. 95.
59. *Ibid.,* pp. 179–180, 97.
60. MacArthur, *Reminiscences,* p. 409.
61. Leckie, *Conflict,* pp. 370–371.
62. MacArthur, *Reminiscences,* pp. 410–443.
63. Eisenhower, *Mandate,* p. 181.
64. Leckie, *Conflict,* p. 369.
65. Hoxie, *Presidency,* p. 5.
66. *Ibid.*
67. *Ibid.*
68. *Ibid.,* p. 5. Hagerty made clear that it was more than just a matter of personal credibility and respect, although these qualities were fundamental. Contrasting the situation with that faced by President Johnson in bringing the North Vietnamese to the negotiating table, Hagerty observed, "This was a lot... different... from what Mr. Johnson inherited. Re-

member, when Mr. Eisenhower came into office, we had military superiority. It was an entirely different world and an entirely different ball game."

69. Berger, *Korean Knot*, p. 169.

70. Eisenhower, *Mandate*, p. 185.

71. Harold Wendell Lady to R. Gordon Hoxie, Oct. 10, 1975, in Center for the Study of the Presidency. This account was recalled from a meeting of President Syngman Rhee, Lieutenant General John B. Coulter, the Deputy United Nations Commander, and Dr. Lady in December 1954 at Rhee's residence in Seoul.

72. *Ibid.*

73. *Ibid.*

74. Eisenhower, *Mandate*, p. 190.

75. Leckie, *Conflict*, p. 387.

76. *Ibid.*, p. 394.

77. Eisenhower, *Mandate*, p. 191.

VIII. Building Peace

1. John Henry Scrivner, "Pioneers into Space: A Biography of Major General Orvil Arson Anderson," unpublished dissertation, University of Oklahoma, Norman, Oklahoma, 1971, pp. 354–355.

2. In this statement Eisenhower declared: "I personally wish to emphasize that I shall regard the Secretary of State as the Cabinet Officer responsible for advising and assisting me in the formulation and control of foreign policy. It will be my practice to employ the Secretary of State as my channel of authority within the executive branch on foreign policy." Jackson, *National Security Council*, pp. 141–142.

3. Eisenhower, *Mandate*, pp. 110–111. In the Senate hearings on his confirmation, Wilson was asked: "Would you make a decision adverse to General Motors?" He responded: "For years I thought what was good for the country was good for General Motors and vice versa." *Ibid.*

4. Ries, *Management*, p. 159.

5. *Ibid.*

6. Eisenhower, *Mandate*, p. 447.

7. Ries, *Management*, p. 166.

8. Hammond, *Organizing*, pp. 302–303.

9. Semiannual Report of the Secretary of Defense, Jan. 1–June 30, 1953, pp. 9–18; *ibid.*, Jan. 1–June 30, 1954, pp. 10–17.

10. Eisenhower, *Mandate*, p. 116.

11. *Ibid.*, p. 99. Forrestal was concerned at an early date about the relationship between the Cabinet and the NSC. On September 22, 1947, he wrote: "I expressed the view that we would have to be most careful to avoid (a) the appearance of either duplicating or replacing the functions of the Cabinet, and (b) giving the public the impression that our foreign policy was completely dominated by a military point of view." Millis, *Forrestal Diaries*, p. 317.

12. Townsend Hoopes, *The Devil and John Foster Dulles* (Boston: Little, Brown and Company, 1973), p. 193.

13. Eisenhower, *Mandate*, p. 131.

14. *Ibid.*

15. *Ibid.*

16. Huntington, *Common Defense*, p. 87. Although Eisenhower was the first President to regularize the attendance of the Secretary of the Treasury at all National Security Council meetings, Forrestal from the outset had grasped the importance of the economic relationship. On September 17, 1947, he declared: "It is apparent that there is going to be a difference between the Budget, some of the White House staff and ourselves on the National Security Council—its functions, its relationship to the President and myself, I regard it as an integral part of the national defense set-up and believe it was so intended by the Congress." Millis, *Forrestal Diaries*, p. 316.

17. Robert Cutler, "The Development of the National Security Council," *Foreign Affairs*, Vol XXXIV, April 1956, p. 452. Frequent participants in Council deliberations also included Harold Stassen, who was named Special Assistant for Disarmament, following the abolition of the Foreign Operations Administration, the director of which had been a statutory member. Also often present was Rear Admiral Lewis L. Strauss, chairman of the Atomic Energy Commission, the Secretaries and the Chiefs of Staff of the Military Services, the ambassador to the United Nations, and the Secretary of Commerce.

18. Cutler, *No Time*, p. 298.

19. *Ibid.*, p. 313. The Operations Coordinating Board resulted from a study of the Jackson Committee (C.D.) initiated by the President the day following his inaugural. It eliminated the Psychological Strategy Board.

20. Dwight D. Eisenhower, *The White House Years, 1956–1961, Waging Peace* (Garden City, N.Y.: Doubleday & Company, 1965), p. 634.

21. *Ibid.*, p. 366; critics of the NSC under Eisenhower have suggested that agreements were reached at the lowest common denominators. Cutler believed these criticisms invalid. Testifying on May 24, 1960, before a Senatorial Committee he declared, "The NSC provides an excellent forum for vigorous discussion. . . ." He did find that working together with the President they had tended to become "a corporate body rather than . . . agency protagonists. . . ." Jackson, *National Security Council*, p. 121. Cutler emphasizes the importance of putting together a team which in a national emergency could effectively move ahead together: "More important than *what* is planned is that the planners *become accustomed* to working and thinking together on hard problems; enabling them when put to the ultimate test—to arrive more surely at a reasonable plan or policy." Cutler, *No Time*, p. 297.

22. Cutler, "Development," p. 444.

23. Hoxie, *White House*, p. 119.

24. Cutler, *No Time*, p. 296.

25. *Ibid.*, p. 311.

26. Hoopes, *Devil*, pp. 193–194.

27. *Ibid.*, p. 195.

28. Eisenhower, *Mandate*, p. 449.

29. Huntington, *Common Defense*, p. 118.

30. Hoopes, *Devil*, pp. 195–196.

31. Eisenhower, *Mandate*, p. 458.

32. *Ibid.*, p. 452.

33. Huntington, *Common Defense*, p. 81.

34. *Ibid.*, p. 65.

35. Eisenhower, *Mandate*, p. 341.

36. Hoopes, *Devil*, p. 211.

37. Eisenhower, *Mandate*, p. 347.

38. Hoopes, *Devil*, p. 201.

39. *Ibid.*, pp. 178–180.

40. Eisenhower, *Waging Peace*, pp. 58–62.

41. *Ibid.*, pp. 62–95.

42. *Ibid.*, p. 58.

43. Hoopes, *Devil*, p. 374.

45. *Ibid.*, p. 90.

46. Eisenhower, *Mandate*, pp. 454–455.

47. *Ibid.*, p. 455.

48. Michael H. Armacost, *The Politics of Weapons Innovation: The Thor-Jupiter Controversy* (New York: Columbia University Press, 1969), p. 76.

49. *Ibid.*

50. *Ibid.*, p. 42.

51. *Ibid.*, pp. 57–58.

52. *Ibid.*, p. 106.

53. *Ibid.*, pp. 49–51; also Eisenhower, *Mandate*, p. 208.

54. Eisenhower, *Mandate*, pp. 219–220.

55. *Ibid.*, p. 205.

56. *Ibid.*, p. 206.

57. Dwight D. Eisenhower, *Public Papers of the Presidents of the United States, 1957* (Washington, D.C.: U.S. Government Printing Office, 1958), pp. 790–793.

58. *Ibid.*, pp. 790–799.

59. *Ibid.*, pp. 807–815.

60. *Ibid.*, p. 361.

61. Eisenhower, *Waging Peace*, p. 244.

62. Dwight D. Eisenhower, *Public Papers of the Presidents of the United States, 1958* (Washington, D.C.: U.S. Government Printing Office, 1959), pp. 7–9.

63. Eisenhower, *Waging Peace*, pp. 244–245.

64. *Ibid.*, p. 206.

65. Senate Committee on Armed Services, *Hearings*, 1958, quoted in Ries, *Management*, p. 176.

66. Ries, *Management*, p. xvii.

67. Eisenhower, *Waging Peace,* p. 246. Eisenhower believed that even his own people in the executive branch did not understand the operations of the NSC. He found the Congress even more filled with misconceptions. He deplored the idea, which he suspected that Congress was advancing, that the NSC should act by "Committee vote." Such procedure, he discerned, would make the NSC subject to Congressional pressures to add or subtract members according to their persuasions. He emphasized that the NSC was and must be purely advisory and that the President could take its advice or "ignore" it.

68. *Ibid.,* p. 248.

69. *Ibid.,* p. 250.

70. Eisenhower, *Public Papers, 1958,* p. 274.

71. *Ibid.,* pp. 269–290.

72. Eisenhower, *Waging Peace,* p. 250.

73. Eisenhower, *Public Papers, 1958,* p. 310.

74. Eisenhower, *Waging Peace,* p. 250.

75. Eisenhower, *Public Papers, 1958,* p. 313.

76. *Ibid.,* pp. 325–326.

77. *Ibid.,* pp. 326–334.

78. Eisenhower, *Waging Peace,* pp. 251–252.

79. Ries, *Management,* p. 181.

80. *Ibid.,* pp. 184–185.

81. Eisenhower, *Waging Peace,* pp. 252–253.

82. *Ibid.,* p. 253.

83. *Ibid.;* also *Annual Report of the Secretary of Defense, July 1, 1958 to June 30, 1959* (Washington, D.C.: U.S. Government Printing Office, 1960), p. 41.

84. *Ibid.*

85. Huntington, "Interservice Competition," p. 52.

86. Eisenhower, *Public Papers, 1958,* p. 334.

IX. *The Final Eisenhower Years*

1. 86th Congress, 2d Session, Senate Committee on Government Operations. Hearings Before the Subcommittee on National Security Policy Making, Part VII (June 28, July 1, 1960), cited in Francis M. Carney and H. Frank Way, Jr., eds., *Politics 1964* (Belmont, Cal.: Wadsworth, 1964), pp. 83–86. In these hearings Senator Henry Jackson voiced opposition to Rockefeller's proposal for a First Secretary for National Security Affairs, or for assigning such a role to the Vice President. Jackson then contended that in the direction of national security affairs there was no substitute for the President. Jackson, *National Security Council,* pp. 21–29.

2. Milton Eisenhower, *President,* pp. 542–561.

3. Letter from Milton S. Eisenhower to R. Gordon Hoxie, March 11, 1975, in Center for the Study of the Presidency.

4. Eisenhower, *Waging Peace*, pp. 635–637.

5. *Ibid.*, p. 638.

6. Henry A. Kissinger, "Nuclear Testing and the Problem of Peace," *Foreign Affairs*, XXXVII, 1, Oct. 1958, pp. 1–17.

7. Henry A. Kissinger, *The Necessity for Choice* (New York: Harper Brothers, 1961), p. 62.

8. Eisenhower, *Mandate*, p. 454.

9. Eisenhower, *Waging Peace*, p. 272.

10. *Ibid.*, p. 276.

11. *Ibid.*, p. 278.

12. *Ibid.*, p. 260–291.

13. *Ibid.*, p. 303.

14. *Ibid.*, p. 304.

15. Letter from eight members of the Committee on Foreign Relations, United States Senate, to the President of the United States, Aug. 25, 1958, in Francis M. Carney and H. Frank Way, Jr., eds., *Politics 1960* (San Francisco: Wadsworth Publishing Company, Inc., 1960), pp. 230–232.

16. Message of the President to the Congress, in *ibid.*, pp. 233–235.

17. Raymond J. Saulnier, "The Eisenhower Economic Policies," *Presidential Studies Quarterly*, V, 1, Winter 1975, p. 34.

18. *Ibid.*

19. Eisenhower, *Waging Peace*, pp. 515–517.

20. *Ibid.*, pp. 526–527.

21. Milton Eisenhower, *President*, pp. 286–287.

22. Eisenhower, *Waging Peace*, pp. 475, 561–563. This treaty strengthened a 1952 agreement, in terms of both United States involvement in Japan's defense and Japan's role as a partner.

23. *Orbis*, IV (Summer 1960), pp. 137–140.

24. President's Address Before a Joint Session of Congress, April 10, 1975, in *The Department of State Bulletin*, LXXII, 1870 (April 28, 1975), p. 533.

25. Arthur E. Adams, *Readings in Soviet Foreign Policy* (Boston: D. C. Heath and Company, 1961), pp. 326–327.

26. Hoxie, *Presidency*, p. 6.

27. Eisenhower, *Mandate*, pp. 503–531.

28. Eisenhower, *Waging Peace*, p. 33.

29. Letter to Anthony Eden, July 31, 1956, in Appendix B, in *ibid.*, p. 664. See also letters of Sept. 2 and Sept. 6, 1956, *ibid.*, pp. 666–671.

30. Appendix A. in *ibid.*, p. 663.

31. J. C. Hurewitz, ed., *Soviet-American Rivalry in the Middle East*, Proceedings of the Academy of Political Science, XXIX, 3 (New York, 1969), 12–16.

32. Eisenhower, *Crusade*, pp. 437–438.

33. Eisenhower, *Waging Peace*, p. 334.

34. Hoxie, *Presidency*, p. 6.

35. N. S. Khrushchev, *Khrushchev in America* (New York: Crosscurrents Press, 1960), p. 9.

36. *Ibid.*, pp. 10–11.

37. *Ibid.*, p. 229.

38. *Ibid.*, p. 199.

39. Eisenhower, *Waging Peace,* p. 448.

40. Khrushchev, *Khrushchev,* p. 220.

41. Eisenhower, *Waging Peace,* p. 560.

42. *Ibid.*, Appendix BB, p. 712.

43. Hoxie, *White House,* p. 120.

44. Eisenhower, *Waging Peace,* p. 713.

45. *Ibid.*, p. 607.

46. *Ibid.*, p. 611.

47. The first Schlesinger poll is detailed in *Life* magazine, Nov. 1, 1948, p. 65; the second in the *New York Times,* July 29, 1962; and the third poll in *Journal of American History,* LVII (June 1970), 105–113.

48. James David Barber, *The Presidential Character: Predicting Performance in the White House* (Englewood Cliffs, N.J.: Prentice-Hall, 1972).

49. R. Gordon Hoxie in 1974 CBS Summer Semester television series.

50. Letter from Curtis P. Nettels to R. Gordon Hoxie, May 5, 1975, in Center for the Study of the Presidency.

51. "The Principal Achievements of President Dwight D. Eisenhower and His Administration," in Center for the Study of the Presidency.

52. Hoxie, *Presidency,* pp. 7–8.

53. *Ibid.*

54. *Ibid.*

55. *Ibid.*, p. 10.

56. Foreword Statement by Dwight D. Eisenhower in Center for the Study of the Presidency.

57. Eisenhower, *Waging Peace,* p. 622.

58. *Ibid.*, p. 327.

59. Dwight D. Eisenhower, *Public Papers of the Presidents of the United States, 1960–61* (Washington, D.C.: U.S. Government Printing Office, 1961), p. 497.

60. *Ibid.*, p. 503.

61. *Ibid.*, p. 513.

62. *Ibid.*, p. 515.

63. *Ibid.*, p. 518.

64. *Ibid.*, p. 597.

65. May 21, 1975, CBS Radio News.

66. *Public Papers, 1960–61,* p. 930.

67. "The President's Prayer," in Center for the Study of the Presidency.

68. McCloy, CBS interview, July 13, 1975.

69. *Ibid.*

70. Curtis P. Nettels, "Washington and Eisenhower," manuscript in Center for the Study of the Presidency.

71. Truman, *Memoirs,* II, pp. 504–506.

72. *Ibid.*, pp. 505–506.

73. *Ibid.*, p. 513.

74. *Ibid.*, p. 521.

75. Dwight D. Eisenhower, *Public Papers of the Presidents of the United States, 1953* (Washington, D.C.: U.S. Government Printing Office, 1960), pp. 179–180.

76. *Ibid.*, p. 186.

77. Eisenhower, *Public Papers, 1953*, pp. 225–226.

78. *Ibid.*, p. 248.

79. *Ibid.*, p. 250.

80. *Ibid.*, pp. 351–354.

81. *Ibid.*, pp. 328–329.

82. Hoxie, *Presidency*, p. 6.

83. Dwight D. Eisenhower, *Public Papers of the Presidents of the United States, 1959* (Washington, D.C.: U.S. Government Printing Office, 1960), pp. 142–143.

84. *Ibid.*, p. 317.

85. *Ibid.*, p. 723.

86. Edward S. Corwin, in Carney and Way, *Politics 1960*, p. 85.

87. Milton Eisenhower, *President*, p. 258.

88. Milton Eisenhower to R. Gordon Hoxie, March 11, 1975.

89. Jules Archer, *Battlefield President* (New York: Julian Messner, 1967), frontispiece.

90. Milton Eisenhower, *President*, p. 66.

91. Archer, *Battlefield President*, pp. 164–165.

92. Parmet, *Eisenhower*, p. 485.

93. *Ibid.*

94. *Ibid.*, p. 559.

95. Elsie Gallagher, ed., *The Quotable Dwight D. Eisenhower* (Anderson, S.C.: Droke House, 1967), p. 33.

96. Eisenhower, *Public Papers, 1953*, p. 239.

97. Eisenhower, *Public Papers, 1960–61*, p. 1043.

98. *Ibid.*, p. 1038.

X. Democracy's Dilemma

1. Alexis de Tocqueville, *Democracy in America*, ed. by Phillips Bradley, Vol. I (New York: Vintage Books, 1954), pp. 243–245.

2. Clare Booth Luce, "Whatever Happened to the American Century?" *Strategic Review*, III, 3, Summer 1975, pp. 14–21.

3. James R. Schlesinger, "The Military and National Purpose," *Air Force Magazine*, Jan. 1976, p. 14.

4. Aleksandr I. Solzhenitsyn, "Letter to the Soviet Leaders," *Religion in Communist Dominated Areas*, XIV, 1, 2, and 3 (1975), p. 4.

5. *New York Times* (editorial), Jan. 30, 1976.

6. Herman Kahn, *On Thermonuclear War* (Princeton: Princeton University Press, 1960), p. 580.

7. Carleton, *Revolution*, pp. 142–143.

8. Henry Paolucci, *War, Peace, and the Presidency* (New York: McGraw-Hill Book Company, 1968), p. 177.

9. Andrew Gyorgy and George D. Blackwood, *Ideologies in World Affairs* (Waltham, Mass.: Blaisdell Publishing Company, 1967), p. 18.

10. *New York Times*, Feb. 5. 1976.

11. Hoxie, *Presidency*, p. 99.

12. *New York Times*, Feb. 5, 1976.

13. Hoxie, *Presidency*, p. 100.

14. Anderson, in Dunn, *Future*, p. 233.

15. Marian D. Irish, "The President's Foreign Policy Machine" in Dunn, *Future*, p. 174.

16. Cronin, *State of the Presidency*, p. 309.

17. *Ibid*.

18. Schlesinger, *Imperial Presidency*, p. 176.

19. Kahan, *Security*, pp. 82–83.

20. Jacob K. Javits, "The Balance in the War Powers Bill," *New York Times*, Feb. 14, 1972.

21. Koenig, *Chief Executive*, p. 220.

22. Arthur M. Schlesinger, Jr., "Is the Presidency Too Powerful?" *Reader's Digest*, Dec. 1975, p. 88.

23. William E. Griffith, "Congress is Wrecking Our Foreign Policy," *Reader's Digest*, Feb. 1976, p. 75.

24. Robert Novak, in Symposium on the Presidency at the University of California at Irvine, Jan. 12, 1976.

25. Griffith, "Congress," p. 74.

26. *New York Times*, Jan. 15, 1976.

27. *Ibid.*, Jan. 20, 1976.

28. *Ibid.*, Feb. 5, 1976.

29. Anderson, in Dunn, *Future*, p. 231.

30. Relyea, "Emergency Powers," p. vi.

31. Samuel Pitt, "The Shrunken Presidency," in *Long Island Press*, Jan. 25, 1976, p. 6.

32. Schlesinger, *Imperial Presidency*, p. 22.

33. *Ibid.*, p. 51.

34. *Ibid.*, p. 65.

35. *Ibid.*, pp. 69–70.

36. Koenig, *Chief Executive*, p. 250.

37. Clinton Rossiter, *The Supreme Court and the Commander in Chief* (Ithaca, N.Y.: Cornell University Press, 1951), p. 129.

38. Aaron Wildavsky, "The Two Presidencies," in *Transaction*, IV (Dec. 1966), pp. 7–14.

39. Michael A. Genovese, "The Supreme Court as a Check upon Presidential Power," *Presidential Studies Quarterly*, VI, 2, Spring 1976.

40. Berle, "Power," p. 80.

41. Griffith, "Congress," pp. 71–76.

42. Herbert S. Parmet, "Power and Reality: John Foster Dulles and Political Diplomacy," in Merli and Wilson, *Makers*, p. 597.

43. Connecticut Walker, "The Power Behind the Powers in Washington," *Parade*, Nov. 30, 1975, p. 18.

44. Koenig, *Chief Executive*, p. 380.

45. Neustadt, *Presidential Power,* p. 34.
46. *Ibid.,* pp. 10–12.
47. Henry M. Jackson, "An Interim Staff Memorandum," Senate Committee on Government Operations, Subcommittee on National Policy Machinery, Dec. 4, 1959, p. 6; also Jackson, *National Security Council.*
48. Padelford and Lincoln, *International Politics,* p. v.
49. Berle, "Power," pp. 75–80.
50. Schlesinger, "Congress," in Tugwell and Cronin, *Presidency,* p. 111.

XI. From Cold War to Détente

1. Questions from Oct. 25, 1975, planning session for Seventh Annual National Student Symposium, Center for the Study of the Presidency.
2. Eisenhower, *Waging Peace,* p. 611.
3. Hoxie, *White House,* pp. 143–144.
4. *Ibid.,* pp. 131–132.
5. *Ibid.,* p. 144.
6. Hoxie, *Presidency,* p. 17.
7. Schlesinger, *Imperial Presidency,* p. 179.
8. George Reedy, *The Twilight of the Presidency* (New York: World Publishing Co., 1970), p. 80.
9. Hoxie, *Presidency,* p. 17.
10. Schlesinger, *Imperial Presidency,* p. 187.
11. Hoxie, *Presidency,* p. 35.
12. *Ibid.,* pp. 30–32, 35–37.
13. Hoxie, *White House,* p. 182.
14. Robert Strausz-Hupé, "National Strategy in a Bi-Polar World," in George B. de Huzar, ed., *National Strategy in an Age of Revolutions* (New York: Frederick A. Praeger, 1959). p. 3.
15. Michael Howard, "The Classical Strategists," in Richard G. Head and Erwin J. Rokke, eds., *American Defense Policy,* 3rd ed. (Baltimore: The Johns Hopkins University Press, 1973), p. 57.
16. Bernard Brodie, ed., *The Absolute Weapon: Atomic Power and World Order* (New York: Harcourt Brace, 1946), pp. 75–76.
17. Curtis P. Nettels, "The Doctrine of Containment," manuscript in Center for the Study of the Presidency.
18. John Lewis Gaddis, "Harry S. Truman and the Origins of Containment," in Merli and Wilson, *Makers,* p. 507.
19. Parmet, "Power," in *ibid.,* pp. 593–594.
20. Hoxie, *White House,* p. 121.
21. Townsend Hoopes, *The Limits of Intervention* (New York: David McKay, 1969).
22. *New York Times,* Jan. 13, 1954.
23. Head and Rokke, *American Defense Policy,* p. 63.
24. *Ibid.*
25. Eisenhower, *Waging Peace,* p. 363.

26. *Ibid.*, pp. 364–365.

27. Parmet, "Power," in Merli and Wilson, *Makers*, p. 507.

28. Bernard Brodie, "Unlimited Weapons and Limited War," in *Reporter*, Nov. 18, 1954.

29. Ambrose, *Rise to Globalism*, pp. 271–272.

30. Joseph A. Bognall, *A Grand and Global Alliance* (Minneapolis: Burgess Publishing Company, 1968), pp. 11–12.

31. *Ibid.*, p. 21.

32. *Ibid.*, p. 40.

33. Robert N. Ginsburgh, *U.S. Military Strategy in the Sixties* (New York: W. W. Norton & Company, 1965), p. 62.

34. *Ibid.*, p. 84.

35. Howard, "Classical Strategists," in Head and Rokke, *American Defense Strategy*, p. 57.

36. Ambrose, *Rise to Globalism*, p. 295.

37. Brown, "New Posture," p. 17.

38. *NATO Handbook*, Nato Information Service, Brussels, Feb. 1975, p. 16.

39. Sir Peter Hill-Norton, "NATO and the Warsaw Pact: The Balance," *NATO Review*, XXIV, 1 (Feb. 1976), pp. 3–5.

40. See Bernard Brodie, *Escalation and the Nuclear Option* (Princeton: Princeton University Press, 1966).

41. *NATO Handbook*, p. 60.

42. *Ibid.*, p. 63.

43. Ambrose, *Rise to Globalism*, p. 306.

44. *Ibid.*

45. *Ibid.*

46. Carney and Way, *Politics 1964.*

47. Ambrose, *Rise to Globalism*, p. 311.

48. Hoopes, *Limits*, quoted in Ambrose, *Rise to Globalism*, p. 329.

49. Ambrose, *Rise to Globalism*, p. 332.

50. Walter Lippmann, "Elephants Can't Beat Mosquitoes in Vietnam," *Washington Post*, Dec. 3, 1967.

51. Hoxie, *Presidency*, p. ix.

52. *Ibid.*, pp. 91–92.

53. Richard M. Nixon, "U.S. Foreign Policy for the 1970's: Building for Peace," *Department of State Bulletin*, LXIV, 1656 (March 22, 1971), 345.

54. Richard M. Nixon, *For a Generation of Peaceful Development* (Washington, D.C.: Agency for International Development, 1971), p. 6.

55. Hoxie, *White House*, p. 13.

56. *Ibid.*, p. 118.

57. Richard M. Nixon, *U.S. Foreign Policy for the 1970's: A New Strategy for Peace* (Washington, D.C.: U.S. Government Printing Office, 1970), p. 19.

58. *New York Times*, May 23, 1971.

59. Peter L. Sargent and Jack H. Harris, *Chinese Assessment of the Superpower Relationship 1972–74* (Vienna, Va.: The BDM Corporation, June 30, 1975), pp. VI-1–6 and VII-1.

60. Richard M. Nixon, *U.S. Foreign Policy for the 1970's: The Emerging Structure of Peace* (Washington, D.C.: U.S. Government Printing Office, 1972), p. 155.

61. Hoxie, *Presidency,* pp. 91–92.

62. Richard M. Nixon, *U.S. Foreign Policy for the 1970's: Shaping a Durable Peace* (Washington, D.C.: U.S. Government Printing Office, 1973), p. 233.

63. Head and Rokke, *American Defense Policy,* p. 65.

64. Nixon, *Emerging Structure,* p. 157.

65. *White Paper 1970 on the Security of the Federal Republic of Germany and on the State of the German Federal Armed Forces* (Bonn, Germany: The Federal Minister of Defense, 1970), p. 6.

66. William S. Stokes, "Whig Conceptions of Executive Power," *Presidential Studies Quarterly,* VI, 2, Spring 1976, p. 16.

67. Dale Vineyard, *The Presidency* (New York: Charles Scribner's Sons, 1971), p. 16.

68. Tex McCrary in WPIX public affairs telecast, Jan. 17, 1976.

69. Kahan, *Security,* p. 29.

70. Ginsburgh, *U.S. Military Strategy,* pp. 63–64.

71. Joseph A. Cernik, "The Current United States Targeting Doctrine of Nuclear Weapons: An Explanation and Analysis," in *Presidential Studies Quarterly,* VI, 2, Spring 1976, p. 62.

72. *Strategic Review,* Winter 1976, p. 4.

73. Helmut Sonnenfeldt, in remarks to Public Members Association of the Foreign Service, Nov. 13, 1975.

74. *New York Times,* Jan. 20, 1976.

75. BDM Corporation, *Critical Situations: 1976–1977* (Vienna, Va.: BDM Corporation, 1975), p. XIII-23.

XII. Command Decision, Continuity, and Crisis Management

1. Morris, *Hamilton,* p. 500.

2. Joseph A. Bognall, *A Grand and Glorious Alliance* (Minneapolis: Burgess Publishing Company, 1968), pp. 11–12.

3. Transcription of oral tapes in the Center for the Study of the Presidency.

4. J. T. Crown, "Fresh Views of John Kennedy's Life and Work," manuscript in the Center for the Study of the Presidency.

5. Transcription of oral tapes in the Center for the Study of the Presidency.

6. Robert F. Kennedy, *Thirteen Days: A Memoir of the Cuban Missile Crisis* (New York: W. W. Norton & Company, 1969), p. 170.

7. *Ibid.,* p. 47.

8. *Ibid.,* pp. 18–20.

9. *Ibid.*

10. R. Gordon Hoxie, "The Office of Commander in Chief: An Historical and Projective View," *Presidential Studies Quarterly,* VI, 4, Fall 1976, pp. 22–23.

11. James A. Nathan and James K. Oliver, *United States Foreign Policy* (Boston: Little Brown and Co., 1976), p. 252.

12. Lyndon B. Johnson, *The Vantage Point: Perspective of the Presidency 1963-1969* (New York: Holt, Rinehart and Winston, 1971), p.34.

13. Hoxie, *Presidency,* p. 12.

14. Johnson, *Vantage Point,* p. 42.

15. Hoxie, *White House,* p. 194.

16. *Ibid.,* p. 115.

17. Transcription of oral tapes in the Center for the Study of the Presidency.

18. *Ibid.*

19. Johnson, *Vantage Point,* p. 32.

20. *Ibid.,* p. xi.

21. *Ibid.,* p. 492.

22. *Ibid.,* p. 509.

23. Koenig, *Chief Executive,* p. 258.

24. *Ibid.,* p. 257.

25. Letter from Major General Robert N. Ginsburgh to R. Gordon Hoxie, Feb. 20, 1976, Center for the Study of the Presidency.

26. Holtzman et al. *v.* Schlesinger et al. 414 U.S. 1304 (1973).

27. Archibald Cox, "The Role of Congress in Constitutional Determination," *University of Cincinnati Law Review,* XI, pp. 199, 204 (1971).

28. Schlesinger, "Congress and the Making of Foreign Policy," in Tugwell and Cronin, *Presidency,* pp. 104-105.

29. Nathan and Oliver, *Foreign Policy,* p. 488.

30. *Ibid.,* p. 520.

31. *Ibid.*

32. Schlesinger, *Imperial Presidency,* p. 179.

33. *Congressional Record, Senate,* April 21, 1977, p. S6177.

34. *Ibid.*

35. *Ibid.*

36. *Ibid.*

37. *Ibid.*

38. *Ibid.*

39. *Ibid.*

40. Herbert Feis, *Trust to Terror: The Onset of the Cold War, 1945-1950* (New York: W. W. Norton & Company, 1970), p. 6.

XIII. Change of Command

1. Thomas A. Bailey, *The American Pageant* (Boston: D. C. Heath and Company, 1961), p. 66.

2. Eugene V. Rostow, "Response," *Virginia Law Review,* LXI, 4, May 1975, p. 803.

3. *Ibid.,* pp. 801-802.

4. *Congressional Record,* Senate, April 21, 1977, p. 6175.

5. *Strategic Review,* Winter 1977, p. 14.

6. *Policy Analysis on Major Issues,* a compilation of papers prepared for the Commission on the Organization of the Senate (Washington, D.C.: U.S. Government Printing Office, 1977), p. 142.

7. *Ibid.,* p. 143.

8. Michael J. Robinson, "Learning by Doing," manuscript in Center for the Study of the Presidency.

9. *New York Times,* Jan. 27, 1977.

10. *Ibid.,* Jan. 28, 1977.

11. Robinson, "Learning," p. 163.

12. *Wall Street Journal,* Jan. 18, 1977.

13. *Ibid.,* Jan. 28, 1977.

14. Eisenhower, *Waging Peace,* p. 634.

15. Jerome A. Kahan, *Security in the Nuclear Age* (Washington, D.C.: The Brookings Institution, 1975), pp. 26–27.

16. Bach and Sulzner, *Perspectives,* p. 24.

17. *Ibid.,* p. 29.

18. Hoxie, *Presidency,* pp. 110–111.

19. Neil Shaheen and Others, *The Pentagon Papers* (New York: Bantam Books, 1971), p. 158.

20. Ernest S. Griffith, *The American Presidency: The Dilemma of Shared Power and Divided Government* (New York: New York University Press, 1976), p. 70.

21. Richard M. Nixon, *U.S. Foreign Policy for the 1970's: A New Strategy for Peace* (Washington, D.C.: U.S. Government Printing Office, 1970), p. 19.

22. *New York Times,* May 13, 1977.

23. *Ibid.*

24. Letter from Brent Scowcroft to R. Gordon Hoxie, March 16, 1977, in Center for the Study of the Presidency.

25. *New York Times,* Jan. 16 and 23, 1977.

26. *Ibid.,* Jan. 28, 1977.

27. Scowcroft to Hoxie, March 16, 1977.

28. *New York Times,* May 14, 1977.

29. *Ibid.*

30. *Ibid.,* May 10, 1977.

31. *Ibid.,* May 14, 1977.

32. Alexander L. George, "The Case for Multiple Advocacy in Making Foreign Policy," *American Political Science Review,* LXVI, 3 (Sept. 1972), 751.

33. I. M. Destler, "National Security Advice to Presidents" (paper prepared for the Conference on Advising the President), Princeton University (Nov. 1, 1975), pp. 110–111.

34. Rose, "President,"p. 15.

35. Stephen Hess, *Organizing the Presidency* (Washington, D.C.: The Brookings Institution, 1976), p. 144.

36. Hoxie, *Presidency*, p. 4.

37. Hoxie, *White House*, p. 148.

38. *Ibid.*

39. Samuel P. Huntington, *The Soldier and the State* (Cambridge, Mass.: Harvard University Press, 1957), pp. 453–455.

40. Peter Lisagor, "Carter's Cabinet Picks," *Long Island Press*, Dec. 13, 1976.

41. Chambers, "Executive Power," p. 29.

42. *New York Times*, Jan. 24, 1977.

43. See Chapter 8.

44. Kenneth H. Bacon, "Can Carter Cut Defense Spending?" *Wall Street Journal*, Dec. 2. 1976.

45. Jackson, *National Security Council*, p. 44.

46. Hoxie, *White House*, pp. 78–79.

47. *Ibid.*, p. 124.

48. *Ibid.*, p. 123.

49. *Ibid.*, p. 130.

50. Rose, "President," p. 16.

51. Hoxie, *White House*, p. 127.

52. *Ibid.*, pp. 180–181.

53. *Ibid.*, p. 132.

54. John C. Campbell, *Defense of the Middle East: Problems of American Policy* (New York: Harper Brothers, 1958), pp. 121–128.

55. Schlesinger, "Congress," pp. 100–113, *passim.*

56. *New York Times*, Jan. 30, 1977.

57. Hoxie, *White House*, p. 127.

58. Seymour H. Fersh, *The View from the White House* (Washington, D.C.: Public Affairs Press, 1961), p. 135.

59. Herbert Feis, *From Trust to Terror: The Onset of the Cold War, 1945–1950* (New York: W. W. Norton & Company, 1970), p. 113.

60. Hoxie, *Frontiers*, p. 155.

61. *Aim Report*, V, 14 (Nov. 22, 1976), p. 3.

62. *Arms Control Report*, U.S. Arms Control and Disarmament Agency Publication 89, released July 1976, p. 7.

63. Griffith, *American Presidency*, p. 70.

64. Koenig, "President," in Dolce and Skau, *Power*, p. 196.

65. Nixon, *U.S. Foreign Policy for the 1970's—A Report to the Congress*, Feb. 18, 1970, pp. 1–13.

66. Nixon, *U.S. Foreign Policy for the 1970's—The Emerging Structure of Peace*, pp. 46–48.

67. *U.S. News and World Report*, June 2, 1975, p. 21.

68. *New York Times*, May 10, 1977.

69. Cf. the following: John Newhouse, *The Story of SALT* (New York: Holt, Rinehart, and Winston, 1973); William R. Kintner and Robert C. Pfaltzgraff, Jr., eds., *Implications for Arms Control in the 1970's* (Pittsburgh: University of Pittsburgh Press, 1973); and Mason Willrich and John B.

Rhinelander, *SALT: The Moscow Agreements and Beyond* (New York: The Free Press, 1974).

70. Colin S. Gray, "Détente, Arms Control and Strategy: Perspective on SALT," *American Political Science Review*, LXX, 4 (Dec. 1976), 1252.

71. Scowcroft to Hoxie, March 16, 1977.

72. Helmut Sonnenfeldt, "The Atlantic Link: A Common Heritage, a Common Challenge," Department of State news release, Feb. 20, 1976.

73. Millis, *Forrestal Diaries*, p. 355.

74. *New York Times*, May 13, 1977.

75. *New York Times*, Jan. 20, 1977.

76. Robert J. Bresler and Robert C. Gray, "The Bargaining Chips and SALT," *Political Science Quarterly*, XCII, 1 (Spring 1977), 74–78.

77. *New York Times*, Jan. 31, 1977.

78. Captain William V. Ruke, USN (Ret.), "The Cruise Missile: Key to Naval Supremacy," *Strategic Review*, V, 1 (Winter 1977), p. 60.

79. *New York Times*, Jan. 31, 1977.

80. *New York Times*, Feb. 6, 1977.

81. C. L. Sulzberger, *New York Times*, Feb. 19, 1977.

82. *Air Force Association Thirtieth Anniversary Annual Report*, Sept. 1, 1975, Sept. 22, 1976, p. 17.

83. Jack Anderson, "President Unruffled by Alarms," *Long Island Press*, Feb. 6, 1977.

84. *New York Times*, Feb. 6, 1977.

85. Scowcroft to Hoxie, March 16, 1977.

86. Ralph Kinney Bennett, "U.S.-Soviet Military Balance: Who's Ahead?" *Reader's Digest*, Sept. 1976, p. 79.

87. George S. Brown, "National Security Policy and the Nation's Armed Services at 200 Years," *Presidential Studies Quarterly*, VI, 4, Fall 1976, p. 8.

88. *Ibid.* Chairman Brown's statement bears some qualifications, however. According to NATO, the Warsaw Pact has 925,000 troops and 15,000 tanks in central Europe; NATO has 777,000 troops and 6,000 tanks. *New York Times*, Dec. 5, 1976. Admiral of the Fleet, Sir Peter Hill-Norton, chairman of NATO's Military Committee, warns: "Unless we are prepared to pay, even at times of economic difficulty, for a stalwart collective defense, then our ability to defend ourselves will be eroded to the point where an early resort to nuclear weapons will become the only option in terms of deterrence." Hill-Norton, "NATO and the Warsaw Pact," p. 5.

89. *Ibid.*

90. *Ibid.*, p. 4.

91. *Ibid.*

92. Gray, "Détente," p. 1246.

93. *Ibid.*, p. 1249.

94. Nixon, *U.S. Foreign Policy for the 1970's—The Emerging Structure of Peace*, p. 49.

95. *U.S. News and World Report*, June 2, 1975, p. 21.

96. *Ibid.*

97. *Department of State Bulletin*, LXXVI, 1958 (Jan. 3, 1977), 9.

98. Gerald R. Ford, "An Agenda for America's Third Century," *Department of State Bulletin*, LXXII, 1872 (May 12, 1975), p. 595.

99. Scowcroft to Hoxie, March 16, 1977.

100. *New York Times*, Feb. 1, 1977.

101. Joseph Lilyveld, "Our New Voice at the U.N.," *New York Times Magazine*, Feb. 6, 1977, p. 62.

102. W. Howard Chase, *Innovation and Management of Change Letter*, XI, 22 (June 5, 1976).

103. *New York Times*, May 24, 1977.

104. *Time*, May 30, 1977, p. 15.

105. *New York Times*, May 25, 1977.

106. *Ibid.*, May 24, 1977.

107. Washington *Star*, May 24, 1977.

108. *Department of State Bulletin*, LXXIV, 1913 (Feb. 23, 1976), p. 231.

109. Seminar on Business and Public Policy, organized by the Center for the Study of the Presidency and Public Members Association of the Foreign Service, Cairo, Egypt, May 17–19, 1976. A similar mission is conducted by the Center with Israel.

110. *Time*, May 30, 1977, p. 23.

111. *New York Times*, May 25, 1977.

112. *Ibid.*

113. *Time*, May 30, 1977, pp. 34, 36.

114. *Ibid.*, p. 36.

115. *New York Times*, Feb. 7, 1977.

116. Marshall Green, "U.S. Responsibility in World Population Issues," *Department of State Bulletin*, LXXV, 1945 (Oct. 4, 1976), p. 423.

117. Marshall Green in Seventh Annual National Student Symposium, Center for the Study of the Presidency, April 23, 1976.

118. *Department of State Bulletin*, LXXIV, 1913 (Feb. 23, 1976), p. 236.

119. *New York Times*, May 23, 1977.

120. Robert Moss, "Let's Look Out for No. 1!" *New York Times Magazine*, May 1, 1977, p. 100.

121. *New York Times*, May 23, 1977.

122. Moss, "Let's Look Out," p. 100.

123. John P. Wemdemuler, ed., "Industrial Democracy in International Perspective," *Annals of the American Academy of Political and Social Science*, 431 (May 1977), viii–ix.

124. *New York Times*, May 23, 1977.

125. Moss, "Let's Look Out," p. 107.

126. Letter from Henry Hall Wilson to President Carter, Feb. 28, 1977, copy in Center for the Study of the Presidency.

127. "Human Rights Policy," PR 194, Bureau of Public Affairs, Department of State.

128. *Ibid.*

129. *U.S. News & World Report*, June 6, 1977, p. 17.

130. *New York Times*, May 23, 1977.

131. *U.S. News & World Report*, June 6, 1977, p. 17.

132. *New York Times*, Aug. 1977.

XIV. Epilogue

1. Michael P. Richards, "The Presidency and the Ratification Controversy," *Presidential Studies Quarterly*, VII, 1 (Winter 1977), 43.

2. Anthony Lewis, "We Have Really Seen the Future and It Works," *New York Times Magazine*, July 4, 1976, p. 82.

3. Robinson, "President," in Bach and Sulzner, *Perspectives*, p. 381.

4. Berle, "Power," p. 80.

5. In Symposium on the Presidency at Princeton, New Jersey, Nov. 1, 1975.

6. Lewis, "We Have Really Seen," pp. 82–85.

7. Rossiter, *American Presidency*, p. 55.

8. James Bryce, *The American Commonwealth*, Vol. I (London: Macmillan and Co., 1889), p. 61.

9. Lewis, "We Have Really Seen," pp. 82–85.

10. Genovese, "Supreme Court," p. 44.

11. *Department of State Bulletin*, LXXIV, 1911 (Feb. 9, 1976), p. 145.

12. *Ibid.*, p. 148.

13. Corwin, *President's Control*, pp. 203–204.

14. Richard M. Kitchum, *The World of George Washington* (New York: American Heritage Printing Company, 1974), pp. 195–196.

15. Corwin, *President's Control*, p. 132.

16. *Ibid.*

17. *Ibid.*, p. 134.

18. *New York Times*, Nov. 28, 1976.

19. *Department of State Bulletin*, LXXIII, 1899 (Nov. 17, 1975), p. 691.

20. Issue Paper, Committee IV, "The United States and the World," The Bicentennial Conference on the United States Constitution, American Academy of Political and Social Science, 1976, p. 11.

21. *Ibid.*

22. *New York Times*, Jan. 28, 1976.

23. *Ibid.*, Nov. 28, 1976.

24. *Ibid.*

25. Aaron Wildavsky, "The Two Presidencies," in Bach and Sulzner, *Perspectives*, p. 396.

26. Anderson, in Dunn, *Future*, p. 233.

27. John C. Hoy and Melvin H. Bernstein, eds., *The Effective President* (Pacific Palisades Cal.: Palisades Publishers, 1976), p. 46.

28. Anderson, in Dunn, *Future*, p. 231.

29. R. Gordon Hoxie, "Note on the Signing of the National Emergencies Act," in *Presidential Studies Quarterly*, VI, 4 (Fall 1976), p. 63.

30. Griffith, *American Presidency*, p. vii.

31. Louis W. Koenig, "We Will Need a Presidency of Substantial Power," *U.S. News and World Report*, Nov. 8, 1976, p. 22.

32. Hoy and Bernstein, *Effective President*, p. 52.

33. *Long Island Sunday Press*, March 28, 1976.

34. Koenig, "President," in Dolce and Skau, *Power*, p. 194.

35. Corwin, *President's Control*, p. 127.

36. *Long Island Press,* Nov. 21, 1976.

37. Bryce, *American Commonwealth,* p. 63.

38. Clark R. Mollenhoff, *The Pentagon* (New York: G. P. Putnam's Sons, 1967), p. 30.

39. Morton H. Halperin, *Bureaucratic Politics and Foreign Policy* (Washington, D.C.: The Brookings Institution, 1974), p. 65.

40. Robert K. Dornan and Ted Risenhoover to R. Gordon Hoxie, July 29, 1977.

41. Halperin, *Bureaucratic Politics,* p. 34.

42. *USSI Report 76-1,* "U.S. Intelligence at the Crossroads" (Washington, D.C.: United States Strategic Institute, 1976), p. 3.

43. *New York Times,* Feb. 13, 1977.

44. *Ibid.,* Jan. 20, 1976.

45. Thomas L. Hughes, *The Fate of Facts in a World of Man: Foreign Policy and Intelligence Making,* Headline Series No. 233, Dec. 1976, Foreign Policy Association.

46. Mollenhoff, *Pentagon,* p. 411.

47. Hughes, *Fate of Facts,* p. 59.

48. Brown, "National Security Policy," p. 4.

49. Marvin Kalb and Bernard Kalb, *Kissinger* (Boston: Little, Brown and Company, 1974), p. 549.

50. Eisenhower, *Waging Peace,* p. 653.

51. *New York Times,* Feb. 9. 1977.

52. Eisenhower, *Waging Peace,* p. 621.

53. Brown, "National Security Policy," p. 5.

54. *Ibid.*

55. George W. Ball, *Diplomacy for a Crowded World* (Boston: Little, Brown and Company, 1976), p. 89.

56. *Ibid.,* p. 92.

57. *Department of State Bulletin,* LXXV, 1908 (Jan. 18, 1976), p. 70.

58. *New York Times,* Jan. 31, 1977.

59. *Ibid.,* Feb. 9, 1977.

60. *Treasury Papers,* II, 6 (Dec. 1976), p. 3.

61. *Long Island Press,* Feb. 13, 1977.

62. *Ibid.*

63. *New York Times,* Feb. 13, 1977.

64. Brown, "National Security Policy," pp. 5-6.

65. *New York Times,* Jan. 22, 1977.

66. *U.S. News and World Report,* Nov. 22, 1976, p. 65.

67. *World Military Expenditures and Arms Transfers, 1966-1975,* U.S. Arms Control and Disarmament Agency Publication 90 (Washington, D.C.: U.S. Government Printing Office, Dec. 1976), pp. 2-6, 51.

68. Sir Peter Hill-Norton, "Crisis Management," *NATO Review,* XXIV, 5 (Oct. 1976), 9.

69. Hoxie, *White House,* pp. 134-135.

70. Albert Speer, *Inside the Third Reich* (New York: The Macmillan Company, 1970), pp. 374-386.

71. *Department of State Bulletin,* LXXV, 1949 (Nov. 1, 1976), 550.

72. Head and Rokke, *American Defense Policy*, p. ix.

73. W. Scott Thompson and Donald D. Frizzell, eds., *The Lessons of Vietnam* (New York: Crane, Russak and Company, Inc., 1977), p. vi.

74. Hoxie, *Presidency*, pp. 114–115.

75. Henry A. Kissinger, "The Future of American Foreign Policy," Bureau of Public Affairs, Department of State, July 6, 1976.

76. *Department of State Bulletin*, LXXVI, 1961 (Jan. 24, 1977), 69–70.

77. *New York Times*, July 4, 1976.

78. Dwight Waldo, "Reflections on Public Morality," *Presidential Studies Quarterly*, V, 1 (Winter 1975), p. 53.

79. Henry Kissinger, "Moral Principles and Practical Needs," *Department of State Bulletin*, LXXV, 1951 (Nov. 15, 1976), p. 598.

80. Elliot L. Richardson, "The Sexless Orgies of Morality," *New York Times Magazine*, Jan. 23, 1977, p. 33.

81. Irving Kristol, "Post Watergate Morality: Too Good for Our Good?" *New York Times Magazine*, Nov. 14, 1976, p. 55.

82. Alexander Böker, "The Intellectual and Moral Aspects of Defence," *NATO Review*, XXIV, 5 (Oct. 1976), p. 14.

83. *Ibid.*, p. 17.

84. *Ibid.*

85. Russell Kirk, "Is American Decadent?" *Imprimis*, V, 1 (Jan. 1976), p. 4.

86. *Department of State Bulletin*, LXXVI, 1963 (Feb. 7, 1977), 107.

87. *New York Times*, Jan. 20, 1976.

88. *Reader's Digest*, Jan. 1976, p. 50.

89. Miller, *Plain Speaking*, pp. 377–378.

90. Koenig, "President," in Dolce and Skau, *Power*, pp. 197–198.

91. Halperin, *Bureaucratic Politics*, p. 82.

92. *New York Times*, Feb. 20, 1977.

93. *Religion in Communist Dominated Press*, XIV, 1, 2, and 3 (1975), p. 18.

94. James Reston, *New York Times*, Feb. 20, 1977.

95. *New York Times*, Feb. 19, 1977.

96. *Ibid.*

97. Drew Middleton, *New York Times*, Feb. 21, 1977.

98. *New York Times*, Feb. 20, 1977.

99. *Ibid.*, Feb. 21, 1977.

100. *Current Policy*, "Panama Canal Treaty Negotiations," No. 9 (revised), Jan. 1977, Bureau of Public Affairs, Office of Media Services, Department of State.

101. *Wall Street Journal*, Feb. 14, 1977.

102. *New York Times*, June 9, 1977.

103. Bryce, *American Commonwealth*, p. 10.

104. C. L. Sulzberger, "No Farce the Second Time," *New York Times*, June 5, 1977.

105. Henry Paolucci, *War, Peace and the Presidency* (New York: McGraw Hill Book Company, 1968), p. 177.

106. Thomas S. Power, *Design for Survival* (New York: Coward-McCann, Inc., 1964), p. 128.

107. *The Air Reservist*, May 1977, p. 3.

108. Department of State News Release, Bureau of Public Affairs, Office of Media Services, April 6, 1976.

109. Luke 11: 21–22.

110. *New York Times*, Aug. 1, 1976.

111. *Department of State Bulletin*, LXVI, 1979 (May 30, 1977), p. 538.

112. Commonwealth Edison Company, *Report of Annual Meeting of Stockholders*, April 20, 1977, p. 10.

113. Allen W. Dulles, *The Craft of Intelligence* (New York: Harper & Row, 1963), p. 264.

114. Eleanor L. Dulles and Robert D. Crane, *Détente: Cold War Strategies in Transition* (New York: Frederick A. Praeger, 1965), p. 8.

115. Harlan Cleveland, *The Obligations of Power* (New York: Harper & Row, 1966), p. 153.

116. *New York Times*, June 1, 1977.

117. *Ibid.*, June 10, 1977.

118. *Ibid.*

119. *Ibid.*

120. Department of State News Release, Bureau of Public Affairs, Office of Media Services, May 10, 1977.

121. Riccards, "Presidency," p. 45.

122. Department of State News Release, Bureau of Public Affairs, Office of Media Services, July 6, 1976.

123. Truman, "The President's Responsibility," p. 4.

124. *Classified Documents News*, II, 1 (March 1977), p. 1.

125. *Ibid.*, I, 2 (second quarter 1975), p. 1.

126. *Congressional Record*, Senate, April 21, 1977, p. S6177.

127. Department of State News Release, Bureau of Public Affairs, Office of Media Services, June 25, 1976.

128. Felix Morley, *The Foreign Policy of the United States* (New York: Alfred A. Knopf, 1951), p. 148.

129. Truman, *Memoirs*, II, p. 478.

130. Eisenhower, *Public Papers, 1957*, p. 16.

131. Eisenhower, *Waging Peace*, p. 327.

132. *Ibid.*

133. Truman, *Public Papers, 1946*, p. 507.

134. *Department of State Bulletin*, LXXVI, 1963 (Feb. 9, 1977), p. 99.

135. R. Gordon Hoxie, "Freedom and Authority, Retrospect and Prospect," in Lyman Bryson, Louis Finkelstein, R. M. MacIver, and Richard McKeon, eds., *Freedom and Authority in Our Time* (New York: Harper & Brothers, 1953), p. 135.

136. Rose, *Managing*, p. 169.

137. Palsits, *Washington's Farewell Address*, pp. 139–159.

138. Kissinger, *Necessity*, pp. 189, 343.

BIBLIOGRAPHY

The chapter notes indicate specifically cited sources. Some of them are included in the following bibliography representing helpful primary sources as well as principal secondary works.

Documentary Sources and Compilations

Administration of National Security. Senate Committee on Governmental Operations. Staff Reports and Hearings, 89th Cong., 1st Sess., 1965.

Air Force Association Thirtieth Anniversary Annual Report, Sept. 1, 1975–Sept. 27, 1976. Washington, D.C.: Air Force Association, 1976.

Arms Control Report. Washington D.C.: U.S. Arms Control and Disarmament Agency, Publication 89, 1976.

Background Information on the Use of United States Armed Forces in Foreign Countries. Committee on Foreign Affairs House Report, 127, 82nd Cong., 1st Sess., 1951.

Background Information on the Use of United States Armed Forces in Foreign Countries. Library of Congress for the House Committee on Foreign Affairs. Committee Print and Revision, 94th Cong., 1st Sess., 1975.

Commonwealth Edison Company. *Report of Annual Meeting of Stockholders.* April 20, 1977.

Congress, The President, and War Powers. House Committee on Foreign Affairs Hearings, 91st Cong., 2nd Sess., 1970.

Congressional Hearings on the European Recovery Program. Senate Committee on Foreign Relations, 80th Cong., 2nd Sess., 1948.

Congressional Hearings before the Subcommittee on National Security Policy Making. Senate Committee on Government Operations, Part VII, 86th Cong., 2nd Sess., June 28–July 1, 1960.

Congressional Record: Containing the Proceedings and Debates. Washington, D.C.: United States Government Printing Office, 1874 to date.

Congressional Oversight of Executive Agreements. Senate Committee on the Judiciary Hearings, 92nd Cong., 2nd Sess., 1972.

The Constitution of the United States of America: Analysis and Interpretation; Annotation of Cases Decided by the Supreme Court of the United States. Senate Document No. 39, 88th Cong., 1st Sess. Washington, D.C.: United States Government Printing Office, 1964.

Department of Defense. *Annual Reports of the Secretary of Defense.* Washington, D.C.: U.S. Government Printing Office, 1948 to date. (For a number of years these were published on a semi-annual basis.)

Department of Defense. *Second Report of the Secretary of Defense and the Annual Reports of the Secretary of the Army, Secretary of the Navy, Secretary of the Air Force for the Fiscal Year 1949.* Washington, D.C.: United States Government Printing Office, 1950.

Documents Relating to the War Powers of Congress, The President's Authority as Commander-in-Chief and War in Indo-China. Senate Committee on Foreign Relations Committee Print, 91st Cong., 2nd Sess., 1970.

Eisenhower, Dwight D. *Public Papers of the Presidents of the United States, 1953–1961.* 8 vols. Washington, D.C.: United States Government Printing Office, 1958–1961.

Emergency Powers Continuation Act. House Committee on the Judiciary Hearings, 82nd Cong., 2nd Sess., 1952.

Emergency Power Statutes. Senate Special Committee on the Termination of the National Emergency Committee Print, 93rd Cong., 1st Sess., 1973.

Ford, Gerald R. *Remarks on the War Powers Act.* Congressional Record, Senate, April 21, 1977.

————. "State of the Union Message." *The New York Times,* Jan. 12, 1977.

Hamilton, Alexander. *The Papers of Alexander Hamilton,* 25 vols. to date. Harold C. Syrett (ed.) and Jacob E. Cooke (assoc. ed.). New York: Columbia University Press, 1961–1977.

Holtzman et al. v. *Schlesinger et al.* 414, U.S. 1304, 1973.

Human Rights. Selected Documents, No. 5, Bureau of Public Affairs, Department of State, 1977.

Jackson, Henry M., Chairman of Senate Committee on Government Operations Sub-Committee on National Policy Machinery Organizing for National Security. *An Interim Staff Memorandum,* Dec. 4, 1959.

Kennedy, John F. *Public Papers of the Presidents of the United States, 1961–1963.* 3 vols. Washington, D.C.: United States Government Printing Office, 1962–1964.

Laird, Melvin R. *Toward a National Security Strategy of Realistic Deterrence.* Statement of Secretary of Defense Melvin R. Laird in the Fiscal Year 1972–73: Defense Program and the 1972 Defense Budget. Washington, D.C.: United States Government Printing Office, 1971.

Legislative Proposals Relating to the War in Southeast Asia. Senate Committee on Foreign Relations Hearings, 92nd Cong., 1st Sess., 1971.

McCormack, John W., et al. *Astronautics and Space Exploration.* Hearings before the Select Committee on Astronautics and Space Exploration, 85th Cong., 2nd Sess. on HR 11881, April 15–May 12, 1958. Washington, D.C.: United States Government Printing Office, 1958.

Military Assistance Program of 1949. Senate Committees on Foreign Relations and Armed Services Hearings, 81st Cong., 1st Sess., 1949. (Considerable on Presidential War Powers)

The Military Situation in the Far East. Senate Committees on Armed Services and Foreign Relations Hearings, 82nd Cong., 1st Sess., 1951. (Includes MacArthur dismissal)

National Emergency. Senate Special Committee on the Termination of the National Emergency Hearings, Parts 1–3, 93rd Cong., 1st Sess., 1973.

National Military Establishment. *First Report of the Secretary of Defense.* Washington, D.C.: United States Government Printing Office, 1948.

National Security Act of 1947. Public Law 253, 80th Cong., 61 Stat. 495; as amended by Department of Defense Reorganization Act of 1958, August 6, 1958, 72 Stat. 514. 50 USC 401.

NATO Handbook. Brussels: NATO Information Service, Feb. 1975.

Nixon, Richard M. *U.S. Foreign Policy for the 1970's: A New Strategy for Peace.* Washington, D.C.: United States Printing Office, 1970.

———. *U.S. Foreign Policy for the 1970's: Building for Peace.* Washington, D.C.: United States Government Printing Office, 1971.

———. *U.S. Foreign Policy for the 1970's: The Emerging Structure of Peace.* Washington, D.C.: United States Government Printing Office, 1972.

———. *U.S. Foreign Policy for the 1970's: Shaping a Durable Peace.* Washington, D.C.: United States Government Printing Office, 1973.

North Atlantic Treaty. Senate Committee on Foreign Relations Hearings, 81st Cong., 1st Sess., 1949.

Palsits, Victor Hugo (ed.). *Washington's Farewell Address.* New York: Arno Press, Inc., 1971.

"Panama Canal Treaty Negotiations." *Current Policy*, No. 9 (revised). Bureau of Public Affairs, Department of State.

Presidential Orders Pertaining to National Emergency. Washington, D.C.: War Information Office, 1942.

To Promote the Defense of the United States. Senate Foreign Relations Committee Hearings, 77th Cong., 1st Sess., 1941.

P. L. 416, 82nd Cong., 2nd Sess., 1952.

Policy Analysis on Major Issues. A compilation of papers prepared for the Commission on Organization of the Senate. Washington, D.C.: United States Government Printing Office, 1977.

Powers of the President as Commander in Chief of the Army and Navy of the United States. Library of Congress, 1956.

Public Papers of the Presidents of the United States. Washington, D.C.: United States Government Printing Office, 1958 to date. (An indispensable series inaugurated by the publication of the 1957 Eisenhower volume).

Relyea, Harold C. *A Brief History of Emergency Powers in the United States.* Prepared for Special Committee on National Emergencies and Delegated Powers, United States Senate. Washington, D.C.: United States Government Printing Office, 1974.

Resolved that Executive Control of Foreign Policy Should be Significantly Curtailed. Library of Congress House Document 90–298, 90th Cong., 2nd Sess., 1968.

Resolved that the Powers of the Presidency Should be Curtailed. Library of Congress House Document 97–273, 93rd Cong., 2nd Sess., 1974.

Richardson, Elliot L. *Annual Defense Department Report, FY 1974.* Washington, D.C.: United States Government Printing Office, 1973.

———. *Statement of Secretary of Defense before the House Armed Services*

Committee on the FY 1974 Defense Budget and FY 1974–1978 Program, April 10, 1973. Washington, D.C.: United States Government Printing Office, 1973.

Russell, Richard B., et al. Hearings before the Senate Committee on Armed Services, 85th Cong., 2nd Sess. on HR 12.541 Defense Department Reorganization Act.

Seizure of the Mayagüez. House Committee on International Relations Hearings, Parts 1–2, 94th Cong., 1st Sess., 1975.

Seminar on Business and Public Policy. Organized by the Center for the Study of the Presidency and Public Members Association of the Foreign Service, Cairo, Egypt, May 17–19, 1976. Papers in the Center for the Study of the Presidency. (A similar program to be conducted in Israel in 1977.)

The State of the Union Messages of the Presidents of the United States. 3 vols. New York: R. R. Bowker Company, 1971.

The Department of State Bulletin. Washington, D.C.: United States Government Printing Office, 1901 to date. (The official weekly record of U.S. foreign policy)

The Steel Seizure Case. House Document 534, 82nd Cong., 2nd Sess., 1952.

Supplemental Foreign Assistance for Fiscal Year 1966: Vietnam. Senate Committee on Foreign Relations Hearings, 89th Cong., 2nd Sess., 1966. (Includes testimony by Secretary of State Dean Rusk, General James Gavin, George Kennan, and General Maxwell Taylor.)

Treaties and Executive Agreements. Senate Judiciary Committee Hearings, 82nd Cong., 2nd Sess., 1952; 83rd Cong., 1st Sess., 1953. (On Bricker Amendment)

Truman, Harry S. Public Papers of the Presidents of the United States, 1945–1953. 8 vols. Washington, D.C.: United States Government Printing Office, 1961–1966.

Unification and Strategy. Report of Investigation by the Committee on Armed Services. House of Representatives Doc. No. 600, 81st Cong., 2nd Sess., 1950.

U.S. Commitments to Foreign Powers. Senate Committee on Foreign Relations Hearings, 90th Cong., 1st Sess., 1967.

U.S. Foreign Policy for the 1970's. Library of Congress for the House Committee on Foreign Affairs. Committee Print, 1971–73. (Analysis of President Nixon's Foreign Policy Reports to Congress)

USSI Report 76-1. "U.S. Intelligence at the Crossroads." Washington, D.C.: United States Strategic Institute, 1976.

United States Foreign Policy 1969–70. A Report of the Secretary of State. Washington, D.C.: United States Government Printing Office, 1971.

United States Foreign Policy 1971. A Report of the Secretary of State. Washington, D.C.: United States Government Printing Office, 1972.

United States Foreign Policy 1972. A Report of the Secretary of State. Washington, D.C.: United States Government Printing Office, 1973.

United States Government Organization Manual. Washington, D.C.: United States Government Printing Office, 1935 to date. (Published annually)

United States Security Agreements and Commitments. Senate Committee on Foreign Relations Hearings, Parts 1-10, 91st Cong., 1st and 2nd Sess., 1969-1970.

Vandenberg, A. H., Jr. (ed.). *The Private Papers of Senator Vandenberg.* Boston: Houghton Mifflin Company, 1952.

War Powers. House Committee on Foreign Affairs Hearings, 93rd Cong., 1st Sess., 1973.

War Powers Legislation. Senate Committee on Foreign Relations Hearings, 92nd Cong., 1st Sess., 1971.

War Powers Legislation. Senate Committee on Foreign Relations Hearings, 93rd Cong., 1st Sess., 1973.

The War Powers Resolution: Relevant Documents, Correspondence, and Reports. House Committee on International Relations. Committee Print, 94th Cong., 1st Sess., 1975.

War Powers: A Test of Compliance. House Committee on International Relations Hearings, 94th Cong., 1st Sess., 1975.

Weekly Compilation of Presidential Documents. Washington, D.C.: United States Government Printing Office, 1965 to date.

White Paper 1970 on the Security of the Federal Republic of Germany and on the State of the German Federal Armed Forces. Bonn, Germany: The Federal Minister of Defense, 1970.

World Military Expenditures and Arms Transfers, 1966–1975. Publication 90. Washington, D.C.: U.S. Arms Control and Disarmament Agency, 1976.

Letters and Manuscripts

Analytical Digest of Testimony before the Senate Military Affairs Committee, Oct. 17 to Dec. 17, 1945, and of the President's Message to the Congress, Dec. 19, 1945. (In Office of Air Force History, Washington, D.C.).

Carter, James E., Jr., to Henry Hall Wilson, March 12, 1977. (Center for the Study of the Presidency).

Crown, J. T. "Fresh Views of John Kennedy's Life and Work." (Center for the Study of the Presidency).

Destler, I. M. "National Security Advice to Presidents." Paper prepared for conference, "Advising the Presidents," Princeton University, 1975.

Eisenhower, Dwight D. "Foreword Statement." (Center for the Study of the Presidency.)

———. "The President's Prayer." (Center for the Study of the Presidency.)

Eisenhower, Milton S. to R. Gordon Hoxie, March 11, 1975. (Center for the Study of the Presidency.)

Ford, Gerald R. "Foreword Statement." (Center for the Study of the Presidency.)

Ginsburgh, Major General Robert N., to R. Gordon Hoxie, Feb. 20, 1976. (Center for the Study of the Presidency.)

Issue Paper, Committee IV, "The United States and the World." The Bicentennial Conference on the United States Constitution. American Academy of Political and Social Science, 1976.

Johnson, U. Alexis. "Interview: President Kennedy and Crisis Management." (Center for the Study of the Presidency.)

Kennan, George. "Interview: President Kennedy and Crisis Management." (Center for the Study of the Presidency.)

Lady, Harold Wendell to R. Gordon Hoxie, Oct. 10, 1975. Account of a meeting between President Syngman Rhee, Lt. General John B. Coulter, Deputy United Nations Commander, and Dr. Lady in Dec. 1954 at Rhee's residence in Seoul, Korea. (Center for the Study of the Presidency.)

Nettels, Curtis P. "Washington and Eisenhower." (Center for the Study of the Presidency.)

————. "The Doctrine of Containment." (Center for the Study of the Presidency.)

————, to R. Gordon Hoxie, May 5, 1975. (Center for the Study of the Presidency.)

Nixon, Richard M., to R. Gordon Hoxie, May 2, 1973. (Center for the Study of the Presidency.)

Nizolek, Michael J. *The Origins of the National Security Act of 1947.* A Senior Thesis submitted to the Faculty of the Department of History, Fordham University, May 1972, New York City. (Center for the Study of the Presidency.)

Questions from Oct. 25, 1975, Planning Session for Seventh Annual National Student Symposium. (Center for the Study of the Presidency.)

Robinson, Michael J. "Learning by Doing." (Center for the Study of the Presidency.)

Scrivener, John Henry. *Pioneers into Space: A Biography of Major General Orvil Arson Anderson.* Unpublished dissertation. Norman: University of Oklahoma, 1971.

Scowcroft, Brent, to R. Gordon Hoxie, March 16, 1977. (Center for the Study of the Presidency.)

Snyder, William P. *Making U.S. National Security Policies.* Carlisle Barracks, Pa.: U.S. Army War College, 1973.

Wilson, Henry Hall, to President Carter, Feb. 28, 1977. (Center for the Study of the Presidency.)

Articles and Essays

Alsop, Joseph. "The Challenge America Must Meet." *Reader's Digest,* Aug. 1975.

Anderson, Jack. "President Unruffled by Alarm." *Long Island Press,* Feb. 6, 1977.

Anderson, John B. "A Republican Looks at the Presidency." In Charles W.

Dunn (ed.), *The Future of the American Presidency*. Morristown, New Jersey: General Learning Press, 1975.

Bacon, Kenneth H. "Can Carter Cut Defense Spending?" *Wall Street Journal*, Dec. 2, 1976.

Bailey, Harry A., Jr. "Controlling the Runaway Presidency." *Public Administration Review*, 35, 5, Sept./Oct. 1975.

Baldwin, Hanson W. "After Vietnam—What Military Strategy in the Far East?" *The New York Times Magazine*, June 9, 1968.

Bennett, Ralph Kinney, and Graham, Daniel O. "U.S. Soviet Military Balance: Who's Ahead?" *Reader's Digest*, 109, 653, Sept. 1976.

Berger, Henry W. "Bi-Partisanship, Senator Taft and the Truman Administration." *Political Science Quarterly*, 90, 2, 1975.

Berle, Adolf A. "Power in Foreign Relations." In Rexford G. Tugwell and Thomas E. Cronin (eds.), *The Presidency Reappraised*. New York: Praeger Publishers, 1974.

Bernstein, Barton, Jr. "Doomsday II." *The New York Times Magazine*. July 27, 1975.

Böker, Alexander. "The Intellectual and Moral Aspects of Defense." *NATO Review*, 24, 5, Oct. 1976.

Bresler, Robert J., and Gray, Robert C. "The Bargaining Chips and SALT." *Political Science Quarterly*, 92, 1, Spring 1977.

Brodie, Bernard. "Unlimited Weapons and Limited War." *Reporter*, Nov. 18, 1954.

Brown, L. Dean. "A New Posture Abroad." *Presidential Studies Quarterly*, V, 4, Fall 1975.

Brown, George S. "National Security Policy and the Nation's Armed Services at 200 Years." *Presidential Studies Quarterly*, VI, 4, Fall 1976.

Burkholder, Donald R. "Caretakers of the Presidential Image." *Presidential Studies Quarterly*, V, I, Winter 1975.

Carter, James Earl, Jr. "Humane Purposes in Foreign Policy." Address at University of Notre Dame, May 22, 1977. News Release, Bureau of Public Affairs, Department of State.

————. "The North Atlantic Alliance." News Release, London, May 10, 1977. Bureau of Public Affairs, Department of State.

Cernik, Joseph A. "The Current United States Targeting Doctrine." *Presidential Studies Quarterly*, VI, 2, Spring 1976.

Chambers, Raymond L. "The Executive Power: A Preliminary Study of the Concept and of the Efficacy of Presidential Directives." *Presidential Studies Quarterly*, VII, 1, Winter 1977.

Chase, W. Howard. *Innovation and Management of Change Letter*. XI, 22, June 5, 1976.

Cox, Archibald. "The Role of Congress in Constitutional Determination." *University of Cincinnati Law Review*, 40, Summer 1971.

Cutler, Robert. "The Development of the National Security Council." *Foreign Affairs*, 34, 3, April 1956.

Drucker, Peter. "How to Make the Presidency Manageable." *Fortune*, Nov. 1974.

Ferrell, Robert H., and McLillan, David. "Dean Acheson, Architect of a Manageable World Order." in Frank J. Merli and Theodore A. Wilson (eds.), *Makers of American Diplomacy*. New York: Charles Scribner's Sons, 1974.

Fisher, Louis. "War Powers: A Need for Legislative Reassertion." In Rexford G. Tugwell and Thomas E. Cronin (eds.), *The Presidency Reappraised*. New York: Praeger Publishers, 1974.

Ford, Gerald R. "An Agenda for America's Third Century." *Department of State Bulletin*, LXII, 1872, May 12, 1975.

Fox, Harrison W., Jr., and Hammond, Susan Webb. "The Growth of Congressional Staffs." In Harvey C. Mansfield (ed.), *Congress Against the President*. Proceedings of the Academy of Political Science, XXXII, 1, 1975.

Fulbright, J. W. "The Decline—and Possible Fall—of Constitutional Democracy in America." In Stanley Bach and George T. Sulzner (eds.), *Perspective on the Presidency*. Lexington, Massachusetts: D. C. Heath and Company, 1974.

Gaddis, John Lewis. "Harry S. Truman and the Origins of Containment." in Frank J. Merli and Theodore A. Wilson (eds.), *American Makers of Diplomacy*. New York: Charles Scribner's Sons, 1974.

Genovese, Michael A. "The Supreme Court as a Check on Presidential Power." *Presidential Studies Quarterly*, VI, 2, Spring 1976.

George, Alexander L. "The Case for Multiple Advocacy in Making Foreign Policy." *American Political Science Review*, LXVI, 3, Sept. 1972.

Ginsburgh, Robert N. "The Challenge to Military Professionalism." In Frank R. Barnett, William C. Mott, and John C. Neff (eds.), *Peace and War in the Modern Age*. Garden City, New York: Doubleday and Company, Inc., 1965.

Graebner, Norman P. "Presidential Power and Foreign Affairs." In Charles W. Dunn (ed.), *The Future of the American Presidency*. Morristown, New Jersey: General Learning Press, 1975.

Gray, Colin S. "Détente, Arms Control and Strategy: Perspective on SALT." *American Political Science Review*, LXX, 4, Dec. 1976.

Green, Marshall. "U.S. Responsibility in World Population Issues." *Department of State Bulletin*, LXXIV, 1913, Feb. 23, 1976.

Greenstein, Fred I. "The Psychological Functions of the Presidency for Citizens." In E. Cornwall, Jr. (ed.), *The American Presidency: Vital Center*. Glenview, Ill.: Scott Foresman, 1966.

Griffith, William E. "Congress Is Wrecking Our Foreign Policy." *Reader's Digest*, Feb. 1976.

Haider, Donald. "Management and the Presidency: from Preparation to Performance." *Presidential Studies Quarterly*, VI, 2, Spring 1976.

Hamilton, Alexander. "Measures of Defense" (1799). In Richard B. Morris, *Alexander Hamilton and the Founding of the Nation*. New York: Dial Press, 1957.

Hammond, Paul Y. "Super Carriers and B-36 Bombers: Appropriations,

Strategy and Politics." In Harold Stein (ed), *American Civil-Military Decisions*. Birmingham: University of Alabama Press, 1963.

Heaphy, Maura E. "Executive Legislative Liaison." *Presidential Studies Quarterly*, V, 1, Fall 1975.

Henkin, Louis. "A More Effective System for Foreign Relations: The Constitutional Framework." *Virginia Law Review*, 61, 4, May 1975.

Hill-Norton, Peter. "Crisis Management." *NATO Review*, XXIV, 5, Oct. 1976.

———. "NATO and the Warsaw Pact: The Balance." *NATO Review*, XXIV, 1, Feb. 1976.

Howard, Michael. "The Classical Strategists." In Richard G. Head and Erwin J. Rokke (eds.), *American Defense Policy*, Third Edition. Baltimore: The Johns Hopkins University Press, 1973.

Hoxie, R. Gordon. "Comments on the Presidency." In Joseph M. Ray (ed.), *The Coattailless Landslide*. El Paso, Texas: Western Press, 1974.

———. "Freedom and Authority, Retrospect and Prospect." In Lyman Bryson, Louis Finkelstein, R. M. MacIver, and Richard McKeon (eds.), *Freedom and Authority in Our Time*. New York: Harper & Brothers, 1953.

———. "Herbert Hoover: Multi-National Man." *Presidential Studies Quarterly*, VII, 1, Winter 1977.

———. "Notes on the Signing of the National Emergencies Act." *Presidential Studies Quarterly*, VI, 4, Fall 1976.

———. "The Office of Commander in Chief: An Historical and Projective View." *Presidential Studies Quarterly*, VI, 4, Fall 1976.

———. "Presidential Greatness." In Philip C. Dolce and George H. Skau, *Power and the Presidency*. New York: Charles Scribner's Sons, 1976.

———. "Who Owns Presidential Papers?" *Presidential Studies Quarterly*, V, 1, Winter 1975.

Huntington, Samuel P. "Interservice Competition and the Political Roles of the Armed Services." *American Political Science Review*, LV, 1, March 1961.

Irish, Marian D. "The President's Foreign Policy Machine." In Charles W. Dunn (ed.), *The Future of the American Presidency*. Morristown, New Jersey: General Learning Press, 1975.

Javits, Jacob K. "The Balance in the War Powers Bill." *The New York Times*, Feb. 14, 1972.

Kirk, Russell. "Is America Decadent?" *Imprimis*, V, 1, Jan. 1976.

Kissinger, Henry A. "The Future of American Foreign Policy." Bureau of Public Affairs, Department of State, July 6, 1976.

———. "Missiles and the Western Alliance." *Foreign Affairs*, XXXVI, 3, April 1958.

———. "Moral Principle and Practical Needs." *Department of State Bulletin*, LXXV, 1951, Nov, 15, 1976.

———. "Nuclear Testing and the Problem of Peace." *Foreign Affairs*, XXXVII, 1, Oct. 1958.

Koenig, Louis W. "The President as Commander in Chief." In Philip C. Dolce and George H. Skau (eds.), *Power and the Presidency*. New York: Charles Scribner's Sons, 1976.

————. "We Will Need a Presidency of Substantial Power." *U.S. News and World Report*, Nov. 8, 1976.

Kristol, Irving. "Post Watergate Morality: Too Good for Our Good?" *The New York Times Magazine*, Nov, 14, 1976.

Lawrence, David. "What Hath Man Wrought?" *U.S. News*, Aug. 17, 1945, reprinted in *U.S. News and World Report*, July 21, 1975.

Lewis, Anthony. "We Have Really Seen the Future and It Works." *The New York Times Magazine*, July 4, 1976.

Lilyveld, Joseph. "Our New Voice at the U.N." *The New York Times Magazine*, Feb. 6, 1977.

Lippmann, Walter. "Elephants Can't Beat Mosquitoes in Vietnam." *Washington Post*, Dec. 3, 1967.

Lisagor, Peter. "Carter's Cabinet Picks." *Long Island Press*, Dec. 13, 1976.

Luce, Clare Booth. "Whatever Happened to the American Century?" *Strategic Review*, III, 3, Summer 1975.

Moss, Robert. "Let's Look Out for No. 1!" *The New York Times Magazine*, May 1, 1977.

Nettels, Curtis P. "Alexander Hamilton and the Presidency." *Presidential Studies Quarterly*, V, 1, 1975.

Neumann, William L. "Roosevelt's Foreign Policy Decisions, 1940–1945." *Modern Age*, XIX, 3, Summer 1975.

Nixon, Richard M. "U.S. Foreign Policy for the 1970's: Building for Peace." *Department of State Bulletin*, LXIV, 1656, March 22, 1971.

Parmet, Herbert S. "Power and Reality: John Foster Dulles and Political Diplomacy." In Frank J. Merli and Theodore A. Wilson (eds.), *Makers of American Diplomacy*. New York: Charles Scribner's Sons, 1974.

Patterson, Thomas G. "The Search for Meaning: George F. Kennan and American Foreign Policy." In Stanley Bach and George T. Sulzner (eds.), *Perspective on the Presidency*. Lexington, Massachusetts: D. C. Heath and Company, 1974.

Pett, Samuel, "The Shrunken Presidency." *Long Island Press*, Jan. 25, 1976.

Riccards, Michael P. "The Presidency and the Ratification Controversy." *Presidential Studies Quarterly*, VII, 1, Winter 1977.

Richardson, Elliot L. "The Sexless Orgies of Morality." *The New York Times Magazine*, Jan. 23, 1977.

Ritkin, R. B. "The Surrender Aboard the USS Missouri Thirty Years Ago." *American Legion Magazine*, Aug. 1975.

Robinson, Donald L. "The President as Commander in Chief." In Stanley Bach and George T. Sulzner (eds.), *Perspectives on the Presidency*. Lexington, Massachusetts: D. C. Heath and Company, 1974.

Roche, John P. "On Being Strident." *Long Island Press*. Feb. 13, 1977.

Rose, Richard. "The President: A Chief but not an Executive." *Presidential Studies Quarterly*, VII, 1, Winter 1977.

Rostow, Eugene V. "Response." *Virginia Law Review*, 6, 4.

Ruke, William V. "The Cruise Missile: Key to Naval Supremacy." *Strategic Review*, V, 1, Winter 1977.

Saulnier, Raymond J. "The Eisenhower Economic Policies." *Presidential Studies Quarterly*, V, 1, Winter 1975.

Schick, Allen. "The Battle of the Budget." In Harvey C. Mansfield, Sr. (ed.), *Congress Against the President*. New York: Proceedings of the Academy of Political Science, XXXII, 1, 1975.

Schlesinger, Arthur M., Jr. "Congress and the Making of Foreign Policy." In Rexford G. Tugwell and Thomas E. Cronin (eds.), *The Presidency Reappraised*. New York: Praeger Publishers, 1974.

———. "Is the Presidency Too Powerful?" *Reader's Digest*, Dec. 1975.

Schlesinger, James R. "The Military and National Purpose." *Air Force Magazine*, January 1976.

Simon, William E. "On Détente." *Treasury Papers*, II, 6, Dec. 1976.

Solzhenitsyn, Aleksandr I. "Letter to the Soviet Leaders." *Religion in Communist Dominated Areas*, XIV, No. 1, 2, 3, 1975.

Sonnenfeldt, Helmut. "The Atlantic Link: A Common Heritage, a Common Challenge." Bureau of Public Affairs, Department of State, Feb. 20, 1976.

Souers, S. W. "Policy Formulation for National Security." *American Political Science Review*, XLIII, 2, June 1949.

Stokes, William S. "Whig Conceptions of Executive Power." *Presidential Studies Quarterly*, VI, 2, Spring 1976.

Strausz-Hupé, Robert. "National Strategy in a Bi-Polar World." George de Huzar (ed.), *National Strategy in an Age of Revolutions*. New York: Frederick A. Praeger, 1959.

Sulzberger, C. L. "No Farce the Second Time." *The New York Times*, June 5, 1977.

Symington, W. Stuart. "Reorganization Plan." *Air Force and Space Digest*, Jan. 1961.

Truman, Harry S. "The President's Responsibility." *Military Review*, XLII, 9, Sept. 1962.

Vance, Cyrus R. "Human Rights Policy." Address delivered at the University of Georgia School of Law, April 30, 1977. PR 194, Bureau of Public Affairs, Department of State, 1977.

Waldo, Dwight. "Reflections on Public Morality." *Presidential Studies Quarterly*, V, 1, Winter 1975.

Walker, Connecticut. "The Power Behind the Powers in Washington." *Parade*, Nov. 30, 1975.

Windmuller, John P. (ed.). "Industrial Democracy in International Perspective." *Annals of the American Academy of Political and Social Science*, 431, May 1977.

Wildavsky, Aaron. "The Two Presidencies." In Stanley Bach and George T. Sulzner (eds.), *Perspectives on the Presidency*, Lexington, Massachusetts: D. C. Heath and Company, 1974.

Wyeth, G. A., Jr. "The National Security Council: Concept of Operations;

ography*277

Organization; Actual Operations." *Journal of International Affairs*, 8, 1954.
Zuckert, Eugene M. "The Service Secretary: Has He a Useful Role in Foreign Affairs?" *Foreign Affairs*, 44, 3, April 1966.

Books

Acheson, Dean. *Present at the Creation: My Years in the State Department.* New York: W. W. Norton & Company, Inc., 1969.
Adams, Arthur E. *Readings in Soviet Foreign Policy.* Boston: D. C. Heath and Company, 1968.
Albion, Robert G., and Connery, Robert H. *Forrestal and the Navy.* New York: Columbia University Press, 1962.
Alperovitz, Gar A. *Atomic Diplomacy: Hiroshima and Potsdam.* New York: Simon and Schuster, 1965.
Ambrose, Stephen E. *Rise to Globalism.* Baltimore: Penguin Books, Inc., 1971.
Anderson, Donald F. *William Howard Taft.* Ithaca, New York: Cornell University Press, 1973.
Archer, Jules. *Battlefield President.* New York: Julian Messner, 1967.
Armacost, Michael H. *The Politics of Weapons Innovation: The Thor-Jupiter Controversy.* New York: Columbia University Press, 1969.
Bach, Stanley and Sulzner, George T. (eds.). *Perspectives on the Presidency.* Lexington, Massachusetts: D. C. Heath and Company, 1974.
Bennett, Frank R., Mott, William C., and Neff, John C. (eds.). *Peace and War in the Modern Age.* Garden City, New York: Doubleday & Company, Inc., 1965.
Bailey, Thomas A. *The American Pageant.* Boston: D. C. Heath and Company, 1961.
———. *Presidential Greatness: The Image and the Man from George Washington to the Present.* New York: Appleton-Century-Crofts, 1966.
Ball, George W. *Diplomacy for a Crowded World.* Boston: Little, Brown and Company, 1976.
Barber, James David. *The Presidential Character, Predicting Performance in the White House.* Englewood Cliffs, New Jersey: Prentice-Hall, Inc., 1972.
BDM Corporation. *Critical Situations: 1976–1977.* Vienna, Virginia: BDM Corporation, 1975.
Berger, Carl. *The Korean Knot.* Philadelphia: University of Pennsylvania Press, 1968.
Bognall, Joseph A. *A Grand and Global Alliance.* Minneapolis: Burgess Publishing Company, 1968.
Brodie, Bernard (ed.). *The Absolute Weapon: Atomic Power and World Order.* New York: Harcourt Brace, 1946.
———. *Escalation and the Nuclear Option.* Princeton, New Jersey: Princeton University Press, 1966.

Brown, Stuart Gerry. *The American Presidency: Leadership, Partisanship, and Popularity.* New York: Macmillan, 1966.

Bryce, James. *The American Commonwealth.* 2 vols. London: Macmillan and Company, 1889.

Burns, James MacGregor. *Roosevelt: the Lion and the Fox.* New York: Harcourt, Brace and Company, 1956.

Califano, J. A. *A Presidential Nation.* New York: Norton, 1975.

Campbell, John C. *Defense of the Middle East: Problems of American Policy.* New York: Harper & Brothers, 1958.

Caraley, Demetrios. *The Politics of Military Unification: A Study of Conflict and the Policy Process.* New York: Columbia University Press, 1966.

Carleton, William G. *The Revolution in American Foreign Policy.* Revised. New York: Random House, Inc., 1957.

Carney, Francis M., and Way, H. Frank (eds.). *Politics 1960.* San Francisco: Wadsworth, 1960.

——. *Politics 1964.* Belmont, California: Wadsworth, 1964.

Clark, J. J. with Reynolds, Clark G. *Carrier Admiral.* New York: David McKay Company, Inc., 1967.

Clark, Keith C. and Legere, L. S. (eds.). *The President and the Management of National Security.* New York: Frederick A. Praeger, 1969.

Cleveland, Harlan. *The Obligations of Power.* New York: Harper & Row, 1966.

Cochran, Burt. *Harry Truman and the Crisis Presidency.* New York: Funk & Wagnalls, 1973.

Commager, Henry Steele. *The Defeat of America: Presidential Power and the National Character.* New York: Simon and Schuster, 1974.

Cooke, Jacob E. (ed.). *The Federalist.* Middletown, Connecticut: Wesleyan University Press, 1961.

Cornwall, E., Jr. (ed.). *The American Presidency: Vital Center.* Glenview, Illinois: Scott Foresman, 1966.

Corwin, Edward S. *The President's Control of Foreign Relations.* Princeton, New Jersey: Princeton University Press, 1917.

——. *The President: Office and Powers, 1787–1957.* New York: New York University Press, 1957.

Cronin, Thomas E. *The State of the Presidency.* Boston: Little, Brown and Company, 1975.

Crown, James Tracey. *The Kennedy Literature: A Bibliographical Essay on John F. Kennedy.* New York: New York University Press, 1968.

Cutler, Robert. *No Time for Rest.* Boston: Little, Brown and Company, 1965.

Daniels, Jonathan. *The Man of Independence.* Philadelphia: Lippincott, 1950.

Dietze, Gottfried. *The Federalist.* Baltimore: The John Hopkins Press, 1960.

Dolce, Philips C., and Skau, G. H. (eds.). *Power and the Presidency.* New York: Charles Scribner's Sons, 1976.

Dulles, Allen W. *The Craft of Intelligence.* New York: Harper & Row, 1963.

Dulles, Eleanor L., and Crane, Robert D. *Détente: Cold War Strategies in Transition.* New York: Frederick A. Praeger, 1965.

Dunn, Charles W. (ed.). *The Future of the American Presidency.* Morristown, New Jersey: General Learning Press, 1975.

Eagleton, Thomas F. *War and Presidential Power: A Chronicle of Congressional Surrender.* New York: Liveright, 1974.

Eisenhower, Dwight D. *Crusade in Europe.* Garden City, New York: Permabooks, 1952.

———. *The White House Years, 1953–1956: Mandate for Change.* Garden City, New York: Doubleday & Company, Inc., 1963.

———. *The White House Years, 1956–1961: Waging Peace.* Garden City, New York: Doubleday and Company, Inc., 1965.

Eisenhower, John S. D. *Strictly Personal.* Garden City, New York: Doubleday & Company, Inc., 1974.

Eisenhower, Milton S. *The President Is Calling.* Garden City, New York: Doubleday & Company, Inc., 1974.

Ekirch, Arthur A. *The Civilian and the Military.* New York: Oxford University Press, 1956.

Emme, Eugene M. *The Impact of Air Power.* New York: Van Nostrand Reinhold Company, 1959.

Farrand, Max. *The Framing of the Constitution of the United States.* New Haven: Yale University Press, 1926.

Feis, Herbert. *The China Tangle: The American Effort in China from Pearl Harbor to the Marshall Mission.* Princeton, New Jersey: Princeton University Press, 1953.

———. *Trust to Terror: The Onset of the Cold War, 1945–1950.* New York: W. W. Norton & Company, 1970.

Fersh, Seymour H. *The View from the White House.* Washington, D.C.: Public Affairs Press, 1961.

Fisher, Louis. *President and Congress: Power and Policy.* New York: The Free Press, 1972.

Gallagher, Elsie (ed.). *The Quotable Dwight D. Eisenhower.* Anderson, South Carolina: Droke House, 1967.

Ginsburgh, Robert N. *U.S. Military Strategy in the Sixties.* New York: W. W. Norton & Company, 1965.

Ginsburgh, Robert N., Hamilton, Richard L., Mulligan, John L., and Ohlinger, John F. (eds.). *The Nixon Doctrine and Military Strategy.* Maxwell Air Force Base, Alabama: Air University, 1971.

Graber, Doris A. *Public Opinion, the President, and Foreign Policy: Four Case Studies from the Formative Years.* New York: Holt, Rinehart & Winston, 1968.

Graff, Henry F. *The Tuesday Cabinet: Deliberation and Decision on Peace and War under Lyndon B. Johnson.* Englewood Cliffs, New Jersey: Prentice-Hall, Inc., 1970.

deGrazia, Alfred, and Stevenson, Thomas H. *World Politics, A Study in International Relations.* New York: Barnes and Noble, Inc., 1962.

Griffith, Ernest S. *The American Presidency: The Dilemma of Shared Power and Divided Government.* New York: New York University Press, 1976.

Gyorgy, Andrew, and Blackwood, George D. *Ideologies in World Affairs.* Waltham, Massachusetts: Blaisdell Publishing Company, 1967.

Halperin, Morton H. *Bureaucratic Politics and Foreign Policy.* Washington, D.C.: The Brookings Institution, 1974.

———. *Limited War in the Nuclear Age.* New York: John Wiley and Sons, 1963.

Hammond, Paul Y. *Organizing for Defense: The American Military Establishment in the Twentieth Century.* Princeton, New Jersey: Princeton University Press, 1961.

Hansen, Harry (ed.). *The World Almanac and Book of Facts for 1950.* New York: New York World Telegram Corporation, 1950.

Hargrove, Erwin C. *The Power of the Modern Presidency.* Philadelphia: Temple University Press, 1974.

Head, Richard G., and Rokke, Erwin J. (eds.). *American Defense Policy.* Third Edition. Baltimore: The Johns Hopkins University Press, 1973.

Hess, Stephen. *Organizing the Presidency.* Washington, D.C.: The Brookings Institution, 1976.

Hirschfield, Robert S. (ed.). *The Power of the Presidency: Concepts and Controversy.* Second Edition. Chicago: Aldine Publishing Company, 1973.

The Holy Bible. King James Version. Cambridge, England: Cambridge University Press.

Hoopes, Townsend. *The Devil and John Foster Dulles.* Boston: Little, Brown and Company, 1973.

———. *The Limits of Intervention.* New York: David McKay, 1969.

Hoover, Herbert. *Memoirs.* 3 volumes. New York: Macmillan Company, 1951–1953.

———. *The Ordeal of Woodrow Wilson.* New York: McGraw-Hill Book Company, 1958.

terHorst, Jerald F. *Gerald Ford and the Future of the Presidency.* New York: The Third Press, 1974.

Hoxie, R. Gordon. *A History of the Faculty of Political Science, Columbia University.* New York: Columbia University Press, 1955.

———. (ed.). *Frontiers for Freedom.* Denver: University of Denver Press, 1952.

———. (ed.). *The Presidency of the 1970's.* New York City: Center for the Study of the Presidency, 1973.

———. (ed.). *The White House: Organization and Observations.* New York City: Center for the Study of the Presidency, 1971.

Hoy, John C., and Berstein, Melvin H. (eds.). *The Effective President.* Pacific Palisades, California: Palisades Publishers, 1976.

Hughes, Thomas L. *The Fate of Facts in a World of Man: Foreign Policy and Intelligence Making.* Headline Series, No. 233. New York: Foreign Policy Association, December 1976.

Huntington, Samuel P. *The Common Defense: Strategic Programs in National Politics.* New York: Columbia University Press, 1961.

———. *The Soldier and the State.* Cambridge, Massachusetts: Harvard University Press, 1957.

Hurewitz, J. C. (ed.). *Soviet-American Rivalry in the Middle East.* New York: Proceedings of the Academy of Political Science, XXIX, 3, 1969.

de Huzar, George B. (ed.). *National Strategy in the Age of Revolution.* New York: Frederick A. Praeger, 1959.

Hyneman, Charles S. *Bureaucracy in a Democracy.* New York: Harper & Brothers, 1950.

Jackson, Henry M. (ed.). *The National Security Council.* Jackson Subcommittee Papers on Policy-Making at the Presidential Level. New York: Frederick A. Praeger, 1965.

Javits, Jacob K. *Who Makes War: The President versus Congress.* New York: William Morrow and Company, Inc., 1973.

Johnson, Lyndon B. *The Vantage Point: Perspective of the Presidency 1963–1969.* New York: Holt, Rinehart and Winston, 1971.

Kahan, Jerome H. *Security in the Nuclear Age.* Washington, D.C.: The Brookings Institution, 1975.

Kahn, Herman. *On Thermonuclear War.* Princeton, New Jersey: Princeton University Press, 1960.

Kalb, Marvin and Kalb, Bernard. *Kissinger.* Boston: Little, Brown and Company, 1974.

Kennan, George F. *Russia, the Atom, and the West.* New York: Harper & Brothers, 1957.

Kennedy, Robert F. *Thirteen Days: A Memoir of the Cuban Missile Crisis.* New York: W. W. Norton & Company, 1969.

Khrushchev, N. S. *Khrushchev in America.* New York: Crosscurrents Press, 1960.

Kimball, Warren F. *Franklin D. Roosevelt and the World Crisis, 1937–1945.* Lexington, Massachusetts: D. C. Heath and Company, 1973.

Kintner, William R., and Pfaltzgraff, Robert C., Jr. (eds.). *Implications for Arms Control in the 1970's.* Pittsburgh: University of Pittsburgh Press, 1973.

Kissinger, Henry A. *The Necessity for Choice: Prospects of American Foreign Policy.* New York: Harper & Brothers, 1961.

———. *Nuclear Weapons and Foreign Policy.* New York: Harper & Brothers, 1957.

Kitchum, Richard M. *The World of George Washington.* New York: The American Heritage Printing Company, 1974.

Koenig, Louis W. *The Chief Executive.* Third Edition. New York: Harcourt, Brace, Jovanovich, Inc., 1975.

———. *The Invisible Presidency.* New York: Rinehart, 1960.

———. *Official Makers of Public Policy: Congress and the Presidency.* Chicago: Scott, Foresman and Company, 1965.

Landecker, Manfred. *The President and Public Opinion: Leadership in Foreign Affairs.* Washington: Public Affairs Press, 1968.

Langsam, Walter C. *The World Since 1919.* Seventh Edition. New York: The Macmillan Company, 1954.

Laski, Harold. *The American Presidency.* New York: Harper & Brothers, 1940.

Leahy, William D. *I Was There.* New York: Whittlesey House, 1950.

Leckie, Robert. *Conflict: The History of the Korean War, 1950–1953.* New York: G. P. Putnam's Sons, 1962.

Luard, Evan T. (ed.). *The Cold War, A Reappraisal*. New York: Frederick A. Praeger, 1964.

Lynn, Naomi B., and McClure, Arthur F. *The Fulbright Demise: Senator J. William Fulbright's View of Presidential Power*. Lewisburg, Pennsylvania: Bucknell University Press, 1973.

Lyons, Eugene. *Herbert Hoover, a Biography*. Garden City, New York: Doubleday and Company, Inc., 1964.

MacArthur, Douglas. *Reminiscences*. New York: McGraw-Hill Book Company, 1964

Mansfield, Harvey C. (ed.). *Congress Against the President*. New York: Proceedings of the Academy of Political Science, XXXII, 1, 1975.

Matloff, Maurice (gen. ed.). *American Military History*. Washington, D.C.: U.S. Government Printing Office, 1969.

May, Ernest R. *"Lessons" of the Past: The Use and Misuse of History in American Foreign Policy*. New York: Oxford University Press, 1973.

————. (ed.). *The Ultimate Decision: The President as Commander in Chief*. New York: George Braziller, 1960.

McCloy, John J. *The Challenge to American Foreign Policy*. Cambridge, Massachusetts: Harvard University Press, 1953.

McNaughton, Frank, and Hehymer, Walter. *This Man Truman*. New York: Whittlesey House, 1945.

Merli, Frank J., and Wilson, Theodore A. (eds.). *Makers of American Diplomacy*. New York: Charles Scribner's Sons, 1974.

Miller, Merle. *Plain Speaking: An Oral Biography of Harry S. Truman*. New York: Berkley Publishing Corporation, 1973.

Millis, Walter. *Arms and Men: A Study in American Military History*. New York: G. P. Putnam's Sons, 1956.

————. (ed.). *The Forrestal Diaries*. New York: The Viking Press, 1951.

Milton, George Fort. *The Use of Presidential Power, 1789–1943*. Boston: Little, Brown, 1946.

Mollenhoff, Clark R. *The Pentagon*. New York: G. P. Putnam's Sons, 1967.

Morgan, Ruth P. *The President and Civil Rights: Policy Making by Executive Order*. New York: St. Martin's Press, 1970.

Morley, Felix. *The Foreign Policy of the United States*. New York: Alfred A. Knopf, 1951.

Morris, Richard B. *Alexander Hamilton and the Founding of the Nation*. New York: Dial Press, 1957.

Nathan, James A., and Oliver, James K. *United States Foreign Policy*. Boston: Little, Brown and Company, 1976.

Neumann, William L. *After Victory: Churchill, Roosevelt, Stalin and the Making of Peace*. New York: Harper & Row, 1967.

Neustadt, Richard E. *Presidential Power: The Politics of Leadership*. New York: John Wiley & Sons, Inc., 1960.

————. *Presidential Power: The Politics of Leadership with Reflections on Johnson and Nixon*. New York: Wiley, 1976.

Newhouse, John. *The Study of SALT*. New York: Holt, Rinehart & Winston, 1973.

Nixon, Richard M. *For a Generation of Peaceful Development*. Washington, D.C.: Agency for International Development, 1971.

———. *U.S. Foreign Policy in the 1970's: Shaping a Durable Peace*. Washington, D.C.: U.S. Government Printing Office, 1973.

O'Brien, L. F. *No Final Victories: Life in Politics from John F. Kennedy to Watergate*. Garden City, New York: Doubleday & Company, Inc., 1974.

Padelford, Norman J., and Lincoln, George A. *International Politics*. New York: The Macmillan Company, 1954.

Paolucci, Henry. *War, Peace, and the Presidency*. New York: McGraw-Hill Book Company, 1968.

Parkes, Henry Bamford, and Carosso, Vincent P. *Recent America*. 2 volumes. New York: Thomas Y. Crowell Company, 1963.

Parmet, Herbert S. *Eisenhower and the American Crusades*. New York: The Macmillan Company, 1972.

Patterson, James T. *Mr. Republican, A Biography of Robert A. Taft*. Boston: Houghton Mifflin Company, 1972.

Phillips, Cabell. *The Truman Presidency*. New York: The Macmillan Company, 1966.

Plischke, Elmer. *Conduct of American Diplomacy*. New York: C. Van Nostrand Company, 1950. (Revised editions 1961, 1967).

Polmar, Norman. *Strategic Weapons: An Introduction*. New York: Crane, Russak & Company, Inc., 1975.

Power, Thomas S. *Design for Survival*. New York: Coward-McCann, Inc., 1964.

Pratt, Julius W. *A History of United States Foreign Policy*. Englewood Cliffs, New Jersey: Prentice-Hall, Inc., 1955.

Price, D. K. (ed.). *The Secretary of State*. Englewood Cliffs, New Jersey: Prentice-Hall, Inc., 1960.

Pringle, Henry R. *Theodore Roosevelt*. New York: Harcourt, Brace and Company, 1931.

Pusey, Merlo J. *The Way We Go to War*. Boston: Houghton Mifflin Company, 1969.

Ray, Joseph M. (ed.). *The Coattailless Landslide*. El Paso, Texas: Western Press, 1974.

Raymond, Jack. *Power at the Pentagon*. New York: Harper & Row, 1964.

Riegel, Robert E., and Long, David F. *The American Story*. 2 volumes. New York: McGraw-Hill Book Company, Inc., 1955.

Ries, John C. *The Management of Defense: Organization and Control of the U.S. Armed Forces*. Baltimore, Maryland: The Johns Hopkins Press, 1964.

Roberts, Charles (ed.). *Has the President Too Much Power?: The Proceedings of a Conference for Journalists sponsored by the Washington Journalism Center*. New York: Harper Brothers Press, 1974.

Robinson, Edgar Eugene, et al. *Powers of the President in Foreign Affairs, 1945–1965: Harry S. Truman, Dwight D. Eisenhower, John F. Kennedy, Lyndon B. Johnson*. San Francisco: Commonwealth Club of California, 1966.

Rogers, Arnold A. *James Forrestal: A Study of Personality, Politics, and Policy.* New York: The Macmillan Company, 1963.

Rositzke, Harry. *The CIA's Secret Operations.* New York: Reader's Digest Press, 1977.

Rossiter, Clinton. *The American Presidency.* New York: The New American Library, 1956.

———. *The American Presidency.* Revised Edition. New York: Harcourt, Brace & World, Inc., 1960.

———. *The Supreme Court and the Commander in Chief.* Ithaca: Cornell University Press, 1951.

Sargent, Peter L., and Harris, Jack H. *Chinese Assessment of the Superpower Relationship 1972–1974.* Vienna, Virginia: The BDM Corporation, 1975.

Schlesinger, Arthur M. *The Rise of Modern America, 1865–1951.* New York: The Macmillan Company, 1951.

———. *The Imperial Presidency.* Boston: Houghton Mifflin Company, 1973.

Schlesinger, Arthur M., Jr. *A Thousand Days: John F. Kennedy in the White House.* Cambridge, Massachusetts: Houghton Mifflin Company, 1965.

Schneider, William, Jr., and Hoeber, Francis P. (eds.). *Arms, Men, and Military Budgets.* New York: Crane, Russak & Company, Inc., 1976.

Seton-Watson, Hugh. *From Lenin to Malenkov: The History of Communism.* New York: Frederick A. Praeger, 1953.

Sievers, Harry J., S.J. (ed.). *Six Presidents from the Empire State.* Tarrytown, New York: Sleepy Hollow Restorations, Inc., 1974.

Sofaer, Abraham D. *War, Foreign Affairs and Constitutional Power: The Origins.* Cambridge, Massachusetts: Ballinger Publishing Company, 1976.

Sorensen, Theodore C. *Decision Making in the White House: The Olive Branch or the Arrows.* New York: Columbia University Press, 1963.

———. *Kennedy.* New York: Harper and Row, 1965.

Stanley, Timothy W. *American Defense and National Security.* Washington, D.C.: Public Affairs Press, 1956.

de Seversky, Alexander P. *America—Too Young to Die.* New York: McGraw-Hill Book Company, Inc., 1961.

Shaheen, Neil, and others. *The Pentagon Papers.* New York: Bantam Books, Inc., 1971.

Smith, Louis. *American Democracy and Military Power.* Chicago: University of Chicago Press, 1951.

Stein, Harold (ed.). *American Civil-Military Decisions.* Birmingham: University of Alabama Press, 1963.

Sulzberger, Arthur O. *The Joint Chiefs of Staff, 1941–1954.* Washington, D.C.: U.S. Marine Corps Institute, 1954.

Taft, William Howard. *The President and His Powers.* New York: Columbia University Press, 1967.

Thompson, W. Scott, and Frizzell, Donaldson D. (eds.). *The Lessons of Vietnam.* New York: Crane, Russak and Company, Inc., 1977.

Tocqueville, Alexis de. *Democracy in America.* Phillips Bradley (ed.). 2 volumes. New York: Vintage Books, 1954.

Truman, Harry S. *Memoirs.* 2 volumes. Garden City, New York: Doubleday & Company, Inc., 1955–1956.

Truman, Margaret. *Harry S. Truman.* New York: William Morrow & Company, Inc., 1973.

Tugwell, Rexford G., and Cronin, Thomas E. (eds.). *The Presidency Reappraised.* New York: Praeger Publishers, 1974.

Turner, Gordon B. *National Security in the Nuclear Age.* New York: Frederick A. Praeger, 1960.

Vineyard, Dale. *The Presidency.* New York: Charles Scribner's Sons, 1971.

Walton, Richard J. *Cold War and Counter-Revolution: The Foreign Policy of John F. Kennedy.* Baltimore, Maryland: Penguin Books, Inc., 1973.

West, J. B. *Upstairs at the White House.* New York: Coward-McCann & Geoghegan, 1973.

White, Leonard D. *The Federalist, A Study in Administrative History; The Jeffersonians, 1801–29; The Jacksonians, 1829–61; and The Republican Era, 1869–1901.* 4 volumes. New York: Macmillan, 1948–1958.

———. *Introduction to the Study of Public Administration.* Third Edition. New York: The Macmillan Company, 1950.

White, Theodore A. *Breach of Faith: The Fall of Richard Nixon.* New York: Atheneum Publishers and Reader's Digest Press, 1975.

Wildavsky, Aaron (ed.). *Perspectives on the Presidency.* Boston: Little, Brown and Company, 1975.

Willrich, Mason, and Rhinelander, John B. *SALT: The Moscow Agreement and Beyond.* New York: The Free Press, 1974.

Yarmolinsky, Adam. *The Military Establishment: Its Impacts on American Society.* New York: Harper & Row, Inc., 1971.

Zacharias, E. M. *Behind Closed Doors: The Secret History of the Cold War.* New York: G. P. Putnam's Sons, 1950.

Newspapers and Periodicals

Administrative Science Quarterly. Ithaca: Cornell University, 1956 to date.

Aim Report. Washington, D.C.: Accuracy in Media, 1971 to date.

Air Force Magazine (formerly *Air Force and Space Digest*). Washington, D.C.: Air Force Association, 1946 to date.

The Air Reservist. Washington, D.C.: Headquarters, United States Air Force, 1954 to date.

The American Archivist. Washington D.C.: Society of American Archives, 1938 to date.

American Historical Review. Washington, D.C.: American Historical Association, 1895 to date.

American Political Science Review. Minasha, Wisconsin: American Political Science Association, 1906 to date.

Annals of the American Academy of Political and Social Science. Philadelphia: American Academy of Political and Social Sciences, 1891 to date.

Atlanta Constitution. Atlanta: Atlanta Newspapers, 1868 to date.

Christian Science Monitor. Boston: Christian Science Membership Society, 1908 to date.

Commanders Digest. Washington, D.C.: Department of Defense, 1957 to date.

Congressional Quarterly Service Weekly Report. Washington, D.C.: Congressional Quarterly, Inc., 1945 to date.

Detroit News. Detroit: Detroit News Inc., 1873 to date.

The Economist. London: The Economist Newspaper Limited, 1843 to date.

Federal Bar Journal. Washington, D.C.: Federal Bar Association, 1931 to date.

Foreign Affairs. New York: Council on Foreign Affairs, 1922 to date.

Fortune. New York: Time Inc., 1930 to date.

Headline Series. New York: Foreign Policy Association, 1935 to date.

Imprimis. Hillsdale, Michigan: Center for Constructive Alternative, 1972 to date.

Innovation and Management of Change Letter. Greenwich, Connecticut: W. Howard Chase Enterprises, 1965 to date.

Journal of American History. Bloomington, Indiana: Organization of American Historians, Indiana University, 1914 to date.

Journal of International Affairs. New York: Columbia University Press, 1947 to date.

Journal of Politics. Gainesville: University of Florida, 1939 to date.

Life Magazine. New York: Time-Life Inc., 1936–1972.

Long Island Press. Jamaica, New York: Long Island Daily Press Publishing Company, 1889–1977.

Modern Age. Bryn Mawr, Pennsylvania: Intercollegiate Studies Institute, Inc., 1956 to date.

National Journal. Washington, D.C.: Government Research Company, 1969 to date.

National Review. Bristol, Connecticut: National Review, Inc., 1955 to date.

NATO Review. Brussels: NATO Information Service, 1953 to date.

Newsday. Garden City, New York: Newsday, Inc., 1940 to date.

Newsweek. New York: Newsweek Inc., 1933 to date.

The New York Times. New York: New York Times Company, 1851 to date. (See *The New York Times Index.* New York: New York Times, 1913 to date. This annual index provides the most comprehensive record of any newspaper.)

New York Daily News. New York: New York News, Inc., 1919–

Orbis. Philadelphia: Foreign Policy Research Institute, 1957 to date.

Parade. New York: Parade Publications, 1941 to date.

Political Quarterly. London: Political Quarterly Publishing Company, Ltd., 1930 to date.

Political Science Quarterly. New York: Academy of Political Science, 1887 to date.

Presidential Studies Quarterly. New York: Center for the Study of the Presidency, 1970 to date.

Prologue, the Journal of the National Archives. Washington, D.C.: National Archives, 1969 to date.

Public Administration Review. Washington, D.C.: American Society for Public Administration, 1940 to date.

Public Opinion Quarterly. New York: Columbia University, 1937 to date.

Reader's Digest. Pleasantville, New York: Reader's Digest Association, 1922 to date.

Religion in Communist Dominated Areas. New York: Research Center for Religion and Human Rights in Closed Societies, Ltd., 1962 to date.

Reporter. New York: Reporter Magazine Company, 1949–1968.

Review of Politics. Notre Dame: University of Notre Dame, 1939 to date.

Strategic Review. Cambridge, Massachusetts: United States Strategic Institute, 1973 to date.

Time Magazine. New York: Time Inc., 1923 to date.

Treasury Papers. Washington, D.C.: Office of Public Affairs; Office of the Secretary of the Treasury, 1975 to date.

U.S. News and World Report. Washington, D.C.: U.S. News and World Report, Inc., 1933 to date.

University of Cincinnati Law Review. Cincinnati, Ohio: University of Cincinnati, 1932 to date.

Virginia Law Review. Charlottesville, Virginia: University of Virginia School of Law, 1913 to date.

Wall Street Journal. New York: Dow Jones & Company, Inc., 1898 to date.

Washington Monthly. Washington, D.C.: Washington Monthly Co., 1969 to date.

Washington Post. Washington, D.C.: Washington Post Company, 1877 to date.

Washington Star. Washington, D.C.: Washington Star Inc., 1952 to date.

INDEX

Congressional relations, *continued*
  war powers in, 17, 27, 31–34, 124,
    269–270, 319, 321–323, 379, 382
Connally, Tom, 20, 58
Connelly, Matthew J., 24
Conolly, Richard L., 165, 192
Constitution, U.S., xv, 4–6, 7, 8, 32,
    33, 35–39, 41–42, 53, 92, 112,
    311, 376, 377, 378, 384, 427
  amendments to, 5, 6, 10, 52,
    113–114, 256, 258, 274, 324
  Constitution, The, 7, 8
containment policy, 15, 69–75, 179,
    192, 202, 288–290, 299, 306, 307,
    345, 422
  antecedents of, 288–289
  collective security (1947–1950)
    and, 70–75, 154
  McArthur's challenge to, 103, 107
conventional forces, weapons, 194,
    202–203, 207, 209, 211, 214, 230,
    296, 298, 347
Coolidge, Calvin, 10, 43, 44
Cooper-Church Amendment,
    269, 423
Coplon, Judith, 109
Corcoran, Thomas G., 20
Corey, Gordon R., 415
Corwin, Edward S., 32, 39, 42–43,
    48–49, 256, 378
Coudert, Frederic R., Jr., 101, 112
Council on Foreign Relations, 203,
    291, 335
counterforce, 287, 306, 307, 308, 422
counterinsurgency, 306, 422
countervalue, 287, 306, 307, 308–
    309, 422
Cousins, Norman, 393
Cox, Archibald, 319
Craig, May, 254
Crommelin, John G., 164, 165, 166
Cronin, Thomas E., 126, 267–269
Crown, James T., 312–313
cruise missiles, 309, 352, 353, 354,
    359, 391, 418, 419
Cuba, 235, 359, 416
Cuban missile crisis (1962), 255,
    261, 268, 278, 298, 307, 312–314,
    316, 322, 335, 336, 338, 347,
    385–386, 392, 400, 410
Cutler, Robert, 21, 142, 144, 150,
    200, 201, 202

Cyprus, 271, 328, 374, 381
Czechoslovakia, 56, 89, 130
  Communist coup in (1948), 73,
    74, 142, 153, 192
  invasion of (1968), 317, 371, 392,
    396, 412

Daniels, Josephus, 131
Dardanelles, 66, 67, 71, 125
Davies, Joseph E., 64
Declaration of Independence, 4
Defense, Department of, 24, 26, 27,
    29, 80, 98, 199, 246, 252, 267,
    291, 294, 313, 330, 339, 344, 380,
    422
  creation of, 81–83, 131–151, 155,
    158–163, 219
  Eisenhower's reorganization of,
    194–198, 209–226
  proposals for reorganization of,
    under Ford and Carter, 338–
    339, 344
  service secretaries in, 159–163,
    196–198, 217, 218, 222–223,
    224–225
Defense Intelligence Agency, 225,
    356, 388
Defense Production Act (1950), 110
Defense Reorganization Act (1949),
    195
Defense Reorganization Act (1958),
    26, 216–226, 228, 243, 253,
    338–339
Defense Secretary, 16, 30, 133–151,
    155, 158–159, 160, 161, 164, 196,
    197–198, 217, 218, 221, 223–226,
    254, 337, 338, 339
de Gaulle, Charles, 241, 295, 296,
    406, 421
Democratic party, 23, 75, 101, 113,
    114, 117, 159, 183, 207, 227, 246,
    252, 266, 293, 327, 328, 343
Denfeld, Louis, 164, 165, 191
Destler, I. M., 335
deterrence, 15, 152, 194, 214, 233,
    242–243, 287, 288, 296, 302, 307,
    394, 424
developing (Third World) nations,
    xviii, 233, 255, 264, 314, 328–
    329, 367–371, 417, 426
Dewey, Thomas E., 77
Diem, Ngo Dinh, 297–298

COMMAND DECISION AND THE PRESIDENCY

by R. GORDON HOXIE

In recent years Congress has passed legislation that seriously weakens the powers of the President to make decisions vital to national security.

In this definitive and ground-breaking work, Dr. Gordon Hoxie recounts the foundations of our national power. He evaluates our current policies and suggests alternatives for the future. Dr. Hoxie answers the question as to whether too much or too little authority has been given the White House, and whether or not Congress has taken unto itself powers that were not intended for it by the designers of the Constitution.

There are startling revelations in this book. No other democratic society has so emasculated the role of the Chief of State in the decade of the 1970's as has the United States. In the past ten years, the Soviet Union has dangerously tilted the strategic balance. A weakened American Presidency is not the proper answer to the power struggle.

As former President Gerald R. Ford says in his Foreword, this book "provides valuable insights into the command decisions in the national security area. . . . [It] will contribute to setting right the proper image of both Harry S Truman and Dwight D. Eisenhower."

This major work evaluates three current strategies: containment, détente and human rights. In the light of these evaluations, the Truman, Eisenhower, Nixon, and Carter doctrines take on new meanings. Eisenhower emerges as the most underestimated American President. Crucial areas of strategic concern—Berlin, Yugoslavia, the Middle East, and southern Africa—are given special focus, as is the Third World. NATO is assessed vis-à-vis the Warsaw Pact.

Dr. Hoxie also evaluates other command decisions from Washington's Delaware crossing to Carter's stoppage of the B-1 two centuries later. These decisions take on new dimension, as do the relationships between foreign policy and domestic issues. In the organization and operations of national strategy in terms of command decision, the roles of the Congress, the National Security Council, the Departments of State and Defense, the armed services, and the intelligence community are all scrutinized, and